Gaze Interaction and Applications of Eye Tracking:

Advances in Assistive Technologies

Päivi Majaranta
University of Tampere, Finland

Hirotaka Aoki
Tokyo Institute of Technology, Japan

Mick Donegan
The ACE Centre, UK

Dan Witzner Hansen
IT University of Copenhagen, Denmark

John Paulin Hansen
IT University of Copenhagen, Denmark

Aulikki Hyrskykari
University of Tampere, Finland

Kari–Jouko Räihä
University of Tampere, Finland

Senior Editorial Director:	Kristin Klinger
Director of Book Publications:	Julia Mosemann
Editorial Director:	Lindsay Johnston
Acquisitions Editor:	Erika Carter
Development Editor:	Hannah Abelbeck
Production Editor:	Sean Woznicki
Typesetters:	Christen Croley, Chris Shearer
Print Coordinator:	Jamie Snavely
Cover Design:	Nick Newcomer

Published in the United States of America by
Medical Information Science Reference (an imprint of IGI Global)
701 E. Chocolate Avenue
Hershey PA 17033
Tel: 717-533-8845
Fax: 717-533-8661
E-mail: cust@igi-global.com
Web site: http://www.igi-global.com

Library of Congress Cataloging-in-Publication Data

Gaze interaction and applications of eye tracking : advances in assistive technologies / Päivi Majaranta ... [et al.].
    p. cm.
  Includes bibliographical references and index.
    ISBN 978-1-61350-098-9 (hardcover) -- ISBN 978-1-61350-099-6 (ebook) -- ISBN 978-1-61350-100-9 (print & perpetual access) 1. Human-computer interaction. 2. Self-help devices for people with disabilities. 3. Computerized instruments. 4. Eye--Movement--Photographic measurements. I. Majaranta, Päivi, 1967-
  QA76.9.H85G397 2012
  004.01'9--dc23
                        2011026203

British Cataloguing in Publication Data
A Cataloguing in Publication record for this book is available from the British Library.

All work contributed to this book is new, previously-unpublished material. The views expressed in this book are those of the authors, but not necessarily of the publisher.

Table of Contents

Section 1
Introduction

Section 2
User Involvement

Section 3
Gaze Interaction and Interface Design Issues

Section 4
Attentive and Gaze-Aware Interfaces

Section 5
Methods and Measures

Section 6
Building an Eye Tracker

Section 7
Future Directions

Foreword

I have been following the work of this book's editors and contributors since I met (most, if not all of) them over a decade ago. At the inaugural ETRA symposium, our keynote speaker, John W. Senders, voiced a cautiously optimistic sentiment about this burgeoning technology and area of research that I think most of us then shared: although the eye tracking Phoenix had arisen anew from the ashes, it was by no means certain how long this new avian being would endure before settling down to build itself a nest of twigs that would then ignite, burning fiercely to consume both nest and bird. Would the work discussed that day matter, to whom, and would the excitement of that day be sustainable? Notwithstanding the fiery myth, COGAIN officially began just a few short years later. The book that you hold in your hands is, I think, proof that the Phoenix has spread its wings.

The COGAIN book, acting as a portal to the abundant knowledge and experience that was gained during COGAIN's lifespan, shows the importance and impact of the advances that have been attained. From eye typing, to computer control, to games, to control of the environment, the book provides a compendium of the work, with a unique focus on assistive technologies for users with disabilities. In so doing, COGAIN poignantly depicts how much an impact the technology has, and to whom the technology matters a great deal.

Along with the passionate efforts put into the COGAIN project, which I had opportunity to witness first-hand during my visits across the pond, the COGAIN book catalogues the catalyst for the technological progress as a combination of camera digitization and miniaturization, increased processing speed, affordability (well, almost anyway), and its usability. For a technological perspective of the progress, I was shown, during one of my visits, the same eye tracker model that Rob Jacob had used before publishing his pioneering work on the Midas Touch problem—the unit looked like a small fridge compared to today's camera-embedded displays, as described in the COGAIN book.

It is a true pleasure to have witnessed the advancements taking shape that you now see inside the COGAIN book. The project has come a long way; by reading its pages, you can learn how to build an eye tracker, write a fixation filter, conduct experiments, and continue to explore new eye tracking research directions. The COGAIN book hints at where these directions may take you. For users with or without disabilities, recent advancements, such as demonstration of the EyePhone and inclusion of forward-facing cameras in cellular phones and tablets, suggest increased mobility, cheaper equipment, and potential for a proliferation of interesting and useful applications. The COGAIN book serves as an invaluable guide for creating future attentive apps on these new, smaller devices.

The COGAIN project clearly cements the importance and impact of eye tracking, and lays the foundation for the future, ensuring that the Phoenix need not start building its nest of twigs any time soon.

Andrew T. Duchowski
Clemson University, January 2011

Andrew T. Duchowski *is a professor of Computer Science at Clemson University. He received his B.Sc. ('90) and Ph.D. ('97) degrees in Computer Science from Simon Fraser University, Burnaby, Canada, and Texas A&M University, College Station, TX, respectively. His research and teaching interests include visual attention and perception, eye movements, computer vision, graphics, and virtual environments. He joined the School of Computing faculty at Clemson in January, 1998. He has since published a corpus of papers and a textbook related to eye tracking research, and has delivered courses and seminars on the subject at international conferences. He maintains Clemson's eye tracking laboratory, and teaches a regular course on eye tracking methodology attracting students from a variety of disciplines across campus.*

Preface

MOTIVATION

The ability to express oneself quickly and efficiently in precise language is fundamental for quality of life. Some people with special needs are not able to carry out interpersonal communication fluently. Producing simple, short sentences may take several minutes, depending on the specific impairment and the communication equipment in use. Similarly, access to the modern information society through the Internet may be severely limited by an inability to use the normal controls of a computer.

Another basic human right is being able to decide where one wishes to be and, equally importantly, where one wishes not to be. In other words, providing means by which people with motor impairments can move about and control their environment is another important goal for improving the quality of life.

Numerous assistive technologies and solutions, targeted at various user groups, have been developed over the years to overcome these problems. This book focuses on communication and control tools based on eye gaze tracking. Eye tracking makes it possible for people who are otherwise totally paralysed to use eye movements and gaze direction as a means to communicate with the outside world. This technology is crucial to users suffering from various types of motor neuron disease (MND), such as ALS or locked-in syndrome. Once thought rare, this impairment is, in fact, quite common: there are nearly 120,000 cases diagnosed worldwide each year. In addition, the technology and interaction methods developed can improve the quality and speed of communication for users with lesser impairments, and eventually for all users. According to Donegan et al. (2009), a new group of disabled users are emerging who are 'choosing to use eye control either to augment or replace their existing method, often because they feel it is a more comfortable, quicker and/or easier way of controlling technology'. In general, our target audience consists of all user groups for whom advanced eye tracking would provide a better interaction method.

Proper tools can improve the quality of life and even life expectancy considerably. With eye typing systems, MND patients have written entire books (Vigand & Vigand, 1997; Martin & Yockey, 2000). In addition to productivity tools (for typing, editing, communication, and control), recent developments have provided access to entertainment applications, such as games played over the Internet, that will bring many everyday pastimes within the reach of this user group. The ultimate challenge could be formulated as a variation of the Turing test: if people are communicating or collaborating at a distance over the Internet, the impairment of one person, ideally, should not be apparent to the others.

Although this objective lies, in general, in the distant future, developments in several fields have taken us closer to reaching it at least in specific cases. First and foremost, the technology has taken enormous steps forward in the last few decades. Eye tracking has a surprisingly long history, going back to the 19th century. For a long time, the techniques used to detect where a person is looking required obtrusive means, such as magnetic coils attached to the cornea. Advances in video-based methods changed this completely, toward the end of the 20th century. Video-based eye tracking, which does not require physical contact with a person, and EOG (eye tracking based on electrodes attached to the face), opened the gates to using eye tracking in augmentative and alternate communication (AAC). Systems for this purpose have been in use since the early 1980s (e.g., Hutchinson, White, Martin, Reichert, & Frey, 1989; Gips, Olivieri, & Tecce, 1993). The last decade has brought much progress in the packaging of the technology. It now has a small footprint and can even be integrated into spectacle frames or embedded within the monitor, making it much easier to install the device in varying environments and to support mobility through mounting of the eye tracker on a wheelchair, for instance.

The extent of this development can be recognised when one considers that some of the earlier devices required manual adjustment of the analogue video by means of a separate control unit: the optics and a camera moved by a servo motor facing the user, and the bulky control unit in another room. Today the digital video image can be analysed in real time inside a system that includes a laptop computer, screen, and video camera embedded in one portable unit. It can be mounted on an arm that can be rotated to any angle to accommodate users who cannot use the equipment in the normal position.

The use of an eye tracking device can open the door to a whole new world for users who have been unable to find an acceptable means of communication. Section 2 of the book presents many such examples, including that of Jayne, a young person in her early twenties with athetoid cerebral palsy. Jayne embraced gaze control technology with the support and encouragement of family, college staff, and friends. Previously, she had rejected other computer control methods. However, after she was given access to an eye tracking system, her prolific e-mail correspondence caused the college server to become 'jammed' on one occasion. 'I get emails now…' her mum says, pausing to reflect. '…endless emails, but I am sure this will calm down'. Secondly she continues, 'I think it's the technology itself. She so hated switches and, I think, felt they were unreliable'. Jayne's notion that switch control was inaccurate was just too hard to shake. 'The more excited she got the more it made presses, whereas it's the other way around for her when she is using gaze control technology. The more excited she gets the less it activates', her mother is quoted as saying. With the exception of gaze control technology, other forms of high-tech communication hadn't just stymied Jayne up to that point; she had rejected them out of hand.

The user base of gaze-based communication and control systems has been growing at an increasing rate. This has several reasons in addition to the advances in technology. Our knowledge of what is required to find a suitable solution for a particular individual has increased. For users with severe impairments, there can hardly ever be off-the-shelf solutions: careful adaptation of the technology to the needs of the user has to be performed on a case-by-case basis. On the other hand, the more we have learnt about individual users, the easier it has become to apply the existing knowledge in finding working solutions for new users. Spreading of information has been important in another sense also: eye tracking devices are not cheap, and people who could make use of them often need financial help in acquiring one. Awareness of the effectiveness of this technology has contributed more and more to the development of eye trackers whose financial support from society would be acceptable.

The early motivation for developing and using eye trackers was psychological research: the need to find the mechanisms that drive eye movement and to discover the process of visual perception. The role of eye trackers in AAC was the first major area where the technology was put to use in interaction with computers. It did not take long, however, before the potential of using point of gaze as an additional input channel in general control of computers was recognised (Jacob, 1991). The eyes provide a natural means for indicating which object on the screen the user wants to manipulate: whatever means are used for issuing a command, the target of the command must be located first – by the user looking at it. Although this sounds natural, the simplicity is deceiving: we do not want the computer to react to everything we look at. Finding natural, fluent, and efficient interaction techniques has given rise to a lot of research, ingenious new interaction techniques, and experiments that tell us how well they work.

Gaze-based interaction can never reach the speed of some other forms of communication, but careful interface design can take these systems a long way. A good example is text entry using gaze, a core element of any tool intended for communication. One natural gaze-based technique uses a soft keyboard on the computer screen, where keys are 'pressed' by looking at them long enough. This is naturally slow, since the threshold for selection of a key cannot be too low, lest false selections become annoyingly frequent. For this reason, it was long thought that this technique could provide text entry rates on the order of 10 words per minute. Here a 'word' is normalised to be a sequence of five characters. To put this in perspective, normal typing on a keyboard reaches entry rates of between 50 and 100 words per minute. In Section 3, we will present several approaches to improving the situation. An ingenious technique called Dasher was introduced by Ward and MacKay (2002). It was based on a totally different paradigm for text entry, not the one familiar from keyboards and typewriters. The paradigm was equally suitable for use with eye gaze and with other input devices, and it allowed text entry rates of close to 30 words per minute. But also with traditional techniques much can be done by carefully adapting them to use via eye gaze. Majaranta, Ahola, and Špakov (2009) show how the text entry rate even with soft keyboards can be almost doubled simply by providing the user with means to control the threshold for key selection. This is one of the many examples throughout the book stressing how important it is to adapt the solutions for each individual user and to provide means for adjusting the settings of one's device oneself.

This combination of different areas – advances of the technology, increased knowledge of the users and their needs, and development of algorithms that facilitate the interaction – make gaze interaction using eye tracking both a challenging and a fascinating field. It is truly multidisciplinary and needs co-operation from both researchers and practitioners.

WHY THIS BOOK

To facilitate bringing together the different stakeholders in this field, the European Union funded a network of Excellence called COGAIN (Communication by Gaze Interaction) in its 6th Framework Programme. The network consisted of 25 partners from universities and research institutes, care centres, end-user organisations, and manufacturers. The partners came from the Czech Republic, Denmark, Finland, France, Germany, Italy, Japan, Lithuania, Spain, Sweden, Switzerland, the UK, and the USA. It was a unique and unprecedented coalition, allowing researchers to get in direct contact with the user community, enabling manufacturers to learn from the latest research and share their extensive experience with researchers, and providing information on the latest technological solutions to the user community.

This book is a result of the work done in COGAIN. In 2004–2009, the project implemented various gaze-operated systems; conducted research; and produced, alongside new hardware and software, many reports and deliverables, containing a great deal of information on eye tracking, gaze estimation, safety issues, gaze-based interfaces, and (especially) gaze-based communication and control. The deliverables of the project are freely available on the Net (http://www.cogain.org/wiki/COGAIN_reports). Although they often represent the most comprehensive account of a specific theme, finding the right deliverable and obtaining the necessary background for reading it may be challenging. We are therefore proud to offer you this 'COGAIN book' that collects the essential knowledge inside the covers of one book in an easy-to-follow, organised format.

The COGAIN book is a collection of self-study materials for people who are interested in the applied use of gaze tracking. The book can also be used as a textbook for courses including an eye tracking module. The book provides basic knowledge of how a gaze tracker works and enough pointers to further readings for a reader who is eager to know more. The book also gives practical hints on building interactive applications that benefit from gaze input and instructions for building a basic eye tracker from off-the-shelf components. Special attention is given to applications targeted at people with disabilities. The book will assist professionals working in the field of assistive technology so that they know the key features of a gaze control system and will be able to make an assessment and select the best system for each client. Examples and case studies are provided to illustrate the issues. The book should be interesting and useful for anyone who has an interest in the subject but is not an expert in all areas, including user interface designers, software engineers, researchers, rehabilitation experts, and assistive technology professionals. Eye tracking brings together diverse skills and technologies and is a truly multidisciplinary area. This book is an attempt to bring the multidisciplinary expertise of the COGAIN Network of Excellence together in written form.

OUTLINE OF THE CONTENT

The book is divided into six thematic sections. They are organised such that the sections that are easier for a novice reader to follow are before the more demanding sections. Sections 2–4 provide practical advice and numerous case studies while sections 5–6 focus on more theoretical and technical information. Each section is complete on its own, and the reader may choose to read only the sections of interest. However, we do recommend first reading the introduction, as it should aid in understanding and putting into context the various thematic sections of the book.

Section 1 describes the area of focus of the book gives an introduction to the basic concepts. Majaranta and Donegan provide with a brief glance at the history of eye tracking and its application area in 'Introduction to Gaze Interaction'. Mulvey introduces basics for 'Eye Anatomy, Eye Movements, and Vision'. Hansen and Majaranta then provide a simple explanation of how a gaze tracking device works in 'Basics of Camera-Based Gaze Tracking'.

Section 2 focuses on end-user-related issues. First, Donegan in 'Features of Gaze Control Systems' discuss the user requirements and key features of a gaze communication and control system from the user's point of view. Then 'A Model for Gaze Control Assessments and Evaluation', by Holmqvist and Buchholz, provides practical advice for assistive technology professionals on how to succeed in finding the right combination of user needs and supporting technology. Pasian, Corno, Signorile, and Farinetti in 'The Impact of Gaze-controlled Technology on Quality of Life' provide several case studies and results from user trials, presenting in detail the process of introducing an eye tracking device to impaired users. Further case studies, with focus on users with the kind of impairments that might at first seem to prevent the use of eye gaze for control, are described by Donegan in 'Participatory Design – the Story of Jayne and Other Complex Cases'. This section should be useful for everybody who works with people with disabilities but also for developers who wish to get a deeper understanding of the target users and their needs.

Section 3 is focused on gaze control applications. It starts by considering the classic area of application of gaze-based interaction: Majaranta reviews in 'Communication and Text Entry by Gaze' both traditional approaches and more recent research on this topic. Skovsgaard, Räihä, and Tall then take a broader look at gaze-based interaction techniques, in 'Computer Control by Gaze'. They take the reader through numerous techniques, citing results related to their efficiency, and discuss as an example one specific field of application: browsing large information spaces, such as the World Wide Web, with eye gaze. In the last chapter, 'Beyond Communication and Control: Environmental Control and Mobility by Gaze', Bates, Castellina, Corno, Novák, and Štěpánková review the challenges and requirements in taking gaze-based interaction beyond communication and control, such as environmental control and mobility by gaze. This field is still in its early stages of development when compared to general interaction and control of a computer. The chapter pins down issues of safety and compatibility with other control systems that need to be taken into account in further development of the solutions. In all three chapters, design issues are discussed in such a way that this part of the book should be useful for anyone interested in implementing a gaze-controlled application, independent of the application area.

Section 4 broadens the perspective from voluntary eye movements used for control to involuntary, natural eye movements. In the first chapter, 'Eye Movements and Attention', Mulvey and Heubner provide an overview of the relationship of eye movements, cognitive processing, and attention – examining visual attention in particular. The chapter looks at what might be possible beyond direct point-and-click gaze control, in inferring subjective states. Vidaurre, Tangermann, Kübler, Müller, and Millán, in 'Brain–Computer Interfaces and Visual Activity', present what is known about the effects of visual stimuli on brain activity as measured via an array of electrodes placed on the scalp. They also discuss the possibilities of brain-controlled interfaces, either with the brain signals as the sole input or in combination with the measured point of gaze. Istance and Hyrskykari close this section with 'Gaze-Aware Systems and Attentive Applications', introducing applications that exploit the information from natural eye movements in the background of the application and do not require the user's intentional changing of gaze behaviour. Gaze-aware applications provide information about where the user's visual attention is targeting. This additional information channel opens gaze tracking to mainstream applications. The chapter offers design tips and discusses lessons learnt from research applications.

Section 5 introduces research methods, metrics, and measures that have emerged within the field associated with the design of gaze interaction systems. Hansen and Aoki start this section with 'Methods and Measures – an Introduction'. Some of the methods are inherited from an engineering approach to system design that can be found within the human factors tradition while others are unique to gaze interaction. In particular, the chapter takes a detailed look at the metrics used in analysis of text entry techniques. MacKenzie discusses, in 'Evaluating Eye Tracking Systems for Computer Input', techniques applicable in general, not just for text entry. The tools range from evaluating throughput and modelling eye movements in pointing tasks by using Fitts' law to collecting subjective opinions via questionnaires. The chapter describes in detail several case studies (experiments and their statistical analyses) that can be used as a model in design and analysis of new interaction techniques. It is well known that eye tracking experiments produce large quantities of data, and this alone may make it tedious to find interesting patterns in gaze behaviour. In the next chapter, 'Gaze Data Analysis: Methods, Tools, Visualisations', Špakov discusses software tools that alleviate this problem by providing overviews of gaze behaviour that can be visually inspected. While most of this book focuses on the use of eye gaze for interaction, the visualisation tools can be equally well applied in traditional usability studies for various visual layouts, such as alternative designs of Web pages. Heikkilä and Ovaska give, in 'Usability Evaluation of Gaze

Interaction', advice on how to carry out an experiment or usability test in a laboratory setting. They, too, discuss several examples of experiments analysed in various contexts. The chapter pays special attention to what should be done to the collected raw data: how to define fixation filters and specify areas of interest as the starting point for visualisations and statistical analyses. Finally, Donegan, Gill, and Oosthuizen take us back from mainstream applications and their analysis to the special issues raised by users with disabilities and consideration of the applications intended for them, in 'A Client-focused Methodology for Gaze-Control Assessment, Implementation, and Evaluation'.

Section 6 takes the reader into the heart of a gaze tracking system. It introduces both the hardware and software part of an eye movement tracking system and explains in detail how such a system works and what is required for the estimation of gaze direction. This section can be seen as a tutorial for readers who wish to build their own gaze tracker. Hansen, Villanueva, Mulvey, and Mardanbegi kick things off with their chapter 'Introduction to Eye and Gaze Trackers', which provides an overview of the main software and hardware components needed for eye tracking. It explains how the joint effect of eye position and head position can be used to determine the estimated point of gaze on the screen. In 'Image Analysis', Droege walks the reader through the many algorithms involved in identifying from a video image the user's eye, the pupil, and a glint caused by an external light source (if used). After these core inputs have been obtained, another set of algorithms are needed for estimating the point of gaze; these are covered by Villanueva, Cabeza, and San Agustin in the chapter 'Gaze Estimation'. A crucial element for making this possible is a geometric modelling of the eyeball, to allow mathematical computation of how light travels through the eyeball and is reflected from the cornea and retina. In 'Eye Tracker Hardware Design', Daunys looks at how to design the hardware components needed in an eye tracker. This involves selecting a suitable camera and processor, choosing the appropriate optical system, and deciding on the illumination of the eye needed for facilitating the image analysis algorithms. The most common source of illumination in use today is infrared light, since it is not visible to the human eye and provides images that are better suited to eye and gaze tracking. Nevertheless, its long-term use may be irritating or cause dryness of the eye. Next, Mulvey, Villanueva, Sliney, Lange, and Donegan present the work done in COGAIN to determine safety limits for exposure to infrared light, in 'Safety Issues and Infrared Light'. Hansen, Mulvey, and Mardanbeigi then wrap up the section by looking at where we can expect eye tracker development to head next, in their 'Discussion and Future Directions' chapter.

Finally, the editors of the book – Donegan, Majaranta, Hansen, Hyrskykari, Aoki, Hansen, and Räihä – sum up the research presented in this book, in 'Conclusion and a Look to the Future'. The closing chapter looks at several themes whose research and development is currently active in the area of gaze interaction and assistive technologies based on eye tracking.

CONCLUSION

The focus of this book is on the use of gaze for interaction. Other common uses of eye trackers are found in psychological studies and usability analysis of visual designs, such as Web pages. There is a wealth of literature and books on both, but on the use of gaze for interaction the knowledge is scattered. A seminal book was published by Duchowski (2003), but thereafter the main sources for new techniques have been the biennial Symposium on Eye Tracking Research and Applications. In addition to bringing the reader up to date with the key developments via a single compendium, another element of the proceedings of the symposia sets these volumes apart from others: the focus on solutions aimed at users with disabilities, without forgetting mainstream applications. The latter is of increasing importance as the algorithms improve, more inexpensive cameras can be used for eye tracking, and the technology can eventually be shipped as commodity goods with modern laptop computers.

This book is a joint effort of key actors in the COGAIN Network of Excellence. Funding from the European Commission ended in 2009, but COGAIN continues its work in the form of the COGAIN Association; see http://www.cogain.org/. The association is open to anyone working in this fascinating field, for sharing knowledge and experiences to help others in the community. The authors of the chapters of this book are donating any proceeds from the book to the association.

We hope you enjoy reading the book and find it useful!

Kari-Jouko Räihä
University of Tampere, Finland

REFERENCES

Donegan, M., Morris, D. J., Corno, F., Signorile, I., Chió, A., Pasian, V., & Holmqvist, E. (2009). Understanding users and their needs. *Universal Access in the Information Society, 8*(4), 259–275. doi:10.1007/s10209-009-0148-1

Duchowski, A. T. (2003). *Eye tracking methodology: Theory and practice*. London, UK: Springer.

Gips, J., Olivieri, C. P., & Tecce, J. J. (1993). Direct control of the computer through electrodes placed around the eyes. In M. J. Smith & G. Salvendy (Eds.), Human–computer interaction: Applications and case studies. *Proceedings of HCI International '93* (pp. 630–635). Amsterdam, The Netherlands: Elsevier.

Hutchinson, T. E., White, K. P. Jr, Martin, W. N., Reichert, K. C., & Frey, L. A. (1989). Human–computer interaction using eye-gaze input. *IEEE Transactions on Systems, Man, and Cybernetics, 19*(6), 1527–1534. doi:10.1109/21.44068

Jacob, R. J. K. (1991). The use of eye movements in human–computer interaction techniques: What you look at is what you get. *ACM Transactions on Information Systems, 9*(3), 152–169. doi:10.1145/123078.128728

Majaranta, P., Ahola, U.-K., & Špakov, O. (2009). Fast gaze typing with an adjustable dwell time. *Proceedings of the 27th International Conference on Human Factors in Computing Systems* (CHI'09) (pp. 357–360). New York, NY: ACM. doi: 10.1145/1518701.1518758

Martin, J., & Yockey, R. (2000). *On any given day*. Winston-Salem, NC: Blair.

Vigand, P., & Vigand, S. (1997). *Only the eyes say yes: A love story*. New York, NY: Arcade.

Ward, D. J., & MacKay, D. J. C. (2002). Fast hands-free writing by gaze direction. *Nature, 418*(6900), 838. doi:10.1038/418838a

Acknowledgment

A large number of institutions and individuals have been involved in making this book happen. The book was conceived during the COGAIN (Communication by Gaze Interaction) project (IST-2003-511598), a Network of Excellence funded by the European Commission in 2004–2009. Much of the content of this book is based on the research articles, technical reports and deliverables produced during the project.

Research institutions, user organizations, eye tracking manufacturers and assistive technology companies have all facilitated the work in one way or the other. The project had 27 official partners representing the different stakeholders:

- University of Tampere, Finland (coordinator)
- Czech Technical University, Czech Republic
- Bispebjerg Hospital, Denmark
- Danish Centre for Technical Aids for Rehabilitation and Education, Denmark
- Danmarks Tekniske Universitet, Denmark
- IT University of Copenhagen, Denmark
- Risø National Laboratory, Denmark
- Metrovision, France
- Technische Universität Dresden, Germany
- University of Koblenz-Landau, Germany
- University of Lübeck, Germany
- Hewlett Packard Italy, Italy
- Politecnico di Torino, Italy
- Tokyo Institute of Technology, Japan
- Siauliu University, Lithuania
- The Public University of Navarre, Spain
- DART Communication and Data Resource Center, Sweden
- Permobil AB, Sweden
- Tobii Technology AB, Sweden
- University of Zürich, Switzerland
- ACE Centre Advisory Trust, UK
- De Montfort University, UK
- Loughborough University, UK
- University of Cambridge, UK

- University of Derby, UK
- EyeTech Digital Systems, USA
- LC Technologies, USA

In addition to EC funding, the work was supported by several research projects as well as core funding coming from the participating universities and industry. Their contributions are gratefully acknowledged.

Many other institutions participated in the work of the project in advisory bodies, including the Board of Industrial Advisors and the Board of User Communities. Altogether hundreds of individuals contributed to the work of the project through its yearly camps, research retreats, workshops, and deliverables. There are too many individuals involved to name each one here; we are grateful to every one of them for carrying the project through, and for their contributions to its operation and, directly or indirectly, to this book.

Managing a project of such a wide scope is no easy task. The link to the European Commission was the coordinator, Kari-Jouko Räihä. The day-to-day operation was in the competent hands of Stina Boedeker (communications officer) and Päivi Majaranta (scientific officer). In addition to managing the regular reporting and monitoring the work done in the work packages, they tirelessly participated in numerous exhibitions and other dissemination events. The strategic decisions were in effect done by the Steering Board, which for the last three years of the project consisted of the following active participants: Fulvio Corno, Gintautas Daunys, Mick Donegan, Bjarne Ersbøll, John Paulin Hansen, Howell Istance, Fiona Mulvey, Kari-Jouko Räihä (chair), Olga Štěpánková, and Arantxa Villanueva. Thank you all, again.

We would like to express our special, sincere thanks to the members of the user community and to those supporting them. They have been kind enough both to be involved in the project, to provide their valuable insight in all phases of the project, and to give their permission to be used as case studies in this book in order to help others. Without the feedback from the actual end users of the eye control technology, all the information in this book would be only academic and of little practical importance. A very special thanks to Sarah Yeo and Kati Lepistö, who cheerfully shared their experiences through the project Web page and literally gave the project a face.

We would also like to thank the many manufacturers of eye gaze systems, from Europe, America and beyond, who generously gave their time and support in many ways, including equipment loans, involvement in exhibitions, contributions at COGAIN meetings and collaboration in our work related to eye gaze safety.

The COGAIN project ended in August 2009. However, the work continues in the form of an association, with Bjarne Ersbøll serving as its first President. In fact, potential royalties of this book will go to the COGAIN Association – a warm thanks to all authors of the book chapters for this and, of course, for the effort they have put in preparing their contributions. We hope this book will serve as impetus for you, the reader, to get involved in the work of the Association: it relies on the continued efforts of individuals volunteering their time. For information on the Association, see www.cogain.org.

Special thanks go also to the publishing team at IGI Global. In particular, we wish to thank Christine Bufton and Hannah Abelbeck for guiding us step by step through this publishing process and for kindly replying to our numerous questions.

We also thank the anonymous reviewers (organised by the publisher) for their constructive comments and ideas for improvements that contributed to the coherence and quality of the book.

Detlev Droege, from the University of Koblenz-Landau, Germany, deserves special thanks for creating a dedicated shared space for the manuscript and for assisting in editing Section 6 of the book. We also thank Diako Mardanbegi from IT University of Copenhagen, Denmark, for his assistance in converting the contributions from LaTeX to Microsoft Word and fine tuning the layout.

Proofreading and language revision of the book chapters was conducted within a very tight schedule by Translatum Oy, Finland.

Päivi Majaranta
University of Tampere, Finland

Hirotaka Aoki
Tokyo Institute of Technology, Japan

Mick Donegan
The ACE Centre, UK

Dan Witzner Hansen
IT University of Copenhagen, Denmark

John Paulin Hansen
IT University of Copenhagen, Denmark

Aulikki Hyrskykari
University of Tampere, Finland

Kari-Jouko Räihä
University of Tampere, Finland

January 2011

Section 1
Introduction

Chapter 1
Introduction to Gaze Interaction

Päivi Majaranta
University of Tampere, Finland

Mick Donegan
ACE Centre, UK

ABSTRACT

Gaze interaction, as understood in this book, provides a means to exploit information from eye gaze behaviour during human-technology interaction. Gaze can either be used as an explicit control method that enables the user to point at and select items, or information from the user's natural gaze behaviour can be exploited subtly in the background as an additional input channel without interfering with normal viewing. This chapter provides a brief introduction to the potential for applied gaze tracking, with special emphasis on its application in assistive technology. It introduces common terms and offers a concise summary of previous research and applications of eye tracking.

INTRODUCTION

Eye tracking systems are used to monitor eye movement and to translate the user's gaze direction into, for example, computer screen coordinates. For people with severe motor disabilities, gaze may be their only means of operating a computer, communicating, writing emails, playing games, or controlling their environment (Donegan et al., 2009). For them, gaze replaces the computer mouse and keyboard as the input method (Scott, 2010). At the other end of the potential user scale,

anyone can benefit from eye-aware applications that adapt their behaviour based on the user's visual attention. If an application is aware of the user's current attentive state or where their visual attention is targeted, it can "know" more about the user's interests and intentions and accordingly react in a more natural way (Jacob, 1991).

This chapter provides a concise summary of previous research and an overview of the potential for applied gaze tracking, which is explored in more detail in the thematic sections of this book. Below, we will first have a quick glance into the history and applications of eye tracking, followed by a brief introduction to currently

DOI: 10.4018/978-1-61350-098-9.ch001

available gaze-based assistive devices. We close by introducing some common terms that recur throughout the book.

BRIEF HISTORY AND BACKGROUND OF MODERN GAZE TRACKING

Early eye tracking systems were used for studying the nature of human eye movements rather than for interaction. First studies on human eye movement were made by direct observation (see Wade & Tatler, 2005, for an extensive review of the history of eye movement research). The early devices were often invasive and uncomfortable as they required the user to wear special instruments or their head position to be fixed by using, for example, a bite bar. The highly cited pioneering work by Yarbus (originally published in 1956 in Russian, reprinted in English in 1967) was conducted using a device with a 'cap' that was "attached by suction to the eyeball". This 'suction device' required that "the cornea is anesthetized, the lids taped apart, and the subject trained to inhibit the natural tendency to move the eyes"

as a precaution to prevent injury on the eye or the device (Yarbus, 1967: quotes taken from the Foreword). A number of experiments on characteristics of eye movements and visual perception were carried out using this device.

The first "non-invasive" eye tracking apparatus, based on photography and light reflected from the cornea, was developed by Dodge and Cline in the early 1900s (Wade & Tatler, 2005). This "Dodge Photochronograph" inspired many later eye tracking devices and is considered the primary ancestor of the current video-based corneal reflection eye tracking systems. The device, and later improved versions of it, were used to categorize numerous basic eye movement properties and types, and laid the foundation for modern eye movement research. Over the years, major effort has been invested into the development of eye tracking technology and more accurate gaze estimation methods (see, e.g., Young & Sheena, 1975; Duchowski, 2003; Li, Babcock, & Parkhurst, 2006; Hansen & Ji, 2010). As a result, usability of modern eye trackers has vastly improved since these early days of eye movement tracking (for examples, see Figures 1 and 2).

Figure 1. Some of the earlier devices required manual adjustment of the analogue video via a separate control unit (on the left; © 1999 TAUCHI. Used with permission). Today, the digital video image can be analyzed in real time through an all-in-one system that includes a laptop, screen and video camera embedded in a single portable unit (on the right; © 2007 COGAIN. Used with permission).

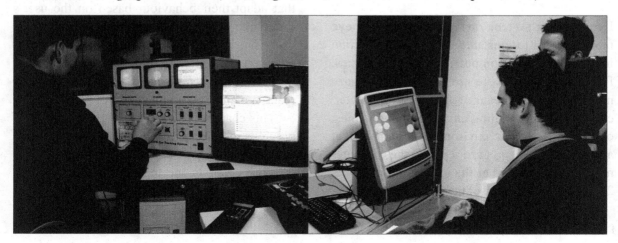

Figure 2. A gaze tracking device tracks the movements of the eye and a computer program maps the user's gaze into co-ordinates of the screen. The information on the user's visual attention ("point of regard") is beneficial for both diagnostic and interactive applications.(© 2001, 2003 TAUCHI, tauchi. cs.uta.fi. Used with permission.)

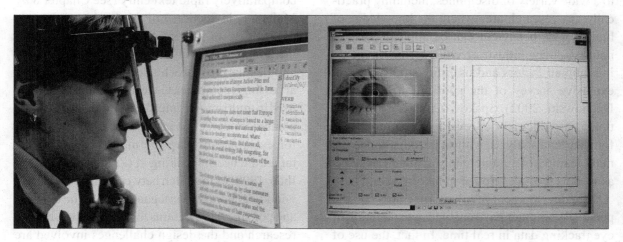

Current eye tracking technologies can be divided into the following categories: electro-oculography (EOG), scleral contact lens/search coil, video-oculography (VOG) or photo-oculography (POG), and video-based combined pupil/corneal reflection techniques (for details, see Duchowski, 2003). Systems that use contact lenses are used mainly for psychological or physiological studies that require extra high accuracy. EOG based systems can be considered impractical for everyday use as they require electrodes to be placed around the eye to measure the skin's electric potential differences, although some EOG systems are successfully employed in augmentative and alternative communication (AAC) (see, e.g., Gips, Olivieri, & Tecce, 1993; Hori, Sakano, & Saitoh, 2006).

Camera (video) based systems are considered least obtrusive and thus best suited to interactive applications (Morimoto, & Mimica, 2005). Video-based techniques using pupil/corneal reflection provide Point of Regard (POR) measurement, meaning that the system can calculate the direction of gaze (Duchowski, 2003). In practice, this enables direct pointing; the user can point with

their eyes by directly looking at the target item on the screen (for a brief, simplified, introduction to basics of gaze tracking see Chapter 3; methods for gaze estimation are explained in detail in Section 6 of this book).

APPLICATIONS OF EYE TRACKING

There are two main categories of eye tracking systems: *diagnostic* and *interactive* (Duchowski, 2003). For diagnostic purposes, gaze tracking provides an objective and quantitative method of recording the viewer's point of regard (Figure 2). Traditionally, information on eye movement has been used by the psychological and medical sciences to study normal human gaze behaviour in various contexts or abnormalities in human (or animal) vision. These include, for example, research on (normal or dyslexic) reading, visual search, scene perception (Rayner, 1995) or even human emotions (Partala & Surakka, 2003). Figure 2 illustrates example uses for eye tracking: on the left, the user's gaze path is tracked while she is reading; on the right, gaze data is being recorded for analysis (software shown on the screen © SensoMotoric Instruments).

Today, the list of uses for eye tracking extends to a wide variety of disciplines, including practically any research area where the knowledge of human gaze behaviour can be applied, such as neuroscience, industrial engineering, marketing, human factors and usability studies (for an extensive survey of the application areas, see Duchowski, 2002). Špakov (Chapter 16 in Section 5) provides a brief review of common tools for gaze data analysis, with an introduction to the main features of commercially available systems as well as tools developed in laboratories.

The development of microprocessors and the personal computer have enabled the collection of eye tracking data in real time. In fact, the use of gaze for computer control has been under investigation since at least the early 1980s (Bolt, 1982). Interactive applications react to the user's gaze at some level. According to Duchowski (2003), the application can be *selective*; the gaze is used as an actual control medium, or *gaze-contingent*; the system is aware of the user's gaze and may adapt its behaviour based on the visual attention of the user. This book focuses on interactive applications that utilize gaze tracking in real time, with special emphasis on its application in assistive technology.

The first interactive applications were, in fact, "eye typing" systems where the user could produce text by using the focus of gaze as a means of input (Ten Kate, Frietman, Willems, Ter Haar Romeny, & Tenkink, 1979; Friedman, Kiliany, Dzmura, & Anderson, 1982; Yamada & Fukuda, 1987; Hutchinson, White, Martin, Reichert, & Frey, 1989). With these early pioneering systems, the keys on the screen needed to be relatively large because of the limited accuracy of the measured point of gaze. The first version of the ERICA system (Hutchinson et al., 1989), for example, had only six selectable items available on screen at a time. Typing was slow as the letters had to be organized in a tree-structured menu hierarchy and several keystrokes were required to enter a single letter (Frey, White, & Hutchinson, 1990). Today, a number of eye typing systems are available and new methods have been developed that enable comparatively rapid text entry (see Chapter 8 by Majaranta in Section 3 of this book).

The use of the eyes as an explicit control medium is a necessity for people with certain disabilities that prevent or hinder them from otherwise accessing a computer. Gaze interaction can also be used in multi-modal interfaces to enhance human-computer interaction in mainstream applications, for example, to warp the mouse cursor on the target the user is looking at (Zhai, Morimoto, & Ihde, 1999) or to switch between applications and windows (Fono & Vertegaal, 2005). The existing and potential applications for gaze control, related research and the design challenges involved are extensively reviewed in Section 3.

Information on user eye behaviour can also be obtained in a more "natural" way by subtly tracking the user's eye movements in the background. Inferring mental states from eye movements can potentially be applied in interactive applications (Salvucci, 1999). Attentive interfaces (Vertegaal, 2003) are an example of this kind of usage. Such gaze-aware interfaces exploit information on the user's area of interest (AOI) to change the application's behaviour depending on the assumed attentive state or assumed intentions of the user. Gaze-aware interfaces are introduced in Section 4.

GAZE TRACKERS FOR ASSISTIVE TECHNOLOGY

Today, ranges of eye tracking systems are available on the market. Most are used for research and diagnostic purposes; only relatively small numbers are developed specifically for people with disabilities. The COGAIN Association maintains a catalogue of currently available systems (see Eye Trackers, 2010). The catalogue includes categorized lists of systems used for assistive technology, systems targeted mainly at research and evaluation, as well as open source and freeware systems that enable the user to convert their web camera into an eye tracker by downloading and installing the required software.

The number of gaze-based communication aids is also on the increase as a rapidly growing group of users are choosing eye control over other control methods (Donegan et al., 2009). From a technical point of view, all eye tracking systems are fairly similar and often use the same basic principles of operation. It is the applications (software such as virtual keyboards) and the accessories (such as modules that enable environmental control) that turn an eye tracking system into an assistive device. A person with a disability can use the system as his or her main communication and control method extensively and in varying conditions. Reliability, robustness and safety are therefore mounting issues, and the availability of (technical) support must be carefully considered in addition to ease of use and general usability.

There are key differences in the currently available gaze control systems that should be taken into account when choosing the best system for each individual user. For example, some systems require the user to maintain a steady head position in order for the eye tracking function to work, rendering them ineffective for users with involuntary head movement. All systems have their individual pros and cons, so it is advisable to make careful comparisons before purchasing a system. The end-user requirements and key features of gaze based assistive devices are discussed in detail in Section 2.

There are three categories of gaze control system available today: (1) all-in-one, (2) dedicated modular, and (3) add-on systems (Donegan, 2010).

All-in-one systems, as the name suggests, provide everything the user needs within a single device. No separate hardware components need be installed by the user and the system is ready for almost immediate use. A potential disadvantage of these systems is that they can be difficult or, in some cases, virtually impossible for the user to update independently. Current examples include the MyTobii P10 (in Figure 1, on the right) by Tobii Technology (www.tobii.com) and SeeTech® Pro by Humanelektronik GmbH (www.see-tech.de).

Dedicated modular systems are communication devices that support a range of input methods in addition to gaze control. The user can choose a specific modality (e.g., touch, via touch-screen control), or a combination of modalities (e.g., multimodal input by using gaze to point at an item and a separate switch to select the item). This is especially beneficial for users with degenerative conditions since they can continue to use a familiar interface and only change the input method to match their current capabilities. Another benefit of such a modular "docking" system is that the communication aid can be bought separately from the gaze module. However, as noted by Donegan (2010), specific modular devices only support the specific eye tracking unit they are designed for. At the time of writing, there is no global cross-compatibility between systems. Therefore, the user should ensure that the communication device itself has all the necessary features required by the user before committing themselves to the purchase of such a modular system, for example, whether or not the device offers full Windows accessibility and sufficient processing power for the Windows applications they wish to use. Current examples of dedicated modular systems include EyeMax by DynaVox Mayer-Johnson (www.dynavoxtech.com) and ECOpoint™ by Prentke Romich Company (www.prentrom.com).

Add-on systems enable any desktop or laptop computer to be used as an eye tracking system. While this may at face value appear to be an ideal choice, key aspects need to be taken into account, such as usability, portability and mounting, which may affect the system's suitability as an assistive device. One should also remember that, while gaze control can, in certain cases, offer an excellent and immediate alternative to direct pointer control using a mouse in certain cases, other users might require special gaze-control enabling software such as the Sensory Software 'Grid' series. Gaze pointing and mouse pointing are not yet on a par; there are inaccuracy and usability issues involved that may prevent using gaze as a direct mouse replacement. We will look at the different ways of solving the user interface and interaction issues involved in gaze control in more detail in Section 3. Current examples of add-on systems include The Eyegaze Edge™ by LC Technologies (www.eyegaze.com), 'TM3' by EyeTech Digital Systems (www.eyetechds.com) and IntelliGaze™ by Alea Technologies (www.alea-technologies.de).

It should be noted that many of the companies mentioned above provide several different models of their eye tracking systems that fall into any of the categories described above. In addition, new systems and companies appear on the market as the demand for gaze-based assistive devices is increasing rapidly.

COMMON TERMS

Even though the terms '*eye*' and '*gaze*' are quite distinctive; the first referring to the human organ and the latter to a fixed look, the terms 'eye tracking' and 'gaze tracking' are often used in the literature as if they were synonyms. Generally, *eye tracking* refers to the procedure of tracking and measuring the movements of the eye. The term 'eye movement tracker', or simply 'eye tracker', refers to a device that follows the eye location over time, while a *gaze tracker* is an eye movement tracker that also determines the viewer's point of gaze (direction or target). In our opinion, the term 'gaze tracking' is more accurate than 'eye tracking' when one is discussing tracking of the direction of gaze, or point of regard. However, 'eye tracking' has become established and is often used in the literature, as it will be in this book, as a general term referring to both the tracking of eye movements and tracking of the user's gaze direction.

In this book, we focus mainly on active monitoring of the eye movements and gaze direction and exploit it in real time as an additional input method for either gaze-controlled or gaze-aware applications. Passive monitoring of eye movements is more useful in diagnostic applications and usability studies that analyse previously recorded eye movement data (Hammoud, 2008). Benefits of recorded eye movement data are discussed in Section 5 of the book, which addresses the analysis of both gaze-controlled and conventional interfaces.

Gaze interaction is similar to human–computer interaction (HCI), but its main interaction method is gaze either instead of or in addition to the more conventional keyboard and mouse. Such an access method can provide opportunities for communication, computer and environmental control for a person with a physical disability who cannot achieve these tasks in any other way. In such cases, the gaze tracker is used as an assistive device.

Eye-aware or *gaze-aware applications* do not require the user to use the eyes or gaze intentionally for control but benefit from natural eye movements. Such *attentive systems* (Vertegaal, 2003) monitor the user's eye movements and gaze direction subtly in the background and use this information only as an additional input for improvement of the application's response to the needs of the user.

By *eye control* we refer to the interactive use of the tracked human gaze position to communicate and control a computer. Similarly to 'eye tracking' versus 'gaze tracking', one may define the difference of eye control from gaze control as referring to systems wherein the mere movement of the eyeball or a blink (Grauman, Betke, Lombardi, Gips, & Bradski, 2003) is used for controlling a computer, for example, by moving the eye from a higher position downward as confirmation for 'yes' or from left to right for 'no'. *Gaze control* involves measuring the direction or point (target) of the gaze. Other common terms for gaze-based control of a computer are *eye input* and *gaze input*.

Gaze pointing, or placing the computer mouse cursor where the user is looking on the computer screen, is an intuitive method that requires little training (Stampe & Reingold, 1995). However, it should be noted that for a severely disabled person who does not have experience with any method of computer control, it may take time to master a gaze pointing system (Gips, DiMattia, Curran, & Olivieri, 1996).

In a gaze-controlled system, the same modality, gaze, is used for both perception and control. This brings with it a very specific challenge: the system should be able to separate intentional commands from casual viewing – to avoid the *Midas touch problem* (Jacob, 1991). The Midas touch problem is a concern for both gaze-controlled and gaze-aware applications. Solutions for avoiding it are discussed in several parts of this book.

CONCLUSION

Eye tracking is no longer a niche technology used exclusively by research laboratories or available only as a last option to a few select users. An increasing number of users with special needs are choosing gaze control over other access methods as their main computer and communication aids, as they feel it is a more efficient, effortless, comfortable and, in certain cases, less painful way of accessing technology compared to the other options available to them (Donegan et al., 2009; Scott, 2010).

The user requirements, design challenges and evaluation of gaze-controlled and gaze-aware applications, as well as implementation issues concerning the eye tracker itself are extensively discussed in the thematic sections of this book. The following two chapters within this section set the basis for the rest of the book by giving an introduction to human vision and eye movement tracking. Both are useful in understanding what makes eye tracking possible and how the characteristics of the eye affect different types of eye movement, as well as the possibilities and challenges involved in modern gaze tracking.

REFERENCES

Bolt, R. A. (1982). Eyes at the interface. *Proceedings of the* SIGCHI *Conference on Human Factors in Computing Systems (CHI '82)* (pp. 360-362). New York, NY: ACM. doi:10.1145/800049.801811

Donegan, M. (2010). Gaze controlled technology – How far have we come? Where are we going? In Wilson, A., & Gow, R. (Eds.), *The eye have it! The use of eye gaze to support communication* (pp. 3–6). Edinburgh, UK: CALL Scotland, The University of Edinburgh.

Donegan, M., Morris, D. J., Corno, F., Signorile, I., Chió, A., Pasian, V., & Holmqvist, E. (2009). Understanding users and their needs. *Universal Access in the Information Society, 8*(4), 259–275. doi:10.1007/s10209-009-0148-1

Duchowski, A. T. (2002). A breadth-first survey of eye tracking applications. *Behavior Research Methods, Instruments, & Computers, 34*(4), 455–470. doi:10.3758/BF03195475

Duchowski, A. T. (2003). *Eye tracking methodology: Theory and practice.* London, UK: Springer-Verlag.

Eye Trackers. (2010). *A catalogue of currently available eye trackers.* Retrieved the COGAIN website: http://www.cogain.org/wiki/Eye_Trackers

Fono, D., & Vertegaal, R. (2005). EyeWindows: Evaluation of eye-controlled zooming windows for focus selection. *Proceedings of the SIGCHI Conference on Human Factors in Computing Systems (CHI '05)* (pp. 151–160). New York, NY: ACM. doi:10.1145/1054972.1054994

Frey, L. A., White, K. P. Jr, & Hutchinson, T. E. (1990). Eye-gaze word processing. *IEEE Transactions on Systems, Man, and Cybernetics, 20*(4), 944–950. doi:10.1109/21.105094

Friedman, M. B., Kiliany, G., Dzmura, M., & Anderson, D. (1982). The eyetracker communication system. *Johns Hopkins APL Technical Digest, 3*(3), 250–252.

Gips, J., DiMattia, P., Curran, F. X., & Olivieri, P. (1996). Using EagleEyes – An electrodes based device for controlling the computer with your eyes – To help people with special needs. In J. Klaus, E. Auff, W. Kremser, & W. Zagler (Eds.), *Proceedings of the 5th International Conference on Computers Helping People with Special Needs (ICCHP '96)* (pp. 630–635). München, Germany: Oldenbourg.

Gips, J., Olivieri, C. P., & Tecce, J. J. (1993). Direct control of the computer through electrodes placed around the eyes. In M. J. Smith & G. Salvendy (Eds.), *Human–computer interaction: Applications and case studies (Proceedings of HCI International '93)* (pp. 630–635). Amsterdam, The Netherlands: Elsevier.

Grauman, K., Betke, M., Lombardi, J., Gips, J., & Bradski, G. R. (2003). Communication via eye blinks and eyebrow raises: Video-based human–computer interfaces. *Universal Access in the Information Society, 2*(4), 359–373. doi:10.1007/s10209-003-0062-x

Hammoud, R. (Ed.). (2008). *Passive eye monitoring: Algorithms, applications and experiments.* Series: Signals and Communication Technology. Berlin, Germany: Springer-Verlag. doi:10.1007/978-3-540-75412-1

Hansen, D. W., & Ji, Q. (2010). In the eye of the beholder: A survey of models for eyes and gaze. *IEEE Transactions on Pattern Analysis and Machine Intelligence, 32*(3), 478–500. doi:10.1109/TPAMI.2009.30

Hori, J., Sakano, K., & Saitoh, Y. (2006). Development of a communication support device controlled by eye movements and voluntary eye blink. *IEICE Transactions on Information and Systems, 89*(6), 1790–1797. doi:10.1093/ietisy/e89-d.6.1790

Hutchinson, T. E., White, K. P. Jr, Martin, W. N., Reichert, K. C., & Frey, L. A. (1989). Human–computer interaction using eye-gaze input. *IEEE Transactions on Systems, Man, and Cybernetics, 19*(6), 1527–1534. doi:10.1109/21.44068

Jacob, R. J. K. (1991). The use of eye movements in human–computer interaction techniques: What you look at is what you get. *ACM Transactions on Information Systems, 9*(3), 152–169. doi:10.1145/123078.128728

Li, D., Babcock, J., & Parkhurst, D. J. (2006). openEyes: A low-cost head-mounted eye-tracking solution. *Proceedings of the 2006 Symposium on Eye-Tracking Research & Applications (ETRA '06),* (pp. 95–100). New York, NY: ACM. doi:10.1145/1117309.1117350

Morimoto, C. H., & Mimica, M. R. M. (2005). Eye gaze tracking techniques for interactive applications. *Computer Vision and Image Understanding, 98*(1), 4–24. doi:10.1016/j.cviu.2004.07.010

Partala, T., & Surakka, V. (2003). Pupil size variation as an indication of affective processing. *International Journal of Human-Computer Studies, 59,* 185–198. doi:10.1016/S1071-5819(03)00017-X

Rayner, K. (1995). Eye movements and cognitive processes in reading, visual search, and scene perception. In Findlay, J. M., Walker, R., & Kentridge, R. W. (Eds.), *Eye movement research: Mechanisms, processes and applications* (pp. 3–22). Amsterdam, The Netherlands: North Holland. doi:10.1016/S0926-907X(05)80003-0

Salvucci, D. D. (1999). Inferring intent in eye-based interfaces: tracing eye movements with process models. *Proceedings of the SIGCHI conference on Human factors in computing systems* (*CHI '99*) (pp. 254–261). New York, NY: ACM. doi:10.1145/302979.303055

Scott, J. (2010). Snapshot of using eye gaze – a professional journey into the world of eye gaze. In Wilson, A., & Gow, R. (Eds.), *The eye have it! The use of eye gaze to support communication* (pp. 7–13). Edinburgh, UK: CALL Scotland, The University of Edinburgh.

Stampe, D. M., & Reingold, E. M. (1995). Selection by looking: A novel computer interface and its application to psychological research. In Findlay, J. M., Walker, R., & Kentridge, R. W. (Eds.), *Eye movement research: mechanisms, processes and applications* (pp. 467–478). Amsterdam, The Netherlands: Elsevier. doi:10.1016/S0926-907X(05)80039-X

Ten Kate, J. H., Frietman, E. E. E., Willems, W., Ter Haar Romeny, B. M., & Tenkink, E. (1979). Eye-switch controlled communication aids. *Proceedings of the 12th International Conference on Medical and Biological Engineering*. Jerusalem, Israel.

Vertegaal, R. (2003). Attentive user interfaces. *Communications of the ACM, 46*(3), 30–33. doi:10.1145/636772.636794

Wade, N. J., & Tatler, B. W. (2005). *The moving tablet of the eye: The origins of modern eye movement research*. Oxford, UK: Oxford University Press.

Yamada, M., & Fukuda, T. (1987). Eye word processor (EWP) and peripheral controller for the ALS patient. *IEE Proceedings Physical Science, Measurement and Instrumentation. Management in Education, 134*(4), 328–330. doi:10.1049/ip-a-1:19870046

Yarbus, A. L. (1967). *Eye movements and vision*. New York, NY: Plenum Press. (Translated from Russian by Basil Haigh. Original Russian edition published in Moscow in 1965.)

Young, L. R., & Sheena, D. (1975). Survey of eye movement recording methods. *Behavior Research Methods, Instruments, & Computers, 7*(5), 397–429. doi:10.3758/BF03201553

Zhai, S., Morimoto, C., & Ihde, S. (1999). Manual and gaze input cascaded (MAGIC) pointing. *Proceedings of the SIGCHI Conference on Human Factors in Computing Systems* (*CHI '99*) (pp. 246–253). New York, NY: ACM. doi:10.1145/302979.303053

Chapter 2
Eye Anatomy, Eye Movements and Vision

Fiona Mulvey
IT University of Copenhagen, Denmark

ABSTRACT

This chapter introduces the basics of eye anatomy, eye movements and vision. It will explain the concepts behind human vision sufficiently for the reader to understand later chapters in the book on human perception and attention, and their relationship to (and potential measurement with) eye movements. We will first describe the path of light from the environment through the structures of the eye and on to the brain, as an introduction to the physiology of vision. We will then describe the image registered by the eye, and the types of movements the eye makes in order to perceive the environment as a cogent whole. This chapter explains how eye movements can be thought of as the interface between the visual world and the brain, and why eye movement data can be analysed not only in terms of the environment, or what is looked at, but also in terms of the brain, or subjective cognitive and emotional states. These two aspects broadly define the scope and applicability of eye movements technology in research and in human computer interaction in later sections of the book.

INTRODUCTION

In order to understand why and how the eye moves, we first need to characterise the image or signal registered by the eye, and how it is processed and organised in the brain. We will see that what is registered is not the same as what is perceived,

and how eye movements relate to both these aspects. This chapter intends to give the reader a good general understanding of vision and the eye. It is not intended to give an exhaustive account of the highly complex structures and functions of the visual system; there are many excellent publications already available for that purpose. Rather, the intention is to outline the basics for a

DOI: 10.4018/978-1-61350-098-9.ch002

multidisciplinary audience who are interested and want to work with eye tracking and gaze-based communication.

As with any area of human anatomy, there is a regrettable amount of specialist terminology which can be daunting to the uninitiated. The reader is advised to bear in mind that long, complicated terminology does not necessarily translate to long, complicated concepts. This chapter will explain the concepts behind human vision sufficiently for the reader to understand later sections in the book on human perception and attention, and their relationship to (and potential measurement with) eye movements. We begin with a description of the path of light energy from the environment through the structures of the eye and on to the brain, as an introduction to the physiology of vision. We will then describe the image registered by the eye, and the types of movements the eye makes in order to perceive the environment as a cogent whole.

PHYSIOLOGY OF VISION

We begin with the major structures light passes through from the environment through the visual system, and trace its path on to the photoreceptive layer of the retina at the back of the eye ball. Figure 1 shows the gross anatomy of the human eye. The first layer which light passes through is the cornea. The cornea is a protective layer around the eyeball which serves to keep the shape of the eye, keep dust and other irritants out, protect the eye from damage, and it also contributes toward the focussing of light towards the retina. It is of fixed shape, translucent, and is responsible for 2/3 of the refracting (or focusing) power of the human eye. The innermost layer of the cornea is the corneal endothelium, a layer responsible for keeping the cornea at the perfect state of hydration for it to remain transparent. It achieves this by regulating flow to and from the 'aqueous humour'; the liquid between the cornea and the iris. Aqueous humour is the next medium light passes through. Its purpose is to keep the cornea under the correct amount of pressure to maintain its shape and it

Figure 1. The gross anatomy of the eye (Adapted from "Schematic diagram of the human eye", 2008. Used under the terms of the GNU Free Documentation License)

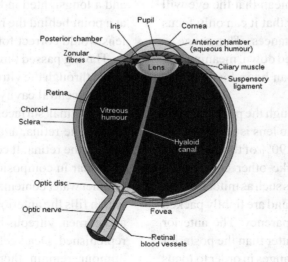

Figure 2. Focusing light from a far away object on the left, and a near object on the right. This changing of the lens shape to focus on objects at varying distances is called accommodation (Adapted from "Focus in an eye", 2007. Used under the terms of the GNU Free Documentation License).

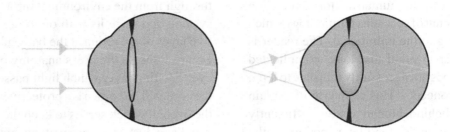

also carries nutrients to the surrounding structures of the anterior chamber, especially the lens.

Having passed through the cornea and anterior chamber, light then passes through the gap in the centre of the iris. The iris is the part of the eye which gives it colour. The function of the iris is to regulate the amount of light entering the eye by contracting and expanding around a central aperture, much like the aperture setting in a photographic camera. Also similar to a camera, the aperture of the iris has an effect on the focal length of the eye. This aperture in the centre of the iris is called the pupil. It can range in size from 1-8mm. The larger the pupil is, the more light gets in, but the shorter the focal length, i.e., the more restricted or narrow the range of distances in focus. This does not necessarily mean that the eye will not see far away, but rather that it can only focus at a reduced range of distances. This range is greater when the iris is closed down, meaning that both near and far objects can be in focus simultaneously.

Light enters the eye through the pupil and then passes through the lens. The lens is composed of water and various proteins. 90% of these proteins are crystallins which, unlike other cells of the body, have no cell organelles such as mitochondria which might obscure light, and are tightly packed together to maintain transparency. The anterior (front) part of the lens is flatter than the posterior (back) surface. Its shape changes in order to focus

on objects at varying distances by means of ciliary muscles which cause it to contract or expand, i.e. make it rounder and thicker, or flatter and thinner (Figure 2). These muscles may deteriorate in some muscular degenerative diseases, which can be an important design factor in gaze control for persons with physical disability.

The lens is responsible for 1/3 of the refractive properties of the eye, and its purpose is to focus light exactly on the retinal surface at the back of the eye. If the lens is not able to attain the perfect shape for this, it commonly focuses light at a point behind the retina, causing short-sightedness, or in front of the retina, causing long-sightedness. Figure 3 shows how the short sighted individual's lens focuses light at a point in front of the retina, and a longsighted individual's lens focuses light at a point behind the retina, and how a corrective lens would correct for this.

Having passed through the lens the light travels on through the vitreous humour, the gel which fills the central cavity of the eye ball, on its way to the retinal surface. This gel stretches all the way to the retina, and is produced by a layer of cells in the retina. It consists mostly of water and is similar in composition to the cornea, but with a higher water content. Unlike the aqueous humour which fills the anterior chamber between the lens and cornea, vitreous humour is not replaced and replenished. Dead cells which enter the vitreous humour remain there forever, often causing

Figure 3. Correction for short-sightedness (left) and long-sightedness (right) using refractive lenses (Adapted from "Myopia", 2007 (left) and "Hypermetropia", 2007 (right). Used under the terms of the GNU Free Documentation License.)

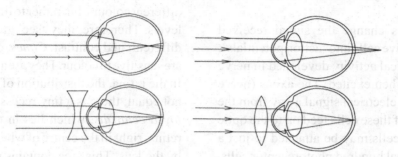

barely perceptible shadows on the retina, which we occasionally see as floating dots in our vision. Vitreous humour gives the eye its shape by putting pressure on the eyeball, much like an inflated balloon. This is important, because an eyeball which is slightly deflated or over inflated has a changed distance between the cornea and the retina, and this has an effect on 'accommodation', that is, the ciliary muscles' action on the lens in response to objects at varying distances. Some pressure is also necessary to maintain the shape of the lens. Some light is lost as it passes through the vitreous humour, hitting dead cells or other bodies.

Finally, having passed through the large chamber of the eyeball, light is focused on the inner surface of the back of the eye; the retina. Understanding the retina and how it operates is essential to understanding why and how the eye moves and how vision is achieved. The human retina lines over two thirds of the inner surface of the eye ball and contains photoreceptive (light-sensitive) cells which respond to light at wavelengths between 350 and 780nm. There are different types of photoreceptive cells, which react to different aspects of the incoming light. Figure 4 shows a schematic diagram of the layers of the retina, with the photoreceptive cells at the outerrmost layer.

The first layer light encounters at the retina contains nerve fibres. Behind this layer are ganglion cells which lead to optic nerve fibres and which pass the signal from the photoreceptive cells on to the brain via the optic nerve. The light thus passes through layers that are involved in the further processing of the signal before actually

Figure 4. The layers of the retina, with light entering from the left (Adapted from "Retine", 2007. Used under the terms of the GNU Free Documentation License)

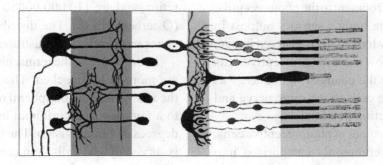

causing the signal in the photoreceptive layer. This is not the case in all animals, but in humans, the photoreceptive layer is behind the conductive cells.

Ganglion cells change the signal received from photoreceptive cells into 'action potentials'; the kind of electrical activity developed in nerve or muscle cells when excited. The axons (nerve fibres which take electrical signal away from the main cell body) of these cells feed on to the optic nerve. Ganglion cells may be attached to just a few or up to several hundred photoreceptor cells. They are actually part of the brain. Having passed through the ganglion cell layer, light travels on through the inner plexiform layer, which contains fibrils linking dendrites (branch-like extensions of the nerve cell which receive information from surrounding cells) from ganglion cells and cells in the inner nuclear layer; on through the inner nuclear layer itself, which contains bipolar cells, horizontal cells and amacrine cells that together are responsible for the input to the ganglion 'junction' like cells; through the outer plexiform layer where the dendrites of horizontal cells synapse (or link together to pass signal) with photoreceptor cells; and through the outer nuclear layer which contains the granules of the rods and cones in the next and final layer; the layer of photoreceptive cells themselves. We will concern ourselves mostly with this final layer, since it has direct relevance for a basic understanding of how and why the eye moves.

The purpose of this chapter is to introduce the major concepts involved to a multidisciplinary audience. Therefore, having briefly followed light on its path from the environment to the photoreceptive cells which form the brain's sensory outpost in the eye, we will now look at the registered image, which is related to how these photoreceptive cells operate, and follow the changed light energy as it travels from these cells to the optic nerve and on to the brain as action potentials.

There are various types of photoreceptive cells, but they are most commonly categorised into two types: rods and cones. *Rods* are sensitive to changes in light and shade, and highly sensitive to movement. They do not respond differently to different colours, but rather to different brightness levels. Therefore, they 'see' greyscale with well differentiated contrast. *Cones*, on the other hand, are sensitive to colour. They are also smaller in size. In the retina, the distribution of rods and cones is not equal; there is a tiny recess of the retina, the *fovea centralis*, which lies in the middle of the retina, right in the centre of where light is focused by the lens. This area contains most of the cones in the retina. It is circular, about 1 to 1.5 mm in diameter. The central 250 μm or so of the fovea centralis has no rods at all, but only cones (Ahnelt, & Pflug, 1986). The rest of the approximately 1,000 square mm of the retina beyond the fovea centralis is largely taken up with rods. Outside the fovea centralis cones are very sparse or absent. This means that colour vision is restricted to the central one or two degrees of vision, while the rest of the 160 deg (w) x 175 deg (h) field of vision for each eye is largely greyscale. So, considering this very restricted part of the visual field in which we register colour information, we can see immediately that in order to perceive colour from the entire visual field, the eye has to move, and the brain remembers the colour registered for each thing the eye stops on. Otherwise, colours would appear to flash on and off with each small movement of the eye. It's important to consider that the *perception* of colour from the entire visual field is due to higher processing of the signal by the brain. The *sensation* of colour is however restricted to central vision[1]. There are 6,400,000 cones in the retina, and are 110,000,000 to 125,000,000 rods (Osterberg, 1935). The distribution of rods and cones in the retina is illustrated in Figure 5.

In the centre of the retina, photoreceptive cells are more tightly packed. The density decreases the further into the peripheral retina we go, down to a fairly constant minimal level outside 5 to 7 degrees of central vision. Thus, peripheral vision is served by less cells than central vision, with a

Figure 5. The distribution of rods and cones in the retina (Osterberg, 1935)

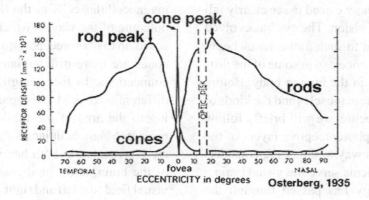

corresponding loss of acuity (you might think of this as analogous to a loss in dpi, or pixels per cm). Further contributing to this, the cells in the fovea are served by so-called 'midget ganglion cells' which link to about 5 or so photoreceptors. The cells in the periphery tend to be served by larger ganglion cells which may link to over one hundred photoreceptors. The loss of acuity due to loss of colour vision, increasing size of photo-receptive cells and decreasing density of photo-receptive cells in peripheral vision, is further exacerbated by the fact that those cells which are there tend to be wired up together to fewer ganglion cells, meaning their individual signals will be transferred on to the brain by an amalgamated signal from one ganglion. Figure 6 illustrates the drop in acuity due to all of these factors.

This brings us to the second important characteristic of the registered image in terms of understanding why the eye moves; only the central degree or so of the viewed scene is registered with high acuity. So, we have characterised the registered image in two important ways; outside of a tiny central portion, it is basically colourless, and of low resolution. This is why although the fovea makes up only a tiny part of the retina, the signal which comes from it, when mapped to the cortex of the brain, takes up over 50% of the area of the cortex involved with visual processing[2]. We would not be able to identify objects or do detailed work based on the majority of our visual

Figure 6. Visual acuity in the human retina in degrees of vision from central vision (Adapted from "AcuityHumanEye", 2009. Used under the terms of the GNU Free Documentation License)

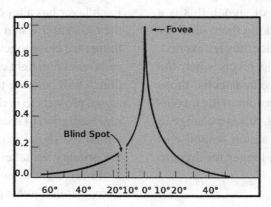

field. In order to do so, we must align our eye so that all objects or areas we need to see clearly fall at the central axis of vision. The eye has evolved to be perfectly suited to such movements, being round, smooth, and connected to some of the fastest moving muscles in the human body. Before going on to look at these muscles and the kinds of movements they execute, we will briefly follow the signal from the photoreceptive layers of the retina as it makes its way to the brain, considering how eye movements serve the visual brain.

Once light energy has passed through the various structures of the retina and is turned into action potentials in the ganglion cells, it is passed through the optic tract to the lateral geniculate nucleus, or LGN, which is found in the thalamus, a region win the very centre of the brain. In terms of evolution, this is a very old part of the brain. Its function is to relay sensory information taken from the environment, send movement signals on to the cerebral cortex and to regulate consciousness and sleep. From the LGN, the signal is sent on to the primary visual cortex, or striate cortex. The LGN has six layers. The inner two of these layers are called magnocellular layers, and the outer four are called parvocellular layers. Here we see the differentiated topography of the retina repeated at a neural level; the magnocellular layers contain the projections from rods, whereas the parvocellular layers contain projections from cones. In a similar fashion to the rods and cones in the retina, the magnocellular cells are large, but respond quickly to changes in brightness of the incoming light (in terms of signal, this is a change in the amplitude), making them ideal for sensing movement rapidly. Once they are excited, they quickly return to resting levels when the stimulus is removed. Parvocellular cells, those responding to changes in the colour of the incoming light (or in terms of signal, this is a change in frequency), are small, their action response is relatively slower and it takes longer for them to return to resting levels.

There are nine times more parvocellular than magnocellular cells in the thalamus. This is an outcome of the way in which ganglion cells are wired up to photoreceptors; as mentioned earlier, cones are more differentiated in their ganglion connections. In fact, ganglion cells are further differentiated as M and P ganglion cells according to the area of the thalamus to which they project. Magnocellular and parvocellular layers are represented in both hemispheres (or halves) of the brain, and signal from the left and right visual field (the left and right of the retinas in each eyeball) is passed on differentially to the right and left hemispheres. The signal from the left visual field (i.e. the left hand side of what both the left and right eye registers) is passed on to the right hemisphere, and the signal from the right visual field is passed on to the left hemisphere. This means that the side of the visual field registered in the parts of the retina which are closest to the nose are transferred to their opposite sides of the brain. In anatomical terms, we use the term ipsilateral to refer to the eye which is on the same side as the visual field in question, and contralateral to refer to the eye which is on the opposite side to the visual field in question. In terms of eye tracking for gaze control, this may be important if the user has visual impairment on one or other side of the visual field. For each half of the LGN, we can trace the projections of the ipsilateral eye (the eye on the same side) to LGN layers 2, 3 and 5, and the projections of the contralateral eye (the eye on the opposite side) to layers 1, 4 and 5. Each layer has a topographical representation of the retina and visual field, in other words, if two things are close together in the viewed scene, the cells receiving light energy reflected by those two things will be close together in the layer that the signal projects to in the brain. This topographical representation of space continues in the next area which the signal is passed to as it is processed; the primary visual cortex.

From the thalamus, the magnocellular and parvocellular layers project signal to the primary visual cortex, also known as V1. This area of the cortex is at the back of the head, in the part of the brain known as the occipital lobe. Here, the central 10 degrees of vision sends signal to 80% of the cells in V1, but the topographical representation of space remains intact. The separation of magno- and parvo-cellular signal into different layers is also present in V1. From the primary visual cortex the signal passes on through two major pathways of vision in humans, the dorsal and ventral visual streams. We will come across these two streams of visual processing again later in the book when we look at some of the measures of cognitive and emotional states, which cognitive psychology suggests may be measurable from eye movements. The dorsal stream is known to be involved with movement and spatial relationships, while the ventral stream is associated with object identification. For a long time, the dorsal stream was thought to be dominated by signal from parvocellular layers of the LGN, i.e. P ganglion cells, i.e. from mostly rods, and mostly peripheral vision. The ventral stream was correspondingly associated with magnocellular layers of the LGN, i.e. M ganglion cells, i.e. mostly cones, and mostly signal from the fovea centralis. There does seem to be a rather modular division of labour, however, there is also evidence of much interconnectedness, so that a purely modular explanation is likely to be a simplification. Some simplifications are, however, useful; there is evidence of measurable differences in the eye movements associated with these two 'where' and 'what' modes of processing.

TYPES OF EYE MOVEMENTS

We will now describe the kinds of movements that the eye makes to sample the visual environment. It is important to bear in mind the nature of the sampled data in terms of the limitations of the retina and the richness of our perception of our world. Despite the limitations of the registered or 'sensed' image, we perceive a rich, detailed and three dimensional world with such apparent accu-

racy that we can extend a hand to catch a moving ball, or recognise a familiar face in a crowd, or even read this text with the perception of a page of clear text when actually only a few letters are clearly identifiable from the registered image at any one time. These rich perceptions are the result of the fact that the eye can move fast, and the brain can put together all the imperfect visual 'samples' gathered by the eye when it is stopped into a highly complex, uninterrupted and continuously updated perception of the environment and the information it contains, unconsciously and seemingly instantly, or at least, exactly as we need it to, with few exceptions. The brain not only reacts to stimulus, but also seeks out the right information at the right time for a subjectively perfect perception of space to move about in, manipulate, and achieve higher order cognitive tasks. There is a lot of processing of this simple registered image. The muscles of the eyeball have to be quick and accurate, and the movements are not just a function of what is contained in the environment but also of what we are trying to do cognitively. Thus, both the spatial and temporal aspects of these movements are important outputs of the actively perceiving brain and eye movements may be thought of as both the primary input, and the primary output of the seeing brain. This connection between eye movements and the external environment, as well as between eye movements and internal, subjective perception, make eye movements unique in terms of providing a direct trace of information between brain and environment, or, brain and computer.

Each eye has six muscles attached to the outer side of the eyeball. These are called the inferior rectus, the superior rectus, the lateral rectus, the medial rectus, the inferior oblique, and the superior oblique. When these muscles are activated, torque is exerted on the globe so that it rotates almost perfectly (with about 1mm of translation – or sideways movement) around a centre point.

The movements made by the eye are classified as: *saccades*, or orienting 'jumps' which direct both eyes concurrently towards intended objects or attention eliciting events; *fixations*, which describe stopping the eye to allow further processing of the currently registered visual stimulus; *smooth pursuit* movements which follow a moving object by matching the speed and direction of the muscle movement to the speed and direction of the moving stimulus; *vergence movements* which serve to bring an object at close range onto both retinas (i.e. what happens if you make yourself go 'cross-eyed' by focusing on your finger in front of your nose) and tiny jittering *microsaccades* which occur during a fixation and are understood to be either biological noise, or serve to function mainly to maintain optimal activation of the photoreceptors, although some research also suggests a relationship to covert (or unconscious) attention (e.g., Martinez-Conde, Macknik, & Hubel, 2004; Hafed, & Clarke, 2002). Not all eye trackers have sufficient accuracy, precision and sample rate to detect microsaccades. Most intended for gaze control purposes currently cannot detect these tiny movements.

There are also the internal movements of the parts of the eye, such as pupil dilation and focussing of the lens. Another type of eye movement, the *vestibulo-ocular reflex*, stabilizes the images on the retina during head movements. For example, if you look at this word, and keep looking at it while turning your head from left to right, your eye will move about in relation to the head, as a reflex action to maintain visual input.

Another reflex movement of the eye is the *optokinetic reflex*, which is similar to both saccades and smooth pursuit, and contains elements of both types of movements. When, for example, looking out of a car window, the eyes can focus on passing railings or fence posts for a brief moment (through smooth pursuit), until it passes out of visual range. As it passes, the optokinetic reflex kicks in and moves the eye back to where it first focused on the fence post (through a saccade) and follow the next one, in succession.

Table 1 summarises the taxonomy of eye movements.

Movements which direct the line of sight to new parts of the visual field, i.e. saccades, are not random, but are elicited by either environmental or cognitive control. This means that the brain sends the eye to focus central vision on certain kinds of stimuli automatically, unconsciously, and uncontrollably, when something which evolution has considered to be important occurs in the environment. This is called exogneous control, meaning outside the individual. During uninterrupted cognitive tasks, where we are using our eyes purposefully to get something done, we have

Table 1. Types of eye movements

Type of eye movement	Common or standard definition
Fixation	>100 ms within 1 degree of vision.
Saccade	Movement to new areas of the visual field greater than 2 degrees.
Microsaccade	Very small movements which occur irregularly during a saccade.
Smooth pursuit	Movement of the eye to follow a moving target with the same velocity and trajectory as the target.
Vergence	Movement of the eyes inward, i.e. in opposite directions, to offset retinal disparity for close objects.
Vestibular ocular reflex (VOR)	Movements to maintain the point of regard during head movements.
Optokinetic reflex	Saccade-smooth pursuit movements to focus on moving scenes.
Accommodation	Changes in the shape of the lens to focus light from objects at varying distances.
Pupil dilation	Changes in the size of the aperture in the iris in order to maintain optimal light levels inside the eye.

conscious control. This is endogenous control, meaning inside the individual. Saccades are fast, ballistic movements; the eye rotates at speeds of up to 500° per second 3-4 times per second (Richardson, & Spivey, 2005). The sensitivity of the eye drops almost to blindness during a saccade (Thiele, Henning, Kubischik, & Hoffmann, 2002). This may sound surprising, considering how often it moves, but consider the consequences if it didn't; the world would jump around with each eye movement, something like what we would register on a video camera if we shake it about while recording. We make up this lost input seamlessly using the brain. Thus, information from the visual world is collected while the eye is stopped. During the periods of about 100-1200ms when the eye is relatively still, the 50,000 or so photoreceptors in the fovea (Tyler, 1997) transmit high acuity visual information.

Measuring eye movements involves examining the number and duration of fixations (which areas were registered by the fovea during relatively still periods), the sequence of locations fixated, often in terms of scanpath (the journey the eye makes travelling over a particular stimulus) or particular areas of interest we want to know were looked at and the speed and length of the jumps made between fixations in order to select further information. Eye trackers may also measure pupil size or compare the movements of the two eyes to calculate the gaze position in a three dimensional space or track which eye might have a speed advantage in reacting to shifts of attention to the periphery. Not all eye trackers are capable of measuring the whole range of eye movements. For point-and-click gaze control purposes, it currently suffices to measure fixations (or dwell times) and saccades (one or other often measured by default, as the distance or time delay between each type of event). There are a number of ways of recording such movements (briefly introduced below). Earliest methods involved attaching equipment to the eye itself, and such methods are still the most accurate. For research purposes, if high temporal

and spatial accuracy are necessary to reliably measure, smooth pursuit, saccade velocity or microsaccadic activity, video cameras and light sources are often mounted onto the head (for an example of a head-mounted eye tracker, see later section of this book on hardware). When natural movement and user comfort is a higher priority than fine accuracy, remote tracking often suffices for research purposes, provided that the temporal resolution and spatial accuracy is reasonably good. In such systems the observer may not even be aware that their eye movements are being recorded. These are also the kinds of eyetrackers most commonly used for gaze interaction today.

REFERENCES

AcuityHumanEye [Image file] (2009). *Wikimedia commons*. Retrieved from http://en.wikipedia.org/wiki/ File:AcuityHumanEye.svg

Ahnelt, P. K., & Pflug, R. (1986). Telodendrial contacts between foveolar cone pedicles in the human retina. *Experientia*, *42*, 298–300. doi:10.1007/BF01942512

Focus in an eye [Image file] (2007). *Wikimedia commons*. Retrieved from http://en.wikipedia.org/wiki/ File:Focus_in_an_eye.svg

Hafed, Z. M., & Clark, J. J. (2003). Detecting patterns of covert attention shifts in psychophysical tasks using microsaccades [Abstract]. *Journal of Vision (Charlottesville, Va.)*, *3*(9), 183. doi:10.1167/3.9.183

Hypermetropia [Image file] (2007). *Wikimedia commons*. Retrieved from http://en.wikipedia.org/wiki/ File:Hypermetropia.svg

Martinez-Conde, S., Macknik, S. L., & Hubel, D. H. (2004). The role of fixational eye movements in visual perception. *Nature Reviews. Neuroscience*, *5*, 229–240. doi:10.1038/nrn1348

Myopia [Image file] (2007). *Wikimedia commons*. Retrieved from http://en.wikipedia.org/wiki/File:Myopia.svg

Osterberg, G. (1935). Topography of the layer of rods and cones in the human retina. *Acta Ophthalmologica, 6*(suppl.), 1–103.

Retine [Image file] (2007). *Wikimedia commons*. Retrieved from http://en.wikipedia.org/wiki/File:Fig_retine.png

Richardson, D. C., & Spivey, M. J. (2005). Eye-tracking: Characteristics and methods, In G. Wnek & G. Bowlin (Eds.) *Encyclopedia of Biomaterials and Biomedical Engineering, 1*(1). Retrieved May 31, 2006, from http://www.dekker.com/sdek/abstract ~db=enc~content=a713554053UT

Schematic diagram of the human eye [Image file] (2008). *Wikimedia commons*. Retrieved from http://commons.wikimedia.org/wiki/File:Schematic_diagram_of_the_human_eye_en.svg

Thiele, A., Henning, P., Kubischik, M., & Hoffmann, K. P. (2002). Neural mechanisms of saccadic suppression. *Science, 295*(5564), 2460–2462. doi:10.1126/science.1068788

Tyler, C. W. (1997). Analysis of human receptor density . In Lakshminarayanan, V. (Ed.), *Basic and clinical applications of vision science* (pp. 83–89). Norwell, MA: Kluwer Academic.

ENDNOTES

[1] This could be a design issue when using gaze control, for example, if changing the colour of objects outside the main area of interest or work area, perhaps to activate a button or display a message, a level of brightness and contrast change is more readily noticed than the equivalent level of colour change.

[2] The cortex is the outermost layer of the brain, from the Latin word for 'bark'.

Chapter 3
Basics of Camera–Based Gaze Tracking

Dan Witzner Hansen
IT University of Copenhagen, Denmark

Päivi Majaranta
University of Tampere, Finland

ABSTRACT

Most of the studies presented in this book use camera-based gaze trackers, used to monitor where the user is looking on screen or in the 3D environment. While a gaze tracker may resemble a blackbox device that miraculously determines the point of gaze, it actually consists of several hardware and software components with specific purposes. This chapter gives a brief introduction to the typical setup, composition and operating principles of eye and gaze tracking and it provides a simplified overview of camera-based gaze trackers that will be of use to all readers of this book.

INTRODUCTION

Most of the studies presented in this book use camera-based gaze trackers, used to monitor where the user is looking on screen or in the 3D environment. Since it is possible to determine where the user is looking on screen, it is also possible to use the tracker interactively, for example through gaze-controlled movement of the cursor.

While a gaze tracker may resemble a blackbox device that miraculously determines the point of

gaze, it in fact consists of several hardware and software components with specific purposes. Camera(s), IR light sources and perhaps a device for rotating the camera(s) according to the user location (pan-tilt) are hardware components often found in current gaze trackers.

Dodge and Cline's "Dodge Photochronograph", introduced in Chapter 1, was perhaps the first camera-based eye tracker (Wade, & Tatler, 2005). Since then, hardware has become smaller, faster and provides better image data; even cheap web cameras can nowadays be used as reasonably good eye trackers (Hansen, & Pece, 2005). The

DOI: 10.4018/978-1-61350-098-9.ch003

technology has, in fact, become so readily available that today there is very little to prevent everyone from having their own eye tracker. Although we have come a long way since Dodge and Cline first proposed their "Photochronograph" and the technology has much improved, most eye trackers used today are, fundamentally, photochronographs. Eye trackers still use corneal reflections and pupil information, but developments in the models used for eye and gaze tracking have lead to fast and accurate gaze trackers that allow user head movement. For a comprehensive review we refer to Hansen & Ji, 2010.

This chapter gives a brief introduction to the typical setup, composition and operating principles of eye and gaze trackers. It provides a simplified overview of camera-based gaze trackers that will be of use to all readers of this book. Advanced readers can find an in-depth description and guidelines for building their own gaze tracker in Section 6.

BASIC SETUP

A typical gaze tracking system *setup* includes a video camera to record the movements of the eye(s) and a computer to analyse the gaze data. In addition, infrared (IR) light sources are often also used to help improve the accuracy of gaze position tracking. The details and reasons for the use of IR are explained below.

With remote systems, the user sits in front of the monitor on which the information is presented and the gaze tracking system maps the user's gaze vector as screen co-ordinates. The gaze position information can then be exploited by any application that has become gaze-aware. Figure 1 shows a fairly typical setup, with the camera placed below the computer screen, IR emitters located on both sides of the camera and a user sitting in front of and looking at the screen. For demonstration purposes, instead of a gaze-aware application, the figure shows the setup screen

Figure 1. The SeeTech system (www.see-tech.de) tracks both eyes, which can be more accurate than single eye tracking (© 2008 COGAIN. Used with permission)

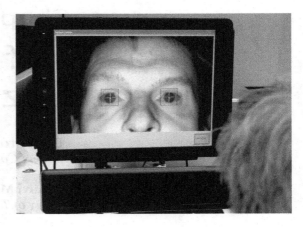

which the user uses to verify that the system is tracking both eyes properly.

Since the tracking is based on eye movements, the system must have an unobstructed view of the eye and the pupil. Remote systems usually have set limits for the optimal distance and angle at which the gaze tracker is able to track the eye reliably. There are also differences between different gaze tracking systems in how much head movement they tolerate and where on the screen they are most accurate. Other potential reasons why the tracker may (momentarily) lose the eye include, for example, varying light conditions, additional reflections caused by glasses or contact lenses, drooping eyelids, heavy makeup, thick glasses, coloured contact lenses, or even narrow framed glasses which can partially block the line of view to the pupil (Goldberg & Wichansky, 2003; Bojko, 2005). Modern trackers have improved substantially in their ability to track almost anybody. However, certain limitations still remain. For example, the user might squint while laughing or accidentally block the camera with their hand. Fortunately, current trackers are often able to resume tracking as soon as the view of the eye(s) is restored.

COMPONENTS OF A CAMERA-BASED GAZE TRACKER

Gaze tracking software usually consists of a component that detects the eyes and tracks their movement within an image, and a component that uses the information from the detected eye to determine where the user is looking (Figure 2, depicts a typical setup). Initially, the gaze tracker captures images from the camera and detects the location of the eye(s) in the image. The user's gaze direction is influenced by their head movements. To counteract this, earlier systems required the head to be fixated using, for example, head rests or bite bars to control head movement. As the hardware became mobile, eye tracking technology developed into the two main types found today, namely head-mounted and remote eye trackers.

Remote eye tracking methods are non-invasive and therefore cause little discomfort to the user. They can sample eye position at up to 500hz or more, although most eye trackers used for gaze control are not quite so responsive, operating at around 50–120hz. Current remote eye trackers have limited mobility. Head-mounted systems are therefore used in mobile situations where the tracker can follow the user. Although coil-based eye tracking is still used for monitoring very fast or very tiny movements and when high temporal and spatial resolution is required, remote tracking is generally preferred, not least because the discomfort of contact lens methods interferes with normal eye movement (Richardson & Spivey, 2005). Coil-based methods are also limited by the need for head fixation or additional methods of determining head orientation.

Cameras and their *lenses* are central to most eye trackers. The eye trackers need high resolution images to obtain high accuracy gaze estimation. The focal length (zoom) of the lens specifies the working distances for the eye tracker. Using a lens with a large focal length (large zoom) provides a close-up image of the eye, while allowing the user to sit further from the camera. When using large focal lengths, however, small head movements can result in large eye movements within the image. Until recently this required a trade-off decision by the manufacturers, who had to choose between allowing the users more freedom of head movement or higher accuracy. Pan-tilt units allow the camera to move and can be used to obtain close-up images of the eye while the user moves their head. Pan-tilt units may not always be sufficiently fast for human head movements and can add to the price

Figure 2. The camera tracks not only the centre of the pupil but also the corneal reflection (Adapted from Goni, Echeto, Villanueva, & Cabeza, 2004)

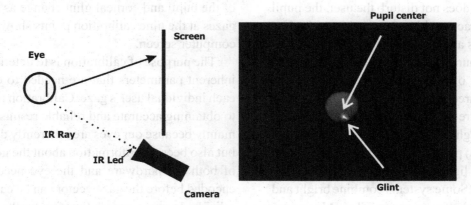

of the eye tracker. The frame rate and latencies of the camera describes how many images are taken per second and how long it takes for the images to be available for further processing. High frame rates and low latencies are preferred as this gives more responsive eye trackers, but these cameras are also more expensive and require better light conditions. Eye positions can be sampled at over 2000 Hz. In recent years cameras have become very cheap (<20 euros), with high resolution (HD quality or better), high frame rates and low latencies. The higher resolution images allow for the use of wider-angle lenses which, in turn, allows for larger head movements while maintaining high accuracy eye images. Higher frame rates means that the eye trackers can be made very responsive (for interactive purposes) and get information on subtle eye movements that only very expensive eye trackers are currently able to capture; and for only a fraction of the price. Within the foreseeable future, price will cease to be a barrier to the emergence of high quality eye trackers for everyday use.

Only one component type remains to be described – light sources. Most gaze trackers use infrared light (IR) to ensure that the point of gaze can be determined during day or night and even when moving the head. However, IR also serves several other purposes in addition to gaze estimation. It ensures that the eye is sufficiently lit for better image analysis without disturbing the user. Since IR does not disturb the user, the pupil does not contract, making eye tracking a lot less problematic as a result.

The light sources generate reflections or 'glints' on the cornea of the eye (see Figure 2, on the right). Gaze direction is calculated by measuring the changing relationship between the moving bright (if the light is aimed on-axis) or dark (light aimed off-axis) pupil of the eye and the reflection of the infrared light source back from the surface of the cornea. (Some systems combine bright and dark pupil for better accuracy, Zhai, Morimoto, & Ihde, 1999.) When looking towards a light

source the location of the glint will, naturally, be very close to the centre of the pupil. As the user gradually looks away from the light source, the distance between the light source and the pupil centre increases. The light source thus actually provides a measure of gaze direction and enables calculation of the gaze direction vector of the eye (and subsequently the translation of the vector into screen co-ordinates). The position of the corneal glint remains relatively constant during rotation of the eye and changes in gaze direction, thus giving a basic eye and head position reference. In practice, however, if the user rotates or turns their head, the corneal glint will correspondingly move. It is therefore difficult to distinguish head movements and eye movements with a single light source. The net-effect of IR light, used primarily for indoor applications, is that it removes the need for an explicit device to estimate head orientation and therefore reduces production costs while also providing better image data. More details on how reflections on the cornea can be used for gaze estimation are provided in Section 6, and the area is reviewed in Hansen & Ji, 2010.

CALIBRATION AND ACCURACY

Calibration, a vital aspect of gaze tracker use, is performed by having the user look at a set of on-screen targets. Figure 3 illustrates how the position of the pupil and corneal glint change as the user gazes at the nine calibration points shown on the computer screen.

The purpose of calibration is to determine the inherent parameters that are needed to estimate each individual user's gaze. Calibration is crucial to obtaining accurate and reliable results. This is mainly because our eyes are inherently different, but also because information about the geometry of both the hardware and the eye needs to be encoded before the gaze vector can be calculated reliably. In some gaze estimation methods, such as those used in most commercial gaze trackers,

Figure 3. An illustration of pupil and corneal reflections as seen by the eye tracker's camera at each of the nine calibration points (left) and an image taken by an eye tracker's video camera (right)(Adapted from Majaranta, Bates & Donegan, 2009)

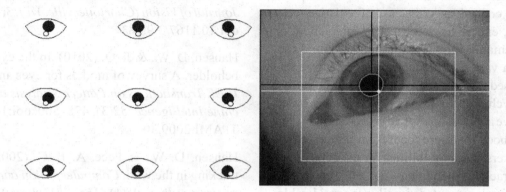

most of the parameters used to encode geometric relationships are known prior to use. The manufacturers have invested time and money in fixing the locations of their hardware (cameras, light sources and monitor) so that their geometric relationships are known. If these parameters are known, then fewer parameters need to be inferred by the calibration process and, therefore, fewer calibration targets are needed. However, the number of calibration targets may change due to the actual gaze estimation method used and for robustness considerations. In cases where the locations of the hardware components are unknown prior to use, more calibration targets would usually be required. However, such solutions often offer more flexibility as to where the cameras and light sources are located and to the mobility of the gaze tracker.

Most current (remote) eye tracking devices claim an accuracy of 0.5 degrees (equivalent to a region of approximately 15 pixels on a 17" display with a resolution of 1024x768 pixels viewed from a distance of 70 cm). The practical accuracy may be less due to 'drifting' where, with continued use, the measured point of gaze drifts away from the actual point of gaze. Drift can have a number of causes, such as light changes or changes in pupil size, but is mainly due to the underlying eye and

gaze models. The effects of drifting can be adjusted and dynamically corrected through prior knowledge of the user interface (e.g. by knowing the locations of buttons, see Stampe & Reingold, 1995) or through various ad-hoc measures. Newer eye-tracking systems have built-in techniques for preventing drift, for example, using the calibration data (Hansen, San Agustin, Villanueva, 2010) or by combining information from both eyes. Binocular gaze trackers usually provide quite robust results and limit drifting, therefore saving the user from continuous recalibration. Ultimately, however, the best way to eliminate drifting is by developing more capable eye and gaze models.

CONCLUSION

Current eye tracking technology provides the means for high-precision tracking of the human eye. This book introduces and describes the current state of the art of the highly multidisciplinary area of gaze-based communication, as presented by top experts in the fields of interface design, e-inclusion and assistive technologies, engineering, computer science and cognitive psychology. As a textbook, the COGAIN book aims to provide a broad but sufficiently thorough insight into eye tracking research and technology within the context of gaze-based communication. This communication can take the form of computer interface control, as in the case of assistive technologies, expert–novice learning interaction, or future human–computer communication and data flow in a variety of conceivable interactive settings based on measures suggested in cognitive neuropsychological research. Most gaze-based interactive applications use a camera-based system and this book therefore focuses on camera-based eye trackers. The possibilities for the application of eye tracking technology in scenarios where information is presented visually are considerable.

REFERENCES

Bojko, A. (2005). Eye tracking in user experience testing: How to make the most of it. *Proceedings of the 14ᵗʰ Annual Conference of the Usability Professionals Association* (UPA), Montreal, Canada. Retrieved from the User Centric, Inc. website: http://www.usercentric.com/publications/2005

Duchowski, A. T. (2003). *Eye tracking methodology: Theory and practice*. London, UK: Springer-Verlag.

Goldberg, J. H., & Wichansky, A. M. (2003). Eye tracking in usability evaluation: A practitioner's guide . In Hyönä, J., Radach, R., & Deubel, H. (Eds.), *The mind's eye: Cognitive and applied aspects of eye movement research* (pp. 493–516). Amsterdam, The Netherlands: North-Holland.

Goni, S., Echeto, J., Villanueva, A., & Cabeza, R. (2004). Robust algorithm for pupil-glint vector detection in a video-oculography eyetracking system. *Proceedings of the 17ᵗʰ International Conference on Pattern* Recognition (ICPR'04) (vol. 4, pp. 941–944). Washington, DC., USA: IEEE Computer Society. doi:10.1109/ICPR.2004.1333928

Hafed, Z. M., & Clark, J. J. (2003). Detecting patterns of covert attention shifts in psychophysical tasks using microsaccades [Abstract]. *Journal of Vision (Charlottesville, Va.)*, *3*(9), 183. doi:10.1167/3.9.183

Hansen, D. W., & Ji, Q. (2010). In the eye of the beholder: A survey of models for eyes and gaze. *IEEE Transactions on Pattern Analysis and Machine Intelligence*, *32*(3), 478–500. doi:10.1109/TPAMI.2009.30

Hansen, D. W., & Pece, A. E. C. (2005). Eye tracking in the wild. *Computer Vision and Image Understanding*, *98*(1), 155–181. doi:10.1016/j.cviu.2004.07.013

Hansen, D. W., San Agustin, J., & Villanueva, A. (2010). Homography normalization for robust gaze estimation in uncalibrated setups. *Proceedings of the 2010 Symposium on Eye-Tracking Research & Applications* (ETRA '10) (pp. 13–20). New York, NY: ACM. doi:10.1145/1743666.1743670

Majaranta, P., Bates, R., & Donegan, M. (2009). Eye tracking. In C. Stephanidis (Ed.), *The universal access handbook* (pp. 36:1–20). CRC Press, Taylor & Francis Group.

Richardson, D. C., & Spivey, M. J. (2004). Eye-tracking: Characteristics and methods . In Wnek, G., & Bowlin, G. L. (Eds.), *Encyclopedia of biomaterials and biomedical engineering* (pp. 568–572). New York, NY: Marcel Dekker, Inc.

Wade, N. J., & Tatler, B. W. (2005). *The moving tablet of the eye: The origins of modern eye movement research*. Oxford, UK: Oxford University Press.

Zhai, S., Morimoto, C., & Ihde, S. (1999). Manual and gaze input cascaded (MAGIC) pointing. *Proceedings of the SIGCHI conference on Human factors in computing systems (CHI '99)*, (pp. 246–253). New York, NY: ACM. doi:10.1145/302979.303053

Section 2
User Involvement

Chapter 4
Features of Gaze Control Systems

Mick Donegan
ACE Centre, UK

ABSTRACT

Severely disabled people will often spend a significant part of their waking day using gaze control. Technology has a positive impact on many areas of their life. What simple features do people who have severe and complex disabilities need to use gaze control technology? In this chapter, we consider features that are enhancing the effective use of this innovative and rapidly growing method of computer control. It also provides practical hints in finding and choosing the best gaze control system for each individual.

INTRODUCTION

Originally, gaze control appealed to people who had eye movement, but very limited movement in other parts of their body. Now, there are a burgeoning number of companies who pitch gaze control systems at the disabled population. Gaze control is a rapidly developing field, in the wake of this wave of innovation it is no longer disregarded by those who have involuntary movement. By broadening its appeal, there are many people who

have severe and complex disabilities that rely on this method of computer control.

In comparison to other methods, participants in the COGAIN project have reported on gaze control offering greater comfort, speed, accuracy, privacy and independence (Donegan et al., 2009). Further in-depth information is presented in the COGAIN report entitled 'D3.2 Report on features of the different systems and development needs' (Donegan et al., 2006a). Inevitably, striking new features will emerge, as this technology continues to seize the imagination of end-users and researchers. This chapter describes a mere sample of the basic features, and principles, as they are at the

DOI: 10.4018/978-1-61350-098-9.ch004

time of writing. Herein it reflects the perspective of those who are new to this field.

CHOOSING THE BEST SYSTEM FOR EACH INDIVIDUAL

The first question to ask is: "which gaze control system is best for me?" In surmising this question, three simple principles are captured by The KEE concept by Donegan and Oosthuizen (2006a). These are as follows:

- **K**nowledge-based: founded on what is known of the user's physical and cognitive abilities;
- **E**nd-user focused: designed to meet the end-users' interests and needs;
- **E**volutionary: ready to change in relation to the end-users response to gaze control technology and software provided.

This concept provides a framework for finding the system that best meets the needs of each individual

Throughout the COGAIN user trials, the prime concern regarding the motor and cognitive skills of users was the demands of involuntary movement. To refer to how and why systems are able to tolerate involuntary movement, please see section 6 of this book. Devices differ in the degree of involuntary movement they do comfortably tolerate. It seems obvious to say that the physical ability of the individual determines how important this is and to what degree. So this feature shall be introduced through a sample of typical gaze control users. The four brief paragraphs that follow present examples of people who have Motor Neurone Disease (MND), Cerebral Palsy (CP), a Spinal Cord Injury and Locked-In Syndrome.

Describing the ways in which gaze control is of real benefit, encounter Jack Orchard, who appears in a video on the LC Technologies (2011) website. In a news item aired on KSDK-TV Jack says "there is so much left to do, so for now, back

to work." Jack experiences Amyotrophic Lateral Sclerosis (ALS), one form of MND. Like anyone else, fulfilling purposeful roles is his "lifeline" (see, LC Technologies, 2011). Evidently, gaze control gives him the means to socially communicate; be creative; and regain independence. Jack is excellent at using his gaze control system and has, in fact, written an entire book with it (Quintero, 2009). Tolerating involuntary movement isn't essential. What is essential, however, is reliability; as Jack's girlfriend says, "as soon as he gets up and is ready he is at his computer". For people whose health is deteriorating, timely and flexible assistance is envisaged, since the software settings and user interface will need to evolve over time

For more information about MND, please see the websites of the MND Association (www.mndassociation.org). For people based in England, please see NHS Choices (www.nhs.uk). The training section of the COGAIN wiki (2011) has online videos related to ALS communication.

By way of contrast, people who have CP have to adopt gaze control systems that support involuntary movement. CP is not a specific disorder or single syndrome; it assumes different forms (Merck Manuals Online, 2001). For example, people who have Athetoid Cerebral Palsy can experience involuntary movement such as a mobile spasm, a fleeting irregular localised contraction or an intermittent tonic spasm, etc. The MyTobii website introduces individuals who have Athetoid CP, evidencing the efficiency of this access method (User Stories, 2011).

Spinal Cord Injury similarly might cause involuntary movement. Sarah has a high cervical injury and good head control. In her case, she prefers to use gaze control over a mouth stick. For her, the particular strengths of gaze control are made clear. It is more comfortable, direct and faster than a mouth stick because of the speed of eye movement. The major weakness of the mouth stick is the need to keep her head still while she waits for a mouse click; which becomes tiring and painful over time (Yeo, 2006). The differences between gaze control systems are often quite subtle and subjective so best to compare several, in order to discern which one is perceived to be the best for the individual.

The COGAIN project has revealed that people who have Locked-In Syndrome work at the limits of gaze control technology. This group are paralyzed in all of their voluntary muscles, except for their eyes. These move in a vertical plane. They experience involuntary eye movement. Further information is available at the website of 'The National Institute of Neurological Disorders and Stroke' at www.ninds.nih.gov. As a result of having complex visual difficulties, it is quite a challenge to be able to direct their gaze and focus on a target. Therefore, it is a matter for researchers and developers to bring an eye gesture recognition switch, already deep in development, commercially into fruition. Used with auditory scanning, such advancement could powerfully optimize complex eye movement.

For improved function, Russell is a prime example of someone who needs to have the versatility of using gaze control and an eye gesture recognition switch. Russell has Locked-In syndrome, poor head control, nystagmus and a strong cough. When he coughs and/or loses head control, he moves slightly, but it becomes nearly impossible for the system to register his eyes. So Russell has to be repositioned. It is this which "takes the time" says his wife, poignantly. However, Russell is always able to accurately look up and down. It is felt that, if this movement could be interpreted as a switch press, it could transform his ability to control the computer, especially when he is susceptible to fatigue (Donegan et al., 2006b, 2009).

As the case of Russell indicates, it is important to be inquisitive about the visual abilities of the individual. During the COGAIN end-user trials, difficulties arose among people who had long eyelashes and/or droopy eyelids; both of which impair pupil visibility. LC Technologies have designed a software feature that responds to droopy eyelids. At times, pupil visibility could be enhanced by moving the monitor from its highest to its lowest position, until eye tracking began, as displayed by the on-screen visual feedback box.

The on-screen visual-feedback box displays how well the eyes are being registered. This resizable utility illustrates when the individual should readjust their position i.e., when the screen is too close or too far away (see Figure 1 as an example) (Donegan et al., 2005).

Figure 1. Visual feedback of the position of the eye (2 black dots) using Sensory Software's The Grid 2

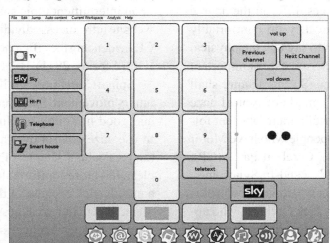

Physical ability over the course of the day ultimately influences the style of system chosen, and how it is to be mounted and positioned, comfort is vital. Lying in bed lets Russell see the screen more easily than being at a table. He is also more relaxed. Instead of twisting to see the monitor screen, the equipment should be placed in the position where the individual feels most at ease. For example, the monitor might be tilted sideways for someone who is side-lying; or be placed above, faced downwards and parallel to someone who is supine.

There is a diverse array of gaze control systems. They appear as: an 'all-in-one' unit in which the computer, camera and monitor are integrated; an 'add-on' unit comprising a camera, infrared emitters and system software which is used on a tablet or a desktop computer; and a unit that docks onto a dedicated communication aid, i.e., a Dynavox EyeMax (Dynavox, 2011). A range of mounting equipment is currently available to suit all such styles, facilitating the use of gaze control in various settings i.e., in the home, classroom, office, or hospital ward.

For example, there are desk stands, mounting arms and wheelchair mounts, etc. When a gaze control system is mounted onto a wheelchair, their width together should be less than a doorway. People who have independent powered mobility need to see ahead clearly (Tuisku et al., 2008). Independent mobility is becoming a requirement of many gaze control users, prompting environmental control features to become an increasingly integral element. College students continue to wish to harness yet greater use of their system while being 'on the move'. Being able to switch between alternative access methods would restore their ability to use their device outdoors. (Donegan et al., 2009). However, mobility is discussed in far greater depth in chapter 10 of section 3 of this book entitled 'Gaze controlled environmental control and mobility', by Bates and colleagues.

It emerged that, having several options for mounting really appealed to many users in the COGAIN project. An individual might be compelled to have bed-rest to protect their skin integrity; or choose to use gaze control in several environments i.e., at home and work. For adaptability, there is the rolling mount. Sticking fluorescent tape onto its black base makes it much easier to see. A clinical scientist might opt for a bespoke mounting solution when convinced that 'off the shelf' options are unsuitable; as in the case of Peter, who had MND; a bespoke mount was tailor made for his TM3 and laptop. For greater ease and independence during transfers, other COGAIN users have commented that they wish for an independent "way to swing the device out of the way" to be invented.

Once the gaze control system is mounted and positioned, it has to acquire information about the individual's eye movement via the calibration process. The individual looks at a specific number of on-screen targets. The physical and cognitive abilities of the individual guide the ways in which the calibration process is to be adapted. Accuracy is refined by using more targets, though a lesser, even the least number would still be functional, depending on the level of accuracy required for the software being used.

Many gaze control systems now offer a choice of a one eye (right or left) and a two eye calibration process. The tracking of one eye only, via a one eye calibration process, has been more accurate for many users including an individual who has Locked-In syndrome, and a divergent squint.

The COGAIN end-user trials discovered that individuals vary in the length of time they need to gaze on a target. Some systems only present the next target once their gaze has been successfully captured, taking the pressure off the person to perform. Adding auditory feedback to signal a successfully calibrated target offers further support. For many highly literate and motivated people, who have good visual control, the calibration process is speedy, automatic and straight forward -"she was up and running very quickly", said one speech and language therapist. However,

31

an automatic calibration process is not designed for all, even when slowed. A modified calibration i.e. one that steps through fewer targets which are adapted (in size, shape, and/or colour) is appreciably more supportive of individuals who have visual and/or learning difficulties. Progressing at the most comfortable pace for the person is considered paramount.

Sometimes the difference between failure and success in the calibration is a narrow one. Often, a weak calibration is strengthened through practice. For example, an individual whose vision was weaker on their left side had a poor, but functional, first calibration. Nevertheless, following a month of practice, recalibrating the gaze control system demonstrated that their control had become noticeably less fleeting. They were able to scan and select cells positioned on the left side more easily.

The calibration might be curtailed because the individual only has vision in a vertical or horizontal plane. In such cases, position the calibration targets where the individual can see, wherever possible. A calibration might fail. The default calibration might work instead. Also, some individuals have several calibrations saved for when their vision fluctuates. These might be ineffective because the individual is experiencing dry eyes, an altered pupil size and/or involuntary movement

Finally, the accuracy of the calibration can be tested while the computer is in use. Ask the individual to look at an object on the screen, and then observe the discrepancy between where the object and the on-screen pointer are. This discrepancy and/or the on-screen pointer might be frustrating for the individual to see. Fortunately, it is often possible to offset weaknesses in the calibration with an appropriate software interface

MATCHING THE SOFTWARE WITH EACH INDIVIDUAL'S INTEREST AND NEEDS

The challenge of controlling the Windows environment might seem impossible for people who have severe and complex disabilities. However, one way it is accessible is via framework software i.e., software that can be tailored in terms of content, layout and style to match the physical and cognitive abilities of the individual. COGAIN Wiki (2011), under User Involvement, presents ideas for customizing framework software. The use of framework software enables the assessment and implementation of gaze control to be user focused, in keeping with the second principle of the KEE concept. It is possible to create an interface that meets the interests and needs of the individual (Donegan & Oosthuizen, 2006a).

With framework software, the first step is to investigate the size of cell that the individual is able to comfortably and accurately access. By choosing the right cell size, the access ability of the individual is less likely to become confused with their cognitive ability.

It is possible to replace the mouse function with either a centralized dwell select feature, or an intentional eye blink. In other words, by dwelling in, or blinking at, a cell, the individual is able to activate a mouse click. When dwelling, the individual should have enough time to think, but not too much time that they become tired or drift off. The length of dwell time, as set in the software settings, might be represented in the form of a clock; a shrinking dot; a highlighted cell; etc. The notion of dwelling is new to most people, and it can be very discouraging to make unwanted selections. Engaging in fun, fail proof activities, therefore, such as playing musical notes by looking at the screen, is an ideal way to introduce this concept.

When the individual is ready to move onto more challenging activities, carefully considering the cell size is still critical. Often the dwell or blink

Figure 2. Bjorn Andre is able to control Windows accurately while lying down

time is extended. The individual needs to be able to visually scan all of the available choices, while not making an accidental selection. Initially, the dwell or blink time might be slow i.e., one and a half seconds. However, in many cases this will speed up as the individual becomes more familiar with the interface. Auditory feedback, such as speaking typed letters aloud, enhances accuracy for some by reducing the amount of alternation between the keyboard and the text input field (text input using gaze and related feedback is discussed in more detail by Majaranta in Chapter 8)

Meanwhile, other people have become very adept at directly controlling the pointer to access the full Windows environment. Of course, this demands a fair degree of accuracy. Such stereotypical users are likely to have good control of their head and eye movement. Having an on-screen magnification feature might hone accuracy when the calibration is not entirely precise. Initially, trying an on-screen magnification feature might be difficult. Nevertheless, persevering with it is worthwhile because it can open up new parts of the Windows environment, such as files and folders. However, for others, an on-screen magnification feature is simply not required

A Windows accessibility on-screen keyboard with direct pointer control might be all that some individuals need, like Bjorn Andre (in Figure 2).

Mouse functions are chosen from a menu of standard mouse functions. Mouse clicks are executed by dwell select or eye blink. Some people might choose to use both. For example, they might use eye blink to navigate the desktop and dwell select to type text. Alternatively, it might be possible to set a short dwell time for a single click, and a longer dwell time for a double click, etc. Filtering out natural, continuous tiny eye movements in the software settings might smooth out and steady the pointer, making targets easier to hit.

Individuals are able to actively pursue interests and fulfil roles, regardless of whether they utilize framework software or direct pointer control. Access to social communication, environmental control and games are some of the activities undertaken by users during the COGAIN project. By completing activities, the salience of certain features of gaze control strike home. For example, Jonathan can't wait to set up a web cam; he says his gaze control system has been "a really great help socially". He also appreciates having the facility to pause his system, so that he can freely move around the screen without triggering commands, which lessens fatigue and creates time to think

BEING READY TO CHANGE AND EVOLVE

Evolutionary, being ready to change in relation to the end-user's response to gaze control technology, and software, is the third and final principle of the KEE concept (Donegan & Oosthuizen, 2006a). It is an entrusted element of providing ongoing support for the successful, long-term use of gaze control. This final principle of the KEE concept (Donegan & Oosthuizen, 2006a) is evidenced in the complementary chapters within this section. All, in their own contrasting styles, explore the issues relating to the assessment and implementation of gaze control technology in greater depth.

REFERENCES

Association, M. N. D. (2011). Life with MND. What is MND? Retrieved from http://www.mndassociation.org/life_with_mnd/what_is_mnd/index.html

Donegan, M., Cotmore, S., Holmqvist, E., Lundalv, M., Buchholz, M., Pasian, V., et al. (2009). Final user trials report. (Deliverable D3.6. Communication by Gaze Interaction (COGAIN), Project IST-2003-511598). Retrieved from the COGAIN Association website: http://www.cogain.org/wiki/COGAIN_Reports

Donegan, M., & Oosthuizen, L. (2006a). The 'KEE' Concept for eye-control and complex disabilities: Knowledge-based, end user-focused and evolutionary. Proceedings of the 2nd Conference on Communication by Gaze Interaction (COGAIN 2006) (pp. 83-87). Retrieved from http://www.cogain.org/conference.

Donegan, M., & Oosthuizen, L. (2006b). Acquired brain injury and eye control technology - What are the key issues? Proceedings of 2006 Communication Matters Annual Conference, Leicester, UK.

Donegan, M., Oosthuizen, L., Bates, R., Daunys, G., Hansen, J. P., Joos, M., et al. (2005). User requirements report with observations of difficulties users are experiencing. (Deliverable D3.1. Communication by Gaze Interaction (COGAIN), Project IST-2003-511598). Retrieved from the COGAIN Association website: http://www.cogain.org/wiki/COGAIN_Reports

Donegan, M., Oosthuizen, L., Bates, R., Istance, H., Holmqvist, E., Lundalv, M., et al. (2006b). Report of user trials and usability studies. (Deliverable D3.3. Communication by Gaze Interaction (COGAIN), Project IST-2003-511598). Retrieved from the COGAIN Association website: http://www.cogain.org/wiki/COGAIN_Reports

Donegan, M., Oozthuizen, L., Daunys, G., Istance, R., Bates, R., Signorile, I., et al. (2006a). Report on features of the different systems and development needs. (Deliverable D3.2. Communication by Gaze Interaction (COGAIN), Project IST-2003-511598). Retrieved from the COGAIN Association website: http://www.cogain.org/wiki/COGAIN_Reports

Dynavox (2011). Products. EyeMax. Say it with your eyes. Retrieved from www.dynavoxtech.com/products/eyemax/

Merck Manuals Online Medical Library. (2001). The Merck Manual for Healthcare Professionals. Pediatrics: Neurologic Disorders in Children: Cerebral Palsy (CP) Syndromes. Retrieved from http://www.merckmanuals.com/professional/sec19.html

Quintero, A. (2009). 'Eye' on technology update. Eyegaze users share their experiences. MDA/ALS Newsmagazine, 14(3), March 2009. MDA Publications. Retrieved from http://www.als-mda.org/publications/als/als14_3.html#eye

Technologies, L. C. (2011). Assistive Technologies. Videos. Eyegaze User Jack Orchard in the news (4:52 min). Retrieved from http://www.eyegaze.com/content/videos

Tuisku, O., Bates, R., Štěpánková, O., Fejtová, M., Novák, P., Istance, H., et al. (2008). A survey of existing 'de-facto' standards and systems of gaze based mobility control. (Deliverable D2.6, Communication by Gaze Interaction (COGAIN), Project IST-2003-511598). Retrieved from the COGAIN Association website: http://www.cogain.org/wiki/COGAIN_Reports

User Stories. (2011). User stories of communicating lives through Tobii. Retrieved from http://www.tobii.com/en/assistive-technology/global/user-stories/

Wiki, C. O. G. A. I. N. (2011). User Involvement. COGAIN: Communication by Gaze Interaction. Retrieved from http://www.cogain.org/wiki/User_Involvement

Yeo, S. (2006). Letter from Sarah (11 April 2006). COGAIN Wiki: User Involvement. Retrieved from the COGAIN website: http://www.cogain.org/wiki/User_Involvement_Users#Sarah

Chapter 5
A Model for Gaze Control Assessments and Evaluation

Eva Holmqvist
DART, Sweden

Margret Buchholz
DART, Sweden

ABSTRACT

Technical aids can contribute towards improved health and satisfaction in life by giving the user increased possibilities for participation in a number of areas of daily life. Assessing people with disabilities that affect their motor, communication and cognitive skills can be a complex matter. The result of an assessment might be the user's only way of independent activity and communication. This stresses the importance of making high quality assessments. This chapter discusses the prerequisites, structure and key elements of a successful gaze control assessment.

INTRODUCTION

Health is more than just not being sick. Health is influenced by the experience of being active, being able to participate and having a sense of connection.

The World Health Organisation stresses the meaning of health in the International Classification of Functioning, Disability and Health (ICF)

DOI: 10.4018/978-1-61350-098-9.ch005

(World Health Organization 2008). It describes the components affecting health from a biological, individual and social perspective, underlining both the environment and participation as highly important factors. Participation can be defined as taking part in meaningful and purposeful activities, as well as interacting with the environment. Technical aids can contribute towards improved health by giving the user increased possibilities for participation in a number of areas of daily life. A person's satisfaction with life depends on how well he or she is able to achieve participation and engage in meaningful activity.

Assessing people with disabilities that affect their motor, communication and cognitive skills can be a complex matter. The result of an assessment might be the user's only way of independent activity and communication. This stresses the importance of making high quality assessments.

An essential prerequisite for high quality assessment is the use of a trans-disciplinary team committed to working towards a shared goal. The team typically comprises a range of professionals such as ICT educational consultants, occupational therapists, speech and language therapists and technicians, although this range will vary. Each team member contributes his or her specific knowledge and experience in relation to the user, the activity, the environment and the technology on an equal basis, and the composition of the team should be based on the outcomes that the team is aiming to achieve for the individual. To achieve effective teamwork the requirements need to be identified and distinct goals set, and the responsibilities of each team member must be made clear.

TAKING A CLIENT-CENTRED APPROACH

A client-centred approach is a basic condition for self-determination and empowerment of the user in all assessment work. Use of an assessment model offers an effective means of ensuring consensus within the team and a high quality outcome. The assessment model referred to here is based on the Canadian Model of Occupational Performance (CMOP) (Townsend, 1997) and has been adapted for the assessment of Assistive Technology (AT). It has resulted in the book "Be active using a computer – possibilities for people with physical disabilities" (Lidström and Zachrisson 2005). The structure of its clinical process is based on the Occupational Performance Process Model (Townsend, 1997), which has a client-centred

perspective. It is easy to follow and is applicable in most cases (Buchholz and Holmqvist 2009). The steps of the process are summarized as follows:

- Identify, describe and prioritize issues
- Select theoretical approaches
- Describe the conditions for the activities
- Describe targeted outcomes and develop an action plan
- Implement plans
- Evaluate outcomes

Identify, Describe and Prioritize Issues

The work of identifying, describing and prioritizing occupational performance issues is, whenever possible, undertaken mainly by the user. The results are used as a foundation for further assessment. To achieve this, we need to listen to the user and ask appropriate questions.

The issues addressed must be specific and describe the limitations in the daily life of the user. The aim is to establish close cooperation between the user and the team members and to work towards a common goal. The user (with support from the team) decides which issues and activities are most important to them. If needed, the interview and discussions with the user should be adapted to meet his or her cognitive and physical abilities. Different approaches are used depending on whether the user is an adult or a child and whether there are cognitive and/or communicative problems. For many users with communicative and cognitive disorders use of the Talking Mats method is useful in helping make the decision-making process easier (Murphy and Cameron 2006).

Select Theoretical Approaches

The theoretical approaches can include theories, models or paradigms and they aim to help clarify further future actions, including assessments and implementations. For example, the ICF, client-centred models, CMOP (Townsend, 1997), laws and praxis models are concerned with the prescription of technical aids and are all potentially applicable.

Describe the Conditions for the Activities

At this point, the team needs to consider the user's abilities as well as factors in the actual environment with respect to the identified activities. It is advisable to examine the strengths and resources of the individual, the environment, the technology and the activity itself. In some cases it can be sufficient simply to ask "why" questions to determine the reasons for certain issues, but often specific tests or observations are necessary for information gathering.

The individual's motivation is central to activity performance. There are also several other factors to consider, such as physical ability, including motor function, speech, vision, hearing and other senses, as well as determining whether the individual has any pain-related problems. One should also be aware of the individual's emotional and social abilities, which can also affect their potential to succeed. It is important to take account of the individual's cognitive abilities, including the ability for abstract thinking, memory, attention and concentration, as well as his or her linguistic skills and perceptual abilities. Visual Impairment (CVI) and crowding are common perceptual problems experienced by people with Cerebral Palsy or other congenital or acquired brain injury. A list of limitations and resources must be drawn up and, based on this, a list of strengths that can be used to overcome the difficulties faced can be identified.

From this general information on the individual, the team continues the assessment by considering the user's prerequisites in regard to the computer control method.

Motor Assessment

The first step is to assess the user's eye movement control. The individual must be able to control his or her eyes to at least some degree. One also needs to assess whether there are any other difficulties that may affect the use of eye gaze systems, such as problems with opening the eyes, tremor, squinting or nystagmus.

Assessment of the user's ability to access the technology should result in a list of useful motor functions and how to make the best use of them. It is recommended that the motor assessment be carried out by a physiotherapist or an occupational therapist, together with an interview with the user in collaboration with the family or others supporting the user, as deemed appropriate. Issues for consideration include identifying whether the user has any motor functions that could serve as a useful alternative to the mouse click. This could be any deliberate active movement of the hand, leg, foot, head or other means of physical control. If possible, the capability to use an emulated mouse click instead of the dwell function (automatic mouse click) can give the user more control. In addition, being able to look at the screen without automatic dwell-select might be less stressful for some users. It might also provide quicker control in some cases. It is also important to know the user's level of strength and coordination, as well as his or her best working position. Can the user hold his or her head, or is there a need for a special headrest, etc?

After completing the motor assessment, the activities that the user has chosen should be analyzed in relation to the use of eye gaze.

Prerequisites of the Technology

When carrying out a gaze control assessment, it is necessary to systematically analyze the characteristics of the gaze control systems available and how well they respond to the user's motor function, cognitive level and the activities that the device will be needed for.

For instance, if the user is not able to look at the whole screen, it is possible to adapt some systems accordingly. Other users may have difficulty in completing a standard calibration due to cognitive problems or extensive spasticity. This may lead to trials with a system with individualized calibration settings, as well as minimising the need to repeat the calibration process.

It might be helpful to know what access methods and technical aids may have been used before and to analyze their strengths and limitations. As always, it is important to ask the user's opinion.

Prerequisites of the Environment

The user environment is a crucial factor affecting the choices made in the assessment process. The availability to the user of funding for technical aids affects their ability to acquire a gaze control system and has a major bearing on the choices that can be made. The availability of competent support within the user's environment is a critical factor that needs to be considered when choosing a gaze control system. A supportive environment is often the key to success.

Ergonomics

Proper ergonomic use of the computer requires a good seating and working position. Adopting a new method of computer access requires a reassessment of seating and positioning. When using a gaze control system, compared with many other access methods, the user does not necessarily need to have as much controlled mobility and muscle function (strength, endurance and muscle tone) but, nonetheless, a good seating and working position is essential. From reported experience, a user who is hypertonic, for example, with a great deal of involuntary movement and perhaps unwanted reflex actions, often seems to be more

relaxed when they are using a gaze control system compared with other methods.

For a good ergonomic position, the key issues are stability, mobility and comfort. The seat, backrest and neck rest of the chair should provide comfortable postural support, allowing for occasional variations in the seating position. Most users need a good neck rest when using a gaze control system. The screen should be positioned at a suitable distance, and the top of the screen should be level with, or slightly lower than, the user's eyes. However, when using a gaze control system, some users may benefit from having the computer screen slightly higher than is generally advised. This forces the user to open his or her eyes more when looking up, which allows the gaze control system to more easily recognise where the user is looking. In these cases, it is important to be attentive to the user's neck in order to avoid pain and to use a good neck rest.

For comfort during extended periods of use, the seating needs to be flexible. The user should be able to change position whenever he or she wishes. An electric wheelchair can enable the seating position to be easily changed. The computer monitor screen must be adjustable for different seated positions, including having the user leaning backwards, whether in an electric wheelchair or lying in bed. This is particularly relevant when using a gaze control system, as it often allows for a wider range of working positions.

The lighting in the user environment is also an important factor to consider when using a gaze control system. Gaze control systems that use infrared light can be affected by ambient light that contains infrared (IR). Sunlight contains infrared, as well as direct light from some light bulbs, especially if the light directly shines into the user's face or into the system's camera. Lighting should be indirect and/or directed from the side. Using a gaze control system outdoors in direct sunlight can be problematic if the sun shines directly onto the screen or into the user's eyes.

Describe Targeted Outcomes and Develop an Action Plan

If issues are clearly defined, goal setting is easier. It is important for the user and the team to agree on the goals and to ensure that they relate to the activities that the user would like to be able to carry out. The goals should be realistic, understandable and measurable.

- Goals...help clarify required measures and action plans. If possible, the user should define the goals, and the problems discussed earlier in the process should affect what goals are set.
- Goals...should be realized through meaningful activities and written down.
- Goals...should be attainable. Long-term goals should be broken down into smaller goals.
- Goals...should be possible to evaluate.
- Goals...affect further actions and are the basis for evaluation.

The team then sets out an action plan, including who is responsible for each part, as well as when, where and how the actions will be carried out. Consensus with the user and his or her environment is the key to a good result!

Implement Plans

Once the goals and action plan are in place, the next task is to carry out an assessment. This will hopefully lead to the recommendation of a technical aid and to the drawing up of training guidelines. Usually there is a need to educate the user, staff and family.

Before the assessment it is advisable to analyze the activities involved. Describe the activities in terms of their complexity and ease. What equipment, materials or other things are needed? In order to be well prepared and to understand the demands on the user, it is important to familia-

rise yourself in advance with the gaze control system and its software. Have everything set up and in order before the user enters the room: the computer on, speakers at a comfortable volume, printer started, and the calibration ready to start. Clear the computer desktop of any unnecessary information. This makes the situation more comfortable for the user and means they do not have to sit through complicated adjustments and settings. Advance preparation and good organization also helps ensure efficient time use. This is especially important if the user has a limited concentration span or tires quickly.

It is often important for key people in the users' own environment to be involved in the assessment. However, having large numbers of people in the assessment room is not recommended. The user must be able to concentrate and must not be put under added pressure. Use video recordings and photos as necessary to enable others to view the training without being present. Some assessment rooms have a one-way screen or cameras and monitors making it possible to follow the assessment from a separate room.

Settings and Lay-Out

The operating system and its various software have several settings that can enhance the use of the system, such as the size and shape of the mouse pointer, sizes of objects, fonts and different targets, as well as the colour settings of the screen. Such adaptations can make it easier for the user to see and distinguish targeted objects and to generally find his or her way around the interface.

Calibration

Before starting a calibration, it is important that the user has seen it demonstrated and knows what is expected of him or her. In some systems it is possible to make an individualized calibration, where the size, colour, location and number of targets can be changed. In some systems it is also possible to use your own pictures, sounds or film clips. This is very useful for children or people with learning disabilities or problems with attention and/or concentration. The calibration process can sometimes take some time to complete. In such cases it can be a good idea to break the task down into short sessions.

Activities/Tasks

When the user tries the gaze control system for the first time, it is advisable to start with simple tasks, preferably activities in which a choice generates a sound only. It is essential during the early stages for the user to be presented with activities that enable him or her to build up their skills with the new tool without making mistakes. To be able to succeed, the choice of activities and software must correspond with the user's interests and abilities. If the demands on the user are too high or low, he or she may lose interest and motivation.

Success is important! Choose a straightforward activity to start with. Note that a simple, non-complex activity does not necessarily mean that the task is childish! Gradually change to more complex activities and have a number of different activities prepared so that you can easily change between activities if the results are better or poorer than expected.

Do not make the sessions too long. Take breaks! Be aware of signs of fatigue – working too hard will only result in mistakes and result in lack of motivation. End the session before this occurs. Most importantly, have fun! Having fun while learning speeds the learning process and makes the user much more motivated.

Introductory Grids

With children or users with cognitive impairment, it is often necessary to prepare personal material for the assessment. The number of cells/choices and the size of targets must be individually adapted to match the user's cognitive skills and gaze control performance.

Music suits all ages. Grids/page sets can be easily changed to suit the user's musical preferences.

The example grid in Figure 1 on the topic of Eurovision songs presents the user with two choices. The user starts the music by looking at their preferred choice. The music changes as soon as he or she looks at another song. A blank cell gives the user a 'resting place', in other words somewhere they can look at on screen without anything happening. If you buy a record, you can convert the music to a suitable file type and load it into any communication software. Images of musicians are often very easy to find on the Internet.

The grid/page set on Figure 2 also presents Eurovision songs, but here there are seven choices.

Figure 3 shows an application for playing instrument loops with the mouse pointer. This is a non-click application which is suitable for initial training and for playing music together.

Figure 4 shows a grid designed for youngsters containing Swedish children's music, for example from the film Pippi Longstocking. Such a grid

Figure 1. Example grid: Eurovision songs. This grid was made in Tobii Communicator (Tobii Technology AB 2010)

Figure 2. Example grid: Eurovision songs with more choices. This grid was made in Tobii Communicator

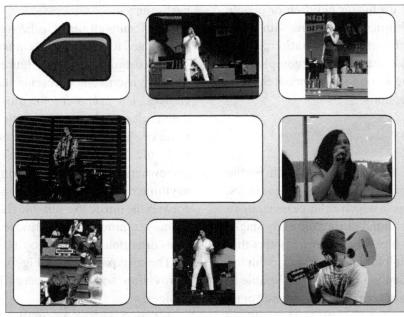

Figure 3. Example grid: Playing musical instrument loops. This grid was made in SAW (Open source assistive technology software 2010)

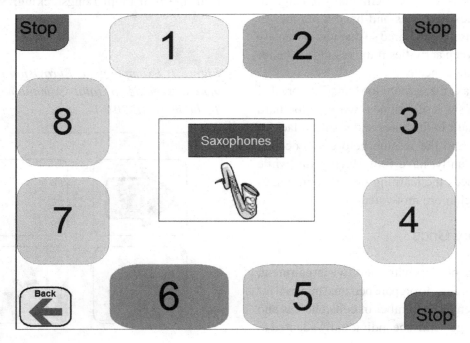

could very easily be adapted to include favourite nursery rhymes.

Figure 5 gives an example of how to make a children's book accessible for a child using a computer. With the arrows, the child can turn the pages backwards and forwards. With the mouth symbol the page is read out loud and the "silent" symbol stops the reading. Using recorded speech is preferable because it makes the story more interesting to the child. There is no action attached to the cell with the picture, so the child can look at the pictures while listening to the story.

Figure 6 shows a grid that has been adapted for the children's game "Simon says". The child looks at the yellow cell and recorded or synthetic speech says: "Simon says that everybody must…" Then the child chooses an activity, for instance "jump!" and everybody in the room plays in the game. It is very important to make this a group activity in which the child is in command.

Figure 7 shows two grids that are designed for an introductory level of communication. Here the user can talk about what he or she likes or dislikes. This gives the user the opportunity to give his or her point of view and the grid can easily be adapted to contain subjects that are relevant to the user.

The first grid in Figure 8 is an example of a simple grid that presents two choices: "It was fun" and "It was boring". This enables a user who is at an early introductory level to participate in evaluating activities.

The second grid in Figure 8 has been designed for evaluating the activities of the session. The user can say "Today I…" and then choose the relevant, appropriate activities, here "played music" and "played Simon says". Then he or she can choose between the following opinions: "It was fun", "It was boring". "It was easy" and "It was hard". This is a useful way to obtain the users opinion (also in writing) and it can be used over and over simply by updating the list of activities.

Figure 4. Example grid: Swedish children's music. This grid was made in Rolltalk Designer (Abilia 2010)

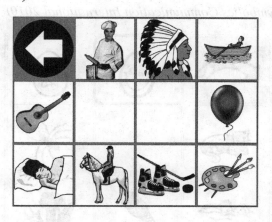

Figure 5. Example grid: Children's book. This grid was made in Rolltalk Designer

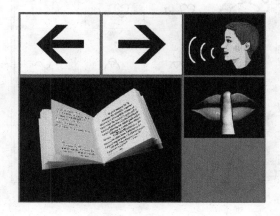

Figure 6. Example grid: Simon says. This grid was made in The Grid (Sensory Software International Ltd 2010) with PCS-symbols (Mayer Johnson 2010)

Figure 7. Example grids: Picture and symbol communication. These grids were made in The Grid with PCS-symbols and Blissymbolics (Blissymbolics Communication International 2010)

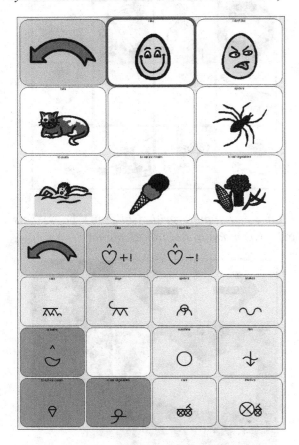

Figure 8. Example grids: Communicating feelings and activities. These grids were made in The Grid with PCS-symbols

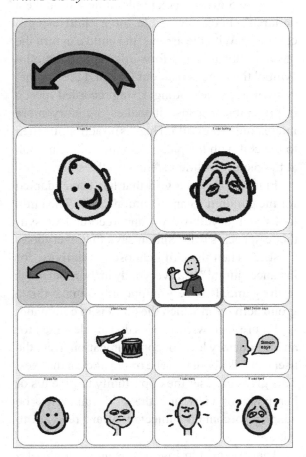

Communication

During the assessment, the team communicates with the user and evaluates the task, settings etc. If the user has a disability that affects their communication skills, it is important to have a low-tech communication aid available. The design of a new communication system should be built on the experiences from previous low- or high-tech solutions. There will always be a need for a well-functioning low-tech alternative for situations when the gaze control system is not available, for example at the beach or while eating.

Choices

The most common way to make a comparison between different computer access methods or settings is to complete the same task using alternative methods or settings, while a score is kept on the time and the errors made. This measuring strategy provides objective information about the user's performance. The opinion of the user is, however, also invaluable. In some cases, a straightforward comparison may not be possible due to varying user performance. In these cases video recordings taken over an extended period of time can be used to analyze the alternatives.

Sometimes the best solution can be to have different access methods or settings for different activities.

It is important not to become swamped by all of the possible technical solutions. The most important thing for the user is that the system works (!), is reliable and demands a minimum amount of maintenance. It does not matter how good a system is in theory, in practice it must be as easy to use as possible and be reliable and functional, with minimal support, in the user's day-to-day life!

Recommendations

Upon ending the assessment the team reports on its findings and gives their recommendations to the user/ staff/ family. They will need to be taught in the use and maintenance of the gaze control system and software. They will probably also need technical support, at least initially.

Evaluate Outcomes

After implementation, the user's functional performance in the targeted activities is evaluated. It is preferable to use evaluation methods where the user takes an active part. Has their functional performance changed? Does the system function satisfactorily? Did any new issues arise? Is there a need for further assessment? There are several evaluation tools that can be used here. If an instrument such as Talking Mats was used initially, it is recommended to carry out the interview again in order to make a comparison. There are also specific instruments concerning user satisfaction with technical aids (these might differ in different countries). Sometimes new issues occur after the initial goals are reached. Technology often gives the user the opportunity for continuous development of his or her functional performance in relation to their changing situation. This necessitates a continuing process with a need for new goal setting based on the user's development.

OUTCOMES AND DISCUSSION

Almost all of DART's users had very severe motor disorders, many of whom also had involuntary head movement. The gaze control computer used, MyTobii, worked to some degree for almost all our users, but not with full functionality in all cases. In our experience to date, other systems we have tried have been more suitable for people who sit still, for example people with ALS or high spinal injuries etc. However, some of the newer gaze control systems on the market, at the time of writing, for example the ALEA IntelliGaze have not been tested at DART within the COGAIN project.

Some users who have tried the MyTobii have in the past experienced problems with the appearance of different pop-up menus, for example turning on and off the dwell function. Today, it is possible to turn off these features. Many have also needed specially adapted on-screen keyboards (colours, sizes etc). The option of having auditory feedback when a choice is made is helpful for most users, especially early on. Functionality was also dependent on the user's visual ability and their seating position, which affects head control and their field of vision. In some cases where the user experiences problems reaching targets in certain parts of the screen (such as those positioned in the corners), it is necessary to allow the user to work only in the area of the screen that they are able to access.

A user needs to have some cognitive understanding of how to use the system; for example, choosing by looking at a picture/symbol. The aim of making adaptations available for people with severe learning disabilities, a very challenging group to find computer access for, is nevertheless very important. Knowledge of how to produce applications that are not too cognitively demanding for users who have learning difficulties is a challenge that needs further attention and work.

We have come across numerous people with severe involuntary movement for whom finding computer access has been almost impossible. For these, gaze control technology has turned out to be the only means of having independent control of any activity (Holmqvist and Buchholz 2009). Some users had experience of other computer control methods prior to using a gaze control system, but these have been difficult for them to manage and much more physically demanding than using eye gaze. Even if the gaze control system may not be a faster option for the user, they are able to work in longer sessions and are able to perform more effectively because it is less tiring. Some users might have difficulty managing a gaze control system effectively during the early stages but, compared with not having any form of independent control at all, gaze control can offer a potential way forward to enhanced opportunities for greater communication and control. Without giving a young person the opportunity to develop their eye control skills, it is impossible to put a limit on what might be achieved given an appropriate system, sufficient time and an appropriate software interface that evolves with the child.

In Sweden today, users who need gaze control systems for communication and/or environmental control have the opportunity of obtaining one as a personal aid. The COGAIN project has helped in highlighting and speeding up this process. We have noticed an increased awareness and interest in the field of gaze control technology, and we feel that user trials have been an important part of the project. There is widespread interest from users who wish to have their own systems at home, school or work.

Considerations when assessing for, and implementing the use of a gaze control system should include the following:

- Possible need for a user-appropriate gaze control system that meets the user's specific physical and visual/perceptual needs. For example, a system that is able to accommodate involuntary head movement and visual problems such as eye tremor.

- Appropriate mounting and positioning of the system in relation to the user's needs, i.e. the system must be positioned for optimal comfort and function for the user. If possible, the mounting system must allow the position of the screen to be adjusted according to the seating position, e g. if the user is laying down or sitting backward in his/her chair. In many cases it is advisable to place the screen slightly higher than normal – this will enhance gaze recognition.

- If a user needs to use the gaze control system in more than one place, for instance in school and at home, one solution in Sweden has been to let the user have two mounting systems and just move the gaze control computer from one place to another.

- Appropriate on-screen visual representation (pictures, symbols, text, foreground/background colours, etc.), i.e. ensure that visual images are presented in a way that is clearly visible and comprehensible to the user.

- Appropriate organization of the images on the screen in relation to the visual abilities of the users to ensure that the visual images are arranged in a way that is most easily understood and controlled

There is also a need for:

- Adaptable calibration procedures. Different users need different features. A range of options is needed to make eye control accessible to more people.

- The development of a wide range of software to support initial trials and training for users with a wide range of physical, visual and cognitive abilities. Software that is already used in schools and for leisure needs to be made accessible by eye control.

- Better integration with Windows and advanced applications.

- Appropriate auditory support and feedback is essential. It is important to ensure that the type of auditory support provided to the user gives them optimal support in relation to their needs and abilities.

REFERENCES

Abilia (2010). *Rolltalk Designer*. Version 6.6.10. Retrieved from http://www.abilia.org.uk/

Blissymbolics Communication International. (2010). *Blissymbolics*. Retrieved from http://www.blissymbolics.org

Buchholz, M., & Holmqvist, E. (2009). Eye gaze assessment with a person having complex needs - the benefits of using an assessment method. *Proceedings of the 5th Conference on Communication by Gaze Interaction (COGAIN 2009)* (pp. 7-11). Copenhagen, Denmark: Technical University of Denmark. Retrieved from http://www.cogain.org/cogain2009/COGAIN2009-Proceedings.pdf

Holmqvist, E., & Buchholz, M. (2009). Clinical experiences from assessment and introduction of eye gaze systems. *Proceedings of the 5th Conference on Communication by Gaze Interaction (COGAIN 2009)* (p. 95). Copenhagen, Denmark: Technical University of Denmark. Retrieved from http://www.cogain.org/cogain2009/COGAIN2009-Proceedings.pdf

Lidström, H., & Zachrisson, G. (Eds.). (2005). *Aktiv med dator - möjligheter för personer med rörelsehinder*. Stockholm, Sweden: Hjälpmedelsintitutet.

Mayer Johnson. (2010). *Picture Communication Symbols*. Retrieved from http://www.mayer-johnson.com/education/symbols/pcs/

Murphy, J., & Cameron, L. (2006). *Talking Mats. A Resource to Enhance Communication*. Stirling, Scotland: University of Stirling.

Open source assistive technology software (2010). *Special Access to Windows, version 5*. Retrieved from http://www.oatsoft.org/Software/SpecialAccessToWindows

Sensory Software International Ltd. (2010). *The Grid 2, version 2.6.30*. Retrieved from http://www.sensorysoftware.com

Tobii Technology, A. B. (2010). *Tobii Communicator, version 4.4.01*. Retrieved from http://www.tobii.com

Townsend, E. (Ed.). (1997). *Enabling Occupation: An Occupational Therapy Perspective. Canadian Association of Occupational Therapists (CAOT)*. Toronto, ON: CAOT Publications.

World Health Organization. (2008). *International classification of functioning, disability and health*. Geneva, Switzerland: World Health Organization.

Chapter 6
The Impact of Gaze Controlled Technology on Quality of Life

Valentina Pasian
ALS Centre, Hospital San Giovani Battista, Italy

Fulvio Corno
Politecnico di Torino, Italy

Isabella Signorile
Politecnico di Torino, Italy

Laura Farinetti
Politecnico di Torino, Italy

ABSTRACT

This chapter presents the process of introducing an eye tracking device to impaired users. It reports results from a gaze control user trial conducted with people for whom gaze control is a necessity due to their current condition or for whom it will soon become a necessity because of a progressive disease. Special attention is paid to the impact of this new communication method on their quality of life.

INTRODUCTION

This chapter reports results from a gaze control user trial conducted with people for whom gaze control is a necessity due to their current condition or for whom it will soon become a necessity because of a progressive disease. Special attention is paid to the impact of this new communication method on their quality of life.

The eye tracking trials in Torino were conducted by the Department of Computer Science of Politecnico di Torino in collaboration with the Department of Neuroscience at the Hospital San Giovanni 'Le Molinette'. The trials were conducted in two stages: in the first stage we tested the Erica eye tracker with amyotrophic lateral sclerosis (ALS) patients using a well-established protocol. In the second phase, still ongoing, we have extended our trials to include other kinds of patients, aiming to collect more qualitative

DOI: 10.4018/978-1-61350-098-9.ch006

information, and we have used both Erica and MyTobii devices.

FIRST PHASE

The hospital San Giovanni Battista 'Le Molinette' in Turin, Italy, hosts the largest specialized ALS center in Italy. The ALS Center comprises a multi-disciplinary team of doctors, speech and language therapists and psychologists. They support approximately three hundred patients with varying stages of ALS. The first phase of the trial took place over a span of 2 years on a significant proportion of Italian ALS patients.

The objective of the trials was to evaluate if and when eye tracking technologies had a positive impact on ALS patients' lives. The emphasis was on the overall quality of life (actual and perceived) and, for this reason; we adopted well-recognized Quality of Life assessment scales (described below) in our study. To have a realistic representation of user satisfaction, we decided to run the trials with off-the-shelf eye-tracking devices and software, so that our results would be repeatable in other environments.

ALS patients have severe mobility impairments, being often confined to bed and dependent on several medical devices. To ease their participation in the trials, as well as to remove a potentially dangerous stress factor, all of the trials were based within each patient's domestic home environment.

Each patient was given the opportunity to use an eye tracking system for several consecutive days (1 or 2 weeks) in order to get accustomed to it and to compensate for the somewhat difficult impact of the first setup. He/she could use the eye tracker in his/her own domestic environment, choosing when to use the system and for which activities.

Methodology

The patients were selected and supported by a 4 person multi-disciplinary team. The team was composed of a neurologist, a psychologist, a speech and language therapist and a computer engineer. The neurologist was primarily involved in selecting the patients and assessing their ability to participate in the trial according to the criteria presented below. The psychologist evaluated the quality of life of the patients throughout the trial and assisted them in the process of accepting the aid and including it in their understanding of their extended abilities. The speech and language therapist trained the patients in the use of the eye tracking device and in related applications. The computer engineer, finally, provided technical support and troubleshooting.

Three contacts were organized during the lending period: an initial contact for basic training in the use of the eye tracker and for a baseline evaluation of the patient's conditions; a mid-period check to reassure the patient that the team was following their progress and to solve potential problems; and a final evaluation of the patient at the end of the trial.

Patients were selected among the whole population of ALS patients in the North-Western regions of Italy (namely, Piemonte, Lombardia, Valle d'Aosta) according to public, transparent and ethically approved recruitment criteria. In particular, the criteria were:

- The patient was unable to speak intelligibly. This included patients without speaking ability or patients who were about to lose this ability. This criterion was applied to ensure suitable patient motivation for participation in the study.
- The patient was able to understand the aim of the study. In particular, he or she should understand that the eye tracker would be taken away after 1-2 weeks, that his/her quality of life will be monitored during the

study, and that the trialed technology may be unstable or experimental.

- The patient was able to give an informed consent.
- The patient should at least have a basic level of computer literacy. This enabled us to rely on previous (pre-illness) knowledge of a basic use of a computer system.

The patients who were trialed had various degrees of impairment of hand function: some of them were still able to use mouse-like devices or special keyboards, while some were already paralyzed in this aspect.

During the *initial meeting*, the psychologist assessed the initial conditions of the patient, with particular emphasis on quality of life, and the speech and language therapist set up the equipment and provided initial training.

The assessment of initial conditions was performed through an interview according to four internationally recognized quantitative scales: quality of life, using the McGill Quality of Life Questionnaire (MQOL) (Cohen, Hassan, Lapointe, & Mount, 1995; Cohen, Mount, Strobel, & Bui, 1996); the Satisfaction With Life Scale (SWLS) (Diener, Emmons, Larsen, & Griffin, 1985; Pavot & Diener, 1993); depression, using the Zung Self-Rating Depression Scale (Zung, 1965); and perception of burden, using the Self-Perceived Burden Scale (Novak & Guest, 1989; Deeken, Taylor, Mangan, Yabroff, & Ingham, 2003). During the same meeting, the speech and language therapist provided initial training to the patient and his/her caregiver(s) on the calibration and use of the eye tracking system, as well as the main applications used in eye tracking mode, such as writing, communicating, using the Internet and accessing Windows functions. The training session usually included other specialized software identified with the help of the computer engineer according to the user's needs and interests.

During the *loan period*, the patient had access to "hotline" support with the psychologist, the speech and language therapist and the computer engineer, depending on his or her needs. This usually included usability issues and technical problems. A mid-period call was also scheduled to check on progress or problems.

At the end of the loan period a *final assessment* meeting was organized in which the same four initial questionnaires were repeated, augmented by two additional specific eye-tracking related questionnaires: the "standard COGAIN questionnaire" (Donegan et al., 2006), and a specific questionnaire developed by the ALS centre focusing on qualitative aspects and feelings, and analyzing the time spent with the system, the training process, subjective satisfaction, and influence on life quality.

Patients Involved

The recruitment criteria identified 16 patients suitable for the trials, amongst whom 12 were men and 4 were women. Their ages ranged from 32 to 78 (the average was 45). The data reported in this paper relates to the trials conducted between April 2006 and August 2007, although the trials still continue with new patients.

The participants presented a wide range of clinical characteristics: 7 patients had lost their respiratory abilities and therefore had a tracheotomy (a procedure by which air is directly pumped into the lungs through a tube installed in the patient's trachea). Out of the 16 in total, 8 patients had a percutaneous endoscopic gastrostomy (PEG), i.e., a feeding tube suitable for those who cannot swallow, administering fluids and nutrition directly into the stomach. Finally, in the trial group, 6 patients were anarthric (i.e., have lost the motor ability enabling them to speak) and another 7 had severe dysarthria (meaning that their language is very difficult to understand).

Since the first informal contact, all patients have shown a strong interest in eye-tracking systems. Most of them had, in fact, already heard about or looked for information about this technology.

Figure 1. A screen shot of iABLE (on the left – © SR LABS. Used with permission) and Pietro (on the right)

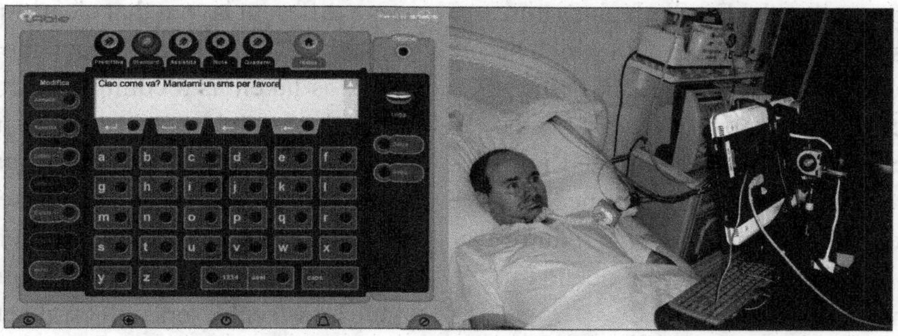

Data Collection

The trials allowed us to gather both quantitative and qualitative data corresponding to the scores in the above-mentioned questionnaires. However, the relatively small sample size prevented us from deriving statistically significant conclusions. Nevertheless, amongst several patients there was clear evidence of a significant positive impact on their quality of life. These positive outcomes are best illustrated by the technology's impact in the following case examples.

Case Study: Marcello

Marcello is 47 and lives at his own home with his family. Prior to the illness Marcello worked as a travelling salesman, frequently travelling the country. At the time of the trial he was using a switch-controlled scanning computer system with an on-screen keyboard controlled by a foot switch. Marcello had previously used the switch scanning system successfully for social communication and for sending emails, but had recently been experiencing considerable problems with the system due to diminishing movement in his feet. Marcello had sought and requested an eye control system, but the Piemonte Regional Government denied him a grant. He later succeeded, thanks to the help of the Italian ALS Association, in raising enough funds to purchase an eye tracker, and purchased a MyTobii with iABLE software (Figure

1). He now uses this system 16 hours a day for communication, writing, emailing, Internet access, telephoning, environmental control, etc. He is also in the process of writing a book in collaboration with other ALS patients who use eye trackers.

Case Study: Pietro

Pietro (in Figure 1, on the right) is 52 years old and lives at home with his wife. Before the illness he was a web designer and, through the use of his gaze control system, has been able to continue in his profession. During the initial trials he was still able to use a mouse (plus a separate switch) as an alternative to gaze control. Pietro does not need a communication aid as he still successfully uses labial movements for communication with his family. He uses numerous programs for his work, and tried them all on the Erica system during the first part of the trial. The results of his initial involvement in the Torino/ALS Centre user trials were positive but, at the time, because he could still use a mouse, he did not need an eye control system. Some time after the initial trial, however, he lost the ability to use a mouse and applied to the Health Service to fund the purchase of an eye tracker. Having done a considerable amount of research and trying a range of systems, Pietro decided that an EyeTech TM3 was the most appropriate for his particular requirements. Before this, he had tried other eye tracking systems but these had proven considerably less effective in controlling his web design programs. As well as the level of accuracy that the EyeTech gives him, Pietro also finds the user interface, with which he accesses the mouse button controls, magnification, etc., particularly appropriate for his needs. In addition, the EyeTech can be 'plugged into' any Windows computer. Because of his need for a powerful system for his graphic design requirements and also for writing music, he needed to buy a specific hi-spec computer.

SECOND PHASE

After the first phase, we changed the methodology of the trials and broadened the range of cases and conditions. In particular, in the second phase we aimed to analyse different types of patients with ALS as well as patients with other disabilities, and to gather information aimed at enabling us to understand their whole Assistive Technology needs. The eye tracker was one of many tools considered with respect to the range of communication and assistive technologies offered.

In this way, we evaluated the actual impact of eye trackers on real patient needs. The results were of a qualitative nature, since we were facing significant variation in patient conditions. This enabled us to establish appropriate practices in the general field of assessment.

The second trial phase was also made possible by the opportunity to adopt a different eye tracker, the MyTobii P10 device, which was more versatile and adaptable to a wider range of cases. This also gave us the opportunity to better compare the differences between the two eye tracking systems used in the two phases of the trials.

The P10 device, lent through the COGAIN project, has been reconfigured thanks to the kind cooperation of the Italian reseller (SR LABS). In particular, SR LABS are selling a much more sophisticated user interface, currently available in Italian only, making the eye tracker more useful and more greatly appreciated by literate and advanced users. The new interface, called iAble, uses a different layout that clearly separates areas "to look at" from areas "to act upon", i.e., where a gaze is taken as a command action. With this separation, much more complex interfaces may be designed and have been integrated in the iAble framework. Depending on the user and on their former computer knowledge, we choose whether to propose the simpler MyTobii grid or the new iAble interface. Users will be able to test both interfaces and to change their choice autonomously during the loan period.

The new eye tracker was immediately appreciated for its substantially easier and less convoluted calibration and initialization procedures, both for the user and the caregiver. These aspects are highly beneficial in terms of establishing a more relaxed approach to the new aid.

As a first partial result of this phase of the trial, all three of the trialled patients with ALS have started the procedure with the relevant Health Service to receive an eye tracker.

Case Study: Marcella

Marcella is around 60 years of age and lives alone. She has a home caregiver, but is left alone each day from 2 p.m. to 8 p.m. Marcella is still able to speak relatively intelligibly, but is no longer able to move. Her only effective movement is via the index finger of her right hand. During the evaluation, Marcella expressed the need to be able to respond to phone calls and to be able to control the remote control of her TV set, on which she relies during the long hours when she is alone. The eye tracker has been tested with her, but she currently refuses to use computer aids, at least whilst she can do without them.

We are currently investigating technical solutions for automatically lifting the phone upon incoming calls and for sending infrared commands to the TV via special remote controls requiring very low activation force. The challenge is to find highly personalized solutions by exploiting low-cost technical components, and by avoiding (as much as possible) solutions requiring a personal computer.

OUTCOMES AND DISCUSSION

While it is important to bear in mind the very brief nature of each trial, the introduction of an eye control system improved the perceived quality of life of many patients, as demonstrated by the following results:

On the whole, the Eyegaze systems used were considered efficient and effective, and facilitated more complex communication. Patients commented that they were able to express more than only their primary needs.

- The ability of the patient to use applications independently, once they had calibrated them successfully, was a positive aspect for all of the patients. This is not possible with all other methods of communication, such as an E-Tran frame, which relies on a communication partner. One patient was able to communicate with a grandchild independently using the eye-control system.
- Patients were impressed with the prediction/vocabulary that enabled faster communication, and the synthesized speech was also well received.

During the COGAIN project, a successful way has been found for electronic engineers and computer engineers to collaborate with doctors and paramedics. We now have a well motivated group who are able to work as a team in an efficient and effective way. The skills of the neurologist have been found to play a key part in highlighting those cases where technical support from the joint team of engineers and allied health professionals is necessary. However, at the same time, the team is finding it increasingly difficult to respond to each individual patient's needs, especially through the utilization of low-cost solutions. This issue is particularly problematic with patients who have progressive illnesses and need multidisciplinary support throughout the *whole course* of the disease, and who need the team to be able to find solutions to the various problems that arise on an ongoing basis. A particularly serious problem with this group is that, in Italy, each patient is only able to receive a new technical aid 2 years following the previous one and, as is well known, the technical requirements of someone with ALS/MND can change many times during such a long period.

The medical team's impressions have been very positive. They felt that the level of satisfaction and engagement gained from eye control was relative to the level of the person's disability. Patients that were unable to speak or move any limb (typical of the middle stage of ALS) were highly motivated to learn a new method of communication and felt that eye control gave them hope. The team felt, following the trials, that eye control is a real option for ALS patients once other methods of control (head-mouse, switches etc.) have failed.

The COGAIN project has helped to raise awareness of the potential benefits of gaze control technology and the sales of these systems are beginning to increase. It is hoped that as more people become aware of the benefits of gaze controlled technology, the funding for these systems will become more commonly available and the necessary support provided by an ever-increasing number of regional health authorities.

REFERENCES

Cohen, S. R., Hassan, S. A., Lapointe, B. J., & Mount, B. M. (1996). Quality of life in HIV disease McGill quality of life questionnaire. *AIDS (London, England)*, *10*, 1421–1427. doi:10.1097/00002030-199610000-00016

Cohen, S. R., Mount, B. M., Strobel, M. G., & Bui, F. (1995). The McGill quality of life questionnaire: A measure of quality of life appropriate for people with advanced disease. A preliminary study of validity and acceptability . *Palliative Medicine*, *9*, 207–219. doi:10.1177/026921639500900306

Deeken, J. F., Taylor, K. L., Mangan, P., Yabroff, K. R., & Ingham, J. M. (2003). Care for the caregivers: A review of self-report instruments developed to measure the burden, needs, and quality of life of informal caregivers. *Journal of Pain and Symptom Management*, *26*(4), 922–953. doi:10.1016/S0885-3924(03)00327-0

Diener, E., Emmons, R., Larsen, J., & Griffin, S. (1985). The satisfaction with life scale. *Journal of Personality Assessment*, *49*(1), 71–75. doi:10.1207/s15327752jpa4901_13

Donegan, M., Oosthuizen, L., Bates, R., Istance, H., Holmqvist, E., Lundalv, M., & Signorile, I. (2006). *Report of user trials and usability studies*. (Deliverable D3.3. Communication by Gaze Interaction (COGAIN), Project IST-2003-511598). Retrieved from the COGAIN Association website: http://www.cogain.org/wiki/COGAIN_Reports

Novak, M., & Guest, C. (1989). Application of a multidimensional caregiver burden inventory. *The Gerontologist*, *29*(6), 798–803. doi:10.1093/geront/29.6.798

Pavot, W., & Diener, E. (1993). Review of the satisfaction with life scale. *Psychological Assessment*, *5*(2), 164–172. doi:10.1037/1040-3590.5.2.164

Zung, W. W. (1965). A self-rating depression scale. *Archives of General Psychiatry, 12*, 63-70. The American Medical Association, Chicago, Illinois. Copyright 1965, American Medical Association.

Chapter 7
Participatory Design:
The Story of Jayne and Other Complex Cases

Mick Donegan
ACE Centre, UK

ABSTRACT

The ACE Centre user trials have involved over a hundred people who have severe and complex physical, cognitive and visual difficulties. Participatory Design methodology underpinned the approach that was adopted, which involved being led by the requirements of the most complex users. Jayne was one of many users through whom we not only developed more effective ways of using the technology, but also more innovative strategies to support its implementation. In this chapter, we describe the process, and outcome of our participatory design approach, through the cases of Jayne and other users.

INTRODUCTION

"...I had an email yesterday from one of the tutors who was saying that you were being disruptive in class and talking too much on your gaze control system... and I thought 'Fantastic!' You haven't had a voice for twenty years and you've suddenly got one and people start complaining that you're speaking too much!..."

DOI: 10.4018/978-1-61350-098-9.ch007

CASE STUDIES

The above comment was made by Tom, a specialist speech and language therapist who works in a college for students who have disabilities. Tom was referring to a student who had started to use a gaze control system, as a result of the COGAIN project. The user was called Jayne. Jayne was one of numerous users involved in the ACE Centre user trials, spanning five years.

The COGAIN project has involved young people and adults who have a wide range of complex physical, cognitive and visual difficulties (Donegan et al., 2005, 2006a, 2006b, 2009). Our approach relied heavily upon Participatory Design methodology, an approach which involved being led by the users (Bødker et al., 1993; Bødker, 1996). In participatory design, users (putative, potential or future) are invited to cooperate with researchers and developers during an innovation process. Potentially, they participate during several stages of an innovation process ie., during the initial exploration and problem definition both to help define the problem and to focus ideas for solution; and during development by evaluating proposed solutions. By adopting this approach, we decided to be led by the requirements of the most complex users. It was felt that, if we could modify the technology to meet the needs of this group, then the scope of our work could benefit many equally (and less) complex users worldwide. Aspects of this work have been conducted in collaboration with other specialist centres of assistive technology.

During the COGAIN user trials, a range of gaze control systems were trialled by the ACE Centre. Whilst many users and those supporting them were keen to know which system was best, this question was, and always will be, impossible to answer. Each of the systems performed in different ways in terms of size, power, how well they dealt with involuntary movement and the user interface, etc. However, whilst it is not possible to answer the question of which is the best system, our users were able to inform us about their requirements. By listening to them, and being led by user requirements, we were able to collaborate with hardware and software developers, other professionals, carers and, of course, the users themselves to proceed through an iterative process that led to more and more of their requirements being met. Jayne was one amid many unique users though whom we not only discovered more effective ways of using the technology, but also more innovative strategies to support its implementation. Below, we describe the process and outcome of participatory design with Jayne and other complex users.

CASE STUDIES

Jayne has embraced gaze control through the encouragement of family, friends and college staff. During a recent visit, the college server had become jammed by a flurry of emails; "I get emails now" her mother says, pausing to reflect; "endless emails, but I'm sure this will calm down". Jayne had previously refused to use all other high-tech methods of computer control. "I think it's the technology itself" says her mother, "she so hated switches and I think felt they were unreliable".

Jayne had made it perfectly clear, for her switch control was simply too erratic. However, this is a successful access method for many other people. For further detailed information, Donegan et al. (2005, Chapter 5) discuss alternative access methods including special switches, mice and keyboards. Tom sees such devices being set up and successfully used by students on a daily basis

It seems that some users associate certain activities with specific methods of computer control. Their choice needs to be knowledge based – guided by what is known of the user's physical and cognitive abilities (Donegan &Oosthuizen, 2006). For example, Michael uses a head switch to control his environment including the television, but, chooses to email and listen to music with his gaze control system. Meanwhile, Jonathan (Brough, 2009) uses a switch to control a camcorder on a pan and tilt base, but, chooses to write; Skype; play games; make PowerPoint presentations; and to visit the MyTobii Community (2011) with his gaze control system

As far as Russell is concerned, his wife says that he is able to converse with his daughter by adopting the voice within his gaze-controlled software. Independently reading and writing emails

Figure 1. Russell's low-tech communication system side A (left) and N

A	B	C		N	O	P	
D	E	F		Q	R	S	
G	H	I		T	U	V	
J	K	L	M	W	X	Y	Z

not only offers him much prized privacy, but it also fuels his passion for cars because he is able to stay in contact with his old work colleagues.

However, in comparison with Michael, Russell has a low-tech communication system. Russell's system is illustrated by Figure 1. It is the size of an A5 sheet of paper. Red capital letters appear on a white background. The first side (on the left) is called A and the second side (on the right) is called N. His communication partner asks "Would you like side A or N?" and Russell looks upwards to confirm his choice. Should he choose side "A" his communication partner asks "would you like row A, D, G or J?" Should he choose row "A" his communication partner asks "would you like letter A, B or C?" and so on and so forth. Russell relies on his low-tech communication system. It is indispensable for activities such as simple environmental control i.e, changing the TV channel.

In fact, many users are, in fact, very reliant upon a low-tech communication system, such as an auditory scan, or an E-TRAN frame. The ACE Centre has observed that there are users, in particular those users who have Locked-In Syndrome such as Russell, for whom it is absolutely critical. In these cases, where gaze control is successful it tends to be chosen for quite specific activities, such as listening to the radio or reading books. Admittedly, the current technology is consistently unable to address all of their needs. It has been found that many people who have Locked-In Syndrome, do retain good control of either an upwards or downwards eye movement. Whilst

such movement is rapid and decisive, the pupil tends to recede behind the eye lid. The concern is that it is quite a challenge for gaze control to interpret such movement. It would be interesting to compare how well an eye gesture recognition switch, once it becomes available, compares with direct gaze control in terms of speed, comfort, accuracy and fatigue.

For many years, eye pointing to vocabulary in a low tech communication book has been invaluable for Jayne (Figure 2). Her low-tech communication book comprises over eighty pages of vocabulary. It is highly adaptable, affordable, portable and reliable. In the summer of 2008, Tom introduced a slightly sceptical but hopeful Jayne to a gaze control system.

Jayne experiences Athetoid Cerebral Palsy (CP), which causes involuntary movement and postural instability. Long and short term goals were identified for the assessment and implementation phases. The first goal set was to simply engage her interest. Previously, Jayne felt very weary and frustrated with high-tech communication. The involuntary movement triggered by other methods of computer control created abject discomfort and sheer exhaustion. Undoubtedly, optimum seating and positioning is important for computer access, yet it was felt that Jayne might have rejected gaze control technology if the process had begun differently, by addressing difficult postural issues. Tom's approach was user focused, guided by what is known of her physical and cognitive abilities, and, it was designed to meet

Figure 2. A contents page from Jayne's low tech communication book

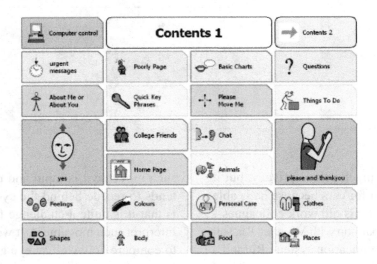

Jayne's interests and needs (Donegan & Oosthuizen, 2006).

It was possible to calibrate the gaze control system once the MyTobii D10, from Tobii Technology, had been positioned so that Jayne felt at ease. Jayne had good vision. A straightforward step through calibration procedure utilizing all areas of the screen was saved. Therefore, Jayne did not need to use the default calibration, nor have several options saved. However, if Jayne had felt under pressure to perform, or been unduly anxious, then naturally difficulties might have arisen. It was necessary to introduce the gaze control system in simple steps to inspire her confidence and increase her motivation.

Following an initial fail proof assessment, Tom loaded a gaze controlled version of Jayne's communication book onto the gaze control system. "Right from the start" Tom says, Jayne had "wanted to use the gaze control system to communicate." Jayne practiced plentifully and, as Tom said, "would happily use the system all of the time if she could". Hansen (2007) asserts that graded practice fosters the interest and prevents the disengagement of people who have progressive degenerative diseases and associated motivational difficulties. New users need to acquire new skills. Grasping the concept of distinguishing between a casual look and a deliberate gaze is essential; while the individual becomes conscious of, and able to direct, their eye movements.

In the early days, Russell was faced with the challenge of increasing his eye stamina; but nowadays, he his able to use his device for up to five hours a day. Whilst Jonathan has built up excellent eye stamina and has refined pointer control, he recalls how exhausting gaze control felt at first. So, he strongly recommends starting off gradually, and emphasises the importance of being shown a good basic demo for encouragement during the early stages. Simple games definitely do assist in developing eye stamina, as do preparatory activities for scrolling within the Internet Browser such as selecting My Documents, scrolling through to My Pictures, selecting open file, choosing a photo and encouraging the user to slide their eyes to the right, left, up and down (read more at MyTobii Community, 2011).

Given the enthusiasm and success achieved by Jayne, it was perhaps made easier for Tom to adopt a flexible approach that was 'ready to change in relation to her response to the technology and the software provided' (Donegan & Oosthuizen, 2006). Tom realized that Jayne was able to access a more compact and portable device by trialling a MyTobii P10 gaze control system. A rolling mount allowed small changes in positioning to be made, gradually, the device was moved into a position that encouraged Jayne to have an improved posture. Her vocabulary cells were made smaller, increasing the content available to her. Of course, the cells could be made larger if they became too effortful or inaccurate for Jayne to access.

During her speech and language therapy sessions, Jayne's grids were frequently updated with additional vocabulary and functions. "It is exactly the same grid; it has just got more environmental controls added and a few more pages" says her speech and language therapy assistant, while adding a sentence bar to each page to open up her vocabulary for emailing purposes. The advantages have been "huge" her mother says, "obviously there is communication, but now there is more spontaneous communication. Plus, Jayne is able to show us her sense of humour! Jayne has increased in confidence; self esteem; and her gaze control system is a source of pride. Jayne absolutely loves controlling her iPod and is able to make her own play list. Jayne is able to use the telephone fairly independently. In the future, we aim to use Skype. Just hearing her voice and not to have someone interpreting what she is saying to me; not always accurately, is a big bonus".

In and around campus, Jayne is freely able to open doors. Tom imagines that the integrated use of environmental control will prompt her to trial independent mobility in the future, if only to adjust her own position. Currently, Jayne prefers to have an attendant assisted wheelchair. For some users there would need to be a suitably designed mobility track, together with an appropriate software interface, for the selection of location and/ or wheelchair position. (Gaze based mobility is discussed in greater depth by Bates and colleagues in Chapter 10 of this book. See also the survey of existing "defacto" standards and systems of gaze

based mobility control by Tuisku et al., 2008. Gaze based mobility is one of the areas for future research as discussed in Chapter 25; a lot of development is required before motor wheelchairs can safely and robustly be steered by the means of gaze alone.)

The COGAIN trial was a valuable experience to such an extent that Tom advanced the case for funding for Jayne to be awarded her own gaze control system, and to attend an additional year of college to consolidate her communication skills. Tom proposed a PowerBox communication aid (www.smartboxat.com) with an ALEA Intelligaze system (www.alea-technologies.de) - light, small and robust enough to be safely wheelchair mounted. For this reason, Jayne is now a spirited gaze control communicator.

All in all, the case study of Jayne illustrates how pivotal it is to receive a high level of support; an individually tailored software interface; to have a can-do attitude; and to be in a positive environment. The ability to secure funding for gaze control systems greatly varies among members of the European Community. It is to be hoped that gaze control systems will become more readily available by raising awareness of the long term benefits; the relative cost savings; and the role it plays in enabling people, who have severe and complex disabilities to enjoy more active lives. This is not only exemplified in the story of Jayne, but is also reflected in the stories of many other users.

With the support of COGAIN, Helen has changed from being a young person who found switch control very difficult and tiring, into being a successful user of gaze control technology. A transformation greatly facilitated by her own determination and the support of her family and school. Helen has a rare metabolic disorder and has extreme difficulty in controlling her movement sufficiently well to be able to operate many of the methods typically used to control a computer. It is probably fair to say that any kind of movement, even speech, has the potential to trigger involuntary movement. For her, speaking or moving any of her limbs is difficult, tiring and uncomfortable.

In primary school, Helen first used gaze control with musical and story activity grids. Helen selected targets of varying sizes so that the most reliable and accurate size of cell could be identified for her. Eventually, when Helen was ready to write words of her own, the computer could not pick up her eye movement well enough for her to be able to select one letter from a whole alphabet of letters. Each letter was too small, so she had to use a grid with larger targets and select a letter by making two hits.

By the time Helen was due to leave primary school, she was excellent at using her own customised grids, often surprising her teaching assistant with her independent use of justification, bold, underline and italics. Today, Helen continues to develop her literacy skills, but, two hit grids remain very important for her. Her accuracy is improving well, but her head control remains difficult. Whilst she is able to accurately hit smaller and smaller targets during practice and leisure activities, in truth, this does not require her to produce a written piece of work. When she is under pressure, and the task becomes more cognitively demanding, larger targets continue to be easier and more accurate to hit. Consistency in the shape, and location of targets, balances speed and accuracy with the time she needs to think.

During her transition from primary to secondary school, Helen's teaching assistant invested a complete term with the staff at her feeder school, in order to transfer her knowledge and skills. Helen's special educational advisory teacher identified that the following are necessary to support teaching assistants who are working with gaze control users: being confident with computers; good training; having time to develop grids (page sets); access to technical support; knowledge of lesson content; and knowledge of other users who have similar difficulties.

OUTCOMES AND DISCUSSION

Taking an overview of the user trials and the individuals involved, it is possible to see that rating a system relates to how well it meets the abilities and needs of each unique user. Whilst the user trials were carried out in a range of different settings, and with a range of different people with different disabilities, there were certain themes and issues which emerged and became highlighted over time. Based on these, we were able to make the following general recommendations, which we believe will enhance the chances of success:

Users should have the opportunity to try a range of different gaze control systems before deciding which one to use. Some suppliers sell one system only. However, our trials have shown that, for some users, any one of several gaze control systems would work successfully. It is recommended that suppliers selling a single system should make sure that customers are aware of the alternatives.

Those users who have the potential to use direct pointer control, as opposed to using specialized framework software such as 'The Grid 2' or 'Tobii Communicator', should have the opportunity to try out direct pointer control on a range of systems, before deciding which system is best for them.

Each assessment or gaze control trial should be planned carefully in advance. The gaze control system used; the type of calibration; the kind of mounting system; and the activities used during the assessment cannot be effectively planned without (a) acquiring advance knowledge of the individual's visual, cognitive and physical abilities; and (b) being end-user focused so that the assessment or trial meets the users' level of motivation, interests and needs (Donegan & Oosthuizen, 2006).

Once a system has been purchased, it is essential that ongoing training is provided for the user and those supporting them i.e., carers and/or personal assistants. Progress should be reviewed regularly, so that the hardware and software can evolve in relation to the user's requirements (Donegan & Oosthuizen, 2006).

During such a review, attention needs to be given to any improvements in the user's level of accuracy with eye control technology. If, for example, they are using a grid-based application and have improved, for example, then the reviewer should consider whether or not they are ready for either (a) a revised, more powerful grid with a greater number of smaller cells; or (b) whether to consider direct pointer control.

REFERENCES

Bødker, S. (1996). Creating conditions for participation: Conflicts and resources in systems design. *Human-Computer Interaction, 11*(3), 215–236. doi:10.1207/s15327051hci1103_2

Bødker, S., Christiansen, E., Ehn, P., Markussen, R., Mogensen, P., & Trigg, R. (1993). *The AT Project: Practical research in cooperative design (DAIMI No. PB-454)*. Aarhus, Denmark: Department of Computer Science, Aarhus University.

Brough, J. (2009). My life and spinal injury by Jonathan Brough. A youtube video. Retrieved from http://www.youtube.com/watch?v=uKSRJflxOJQ

Donegan, M., Cotmore, S., Holmqvist, E., Buchholz, M., Lundalv, M., Pasian, V., et al. (2009). Final user trials report. (Deliverable D3.6. Communication by Gaze Interaction (COGAIN), Project IST-2003-511598). Retrieved from the COGAIN Association website: http://www. cogain.org/wiki/COGAIN_Reports

Donegan, M., & Oosthuizen, L. (2006). The 'KEE' concept for eye-control and complex disabilities: Knowledge-based, end user-focused and evolutionary. Proceedings of the 2nd Conference on Communication by Gaze Interaction (COGAIN 2006), Turin, Italy (pp. 83–87). Retrieved from the COGAIN Association website: http://www. cogain.org/conference

Donegan, M., Oosthuizen, L., Bates, R., Daunys, G., Hansen, J. P., Joos, M., et al. (2005). User requirements report with observations of difficulties users are experiencing. (Deliverable D3.1. Communication by Gaze Interaction (COGAIN), Project IST-2003-511598). Retrieved from the COGAIN Association website: http://www. cogain.org/wiki/COGAIN_Reports

Donegan, M., Oosthuizen, L., Bates, R., Istance, H., Holmqvist, E., Lundalv, M., et al. (2006b) Report of user trials and usability studies. (Deliverable D3.3. Communication by Gaze Interaction (COGAIN), Project IST-2003-511598). Retrieved from the COGAIN Association website: http:// www.cogain.org/wiki/COGAIN_Reports

Donegan, M., Oozthuizen, L., Daunys, G., Istance, R., Bates, R., Signorile, I., et al. (2006a). Report on features of the different systems and development needs. (Deliverable D3.2. Communication by Gaze Interaction (COGAIN), Project IST-2003-511598). Retrieved from the COGAIN Association website: http://www.cogain.org/wiki/ COGAIN_Reports

Hansen, J. P. (2007). Communication by gaze interaction with computers. Nordic Conference on Motor Neuron Disease (MND) and Meeting of ALS/ MND alliance. Oslo, Norway. (The talk is available as a Youtube video: "Communication by gaze interaction with computers". Retrieved from http:// www.youtube.com/watch?v=lL9kuCbWnpk)

MyTobii Community. (2001). Retrieved from www.mytobiicommunity.com

Tuisku, O., Bates, R., Stepankova, O., Fejtova, M., Novak, P., Istance, H., et al. (2008). A survey of existing 'de-facto' standards and systems of gaze based mobility control. (Deliverable D2.6. Communication by Gaze Interaction (COGAIN), Project IST-2003-511598). Retrieved from the COGAIN Association website: http://www. cogain.org/wiki/COGAIN_Reports

Section 3
Gaze Interaction and Interface Design Issues

Chapter 8
Communication and Text Entry by Gaze

Päivi Majaranta
University of Tampere, Finland

ABSTRACT

There are several ways to write by gaze. In a typical setup, gaze direction is used to point and dwell-select letters on an on-screen keyboard. Alternatively, if the person cannot fixate, the eyes can be used as switches using blinks or rough gestures to select items. This chapter introduces different ways to enter text by gaze and reviews related research. We will discuss techniques to enhance text entry by gaze, such as word and letter prediction, and show how the possibility of adjusting the duration of the dwell time affects learning and typing speed. In addition, design issues such as keyboard layout and feedback are raised, with practical examples and guidelines that may aid in designing interfaces for gaze-based text entry.

INTRODUCTION

Serious accident, disease, or a brainstem stroke may lead to a state wherein one is unable to move or talk. Often the eyes still function, even though the person is otherwise totally paralysed. In this situation, the movement of the eyes or the gaze direction can be used as means of communication. For example, the doctor may ask the patient to look up as a sign of agreement. One can also use

a communication frame with pictures or letters attached to it. By looking at the letters, the disabled person can spell out words. The conversation partner interprets the eye movements into words and sentences. In Figure 1, a boy communicates with his mother. He looks at first the letter, then the corresponding colour of button. The grouping of the letters makes it easier for the helper to distinguish the targets from each other, so there is no need to separate targets that are near each other. Feedback is given by speaking out the letter. More examples of non-electronic communication

DOI: 10.4018/978-1-61350-098-9.ch008

Figure 1. The person on the other side of the E-TRAN gaze communication frame acts as a human eye tracker and interprets the gaze direction through the transparent board. A letter is chosen by first looking at it, then looking at the colour of button that corresponds to the colour of the letter. Downloadable gaze communication frame templates, along with instructions for making and using them, are available at the COGAIN website (Eye Gaze Communication Board, 2010). Photo © 2005 COGAIN. Used with permission

aids are given by Goossens' and Crain (1987) or Scott (1998).

An advanced method of tracking the gaze direction is to use an eye tracking device that allows entering text and controlling a computer independently. An eye tracker, typically placed under the screen, follows the eye movements of a person looking at the screen. A computer program interprets the gaze direction and maps it to individual keys on the virtual keyboard. Gaze direction is used for pointing. The letter focused on can then be selected either via a separate switch (e.g., a key on the keyboard) or by staring at the letter with the focus, in which case dwell time is used for selection.

There are several ways to write by gaze. If the person cannot fixate, the eyes can be used as switches. In this case, rough glances up or down, or blinks, can then be used to select items. One can also write by gaze gestures; for example, a glance to the right and then down could form the letter 'T'. Some systems, such as Dasher (Ward & MacKay, 2000), are based on a language model. Dasher can predict the letters the user wants to write next. The more probable letters are given more screen space than the less probable choices, which makes them easier and faster to hit by gaze. Different ways to enter text by gaze are introduced below. We will also discuss techniques to enhance text entry by gaze and show how the possibility of adjusting the duration of the dwell time affects learning and typing speed. In addition, we provide practical examples and guidelines that may aid in designing interfaces for gaze-based text entry. This chapter is largely adapted from the doctoral thesis by Majaranta (2009); the thesis is freely available in electronic form online (link listed in references) for any reader who wishes to access full details of the research summarised below.

GAZE-BASED TEXT ENTRY METHODS

Systems that utilise eye tracking for text entry have existed since the 1970s (Majaranta & Räihä, 2002). We have categorised text entry methods into four classes according to input technique, following the categorisation introduced by Majaranta and Räihä (2007). The most common method of entering text by gaze is by using 1) *direct gaze pointing* to select letters from an on-screen keyboard. This is often called '*gaze typing*' (or '*eye typing*'), as the user enters text by 'pressing' keys on a virtual keyboard one at a time. Prolonged dwelling (fixation) is used to point at (and select) the letters. Text entry by 2) *discrete gaze gestures* is based on a gesture alphabet in which each character is formed by its own sequence of gaze strokes (saccades). Text entry via 3) *continuous gaze gestures*, or '*gaze writing*' (note the difference from 'gaze typing'), allows mode-free control via eye movements (allowing smooth-pursuit-type eye movement). A similar categorisation is used by Bee and André (2008), who distinguished among three types of gaze-based text entry methods: typing, gesturing, and continuous writing. We also add a separate class, for text entry by 4) *eye switches*. Using the eyes as simple switches enables gaze-based text entry by people who have only limited eye movement (e.g., can move their eyes only vertically) or have trouble fixating (Chapman, 1991; Donegan et al., 2005). The four different methods are described below.

Text Entry by Direct Gaze Pointing

The most common way to use gaze for text entry is direct pointing by looking at the desired letter on the virtual keyboard (see Figure 2). The user focuses (fixates) on the desired letter by looking it. The system gives feedback on the item in focus, for example, by highlighting the item or by moving a 'gaze cursor' over the key in focus. The item focused on can then be selected by means of a separate switch, a blink, or any muscle

activity. If no muscle control is available to the user, the letter can be selected by dwell time: the user needs to fixate on the key for longer than a predefined threshold time (typically, 500–1,000 ms) in order for the key to be selected. The letter typed appears in the text field, and the system may also give feedback on successful selection by speaking the letter or playing a 'click' sound (as discussed below).

Dwell-time-based eye typing can be slow, typically below 10 wpm, because dwell time durations set a limit to the maximum typing speed (Majaranta & Räihä, 2007). People need time for cognitive processing, to think about what to type next, to search for the next key on the keyboard, to correct errors, etc. However, experienced users may require considerably shorter dwell times (as low as 200–300 ms), which, naturally, increases the text entry rate correspondingly (up to about 20 wpm) (Majaranta, Ahola, & Špakov, 2009).

Figure 2. The typing interface of the LC Eyegaze (http://www.eyegaze.com/) system, using direct pointing. Photo © 2005 COGAIN (used with permission)

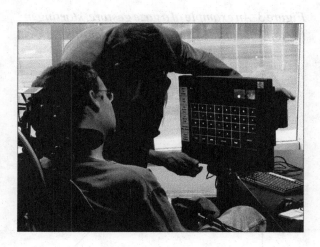

Text Entry by Discrete Gaze Gestures

In direct pointing, the user exploits fixations to point at and dwell on the target characters on the screen. Gaze gestures are based on a sequence of saccades: the user initiates a command by making a sequence of 'eye strokes' in a certain order. Figure 3 shows an example gesture. A gesture does not require dwell time, though dwell can be used to start a gesture or separate several gestures from each other. Making a gaze gesture still requires a brief stop (fixation) between the strokes (saccades).

A gaze gesture can be independent of the screen location and rely only on relative changes in the direction of gaze, or it may rely on certain locations (hot spots or target areas) on or off the screen. Using off-screen targets saves the actual screen space for other purposes (Isokoski, 2000). Gestures that are not bound to certain locations (on the screen) but are based on relative change in the direction of gaze are insensitive to accuracy problems and calibration shifting (Drewes & Schmidt, 2007). They are especially useful with small screens and in mobile situations involving mobile trackers (Bulling, Roggen, & Tröster, 2008). Obviously, gaze gestures that are used in free viewing situations should be complex enough

Figure 3. An example of a gaze gesture, starting in the top left corner, with a gazing order of SE, W, N

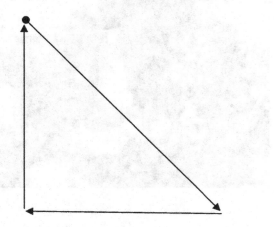

to differ from natural gaze patterns but still simple enough that people can easily learn and remember them.

An example of a gesture-based text entry system, EyeWrite (Wobbrock, Rubinstein, Sawyer, & Duchowski, 2008) and its alphabet, is given in Figure 4. The user enters characters by drawing letter-like gestures in a small dedicated window. The advantage of a separate input window is that there is no danger of the stroke overlapping with other user interface objects, which ensures robust interpretation of the gestures. The window also enables dynamic feedback while the user enters the strokes needed for each gesture. As soon as the gaze enters the active area, an arch is drawn there to illustrate a successful stroke and the target character recognised is shown in the final target area. The user draws the letters by moving the gaze (cursor) from one corner to another. For example, the letter 't' is entered by moving the cursor (gaze) from the top left corner to the top right corner, then to the bottom right corner (see Figure 4). The interpreted character is sent to a separate text input window, which has the focus (e.g., Notepad). No dwelling in the corner area is needed; the stroke is recognised as soon as the cursor crosses the line delimiting the corner area. The system is highly resistant to noise in input (inaccuracy in eye tracking). Therefore, the input window can be quite small, which is an advantage in gaze-controlled interfaces as compared to, for example, the more common QWERTY virtual keyboard that occupies most of the screen space. On the other hand, learning the gesture-based alphabet takes time. Furthermore, even if the gesture-based system does not require dwell time, the requirement of several strokes for each character involves time and may negate any advantage saved by not using dwell. Wobbrock et al. (2008) compared EyeWrite with an on-screen keyboard based on direct gaze pointing and dwell time in a longitudinal experiment. The average speed was 4.87 wpm for EyeWrite and 7.03 wpm for the on-screen keyboard. There were fewer errors left in text with EyeWrite, but there was

Figure 4. Screen capture of EyeWrite (Wobbrock et al., 2008) and its gesture-based alphabet (EyeWrite is available for free download, see EyeWrite, 2010)

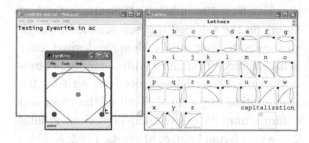

no significant difference in the number of errors corrected during entry.

Other examples of gaze-based text entry systems that exploit discrete gaze gestures include VisionKey, by Kahn, Heynen, and Snuggs (1999); the Minimal Device Independent Text Input Method (MDITIM), by Isokoski (2000); iWrite and StarWrite, by Urbina and Huckauf (2007); Eye-S, by Porta and Turina (2008); and Quikwriting, adapted for gaze by Bee and André (2008). More information and a detailed description of each are given by Majaranta (2009) and on COGAIN's Web site (http://www.cogain.org/).

Text Entry by Continuous Pointing Gestures

Most of our eye movements are based on fixations and saccades, where we look at things by stopping our gaze on the target and then 'jump' to the next target by moving our gaze to it. Continuous pointing gestures often resemble a smooth-pursuit type of eye movement, where the eye smoothly follows a moving target. Even if we move our gaze in saccadic jumps from one target to another, continuous writing is still useful for text entry by gaze. Our eyes are always on (if not closed) so can be compared to a pencil that is never lifted from the paper. Our eyes also move constantly; it is not natural for us to hold our gaze for long on a target. Even if we keep looking at one object, we

usually make small saccades within (and around) the object.

The best-known example of gaze-based text entry that exploits continuous pointing gestures is Dasher, developed by Ward and MacKay (2002). It is a zooming interface that dynamically changes as the user writes with it. In the beginning, all letters are located in a column on the right side of the screen, in alphabetical order. The user writes by pointing (looking) at the desired character. Immediately, the letter focused upon starts to move to the left and the area around it grows bigger (see Figure 5). Simultaneously, other letters start to move in smooth animation to the left and the language model of the system predicts the most probable next letters. The areas of the next most probable characters start to grow (as compared to other, less probable letters) within the chosen region. This brings the most probable next letters closer to the current cursor position, thus minimising distance and time for selection of the next letter(s). The letter is typed when it crosses the vertical line at the centre of the screen. Cancelling the last letter is done by looking to the left; the letter then moves back to the right side of the screen. Dasher's mode-free continuous operation makes it especially suitable for gaze, since only one bit of information is required: the direction

Figure 5. Dasher (Ward & MacKay, 2002) allows gaze writing using continuous pointing gestures

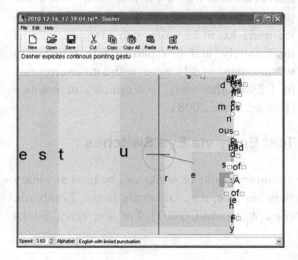

of gaze. No additional switches or dwell times are needed to make a selection or to cancel. It is also possible to select several characters with one gesture, which can significantly speed up writing. In fact, Dasher has been referred to as the world's fastest method of entering text by gaze, enabling a gaze writing speed of 10–25 wpm after a couple of hours' practice (Tuisku, Majaranta, Isokoski, & Räihä, 2008; Ward & MacKay, 2002), up to a world record speed of 34 wpm by an expert user (Ward & MacKay, 2002). However, as noted by Tuisku et al. (2008), Dasher may be a bit confusing in the beginning and mastering it takes some time.

Another example of a system based on continuous pointing gestures and zooming is the Stargazer developed by Hansen, Skovsgaard, Hansen, and Møllenbach (2008). In Stargazer, the user zooms on the z-axis and panning occurs on the x- and y-axis. At the beginning, all characters are positioned in the space in a circular form in a familiar (alphabetical) order around the central area. The user navigates ('flies') in the 3D space of characters by looking at the desired character. The 3D cursor points in the direction of navigation and the display pans toward the target character, which starts to move toward the centre of the screen. The target character will also start to grow bigger, indicating that the user is approaching it. Selection is performed by 'flying' through the target letter. The user is always returned to the initial view after a selection is made. Stargazer has been tested with a low-resolution (low-accuracy) tracker, with reasonably good results. Novice users learnt to write with Stargazer almost immediately, and test participants achieved a writing speed of 8.16 wpm, with a mean error rate of 1.23%, after only five minutes of practice (Hansen et al., 2008).

Text Entry via Eye Switches

Voluntary blinks or winks can be used as binary switches (see, e.g., Grauman, Betke, Lombardi, Gips, & Bradski, 2003). For text entry, blinks are usually combined with a scanning technique, with letters organised into a matrix. The system moves the focus automatically by scanning the alphabet matrix line by line. The highlighted line is selected by a blink. Then the individual letters on the selected line are scanned through and again the user blinks when the desired letter is highlighted. Text entry with scanning is obviously slow, since the user needs to wait for the scan routine to go through all of the rows and columns until the desired item is reached: around 2–6 wpm (Beukelman & Mirenda, 1992; Koester & Levine, 1994).

In addition to blinks, coarse eye movements can be used as switches. The Eye-Switch Controlled Communication Aids of Ten Kate, Frietman, Willems, Ter Haar Romeny, and Tenkink (1979) used large (about 15-degree) eye movements to the left and to the right as switches that could be used to start the scanning routine and to select the item currently focused upon. Eye switches can also be used as an eye-operated joystick: the user moves the cursor or shifts focus from item to item by looking left, right, up, or down. For example, the I4Control system (Fejtová, Fejt, & Lhotská, 2004) achieves text entry via eye switches by moving the mouse cursor over the desired key on an on-screen keyboard and selecting the key with a blink. The four different eye movements recognised by I4Control are activated by a glance in the corresponding direction. As long as the user looks up, the eye joystick is held in the up position. The central position (looking directly ahead) is used as a home position where no commands are issued.

COMMUNICATION VS. TEXT ENTRY

Communication is more than just production of text, and eye typing feels especially slow in face-to-face communication situations, since its entry rate (only a few words per minute) is far below that of human speech (150–250 wpm). The goal of the user is not just to type letters but to produce phrases and sentences. Writing a message letter by letter by eye is relatively slow. Phrases for everyday usage could and should be included in the program. The system should support editable phrases, because the needs of disabled users vary greatly. Since not all of the phrases can be visible at a time, they can be arranged in a tree structure. For example, in the phrase selection menu of LC Eyegaze, the person can first select a topic for the discussion and then access ready-made phrases related to the selected topic (Chapman, 1991).

The gaze communication system may also have a sentence buffer for predefined strings that can be joined together. The Eyetracker communication system developed by Friedman, Kiliany, Dzmura, and Anderson (1982) provides the option of first selecting a standard phrase (e.g., 'please give me') and then completing it with another ('a drink of water'). Ready-made greetings and phrases can speed up everyday communication, and a speech synthesiser can give the user a voice and the ability to speak aloud. However, the synthesised voice may not feel 'right' if it does not match the user's age and gender (Friedman et al., 1982).

Not all disabled people are able to read or write; instead, some use pictures and icons for communication. Therefore, it is useful for an eye-gaze-based communication system to support pictures in addition to text. Examples are PCS (Picture Communication Symbols), Minspeak, and Bliss; for more information about picture- and icon-based communication, see, e.g., the work of MacDonald (1998).

The natural eye-to-eye contact of typical communication is broken when the user needs to look at the computer screen during the intercourse. Because of this loss of facial communication, a see-through communication board (Goossens' & Crain, 1987; Scott, 1998) may actually feel more natural for everyday communication, since the people involved maintain a face-to-face connection (see Figure 1). The communication board can also be used everywhere, and it is always reliable

and does not 'crash'. Besides, an experienced human interpreter is a far more effective word predictor than any of the computer-based systems, which do not understand conversational context and situation and are not able to understand humour, etc. After years of practice, one may learn the locations of letters and therefore not need the board anymore; each letter has its position in thin air (Majaranta, 2004). There is still a need for more effective textual gaze communication, if we wish the eye tracker to reach the efficiency of a human interpreter.

METHODS TO SPEED UP TEXT ENTRY

Text entry by gaze is fairly slow, achieving a typing speed of only a few words per minute to around, at most, 10–15 wpm. Because the dwell time duration sets a maximum limit to the text entry rate, several attempts have been made to develop dwell-time-free systems (as introduced above). However, since dwell time has often been replaced with methods requiring extra saccades that increase the keystrokes required per character (KSPC) (as in gaze-gesture-based systems), only a minimal speed gain is obtained, if any.

Language models and character and word prediction can provide methods for more efficient text entry. Salvucci (1999) developed advanced methods wherein the user can look around the virtual keyboard and select by direct pointing without a dwell time delay. The system analyses the gaze path and tries to map the fixations to letters. It uses a dictionary and predefined grammar of how the letters follow each other when judging whether the fixations belong to the word or not. In an experiment with seven novice participants, Salvucci found that participants 'typed' with an average speed of 822 ms per character, which equates to about 15 wpm. Typing rates spanned an average of about 28 wpm (430 ms per character) for the fastest participant to about 9 wpm (1,272 ms per character) with the slowest participant. The fairly long times needed per character are most probably caused by the long search time needed by a novice who has no previous experience of on-screen keyboards. It would be interesting to repeat Salvucci's experiment to find out how rapidly true experts can glance from character to character and what their pointing accuracy is.

In the following section, we briefly introduce common ways to implement word and character prediction in gaze-based text entry systems and related research.

Predicted Word Lists

A common way to implement word prediction is to present a list of predicted words for the user. The words are based on the letters the user has written so far. The list is dynamically adjusted as more letters are written and the number of possible continuations of the word decreases. GazeTalk (Hansen, Hansen, & Johansen, 2001; an updated version is illustrated in Figure 6) provides both letter and word prediction (Hansen, Johansen, Hansen, Itoh, & Mashino, 2003). The six cells toward the bottom right contain the six most likely letters to continue the word that is being entered (shown in the two top cells at left). The leftmost cell in the middle row provides shorthand access to the eight most likely completions: with activation of that button, the screen changes into one where those words populate the cells on the two bottom rows. If none of the suggested continuations (words or letters) is correct, the user has access to the button labelled 'ABCD...' for populating the bottom-row cells with the next options in the hierarchy.

In Figure 6, the user has entered 'Gr'; on the basis of those two letters, GazeTalk has predicted a list of potential words: 'Great', 'Granted', 'Greg', etc. Many systems support adaptive learning, meaning that new words written by the user are automatically inserted into the vocabulary and

Figure 6. GazeTalk (Hansen et al., 2001) provides both word and letter prediction features. GazeTalk's new interface shows a preview of the next character layout within the cell that is currently being selected. Therefore, the user can proceed directly to the correct cell after the current letter has been selected and hence save the search time needed for locating the cell for the next letter

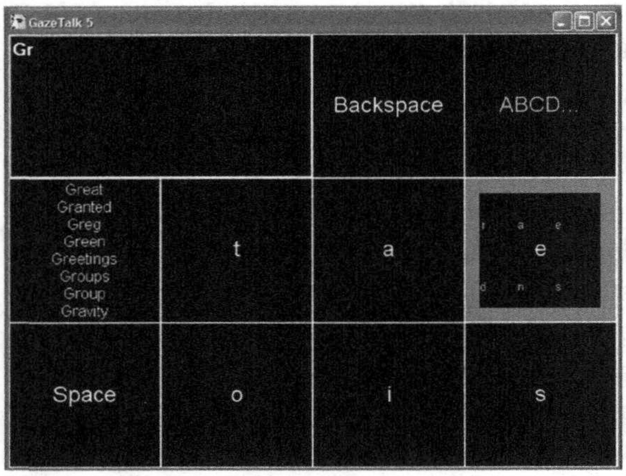

the probabilities for existing words are adjusted on the basis of their usage statistics.

Word continuations are predicted on the basis of the letters typed so far. After a space, the situation is trickier. A simple way to implement the prediction after a space is to show the next probable word candidates from the most frequent general words such as 'the', 'of', and 'an' (MacKenzie & Zhang, 2008). Another solution is to use semantic information from the previous text; for example, 'my name' continues with 'is' typically.

Character Prediction

In addition to providing the list of predicted words, GazeTalk uses character prediction for dynamically changing the characters shown in the cells that contain the most probable next letters. In Figure 6, one of the most likely next letters after 'Gr' is 'e', which is being selected in Figure 6 (hence the highlighting in its background).

In an experiment by Hansen et al. (2003), novice participants found the dynamic, predictive layout confusing. Since the order of the letters was constantly changing, they had to search for the desired letter every time the display changed: they found it confusing that the same letter was not always shown in the same location (the same cell). Therefore, the developers decided to set 'home positions' for all letters so that they could be found in the same cell unless a letter with higher probability shares the same home.

Recently, the developers of GazeTalk further improved the dynamic layout. They implemented a new interface that shows a preview of the layout within the key that is selected, so that the user can proceed directly to the correct cell when the cells are reoccupied with the letters after the current selection. Note the small yellow letters around the 'e' in the selected cell in Figure 6. To my knowledge, at the time of writing, this new layout with the character preview has not yet been tested with users, even though it has been publicly available for a while (with free download via the Web).

GazeTalk fills the cells with new (most probable next) letters every time the user types a letter. Another approach is to show all letters at once, by placing several of them in each cell. The user can then type by simply selecting the cell containing the desired letter, and, on the basis of the underlying language model, the program decides which of the possible letter combinations is most likely the word the user wants to write. This approach is similar to the predictive text entry used in mobile phones (such as T9). This way, the number of keystrokes required per character can be reduced significantly.

Dasher takes the character prediction feature a step further. Dasher's prediction includes all characters, not only letters (Ward, Blackwell, & MacKay, 2000). Here, common punctuation marks are given more space than rarely used punctuation. With Dasher, the user can select several characters, whole words, or sometimes small phrases all at once. They are also all shown near the current gaze point, so that the user does not need to glance through a separate list.

The Cost of the Additional Cognitive and Perception Load

Word prediction, or word completion, is especially useful with highly ambiguous keyboards that have only a few buttons. Such keyboards can provide efficient text entry with low motor or accuracy demands (Harbusch & Kühn, 2003), because, using the word prediction feature, one can reduce the number of keystrokes required to write the word. One should, however, keep in mind the additional cost of perceptual and cognitive load, caused by shifting the focus from the keyboard to the word list and the repeated scanning of the list. Because of the added cost of scanning the list, the actual benefit may be smaller than expected from simply calculating the potential keystroke savings. In some cases, the use of word prediction may even decrease the text entry rate. Koester and Levine (1994) had both able-bodied participants and disabled ones (suffering from spinal cord injuries) transcribe text with and without the word prediction feature. They found modest enhancements for the able-bodied participants, but the cognitive cost of much slower list search times for the injured participants was so high that in their case the word prediction feature had a negative effect on performance. Therefore, one should carefully consider the implementation and layout. For example, one may want to optimise the list of predicted words to better match the current context or vocabulary of the user and let the users adjust the number of items shown in the list to match their perceptual capabilities and preferences. Trnka, McCaw, Yarrington, McCoy, & Pennington (2008) compared two different word prediction methods with a letter-by-letter text entry system. They found that word prediction can improve text entry rates, and that a more accurate prediction system gives better results. This is partly an effect of greater utilisation of the prediction feature: if the prediction is accurate, people trust it and use it more. In gaze-based interfaces, the space taken by the word lists is also an issue worth considering; if the words are located within separate buttons, those buttons reserve precious screen space.

MacKenzie and Zhang (2008) compared word and letter prediction in a gaze typing system. Their system predicted the next probable words and showed them on buttons located below the text input field. In addition to word prediction, they experimented with character prediction in an on-screen keyboard. When the user typed a character, the system highlighted the three most probable next letters on the keyboard (by drawing a coloured circle around the next probable keys). They expected the highlighting to speed up letter selection if the desired letter is one of the highlighted letters, since the search task is reduced from 26 to three characters. Naturally, if the desired letter is not among the highlighted letters, the effect may be negative. They also used the predicted letters for improving the accuracy of their fixation algorithm: they adjusted the measured point of gaze by correcting drift according to the probabilities of letters (keys) near the measured gaze point. They compared the letter and word prediction with two button sizes (small and large) in an experiment with 10 participants. Entry speed ranged from 10.8 wpm to 12.3 wpm. The results show that letter prediction was about 10% faster than word prediction when small buttons were used. With large buttons, word prediction was about 10% faster than with small buttons, probably because the larger size made it easier to recognise the predicted words. With large buttons, there was little or no improvement in entry speed. MacKenzie and Zhang concluded that letter prediction was as good as word prediction, or even better in some cases. Hence, there is potential in such letter prediction, especially with an unfamiliar layout (the experiment's participants were familiar with QWERTY).

INTERFACE DESIGN ISSUES: LAYOUT AND FEEDBACK

Layout

Typically, with a 'flat' keyboard layout design where all characters are visible, only one keystroke per character is needed, since most letters can be directly pointed at and selected. Having all characters visible at the same time requires space. The keys on the virtual keyboard must be big enough to accommodate the accuracy limitations of eye tracking devices.

Sometimes the full keyboard cannot be shown at once, on account of accuracy and calibration issues. In such a case, only a few keys can be shown at a time, which prevents the use of full-size keyboards such as a full QWERTY keyboard. Similarly to the use of several key presses to enter a letter in the multi-tap method for mobile phones, large on-screen keys can be selected repeatedly to enter a character, which increases the KSPC rate. For example, the first version of the ERICA system (Hutchinson, White, Martin, Reichert, & Frey, 1989) had only six selectable items available on the screen at a time. The letters were organised in a tree-structured menu hierarchy. The user selected first a group of letters, then either another group of letters or the single target letter. Typing was slow – it took from two to four menu selections to select a single letter, meaning that several keystrokes were needed for entry of one character. Letters were arranged in the hierarchy on the basis of word frequencies, so that the expected number of steps for text entry was minimised (Frey, White, & Hutchinson, 1990).

Layouts with large keys are still needed and used in today's systems. Even though the state-of-the-art eye trackers are fairly accurate (to 0.5–1 degrees), the so-called low-cost systems still do not reach the accuracy levels needed for a QWERTY keyboard. An example of such a system is GazeTalk (Hansen et al., 2001), developed with a standard Web camera in mind. Big buttons enable easy selection even with inaccurate pointing devices. In addition, some medical conditions cause involuntary head movements or eye tremor that may prevent good calibration or may even restrict eye movements to one direction only (Donegan et al., 2005; see also the chapters in the 'User Involvement' section of this book for examples of the challenges and solutions for different medical conditions).

Feedback

Appropriate feedback is especially important when the same modality is used for both control and perception. When gaze is used to control an application and select objects on the screen, gaze is engaged in the input process: the user needs to look at an object to select it. This means that the user cannot simultaneously control an object and view the effects of the action, unless the effect appears on the object itself. For example, if the user is entering text by gaze, he or she cannot see the text appear in the text input field while simultaneously selecting a letter by 'eye pressing' a key on an on-screen keyboard. To review the text written so far, the user needs to move the gaze from the on-screen keyboard to the typed text field. This looking back and forth can become excessive, especially as novices in particular often shift their gaze between the keyboard and the text input field to review the text written so far (Bates, 2002). This shifting can be reduced by adding auditory feedback, such as an audible 'click' or pronunciation of each letter as it is written. Experienced users learn to cope with having to use the same modality for input (control) and output (feedback); they complete the task (e.g., scrolling) before gazing at the results (ibid.).

There is a noteworthy difference between using dwell time as an activation command in comparison to, for example, a button click. With a button click, the user makes the selection and defines the exact moment when the selection is made. Using dwell time, the user only initiates the action; the system makes the actual selection after a predefined interval. Therefore, general guidelines on feedback in graphical user interfaces may not be suitable as such.

Majaranta, MacKenzie, Aula, and Räihä (2006) conducted three experiments to study the effects of feedback and dwell time on eye typing speed and accuracy. Their results show that the type of feedback significantly affects typing speed, accuracy, gaze behaviour, and subjective experience. For example, visual feedback in combination with a short audible 'click' significantly facilitates eye typing. Compared with plain visual feedback, added auditory feedback significantly increases typing speed and reduces errors. It not only confirms selection but also supports the typing rhythm. Also, most participants in the experiment preferred combined visual and auditory feedback over other feedback modes tested (visual only, speech only, and combined visual and spoken feedback).

Spoken feedback can be useful for novices using long dwell times: speaking out the letters as they are typed significantly helps in reducing errors. However, with short dwell times, spoken feedback is problematic since speaking a letter takes time. As our experiment demonstrated, people tend to pause to listen to the speech. This not only decreases the typing speed but also introduces double-entry errors: the same letter is unintentionally typed twice.

For novices, it may be useful to give extra feedback on the dwell time progress. This can be done through animation or by giving two-level feedback: first on the focus and then, after the dwell time has elapsed, feedback on selection. This gives users an opportunity to cancel the selection before the dwell time runs out. It is not natural to fixate on a target for a long time. Animated feedback helps in maintaining focus on the target. When a short dwell time is used, there is no time to give extra feedback to the user. With short dwell times, the participants found the two-level feedback confusing and distracting.

The feedback should be matched with the dwell time. Short dwell times require simplified feedback, while long dwell times allow extra information on the eye typing process. The same dwell time (e.g., 500-ms) may be 'short' for one user and 'long' for another. Therefore, the user should be able to adjust the dwell time duration as well as the feedback parameters and attributes.

Showing the feedback at the centre of the focused item, rather than the actual (potentially slightly inaccurate) position of the gaze, seems to be especially useful for some users (Donegan at al., 2006). When the feedback is shown at the centre of a gaze-responsive button, the calibration appears perfect to the user, encouraging the user to feel confident when using gaze.

CONCLUSION

This chapter provided a brief overview of the existing methods of gaze-based text entry and of related research. People with communication difficulties can benefit greatly from the use of eye tracking technology (for examples and case studies, see the 'User Involvement' section of this book). As the technology develops and the prices of the systems slowly come down, eye tracking is becoming a realistic option for a much wider group of users than previously expected.

Even though gaze-based text entry has existed and been in use for decades, there is still plenty of room for further research on the design issues. The research briefly reviewed above showed that design issues such as feedback and layout can significantly affect user performance and satisfaction. However, there are aspects of text entry that still merit further research, such as increasing the communication speed in face-to-face conversation situations or improving methods for editing text by gaze – addressing the question of how can one modify and format already written text efficiently and effortlessly by gaze alone.

ACKNOWLEDGMENT

This chapter is largely based on my doctoral thesis (Majaranta, 2009), which, in turn, was based on several co-authored research articles. Therefore, I want to express my sincere gratitude to all of my original co-authors: Kari-Jouko Räihä, I. Scott MacKenzie, Anne Aula, Oleg Špakov, Outi Tuisku, Ulla-Kaija Ahola, Niina Majaranta, Richard Bates, Mick Donegan, Gintautas Daunys, and Poika Isokoski.

REFERENCES

Bates, R. (2002). Have patience with your eye mouse! Eye-gaze interaction with computers can work. *Proceedings of the 1st Cambridge Workshop on Universal Access and Assistive Technology (CWUAAT '02)* (pp. 33–38). Retrieved from http://www.cse.dmu.ac.uk/~rbates/Bates7.pdf

Bee, N., & André, E. (2008). Writing with your eye: A dwell time free writing system adapted to the nature of human eye gaze. *Perception in multimodal dialogue systems* (pp. 111–122). Berlin/Heidelberg, Germany: Springer. LNCS 5078/2008, doi:10.1007/978-3-540-69369-7_13

Beukelman, D. R., & Mirenda, P. (1992). *Augmentative and alternative communication: Management of severe communication disorders in children and adults*. Baltimore, MD: Paul H. Brookes Publishing Co.

Bulling, A., Roggen, D., & Tröster, G. (2008). It's in your eyes – Towards context-awareness and mobile HCI using wearable EOG goggles. *Proceedings of the 10th International Conference on Ubiquitous Computing (UbiComp '08)* (pp. 84–93). New York, NY: ACM. doi:10.1145/1409635.1409647

Chapman, J. E. (1991). Use of an eye-operated computer system in locked-in syndrome. *Proceedings of the CSUN's 6th Annual International Conference on Technology and Persons with Disabilities (CSUN '91),* Los Angeles, CA.

Donegan, M., Oosthuizen, L., Bates, R., Daunys, G., Hansen, J. P., & Joos, M. …Signorile, I. (2005). *User requirements report with observations of difficulties users are experiencing.* (Deliverable D3.1. Communication by Gaze Interaction (COGAIN), Project IST-2003-511598). Retrieved from the COGAIN Association website: http://www.cogain.org/wiki/COGAIN_Reports

Donegan, M., Oosthuizen, L., Bates, R., Istance, H., Holmqvist, E., & Lundalv, M. …Signorile, I. (2006). *Report of user trials and usability studies.* (Deliverable D3.3. Communication by Gaze Interaction (COGAIN), Project IST-2003-511598). Retrieved from the COGAIN Association website: http://www.cogain.org/wiki/COGAIN_Reports

Drewes, H., & Schmidt, A. (2007). Interacting with the computer using gaze gestures. In C. Baranauskas, P. Palanque, J. Abascal, & S. D. J. Barbosa (Eds.), *Human–Computer Interaction (INTERACT 2007)* (LNCS 4663, pp. 475–488). Berlin, Germany: Springer-Verlag. doi:10.1007/978-3-540-74800-7_43

Eye Gaze Communication Board. (2010). *COGAIN Wiki.* Retrieved from the COGAIN website: http://www.cogain.org/wiki/Eye_Gaze_Communication_Board

EyeWrite. (2010). Retrieved December, 2010, from http://depts.washington.edu/ewrite/eyewrite.html

Fejtová, M., Fejt, J., & Lhotská, L. (2004). Controlling a PC by eye movements: The MEMREC project. In K. Miesenberger, J. Klaus, W. Zagler, & D. Burger (Eds.), *Proceedings of the 9th International Conference on Computers Helping People with Special Needs (ICCHP '04)* (LNCS 3118, pp. 770–773). Berlin/Heidelberg, Germany: Springer. doi: 10.1007/978-3-540-27817-7_114

Frey, L. A., White, K. P. Jr., & Hutchinson, T. E. (1990). Eye-gaze word processing. *IEEE Transactions on Systems, Man, and Cybernetics, 20*(4), 944–950. doi:10.1109/21.105094

Friedman, M. B., Kiliany, G., Dzmura, M., & Anderson, D. (1982). The eyetracker communication system. *Johns Hopkins APL Technical Digest, 3*(3), 250–252.

Goossens', C. A., & Crain, S. S. (1987). Overview of nonelectronic eye gaze communication techniques. *Augmentative and Alternative Communication, 3,* 77–89. doi:10.1080/07434618712331274309

Grauman, K., Betke, M., Lombardi, J., Gips, J., & Bradski, G. R. (2003). Communication via eye blinks and eyebrow raises: Video-based human–computer interfaces. *Universal Access in the Information Society, 2*(4), 359–373. doi:10.1007/s10209-003-0062-x

Hansen, D. W., Skovsgaard, H. H., Hansen, J. P., & Møllenbach, E. (2008). Noise tolerant selection by gaze-controlled pan and zoom in 3D. *Proceedings of the 2008 Symposium on Eye Tracking Research & Applications (ETRA '08)* (pp. 205–212). New York, NY: ACM. doi:10.1145/1344471.1344521

Hansen, J. P., Hansen, D. W., & Johansen, A. (2001). Bringing gaze-based interaction back to basics. *Universal Access in HCI (UAHCI 2001): Towards an Information Society for All, 3,* 325–329. Mahwah, NJ: Lawrence Erlbaum.

Hansen, J. P., Johansen, A. S., Hansen, D. W., Itoh, K., & Mashino, S. (2003). *Language technology in a predictive, restricted on-screen keyboard with ambiguous layout for severely disabled people*. Presented at the Workshop on Language Modeling for Text Entry Methods (EACL '03), Budapest, Hungary. Retrieved from http://www.it-c.dk/research/EyeGazeInteraction/Papers/Hansen_et_al_2003a.pdf

Harbusch, K., & Kühn, M. (2003). Towards an adaptive communication aid with text input from ambiguous keyboards. *Proceedings of the 10th Conference of the European Chapter of the Association for Computational Linguistics* (vol. 2, pp. 207–210). Morristown, NJ: European Chapter Meeting of the Association for Computational Linguistics.

Hutchinson, T. E., White, K. P. Jr, Martin, W. N., Reichert, K. C., & Frey, L. A. (1989). Human–computer interaction using eye-gaze input. *IEEE Transactions on Systems, Man, and Cybernetics*, *19*(6), 1527–1534. doi:10.1109/21.44068

Isokoski, P. (2000). Text input methods for eye trackers using off-screen targets. *Proceedings of the 2000 Symposium on Eye Tracking Research & Applications (ETRA '00)* (pp. 15–21). New York, NY: ACM. doi:10.1145/355017.355020.

Kahn, D. A., Heynen, J., & Snuggs, G. L. (1999). Eye-controlled computing: The VisionKey experience. *Proceedings of the 14th International Conference on Technology and Persons with Disabilities* (CSUN '99), Los Angeles, CA.

Koester, H. H., & Levine, S. P. (1994). Modeling the speed of text entry with a word prediction interface. *IEEE Transactions on Rehabilitation Engineering*, *2*(3), 177–187. doi:10.1109/86.331567

MacDonald, A. (1998). Symbol systems . In Wilson, A. (Ed.), *Augmentative communication in practice: An introduction* (2nd ed., pp. 19–26). Edinburgh, UK: CALL Centre, University of Edinburgh.

MacKenzie, I. S., & Zhang, X. (2008). Eye typing using word and letter prediction and a fixation algorithm. *Proceedings of the 2008 Symposium on Eye-Tracking Research & Applications (ETRA '08)* (pp. 55–58). New York, NY: ACM. doi:10.1145/1344471.1344484

Majaranta, P. (2004, October 2). *Visiting Kati*. Retrieved from the COGAIN website: http://www.cogain.org/wiki/Visiting_Kati

Majaranta, P. (2009). Text entry by eye gaze. *Dissertations in interactive technology, number 11*. Retrieved from the University of Tampere website: http://acta.uta.fi/teos.php?id=11211

Majaranta, P., Ahola, U.-K., & Špakov, O. (2009). Fast gaze typing with an adjustable dwell time. *Proceedings of the 27th International Conference on Human Factors in Computing Systems (CHI '09)* (pp. 357–360). New York, NY: ACM. doi:10.1145/1518701.1518758

Majaranta, P., MacKenzie, I. S., Aula, A., & Räihä, K.-J. (2006). Effects of feedback and dwell time on eye typing speed and accuracy. *Universal Access in the Information Society*, *5*(2), 199–208. doi:10.1007/s10209-006-0034-z

Majaranta, P., & Räihä, K.-J. (2002). 20 years of eye typing: Systems and design issues. *Proceedings of the 2002 Symposium on Eye Tracking Research and Applications (ETRA '02)* (pp. 15–22). New York, NY: ACM. doi:10.1145/507072.507076

Majaranta, P., & Räihä, K.-J. (2007). Text entry by gaze: Utilizing eye-tracking . In MacKenzie, I. S., & Tanaka-Ishii, K. (Eds.), *Text entry systems: Mobility, accessibility, universality* (pp. 175–187). San Francisco, CA: Morgan Kaufmann.

Porta, M., & Turina, M. (2008). Eye-S: A full-screen input modality for pure eye-based communication. *Proceedings of the 2008 Symposium on Eye Tracking Research and Applications (ETRA '08)* (pp. 27–34). New York, NY: ACM. doi:10.1145/1344471.1344477

Salvucci, D. D. (1999). Inferring intent in eye-based interfaces: Tracing eye movements with process models. *Proceedings of the SIGCHI Conference on Human Factors in Computing Systems (CHI '99)* (pp. 254–261). New York, NY: ACM. doi:10.1145/302979.303055

Scott, J. (1998). Low tech methods of augmentative communication. In Wilson, A. (Ed.), *Augmentative communication in practice: an introduction* (2nd ed., pp. 13–18). Edinburgh, UK: CALL Centre, University of Edinburgh.

Ten Kate, J. H., Frietman, E. E. E., Willems, W., Ter Haar Romeny, B. M., & Tenkink, E. (1979). Eye-switch controlled communication aids. *Proceedings of the 12th International Conference on Medical and Biological Engineering*, Jerusalem, Israel.

Trnka, K., McCaw, J., Yarrington, D., McCoy, K. F., & Pennington, C. (2008). Word prediction and communication rate in AAC. *Proceedings of the 4th IASTED International Conference on Telehealth and Assistive Technologies (Telehealth/AT '08)* (pp. 19–24). Anaheim, CA: ACTA Press.

Tuisku, O., Majaranta, P., Isokoski, P., & Räihä, K.-J. (2008). Now Dasher! Dash away! Longitudinal study of fast text entry by eye gaze. *Proceedings of the 2008 Symposium on Eye Tracking Research & Applications (ETRA '08)* (pp. 19–26). New York, NY: ACM. doi:10.1145/1344471.1344476

Urbina, M. H., & Huckauf, A. (2007). Dwell time free eye typing approaches. *Proceedings of the 3rd Conference on Communication by Gaze Interaction (COGAIN 2007)* (pp. 65–70). Leicester, UK: De Montfort University. Retrieved from the COGAIN website: http://www.cogain.org/conference

Ward, D. J., Blackwell, A. F., & MacKay, D. J. C. (2000). Dasher – A data entry interface using continuous gestures and language models. *Proceedings of the 13th Annual ACM Symposium on User Interface Software and Technology (UIST '00)* (pp. 129–137). New York, NY: ACM. doi:10.1145/354401.354427

Ward, D. J., & MacKay, D. J. C. (2002). Fast hands-free writing by gaze direction. *Nature*, *418*(6900), 838. doi:10.1038/418838a

Wobbrock, J. O., Rubinstein, J., Sawyer, M. W., & Duchowski, A. T. (2008). Longitudinal evaluation of discrete consecutive gaze gestures for text entry. *Proceedings of the 2008 Symposium on Eye Tracking Research & Applications (ETRA '08)* (pp. 11–18). New York, NY: ACM. doi:10.1145/1344471.1344475

Chapter 9
Computer Control by Gaze

Henrik Skovsgaard
IT University of Copenhagen, Denmark

Kari-Jouko Räihä
University of Tampere, Finland

Martin Tall
Duke University, USA

ABSTRACT

This chapter provides an overview of gaze-based interaction techniques. We will first explore specific techniques intended to make target selection easier and to avoid the Midas touch problem. We will then take a look at techniques that do not require the use of special widgets in the interface but instead manipulate the rendering on the basis of eye gaze to facilitate the selection of small targets. Dwell-based interaction makes use of fixations; recent research has looked into the other option, using saccades as the basis for eye gestures. We will also discuss examples of how eye gaze has been used with other input modalities (blinks and winks, keyboard and mouse, facial gestures, head movements, and speech) to speed up interaction. Finally, we will discuss examples of interaction techniques in the context of a specific area of application: navigating information spaces.

INTRODUCTION

Users of a standard PC need to be able to perform point-and-select operations to interact with the modern graphical user interface. Interaction with interface elements such as icons and buttons is often performed with a conventional mouse, a task that has been mastered by most able-bodied users. The advantage with the conventional mouse is that with this device there is virtually no noise between the physical movement of the device and the movement of the on-screen cursor. This allows selection of very small targets in a windowed environment down to the finest levels, to the pixel.

Users with motor disabilities who are not able to use and control a conventional mouse

DOI: 10.4018/978-1-61350-098-9.ch009

need alternative input devices for performing point-and-select operations to gain access to the graphical user interface. Eye trackers are feasible input devices for users who retain control of their eye movements. Eye gaze has several desirable characteristics, such as natural and fast pointing (Sibert & Jacob, 2000). However, most graphical user interfaces are not designed for use with these alternative input devices, which often have limited accuracy or may require unnatural selection techniques that interfere with access to mainstream GUIs.

Gaze tracking is well suited to pointing because humans naturally tend to direct their eyes in the direction of the target of interest. On the other hand, gaze tracking with no additional input modalities is not very suitable for selection, since humans tend to look at objects of interest to explore them independently of their intention to select them (Jacob, 1991, 1993). It therefore cannot be assumed that the user wants to perform an operation on every object that has been looked at. The speed of eye movements can, in fact, turn into a disadvantage: while it is extremely fast to turn attention to the target of interest, perceiving that item cognitively may well take enough time that the system interprets the lack of activity as an indication of expected system action. Finding a proper balance here is one of the main themes of research in this field.

The methods for computer control by gaze interaction can be divided into two main categories: either the eye tracker is simply used to control the mouse in the normal graphical user interface or a custom interface is constructed. In the first case of mouse control (the so-called eye mouse; see Bates & Istance, 2003), the main problem is that there is no universal method for issuing mouse clicks. The most common method to distinguish inspections from selections is to set a time threshold (i.e., dwell time), with a click issued after the duration of the fixation exceeds a specified amount of time. The use of dwell time may lead to unintentional activations resulting from fixations used for in-

spection being confused for a selection. This issue is referred to as the Midas touch problem (Jacob, 1991). Increasing the dwell time leads to slow and unnatural interaction, whereas a short dwell time leads to an increase in unintentional activations, which may cause frustration. Dwell-based activation therefore typically faces the classic speed-accuracy trade-off: the faster the interaction, the higher the number of erroneous actions.

These problems have led to the creation of several customised interfaces that are built to accommodate the special needs of target acquisition by eye gaze. The limited precision of gaze interaction restricts the possibilities for target selection *per se* and has resulted in a number of research projects exploring this issue. Most of these have addressed the problem by means of signal smoothing and effectively manipulating the target area with so-called zooming and distortion interfaces.

In this chapter, we will first explore specific techniques for gaze-based interaction, intended to make target selection easier and to avoid the Midas touch problem. We will then take a look at techniques that do not require the use of special widgets in the interface but instead manipulate the rendering on the basis of eye gaze (so-called gaze-contingent interfaces) to facilitate the selection of small targets. Dwell-based interaction makes use of fixations; recent research has looked into the other option, using saccades as the basis for eye gestures. We will also discuss examples of how eye gaze has been used with other input modalities (blinks and winks, keyboard and mouse, facial gestures, head movements, and speech) to speed up interaction. Finally, we will discuss examples of interaction techniques in the context of a specific area of application: navigating information spaces.

DWELL-BASED SELECTION

In dwell-based interaction, fixating for a pre-specified time threshold on a certain location will make the system issue an activation at that location. As discussed in the preceding chapter, on text entry by eye gaze, dwelling is the most common technique for performing selections in gaze typing applications. Dwell-based activation is also the most popular technique in other areas of application, such as drawing applications (Hornof & Cavender, 2005).

Finding the optimal dwell time for issuing activations comes with a trade-off, as the interaction seems to be unnatural if waiting time increases and, on the other hand, fast interaction leads to unintentional activations (Jacob, 1995). Often the best solution may be to leave control of the dwell threshold to the user, as experiments with text entry have shown (Majaranta, Ahola, & Špakov, 2009). This allows novice users to utilise longer dwell times in the beginning and reduce the threshold as they grow more skilled and confident with the selection method.

Another possibility is to adjust the dwell time automatically, within the application, as users become more skilled. This was studied for an eye typing application by Špakov and Miniotas (2004). They found that as the users grew more experienced, they tended to leave the selected keys sooner than novice users did. As a consequence, this exit time could be used as an indication of experience, and, correspondingly, the dwell time could be automatically reduced for experienced users. It was found that the algorithm was able to reduce the initial dwell time (600 ms) automatically to a level that was, in general, similar to the one chosen as most convenient by each participant when the participant was allowed to set the dwell time manually. Thus the approach was successful in this case. However, Huckauf and Urbina (2008b) point out that adaptive dwell time involves a lot of training (of the user, application, and algorithm) to distinguish intended from unintended selections.

Basic dwell-based interaction works well in applications specifically developed with eye gaze in mind. Then the designer can take the inaccuracy of eye trackers into account by making the selectable objects (such as keys on the soft keyboard or icons in a palette) large enough. For general access to a windowing environment, the small size of the graphical elements easily becomes an issue.

Lankford (2000) explored true integration of the Windows environment with the Eye-gaze Response Interface Computer Aid (ERICA) system. Experimenting with dwell-based gaze clicking, Lankford found that many targets, such as the small buttons in the window's title bar used to minimise and maximise, were hard to select. Moreover, positioning the caret in the desired position in the text was difficult, since the density of letters was so high. In order to have the system work reliably, Lankford experimented with changing the screen resolution to the lowest possible. In addition, text on the screen was magnified 200%. These changes reduced the amount of space on the screen to a minimum, but even with this set-up the users would still need repeated attempts to hit the targets. The solution adopted by Lankford was effectively increasing target size by magnifying a small region of the Windows desktop around the detected fixation. This is an example of zooming techniques, which we will return to later.

DEDICATED INTERFACE WIDGETS

Thus far, we have assumed that the interface widgets behave in a manner familiar from mouse-based interaction. For instance, a button is pressed by clicking anywhere within its predefined area. In gaze-based interaction, this does not always need to be the case. The text entry technique of MacKenzie and Zhang (2008) discussed in the previous chapter modifies the selection area of each soft key on the keyboard dynamically, on the basis of the probability of the key (i.e., letter), given the portion of the word already typed. Characters that are more likely to follow this beginning have a larger effective selection area, although all keys are always rendered in the same size.

Another possibility is to have different viewing and selection areas for the buttons. The Quick

Figure 1. Two-step fixation method: selection area to the right of each button (© 2003 Takehiko Ohno. Used with permission)

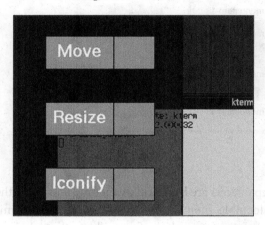

Glance selection method (Ohno, 1998; Ohno & Mukawa, 2003) aims to solve the Midas touch problem by using a specific selection area next to each interface widget (see Figure 1); to activate the function, one must fixate on the special selection area. There are two major advantages with this. First, the user can inspect the menu items without worrying about accidental activations. Second, advanced users can head for the activation area directly without even reading the menu text, just as many people know the order and location of items in the Windows Start menu, for instance. The downside of the technique is the amount of screen real estate used to display the tools. Moreover, accidental activations may still occur.

More recent research has used dynamically appearing interface components based on a two-step activation process. This allows for greater utilisation of screen real estate and lower error rates. However, the reduction in selection errors comes at the expense of increased selection time.

Figure 2 shows the implementation (Tall, 2008) of a type of button similar to that in Figure 1, but now with dynamic activation. When the user dwells on the button in its initial state, the selection component appears to the right of the object of interest and the selection is confirmed with an additional dwell on its selection component.

Tall (2008) experimented with various dwell time thresholds. The middle settings (300 ms for dwelling in the initial state to make the activation area visible, and another 300 ms to make the selection in the activation area) minimised the number of errors. In a small experiment with nine tasks, the selection time per task was slightly more than 1 s, on average. This is not much more than the times obtained by Ohno (1998) in the best case, which is an encouraging result.

SUPPORTING ACCESS TO SMALL TARGETS

By and large, the approaches for making small interface elements better accessible to eye gaze are based on zooming. Zooming, however, can take many forms. Next we will present solutions that use semantic zooming (a technique where

Figure 2. Dynamic two-step fixation method: selection area appears on the basis of dwell and gives feedback on activation status (© 2008 Martin Tall. Used with permission)

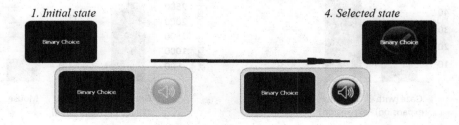

Figure 3. Expanding menu items upon gaze fixation (© 2005 Oleg Špakov. Used with permission)

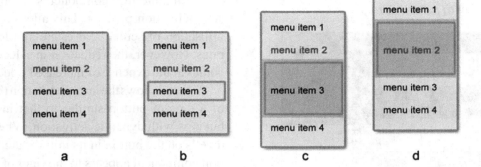

the appearance of objects is adjusted based on scale) and various forms of non-semantic, graphical zooming: providing the zoomed image in a separate window, zooming dynamically in the same window, and using a fisheye view.

Semantic Zooming

Špakov and Miniotas (2005) developed a technique for selecting items with eye gaze from a standard-sized menu. In their technique, fixating on a menu item makes the surrounding area expand to accommodate the inaccuracy of eye trackers (see Figure 3).

The technique is related to the special interface widgets discussed in the previous section, except that semantic zooming does not require any additional activation. In this case, the menu item expansions are based on dwell time and make the selectable menu items easily accessible. Similarly to customised interface widgets, the technique reduces errors at the cost of increased interaction time as shown in Figure 4. The trade-off for more accurate selection leads to an average increase in selection time by 39%.

Web browsing is another example of densely placed targets. Accuracy may therefore become an issue during browsing. If multiple links are placed close to the point of gaze, the possible targets can be splayed out, as is done by the Web browser in MyTobii (2009). The main idea of displaying links sufficiently far apart is to effect a reduction in erroneous selections with large, easily selectable proxies (see Figure 5).

Figure 4. Error rate (left) and selection time (right) for three conditions: gaze interaction with menu expansion, gaze interaction without menu expansion, and mouse interaction (Adapted from the work of Špakov and Miniotas, 2005)

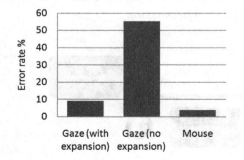
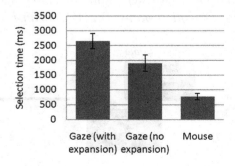

Figure 5. Semantic zooming in Web browsing

Graphical Zooming

Zooming in a Separate Window

A natural way of improving access to arbitrary graphical user interfaces is to provide a separate window that shows an enlarged image of part of the screen. This is illustrated in Figure 6 (Istance,

Spinner, & Howarth, 1996). An area around the measured focus of the gaze is shown in a special panel. The same panel contains gaze-activated buttons for operations that correspond to those that can be issued with a mouse.

An advantage of this technique is that it is general (that is, does not depend on a particular interface element) and fairly easy to implement. Lankford (2000) came up with a similar solution to overcome the accuracy problems that he had encountered with a non-zooming interface. Yet another application of this approach was studied by Pomplun, Ivanovic, Reingold, and Shen (2001). They employ two windows, of equal size, with one displaying the information-dense image and the second displaying an enlarged version of a sub-image taken from the original image. When the user is looking around in the original image, a highlighted square follows the user's gaze and serves as a selection marker for the sub-image. When the user gazes in the second window, a magnified version of the highlighted square is shown.

Figure 6. The Zoompad interface. The bottom part of the view on the right shows the placement of the zoomed content and the gaze-controlled buttons for interaction. The insert on the left shows how the standard interface buttons would look when zoomed in (Istance et al., 1996). (© 1996 Howell Istance. Used with permission)

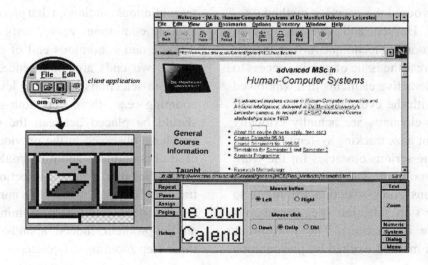

Pomplun et al. (2001) compared gaze control to a standard mouse. More magnifications were triggered by the gaze condition than by the mouse condition, which led to a higher error rate. On the other hand, response time was only slightly longer in the gaze-based condition, and the overall performance was encouraging, in view of the fact that the comparison was with a standard interface device.

Direct Interaction with Zooming

As seen above, indirect interaction by providing a zoomed image and interaction buttons in a separate window achieves the goal of avoiding errors, but usually at a cost to efficiency. Early work by Bates (1999) suggested that continuous direct interaction, with no additional on-screen element, could improve the performance of gaze-based pointing. Bates and Istance (2002) investigated in more detail direct gaze-based pointing with a standard graphical user interface. They compared direct interaction with a standard eye mouse, a zooming eye mouse, and a head mouse (baseline). Direct interaction with a standard eye mouse proved more difficult than the head mouse, but the addition of the zoom enhancement improved performance such that it surpassed that of the head mouse. No measurable effect on physical effort was found in comparison with the head mouse, but subjective assessments favoured the zooming method.

Skovsgaard, Hansen, and Mateo (2008) investigated the zooming technique further. In their work, they address the issue of gaining access to the smallest interactive elements in a windowed environment with the eyes only. Only a few of the interactive elements are actually critically small for current gaze tracking systems, but they still can become serious obstacles for the work flow without zooming. The study compared a novel continuous zoom-selection technique to traditional two-step selection (i.e., continuous versus discrete interaction). The continuous zoom-selection method worked by presenting a window centred on the user's point of regard, and a smooth animation showed the content of the window gradually increasing in size. The zoom functionality allowed for runtime course corrections during the selection process proportional to the current level of magnification.

Performing selections with direct zooming was found to be significantly faster than using the two-step discrete interaction technique. Subjective evaluations from the users indicated that the two-step technique might be more fatiguing, since it (in this implementation) required double the number of clicks. In terms of accuracy, the two-step selection technique performed significantly better than the novel zoom-selection technique, but taking the longer selection time for the two-step technique into account, Skovsgaard et al. (2008) found essentially the same overall efficiency for the two techniques.

The findings of these experiments indicate that the two selection techniques could complement each other in gaze interactive systems. Zoom selections are the fastest method and can with no problem handle icons larger than 32 × 32 pixels. The user could engage the two-step technique as a second option when needed if the targets are very small or the tracker becomes inaccurate.

In a follow-up study, Skovsgaard, Mateo, Flach, and Hansen (2010) developed a framework that organised all of the zoom tools in a discrete-to-continuous continuum that placed the two-step and the continuous zoom, respectively, on the discrete and continuous end of the continuum. These two ends are, in essence, the extremes of zoom selections, and other levels of discrete zooming (e.g., three-step, four-step, five-step) should be placed between the extremes. The problems observed in the previous study in the case of continuous zooming could be attributed to the fact that it turned selection more into a tracking-like task, which felt unnatural for this type of action. Multi-step zooming could alleviate the problem. Indeed, a study that compared three-step zooming to two-step zooming found it to be equally fast but significantly more accurate (Skovsgaard et al., 2010).

Distortion-Based Interfaces

Ashmore, Duchowski, and Shoemaker (2005) evaluated a fisheye-lens technique that is related to direct zooming but based on distortion. The basic idea with the fisheye lens is to magnify the display locally at the point of the user's gaze and thereby facilitate eye pointing and selection of the magnified (expanded) targets. The key innovation of the gaze-contingent fisheye control is to hide the fisheye lens during visual search and morph the fisheye into view as soon as the eye movement indicates change from saccadic movement to fixation on a target of interest. This would allow the user to maintain an overview of the desktop during visual search and have the fisheye present only when needed.

In a controlled experiment, no significant effect was found on error rates (incorrect selections) (Ashmore et al., 2005). Nevertheless, in terms of speed and accuracy the fisheye-on-demand condition was found to perform significantly better than the omnipresent condition (fisheye continuously slaved to the user's gaze) and non-existent condition (no usage of target expansion). The fisheye technique is suitable for performing visual inspection tasks such as quality control, medical x-ray examination, and satellite imaging. On the downside, the nature of the lens distorts the image, which breaks the original spatial relationship between items in the display. It would be interesting to carry out a comparison of the fisheye technique and the various zooming techniques.

GESTURE-BASED ACTIVATIONS

Thus far we have discussed the use of fixations for selection. The use of fixations is motivated by the fact that users need to spot the target visually before selecting it; thus, target acquisition in the application can naturally follow target acquisition by the visual system. However, the nature of fixations lead them to take much more time than the other basic form of eye movements, saccades. Recent research has therefore put increasing effort into studying the possibilities of gaze gestures (sequences of saccades) in target acquisition. In addition to being potentially fast, gaze gestures have the advantage that they have the potential to avoid the Midas touch problem, when the initial point of gaze in a gaze gesture is not significant.

The chapter on eye typing has presented some examples of using gestures for text entry. Juang, Jasen, Katrekar, Ahn, and Duchowski (2005) carried out one of the earliest studies on gesture-based activations. They investigated the use of eye gestures for navigating large document collections, such as Web sites. When the user's gaze moved from the centre of the screen and passed through one of the four off-screen hot spots, the system interpreted the movement as one of four commands independently of fixations. The four simple commands that could be issued on a Web page were page up and page down (with vertical, up or down gestures) and forward and backward page flipping (with horizontal, left and right gestures).

Juang et al. (2005) implemented only a proof of concept, not a full gaze-operated Web browser. In a study of the prototype, two participants out of 15 had problems with interacting as intended, but the other 13 were almost as fast and error-free with gaze as with the mouse. In addition, they offered enthusiastic subjective comments, such as 'an amazing experience' and 'a great innovation'. Juang et al. also suggest several ways to enhance the use of gestures. For instance, the length of the gesture could be used to determine the amount of scrolling, instead of a fixed scrolling distance being used. Combined with dwell-based selection, dwelling on a link (with no particular threshold, only so that the tracker can detect the fixation), followed by a glance at the hot spot on the right, could be used for following a link. These ideas were not implemented. Later, we will briefly look at the various fully implemented gaze-based browsers on the market.

Single-stroke gestures are designed to be carried out with one saccade only. Møllenbach, Lillholm, Gail, and Hansen (2010) studied the characteristics of single-stroke gestures in detail. The interface consisted of four peripheral initiation areas, which were immediately activated when looked at, and the centre of the screen, which was unaffected by gaze. Selections were completed by glancing from a peripheral initiation field to the opposite side of the screen in a single stroke, hence the concept of single strokes. The single-stroke gestures were explored in four directions (vertical: up, down; horizontal: left, right), the effect of stroke length was examined (by varying the size of the areas), and the effect of sampling rate was also explored (by using different eye trackers). The main finding of Møllenbach et al. was that all of these parameters had a statistically significant effect on the gesture completion speed. This clearly points to the need for careful interface and interaction design when gestures are used for activation.

It would be appealing if a gaze gesture could be issued whenever and wherever the user wishes. What would the gestures then need to be like in order to be distinguishable from normal browsing of the screen? This was studied by Drewes and Schmidt (2007). Their gesture detection algorithm distinguished among horizontal, vertical, and diagonal movements within a rectangular area on the screen. In their experiment, the size of that area (and therefore the length of gestures) did not have a significant effect on the speed of gestures. They

then recorded and examined normal Web surfing for half an hour and mapped the saccades to the same kind of strokes identified by their algorithm. Naturally, all short stroke sequences were found in the gaze point stream, caused by simple browsing and looking around. Therefore, they could not be used as universal gestures to invoke commands. Drewes and Schmidt did, however, find some four-legged gestures (sequences of four strokes) that occurred only rarely, if at all. These could be good candidates for gestures that can be automatically distinguished from general browsing.

As an opposite example, Istance, Hyrskykari, Immonen, Mansikkamaa, and Vickers (2010) designed custom gaze gestures to be used with a game: World of Warcraft. In addition to the gaze gestures, they also implemented their own algorithm for detecting the gestures, instead of relying on default events produced by the eye tracker. As a result, the gestures could be registered quickly and with good accuracy.

How fast are gaze gestures? This is an interesting issue, particularly since the published results vary greatly. Some results are collected in Table 1. The last column shows the number of strokes (legs) used in the gesture, and the second column shows the average time per stroke (duration of full gesture divided by number of strokes).

There are several explanations for such huge differences. A critical issue is what is included when one computes the duration of a gesture. Does it start from the beginning of the preceding fixation or from the first gaze point that does not belong to the preceding fixation? Similarly, does it end with the first gaze point in a specific area

Table 1. Times measured for single gaze strokes (as part of longer gestures)

Source	Average duration of single stroke	Number of strokes in full gesture
Møllenbach et al.(2010)	79–270 ms	1
Istance et al. (2010)	247–293 ms	2–3
Drewes and Schmidt (2007)	557 ms	4
Heikkilä and Räihä (2009)	824–1,190 ms	2–4

(whether fixated or not), the first gaze point of the ending fixation, the gaze point that allows the fixation to be detected, or the last gaze point that belongs to the ending fixation? Another critical factor is what is required from the gesture. Does it need to cross a line between two areas, or move between the areas (fixating on them), or follow a specific pattern? In the latter case, is the pattern visible on the screen, or does it need to be imagined by the person issuing the gesture? Such factors explain the much longer times obtained by Heikkilä and Räihä, who requested the participants in their experiment to produce images like lines, rectangles, and circles with eye gaze, motivated by the intention to use gestures in a drawing application. The desire to perform the task accurately slowed down the participants in this experiment. Again, these results point to the need for and possibilities of careful design of application-specific gestures, as the good performance obtained in some of the recent studies testifies.

Heikkilä and Räihä (2009) provide a survey of the various uses of gestures in gaze-based interfaces, in terms of both the applications and the types of gestures used.

BEYOND LEFT CLICKS

The preceding sections have presented a number of techniques for activating interface elements. Life is, however, more than pointing and clicking. Fluent use of graphical user interfaces involves issuing commands such as right clicks to access a context-dependent menu, dragging items while keeping the mouse button depressed, and so on. In this section, we take a look at techniques developed for more complicated interaction than just pointing and clicking.

Pie menus are a familiar concept from mouse-based interaction that is known to perform well and is fast in practice, especially when combined with marking menus that do not even require

rendering on the screen (Kurtenbach, Sellen, & Buxton, 1993). Pie menus have also been used successfully with gaze-based interaction (Huckauf & Urbina, 2008a, 2008b). Huckauf and Urbina (2008a) propose gaze-controlled pies as a universal interaction technique, demonstrating their use both for eye typing and in desktop navigation. In the latter case, for instance, their five-section pies contained desktop files and folders, and the functionality implemented included standard operations such as creating, moving, or deleting new files and folders. The items were organised in a three-level hierarchy to increase the number of selectable objects or actions that could be taken. Navigating in the pie-menu hierarchy or selecting items was set to take place after a dwell of 700 ms. An informal user study with six participants elicited positive comments and showed that all participants were able to carry out the interaction tasks in the experiment.

Later work has focused on the optimal number of slices and established six slices in a full pie as a good number, making it easy for users to distinguish the pie sectors from one another (Urbina, Lorenz, & Huckauf, 2010). On the other hand, Kammerer, Scheiter, and Beinhauer (2008) found that a half-pie with only half of the circle works better than a full pie. Their design did, however, have other differences as well: menus in sub-hierarchies did not open as new pies centred along the edge of the previous circle; instead, all hierarchies were shown with the same centre but with increasing radius of the circle.

Of particular interest is the study by Urbina et al. (2010) that compared dwell-based and gesture-based selections. Instead of dwelling in a pie segment for activation, another possibility is to use simple crossing of the border of the visible circle as indication of selection. This resembles the idea of the original marking menus: experienced users could now simply glance in the direction of an item they already were familiar with, whereas novice users could inspect the pie freely before making the selection. The experiment carried out by Urbina et al. showed no speed advantage for the 'selection by borders' method, but it reduced errors to half. In their paper, they point out that further improvements might be obtained by varying the location of the lower pie hierarchies; in the study, they appeared in fixed locations (centred at the border of the circle), obviously diminishing the advantage of the quick glance beyond the border.

Another setting in which diverse forms of interaction are needed is virtual worlds, such as Second Life. In that context, the users need to carry out a variety of actions for looking around, moving within the environment, and launching events. If everything were carried out with just normal dwell, the Midas Touch problem would be prominent. Istance, Bates, Hyrskykari, and Vickers (2008) solved this in the Snap Clutch technique, using four modes, each activated by a quick glance beyond one of the borders of the screen. The modes were used for locomotion and camera control, in-world object manipulation, application control, and communication. In application control, for instance, a dwell could be used to issue a mouse-down event. Then another dwell indicated where the action was to take place, and a saccade would then generate a mouse-up event, activating the action. Such a multi-step process proved crucial where an application has controls in one part of the screen and their effect takes place in another part. In mouse-based control, the mouse cursor can be placed on the control first and the effect of the operation can be viewed when the mouse button is pressed. With gaze-based control, gaze cannot be used simultaneously for both, so breaking the sequence into its components is necessary.

A significant advantage of Snap Clutch is that the modes implemented are independent of the underlying application: they can be used in other contexts as they are. The motivation for the original work was to provide interaction techniques for users with disabilities that would make it as easy for them to interact in the virtual world as it was for able-bodied users. This goal was not quite achieved (except for locomotion), and further

work has pinned down the elements that could be improved most and suggested alternative designs (Istance, Hyrskykari, Vickers, & Ali, 2008). These include additional feedback using a green strip at the edge of the screen to indicate the active mode, and addition of several other modes.

Porta, Ravarelli, and Spagnoli (2010) suggested another solution with modes. They introduced a modified cursor control called ceCursor that could be moved in four directions by dwelling in one of the four arms pointing out of the star-shaped widget (see Figure 7). Dwelling on one of the four arms forces the cursor to move smoothly on the desktop or jump in discrete steps from icon to icon. Selections are made with a simple dwell in the centre of the star. An interesting feature is the hot spot replicated in the activated arms. This ensures that the user will always know what is underneath the centre hot spot. Although this is not considered to be natural interaction, the ceCursor control facilitates fine-grained positioning.

Facilitating access to small targets by means of cursor manipulation was also studied by Zhang, Ren, and Zha (2008). They introduced three methods for modulating the cursor trajectories to counteract the eye jitter and instability of gaze pointing: force field, speed reduction, and warp-

Figure 7. ceCursor moving to the right, with the centre area replicated in the arm of the star. A small red circle in the centre marks the hot spot (Porta et al., 2010). (© 2010 ACM. Used with permission)

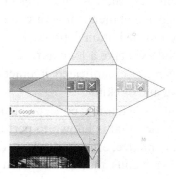

ing to target centre. The force-field method created a force point in the target centre such that, while within the target area, the cursor was attracted toward the target centre. The speed-reduction method was a variant of the force-field method in which, in addition to use of the target centre as a force point, the speed of the cursor was reduced while it was within the target area. The goal of the speed-reduction method was to prevent eye jitter from unintentionally interrupting dwell time by moving the cursor outside the target area. The warping-to-target-centre method moved the cursor to the target centre as soon as the cursor entered the target area and held it there while the gaze was within the target area. The evaluation by Zhang et al. showed that force field and speed reduction significantly alleviated the instability of the eye cursor, improving performance of dwell-based gaze pointing tasks. However, warping to target centre did not help, most likely because of the dramatic unnatural movement of the eye cursor.

USING EYE GAZE IN COMBINATION WITH OTHER MODALITIES

So far, we have looked at interaction techniques that are suitable for use with gaze as the only modality. We will now turn our attention to techniques wherein the use of gaze can be supported by a multi-modal approach or used to enhance traditional techniques with other input channels.

Blinks, Winks, and Pupil Dilation

Since the eyes are used for selection, it seems a natural idea to use them for more than just the point of gaze. Blinking (closing both eyes) or winking (closing just one eye) can be used for triggering a mouse click event. However, winking is not easy for some people, and intentional blinking would need to be separated from natural blinking. This could be done with prolonged blinks for activating

events, but at the expense of speed of interaction. Moreover, as Huckauf and Urbina (2008b) point out, blinking may affect the vergence of the eyes. Overall, selection by blinking may prove strenuous for the eye muscles. Selection by blinking is supported by several manufacturers of eye tracking systems and has been used in research prototypes (e.g., Grauman, Betke, Lombardi, Gips, & Bradski, 2003). However, using blinking and winking for selections has not gained popularity comparable to that of dwell-based selections.

Another rarely used attribute of the eyes is pupil dilation. There is a good reason for this: it is hard to control pupil size voluntarily, and to distinguish voluntary changes in pupil size from involuntary changes in pupil dilation that can be prompted by many factors (such as excitement and image brightness). However, Ekman, Poikola, Mäkäräinen, Takala, and Hämäläinen (2008) showed that voluntary pupil size control is possible, and changes in pupil size can be detected on a statistically significant level, especially with properly designed feedback. Ekman, Poikola, and Mäkäräinen (2008) then explored the use of pupil size as a control mechanism in a game, where the interaction was carefully designed so that voluntary pupil changes were coupled with actions designed to instigate positive arousal. Thus both voluntary and involuntary pupil dilations contributed to the change detected in pupil size.

Keyboard and Mouse

The Zoompad prototype in Figure 6 showed how a dedicated area of the screen was reserved to display various controls such as gaze-sensitive buttons to generate mouse events and a magnification window. A similar technique can be applied without reservation of any additional screen real estate if gaze is used in conjunction with the conventional mouse and keyboard.

Figure 8. The EyePoint selection method (Kumar et al., 2007) uses a two-step process, first fixating on a target and then pressing a keyboard shortcut. This will bring up a zoomed-in view around the last fixation, which allows higher tolerance for eye tracker noise. The user fixates on the target again and releases the button, which issues a simulated mouse click in the position of the current fixation (© 2007 ACM. Used with permission)

Keyboard

Combination of gaze interaction with input from the keyboard was implemented in the multi-modal EyePoint prototype (Kumar, Paepcke, & Winograd, 2007). Figure 8 illustrates the sequence of actions being performed to click on a specific link on a Web page. First, the user locates the target of interest with the gaze. Second, pressing a key on the keyboard brings up a magnified view of the region that was looked at. Third, the user locates the target in the magnified window and releases the keyboard key to issue the click. In the final step with the prototype, the magnification allows for more accurate selections since the effective width of the target is increased – a feature inspired by the two-step technique of Lankford (2000).

In a controlled experiment, EyePoint was found to be slower and less accurate than a standard mouse in a pure pointing task. However, in a more realistic task that combined pointing and typing, EyePoint was slightly but significantly faster than using the mouse. In this case, the fact that participants could keep their hands on the keyboard without a need to reach for the mouse compensated for the intrinsic slowness of the two-step technique. Error rates remained considerably higher for EyePoint in comparison to the mouse.

In addition to pointing and clicking, another extremely frequent operation in a windowed interface is switching between applications and between windows. This, too, can be supported by eye gaze. Figure 9 shows how the EyeExposé prototype manipulates the window-switching solution in the Windows operating system. The

Figure 9. The EyeExposé window selection method (Kumar, 2007) supports fast application-switching. The interaction combines the use of keyboard input and gaze pointing (© 2007 Manu Kumar. Used with permission)

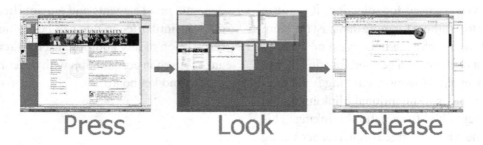

prototype has modified the normal 'press–release–mouse click' sequence and replaced it with a 'press–look–release'. The potential for saving time during interaction is obvious, and accuracy should not be an issue, as the proxies of the miniaturised windows tend to be fairly large.

If there are no overlapping windows (i.e., windows are placed side by side), the switching operation can be further simplified. Gazing at a specific window for a predefined time can then enlarge and put the focus on the window of interest and decrease the size of all unattended windows. This was implemented in the EyeWindow system (see Figure 10) by Fono and Vertegaal (2005).

In their study, Fono and Vertegaal (2005) found that eye tracking with automatic activation was about twice as fast as use of a mouse with special keyboard keys. Eye tracking with key activation was more than 70% faster than manual conditions and was preferred by most participants.

Møllenbach, Stefansson, and Hansen (2008) evaluated mouse and gaze interaction in two zoomable, multi-scaled information spaces: one large with 2000 nodes designed for a searching and browsing task, and a second designed for precision zooming in a target selection task. For control, mouse and gaze were used to control panning and two keys on a standard keyboard were used for zooming in and out, respectively.

Their study compared the navigation with gaze and mouse and the results indicated that the performance between gaze and mouse were indistinguishable. However, in the selection task, gaze control proved 16% faster than mouse control. Møllenbach et al. conclude how gaze-controlled pan/zoom-navigation is a viable alternative to the traditional mouse control during inspection and target exploration in multi-scaled environments.

Mouse

EyePoint illustrated how the use of dedicated keys in conjunction with eye gaze can support accurate selections with zooming. The earliest technique that combined the use of eye gaze and traditional input devices was MAGIC pointing, from Zhai, Morimoto, and Ihde (1999). In MAGIC pointing, the mouse pointer is automatically warped to the vicinity of a selectable object if the user's gaze is within a specified spatial threshold of the object. The final fine-grained movement of the mouse pointer is done with the physical mouse. Zhai et al. found in their experiment that the participants liked the technique and it was slightly faster than use of the mouse alone. No differences in accuracy (i.e., incorrect selections) were found. This is an example of a technique that falls between the somewhat grey area of explicit computer control and attentive interfaces. Moving the mouse

Figure 10. EyeWindow by Fono and Vertegaal (2005). On the left, gazing at the bottom right window makes it bigger and moves the focus to that window, so that (on the right) typing can continue without removal of the hands from the keyboard (© 2005 ACM. Used with permission)

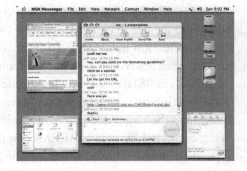 

pointer can be so indiscernible that the user may not realise that the eyes are actually used for control. The technique is discussed in more detail in the chapter on attentive interfaces by Istance and Hyrskykari.

Räihä and Špakov (2009) developed a related technique to be used with multiple monitors. To overcome the long mouse movements in such settings, it has been suggested that multiple mouse pointers could be used, all controlled with a single mouse simultaneously and in synchrony (Kobayashi & Igarashi, 2008). Selecting with such a technique is ambiguous if several mouse pointers are present at the same time (i.e., multiple cursors on top of selectable targets). Räihä and Špakov suggested the use of eye gaze to select the active pointer. The pointer closest to the user's point of gaze was active and the underlying target received the mouse click. In an experiment with two monitors, the method improved target-acquisition times over long distance (when the target was on a different monitor than the previously active pointer). Users preferred the condition in which each monitor had one mouse pointer and eye gaze was used to indicate the active monitor. Blanch and Ortega (2009) suggested a similar technique with even greater speed improvements.

Facial Muscles (EMG)

One user group that benefits from computer control by gaze is people with quadriplegia. For them, use of the other facial muscles (in addition to eye muscles) could provide additional control mechanisms. Extensive studies on use of frowning (movement of the muscles of the forehead) together with eye gaze were carried out by Surakka and his group (Partala, Aula, & Surakka, 2001; Surakka, Illi, & Isokoski, 2004). Muscle activity was measured with two electrodes attached to the forehead. In summary, their results showed that for short movement distances (6 cm on a normal screen), interaction with the mouse was faster for able-bodied participants, but with longer dis-

tances (starting with 12 cm) gaze-based looking and frowning was not significantly slower than the mouse. In fact, with the longest distances the results indicate that the new technique could even beat the mouse. Not surprisingly, the speed of eye movements could compensate for the loss in selection speed from frowning. As usual in gaze-based interaction, the mouse is superior in selection accuracy but the accuracy of selection by gaze can be improved with sufficiently large targets.

In follow-up studies, Surakka, Isokoski, Illi, and Salminen (2005) found that selection by smiling was significantly faster and less error-prone than selection by frowning. In a study by Junker and Hansen (2006) with three participants in a real application environment (producing text with GazeTalk), the mouse was again fastest, but selection by frowning was more efficient (in words per minute) than dwell-based selection was. Mateo, San Agustin, and Hansen (2008) measured EMG signals, using a Cyberlink™ headband that reacted to a variety of muscle movements, such as frowning or biting (movement of the jaw). They found a speed advantage for gaze even with shorter distances than those reported by Surakka et al. (2004), but at the cost of some missed selections due to problems with the EMG technology used. San Agustin, Mateo, Hansen, and Villanueva (2009) found the combination of gaze for pointing and EMG for selection (using the same Cyberlink™ system) to be the fastest technique among the video game controllers they used in their experiment, including a traditional mouse.

Grauman et al. (2003) compared selection by blinking and selection by raising the eyebrows and found the former to be more accurate (95.6% vs. 89.0% detection accuracy). To improve overall selection accuracy, Chin, Barreto, Cremades, and Adjouadi (2008) developed a technique in which gaze positioning on the coarse scale was done by looking at the target and inaccuracies in tracking were corrected by means of EMG signals from four electrodes. This allowed binding muscle movements to different actions, such as a left jaw clench for moving the cursor to the left, raising the eyebrows for moving the cursor up, and so on. A click was activated by a full bite action (clenching of both the left and right jaw). Their experiment showed a significant improvement in selection accuracy, though (as might be expected) at the cost of increased selection time. In another attempt to improve accuracy, especially in noisy environments, Ariz et al. (2009) implemented a scheme wherein EMG signals for selection were reacted to during fixations only. This, too, reduced incorrect (unintended) selections significantly while increasing selection time.

Head

An interesting solution was suggested by Adams, Witkowski, and Spence (2008), who used body movements together with eye movements. In particular, since it is natural for humans to move closer to a target that they want to inspect in greater detail, they used the screen to eye distance to control zooming of the view. The setting for their experiment was Google Earth, where participants needed to navigate to a given destination. They compared four methods of zooming: by head movement, by staring, by mouse, and by mouse but with gaze for panning. Looking at the edges of the screen activated panning; the pan region was less than 15% of the screen real estate in all directions. Zooming could be activated in the centre area by one of the four techniques. In staring-to-zoom, for instance, fixating within the centre area caused zooming in at a comfortable rate and also panning to place the fixation location at the centre. Visually scanning the centre area stopped the zooming. Glancing at the eye tracker below the screen triggered zooming out.

The goal of this design was to create an interaction technique that is natural for the application in question. The initial experience with the new head-to-zoom technique was not encouraging: it took considerably more time for the participants to get comfortable with. However, in a navigation task repeated several times, performance was similar for all techniques by the third trial. In a search task mouse-based techniques were better than those that used gaze or head distance for zooming.

The time for becoming familiarised with the head-to-zoom technique was attributed to limitations of the eye tracking technology: if the user moves too close to the tracker, the eyes are lost from the video image and the gaze point cannot be computed. This stalled the zooming on the screen although the user might still have been physically moving. This resulted in sensations of nausea for some participants. With practice, the participants learned the range in which the eye tracker could be operated, which is indicated by the results in the third trial.

A similar idea was proposed by Lepinski and Vertegaal (2007) and implemented with a low-cost Web camera. However, only anecdotal evaluation results were published.

Speech

Combining gaze with speech is another attractive option. It was pioneered early on by Bolt (1984) in his seminal Put-That-There system. It initially used pointing gestures for indicating the target and spoken commands to cause actions, but gaze was soon added as an additional modality to compensate for the inaccuracy of pointing gestures. Neither gaze nor gestures alone was accurate enough for the system, but when the two approaches were fused the overall robustness improved.

New issues emerge when gaze is used for pointing and another modality for selection. Kaur et al. (2003) implemented an application in the spirit of the Put-That-There system. The task was to look at an object on the screen and say: 'Move it', look at the destination and say: 'there'. The research question in the study by Kaur et al. was to identify the object that the participant was manipulating. The result was, in general, that the best fixation to use as the identifying fixation started before uttering of the command – which is natural, since the user can be expected to inspect the object first. However, the time difference was considerable; the fixation took place, on average, 630 ms before the onset of speech. Moreover, individual variation was low but inter-participant variation was quite high. Therefore, no general threshold seemed to work well; instead, the timing had to be set separately for each user if reliable operation (close to 95% accuracy) was to be achieved. In another multi-modal synchronisation study, Kumar, Klingner, Puranik, Winograd, and Paepcke (2008) considered the timing of fixations and selection by a key press on the keyboard. They found an opposite result: users tended to press the key before the fixation had been detected. An improved fixation detection algorithm amended this.

Miniotas, Špakov, Tugoy, and MacKenzie (2006) used speech to reduce inaccuracies in selection by gaze alone when the targets were small and densely placed. They highlighted with different colours all selectable objects within a 100-pixel threshold distance from the measured point of gaze. Selection was done with the standard dwell method. The neighbours to the object most likely to be selected would be highlighted in different colours. Here, an unwanted object at the point of gaze could be omitted by saying aloud the name of the colour used for highlighting. This method both improved selection speed and decreased errors. However, the dwell times used in the experiment were rather long (1,000 ms and up).

Another study, by Kammerer et al. (2008), compared the use of gaze only and gaze plus speech in the context of pie menus. Selection by speech took place when the user uttered the word 'click'. No speed advantage for the multi-modal condition was found; the dwell time used in the experiment was 750 ms. Similarly, in a study by O'Donovan, Ward, Hodgins, and Sundstedt (2009), using gaze and voice commands was found to perform significantly worse than the mouse and keyboard in a game application. However,

users did feel more immersed when using gaze and voice. Clearly, the traditional performance metrics are not always the only issues to consider.

BROWSING AND NAVIGATION OF INFORMATION SPACES

We have discussed a number of techniques for computer control by gaze. They have been developed and studied mostly in specially designed contexts and dedicated applications. Let us close this chapter by focusing on one specific application area: browsing and navigating information spaces. They can take many forms: 3D worlds, Google Earth, collections of pages and documents, and the World Wide Web. We have already addressed Google Earth; here, we will discuss other interesting initiatives for using gaze as an alternative input device.

3D Worlds

An early study of navigation in a virtual world was carried out by Tanriverdi and Jacob (2000). They used an eye tracker in combination with a head-mounted display. The user could navigate in the 3D world simply by looking around. When a 3D object in the world got the user's visual attention, it was smoothly moved closer to the user. The opacity of the object's front panel was also removed, so that its inside could be inspected. Looking elsewhere would make the object retract and become opaque again. When compared to more conventional 3D pointing, the interaction based on eye movements was faster, but participants had more trouble in recalling spatial information than when they navigated by hand. The study did not find any significant differences in subjective preferences.

Navigation in Second Life (Istance, Bates, et al., 2008; Istance, Hyrskykari, et al., 2008) has been discussed above. Castellina and Forno (2008) compared several gaze-based interaction techniques both for interacting in a virtual world and for playing a 3D game. For the non-shooting tasks in the virtual world, the most accurate technique turned out to be having semi-transparent virtual buttons at the edges of the screen. The buttons on the left and right rotated the camera, while the buttons at the top and bottom moved the avatar forward and backward. With dwell-based button selections, the number of navigation errors decreased in comparison to 'direct gaze control', where forward movement was activated by dwelling in the centre of the screen. However, the latter resulted in faster performance when the task did not involve much searching and navigation.

Collections of Documents and Pages

Figure 11 shows the experimental software ('GazeSpace') used by Laqua, Bandara, and Sasse (2007). The screen consists of seven information panes. The content of the central pane is exposed and can be read normally. When the user shifted attention to one of the surrounding navigation elements, its borders were first highlighted (bolded and coloured), and after a threshold was reached, it swapped places with the element in the centre. Two techniques for interest accumulation were compared. In the static interest accumulation algorithm, gaze points on an element were tallied cumulatively until one element was chosen, at which point all tallies were cleared. In the dynamic algorithm, the number of gaze points would decay dynamically when interest moved elsewhere. For instance, if 50 gaze points were collected after the last gaze point that landed on an element, the tally for that element would be decreased by 50%.

The experiment carried out showed that users mainly had positive comments about GazeSpace. They felt the interaction to be natural, although some complained about excessively high thresholds causing interaction to be too slow. Interestingly, no difference was found between the two interest collection algorithms. Users did not always notice that different algorithms were used.

Another approach was suggested by Numajiri, Nakamura, and Kuno (2002). Their Speed Browser pushes information, each page in a separate window, into view from the bottom of the screen. Three columns of windows are used. If the user scans their content quickly, the windows move at a high speed, but if the scanning speed slows down, also the movement of the windows is slowed down. If the eyes fixate on an element in a window, move-

Figure 11. GazeSpace by Laqua et al., 2007 (© 2007 Sven Laqua. Used with permission)

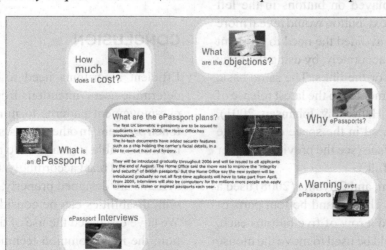

ment is stopped and the window is blown up at the centre of the screen. A key press is required to get the windows moving again.

An obvious limitation of both GazeSpace and Speed Browser is that they do not scale well to large information spaces, such as the Web, where the user needs more control for selecting the visible content. Techniques applicable in that context are reviewed next.

Interacting on the World Wide Web

The Web is, obviously, an important and challenging environment for people who need to rely on gaze for their communication with computers. An eye mouse can, of course, be used for Web navigation (see, e.g., Gips, DiMattia, Curran, Lees, & Gates, 2002), but the problems with accuracy and targets (links) that are close to each other need special attention.

Castellina and Corno (2007) implemented a special Web browser for gaze interaction. In their design, all links on a Web page were tagged with a number (that could consist of several digits, in the case of more than nine visible links). The left pane of the browser had a soft numeric pad, and links could be chosen by dialling in the corresponding number with consecutive dwells. In an alternative design, the names (text) of five links could be displayed on buttons in the left pane; selecting a 'Next' button would reveal more links. Both designs avoided the need to pinpoint a small textual link accurately, by using the large buttons as proxies for the links. The same basic idea has been implemented in the latest release of GazeTalk (Hansen, Hansen, & Johansen, 2001), where links are placed in the space of the large buttons of the interface (see the previous chapter for details of GazeTalk).

Abe, Owada, Ohi, and Ohyama (2008) used a stepping approach. The top and bottom parts of the screen contained a row of five buttons each. The top buttons could be used to move the mouse cursor from a selectable object (such as a link,

radio button, or text box) to the next, in all four directions. This helped to decrease the number of steps in navigation when there are many objects, such as links, on the page. The fifth button then initiated an action, such as following a link. There was also a 'fast forward' option available, which could make the cursor jump in steps of five or ten objects. Along the bottom edge were three menus (selected by toggling among the three options). The menus provided operations for scrolling, accessing browsing history, refreshing the view, and bringing up a soft keyboard where keys were again selected by stepping through them. The advantages of the browser by Abe et al. include that it was usable with a low-accuracy tracker based on a Web cam and that it supported the most common functions needed for working with the Web, not only browsing by following links.

Perhaps the most elegant solutions for browsing are those based on semantic zooming, such as the one shown in Figure 5. The advantage there is that not all links need to be blown up in the interface, only those that are relevant when the browser cannot be sure which link the user has intended to select.

Finally, the ideas discussed here could be well combined with those of Juang et al. (2005), who used gaze gestures for simple back-and-forth navigation and up-and-down scrolling.

CONCLUSION

Efficient algorithms need to be developed to determine users' intentions from spatiotemporal eye-movement patterns to minimise the Midas touch problem. In other words, software solutions need to be able to analyse the users' gaze on the monitor and react accordingly. If gaze-controlled systems are designed properly, the life of people with disabilities can be considerably improved. We have discussed the use of dwell-based selection, the most common technique in use today. In addition, the approaches covered included specially designed interface widgets, variations of zooming, the use of gestures, and multi-modal interaction. We looked at browsing of information spaces as an example of an area where many of the techniques have been put to use.

Another interesting area of application is the use of gaze control in games. We have covered only a few examples above, but a comprehensive survey was published by Isokoski, Joos, Špakov, and Martin (2009), and it makes for interesting reading in the light of the different interaction techniques used. Quite recent work includes the use of eye gaze for playing World of Warcraft (Istance, Hyrskykari, Vickers, & Chaves, 2009; Istance, Vickers, & Hyrskykari, 2009; Istance et al., 2010).

How fast can computer control by eye gaze get? We have seen many examples illustrating how gaze can often be comparable in efficiency to control by mouse, and sometimes even faster (e.g., Dorr, Pomarjanschi, & Barth, 2009), but often the biggest difference is in interaction accuracy: selections are not always recognised correctly. They may be missed altogether or be associated with an incorrect object. Several techniques have been tested, and many are in production use, but there is still room for improvement, to find the proper balance of operation efficiency, accuracy, and user satisfaction.

REFERENCES

Abe, K., Owada, K., Ohi, S., & Ohyama, M. (2008). A system for Web browsing by eye-gaze input. *Electronics and Communications in Japan, 91*(5), 11–18. doi:10.1002/ecj.10110

Adams, N., Witkowski, M., & Spence, R. (2008). The inspection of very large images by eye-gaze control. *Proceedings of the Working Conference on Advanced Visual Interfaces (AVI '08)* (pp. 111–118). New York, NY: ACM. doi:10.1145/1385569.1385589

Ariz, M., Navallas, J., Villanueva, A., San Agustin, J., Cabeza, R., & Tall, M. (2009). Optimizing the interoperability between a VOG and a EMG system. *Proceedings of the 5th Conference on Communication by Gaze Interaction (COGAIN 2009)* (pp. 43–48). Copenhagen, Denmark: DTU. Retrieved from the COGAIN website: http://www.cogain.org/conference

Ashmore, M., Duchowski, A. T., & Shoemaker, G. (2005). Efficient eye pointing with a fisheye lens. *Proceedings of Graphics Interface 2005 (GI '05)* (pp. 203–210). Ontario, Canada: Canadian Human–Computer Communications Society (CHCCS).

Bates, R. (1999). Multimodal eye-based interaction for zoomed target selection on a standard graphical user interface. In M. A. Sasse & C. Johnson (Eds.), *Human–Computer Interaction (INTERACT '99)* (vol. II, pp. 7–8). Amsterdam, The Netherlands: IOS Press.

Bates, R., & Istance, H. (2002). Zooming interfaces! Enhancing the performance of eye controlled pointing devices. *Proceedings of the 5th International ACM Conference on Assistive Technologies (ASSETS 2002)* (pp. 119–126). New York, NY: ACM. doi:10.1145/638249.638272

Bates, R., & Istance, H. O. (2003). Why are eye mice unpopular? A detailed comparison of head and eye controlled assistive technology pointing devices. *Universal Access in the Information Society, 2*(3), 280–290. doi:10.1007/s10209-003-0053-y

Blanch, R., & Ortega, M. (2009). Rake cursor: Improving pointing performance with concurrent input channels. *Proceedings of the 27th International Conference on Human Factors in Computing Systems (CHI '09)* (pp. 1415–1418). New York, NY: ACM. doi:10.1145/1518701.1518914

Bolt, R. A. (1984). *Human interface: Where people and computers meet*. New York, NY: Wiley.

Castellina, E., & Corno, F. (2007). Accessible Web surfing through gaze interaction. *Proceedings of the 3rd Conference on Communication by Gaze Interaction* (*COGAIN 2007*) (pp. 74–77). Leicester, UK: De Montfort University. Retrieved from the COGAIN website: http://www.cogain.org/conference

Castellina, E., & Corno, F. (2008). Multimodal gaze interaction in 3D virtual environments. *Proceedings of the 4th Conference on Communication by Gaze Interaction* (*COGAIN 2008*) (pp. 33–37). Prague, Czech Republic: Czech Technical University. Retrieved from the COGAIN website: http://www.cogain.org/conference

Chin, C. A., Barreto, A., Cremades, J. G., & Adjouadi, M. (2008). Integrated electromyogram and eye-gaze tracking cursor control system for computer users with motor disabilities. *Journal of Rehabilitation Research and Development*, *45*(1), 161–174. doi:10.1682/JRRD.2007.03.0050

Dorr, M., Pomarjanschi, L., & Barth, E. (2009). Gaze beats mouse: A case study on a gaze-controlled breakout. *PsychNology Journal*, *7*(2), 197–211.

Drewes, H., & Schmidt, A. (2007). Interacting with the computer using gaze gestures. In C. Baranauskas, P. Palanque, J. Abascal, & S. D. J. Barbosa (Eds.), *Human–Computer Interaction (INTERACT '07)* (LNCS 4663, pp. 475–488). Berlin, Germany: Springer. doi:10.1007/978-3-540-74800-7_43

Ekman, I., Poikola, A., & Mäkäräinen, M. (2008). *Invisible Eni* – Using gaze and pupil size to control a game. *Extended Abstracts on Human Factors in Computing Systems (CHI '08)* (pp. 3135–3140). New York, NY: ACM. doi:10.1145/1358628.1358820

Ekman, I., Poikola, A., Mäkäräinen, M., Takala, T., & Hämäläinen, P. (2008). Voluntary pupil size change as control in eyes only interaction. *Proceedings of the 2008 Symposium on Eye-Tracking Research & Applications* (*ETRA '08*) (pp. 115–118). New York, NY: ACM. doi:10.1145/1344471.1344501

Fono, D., & Vertegaal, R. (2005). EyeWindows: Evaluation of eye-controlled zooming windows for focus selection. *Proceedings of the SIGCHI Conference on Human Factors in Computing Systems (CHI '05)* (pp. 151–160). New York, NY: ACM. doi:10.1145/1054972.1054994

Gips, J., DiMattia, P. A., Curran, M., Lees, D., & Gates, M. (2002). Accessing Internet courses by eye movement and head movement. In K. Miesenberger, J. Klaus, & W. Zagler (Eds.), *Computers Helping People with Special Needs* (LNCS 2398, pp. 291–308). Berlin, Germany: Springer. doi:10.1007/3-540-45491-8_48

Grauman, K., Betke, M., Lombardi, J., Gips, J., & Bradski, G. R. (2003). Communication via eye blinks and eyebrow raises: Video-based human–computer interfaces. *Universal Access in the Information Society*, *2*(4), 359–373. doi:10.1007/s10209-003-0062-x

Hansen, J. P., Hansen, D., & Johansen, A. (2001). Bringing gaze-based interaction back to basics. *Universal Access in HCI (UAHCI 2001): Towards an Information Society for All* (vol. 3, pp. 325–329). Mahwah, NJ: Lawrence Erlbaum.

Heikkilä, H., & Räihä, K.-J. (2009). Speed and accuracy of gaze gestures. *Journal of Eye Movement Research*, *3*(2):1, 1–14.

Hornof, A. J., & Cavender, A. (2005). EyeDraw: Enabling children with severe motor impairments to draw with their eyes. *Proceedings of the SIGCHI Conference on Human Factors in Computing Systems (CHI '05)* (pp. 161–170). New York, NY: ACM. doi:10.1145/1054972.1054995

Huckauf, A., & Urbina, M. H. (2008a). Gazing with pEYEs: Towards a universal input for various applications. *Proceedings of the 2008 Symposium on Eye-Tracking Research & Applications* (*ETRA '08*) (pp. 51–54). New York, NY: ACM. doi:10.1145/1344471.1344483

Huckauf, A., & Urbina, M. H. (2008b). On object selection in gaze controlled environments. *Journal of Eye Movement Research, 2*(4):4, 1–7.

Isokoski, P., Joos, M., Špakov, O., & Martin, B. (2009). Gaze controlled games. *Universal Access in the Information Society, 8*(4), 323–337. doi:10.1007/s10209-009-0146-3

Istance, H., Bates, R., Hyrskykari, A., & Vickers, S. (2008). Snap Clutch, a moded approach to solving the Midas touch problem. *Proceedings of the 2008 Symposium on Eye-Tracking Research & Applications* (*ETRA '08*) (pp. 221–228). New York, NY: ACM. doi:10.1145/1344471.1344523

Istance, H., Hyrskykari, A., Immonen, L., Mansikkamaa, S., & Vickers, S. (2010). Designing gaze gestures for gaming: An investigation of performance. *Proceedings of the 2010 Symposium on Eye-Tracking Research & Applications* (*ETRA '10*) (pp. 323–330). New York, NY: ACM. doi:10.1145/1743666.1743740

Istance, H., Hyrskykari, A., Vickers, S., & Ali, N. (2008). User performance of gaze-based interaction with on-line virtual communities. *Proceedings of the 4th Conference on Communication by Gaze Interaction* (*COGAIN 2008*) (pp. 28–32). Prague, Czech Republic: Czech Technical University. Retrieved from the COGAIN website: http://www.cogain.org/conference

Istance, H., Hyrskykari, A., Vickers, S., & Chaves, T. (2009). For your eyes only: Controlling 3D online games by eye-gaze. In T. Gross, J. Gulliksen, P. Kotzé, L. Oestreicher, P. Palanque, R. O. Prates, & M. Winckler (Eds.), *Human–Computer Interaction (INTERACT 2009)* (LNCS 5726, pp. 314–327). Berlin, Germany: Springer. doi:10.1007/978-3-642-03655-2_36

Istance, H., Vickers, S., & Hyrskykari, A. (2009). Gaze-based interaction with massively multiplayer on-line games. *Extended Abstracts of the 27th International Conference on Human Factors in Computing Systems* (*CHI '09*) (pp. 4381–4386). New York, NY: ACM. doi:10.1145/1520340.1520670

Istance, H. O., Spinner, C., & Howarth, P. A. (1996). Providing motor impaired users with access to standard Graphical User Interface (GUI) software via eye-based interaction. *Proceedings of the 1st European Conference on Disability, Virtual Reality and Associated Technologies* (*ECDVRAT 96*) (pp. 109–116). Reading, UK: University of Reading.

Jacob, R. J. K. (1991). The use of eye movements in human–computer interaction techniques: What you look at is what you get. *ACM Transactions on Information Systems, 9*(2), 152–169. doi:10.1145/123078.128728

Jacob, R. J. K. (1993). What you look at is what you get. *Computer, 26*(7), 65–66. doi:10.1109/MC.1993.274943

Jacob, R. J. K. (1995). Eye tracking in advanced interface design . In Barfield, W., & Furness, T. A. III, (Eds.), *Virtual environment and advanced interface design* (pp. 258–288). New York, NY: Oxford University Press.

Juang, K., Jasen, F., Katrekar, A., Ahn, J., & Duchowski, A. T. (2005). *Use of eye movement gestures for Web browsing*. Retrieved from the Clemson University website: http://andrewd.ces.clemson.edu/courses/cpsc412/fall05/teams/reports/group2.pdf

Junker, A. M., & Hansen, J. P. (2006). Gaze pointing and facial EMG clicking. *Proceedings of the 2nd Conference on Communication by Gaze Interaction* (*COGAIN 2006*) (pp. 42–45). Turin, Italy: Politecnico di Torino. Retrieved from the COGAIN website: http://www.cogain.org/conference

Kammerer, Y., Scheiter, K., & Beinhauer, W. (2008). Looking my way through the menu: The impact of menu design and multimodal input on gaze-based menu selection. *Proceedings of the 2008 Symposium on Eye-Tracking Research & Applications* (*ETRA '08*) (pp. 213–220). New York, NY: ACM. doi:10.1145/1344471.1344522

Kaur, M., Tremaine, M., Huang, N., Wilder, J., Gacovski, Z., Flippo, F., & Mantravadi, C. S. (2003). Where is "*it*"? Event synchronization in gaze-speech input systems. *Proceedings of the 5th International Conference on Multimodal Interfaces* (*ICMI '03*) (pp. 151–158). New York, NY: ACM. doi:10.1145/958432.958463

Kobayashi, M., & Igarashi, T. (2008). Ninja cursors: Using multiple cursors to assist target acquisition on large screens. *Proceedings of the 26th Annual SIGCHI Conference on Human Factors in Computing Systems* (*CHI '08*) (pp. 949–958). New York, NY: ACM. doi:10.1145/1357054.1357201

Kumar, M. (2007). *Gaze-enhanced user interface design* (Doctoral dissertation, Stanford University). Retrieved from https://hci.stanford.edu/research/GUIDe/publications/Manu Kumar Dissertation - Gaze-enhanced User Interface Design.pdf

Kumar, M., Klingner, J., Puranik, R., Winograd, T., & Paepcke, A. (2008). Improving the accuracy of gaze input for interaction. *Proceedings of the 2008 Symposium on Eye-Tracking Research & Applications* (*ETRA '08*) (pp. 65–68). New York, NY: ACM. doi:10.1145/1344471.1344488

Kumar, M., Paepcke, A., & Winograd, T. (2007). EyePoint: Practical pointing and selection using gaze and keyboard. *Proceedings of the SIGCHI Conference on Human Factors in Computing Systems* (*CHI '07*) (pp. 421–430). New York, NY: ACM. doi:10.1145/1240624.1240692

Kurtenbach, G. P., Sellen, A. J., & Buxton, W. A. S. (1993). An empirical evaluation of some articulatory and cognitive aspects of marking menus. *Human-Computer Interaction, 8*(1), 1–23. doi:10.1207/s15327051hci0801_1

Lankford, C. (2000). Effective eye-gaze input into Windows. *Proceedings of the 2000 Symposium on Eye Tracking Research & Applications* (*ETRA '00*) (pp. 23–27). New York, NY: ACM. doi:10.1145/355017.355021

Laqua, S., Bandara, U., & Sasse, M. (2007). GazeSpace: Eye gaze controlled content spaces. *Proceedings of the 21st British HCI Group Annual Conference on People and Computers* (*BCS-HCI '07*) (vol. 2, pp. 55–58). Swindon, UK: British Computer Society.

Lepinski, G. J., & Vertegaal, R. (2007). Using face position for low cost input, long range and oculomotor impaired users. *Proceedings of the 3rd Conference on Communication by Gaze Interaction* (*COGAIN '07*) (pp. 71–73). Leicester, UK: De Montfort University. Retrieved from the COGAIN website: http://www.cogain.org/conference

MacKenzie, I. S., & Zhang, X. (2008). Eye typing using word and letter prediction and a fixation algorithm. *Proceedings of the 2008 Symposium on Eye-Tracking Research & Applications* (*ETRA '08*) (pp. 55–58). New York, NY: ACM. doi:10.1145/1344471.1344484

Majaranta, P., Ahola, U.-K., & Špakov, O. (2009). Fast gaze typing with an adjustable dwell time. *Proceedings of the 27th International Conference on Human Factors in Computing Systems* (*CHI '09*) (pp. 357–360). New York, NY: ACM. doi:10.1145/1518701.1518758

Mateo, J. C., San Agustin, J., & Hansen, J. P. (2008). Gaze beats mouse: Hands-free selection by combining gaze and EMG. *Extended Abstracts on Human Factors in Computing Systems* (*CHI '08*) (pp. 3039–3044). New York, NY: ACM. doi:10.1145/1358628.1358804

Miniotas, D., Špakov, O., Tugoy, I., & MacKenzie, I. S. (2006). Speech-augmented eye gaze interaction with small closely spaced targets. *Proceedings of the 2006 Symposium on Eye-Tracking Research & Applications* (*ETRA '06*) (pp. 67–72). New York, NY: ACM. doi:10.1145/1117309.1117345

Møllenbach, E., Lillholm, M., Gail, A., & Hansen, J. P. (2010). Single gaze gestures. *Proceedings of the 2010 Symposium on Eye-Tracking Research & Applications* (*ETRA '10*) (pp. 177–180). New York, NY: ACM. doi:10.1145/1743666.1743710

Møllenbach, E., Stefansson, T., & Hansen, J. P. (2008). All eyes on the monitor: Gaze based interaction in zoomable, multi-scaled information-spaces. *Proceedings of the 13th International Conference on Intelligent User Interfaces* (*IUI '08*) (pp. 373–376). New York, NY: ACM. doi:10.1145/1378773.1378833

MyTobii. (2009). *User Manual: MyTobii, Version 2.3*. Danderyd, Sweden: Tobii Technology.

Numajiri, T., Nakamura, A., & Kuno, Y. (2002). Speed Browser controlled by eye movements. *Proceedings of the IEEE International Conference on Multimedia & Expo* (*ICME 2002*) (vol. 1, pp. 741–744). Washington, DC., USA: IEEE. doi:10.1109/ICME.2002.1035888

O'Donovan, J., Ward, J., Hodgins, S., & Sundstedt, V. (2009). Rabbit Run: Gaze and voice based game interaction. *The 9th Irish Eurographics Workshop*. Presented at Eurographics Ireland 2009 (EGIrl '09), Dublin, Ireland. Retrieved from http://gv2. cs.tcd.ie/egirl09/papers/07.pdf

Ohno, T. (1998). Features of eye gaze interface for selection tasks. *Proceedings of the 3rd Asia Pacific Computer Human Interaction* (*APCHI '98*) (pp. 176–181). Washington, DC., USA: IEEE. doi:10.1109/APCHI.1998.704190

Ohno, T., & Mukawa, N. (2003). Gaze-based interaction for anyone, anytime. *Proceedings of HCI International 2003* (vol. 4, 1452–1456). Mahwah, NJ: Lawrence Erlbaum.

Partala, T., Aula, A., & Surakka, V. (2001). Combined voluntary gaze direction and facial muscle activity as a new pointing technique. In M. Hirose (Ed.), *Human–Computer Interaction (INTERACT '01)* (pp. 100–107). Amsterdam, The Netherlands: IOS Press.

Pomplun, M., Ivanovic, N., Reingold, E., & Shen, J. (2001). Empirical evaluation of a novel gaze-controlled zooming interface. *Proceedings of HCI International 2001* (vol. 1). Mahwah, NJ: Lawrence Erlbaum.

Porta, M., Ravarelli, A., & Spagnoli, G. (2010). *ceCursor*, a contextual eye cursor for general pointing in windows environments. *Proceedings of the 2010 Symposium on Eye-Tracking Research & Applications* (*ETRA '10*) (pp. 331–337). New York, NY: ACM. doi:10.1145/1743666.1743741

Räihä, K., & Špakov, O. (2009). Disambiguating Ninja cursors with eye gaze. *Proceedings of the 27th International Conference on Human Factors in Computing Systems* (*CHI '09*) (pp. 1411–1414). New York, NY: ACM. doi:10.1145/1518701.1518913

San Agustin, J., Mateo, J. C., Hansen, J. P., & Villanueva, A. (2009). Evaluation of the potential of gaze input for game interaction. *PsychNology Journal*, 7(2), 213–236.

Sibert, L. E., & Jacob, R. J. K. (2000). Evaluation of eye gaze interaction. *Proceedings of the SIG-CHI Conference on Human Factors in Computing Systems* (*CHI '00*) (pp. 281–288). New York, NY: ACM. doi:10.1145/332040.332445

Skovsgaard, H., Mateo, J. C., Flach, J. M., & Hansen, J. P. (2010). Small-target selection with gaze alone. *Proceedings of the 2010 Symposium on Eye-Tracking Research & Applications* (*ETRA '10*) (pp. 145–148). New York, NY: ACM. doi:10.1145/1743666.1743702

Skovsgaard, H. H. T., Hansen, J. P., & Mateo, J. C. (2008). How can tiny buttons be hit using gaze only? *Proceedings of the 4th Conference on Communication by Gaze Interaction* (*COGAIN 2008*) (pp. 38–42). Prague, Czech Republic: Czech Technical University. Retrieved from the COGAIN website: http://www.cogain.org/conference

Špakov, O., & Miniotas, D. (2004). On-line adjustment of dwell time for target selection by gaze. *Proceedings of the 3rd Nordic Conference on Human–Computer Interaction* (*NordiCHI '04*) (pp. 203–206). New York, NY: ACM. doi:10.1145/1028014.1028045

Špakov, O., & Miniotas, D. (2005). Gaze-based selection of standard-size menu items. *Proceedings of the 7th International Conference on Multimodal Interfaces* (*ICMI'05*) (pp. 124–128). New York, NY: ACM. doi:10.1145/1088463.1088486

Surakka, V., Illi, M., & Isokoski, P. (2004). Gazing and frowning as a new human–computer interaction technique. *ACM Transactions on Applied Perception*, *1*(1), 40–56. doi:10.1145/1008722.1008726

Surakka, V., Isokoski, P., Illi, M., & Salminen, K. (2005). Is it better to gaze and frown or gaze and smile when controlling user interfaces? *Proceedings of HCI International 2005*. CD-ROM. Mahwah, NJ: Lawrence Erlbaum.

Tall, M. (2008). NeoVisus: Gaze driven interface components. *Proceedings of the 4th Conference on Communication by Gaze Interaction* (*COGAIN 2008*) (pp. 48–52). Prague, Czech Republic: Czech Technical University. Retrieved from the COGAIN website: http://www.cogain.org/conference

Tanriverdi, V., & Jacob, R. J. K. (2000). Interacting with eye movements in virtual environments. *Proceedings of the SIGCHI Conference on Human Factors in Computing Systems* (*CHI '00*) (pp. 265–272). New York, NY: ACM. doi:10.1145/332040.332443

Urbina, M. H., Lorenz, M., & Huckauf, A. (2010). Pies with EYEs: The limits of hierarchical pie menus in gaze control. *Proceedings of the 2010 Symposium on Eye-Tracking Research & Applications* (*ETRA '10*) (pp. 93–96). New York, NY: ACM. doi:10.1145/1743666.1743689

Zhai, S., Morimoto, C., & Ihde, S. (1999). Manual and gaze input cascaded (MAGIC) pointing. *Proceedings of the SIGCHI Conference on Human Factors in Computing Systems* (*CHI '99*) (pp. 246–253). New York, NY: ACM. doi:10.1145/302979.303053

Zhang, X., Ren, X., & Zha, H. (2008). Improving eye cursor's stability for eye pointing tasks. *Proceedings of the 26th Annual SIGCHI Conference on Human Factors in Computing Systems* (*CHI '08*) (pp. 525–534). New York, NY: ACM. doi:10.1145/1357054.1357139

Chapter 10
Beyond Communication and Control:
Environmental Control and Mobility by Gaze

Richard Bates
De Montfort University, UK

Emiliano Castellina
Politecnico di Torino, Italy

Fulvio Corno
Politecnico di Torino, Italy

Petr Novák
Czech Technical University, Czech Republic

Olga Štěpánková
Czech Technical University, Czech Republic

ABSTRACT

This chapter reviews the challenges and requirements in taking gaze-based interaction beyond communication and control, such as environmental control and mobility by gaze. The chapter is divided into two sections: the first section is devoted to environment control and the second to mobility control. Each section starts by introducing its necessary underlying notions and definitions and proceeds by explaining the main arguments for the development of environmental and mobility control and examining the general problems with these areas and of those domain-specific problems related to gaze control. While special attention is devoted to standardization when environment control is at issue, user safety is the priority in mobility control. A brief review of existing commercial or advanced research solutions offered for domotic and mobility control is given for both sections, as is a review of current open research issues. Finally, some promising academic prototypes are described, along with the ways in which their developers are trying to solve some of the problems identified.

DOI: 10.4018/978-1-61350-098-9.ch010

INTRODUCTION

This chapter is divided into two sections, which share a similar structure – the first section is devoted to environment control and the second to mobility control. Each section starts by introducing its necessary underlying notions and definitions – namely, intelligent domotic environments, gaze-based mobility, and mobile gaze tracking – and proceeds by explaining the main arguments for the development of environmental and mobility control and examining the general problems with these areas and of those domain-specific problems related to gaze control. While special attention is devoted to standardisation when environment control is at issue, user safety is the priority in mobility control. A brief review of existing commercial or advanced research solutions offered for domotic and mobility control is given for both sections, as is a review of current open research issues. Finally, some promising academic prototypes are described, along with the ways in which their developers are trying to solve some of the problems identified.

The Need for Gaze-Based Environment Control

Domotic systems ('domotic' is a portmanteau from the Latin word for home, 'domus', and 'informatics'), also known as home automation systems, smart home systems, or environmental control systems, have been available on the market for several years. However, only recently have they started to spread to residential buildings, thanks to the increasing availability of low-cost devices and the drive from newly emerging needs for house comfort, energy savings, security, communication, and multimedia services. The aim of smart home systems is:

- to reduce the day-to-day home operation work load of the occupants, and
- to enable the disabled occupants of a home to live as *autonomously* as possible.

Personal environmental control can be considered to be a comprehensive and effective aid, adaptable to the functional capabilities of the users and to their desired actions. When a user has a physical disability, that user might not be capable of physically manipulating all or some objects in the environment. Thus, an environmental control system moves from being a useful labour-saving device to a personal necessity for independent living, by enhancing and extending the abilities of a disabled user and allowing independence to be maintained. An environmental control system may be the sole and only way by which such persons can control their environment. Such personal autonomy over their environment has the benefit of reducing the reliance on the continuous help of a family member or other carer, and increasing the self-esteem of the users, as they can control the world around them.

The Need for Gaze-Based Mobility Control

In addition to environmental control, another significant requirement for assistive technology for many people with physical difficulties is that of *powered mobility control*. Without a self-controlled powered wheelchair, many people with disabilities are totally reliant on other people – not only to take them to a desired location but also in relation to their position once they get there. The freedom to come and go as we please, and its many benefits, is something that non-disabled people can take for granted. However, for people with mobility impairments, there are several specific benefits that are worth noting, including the following:

- Firstly, powered mobility, whether for adults (Evans, Frank, Neophytou, & de Souza, 2007) or for young children (Bottos, Bolcati, Sciuto, Ruggeri, & Feliciangeli, 2001), can considerably increase independence.

- Secondly, there can be significant benefits in terms of learning and rehabilitation. It has long been accepted that exploration is an essential element of learning (Papert, 1980; Piaget & Inhelder, 1967), whether through the manipulation of objects or through the exploration of a physical environment. Exploration is a building block of human development. The benefits of exploration through 'self-directed mobility', even for adults and children with severe and multiple impairments, are described by, for example, Iles and Shouksmith (1997) and Nilsson and Nyberg (1998), the latter of whom claim:

"The individuals' alertness rose, their understanding of simple cause-and-effect relationships were developed, and they began to use their hands in explorative behaviour with objects and [the] environment."

Acknowledgement of such benefits has become so well established that several 'smart wheelchairs' have been developed to enable powered mobility for all, even if they need to be used in a safe environment and under controlled conditions. Smart wheelchairs usually employ sonar, infrared, or other sensors to detect obstacles (Mandel, Huebner, & Vierhuff, 2005) and can modify the users' intended commands to ensure that they can move around safely – e.g., by stopping automatically before a collision can occur. Benefits of smart wheelchairs have been examined in several research papers (Hardy, 2004; Iles & Shouksmith, 1987), and, for example, Odor and Watson (1994) have already emphasised the impact of powered mobility by describing it as '*an effective motivator in situations where other stimuli have failed*' (p. 167). The authors reported that this motivation led to the development of exploratory behaviour, self-directed mobility, assertiveness, and persistence. They also reported improvements in social skills, asserting that, through taking advantage of the opportunities to explore, there were clear gains in social interaction. Other reported gains included improved posture, muscle tone, and physical skills.

Depending on individual needs, then, the benefits of 'self-directed mobility' can include enhanced opportunities for independence, learning, motivation, social skills, and even physical benefits. Independent powered mobility should, therefore, be available to as many mobility-impaired people as possible. In terms of its ability to enable individuals to decide where they wish to be and, equally importantly, where they *do not* wish to be, *it can be regarded as a basic human right*.

GAZE-BASED ENVIRONMENT CONTROL

Intelligent Domotic Environments

Many research groups are currently involved in the development of new architectures, protocols, appliances, and devices (Jiang, Liu, & Yang, 2004) for smart homes. Also, commercial solutions are increasing their presence in the market, and many brands are proposing very sophisticated domotic systems; see Table 1 for some examples.

Much research work is evolving toward the concept of the *intelligent domotic environment*, by adopting either centralised or distributed approaches that extend current domotic systems with suitable devices or agents. The decreasing cost of hardware, together with the constant increase in computation power and connection capabilities, is a major driving force that is currently drawing research efforts toward systems based on simple, embedded PCs able to bridge the interconnection gap between domotic systems and to bring intelligence to homes. DomoNet (Miori, Tarrini, & Manca, 2006) represents an interesting framework for domotic interoperability based on Web Services, XML, and Internet protocols. Instead, Bonino, Castellina, and Corno (2008) describe a system that models the home environment and the domotic devices with a proper ontology, DogOnt (Bonino & Corno, 2008), and leverages informa-

Table 1. Some examples of commercial domotic products

Product	Web page / other reference	Comments
BTicino MyHome	http://www.myhome-bticino.it/	BTicino is among the most important producers of low-voltage devices for power delivery, communication, and environmental control
EIB/KNX	http://www.knx.org/	KNX is an international standard that combines and supersedes three previous European standards (BatiBus, EIB, and EHS)
ZigBee Home Automation	http://www.zigbee.org/	ZigBee is the result of a joint effort of more than 20 international partners
X10	http://www.x10.com/	X10 is an open international standard for domotic devices, mainly based on power line communication
LonWorks	http://www.echelon.com/	LonWorks is a communication technology based on a bus developed by Echelon Corporation

tion encoded in such a model to support device generalisation (e.g., treating a dimmer lamp as a simple lamp), device functionality, and device state description.

An intelligent domotic environment (IDE; see Figure 1) is usually composed of one (in this case, interoperation may not be needed but intelligence still needs to be supported) or more domotic systems, complemented by a variable set of (smart) home appliances (e.g., plugs, lights, doors, and shutter actuators) and by a home gateway that allows implementation of interoperation policies and provision of intelligent behaviours. Domotic systems usually include a so-called network-level gateway that allows one to tunnel low-level protocol messages over more versatile, application-independent, interconnection technologies – e.g., TCP/IP over Ethernet, LANs, or

Figure 1. Intelligent domotic environment

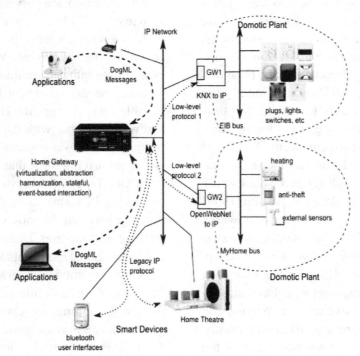

home Wi-Fi. These gateways are not suitable for implementing features needed by IDEs, as they have reduced computation power and are usually closed; i.e., they cannot be programmed to provide more than factory default functionality. However, they play a significant role in the IDE architecture, as they offer an easily exploited access point to domotic systems.

Appliances can be either 'dumb' devices that can only be controlled by switching on and off the power points to which they are connected, or 'smart' devices able to provide complex functionality and to control (or be controlled by) other devices, through a specific, often IP-based, communication protocol.

An intelligent and programmable home gateway is the key component for achieving interoperation and intelligence in IDEs; it is designed to respond to different requirements, ranging from simple bridging of network-specific protocols to complex interaction support. These requirements can be attributed to three complexity levels: level-1 priorities include all of the features needed to control different domotic systems, using a single, high-level, communication protocol and a single access point; level-2 priorities refer to all functions needed for defining inter-network automation scenarios and allowing inter-network control (e.g., to enable a Konnex switch to control an OpenWebNet light); and level-3 requirements are related to intelligent behaviours, to user modelling, and to adaptation. Table 2, taken from the work of Bonino et al. (2009), summarises the requirements, grouped by priority.

The challenge of intuitive and comprehensive gaze-based environmental control systems requires innovative solutions in different fields: user interaction, domotic system control, and image processing. The currently available solutions can be seen as isolated attempts to tackle smaller portions of the problem space and provide interesting solutions in each sub-domain. Recently, some

Table 2. Requirements for home gateways in IDEs (Bonino et al., 2008)

Priority	Requirement	Description
R1 Interoperability	R1.1 Domotic network connection	Interconnection of several domotic networks.
	R1.2 Basic interoperability	Translation/forwarding of messages across different networks.
	R1.3 High-level network protocol	Technology-independent, high-level network protocol allowing neutral access to domotic networks.
	R1.4 API	Public API to allow external services to interact easily with home devices.
R2 Automation	R2.1 Modelling	Abstract models to describe the house devices and their states and functions, to support effective user interaction and to provide the basis for home intelligence.
	R2.2 Complex scenarios	Ability to define and operate in scenarios involving different networks / components.
R3 Intelligence	R3.1 Off-line intelligence	Ability to detect misconfiguration, structural problems, security issues, etc.
	R3.2 On-line intelligence	Ability to implement runtime policies such as energy savings or fire prevention.
	R3.3 Adaptation	Learning of frequent interaction patterns to simplify users' everyday activities.
	R3.4 Context-based intelligence	Proactive behaviour driven by the current house state and context aimed at reaching of specific goals such as safety, energy savings, and robustness to failures.

research on gaze-controlled intelligent environments has been published. In these studies, two main interaction modalities are foreseen: direct interaction and mediated interaction. In direct interaction paradigms, gaze is used to select and control devices and appliances either with head-mounted devices that can recognise objects (Shi, Gale, & Purdy, 2006) or through intelligent devices that can detect when people are staring at them (Vertegaal, Mamuji, Sohn, & Cheng, 2005). This natural solution is not as innocent as it may seem at first glance: sometimes it is not clear whether the user is just observing an object to learn more about it or intends to start a function. This second option raises the problem referred to as the Midas touch (Jacob, 1991). It is bypassed in mediated interaction, when the user is expected to issue requests by gaze through a control panel of a software application (hosted on desktop or portable PCs) that makes it possible to control all home appliances and devices (Bonino & Garbo, 2006). A survey of integrated gaze-controlled environments is provided by Bonino et al. (2009). The systems described aim at tackling gaze-based home automation as a whole, exploiting state-of-the-art technologies and trying to integrate interaction modalities that are currently supported and that may be supported in the near future.

Mixing interaction by gaze and home automation requires an open and extensible logic architecture for easily supporting different interaction modalities, on one side, and different domotic systems and devices, on the other. Several elements have to be in some way mediated, including different communication protocols, different means of communication, and different interface objects. Mediation implies, in a sense, centralisation – i.e., defining a logic hub in which specific, low-level aspects are unified and harmonised into a common high-level specification. There are three possible methods of integrating gaze control into such systems:

1. Using gaze as a means of controlling the existing system without modification
2. Bypassing the existing interface and replacing the system interface with a gaze-friendly custom interface for the central domotic system
3. Bypassing the core system and integrating gaze control into the protocols for communication with the environment

In order to know how gaze control may be integrated with any of these three methods, we need to know what types of interfaces are currently *de facto* standards so that we may determine whether we can directly control these interfaces via gaze (option 1) or can replace them with gaze-friendly interfaces (option 2). We also need to know what communication protocols are *de facto* standards, so that we can bypass the core domotic system and control the environment actuators directly (option 3).

User Interface Recommendation

Corno et al. (2007) have provided a set of guidelines for development of domotic control interfaces based on gaze interaction. The primary goal was to promote safety and accessibility whilst keeping in mind the specific problems of gaze interaction. The guidelines (see Table 3) are grouped into four main categories:

- **The control application's safety:** guidelines concerning the behaviour of the application in critical conditions, such as alarms and emergencies.
- **Input methods for the control application:** guidelines related to the input methods and the relevant issues that the control applications have to (or should) support.
- **The control application's operative features:** guidelines defined not only for the gaze-based control application but also with an impact on the domotic gateways.

Table 3. Summary of COGAIN recommendations for gaze-based environmental control (Corno et al., 2007)

Category		Guideline	PL
Control applications' safety	1.1	Provide fast, easy-to-understand, and multi-modal alarm notification	1
	1.2	Provide the user with only a few clear options for handling of alarm events	2
	1.3	Provide a default safety action to overcome an alarm event	1
	1.4	Provide a confirmation request for critical and possibly dangerous operations	1
	1.5	Provide a STOP function that interrupts any operation	1
Input methods for control application	2.1	Provide a connection with the COGAIN-ETU driver	1
	2.2	Support several input methods	2
	2.3	Provide reconfigurable layout	2
	2.4	Support use of several input methods at the same time	2
	2.5	Manage the loss of input control by providing automated default actions	2
Control applications' operative features	3.1	Respond to environment control events and commands at the right time	1
	3.2	Manage events with different time-critical priority	1
	3.3	Execute commands with different priority	1
	3.4	Provide feedback when automated operations and commands are being executed	2
	3.5	Manage scenarios	2
	3.6	Communicate the current status of any device and appliance	2
Control applications' usability	4.1	Provide a clear visualisation of what is happening in the house	1
	4.2	Provide a graceful and intelligible interface	2
	4.3	Provide a visualisation of the status and location of the house devices	2
	4.4	Use colours, icons, and text to highlight a change of status	2
	4.5	Provide an easy-to-learn selection method	2

- **The control application's usability:** guidelines concerning the graphical user interface and the interaction patterns of the control applications.

  Each guideline has a priority level (PL):

  - **Priority level 1:** the guideline has to be implemented by the applications.
  - **Priority level 2:** the guideline should be implemented by the applications.

Examples of Commercial Control Applications

This section presents a brief description of some commercial applications that include an interface for environmental control based on gaze interaction. Typically, these applications are bundled with the eye tracking systems.

LC Technologies provide a basic gaze-controlled 'Lights and Appliances' program, which includes their own computer-controlled switching equipment. This system provides basic control of lights and appliances anywhere in the home. To use the system, the user turns appliances on and off by looking at a bank of switches displayed on the screen, with commands sent to home sockets and light switches via the main electricity wiring according to the X10 protocol.

The *ERICA EnviroMate* system offers essentially the same basic functionality as the LC Technologies system, by presenting the user with a grid of buttons related to environmental objects, with a mains-borne X10 communication system.

In addition, the user may control an infrared transmitter that can be programmed with a television remote control and issue other commands to control IR domestic environments.

iAble on MyTobii: SR Labs (http://www.srlabs. it/en/) is an Italian company that is developing the 'iAble' suite of software applications for the MyTobii eye tracker. iAble includes also a domotic control interface that allows the user to command the domestic devices by remote control. This module provides remote control of external devices through infrared signals. The main screen of the application module is composed of a grid of elements that serve the principal needs of the user.

Examples of Research Applications

DOGEYE

DOGEYE (see Figure 2), described by Corno, Castellina, and Razzak (2009), has been designed with two main constraints: interacting with the DOG platform (Bonino et al., 2008) and being compliant with COGAIN user interface requirements (see Table 3).

DOGEYE is the first step toward fulfilling interface design guidelines to produce a fully compliant gaze-driven domotic system for users and to create a reference implementation of the COGAIN recommendations. It fulfils most of the requirements on priority level 1 in the design guidelines and also implements some priority-level-2 guidelines. It also focuses on developing new techniques that will enable users to use the interface with comfort and enhance the performance of the overall system.

Direct Gaze: The Attention Responsive Technology Interface

The ART (Attention Responsive Technology) interface described by Shi, Gale, and Purdy (2006) aims to facilitate interaction with the user's environment by developing a system that responds

Figure 2. DOGEYE interface

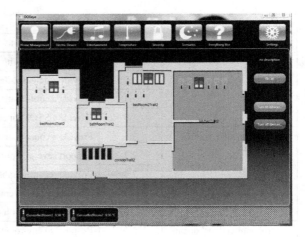

directly to user gaze, enabling interaction with the environment by responding appropriately to the user's 'attention'. In the system, 'attention' is anticipated by means of gaze tracking, with elements of the environment subsequently actuated and controlled by gaze alone via the environmental control system.

The system utilises a combination of computer recognition and eye tracking technology to gauge the users' attention in relation to controllable objects within their environment. It uses this information to predict the user's possible intention, then responds intelligently to facilitate interaction with the device in question.

Figure 3 shows the principle of operation and the control interface. Here the user looks at a controllable object (1), the interface responds by offering only the appropriate controls (2), and the user operates the object by using a custom control interface (3). The advantage of the system is that any domestic object is selected purely by looking at it directly. The disadvantage is that, in the current stage of development, some level of indirect manipulation of the vision controller is required for changing the properties of that object.

Figure 3. ART principle of operation and control interface (© Richard Bates. Used with permission)

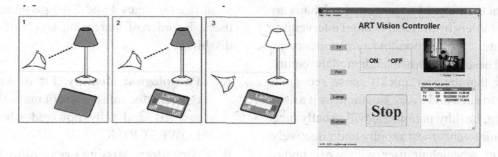

The Czech Technical University System

Štěpánková and Novák (2009) describe an interface that mediates communication between simple input devices (connected to the computer through standard input – for example, USB, RS232, LAN, or Bluetooth) and selected household appliances to be controlled. Figure 4 shows examples of control dialogs used in the system. The system devotes specific attention to problems of usability: it uses a consistent, uniform interface design with the same type of buttons and the same layout structure no matter the appliance controlled.

GAZE-BASED MOBILITY CONTROL

It is important to distinguish between two closely related notions: '*gaze-based mobility*' and '*mobile*

gaze tracking'. The first means, in essence, control of a wheelchair by gaze (the same as 'mobility control'), and the second refers to being able to use an eye tracker for communication (and control of a computer, the environment, and so on) while on the move and possibly outdoors. Obviously, mobile gaze tracking is a necessary prerequisite for gaze-based mobility. Currently there is no fully satisfactory solution for mobile gaze tracking, and research into gaze-based mobility is continuing. The current state of the art is carefully described by Tuisku et al. (2008) and Bates et al. (2009). These research reports pay specific attention to safety, which seems to be a critical issue of gaze-based mobility. A clear explanation for this concern is provided by the report 'Power Wheelchairs and User Safety', prepared in 2003 by the National Institute for Rehabilitation Engineering (NIRE, 2003). This document states, on page 4:

Figure 4. The Czech Technical University system (© 2010 Petr Novák. Used with permission)

Wheelchair Control Methods are also very significant to safety. Most power wheelchairs are controlled solely by the user, without intervention by computers, terrain monitors gyroscopes or autopilots. These power wheelchair models require, for safety, that the user quickly sense, recognize and react to each and every situation, as it arises. The young, healthy paraplegic will usually meet these requirements most rapidly and effectively. The power wheelchair user with weak and/or slow-moving hand responses is more likely to have accidents and may be more severely injured. An ALTERNATIVE is available in some more costly power wheelchair models. This is the addition of computer-controlled systems that constantly monitor and correct for: wheelchair position and attitude; forward terrain variations; up and down stairway variations; user commands; and overall wheelchair performance. *In theory*, these power wheelchairs are much safer to operate than those without computer oversight. *In practice*, however, these power wheelchairs are sometimes more dangerous than non-computer wheelchairs. Serious accidents sometimes result from sensing or computer system failures. The failures may be subtle ones not recognized by the wheelchair user. Or, they can be in the form of a sudden, unexpected total failure of the wheelchair computer system, which may result in an accident when occurring at a critical time. Disregarding cost factors and considering safety issues alone, it is difficult to recommend the use of power wheelchairs that have – or that lack – computer monitoring and control capabilities. This type decision is best made with advice, on an individual basis, by each patient's physician, therapist or mobility trainer. *A "Dead-Man's" safety control to automatically stop and brake the wheelchair if the user should let go of the wheelchair control stick or slump in his seat, can protect against accidents due to sudden loss of manual control or due to fainting or seizure. This feature is highly recommended and was included in most power wheelchairs dispensed by this Institute.*

The same document (NIRE, 2003) clearly identifies on pages 4 and 5 the particular risk to users, in order of increasing levels of physical disability:

A. **Paraplegics: Healthy, Fit & Active** are typically the safest users of manual, power-assisted, and fully powered wheelchairs. LOWEST RISK.

B. **Amputees: Missing Legs and/or Arms** *but with active upper bodies* are usually safe users of power wheelchairs, depending on the type of control devices used. If planned and implemented properly, then LOW RISK.

C. **People with Weak or Poorly Controlled Upper Bodies** *using standard joystick* to reliably control power wheelchairs. This category may include some people with Cerebral Palsy, some with Multiple Sclerosis, some with Parkinson Disease, and people with many other conditions. Some of these conditions may cause impaired eyesight, slowed reflexes and/or impaired judgment. All should be fully screened for such functional deficits just as for automobile driving safety. MODERATE RISK.

D. **People with Little or No Upper Body Movement**, *using special quad controls* such as mouth joystick, puff & sip breath control, or gyroscopic (inertial) wheelchair controls. HIGH RISK.

E. **Paralyzed Small People: Children and "Very Small" Adults** *in special seats* or carriers often need a power wheelchair, most of all when significantly paralyzed. Depending on mechanical implementations, individual conditions, and personalized mobility and safety training, these people are at HIGH RISK.

Most gaze control users are constrained by limitations described in group D and, consequently, have to be characterised as high-risk users. It is not rare that they also suffer from several additional conditions mentioned in group C or from various cognitive impairments (resulting, for example, from brain damage). In general, combination of any high-risk solutions multiplies the potential danger. That is why powered mobility with gaze control, which still remains potentially unreliable (e.g., because of its dependence on unstable light conditions), increases the potential hazard greatly.

The safety of the user must always be the top priority in the design of any new type of assistive product. Is it worth trying to produce a gaze-controlled wheelchair? What are the significant benefits offered to its users that tempt us to fight the related danger by designing various sophisticated solutions? We have tried to answer these questions in the section 'The need for gaze-based mobility control', introducing this chapter, and we have concluded that 'self-directed mobility' should be regarded as a basic human right. With this in mind, we find that it seems to be our duty to search for an appropriate solution for this task and to apply the recent results of technical development such that its risk is made sufficiently low through diligent thought and development with the needs of the user, and consultation of that user, in mind.

Characteristics of Gaze-Based Mobility Safety

Existing wheelchair control systems range from the hand- or joystick-driven (the most conventional and most widely adopted) through sip–puff switches all the way to face pointing. All of these modes have their own potential hazards stemming from the basic principles of control applied and influencing their characteristics: reaction speed, reliability, or the precision with which they can be positioned. All this is made even more complex by relatively slow reaction time due to inertia of the standard powered mobility platforms, which have considerable movement power and speed (typically, platforms range from 100 kg to 300 kg plus the user's weight and use a speed of 4–6

km per hour). As a result, the wheelchair cannot stop or change direction on the spot. For a similar reason, even a small control command, either voluntary or involuntary, can result in a large and powerful effect that may cause injury or hazard.

It is expected that the following questions of the quality of hand control by the user will be answered during the procedure for analysis of the user-centric safety issue for a wheelchair *controlled by hand with a joystick*:

- Can the user control hand movement adequately for controlling mobility sufficiently accurately to manoeuvre safety and also accomplish the desired movement?
- Can the user position the joystick in the 'off' or 'stationary / no movement' position in an accurate and repeatable fashion, or remove the hand from the joystick sufficiently rapidly, to stop movement?
- Does the user have sufficient hand control to stop the movement in an emergency?
- What happens with the user's motor function (this may involve spasticity or difficulties in physically reacting), and how does the user react, in an emergency?

In addition, the systems themselves have characteristics that may give rise to, or compensate for, potential hazards and safety issues. For example, with hand control again:

- Is the joystick measuring hand position accurately and reliably, and is it communicating the control demands of the user to the control system accurately?
- Does the joystick / controller system employ algorithms that compensate for inaccurate user input – such as damping against involuntary hand movements?
- Does the mobility platform (electric wheelchair, power chair, or the like) have collision detection and obstacle avoidance to aid the user?

Figure 5. 'Eyes down' (left) and 'eyes up' (right) gaze mobility control interfaces (© Richard Bates. Used with permission)

We should proceed analogously when gaze control is used. Under these conditions, the problem gains a new dimension arising from the uncertain nature of measurement of gaze and the inherent inaccuracies of gaze pointing. Bates et al. (2009) applied this approach and offer a very detailed list of the main suggested characteristics and safety descriptions required for any gaze-driven mobility system. These characteristics were compiled from contributions by the gaze-driven mobility research groups associated with COGAIN. The aim with the set of characteristics briefly reviewed in the next section is to determine which issues and characteristics are most important for safe gaze-based mobility control.

The User Interface

Wheelchair user interfaces may be divided into two main types: 'eyes up' and 'eyes down' user interfaces, as introduced by Tuisku et al. (2008). In an 'eyes down' interface, the user applies indirect control to the wheelchair by using a computer screen (and on-screen buttons) attached to the wheelchair – this forces the user to look down at a screen while moving. This solution is probably the one that is most easily achieved but is not the safest. The direct control mode can be applied as well – in such a case, the world around the user is the interface (in other words, there is no computer screen) and users simply look where they wish to go. The resulting 'eyes up' solution seems much more natural at first glance, but it raises the Midas touch problem, which has to be addressed in this context. Both approaches are illustrated in Figure 5 (reprinted from the work of Tuisku et al., 2008).

'Eyes Down' Wheelchair User Interface

The 'eyes down' interface relies on a screen placed within the view of the user (typically in front and over the lap of the user) with the user indicating control commands on the screen via a gaze-driven pointer and usually large on-screen buttons indicating the desired direction etc. In examination of the safety aspects of such a design, attention has to be paid to the placement and properties of the control screen, the way wheelchair movement is initiated and stopped (also in case of an emergency), and the precision with which the wheelchair follows the commands indicated. Bates et al. (2009) summarise 18 requirements related to these topics, such as: '*The computer screen must be visible in all light conditions (e.g. bright sunlight either indoors or outdoors) and has to be equipped by anti-glare or anti-reflection features and by a backlight for low-light conditions.*'

'Eyes Up' Wheelchair User Interface

The 'eyes up' interface relies on moving the mobility platform via gaze commands without a screen. A clear advantage of this choice is that users may look where they are going at all times if they wish. On the other hand, there are no easy methods for communicating with the controlling computer and receiving feedback. Six safety-related aspects are identified by Bates et al. (2009) – those with the highest priority appear both in 'eyes down' and in 'eyes up' user interfaces – for example: '*A carer or assistant must be able to stop the wheelchair in an emergency.*'

Indoor or Outdoor Usage

Indoor and, especially, outdoor usage present specific safety issues, ranging from operation of the gaze tracking system in varying lighting conditions to navigation of obstacles in indoor and outdoor environments. Bates et al. (2009) identify eight recommendations. For example, '*gaze tracking has to be reliable even when under vibration due to traversing uneven ground or when subject to 50 Hz / 60 Hz light strobing from non-incandescent sources*'.

System Response Times

System response times are defined as the time between the user gazing at a control and the actual movement response from the mobility platform. If the user is to perceive a feeling of being 'in control' of the system, the response time should be rather short. These times are critical, as the system must accommodate two contradictory conditions; namely, it has to react as rapidly as possible to emergency commands but must also apply appropriate deceleration if it is to avoid tipping the user from the platform.

Additional Safety Devices

Additional safety devices such as collision detection and curb/step and incline detection may be used to ease user navigation by reducing the control load placed on the user. Typically these take the form of ultrasonic, laser, and vision-based object detection and object-proximity-related systems. All of them have to warn the user of tipping possibilities before these reach a danger point – such a feature significantly increases the user's feeling of safety. And this is an important issue influencing the user's comfort: a system that is not perceived as reliable is not used!

Intelligence of the Control Algorithm

Additional intelligence in the control algorithms of the mobility platform may be employed to aid users with mobility and reduce their control work load by offering means for automatic object avoidance and route-finding. Although the intelligence of these systems goes above and beyond that of the simpler additional safety devices mentioned above, it still must allow the user full control in an emergency.

Example Safety Scenarios

The safety recommendations for gaze-based mobility must try to cover the situations that can arise in use of the system being considered. That is why they can be best explained through description of some realistic situations and problems that can appear under certain conditions. This is the approach taken by Bates et al. (2009). We will next quote four of these scenarios that provide detailed reasoning for the safety recommendations that should be followed in the design of the eye-controlled mobile platforms (material below comes directly from the work of Bates et al.).

Moving and Turning to Look Out of the Window

The user is sitting on their mobility platform, they have a high-level of paralysis and use gaze to interact and communicate. They have experience in using gaze control. They wish to turn 120 degrees to face a nearby window, and then move approximately 1 metre to go to the window. They use an 'eyes down' interface for both gaze communication and mobility control. The user first gazes onto their interface and disengages their communication control interface (which fills the entire screen due to the need for large onscreen buttons) and displays their mobility control interface. The interface shows 10 arrows as in Figure 6.

The user gazes at the rotate left arrow (top left arrow, Figure 6) and invokes a dwell click. The chair starts to rotate anticlockwise on its axis and as long as the user keeps dwelling the chair will rotate. As the chair rotates the user cannot take their gaze away from the eyes down interface and the chair bumps into a chair on the users left that they could not see (many users of gaze cannot turn their head due to paralysis and so cannot 'look around'). The user takes their gaze away from the arrow and motion stops. They see the obstacle and repeat their gaze commands to avoid the chair. They are now facing the window and must travel 1 metre toward it. They gaze and dwell

on the uppermost arrow (Figure 6) to engage forward motion. They move forward toward the window at a slow but increasing speed based on the acceleration profile of their mobility platform. They observe the window in the periphery of their vision and then look directly at the window to see how far away it is. This stops forward motion. They then gaze back again at the forward arrow and move forward until they touch the window with their feet (however, as many people with paralysis have reduced or no sensation in their feet, the user does not realize this contact with the window). The user is happy with their position and disengages their mobility control interface and displays their communication control interface.

Key Notes

- *By needing to disengage their communication interface to display their mobility interface, the user is temporarily without communication during mobility.* The user may wish or need to communicate during motion, this should be allowed.
- *By needing to continually dwell their gaze on the interface to activate and maintain motion the user cannot see where they are going.* The user needs some method of

Figure 6. Direction arrows on a gaze mobility control interface (© Richard Bates. Used with permission)

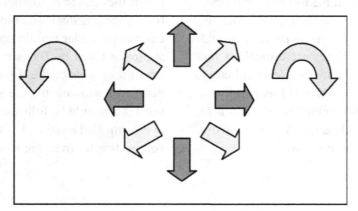

maintaining motion (safely) and being able to look up from the control interface.

- *There is no collision detection so the user first bumps into a chair, and then ends the manoeuvre with their feet in contact with the window* – this is undesirable and may cause injury.

Safety Recommendations

- The mobility control system should allow the user to look up from the interface when moving, or only move in small increments and then stop to allow the user to view their surroundings. This would have prevented the user colliding with the chair as they would have been able to see it come into view as the chair rotated.
- The mobility platform should incorporate collision detection to prevent or alert the user of possible obstacles.

Going Outside

The user is sitting on their mobility platform, they have a high-level of paralysis and use gaze to control their mobility. They use a common IR gaze tracker as their sole means of communication and control and use an 'eyes down' interface. They wish to go out from indoors to a safe level patio area through a wide doorway. The sun is shining. (Nearly all gaze tracking systems use IR light sources and cameras – exposure to additional strong IR incidental light (such as sunlight) can dramatically decrease accuracy, hinder or even stop operation of these systems.)

The user engages their mobility driving interface and starts motion out through the doors. As the user approaches the open door to the outside bright daylight falls onto the face of the user. This causes the gaze tracker to have degraded performance such that the gaze of the user on the interface now has an offset and the gaze driven pointer moves off the 'forward' motion arrow and

onto an adjacent control. Motion changes direction and the user compensates by gazing slightly 'off target' to bring the cursor back onto the forward motion arrow. Motion resumes. The user now passes into full sunshine. Additional IR light now stops accurate operation of the gaze tracker and the gaze pointer on the interface is displaced erratically, causing the involuntary selection of several different movement commands. The user is moved involuntarily and placed in a dangerous situation. The user executes an emergency stop command. Due to the IR light the gaze tracker stops working and the user is stranded without mobility or communication.

Key Notes

- *Moderate incidental IR illumination (caused by bright indoor incandescent lights or sunlight) can degrade gaze tracking accuracy.* This inaccuracy must be allowed for by safety systems detecting reduced gaze accuracy.
- *Loss of gaze tracking due to mobility causing change in environment can also lead to loss of gaze communication.* Tracking should have fallback operation to allow limited control or communication in an emergency.

Safety Recommendations

- The mobility control system must allow for degradation in gaze tracking performance. This can be the detection of the reduction in quality of gaze tracking leading to the control system reducing motion speed or direction for safety. This may also require the interface target sizes to be increased to aid selection for safety. This degradation must be accommodated by the system to the point where even under very difficult tracking conditions the system still allows basic commands to be made by gaze, for example looking left and right only. Here the interface would only show yes/no commands in response to extreme left and right gazing.

- If gaze tracking is highly degraded to the point of loss of control the system must alert the user, and allow the user to alert a third party or caregiver, or perform other automated commands to aid the user.
- An emergency stop system must be in place to monitor gaze tracking accuracy and operation.
- A system could automatically reduce speed or stop (maybe as a choice depending on the user's capabilities) when degradation in gaze tracking performance may affect driving safety.

An 'Eyes Up' Journey

The user is sitting on their mobility platform, they have a high-level of paralysis and use gaze to control their mobility. They use an 'eyes up' interface meaning they gaze directly in the direction they wish to travel. They wish to go out from indoors to visit the house next door. The gaze tracking system they use is not reliant on constant IR illumination levels and can tolerate some sunlight. It has automatic collision detection and avoidance.

The user then attempts to engage 'eyes up' mobility via their chosen method (such as a gaze gesture of eyes looking left, right, and then up, for example); this fails and a second attempt is made which is successful. Previously the user had engaged this command involuntarily when gazing around a room and is aware of this problem. The mobility platform starts to move forward in line with their line of gaze from the platform. The user is distracted by the telephone ringing; they briefly gaze at the distraction. This causes the mobility platform to also turn and move toward the distraction. The user corrects this motion by gazing at the door and the mobility platform moves through the door using collision detection and navigation

to pass through the door easily. The accuracy of gaze tracking is now reduced but operational in sunlight, and the platform now automatically reduces speed to compensate for the reduction in control accuracy. The user manages to navigate to the pavement but is once again distracted by passing cars and pedestrians. This causes their gaze to wander from the chosen path for short intervals, making their journey wander across the pavement to such an extent that the wheels of the mobility platform become dangerously close to the edge of the pavement and near to the road. The chair detects this proximity and stops. The user now must manoeuvre very carefully to reverse the chair from the situation. They then continue along the path to their destination.

Key Notes

- *Eyes up interfaces require a positive and unambiguous command set to control basic operations such as engage/disengage.*
- *Eyes up interfaces require a complex sequence of gaze gestures from the user to give unambiguous commands to the system.*
- *Eyes up interfaces are prone to user distraction causing unwanted movement commands.*

Safety Recommendations

- The system must be capable of being taught the gaze gestures preferred by the user that result in commands.
- The mobility control system must attempt to disambiguate random or deliberate sudden gaze movements from *gaze* movements directing the movement path to follow. This may be accomplished via averaging of gaze direction – typically when following the gaze of the user, that user will gaze predominately in the direction where they wish to travel, and other short gaze deviations must be ignored.

A Predefined Journey

There are systems that allow a user to follow a predefined track, as if they were driving a train along rails. An example is a Swedish system for users who are not able to drive on their own, due to motor or cognitive problems. It is sold by Permobil (http://www.permobil.com/) and comprises of a metal tape laid into or on the floor as a track, and the wheelchair can only follow these tracks. The user only needs to touch a button to move the chair, and release it to stop (or press again). For some eye gaze users, who are not able to drive a chair by themselves safely, this is an alternative to 'go anywhere' or 'free' driving, and allows them to be able to go between different rooms and in different directions by using tracks like this. They can choose by eye gaze the speed and track if they want to go to another room, for instance.

The user is sitting in their living room, and wishes to go to the kitchen which is situated along a corridor. On their gaze interface they select the track to the kitchen and then gaze at the 'drive' command on their interface. The wheelchair turns and starts to follow the track at a low safe speed. The user is required to repeatedly gaze at the 'drive' button on their interface every 2 seconds to continue driving. This allows them to look around whilst moving, but also requires them to continually 'approve' the movement. If they do not 'approve' the movement then the chair will automatically stop after 2 seconds.

The user notices an obstacle in their path – a discarded toy left by one of their children for example. The chair has no collision avoidance and so if the user did not notice the obstacle then the chair may drive into it and stop, possibly leaving the user stranded. They stop looking at the 'approve' command and the chair stops, they then can call for help for the obstacle to be removed, or they can ask the chair to turn around and return to the living room, but due to the track-following nature of the chair, they cannot manoeuvre around the obstacle.

Key Notes

- *The interface requires a positive and unambiguous command to allow movement.*
- *The track following method allows users who cannot steer their chair easily to still retain control over their movement.*
- *Their movement is predefined so they have only limited movement options.*
- *They cannot negotiate away from the track.*

Safety Recommendations

- The system must require continual user input / acknowledgement to maintain motion.
- The system is vulnerable to obstacles on the predefined path.

Research Applications and Prototypes

The review presented problems that have to be faced during the design and development of gaze-based mobility control, and proves that we are dealing with a truly challenging research issue. The first experiments attempting to offer a solution can be traced back to 1995. Let us characterise briefly several interesting solutions as they have appeared over the last 15 years. All of them are dealt with in more detail by Bates et al. (2009).

The first serious attempt at work toward gaze-based mobility control was the Wheelesley (Yanco, 1998; Yanco & Gips, 1997, Yanco, Hazel, Peacock, Smith, & Wintermute, 1995). In this project, a semi-autonomous robotic wheelchair is controlled by the EOG EagleEyes system (Gips, Olivieri, & Tecce, 1993) with the 'eyes down' mode. The user has to look at the desired direction arrow in the interface in order to generate a dwell click and initial movement. Safety is a concern, and large stop targets are placed in the simple interface. There are two levels of control; high-level directional commands from the user (such as 'go forward' commands) and low-level computer-controlled routines (such as collision detection). The system can also act on some correctional input from head movements, which, although not essential, offer extra means to ensure corrections for accuracy drift. Low-level control is provided by a Wheelesley system that allows the user to tell the platform where to move. The system has sensors that can detect obstacles and can avoid these obstacles in spite of user commands. For example, the user may command a forward movement but the platform will stop if an object is detected in front of the chair.

The SIAMO (a Spanish acronym for 'Integral System for Assisted Mobility') wheelchair project was reported on in a series of studies conducted by Barea and his colleagues (e.g., Barea, Boquete, Mazo, & López, 2002). Again, the user provides the control signals through EOG. A significant advantage of this approach is that it removes any need for a camera-based tracking system and makes the system suitable for use in any lighting conditions (indoors or even outdoors in bright sunshine). The system consists of a standard electric wheelchair, an on-board computer, sensors, and a graphical user interface. The user interface of the on-screen computer presents buttons for forward, backward, left, right, and stop, and the user is given three, differing control options, selected by unambiguous gaze gestures: 'eyes down' for direct access guidance and for automatic and semiautomatic 'scan' but 'eyes up' for continuous control. Selection of commands with 'eyes down' is typically by dwell clicking, with commands initiated via a secondary 'tick' to validate them. Stop commands are customisable; for example, one might use a blink of an eye to stop the wheelchair. Local environmental sensing is achieved by a mixture of ultrasonic sensors, infrared sensors, active laser sensors, and a passive vision system based on artificial landmarks. Automatic navigation is possible by using the passive vision system and a predefined map of the local environment, with step/kerb detection from ultrasonic sensors.

The semi-autonomous system developed by Jarvis (2003) is probably the most comprehensive system suitable for outdoors use. It uses an eye gaze tracking system located remotely from a four-wheel-drive rough-terrain wheelchair system. The system attempts to relieve the user of as much of the control load as possible by using extensive environmental sensing systems and computer processing. Top-level control is provided by the human operator (with the aim of this being the user in the chair at a later date), whose actions are defined as 'user intentions', which are then evaluated and executed by the system. A certain level of safety is provided by the low-level control systems that can be configured to operate even if other control input is absent by, for example, slowing the chair to a halt when control is lost. All control is executed through the sophisticated environmental tracking and evaluation systems, with the user rarely in direct control. This level of autonomy aids the user but can give rise to safety issues because the user is not typically in full direct control of the mobility platform.

The Magic Key system (Figueiredo, Nunes, Caetano, & Gomes, 2008) uses an adapted standard Web camera (sensitive to near IR) with supplemental IR light to track the gaze of a user. This system has been adapted and extended to wheelchair control by providing both an 'eyes down' and later an 'eyes up' interface. The wheelchair interface is composed of PIC controllers replacing the potentiometers of the chair; this way, almost any chair may be controlled, although with such a simple interface there can be no knowledge of the actual location of the chair. Collision detection systems and other supporting systems are not used, leaving a simple but effective system. In the system, a Web camera is placed on the chair in front of the user. Initially an 'eyes down' interface was used, but this was rejected and replaced by an 'eyes up' system to allow users to look where they are travelling. Control commands are executed by blinks of either eye.

Figure 7. Example convergence distance measurements with a Tobii X120 (© Richard Bates. Used with permission)

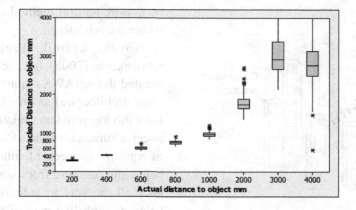

Rolltalk (Falck Igel, 2007) is a communication aid for people with speech disabilities. This system also lets a person operate various wheelchair functions (driving and adjusting seating positions); control the environment; and use mobile phones and the Internet, including e-mail. Rolltalk supports a variety of input devices: touch, switches, head-mouse, etc. It can also be delivered with an IntelliGaze or ERICA eye tracking system. Rolltalk Workshop software is also MyTobii compatible. Rolltalk is independent of the eye tracker system, but it is tightly integrated with those mentioned above. The Rolltalk wheelchair controller can be mounted on the most common wheelchair models sold in the Nordic countries.

The Eye Drive system, proposed by De Montfort University, uses a gaze tracking system coupled to a power chair. The system is 'eyes up' and has no screen or visible interface in front of the user. Any high-accuracy binocular eye tracking system that can be chair-mounted can be used, with the system tracking the gaze of the user in the world in front of the chair. Users gaze where they wish to travel whilst the system tracks gaze direction and also gaze convergence distance in order to determine not only which direction they wish to travel but also how far, or when they have reached their desired destination and need to stop.

Accurate measurement of convergence distance increases in difficulty with increasing distance from the user, on account of the ever-smaller changes in angular convergence with increasing distance. Preliminary evaluations using a Tobii X120 binocular gaze tracker have shown that reliable distance measurements can be made up to three metres in front of the user (see Figure 7).

For the above figure, an experienced gaze tracking user was asked to gaze at paper targets placed 200, 400, 600, 800, 1000, 2000, 3000, and 4000 mm away, with box plots calculated for the tracked convergence distance. Near-to-user distances correlated with accurate results, as the gaze convergence is substantial, with reliable tracking up to 3 m, while the convergence angle measurement became unreliable at 4 m and beyond. It is possible that, with increases in the accuracy of gaze tracking technology, greater distances may be measured accurately. However, the system is usable with current technology, since a simple measurement of gaze direction can be used to initiate travel in any direction, with convergence measurement being utilised as the user comes within 3 m of the desired destination.

In an extension to this system, virtual command volumes can be placed in space in front of the user. By learning the location of these, the user may

Figure 8. Eye Drive command volumes concept (© Richard Bates. Used with permission)

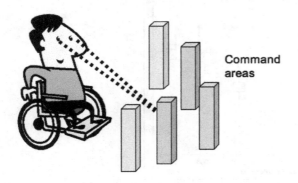

Command areas

gaze at a command area to enable various control actions, such as 'start moving' or 'stop' (see Figure 8). For disambiguation of normal gazing around in the world from deliberate command gazing, the commands may be initiated similarly to those in conventional gaze interaction, with selection of the command by means of a gaze dwell, a gaze gesture, or a supporting modality such as a simple switch. The location of these command volumes must be learnt by the user (or the system must learn suitable and comfortable volume locations as specified by the user), and they may be used for more than mobility – for example, also for speech output and communication or actuation of environmental controls around the user. The disadvantage of this system is that the user must learn the volume locations and learn to converge voluntarily at these volumes, but the advantage

in this approach is that it is 'eyes up' (there is no obtrusive screen in front of the user) and it may be a more natural method of control – we look where we wish to go.

Novák, Krajník, Přeučil, Fejtová, and Štěpánková (2008) have designed and implemented the SmAWA (smart autonomous wheelchair architecture) as an experimental platform for studying problems related to interaction between a human user and a machine exhibiting any of various degrees of autonomous intelligent behaviour, ranging from simple collision avoidance all the way to autonomous path planning using a graph-like map of the environment that the system creates on-line. The intelligence of the system is achieved through sophisticated interpretation of sensor data by an on-board computer that uses a dynamically built model/map of the environment and recent results from the field of intelligent mobile robotics (Košnar, Krajník, & Přeučil, 2008; Krajník & Přeučil, 2008). The SmAWA solution can be combined with various input devices. It has been tested in a setting with the wheelchair fully controlled either by the I4Control® system (Fejtová, Novák, Fejt, & Štěpánková, 2006) for gaze interaction (see Figure 9) or by a joystick as a single input. This combination offered both 'eyes down' and 'eyes up' operation, and it has been used both indoors and outdoors. Combination of the 'eyes down' and 'eyes up' modes seems to be a feasible and attractive solution for mobility control in the

Figure 9. The smart wheelchair controlled by the I4Control® system (© 2010 Petr Novák. Used with permission)

context of the SmAWA system: the user can start by selecting high-level goals in 'eyes down' mode. As soon as this selection is confirmed, the user is free to observe the environment and to apply 'eyes up' mode in the event that any type of intervention is deemed necessary.

A Way Forward

Levels of Control

One potential way forward would be to implement modes or levels of control, ranging from small and safe incremental movements to full dynamic control in real time. In general, control signals for a wheelchair can be interpreted in three, different modes – namely:

1. The *continuous mode* maps the signals provided by the user to the set of control signals for the wheelchair.
2. The other two modes (*direct access* and *scanning mode*) rely on a computer user interface that offers a menu containing various wheelchair commands. The user is expected to indicate the choice by using one of the available control signals.

There seems to be no reason gaze control could not be applied as an input device for one of the modes listed under item 2 while the system also utilises all of the safety precautions implemented with other input devices as reviewed above and uses these, for example, in combination with muscle control. Application of the continuous mode (1) may be more difficult, because there is a danger of misinterpretation of involuntary eye movements. Even this mode is worthy of consideration, provided that eye movement is used to command initiation of only a very small movement (one small motion at a time) or independent input is used for confirmation of the control command.

Full safety of the human user has to be guaranteed. This may seem easy in a laboratory setting,

but what will happen if the user suddenly looks elsewhere (toward the source of a suspicious noise), reaches a place with poor or unfavourable light conditions (and the system loses the control signal), or is forced to close the eyes because of irritation (dust, strong light, etc.)?

It is clear that in real-world conditions the gaze-controlled wheelchair cannot rely only and completely on its user. Experiments with other types of input signals prove that recent developments in autonomous robotics offer interesting means that can be incorporated into a wheelchair control system. One can envision various operation modes, ranging from the case in which it is primarily the user who is in charge of the system, which is equipped with some collision avoidance solution, through to the situation in which the chair moves autonomously to the destination that was described by means of gaze interaction. All of the modes could be used by the same user, each for a different purpose – the user could be in charge when the wheelchair is exploring a new, unknown environment and simultaneously collecting experience that can be reused later in the autonomous mode.

A Way Forward

User Ambitions and Bringing Gaze Control Closer

This chapter has set out the need for gaze-based mobility systems for users' well-being, showing that control over one's own mobility is a human right and should be enabled wherever possible. However, throughout the work of COGAIN and others on gaze control, it has been consistently found that gaze is not a fully reliable modality for accurate and consistent pointing, even under relatively controlled laboratory or domestic conditions. Therefore, providing that desired mobility control to users also puts those users at increased risk due to the vagaries of gaze control. As powerful mobility platforms are capable of exerting high levels of force in the immediate vicinity of people, their malfunction could cause serious harm to the user and to other people. Therefore, such platforms have to be considered safety-critical systems whose users often rely completely on the correct behaviour of the technical systems: if, for example, the user of the wheelchair instructs the vehicle to go to the door, the dependable execution of this operation may be life-critical and failure would not be an acceptable option. Accordingly, enablement, safety, and reliability are key issues.

Although the survey presented has shown that gaze control of wheelchairs is still essentially confined to the research laboratory, this is often because researchers' ambition is to provide full dynamic control – similar to conventional joystick control. However, a way may be found to bring about more widespread usage of gaze control by examining user needs in the short term. It is important to note that most users will have no control whatsoever of their mobility, so even small levels of control are certain to bring an improvement in quality of life. Hence, the user ambition of simply being able to turn a few degrees within the home living room and perhaps look out a window or face a visitor should not be ignored as a way forward. It should be possible to create a simple and reliable gaze-driven interface that allows limited, small, and hence relatively safe movements that would go some way to satisfying user ambitions. This could be confined to the home and other known environments where safety can be addressed. Movement could be accomplished with small motions, one at a time, with some pre-movement confirmation systems to prevent inadvertent movements. A simple interface could be adopted as a short-term solution, with an example being the interface in the Wheelesley system (Yanco, 1997), offering simple and clear movement symbols and a failsafe go/no-go command structure.

Absence of gaze-driven mobility is mainly due to safety concerns associated with the technology and with the methods of gaze control that could be used. The user groups that may have the most to gain from gaze-driven mobility are those same groups who are the most vulnerable to accidents when mobile. It would not be acceptable to put any user at increased risk; hence, Tuisku et al. (2008) have provided a list of the highest-priority safety guidelines, which COGAIN would wish all developers of mobility platforms to adhere to, and to exceed. Only then will gaze control of personal mobility be more safely available to all. These guidelines are based on certain safety scenarios that point to numerous problems that will have to be resolved first: Automatic collision detection seems to be a must. But a great deal of further research and testing is necessary to ensure that the final products meet the basic requirements, namely:

- The system has to be able to recognise diminishing quality in the gaze data provided and modify its behaviour appropriately to ensure safety.
- Both the user and the carer or assistant must be able to stop the wheelchair safely in case of emergency.

CONCLUSION

We believe that there are three types of personal needs that may be addressed by gaze control. The first is communication via gaze-driven text entry or speech generation systems, the second is gaze control of a personal environment, and the final element is gaze control of personal mobility. Collectively, these give the user communication, environment, and mobility control. To build such complex systems, a number of techniques, from different domains, including artificial intelligence, will have to be applied and the corresponding technical problems will have to be resolved. The other problem dimension is related to the need to tailor the resulting systems for the specific user and to find suitable control modes. It is clear that development of these ideas has to proceed in close co-operation with end users and their communities and must build on the most recent technological developments. While gaze-based environmental control is already becoming a reality, a number of issues remain to be solved in the field of gaze-driven mobility. It is hoped that, if current rates of development are maintained, gaze-driven mobility may become mainstream within the next 10 years and, so, finally benefit the many users who currently have little or no control of their mobility.

ACKNOWLEDGMENT

Petr Novak and Olga Štepánková have been partially supported by the Ministry of Education, Youth and Sport of the Czech Republic with the grant No. MSM6840770012 entitled "Transdisciplinary Research in Biomedical Engineering II".

REFERENCES

Barea, R., Boquete, L., Mazo, M., & López, E. (2002). Wheelchair guidance strategies using EOG. *Journal of Intelligent & Robotic Systems*, *34*(3), 279–299. doi:10.1023/A:1016359503796

Bates, R., Štěpánková, O., Corno, F., Brynildsen, O. M., Donegan, M., Novák, P., & Majaranta, P. (2009). *Recommendations on safety issues involved in gaze based mobility control*. Deliverable D2.7. Communication by Gaze Interaction (COGAIN), Project IST-2003-511598. Retrieved from http://www.cogain.org/wiki/COGAIN_Reports

Bonino, D., Castellina, E., & Corno, F. (2008). The DOG gateway: Enabling ontology-based intelligent domotic environments. *IEEE Transactions on Consumer Electronics*, *54*(4), 1656–1664. doi:10.1109/TCE.2008.4711217

Bonino, D., Castellina, E., Corno, F., Gale, A., Garbo, A., Purdy, K., & Shi, F. (2009). A blueprint for integrated eye-controlled environments. *Universal Access in the Information Society*, *8*(4), 311–321. doi:10.1007/s10209-009-0145-4

Bonino, D., & Corno, F. (2008). DogOnt – Ontology modeling for intelligent domotic environments. In A. Sheth, S. Staab, M. Dean, M. Paolucci, D. Maynard, T. Finin, & K. Thirunarayan (Eds.), *The Semantic Web. Proceedings of the 7th International Semantic Web Conference* (*ISWC 2008*) (LNCS 5318, pp. 790–803). Berlin, Germany: Springer-Verlag. doi:10.1007/978-3-540-88564-1_51

Bonino, D., & Garbo, A. (2006). An accessible control application for domotic environments. In A. Maña & V. Lotz (Eds.), Developing Ambient Intelligence. *Proceedings of the 1st International Conference on Ambient Intelligence Developments* (*AmID '06*) (pp. 11–27). Paris, France: Springer. doi:10.1007/978-2-287-47610-5_2

Bottos, M., Bolcati, C., Sciuto, L., Ruggeri, C., & Feliciangeli, A. (2001). Powered wheelchairs and independence in young children with tetraplegia. *Developmental Medicine and Child Neurology*, *43*(11), 769–777. doi:10.1017/S0012162201001402

Corno, F., Castellina, E., Bates, R., Majaranta, P., Istance, H., & Donegan, M. (2007). *Draft standards for Gaze based environmental control*. Deliverable D2.5. Communication by Gaze Interaction (COGAIN), Project IST-2003-511598. Retrieved from http://www.cogain.org/wiki/COGAIN_Reports

Corno, F., Castellina, E., & Razzak, F. (2009). Environmental control application compliant with COGAIN guidelines. *Proceedings of the 5th Conference on Communication by Gaze Interaction* (*COGAIN 2009*) (pp. 31–34). Copenhagen, Denmark: DTU. Retrieved from the COGAIN website: http://www.cogain.org/conference

Evans, S., Frank, A. O., Neophytou, C., & de Souza, L. (2007). Older adults' use of, and satisfaction with, electric powered indoor/outdoor wheelchairs. *Age and Ageing, 36*(4), 431–435. doi:10.1093/ageing/afm034

Falck Igel. (2007). *Rolltalk: A product overview* (brochure). Retrieved from http://www.falckigel.com/userfiles/4129/Compact_Rolltalk_overview.pdf

Fejtová, M., Novák, P., Fejt, J., & Štěpánková, O. (2006). When can eyes make up for hands? *Proceedings of the 2nd Conference on Communication by Gaze Interaction* (*COGAIN 2006*) (pp. 46–49). Turin, Italy: Politecnico di Torino. Retrieved from the COGAIN website: http://www.cogain.org/conference

Figueiredo, L., Nunes, T., Caetano, F., & Gomes, A. (2008). Magic Environment. In *Proceedings of the 4th Conference on Communication by Gaze Interaction* (*COGAIN 2008*) (pp. 15–18). Prague, Czech Republic: Czech Technical University. Retrieved from the COGAIN website: http://www.cogain.org/conference

Gips, J., Olivieri, P., & Tecce, J. J. (1993). Direct control of the computer through electrodes placed around the eyes. In M. J. Smith & G. Salvendy (Eds.), *Human–computer interaction: Applications and case studies*, 630–635. New York: Elsevier.

Hardy, P. (2004). Powered wheelchair mobility: An occupational performance evaluation perspective. *Australian Occupational Therapy Journal, 51*(1), 34–42. doi:10.1111/j.1440-1630.2004.00413.x

Iles, G. H., & Shouksmith, G. (1987). *A study of the importance of independent mobility in severely physically disabled children.* Palmerston North, New Zealand: Department of Psychology, Massey University.

Jacob, R. J. K. (1991). The use of eye movements in human–computer interaction techniques: What you look at is what you get. *ACM Transactions on Information Systems, 9*(3), 152–169. doi:10.1145/123078.128728

Jarvis, R. (2003). A go where you look tele-autonomous rough terrain mobile robot. In B. Siciliano & P. Dario (Eds.), *Springer Tracts in Advanced Robotics: Vol. 5. Experimental Robotics 8, Proceedings of the 8th International Symposium* (*ISER 2002*) (pp. 624–633). Berlin/Heidelberg: Springer.

Jiang, L., Liu, D., & Yang, B. (2004). Smart home research. *Proceedings of the 2004 International Conference on Machine Learning and Cybernetics* (vol. 2, pp. 659–663). Berlin/Heidelberg: Springer.

Košnar, K., Krajník, T., & Přeučil, L. (2008). Visual topological mapping. *Proceedings of the European Robotics Symposium 2008.* Springer Tracts in Advanced Robotics, 44/2008, 333–342. Berlin/Heidelberg: Springer. doi:10.1007/978-3-540-78317-6_34

Krajník, T., & Přeučil, L. (2008). A simple visual navigation system with convergence property. *Proceedings of the European Robotics Symposium 2008.* Springer Tracts in Advanced Robotics, 44/2008, 282–292. Berlin/Heidelberg: Springer. doi:10.1007/978-3-540-78317-6_29

Mandel, C., Huebner, K., & Vierhuff, T. (2005). Towards an autonomous wheelchair: Cognitive aspects in service robotics. *Proceedings of Towards Autonomous Robotic Systems* (*TAROS 2005*), London, UK (pp. 165–172). Retrieved from http://www.iis.ee.ic.ac.uk/~taros05/papers/mandel.pdf

Miori, V., Tarrini, L., & Manca, M. (2006). DomoNet: A framework and a prototype for interoperability of domotic middlewares based on XML and Web Services. *Digest of Technical Papers, International Conference on Consumer Electronics* (*ICCE'06*) (pp. 117–118). Washington, DC., USA: IEEE. doi:10.1109/ICCE.2006.1598338

Nilsson, L., & Nyberg, P. (1998). Training in powered wheelchair, benefits for individuals at an early developmental level. *Proceedings of the 12ᵗʰ International Congress of the World Federation of Occupational Therapists* (*WFOT 1998*), Montreal, Canada.

NIRE. (2003). *Power wheelchairs and user safety.* National Institute for Rehabilitation Engineering. Retrieved from http://www.abledata.com/abledata_docs/PowerChair-Safety.pdf

Novák, P., Krajník, T., Přeučil, L., Fejtová, M., & Štěpánková, O. (2008). AI support for a gaze controlled wheelchair. *Proceedings of the 4ᵗʰ Conference on Communication by Gaze Interaction* (*COGAIN 2008*) (pp. 46–49). Prague, Czech Republic: Czech Technical University. Retrieved from the COGAIN website: http://www.cogain.org/conference

Odor, P., & Watson, M. (1994). *Learning through smart wheelchairs: A formative evaluation of the effective use of the CALL Centre's smart wheelchairs as parts of children's emerging mobility, communication, education, and personal development.* Edinburgh, UK: CALL Centre, University of Edinburgh. Retrieved from http://callcentre.education.ed.ac.uk/downloads/learning_sw/Learning_SW_Complete.pdf

Papert, S. (1980). *Mindstorms: Children, computers and powerful ideas.* New York, NY: Basic Books.

Piaget, J., & Inhelder, B. (1967). *The child's conception of space* (see especially Chapter 8, 'Systems of Reference and Horizontal–Vertical Coordinates', pp. 375–418). New York, NY: Norton.

Shi, F., Gale, A., & Purdy, K. (2006). Direct gaze-based environmental controls. *Proceedings of the 2ⁿᵈ Conference on Communication by Gaze Interaction* (*COGAIN 2006*) (pp. 36–41). Turin, Italy: Politecnico di Torino. Retrieved from the COGAIN website: http://www.cogain.org/conference

Štěpánková, O., & Novák, P. (2009). Home and environment control. *Proceedings of the 5ᵗʰ Conference on Communication by Gaze Interaction* (*COGAIN 2009*) (pp. 35–38). Copenhagen, Denmark: DTU. Retrieved from the COGAIN website: http://www.cogain.org/conference

Tuisku, O., Bates, R., Štěpánková, O., Fejtová, M., Novák, P., Istance, H., & Majaranta, P. (2008). *A survey of existing 'de-facto' standards and systems of gaze based mobility control.* Deliverable D2.6. Communication by Gaze Interaction (COGAIN), Project IST-2003-511598. Retrieved from http://www.cogain.org/wiki/COGAIN_Reports

Vertegaal, R., Mamuji, A., Sohn, C., & Cheng, D. (2005). Media eyepliances: Using eye tracking for remote control focus selection of appliances. *Extended Abstracts of the SIGCHI Conference on Human Factors in Computing Systems* (*CHI'05*) (pp. 1861–1864). New York, NY: ACM. doi:10.1145/1056808.1057041

Yanco, H. A. (1998). Wheelesley: A robotic wheelchair system: Indoor navigation and user interface. In V. O. Mittal, H. A. Yanco, J. Aronis, & R. Simpson (Eds.), *Assistive Technology and Artificial Intelligence, Applications in Robotics, User Interfaces and Natural Language Processing* (LNCS 1458, pp. 256–268). London, UK: Springer. doi: 10.1007/BFb0055983

Yanco, H. A., & Gips, J. (1997). Preliminary investigation of a semi-autonomous robotic wheelchair directed through electrodes. *Proceedings of the Rehabilitation Engineering Society of North America Annual Conference* (*RESNA'97*) (pp. 414–416). Arlington, VA: RESNA. Retrieved from http://www.cs.bc.edu/~gips/yanco-gips-resna97.pdf

Yanco, H. A., Hazel, A., Peacock, A., Smith, S., & Wintermute, H. (1995). Initial report on Wheelesley: A robotic wheelchair system. *Proceedings of the Workshop on Developing AI Applications for the Disabled* (*IJCAI'95*), from the International Joint Conference on Artificial Intelligence, Montreal, Canada. Retrieved from http://www.cs.uml.edu/~holly/publications/PDF/ijcai95.pdf

Section 4
Attentive and Gaze–Aware Interfaces

Chapter 11
Eye Movements and Attention

Fiona Mulvey
IT University of Copenhagen, Denmark

Michael Heubner
Technische Universität Dresden, Germany

ABSTRACT

When it comes to measuring attention, or quantifying it in any way, it is not easy to pin down what exactly we measure. Advances in technology have enabled the construction of complex models of certain aspects of attention and identified many of the structures and factors involved in the changing nature of attention. In this chapter, we will go with a working definition of attention as the concentration or focusing of mental effort on sensory or internal mental events. In terms of eye movements, we are mainly concerned with visual attention, pertaining to events and external stimuli in the environment, but not exclusively so. Eye movements may also offer an opportunity to measure internal or subjective events and states. This chapter will look at what might be possible beyond direct, point and click gaze control, in inferring subjective states. The aim is to identify and explain those measures from cognitive psychology which are most promising in terms of future technologies for gaze based human computer interaction.

INTRODUCTION

In 1890, William James defined attention as:

"The taking possession of the mind, in clear and vivid form, of one out of what seem several simultaneously possible objects or trains of thought. Focalization, concentration of consciousness are

of its essence. It implies withdrawal from some things in order to deal effectively with others." (1890)

Despite great advances in the methods of cognitive psychology and neuroscience since this definition was formulated, our definition of what attention is has not greatly changed in the interim. When it comes to measuring attention, or quantifying it in any way, it is not easy to pin down what

DOI: 10.4018/978-1-61350-098-9.ch011

exactly we measure. Advances in technology have enabled the construction of complex models of certain aspects of attention and identified many of the structures and factors involved in the changing nature of attention. However, dependant concepts such as consciousness, attentional control and processing capacity (as implied in James' definition above) are still debated. In this chapter, we will go with a working definition of attention as the concentration or focusing of mental effort on sensory or internal mental events. In terms of eye movements, we are mainly concerned with visual attention, pertaining to events and external stimuli in the environment, but not exclusively so. Eye movements may also offer an opportunity to measure internal or subjective events and states, and it is this aspect of eye movements as a major output of the seeing brain with a potential trace of internal cognitive states which we will now address. The purpose of including this in a book on gaze control is that these measures point towards a future use of eye movements in human computer interaction as a means of characterising the individual user, on a moment-to-moment basis. Eye movements, therefore, potentially offer a rich stream of information from the individual to the computer. Currently, human computer interaction is dominated by information flowing in the opposite direction.

Eye movements are a relatively direct and unobtrusively observable output of the active brain, with the added possibility of a direct measure of the visual stimulus registered and sent on to the perceiving brain on a moment-to-moment basis. The sensory registration of light by the eye is the basis of, but is vastly different to, the world perceived; perception is much more than simply vision. It is the ongoing selection and processing of samples of information in order to build and maintain a detailed and effective representation of reality, using limited sense organs. The way in which we achieve this is by a process of active vision. As we have seen in the introduction to this book, the image registered by the eye is severely limited. Therefore, when we perceive reality, we are actively processing rudimentary samples of the visual world in order to maintain an internal, rich and stable world which we can move around in and manipulate according to our current goals.

Having confronted the limitations of the image registered by the retina, we know that extensive elaboration takes place between registration and perception. However, it is often the case that information is ignored, rather than elaborated, in order to maintain a stable reality. For example, during saccadic suppression the light registered on the retina is not processed further. Because the eye is limited in terms of having only a small central area of high acuity vision, and because research methods (including direct measurement of receptor response) have resulted in quite a detailed model of the retina's structure and sensitivity to light, we can estimate the registered image during the stable periods of fixation with relatively high spatial accuracy. Of course, the validity of these measures varies depending on the limitations of the particular eye tracker used. Alongside this, we must take into consideration the limited angle of high acuity vision. These two factors mean that the eye needs to move to see the entirety of even relatively small objects or areas of interest in maximum detail. If we measure, therefore, the movements of the eye on a given stimulus during a given task, we have an information-rich trace of the active vision process, as the eye is directed to what is relevant to the purposes of the viewer, as higher processes direct it, or as the stimulus itself takes control and attracts the eye to changes in the environment by reflex. Within the eye movement trace, we have behavioural information directly related to the changing attentional states of the viewer. So far, in interactive settings, eye movements have been used largely as a means of controlling an interface. This chapter will look at what might be possible beyond direct, point and click gaze control, in inferring subjective states. The aim is to identify and explain those measures from cognitive psychology which are most promising in terms of future technologies for gaze based human computer interaction. We will explain attention using a levels of processing approach. The approach is not undisputed, although it is now widely accepted in cognitive and neuropsychological literature and has a long and diverse history central to the field of cognitive science.

PRELIMINARY CONSIDERATIONS AND TECHNICAL LIMITATIONS

Eye movements have long been used as a tool in investigating a broad spectrum of behaviours including reading (e.g. Rayner, Juhasz, Ashby & Clifton, 2003; Tinker, 1946), scene perception (e.g. Pomplum, Ritter, & Velichkovsky 1996), learning (e.g. Rehder &Hoffman, 2005) face perception (e.g. Althoff & Cohen, 1999) mental imagery (e.g. Laeng &Teodorescu, 2002); motor control, cognition and memory (e.g. Leigh & Kennard, 2004).

The introduction section of this book provides an overview of the various types of movements the eye makes and how light is sensed. To recap briefly, stops of the eye are called fixations, movements to new areas in the visual space are called saccades, and movement to follow a moving target is called smooth pursuit (see Table 1 in Chapter 2 of Section 1 for a summary of the various types of eye movements). We measure all of these movements by applying parameters to a data stream containing x, y (and, rarely, z) points in space which represent the centre of an area that the eye is directed towards on a distant plane (or volume, in the case of 3d tracking) at a given regular temporal interval. Herein is our first consideration in the analysis of the data we actually record; we measure at a given temporal interval. This interval gap (or sample rate) may be more or less fine, whereas the eye is moving all the time. Some movements (e.g. micro-saccades) are so fast and tiny that only eye trackers with the

highest temporal and spatial precision (upwards of $500 Hz$) can measure them to any degree of accuracy. All eye movement data is therefore an abstraction or sampling of actual eye movement, and more frequent sampling of gaze direction would thus give a better representation of actual events. However, the sampling rate is not the only topic of concern here; accuracy, in terms of how the geometry is applied to the inference of gaze position, the quality of the image of the eye used to calculate the geometry, and how well matched the two are, as well as considerations such as the match between the actual eye being observed and the implicit model of the eye incorporated into system calculations and what lighting conditions are present at recording, all have a bearing on how the data should be treated, what kinds of noise might be present, and what kind of inferences about the actual eye movement can be validly reported. Relatively sparse sampling and low accuracy and precision may suffice to direct gaze towards on-screen buttons comfortably, but measurement of many of the cognitive processes suggested within literature to be reflected in eye movements require more spatial and temporal accuracy and a higher definition image of the eye. Likewise, measurement of the minute changes in pupil size discussed in this chapter are viable only using a high sample rate and a high quality camera. Any intended study of eye movements should match the variables of interest with the capabilities of the eye tracker used. If one is interested in observing, for example, micro-saccades and covert attention, a very high sample rate, accuracy and precision will be required of the eye tracker, likely far in advance of those typically used for gaze control. This chapter is therefore about what the limits of currently available gaze control systems might be in terms of measuring mental states, and how future technologies might take best advantage of what basic research into eye movements and cognition has discovered.

Smooth pursuit movements are particularly difficult to differentiate from fixations and saccades even at high sample rates; at sample rates less than 1000 Hz the measurement of smooth pursuit is currently not viable unless the speed and trajectory of moving stimuli is known and some sort of 'mash up' of eye and stimulus movement is possible (e.g. in virtual reality or computer generated animation). Such an approach takes advantage of the fact that smooth pursuit movements require a moving stimulus and are qualitatively different from saccades. The quality of the estimation of gaze direction will be influenced by the sample rate, depending on how an 'average' of samples across a given fixed minimum duration and spatial range is calculated as the fixation point; i.e. the fixation detection algorithm. Most eye trackers intended for research provide a description of the fixation detection algorithm and access to the 'raw' sample data, i.e. without any pre-processing or 'smoothing' of the data, however this is not always the case. In terms of developing measures of internal processing or subjective states, access to raw data is at least desirable, if not essential. In practice, it is important to match the specifications of the eye tracking system to the temporal and spatial parameters of the eye behaviours of interest. It is not unknown for research to be reported where the relationship claimed between eye movements and subjective states deny the basic limitations of the hardware or experimental methods used. Finally, the method chosen for identifying fixations and saccades from sample data must be considered, as this too has a large effect on what can be validly inferred. For example, if we find research suggesting that a particular group (such as novice users) have shorter fixations while performing a given task, and we want to use that as a potential indicator in an interactive scenario, we need to make sure we are not setting too high a minimum duration in our mathematical definition of fixation, and also that we have a sufficiently fast sample rate to register the short stops or short saccades that the eye makes. Likewise, if we are assessing research which claims that pupil size is related to arousal, we first need to check that the experi-

mental procedures are controlled for ambient and stimulus brightness, since pupil size is first and foremost a result of the amount of light getting into the eye. It should be clear from these points that anyone wishing to apply eye movements to interactive interfaces or to the measurement of usability or any other domain where measures of human cognitive processes are inferred, must first and foremost have a good general knowledge of the hardware and theory behind the measurement of eye movements. The hardware chapter of this book (see Daunys, Chapter 22) provides a good starting point.

In order to focus on elements of a visual scene, the eye moves so that salient aspects of the environment fall on a small area in the centre of the retina (the 'fovea'). Changing features in the surrounding environment, such as movement or noise, are extrapolated from input to peripheral vision and reacted to quickly with a redirection of the locus of attention, usually with an eye movement towards the source of the stimulation. Depending on current goals and current environmental events, the eye will move in response to either 'bottom up' (stimulus driven) or 'top down' (goal driven) control. Top down control indicates a higher level of processing and a more focused level of attention. These levels of attention, one being generally concerned with spatial relationships and the other with object identification, are variously referred to in literature as where-what, global-local, dorsal-ventral and ambient-focal processing. There are many more terms and permutations of this concept of separate processing streams for vision. The division of visual processing into these two separate systems is generally accepted in cognitive and neuropsychological research, with extensive theoretical and physiological support. However, attention is a complex concept, and its clear differentiation into two or more distinct levels is likely an over-simplification, albeit a useful one. This chapter is concerned with what directions psychological research has suggested towards the measurement of an individual's active attentional states and internal processes from eye movements, and what this might contribute towards the development of new measures for real-time analysis of eye movement data in human-computer interactive settings.

The eye remains in constant motion in order to sample information from all relevant areas in the environment. What is relevant in the environment can be either reflex-inducing stimulation triggered by events in the environment (movement, sudden flashes or changes in colour) under the control of structures which are, in terms of human evolution, older, or, can be more cognitively controlled behaviours which serve higher order processes such as object identification, under the control of brain structures which evolved later in the human brain. These two types of eye movement control are represented by two separate structures or streams of processing in the brain; the dorsal and ventral streams of the visual system (Figure 1). The hypothesis of two streams of processing for human vision is now largely accepted in cognitive and neuropsychological research, but it is also criticized as likely being an over simplification.

Figure 1. The Dorsal Stream (green) and ventral stream (purple) of the human visual system (Adapted from "Ventral-dorsal streams", 2007. Used under the terms of the GNU Free Documentation License)

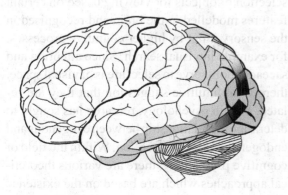

ATTENTION

There is an implicit assumption that where one looks is directly related to whatever has captured attention, and although this assumption has been challenged, in that attention can momentarily divert from where one looks (e.g. Hafed & Clark, 2002), or, for example, that one can attend to a memory while 'staring into space', in general, the eye is directed towards things in the visual world that we are currently attending to, are about to attend to, or have just attended to. Posner (1980) proposed that attention needs to be directed towards the destination of a saccade before the saccade can be programmed, and that this involves a covert (or implicit) attention shift without an overt (or explicit) eye movement. This argument is somewhat supported by the observation that moving a target after a saccade towards it is initiated has no effect on the location of the subsequent fixation - the destination site is not revisable - i.e. saccades are ballistic movements. However, fixations to the locus of attention are found to occur immediately following a shift in covert attention, within a fraction of a second, so that fixations are generally accepted as a viable measure of the locus of attention, usually with close temporal coupling. While it is important to remember that there is more going on in perception than we can directly observe in eye movements or even by combining eye movements with brain imaging, it is also important to realise that eye movements are particularly useful since we can know the spatial co-ordinates (and hence the sensory content) of the area targeted by the eye, something we cannot do for any other sense organ.

How eye movements relate to cognition, and what we might be able to tell about the inner world of the thinking brain from the analysis of eye movement parameters, is not yet entirely clear. There is little doubt that parameters such as fixation duration and saccade amplitude do have a relationship to cognitive processes, but we are now only beginning to understand the nature of this relationship and the parameters in which it seems to exist. Research has suggested many relationships, which we can observe, but struggle to integrate into old models. For example, there is a recurring finding that patterns of eye movements occurring during the perception of an image are replicated while remembering that image (de'Sperati 2003). This result has, however, been challenged. It was observations such as this which led researchers to believe that there may be more to the eye than simply being a window through which the brain looks out on the visual world, the data we seek out from the visual world as we manipulate ourselves around it is the result of an active process of continuously updating and rebuilding an internal 3D world. The eye is not just a passive observer scanning the visual space, it is moving purposefully.

The world we perceive is much richer than the flat image which the eye registers. The natural degradation in the image quality from central vision outwards can be thought of as a first, physical filter of available visual information, where the objects in line with the orientation of the eye are given preference. Thus we can respond to the environment and our aims within it by changing the sampling behaviour of the eye, reorienting the eye, looking at a particular area for longer or shorter periods of time, and so on. One of the major results of eye tracking research has been the possibility to observe and verify that the process of visual perception is *active*.

The information internalised while building a percept of a stimulus from the external world is often described as a 'mental image'. The mental image represents the product of perceptual and cognitive processing during and following the viewing process. Mental images have been the subject of experimental research for over 30 years, with consistent findings that there are close spatial relationships between a stimulus object/scene and its subsequent internal representation. Although the existence of mental images as 'pictures in the brain' was hotly debated and severely criticised

(Pylyshyn 2003), the close relationship between scan-paths while viewing and while remembering the same scene/object suggested a close relationship between eye movements and internal processes. This suggested to many researchers that cognitive processes are linked to the *strategic* pattern of eye movements. Such findings coincided with other research findings that fixation durations seem to be related to cognitive load and many similar findings from disparate areas of research described in this chapter.

Attention is competed for and distributed variously to exogenous (externally controlled) and endogenous (internally controlled) events; we can attend to some but not all of these events. We have a certain amount of control over which events we attend to, and many practiced or familiar situations require little attention and can be performed automatically with some minimal monitoring. We are conscious only of those things which we have attended, and there are various levels of attention which are more or less conscious and require more or less mental effort.

Levels of Attentional Processing

Exogenous control of eye movements results from salient new objects or areas in the environment capturing attention and the eyes, even if those objects are irrelevant to the current task (Theeuwes, Kramer, Hahn, & Irwin, 1998; Theeuwes, & Burger, 1998; Theeuwes, 1995; 1994). Endogenous control, on the other hand, describes the selection of objects for viewing based on certain features modelled in the brain and recognised in the sensory input by higher cognitive processes, for example in visual search. Since attention and saccades both serve to select areas of visual space, there is an intuitive suggestion that they are related. Within psychology, research has sought to determine the relationship between exogenous and endogenous shifts in attention. Within the field of cognitive psychology, there are various theoretical approaches which are based on the existence of two modes of visual processing, variously referred to as what-where, ambient-focal, and foveal-ambient, examining-noticing, or figural-spatial (see for example Held, Ingle, Schneider, Trevarthen, 1967; Hoffman, 1999; Norman, 2002; Velichkovsky, 1982). One of these concepts was developed by Trevarthen in 1968 by distinguishing between ambient and focal visual processing; focal processing was associated with the eyes moving within the central 5° of visual angle, i.e., within the area projected onto the fovea. This theoretical separation of vision into two processes is supported by the existence of two distinct pathways for vision in the brain (Goodale & Milner, 1992, Ungerleider & Mishkin, 1982). Dorsal stream functions are related to spatial perception and the control of visually guided movements (Mishkin, Ungerleider, Macko, 1983), while ventral stream functions are related to stimulus identification.

Findlay and Walker (1999) suggest a fixate-move control system, which initiates saccadic eye movements. The "move" command in the model is controlled by both automatic, low-level processes and by higher-level, voluntary and cognitively driven goals. Two systems are suggested to control saccadic eye movements; a spatial system that controls where the eye will move to and a temporal system that controls when a saccade is initiated. Similarly, Hoffman (1999) found evidence of a two-stage model of visual search. A preattentive stage serves to locate objects in the environment; a following second stage relates to attentive processing of objects in the environment. The number of objects processed concurrently in this second stage is limited and this results in a bottleneck in visual processing. While fixating during attentive processing, the fixation duration is under voluntary control until some pre-attentive, reflex-like response to the environment interrupts it. Such an interruption leads in general to a decrease in fixation duration, or, looked at another way, and considering the comparatively stable duration of saccades, an increase in number of fixations. The eye movements of subjects completing a visual search-and-comparison task suggest two phases of processing which have been differentiated on the basis of the duration of fixation. In the initial phase of viewing, when the viewer is assumed to search for the relevant object or scene characteristics, fixation duration is mainly a function of spatial density. Following this initial phase and during task completion, cognitive work is characterised by hypothesis generation and testing. In this later phase, fixation durations are influenced by task complexity and decision-making processes.

Exogenous control is most evident in dynamic scenes, where movement or change in peripheral vision frequently capture attention (Velichkovsky, 2002). Saccades initiated by endogenous control mechanisms are reported to be slower than those initiated involuntarily by exogenous control. Cue-target onset delays in exogenous control are as quick as 100ms, while endogenous, goal-driven saccades can have cue-target delays of 275-400ms (see Kean & Lambert 2003). Although exogenous control mechanisms may elicit non-goal oriented eye movements, endogenous control of eye movements can be thought of as covert attentional strategies or "central decisions" (Posner 1980) governing a measurable overt behaviour.

Consistent with this view, dorsal stream structures (e.g., areas in the posterior parietal cortex) contain neurons sensitive to direction of movement and shifts of spatial attention (Maunsell &Newsome, 1987), whereas ventral stream structures (e.g., areas in the infero-temporal cortex) contain neurons sensitive to shape, colour, and texture (Desimone, Schilen, Moran & Ungerleider, 1985). Related research found that individual differences in visuospatial abilities reflect individual differences in the efficiency with which the dorsal and ventral streams process information (Chen, Myerson, Hale, Simon, 2000). In 1996, Velichkovsky, Pomplun, and Rieser suggested that parameters of fixation durations could be used to infer levels of attention. Later research also incorporated saccade amplitude in differentiating between focal and ambient processing (Unema, Pannasch,

Joos, & Velichkovsky 2005). Research from free viewing picture tasks suggested that specific combinations of eye movement parameters are indicative of an involvement of either of the two processing streams (Velichkovsky, Rothert, Kopf, Dornhoefer, & Joos, 2002; Unema et al. 2005; Velichkovsky, Joos, Helmert, Pannasch, 2005).

Such research has suggested parameters for the temporal analysis of levels of attention while viewing a scene. Focal processing was associated with longer fixations followed by shorter saccades, and ambient processing was identified as shorter fixations followed by longer saccades to areas outside the foveal range (Unema et al., 2005; Velichkovsky, 2002; Velichkovsky et al. 2000). This was supported by the analysis of memory representations related to these two modes. Areas of a visual scene corresponding to a presumably focal mode of processing were remembered more frequently than areas similarly fixated in the course of a presumed ambient exploration (Velichkovsky et al., 2005). This research suggests that it is possible to distinguish between pre-attentive, or ambient scanning and more focused cognitive elaboration using parameters of fixation duration and saccade amplitude. Practically speaking, such measures could be applied and tested without having to know the exact locations of fixations (Velichkovsky et al, 2000). So what might this mean for gaze interaction? Well, it could mean that the online processing of fixation durations and saccade amplitudes could predict whether the user identified the object at the point of regard, whether they were likely to remember the content of their point of regard, and whether they were engaged in the process of, for example, orienting to the visual space, versus analyzing the stimulus content for relevant material. Such measures could greatly enhance the flow of information from human to computer. Current interaction scenarios typically rely largely on information flowing in the opposite direction.

Parameters such as those outlined above allow for a sufficient amount of individual and task dependent variance to be applied to the investi-gation of individual differences in cognition and inter-individual, task-based visual strategies. For example, Miall and Tchalenko (2001) showed that an artist's eye movement patterns were different when looking at an object in order to draw it as compared to their normal eye movements, and had longer fixation durations than novices when drawing an object. Such measures which could trace the changes in attentional states of a user would be valuable in the design of intelligent interfaces that respond to the user's cognitive state, level of expertise and even perceptual styles. There is a vast amount of scientific literature from which to draw on, however, much of this remains theory and has not been applied or even tested in an applied setting. The application of such theory requires a multi-disciplinary approach and the potential benefits of such an approach are significant.

There is considerable scope for further eye movement research involving the application and testing of the findings of cognitive and neuropsy-chology to human computer interaction scenarios. Although many measures have been found to co-vary with level of attention, a concerted effort to collate and validate findings in terms of general models is also necessary. Inferential statistical methodologies, which necessarily control for many variables while measuring specific ones, may be insufficient to fully explain the complexity reflected here. It is likely that in order to obtain full potential from studies in cognitive neuropsy-chology for the development of human computer interaction, more powerful analysis methods must be applied to the task of concurrently investigating eye movement and individual parameters with respect to stimulus characteristics.

EYE MOVEMENTS AND SUBJECTIVE STATES

The theoretical basis for the relationship between eye movements and subjective states has a long history. Buswell (1935) produced some of the earliest 2-dimensional scan paths of subjects inspecting pictures. He measured the duration of fixations in order to identify areas of interest and found that fixations would centre on informative areas, leaving blank or uninformative areas uninspected. He also compared the fixation durations of art students on works of art with those of other people and found that art training had a tendency to result in shorter fixations. Areas fixated depended on the attributes of the stimulus as well as the goals of the observer, and fixation durations increased with longer viewing times. He suggested that the initial stage of inspection involves a general survey of the scene, followed by a more detailed study of selected regions. Following this, Yarbus (1967) reported, firstly, that people tended to look longer at the most informative regions in a scene and, secondly, that he could influence the places where the eye stopped on a scene by asking viewers to make different judgements on its content. Furthermore, longer viewing periods were not associated with examining secondary elements in a scene, but were instead used to re-examine what were considered the most important areas. Treisman (1964) proposed that perceptual processing involved a hierarchy of levels of analysis, whereby stimuli were first analysed at a sensory level and later analysed for identification and meaning. Craik and Lockhart (1972) also proposed that perception involves an ongoing combination of bottom-up, stimulus driven and top-down (endogenous, internally driven), conceptually driven processing. We will now look at several ways in which these processes have been identified in patterns of eye movement behaviour.

Eye Movements Signaling the Intention to (Inter)Act

Even the most basic actions, such as picking up a cup of tea from one's desk or walking up the stairs in a shopping centre, require perfect co-operation of highly complex sensory-motor processes. The complexity of these operations is due to the great dynamic change both in our environment and within our own bodies. Our sensory-motor

system needs to adapt to alterations in the position and orientation of target objects as well as to permanent changes in our own posture (Milner & Goodale, 2006). In order to enable goal-directed operations, the cognitive representations of target objects, their position and parts of our corpus have to be updated frequently, primarily based on visual input (Ballard, Hayhoe, Pook, & Rao, 1997). Various authors therefore emphasize that eye movements play an important role in the visual guidance of actions (Findlay & Gilchrist, 2003). In the context of gaze interaction, where the intent to affect some change in the interface is even more directly related to eye position, an understanding of and sensitivity to the relationship between the eye and the intention to act is paramount. The aim of the following section is to introduce empirical findings supporting a close spatio-temporal relationship between eye movements and action and outline the theoretical accounts offered in literature. An introduction to related research on the neurophysiological bases of visually guided actions follows. Such research has direct relevance in designing for users with neurodegenerative disease as well as for the general populous.

Selecting Objects for Action with the Eye

Usually, we look directly at objects before reaching for them, thus bringing them into the centre of our visual field. In eye-hand action sequences, the first large saccade towards the target object is typically finished when the hand starts to move. This is followed by a second so-called correction saccade which centers the image of the object more exactly onto the fovea (Milner & Goodale, 2006). When we want to grasp for an object, we first fixate it and then direct our hand to the centre of the fixation coordinate frame. According to Ballard et al. (1997), in action sequences cognitive representations are thus coupled to points in space, i.e. objects in our environment. This implies that in order to update and maintain cognitive representations of the space we are in and the objects in it, we have to permanently scan the environment. According to the "passive vision" approach, where the movements of the eye are modelled as passive responses to events in the environment, information about objects in the environment not currently fixated can be retrieved from memory. However, this implies some kind of storage capacity large enough to maintain high-resolution image of the changing visual scene. Several authors argue that this assumes unreasonably high computational costs on processing and memory systems. The argument is that it would not only require capacities for far too great an amount of information in storage, it would also be bad neurological economics to need so much storage for vision. From an evolutionary point of view, a first principle in modelling the functional architecture of the brain is to reduce processing load, i.e. to favour explanations or strategies which have lower processing demands for the human brain. It follows that the visual guidance of actions should not rely too heavily on visual memory. Actions might then be primarily guided by information gathered at the time it is needed rather than being stored cumulatively until needed. This would mean that goal-directed saccades, where the eye moves in response to cognitive control, rather than stimulus events, are deep-seated within action sequences and hence this eye movement data can reveal the strategic collection and processing of information for current cognitive goals as they are executed. Relevant stimuli are actively sought out by the brain as they are needed in the reasoning process during visually based cognitive tasks. In terms of gaze-based interaction, the significance of the eye seeking out information exactly as it is needed may be that there are quantifiable limitations on what kind of gaze-contingent display changes are possible without disrupting perceptual flow, or, in the case that the eye essentially replaces the hand for point-and-click tasks, that the intention to act on a stimulus with the eye is likely to be realized as the first fixation towards the object is completed. Such suppositions require testing in an applied setting.

Ballard, Hayho, Li, & Whitehead (1992) provide empirical support for an active process in eye movements. In one study, participants were required to copy a pattern of coloured blocks displayed on a computer screen by moving elements from a resource area to a workspace with click and drag actions (see Figure 2). The relevance of this task was that subjects were required to move an object from one space to another according to some higher cognitive goal. Both hand and eye movements were tracked. The question was would the hand move first, presumably relying on memory to direct the target location, or would the eye move first, to refine location information at exactly the time needed. Analysis of subjects' eye movements revealed that many more saccades had been executed while moving an object than one would think necessary. It would be reasonable to expect something along the lines of the following sequence of operations: 1) click the block that is to be moved, 2) fixate the target location, and 3) move the block onto the target space. In contrast, Ballard et al. observed that participants often began moving the block without having first gazed at its target position. 'Monitoring' eye movements, i.e. movements switching between the object and the target area, occurred while moving the object. The authors conclude that object related representations are computed as late as possible

Figure 2. The 'blocks' task studied by Ballard et al. 1992

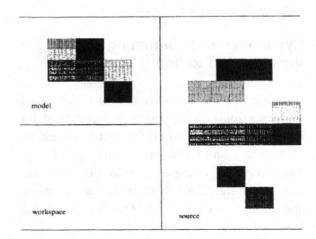

and the crucial information is sampled by frequent eye movements between the object and the target space, rather than retrieved from memory. Ballard et al. call this a "minimal memory strategy" (1992, p. 338).

There are substantial similarities between the "block-task" developed by Ballard et al. and how users behave when interacting with a graphic interface. Frequent operations common to both contexts are the selection, activation and movement of objects with an on-screen mouse or cursor. So, if, based on the evidence above, we favour a view of the active brain selecting samples of visual space exactly when the information is needed for action, over one of the passive eye collecting visual information for storage, the next question is, what if the eye was 'helped' towards relevant information in the visual space at the right time? How might that effect problem solving in tasks such as those used by Ballard et al.? Velichkovsky and colleagues (1996) applied a similar task to test whether the display of a cooperating partner's eye movement information had a beneficial effect on partners' performance during conjoint problem solving. Partners had to solve puzzles on a computer screen. One of the pair knew the solution to the problem task but could not act on the puzzle; the other partner was able to act without knowing the solution. Alongside the exchange of verbal commands, information on partners' gaze positions were projected onto the workspace of each partner. The authors found that the display of partners' eye movements not only changed communication patterns but also led to improved performance in cooperative tasks. These findings suggest that there may be an intuitive awareness of some indicative value of gaze positions for individuals' intentions, and users or learners could explicitly use gaze information in order to instruct another or follow another's instructions. For human computer interaction, there are obvious research and application domains. For example, in computer-based learning tasks, how might the recorded scan path of an expert solving a task or assessing some visual information help a beginner, assuming the expert

has learned to fixate exactly the right information to solve the task, at exactly the right time? Might this improve learning performance? In terms of intelligent interfaces, the relevant point here is that we could compare a person's eye movement behaviour either to that of an expert, in order to assess the level of expertise, or to themselves over time, as a measure of learning.

To further understand the temporal relationship between eye movements and the intention to act, a series of studies by Land and colleagues (Land & Furneaux, 1997; Land, Mennie, & Rusted, 1999) studied eye-action sequences outside the lab in free-viewing 3d spaces. These studies recorded eye movements in people carrying out everyday actions. They found that eye movements usually precede and initiate actions rather than passively monitoring the progression of operations. For example, while people play table tennis their gaze does not follow the movement of the ball as one might expect, but rather eye movements anticipate the balls' trajectory (Land & Furneaux, 1997). In a seminal study, Land et al. (1999) analyzed subjects' eye movements while they prepared a cup of tea (see Figure 3). Having divided the whole action sequence into basic action units (e.g. 'find the kettle' and 'transport to sink' etc.), the temporal relationship between action and eye movements was analyzed. They found that the objects neces-

Figure 3. Participant preparing tea while eye movements and actions are tracked (imported from Land et al., 1999, used with permission)

sary for completing an action subsequence are fixated just before the manipulation starts. The eye movement to the target object preceded an action on the object by approximately 0.6 seconds.

These findings suggest that eye movements are highly indicative of individuals' intentions to act upon objects in the visual space. Such findings are relevant for the development of eye trackers for environmental control, or for the control of a wheelchair. The question of whether it may be possible to develop attentive interfaces, which use algorithms to analyse gaze behaviour in order to infer and support users' subsequent actions, remains a subject of current research. However, it must be noted that a large proportion of fixations are not directly related to performed actions, since we are not always performing action sequences. Therefore, in order to infer the user's intentions to act, the challenge of reliably separating action-related from non-action-related eye movements must first be met. This problem is highly related to the differentiation of 'where' and 'what' eye movements, as discussed earlier in this chapter.

Eye Movements and Mental Load

The concept of mental load has gained broad attention since the 1940s under the auspices of workload analyses. Mental load was assessed in the context of human-machine systems in order to optimize task demands and facilitate an increasing automation of work tasks (Manzey, 1998). The term 'mental load' describes the effort that intellectual tasks require from the human information processing system (Gopher & Donchin, 1986). Since the mental resources available for processing information are limited, performing several mental operations concurrently leads to high mental load (Mulder, 1986). The objective level of mental load induced by a task increases with the number of distinct processing subsystems involved in task completion (e.g. systems underlying operations such as reception, recoding, emission, storing). Besides these structural aspects, the intensity

of system activation determines the mental load (Kahneman, 1973). The level of system activation is directly associated with the psychophysiological arousal that accompanies the completion of certain tasks, ranging from states of very low activation for mundane or automated tasks, to states of highest arousal for difficult or complex tasks (Manzey, 1998). The relevant finding for application to human computer interaction may be that as tasks become more familiar or routinised, or are new and difficult for the viewer, indicators of a reduction or increase in processing load may be embedded in the eye movement data. This would represent a rich trace of the subjective learning experience for the modelling of individual users, as well as a useful measure for usability studies assessing and comparing the relative ease of use of an interface.

In terms of the subjective experience of cognitive functioning, mental load expresses itself as a feeling of stress brought on by intellectual effort (Gopher & Donchin, 1986). The subjective stress level depends on task load (i.e. the inherent difficulty of the task) as well as on factors within the individual (Manzey, 1998). Lowest levels of subjective stress are reported for tasks of medium difficulty, which are assumed to cause medium levels of psychophysiological arousal (Fischer, Langner, Birbaumer, & Brocke, 2008). It becomes apparent that the concept of mental load describes a complex interaction between factors within the individual and the characteristics of the task at hand. In psychophysiological studies, various indicators which co-vary substantially with mental load were identified in the central and peripheral nervous system. Alongside changes in brain activity (e.g. in the spontaneous EEG, Kramer, 1991; and in event-related potentials, Kramer, Sirevaag, & Hughes, 1988), cardiovascular activity (Ohsuga, Shimono, & Genno, 2001) and electro dermal activity (Cacioppo & Sandman, 1978), mental load is accompanied by specific changes in eye movement parameters. In the following section the relationship between mental load and measures of fixations, saccades, blinks and pupillary movements will be discussed in order to assess the indicative value of the individual parameters for inferring users' levels of stress and attention in cognitive tasks.

The Effect of Mental Load on Fixations and Saccades

Studies measuring the fixation durations of subjects performing tasks of varying difficulty indicate that changes in fixation duration are related to different levels of task-dependent mental workload (e.g. De Rivecourt, Kuperus, Post, & Mulder, 2008). However, the direction of the effect varies across the different studies. Whether fixation duration is lengthened or shortened by increasing mental load seems to depend on task characteristics. In tasks requiring rapid responses, greater mental effort results in shorter fixation durations. This effect was shown while driving a car (Miura, 1986; Unema & Rötting, 1990) and piloting an airplane (Gerathewohl et al., 1978). The decrease in fixation duration is explained by the high level of activation typical for these tasks (Starger & Angus, 1978). In contrast, results showing increased load to be accompanied by longer fixations are also reported. Typically, this effect occurs in tasks involving higher cognitive processes, such as reading texts of increasing complexity (Rayner, 1978, 1982). Users controlling a computer interface will engage in higher cognitive processes, e.g. reading information on the display, understanding the interface structure and engaging in normal computer usage for work or entertainment, switching between looking to see and looking to control. We can assume a situation of high mental load, expecting that mental load will be accompanied by longer fixations. However, it is worth bearing in mind that interaction techniques based on a dwell time click will systematically alter an individual's fixation durations, so that a method of reliably differentiating fixating to see and fixating to control is essential for any eye

movement based analysis of mental load in gaze control scenarios.

In terms of saccades, two parameters have been found to be affected by changes in mental load: saccade amplitude and saccade velocity. The average saccade amplitude is, to a large extent, dependent on characteristics of the visual environment and correlates with the functional field of view (FFOV, Mackworth, 1965). The FFOV is the area of the visual field around the fixation point from which individuals are able to extract and process information in order to explore the scene (Saida & Ikeda, 1979). It describes the distance from the centre of foveal vision at which objects can be reliably identified (Mackworth, 1965). Outside this area visual stimuli can still be processed, however, the ability to reliably recognize objects is considerably limited or absent.

The FFOV has been found to alter in size with changes in processing load (Joos, Rötting, & Velichkovsky, 2002). Increasing mental load leads to a smaller FFOV. This effect is reflected by a decrease in the amplitudes of saccades. May, Kennedy, Williams, Dunlap and Brannan (1990) tested the influence of task difficulty on the extent of saccadic jumps. Their participants were asked to listen to random tone sequences consisting of high, medium and low tone pitches. The task was to count the tones following a fixed pattern. Three levels of difficulty were applied. In the easiest condition, subjects simply responded to every fourth tone. In the medium difficulty condition, a response was required after every fourth deep and every fourth medium tone. In the most difficult condition, a response after every fourth high tone had to be made in addition to the requirements of condition two. Data analysis revealed that alongside a substantial drop in subjects' performance in the high workload condition, there was a significant decrease in saccadic amplitude with increasing task difficulty. Although extensive practice could compensate for the effects of task difficulty on performance, the differences in saccadic range remained stable. This suggests that saccadic amplitudes represent an indicator of mental load unaffected by practice and affected by auditory as well as visual stimulation. May et al. used a strictly controlled experimental setup in their laboratory study. However, numerous other factors affecting saccadic amplitudes challenge the usefulness of this parameter as an indicator of mental load outside the lab.

Saccade velocity has also been investigated in relation to mental load. Dichgans et al. (1973) demonstrated that increasing task demands were accompanied by faster saccades. This finding was replicated in driving simulation tasks of changing complexity. In a recent study, Di Stasi and colleagues found saccadic peak velocity to be an adequate indicator of mental load in participants interacting with computer interfaces (Di Stasi, Alvarez, Antoli, Gea, & Cañas, submitted). According to Galley (1989, 1998) changes in parameters of saccadic velocity reflect varying levels of activation and vigilance. He found that subjects working on a tiring and boring task showed a decrease in saccadic velocity. Also, the relaxing effect of benzodiazepines and alcohol leads to saccadic slowing (Galley, 1998). However, saccadic velocity is also systematically related to saccadic extent (peak velocity is supposed to be log-linearly dependent on saccadic amplitude), with the fastest movements being those to the periphery of the visual field. This must be controlled for in order to extricate changes in velocity due to distance from changes due to levels of activation. So far, the number of studies addressing the relationship between saccadic velocity and psychological phenomena is small. However, in light of the increasing availability and decreasing cost of eye-trackers that provide information on saccadic velocities by default, there is considerable scope for addressing the relationship in everyday computer usage. It is worth noting that the measurement of saccadic velocity requires a sufficiently fast sample rate.

The Effect of Mental Load on Blinking Rate

A blink is a temporary closure of the eye lids. Reflexive blinks protect the eye from potentially harmful stimuli or foreign bodies. They can be elicited by mechanical or chemical irritation, intense light or noise. In contrast, spontaneous blinks occur without external stimulation. Spontaneous blinks prevent the cornea from drying out by covering the eye periodically with tear fluid (Galley, 2001). Beyond the first line of physiological and protective functions, individuals' blinking behaviour is indicative of a number of mental processes. As already illustrated in the introduction chapter, blinks interrupt visual perception for approximately 150 ms. To allow for optimal information processing, blinks, when voluntary, should occur when disruption of information uptake is minimally adversarial. This suggests that the inhibition of blinks depends on both visual load and task characteristics. Reduced activation of the processing system leads to a decrease in inhibition mechanisms (Fukuda, Stern, Brown, & Russo, 2005). Empirical evidence for this relationship stems from a study by Holland and Tarlow (1972). In order to prevent interference from visual stimuli, two non-visual tasks were used. Participants were required to remember sequences of digits containing four, six, or eight elements for a period of 70 seconds. The sequences had to be subsequently recalled. A second task consisted of arithmetic problems at two difficulty levels. During both tasks, participants gazed at a fixed point. Analysis of blinking rate revealed a decrease in blinks while retaining long digit sequences as well as during the arithmetic tasks of high difficulty. The authors conclude that increases in mental load lead to decreasing blinking rates independent of the visual environment. In contrast, emotional activation and stress are accompanied by increased blinking (see Tecce, 1992). Frequent blinks reflect particularly negative feelings, whereas blink rate slows in relaxed and pleasant states. For the integration of eye movements into human computer interaction scenarios, blink rate may be an interesting measure since, compared to pupil response, it is relatively unaffected by bottom-up properties of the stimulus and is reliably measurable by even the most rudimentary eye tracking systems. Depending on the way in which eye position is inferred from the eye image, blinks have an easily recognisable trace in the data, often displaying very fast changes in the y axis, or vertical movements of both eyes followed by eye loss for a fraction of a second. This is due to the apparent transformation of the pupil just as the lid covers it as the eye closes. Blinking rates may prove useful for low cost or low quality eye trackers.

Mental Load and Pupil Response

Pupil response has been extensively investigated with respect to mental load. Beatty (1982) reviewed studies examining changes in pupil size in various dimensions of mental load, e.g. perception, arithmetic, speech and memory. The reviewed studies consistently supported a close relationship between mental load and pupil size. A stable finding is that increased processing load, usually induced by growing task complexity, leads to pupil dilatation (Hess & Polt, 1964; Verney, Granholm, & Dionisio, 2001). The pupil continuously dilates following task onset and reaches a maximum after 700-1200 ms before returning to baseline level. The amplitude of this reaction correlates positively with task difficulty and complexity. The latency of the cognitively induced pupil response is 100-200 ms (Manzey, 1998). This is clearly shorter than the light reflex, which has a peak response from 0.5 to 1.0 sec after presentation of a bright light, suggesting an adequate differentiation of the two reactions, providing the system used has sufficient temporal resolution and eye image quality (Beatty & Lucero-Wagoner, 2000). However, the detection of task-evoked changes in pupil size remains challenging (Lin, Zhang, & Watson, 2003).

Alterations in pupil diameter caused by cognitive processes are often smaller (typically less than 0.5 mm) than light regulative changes (Beatty & Lucero-Wagoner, 2000). Individual differences affecting the size of the pupil are state of health (Moeller & Maxner, 2007) and age (Loewenfeld, 1972). Controlling for these nuisance factors as well as for lighting conditions and changes in the distance between pupil and eye tracking camera is essential for the detection of arousal through pupil behaviour. Mental load, if correctly measured, is potentially very useful when adapting systems to human processing limitations. Parameters of eye movements have been shown relate to mental load. However, results indicate that the direction of the effects is strongly task dependent. In natural settings there is a significant confounding effect between cognitive and non-cognitive influences on eye movement parameters. In spite of the constraints, the analysis of these parameters or their combination (Marshall, 2007) can potentially provide a viable measure of task demands. The development of such measures requires a validation of eye movement parameters with the concurrent application of other methods such as verbal reports.

Influence of Emotions on Attention and Eye Movement Behaviour

Emotions are states of high personal importance. Meaningful events are usually accompanied by emotional reactions. Although most people can offer some definition of emotions (Shaver, Schwartz, Kirson, & O'Connor, 1987), theorists have so far agreed only to a working definition, involving a limited number of agreed characteristics (Reisenzein, 2007). According to this, emotions are usually conscious episodic mental states, e.g. happiness, sadness, fear, hope, relief and anger, which are directed at or elicited by objects, individuals or situations. Emotional states are characterised by specific subjective feelings and are accompanied by physiological changes, expressions and actions (Reisenzein & Horstmann, 2006).

From an evolutionary-functional perspective, emotions are adaptive states which allow flexible reactions to the various demands of the environment, e.g. reflexive escape actions or actively seeking social support in situations of threat (Öhman, Flykt, & Lundqvist, 2000). Although the major function of affective reactions involve the regulation of behaviour, virtually all types of cognitive processes are also influenced by emotional states (Storbeck & Clore, 2007). In terms of the interplay between emotions and attentional processes, Izard (1979, p. 163) states that "a particular emotion sensitizes the organism to particular features of its environment [and] ensures a readiness to respond to events of significance to the organism's survival and adaptation." Emotionality is affected by whether objects satisfy or frustrate current motives and hence whether those objects require special attention (Schwarz & Clore, 1983). An attentional system especially efficient in detecting and processing emotional stimuli is therefore adaptive, enabling the quick evaluation of objects and events with respect to one's safety and well-being and prompt initiation of adaptive or defensive behaviour.

The following section describes research summarising the various levels and characteristics of emotional influence on attentional mechanisms suggested in literature. We will focus firstly on the influence of emotional stimuli on orienting behaviours and attentional breadth from the bottom up (i.e. stimuli which provoke emotional responses in the observer). Secondly, we will assess literature on the top-down modulation of attention by latent emotional states such as moods and emotional dispositions. There is currently a lot of interest in measuring emotion from eye movements, however, as we shall see, not all claims are supported by the literature.

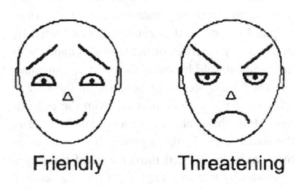

Figure 4. Schematic Faces Used in the Study by Öhman et al. (2001)

Bottom-Up Capturing of Attention by Emotional Stimuli

Research on the perception of emotional faces (see Figure 4) shows that angry and threatening faces, in particular, are detected faster than neutral faces (Öhman, Lundqvist, & Esteves, 2001; Fox et al., 2000). This effect was replicated with other threatening stimuli, such as pictures of snakes and spiders (Öhman et al., 2000). These findings support the idea that attention is particularly biased towards negative stimuli due to their relevance to the individual's well-being (Öhman et al., 2001). However, the results of Calvo and Lang (2004) challenge the negativity hypothesis. They found that participants watching neutral and emotionally arousing photographs showed a similar attentional bias for positive and negative pictures over neutral stimuli. These findings indicate that emotional stimuli generally capture attention. However, the strength of the effect seems to depend on other factors such as general emotional arousal and thematic relevance.

To further explain the phenomenon, Calvo and Lang (2004) and Calvo, Nummenmaa and Hyona (2007) recorded eye movements while participants viewed various emotionally arousing images. Analysis of gaze data revealed that the probability of the first fixation landing on a stimulus was increased when presented with emotional as compared to neutral stimuli. Shorter fixations were required to adequately identify emotional scenes, in comparison to neutral scenes. Despite the greater efficiency in processing emotional information, individuals tend to fixate emotional stimuli longer during first-pass perception (Calvo & Lang, 2004; Nummenmaa, Hyona, & Calvo, 2006), supporting the idea that attention is literally captured by emotional content. An attentional bias towards emotional stimuli can be observed even when participants are instructed to ignore them, underlining the involuntary, reflex-like nature of the phenomenon (Nummenmaa et al., 2006).

As well as influencing the direction of attention, emotional stimuli have been found to alter attention to central vs. peripheral visual cues (Derryberry & Tucker, 1994). This effect is particularly evident in the phenomenon known as weapon focusing (see e.g. Kramer, Buckhout, & Eugenio, 1990). In this literature, victims' attention during crimes is usually focused narrowly on any weapons present (e.g. guns, knives), while peripheral details of the scene are given less attention (Kramer et al., 1990). In a study by Loftus, Loftus and Messo (1987) subjects watched two versions of a fast-food restaurant scene. In one version, the customer hands a cheque to the cashier, who then returns their change. In the weapon version, the same "customer" points a gun at the cashier who is returning money. The only difference between the scenes was the object that the customer targets at the cashier, gun vs. cheque. Analysis of participants' gaze behaviour revealed more and longer fixations on the gun compared to the cheque. Furthermore, subjects in the weapon condition had degraded memory of peripheral details of the scene (e.g. appearance of the customer). The authors conclude that the central feature in the threatening scene, the weapon, captured the majority of attentional resources and left fewer resources for encoding the rest of the scene. Better recall for central compared to peripheral details was also shown for pictures showing accidents with injured

persons (Christianson, Loftus, Hoffman, & Loftus, 1991). According to Christianson and colleagues, the arousal component of emotional stimuli elicits more attention to central rather than peripheral details. However, the mechanisms underlying this effect are not yet sufficiently understood (Christianson et al., 1991). In terms of gaze interaction, such findings have relevance for the design of interactive strategies, for example the strategic analysis of eye movements during game play in virtual environments, or identifying what is most emotionally arousing to an individual on screen.

These studies provide broad evidence in support of the thesis that emotional stimuli capture individuals' attention quicker and more often than neutral stimuli. Emotional capturing leads to a) increased orienting of gaze direction towards the emotional stimulus and b) improved processing of central cues within emotional scenes at the expense of attention towards peripheral details.

In summary, a large number of empirical studies demonstrate an influence of emotions on attentional processes. The reported research supports the attentional capturing hypothesis. The implementation of "emotion detection" algorithms in attentional interfaces would constitute a promising extension of this technology. However, attempts to develop emotion detection tools are confronted with a lack of empirical findings and significant challenges to be overcome in terms of either careful monitoring or controlling for environmental factors. Pupil size changes seem to be promising in the literature, but require highly controlled settings and a good quality image of the eye. More scientifically rigorous research is clearly needed in this area to clarify and validate the claims made. Although it seems clear that emotional states do affect eye movement behaviour and indeed cognitive processing in general, there is nothing clear about the nature of the effect and certainly no indication from a scientific point of view that eye movements can have any diagnostic function in terms of which emotion is being felt by the viewer. It seems viable, based on current theory, to recognise emotional arousal under controlled settings, however, there is no theoretical or empirical basis for claims that emotions can be differentiated based on eye movement parameters.

SUMMARY

In this chapter we have seen that many disparate studies have come to similar conclusions regarding the relationship between eye movements, attention and subjective states of the viewer. It seems that eye movements can offer a means of measuring something about the private cognitive life of the viewer, on a moment-to-moment basis. The development and application of such theories to human computer interaction requires a concerted approach to collate these findings meaningfully and construct clear parameters for the application and reliability of such measures in real world settings. Many of the studies outlined above have overlapping results. However, how these factors relate to each other in a cogent model of human perception is unclear. It is difficult to imagine how the traditional approaches of the experimental method alone (i.e. hypothesis testing with inferential statistics) will lead to a sufficiently complex model of all the variables implicated in measuring internal states. Much work is currently being carried out on bringing together brain and eye movement measures with computational modelling techniques, machine learning and more complex analysis methods capable of handling many sources of data of differing quality and temporal resolution. Nonetheless, the unique properties of eye movement measures, both as a direct output of the active brain and a means of tracing the sensory input to the visual system, as well as the decrease in price and increase in application domains of eye tracking technology, indicate that the popularity of eye movement as a key area of interest in human-computer interaction will continue to grow. The practice of improving interface design and usability through the application of eye movement theory to real world

scenarios has already begun. Such an integrated approach is necessary to realise the full potential of eye movement data as a rich source of internal processing measures in the flow of information from human user to intelligent, attentive interfaces.

ACKNOWLEDGMENT

We would like to thank Markus Joos of Interactive Minds Dresden and Sebastian Pannasch of TU-Dresden for providing helpful comments on and suggestions for earlier versions of this manuscript.

REFERENCES

Althoff, R. R., & Cohen, N. J. (1999). Eye-movement-based memory effect: A reprocessing effect in face perception. *Journal of Experimental Psychology. Learning, Memory, and Cognition, 25*(4), 997–1010. doi:10.1037/0278-7393.25.4.997

Andreassi, J. L. (2007). *Psychophysiology: Human behavior and physiological response (5 ed.)*. Mahwah, New Jersey: Lawrence Erlbaum Associates.

Ballard, D. H., Hayhoe, M. M., Li, F., & Whitehead, S. D. (1992). Hand-eye coordination during sequential tasks. *Philosophical Transactions of the Royal Society of London. Series B, Biological Sciences, 337*(1281), 331–339. doi:10.1098/rstb.1992.0111

Ballard, D. H., Hayhoe, M. M., Pook, P. K., & Rao, R. P. (1997). Deictic codes for the embodiment of cognition. *The Behavioral and Brain Sciences, 20*(4), 723–767. doi:10.1017/S0140525X97001611

Beatty, J. (1982). Task-evoked pupillary responses, processing load, and the structure of processing resources. *Psychological Bulletin, 91*(2), 276–292. doi:10.1037/0033-2909.91.2.276

Beatty, J., & Lucero-Wagoner, B. (2000). The pupillary system. In Cacioppo, J. T., Tassinary, L. G., & Berntson, G. G. (Eds.), *Handbook of Psychophysiology, 2* (pp. 142–162). New York, NY: Cambridge University Press.

Buswell, G. T. (1935). *How people look at pictures*. Chicago, IL: University of Chicago Press.

Cacioppo, J. T., & Sandman, C. A. (1978). Physiological differentiation of sensory and cognitive tasks as a function of warning, processing demands, and reported unpleasantness. *Biological Psychology, 6*(3), 181–192. doi:10.1016/0301-0511(78)90020-0

Calvo, M. G., & Lang, P. J. (2004). Gaze patterns when looking at emotional pictures: Motivationally biased attention. *Motivation and Emotion, 28*(3), 221–243. doi:10.1023/B:MOEM.0000040153.26156.ed

Calvo, M. G., Nummenmaa, L., & Hyona, J. (2007). Emotional and neutral scenes in competition: Orienting, efficiency, and identification. *Quarterly Journal of Experimental Psychology, 60*(12), 1585–1593. doi:10.1080/17470210701515868

Chen, J., Myerson, J., Hale, S., & Simon, A. (2000). Behavioural evidence for brain-based ability factors in visuospatial information processing. *Neuropsychologia, 38*, 380–387. doi:10.1016/S0028-3932(99)00095-0

Christianson, S. A., Loftus, E. F., Hoffman, H., & Loftus, G. R. (1991). Eye fixations and memory for emotional events. *Journal of Experimental Psychology. Learning, Memory, and Cognition, 17*(4), 693–701. doi:10.1037/0278-7393.17.4.693

Cohen, Y. E., & Andersen, R. A. (2002). A common reference frame for movement plans in the posterior parietal cortex. *Nature Reviews. Neuroscience, 3*(7), 553–562. doi:10.1038/nrn873

Craik, F. I. M., & Lockhart, R. (1972). Levels of processing: A framework for memory research. *Journal of Verbal Learning and Verbal Behavior, 11*, 671–684. doi:10.1016/S0022-5371(72)80001-X

De Rivecourt, M., Kuperus, M. N., Post, W. J., & Mulder, L. J. (2008). Cardiovascular and eye activity measures as indices for momentary changes in mental effort during simulated flight. *Ergonomics, 51*(9), 1295–1319. doi:10.1080/00140130802120267

de'Sperati, C. (2003). The inner working of dynamic visuo-spatial imagery as revealed by spontaneous eye movements. In Hyönä, J., Radach, R., & Deubel, H. (Eds.), *The mind's eye: Cognitive and applied aspects of eye movement research*. Amsterdam, The Netherlands: Elsevier Science.

Derryberry, D., & Reed, M. A. (1998). Anxiety and attentional focusing: Trait, state and hemispheric influences. *Personality and Individual Differences, 25*, 745–761. doi:10.1016/S0191-8869(98)00117-2

Derryberry, D., & Tucker, D. M. (1994). Motivating the focus of attention. In Niedenthal, P. M., & Kitayama, S. (Eds.), *The heart's eye: Emotional influences in perception and attention*. San Diego, CA: Academic Press.

Desimone, R., Schilen, S. J., Moran, J., & Ungerleider, L. G. (1985). Contour, color and shape analysis beyond the striate cortex. *Vision Research, 25*, 441–452. doi:10.1016/0042-6989(85)90069-0

Di Stasi, L. L., Alvarez, V., Antoli, A., Gea, M., & Cañas, J. J. (n. d.). A neurousability approach to evaluate cognitive load in hypermedia interactions. *Interacting with Computers*.

Dichgans, J., Nauck, B., & Wolpert, E. (1973). The influence of attention, vigilance and stimulus area on optokinetic and vestibular nystagmus and voluntary saccades. In Zikmund, V. (Ed.), *The oculomotor system and brain functions* (pp. 279–294). London, UK: Butterworths.

Easterbrook, J. A. (1959). The effect of emotion on cue utilization and the organization of behavior. *Psychological Review, 66*(3), 183–201. doi:10.1037/h0047707

Findlay, J. M., & Gilchrist, I. D. (2003). *Active vision: The psychology of looking and seeing*. Oxford, UK: Oxford University Press.

Findlay, J. M., & Walker, R. (1999). A model of saccade generation based on parallel processing and competitive inhibition. *The Behavioral and Brain Sciences, 22*, 348–362. doi:10.1017/S0140525X99002150

Fischer, T., Langner, R., Birbaumer, N., & Brocke, B. (2008). Arousal and attention: Self-chosen stimulation optimizes cortical excitability and minimizes compensatory effort. *Journal of Cognitive Neuroscience, 20*(8), 1443–1453. doi:10.1162/jocn.2008.20101

Fox, E., Lester, V., Russo, R., Bowles, R. J., Pichler, A., & Dutton, K. (2000). Facial expressions of emotion: Are angry faces detected more efficiently? *Cognition and Emotion, 14*(1), 61–92. doi:10.1080/026999300378996

Fredrickson, B. L. (2001). The role of positive emotions in positive psychology - The broaden-and-build theory of positive emotions. *The American Psychologist, 56*(3), 218–226. doi:10.1037/0003-066X.56.3.218

Fredrickson, B. L., & Branigan, C. (2005). Positive emotions broaden the scope of attention and thought-action repertoires. *Cognition and Emotion, 19*(3), 313–332. doi:10.1080/02699930441000238

Fukuda, K., Stern, J. A., Brown, T. B., & Russo, M. B. (2005). Cognition, blinks, eye movements, and pupillary movements during performance of a running memory task. *Aviation, Space, and Environmental Medicine, 76*(7Suppl), C75–C85.

Galley, N. (1989). Saccadic eye movement velocity as an indicator of (de)activation. A review and some speculations. *Journal of Psychophysiology, 3*, 229–244.

Galley, N. (1998). An enquiry into the relationship between activation and performance using saccadic eye movement parameters. *Ergonomics, 41*(5), 698–720. doi:10.1080/001401398186865

Galley, N. (2001). Physiologische Grundlagen, Meßmethoden und Indikatorfunktion der okulomotorischen Aktivität. In F. Rösler (Ed.), *Enzyklopädie der Psychologie, Band 4: Biologische Psychologie* (pp. 237-315). Göttingen: Hogrefe.

Gasper, K., & Clore, G. L. (2002). Attending to the big picture: Mood and global versus local processing of visual information. *Psychological Science, 13*(1), 34–40. doi:10.1111/1467-9280.00406

Gerathewohl, S. J., Brown, E. L., Burke, J. E., Kimball, K. A., Lowe, W. F., & Stackhouse, S. P. (1978). Inflight measurement of pilot workload: A panel discussion. *Aviation, Space, and Environmental Medicine, 49*(6), 810–822.

Goodale, M. A., & Milner, D. A. (1992). Separate visual pathways for perception and action. *Trends in Neurosciences, 15*, 20–25. doi:10.1016/0166-2236(92)90344-8

Gopher, D., & Donchin, E. (1986). Workload - An examination of the concept. In K. R. Boff, L. Kaufman & J. P. Thomas (Eds.), *The handbook of perception and human performance. Cognitive processes and performance* (vol. 2, pp. 41:1–49). New York, NY: Wiley.

Hafed, Z., & Clark, J. (2002). Microsaccades as an overt measure of covert attention shifts. *Vision Research, 42*, 2533–2545. doi:10.1016/S0042-6989(02)00263-8

Held, R., Ingle, D., Schneider, G., & Trevarthen, C. (1967). Locating and identifying: Two modes of visual processing, A symposium. *Psychologische Forschung, 31*, 42–43. doi:10.1007/BF00422384

Hess, E. H. (1972). Pupillometrics. In Greenfield, N. S., & Sternbach, R. A. (Eds.), *Handbook of psychophysiology* (pp. 491–531). New York, NY: Holt, Rinehart & Winston.

Hess, E. H., & Polt, J. M. (1964). Pupil size in relation to mental activity during simple problem-solving. *Science, 143*(361), 1190–1192. doi:10.1126/science.143.3611.1190

Hoffman, J. E. (1999). Stages of processing in visual search and attention. In Challis, B. H., & Velichkovsky, B. M. (Eds.), *Stratification in cognition and consciousness* (pp. 43–71). Amsterdam, Philadelphia: John Benjamins.

Holland, M. K., & Tarlow, G. (1972). Blinking and mental load. *Psychological Reports, 31*(1), 119–127.

Izard, C. E. (1979). Emotions as motivations: An evolutionary-developmental perspective. In H. E. Howe & R. A. Dienstbier (Eds.), *Nebraska Symposium on Motivation 1978* (pp. 163–200). Lincoln, NE: University of Nebraska Press.

James, W. (1890). *The principles of psychology, with introduction by George A. Miller (1983)*. Cambridge, MA: Harvard University Press.

Joos, M., Rötting, M., & Velichkovsky, B. M. (2002). Die Bewegungen des menschlichen Auges: Fakten, Methoden, innovative Anwendungen. In Rickheit, G., Herrmann, T., & Deutsch, W. (Eds.), *Psycholinguistics* (pp. 142–168). Berlin, NY: Walter de Gruyter.

Kahneman, D. (1973). *Attention and effort*. Englewood Cliffs, N.J.: Prentice Hall.

Kimchi, R., & Palmer, S. E. (1982). Form and texture in hierarchically constructed patterns. *Journal of Experimental Psychology. Human Perception and Performance, 8*(4), 521–535. doi:10.1037/0096-1523.8.4.521

Kramer, A. F. (1991). Physiological metrics of mental workload: A review of recent progress. In Damos, D. (Ed.), *Multiple task performance* (pp. 279–328). London, UK: Taylor & Francis.

Kramer, A. F., Sirevaag, E. J., & Hughes, P. R. (1988). Effects of foveal task load on visual-spatial attention - event-related brain potentials and performance. *Psychophysiology, 25*(5), 512–531. doi:10.1111/j.1469-8986.1988.tb01887.x

Kramer, T. H., Buckhout, R., & Eugenio, P. (1990). Weapon focus, arousal, and eyewitness memory - Attention must be paid. *Law and Human Behavior, 14*(2), 167–184. doi:10.1007/BF01062971

Laeng, B., & Teodorescu, D. (2002). Eye scanpaths during visual imagery re-enact those of perception of the same visual scene. *Cognitive Science, 26*, 207–231. doi:10.1207/s15516709cog2602_3

Land, M. F., & Furneaux, S. (1997). The knowledge base of the oculomotor system. *Philosophical Transactions of the Royal Society of London. Series B, Biological Sciences, 352*(1358), 1231–1239. doi:10.1098/rstb.1997.0105

Land, M. F., Mennie, N., & Rusted, J. (1999). The roles of vision and eye movements in the control of activities of daily living. *Perception, 28*(11), 1311–1328. doi:10.1068/p2935

Leigh, R. J., & Kennard, C. (2004). Using saccades as a research tool in the clinical neurosciences. *Brain, 127*, 460–477. doi:10.1093/brain/awh035

Lin, Y., Zhang, W. J., & Watson, L. G. (2003). Using eye movement parameters for evaluating human-machine interface frameworks under normal control operation and fault detection situations. *International Journal of Human-Computer Studies, 59*(6), 837–873. doi:10.1016/S1071-5819(03)00122-8

Loewenfeld, I. E. (1972). Pupillary changes related to age. In Thompson, H. S., Daroff, R., Frisén, L., Glaser, J. S., & Sanders, M. D. (Eds.), *Topics in neuro-ophthalmology* (pp. 124–150). Baltimore, MD: Williams and Wilkins.

Loftus, E. F., Loftus, G. R., & Messo, J. (1987). Some facts about weapon focus. *Law and Human Behavior, 11*(1), 55–62. doi:10.1007/BF01044839

Mackworth, N. H. (1965). Visual noise causes tunnel vision. *Psychonomic Science, 3,* 67–68.

Manzey, D. (1998). Psychophysiologie mentaler Beanspruchung. In F. Rösler (Ed.), *Ergebnisse und Anwendungen der psychophysiologie. Enzyklopädie der Psychologie* (vol. C/I/5, pp. 799–864). Göttingen, Germany: Hogrefe.

Marshall, S. P. (2007). Identifying cognitive state from eye metrics. *Aviation, Space, and Environmental Medicine, 78*(5Suppl), B165–B175.

Maunsell, J. H. R., & Newsome, W. T. (1987). Visual processing in monkey extrastriate cortex. *Annual Review of Neuroscience, 10,* 363–401. doi:10.1146/annurev.ne.10.030187.002051

May, J. G., Kennedy, R. S., Williams, M. C., Dunlap, W. P., & Brannan, J. R. (1990). Eye movement indices of mental workload. *Acta Psychologica, 75,* 75–89. doi:10.1016/0001-6918(90)90067-P

Miall, R. C., & Tchalenko, J. (2001). A painter's eye movements: A study of eye and hand movement during portrait drawing. *Leonardo, 34,* 35–40. doi:10.1162/002409401300052488

Milner, A. D., & Goodale, M. A. (2006). *The visual brain in action (2 ed.).* Oxford, UK: Oxford University Press.

Mishkin, M., Ungerleider, L. G., & Macko, K. A. (1983). Object vision and spatial vision: Two cortical pathways. *Trends in Neurosciences, 6,* 414–417. doi:10.1016/0166-2236(83)90190-X

Miura, T. (1986). Coping with situational demands: A study of eye movements and peripheral vision performance. In Gale, A. G., Freeman, M. H., Haslegrave, C. M., Smith, P., & Tayler, S. P. (Eds.), *Vision in vehicles* (pp. 205–216). Amsterdam, The Netherlands: Elsevier.

Moeller, J. J., & Maxner, C. E. (2007). The dilated pupil: An update. *Current Neurology and Neuroscience Reports, 7*(5), 417–422. doi:10.1007/s11910-007-0064-9

Mountcastle, V. B., Lynch, J. C., Georgopoulos, A., Sakata, H., & Acuna, C. (1975). Posterior parietal association cortex of the monkey: Command functions for operations within extrapersonal space. *Journal of Neurophysiology, 38*(4), 871–908.

Mulder, G. (1986). The concept and measurement of mental effort. In Hockey, C. R. J., Gaillard, A. W. K., & Coles, M. G. H. (Eds.), *Energetical issues in research on human information processing* (pp. 175–198). Dordrecht, The Netherlands: Martinus Nijhoff.

Norman, J. (2002). Two visual systems and two theories of perception. *The Behavioral and Brain Sciences, 25*(1), 73–144.

Nummenmaa, L., Hyona, J., & Calvo, M. G. (2006). Eye movement assessment of selective attentional capture by emotional pictures. *Emotion (Washington, D.C.), 6*(2), 257–268. doi:10.1037/1528-3542.6.2.257

Öhman, A., Flykt, A., & Lundqvist, D. (2000). Unconscious emotion: Evolutionary perspectives, psychophysiological data and neuro-psychological mechanisms. In Lane, R., & Nadel, R. (Eds.), *Cognitive neuroscience of emotion* (pp. 296–327). New York, NY: Oxford University Press.

Öhman, A., Lundqvist, D., & Esteves, F. (2001). The face in the crowd revisited: A threat advantage with schematic stimuli. *Journal of Personality and Social Psychology, 80,* 381–396. doi:10.1037/0022-3514.80.3.381

Ohsuga, M., Shimono, F., & Genno, H. (2001). Assessment of phasic work stress using autonomic indices. *International Journal of Psychophysiology, 40*(3), 211–220. doi:10.1016/S0167-8760(00)00189-6

Pomplun, M., Ritter, H., & Velichkovsky, B. (1996). Disambiguating complex visual information: Towards communication of personal views of a scene. *Perception, 25*(8), 931–948. doi:10.1068/p250931

Posner, M. I. (1980). Orienting of attention. *The Quarterly Journal of Experimental Psychology, 32*, 3–25. doi:10.1080/00335558008248231

Pylyshyn, Z. (2003). Return of the mental image: Are there really pictures in the brain? *Trends in Cognitive Sciences, 7*(3). doi:10.1016/S1364-6613(03)00003-2

Rayner, K. (1978). Eye-movements in reading and information-processing. *Psychological Bulletin, 85*(3), 618–660. doi:10.1037/0033-2909.85.3.618

Rayner, K. (1982). Visual selection in reading, picture perception and visual search. In Bouma, H., & Bouwhuis, D. G. (Eds.), *Attention and performance* (pp. 67–96). Hillsdale, NJ: Lawrence Erlbaum.

Rayner, K., Juhasz, B., Ashby, J., & Clifton, C. (2003). Inhibition of saccade return in reading. *Vision Research, 43*, 1027–1034. doi:10.1016/S0042-6989(03)00076-2

Rehder, B., & Hoffman, A. B. (2005). Thirty-something categorization results explained: Selective attention, eyetracking, and models of category learning. *Journal of Experimental Psychology. Learning, Memory, and Cognition, 31*(5), 811–829. doi:10.1037/0278-7393.31.5.811

Reisenzein, R. (2007). What is a definition of emotion? And are emotions mental behavioral processes? *Social Science Information Sur Les Sciences Sociales, 46*(3), 424–428.

Reisenzein, R., & Horstmann, G. (2006). Emotion. In Spada, H. (Ed.), *Lehrbuch Allgemeine Psychologie* (*Vol. 3*). Bern: Huber.

Rowe, G., Hirsh, J. B., & Anderson, A. K. (2007). Positive affect increases the breadth of attentional selection. *Proceedings of the National Academy of Sciences of the United States of America, 104*(1), 383–388. doi:10.1073/pnas.0605198104

Saida, S., & Ikeda, M. (1979). Useful visual field size for pattern perception. *Perception & Psychophysics, 25*(2), 119–125. doi:10.3758/BF03198797

Schwarz, N., & Clore, G. L. (1983). Mood, misattribution, and judgements of well-being: Informative and directive functions of affective states. *Journal of Personality and Social Psychology, 45*, 513–523. doi:10.1037/0022-3514.45.3.513

Shaver, P., Schwartz, J., Kirson, D., & O'Connor, C. (1987). Emotion knowledge - Further exploration of a prototype approach. *Journal of Personality and Social Psychology, 52*(6), 1061–1086. doi:10.1037/0022-3514.52.6.1061

Starger, P., & Angus, R. (1978). Locating crash sites in simulated air-to-ground visual search. *Human Factors, 20*, 453–466.

Storbeck, J., & Clore, G. L. (2007). On the interdependence of cognition and emotion. *Cognition and Emotion, 21*(6), 1212–1237. doi:10.1080/02699930701438020

Tecce, J. J. (1992). Psychology, physiology and experimental psychology. In *McGraw - Hill yearbook of science & technology* (pp. 375–377). New York, NY: McGraw - Hill.

Theeuwes, J. (1994). Endogenous and exogenous control of visual selection. *Perception, 23*, 429–440. doi:10.1068/p230429

Theeuwes, J. (1995). Perceptual selectivity for color and form: On the nature of the interference effect. In Kramer, A. F., Coles, M. G. H., & Logan, G. D. (Eds.), *Converging operations in the study of visual attention* (pp. 297–314). Washington, DC, USA: American Psychological Association.

Theeuwes, J., & Burger, R. (1998). Attentional control during visual search: The effect of irrelevant singletons. *Journal of Experimental Psychology. Human Perception and Performance, 24*, 1342–1353. doi:10.1037/0096-1523.24.5.1342

Theeuwes, J., Kramer, A. F., Hahn, S., & Irwin, D. E. (1998). Our eyes do not always go where we want them to go: Capture of the eyes by new objects. *Psychological Science*, *9*, 379–385. doi:10.1111/1467-9280.00071

Tinker, M. A. (1946). The study of eye movements in reading. *Psychological Bulletin*, *43*, 93–120. doi:10.1037/h0063378

Treisman, A. M. (1964). Selective attention in man. *British Medical Bulletin*, *20*, 12–16.

Trevarthen, C. (1967). Two visual systems in primates. *Psychologische Forschung*, *31*, 321–337.

Unema, P., Pannasch, S., Joos, M., & Velichkovsky, B. M. (2005). Time-course of information processing during scene perception: The relationship between saccade amplitude and fixation duration. *Visual Cognition*, *12*(3), 473–494. doi:10.1080/13506280444000409

Unema, P. J. A., & Rötting, M. (1990). Differences in eye movements and mental workload between experienced and inexperienced motor-vehicle drivers. In Brogan, D. (Ed.), *Visual search* (pp. 193–202). London, UK: Taylor & Francis.

Ungerleider, L. G., & Mishkin, M. (1982). Two cortical visual systems. In Ingle, D. J., Goodale, M. A., & Mansfield, R. J. W. (Eds.), *Analysis of visual behaviour*. Cambridge, MA: MIT Press.

Velichkovsky, B. M. (1982). Visual cognition and its spatial-temporal context. In Klix, F., Hoffmann, J., & Meer, E. v. (Eds.), *Cognitive research in psychology* (pp. 63–79). Amsterdam, The Netherlands: North Holland.

Velichkovsky, B. M. (1999). From levels of processing to stratification of cognition. In Challis, B. H., & Velichkovsky, B. M. (Eds.), *Stratification in cognition and consciousness* (pp. 203–226). Amsterdam, Philadelphia: John Benjamins.

Velichkovsky, B. M. (2002). Heterarchy of cognition: The depths and the highs of a framework for memory research. *Memory (Hove, England)*, *15*(6), 126–149.

Velichkovsky, B. M., Joos, M., Helmert, J. R., & Pannasch, S. (2005). Two visual systems and their eye movements: Evidence from static and dynamic scene perception. In B. G. Bara, L. Barsalou & M. Bucciarelli (Eds.), *Proceedings of the 27th Annual Conference of the Cognitive Science Society* (pp. 2283–2288). Mahwah, NJ: Erlbaum.

Velichkovsky, B. M., Pomplun, M., & Rieser, J. (1996). Attention and communication: Eye-movement-based research paradigms. In Stiel, S., & Freksa, C. (Eds.), *Visual attention and cognition* (pp. 125–154). Amsterdam, New York: Elsevier Science Publisher. doi:10.1016/S0166-4115(96)80074-4

Ventral-dorsal streams [Image file] (2007). *Wikimedia commons*. Retrieved from http://en.wikipedia.org/wiki/File:Ventral-dorsal_streams.svg

Verney, S. P., Granholm, E., & Dionisio, D. P. (2001). Pupillary responses and processing resources on the visual backward masking task. *Psychophysiology*, *38*(1), 76–83. doi:10.1111/1469-8986.3810076

Weiskrantz, L. (1986). *Blindsight: A case study and implications*. Oxford, UK: Oxford University Press.

Yarbus, A. L. (1967). *Role of eye movements in the visual process*. New York, NY: Plenum Press.

Chapter 12
Brain–Computer Interfaces and Visual Activity

Carmen Vidaurre
Berlin Institute of Technology, Germany

Andrea Kübler
Universität Würzburg, Germany

Michael Tangermann
Berlin Institute of Technology, Germany

Klaus-Robert Müller
Berlin Institute of Technology, Germany

José del R. Millán
Swiss Federal Institute of Technology Lausanne, Switzerland

ABSTRACT

There is growing interest in the use of brain signals for communication and operation of devices – in particular, for physically disabled people. Brain states can be detected and translated into actions such as selecting a letter from a virtual keyboard, playing a video game, or moving a robot arm. This chapter presents what is known about the effects of visual stimuli on brain activity and introduces means of monitoring brain activity. Possibilities of brain-controlled interfaces, either with the brain signals as the sole input or in combination with the measured point of gaze, are discussed.

INTRODUCTION

Brain states can be detected and translated into actions such as selecting a letter from a virtual keyboard, playing a video game, or moving a robot arm. Such devices, which do not require the user to perform any physical action, are called brain–computer interfaces (BCIs) or brain–machine interfaces (BMIs). Although brain–computer interfaces and brain–machine interfaces involve the same kind of interface technology, it is agreed for purposes of precision in nomenclature that the latter are based upon invasive signals whereas the former rely upon non-invasive signals. For this reason, the term 'BCI' will be used in this chapter.

DOI: 10.4018/978-1-61350-098-9.ch012

It is important to remark that, although the main application of BCI technology has been centred in providing a new communication channel for patients with severe neuromuscular disabilities (Kübler et al., 2011), it is also a powerful tool for contribution to a better understanding of the brain and it provides a novel communication channel for human–machine interaction. Also, BCI prototypes have only been developed recently, but the basic ideas were already put forward in the 1970s. Initial successful experiments were based on analysis of the brain's electrical activity – namely, the visual evoked potential – generated in response to changes in gaze direction (Vidal, 1977).

We also wish to remark that some of the text included in this introduction has been extracted from the introductory chapter of the book *Towards Brain–Computer Interfacing* (Kübler & Müller, 2007). The curious reader is enthusiastically referred to this book, as it provides a still-timely overview of the BCI field (Dornhege et al., 2007).

Principles of BCI Systems

BCI research for communication and control is now possible because of both the neuro-scientific advances concerning the functioning of the brain and the powerful computing possibilities of current computers. Also, there is a growing awareness of the needs, problems, and potential of people with disabilities, as testified by the appearance of this book. No less important is the opportunity that BCI offers to investigate brain activity as an independent variable, in comparison to traditional psycho-physiological experiments. In the latter, the subjects are presented with a task or stimuli (independent variables) and the related brain activity is measured (dependent variable). Conversely, with neuro-feedback by means of a BCI, subjects can learn to deliberately increase or decrease brain activity (independent variable) and changes in behaviour can be measured accordingly (dependent variable).

An often overlooked direction of BCI applications beyond clinical and basic research aspects is the yet unexplored use of a BCI as an additional independent channel of human–machine interaction. In particular, brain signals can provide direct access to aspects of human brain state such as cognitive work load, alertness, task involvement, emotion, or concentration. The monitoring of these will allow for a novel technology that directly adapts a human–machine interface design to the inferred brain state in real time. Furthermore, BCI technology will in the near future be able to serve as an add-on in the development of new computer games – for example, fantasy games that require the brain-controlled mastering of a task for advancing to the next game level, where from our point of view there is great potential for the combination of gaze tracking and BCI technology. However, unlike in the field of gaze tracking, sensors are the bottleneck of today's invasive and non-invasive BCIs: invasive sensors can last only a limited time before they lose signal, and non-invasive sensors might need a long preparation time because of the use of conductive gel, depending on the number of electrodes used. In any case, the gel has to be removed later with soap and water, which makes the procedure uncomfortable, especially for patients.

Current BCI technology can be divided into two different approaches, although more or less all BCI systems rely primarily on a mixture of the two. The first approach is based on neuro-feedback and operant conditioning. Bio-feedback is a procedure that, by means of feedback on a (seemingly) autonomous parameter, is aimed at acquiring voluntary control over this parameter. Participants receive visual, auditory, or tactile information about their cardiovascular activity (heart rate or blood pressure), temperature, skin conductance, muscular activity, electrical brain activity (as shown by EEG or MEG signals), or blood-oxygen-level-dependent (BOLD) response (with functional magnetic resonance imaging (fMRI) or functional near-infrared spectroscopy (fNIRS)) and learn to regulate it voluntarily. When bio-feedback involves the control of neural signals, it is called neuro-feedback. In any case, the participants are presented with the task of either increasing or decreasing the activity of interest. By means of the feedback signal, participants receive continuous information about the alteration of the activity and success in the task is positively reinforced. Depending on the signal of interest and instruction, more or less extensive subject training is required for gaining sufficient voluntary control.

The second approach is the machine learning procedure, which infers the statistical signature of specific brain states or intentions within a calibration session. The training in this case occurs in the machine, in the form of a learning algorithm. Its parameters are individually fitted to the participant. Because of the great diversity of the signals (even from the same person), the learning algorithms require examples from which they can infer the underlying statistical structure of the relevant brain state. In the typical approach, users first repeatedly produce a specific brain state during a calibration session (without feedback) that is used for extraction of spatio-temporal patterns of the brain states, which will later be detected in a feedback session. Machine learning approaches can be usefully employed in an exploratory scenario, where 1) a new paradigm is tested that also could generate unexpected neurophysiological signals, 2) a hypothesis about underlying task-relevant brain processes is generated automatically by the learning machine through feature extraction, and 3) the paradigm can be refined and thus a better understanding of the brain processes can be achieved. For example, the weights of a classifier might give an idea of the importance of the features in the classification task (if all features have similar magnitudes): close to zero weights indicate that features are not relevant for the classification. The spatial location (see Figure 2) or the frequency content of the relevant features might aid in understanding the neuro-physiological processes underlying the task.

Figure 1 shows the general architecture of a brain-actuated robot. The brain's electrical activity is recorded with a portable device. These raw signals are first processed and transformed, for extraction of relevant features that are then transferred to mathematical models. These models compute, after a training process, the appropriate mental commands to control devices, from robot

Figure 1. General architecture of a brain—computer interface for controlling robotics devices

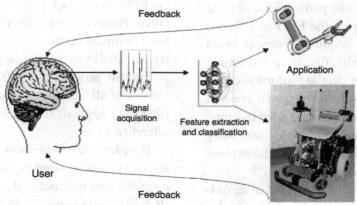

Figure 2. The placement of scalp electrodes as an extension to the 10/20 international system

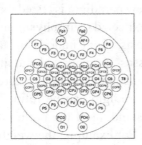

arms to vehicles. Finally, visual feedback, and maybe other kinds, such as haptic or auditory feedback, informs the user about the performance of the brain-actuated robot, to allow learning of appropriate mental control strategies and making of rapid changes to achieve the task. A BCI may monitor brain activity via a variety of methods, which can be broadly classified as invasive and non-invasive.

Means of Monitoring Brain Activity

Non-Invasive BCI Systems

Most non-invasive BCI systems use electroencephalogram (EEG) signals – i.e., the electrical brain activity recorded from electrodes placed on the scalp (see Figure 2). The main source of the EEG is the synchronous activity of thousands of cortical neurons (those perpendicular to the scalp surface). Measuring the EEG is a simple non-invasive way to acquire electrical brain activity information with fine time resolution, but it does not provide detailed information on the activity of single neurons (or small areas of the brain). Moreover, it is characterised by small signal amplitudes (a few microvolts) and noisy measurements (especially if recording takes place outside laboratory conditions).

EEG signals are a valuable method of recording cortical activity with a very good time resolu-tion. However, they are also characterised by a poor signal-to-noise ratio and spatial resolution. Fortunately, their quality is greatly improved by means of spatial filters. One example is the common average reference (CAR), which consists in removing the average activity over all of the electrodes. Laplacian or bipolar filters are also very common. A Laplacian filter is obtained by referencing an electrode to the mean of its four nearest neighbouring electrodes (the mean activity of these four electrodes is subtracted from the activity of the electrode to be referenced). A bipolar filter is computed as the difference of the electrodes in anterior and posterior directions. A more sophisticated spatial filter is called surface Laplacian (SL) derivation. This requires a large number of electrodes (normally 64–128). The SL estimate yields new potentials that represent better the cortical activity with its origin in sources radial to the scalp.

Another possibility is to use a data-driven approach to construct common spatial patterns (CSP), which finds spatial filters that are optimal for discrimination of two populations of EEG signals. CSP is based on the simultaneous diagonalisation of two matrices – the variance matrices of the two populations – and finds directions – i.e., spatial filters – with the biggest difference in variance between the two classes. Unlike the other spatial filtering methods, a band-pass filter focusing on the rhythms of interest is applied to the EEG signals before the computation of CSP. Often, electrodes are referenced to the ear (mastoid) or linked mastoids. The reference potential is calculated by averaging the potentials measured in the two earlobes and is subtracted from the activity of all electrodes. However, when spatial filters are applied, the transformed signals are reference-free.

Besides electrical activity (EEG), neural activity produces other types of signals, such as magnetic and metabolic, that could be used in a BCI. Magnetic fields can be recorded with magnetoencephalography (MEG), while the brain's metabolic activity – reflected in changes of the blood oxygenation level or concentration of metabolites (e.g., glucose) – can be observed with positron emission tomography (PET), functional magnetic resonance imaging, and optical imaging.

To date, MEG has been used only in laboratory settings and consequently is not suitable for a BCI for communication and control in the patient's home environment. The advantages of MEG as compared to EEG are better spatial resolution, leading to precise localisation of cortical activation related to a specific task or sensory stimulation, and higher signal-to-noise ratio, especially for higher-frequency activity such as gamma-band activity. MEG is therefore a viable tool for short-term intervention and rehabilitation. In a study with three tetraplegic patients after cervical spinal cord injury, Kauhanen and colleagues (2006) achieved the same classification accuracies in MEG data as in EEG data. The patient's task was to attempt finger movement, and data were analysed offline. Lal and colleagues showed that regulation of the magnetic activity of the brain by means of motor imagery can be used to select letters on a computer screen, but participants were still not provided with online feedback of MEG activity; instead, they were provided with feedback on results – that is, a smiling face after correct classification or selection of the correct letter (Lal et al., 2005). A closed-loop online-feedback motor-imagery-based BCI with MEG was implemented by Mellinger and colleagues (Mellinger et al., 2007). Learning to regulate brain activity by means of MEG feedback and the accuracies gained were comparable to EEG. MEG may be used to localise the focus of activity during motor imagery if EEG provides no clear results.

Currently, MEG feedback during motor imagery is used to train chronic stroke patients to reactivate the paralysed limb when not the entire motor cortex or all pyramidal tracts are lesioned. Chronic stroke patients undergo MEG feedback training such that an orthosis is attached to the paralysed limb, which opens and closes the hand (Buch et al., 2008). Motor imagery opens the orthosis while relaxation (thinking of nothing) closes it. This training provides the patients with self-induced sensory feedback for the paralysed limb, the idea behind this being that activation of a sensorimotor network enables patients to relearn motor functions.

For the past approximately ten years it has been possible to use the blood-oxygen-level-dependent response as input signal for a BCI. The local concentration of de-oxygenated haemoglobin in brain tissue depends on neuronal activity and metabolism, and changes can be measured with functional magnetic resonance imaging; fMRI allows spatial resolution in the range of millimetres and provides for more precise allocation of neuronal activity than does EEG. Additionally, activation in subcortical areas can be recorded. With recent advances in acquisition techniques, computing power, and algorithms, the functional sensitivity and speed of fMRI have increased considerably and the delay in feedback could be reduced to below two seconds, improving the conditions for feedback experiments. Target areas for feedback were sensory and motor areas, the parahippocampal area, and the affective and cognitive subdivisions of the anterior cingulate cortex (ACC). Learning of self-regulation of the BOLD response was reported in all studies that included subject training to regulate said response, and some reported behavioural effects in relation to activation or deactivation of target areas. Owen and colleagues successfully distinguished activation patterns associated with motor imagery (playing tennis) and spatial navigation (through one's own house, starting at the front door) in a patient diagnosed as being in a persistent vegetative state and could thus show that she was consciously aware (Owen et al., 2006). Recently, this approach was used with 'yes'/'no' answers being provided by healthy subjects and a few patients diagnosed as being in a vegetative state, again showing that the participants were consciously aware and, accordingly, falsely diagnosed. Currently, the use of BCIs to improve the detection of consciousness and to provide non-responsive patients with a simple and robust means of communication is under investigation (see http://www.decoderproject.eu/).

The advantage of fMRI over EEG is in its 3D spatial resolution. However, fMRI is expensive and tied to the laboratory. Functional near-infrared spectroscopy offers comparable spatial resolution, albeit restricted to cortical areas (depth: 1–3 cm), with much less technical effort and cost. Moreover, the NIRS-BCI is portable and could, therefore, be used in a patient's home environment. The fNIRS-BCI system presented by Sitaram and colleagues incorporates the so-called continuous wave technique. Regional brain activation is accompanied by increases in regional cerebral blood flow (rCBF) and the regional cerebral oxygen metabolic rate (rCMRO2). The increase of rCBF exceeds that of rCMRO2, resulting in a decrease of deoxygenated haemoglobin in venous blood. So the ratio of oxygenated to de-oxygenated haemoglobin is expected to increase in active brain areas and is measured with NIRS. The continuous wave approach uses multiple pairs, or channels, of light sources and light detectors operating at two or more discrete wavelengths. The light source may be a laser or a light-emitting diode (LED). The optical parameter measured is attenuation of light intensity due to absorption by the intermediate tissue. The changes in concentration of oxygenated and de-oxygenated haemoglobin are computed from the changes in the light intensity at different wavelengths (Sitaram et al., 2007). Bauernfeind and colleagues presented a working NIRS-BCI wherein users performed arithmetic operations to control the system (Bauernfeind, Leeb, Wriessnegger, & Pfurtscheller, 2008).

Invasive BCI Systems

In invasive BCI systems, the activity of single or a few neurons (their spiking rate) is recorded from microelectrodes implanted in the brain. In a series of experiments with rats and monkeys, researchers have monitored different areas of the cortex related to execution and planning of movements – the motor, pre-motor, and posterior parietal cortex. From real-time analysis of the activity of the neuronal population, it has been possible to determine a monkey's movement intention, predict the animal's hand trajectory, and drive a computer cursor to desired targets. In patients with severe motor impairment due to high spinal cord injury or neurodegenerative disease, the first steps have been made toward invasive approaches. In two studies (Kennedy, Bakay, Moore, Adams, & Goldwaithe, 2000; Hochberg et al., 2006), patients were eventually able to drive a cursor and write messages. The performance, however, was only similar to that achieved with non-invasive BCI systems. Less invasive approaches are based on the analysis of electrocorticogram (ECoG) signals from electrodes placed subdurally or epidurally on the cortical surface. ECoG signals are less noisy than EEG signals are and also have higher spatial resolution. EcoG, however, requires surgery.

Given the risks generated by permanent surgically implanted devices in the brain, and the associated ethical concerns, below we will concentrate only on non-invasive approaches – in particular, electrical brain signals as measured by EEG.

EEG-BASED BRAIN-COMPUTER INTERFACES

Methodologies

The brain reacts characteristically to external sensory stimulation such as flashes or tones with so-called evoked potentials reflecting synchronous discharge of cell assemblies. Evoked potentials are, in principle, easy to pick up with scalp electrodes and have been widely used in the context of BCIs. The necessity of external stimulation does, however, restrict the applicability of evoked potentials to a limited range of tasks. Despite this, evoked potentials are the type of signals most commonly used to develop BCI applications (spelling, Internet browsing, gaming, painting, and photo browsing). Another suitable alternative for interaction is to analyse components associated with spontaneous 'intentional' mental activity. This is particularly the case for control of robotics devices.

Spontaneous BCIs are based on the analysis of EEG phenomena associated with various aspects of brain function related to mental tasks carried out by the subject at his or her own will. This kind of BCI can exploit two kinds of spontaneous or endogenous brain signals: slow potential shifts and variations of rhythmic activity. The latter are variations in the power of specific frequency bands of the EEG. It should be noted that eye movements and breathing may cause considerable artefacts in slow potentials while muscular tension – in the face and neck – can generate artefacts in higher frequencies and affect EEG rhythms. Another characteristic worthy of note is that a change in EEG rhythms is observable only after 0.5 seconds (response latency).

Slow Cortical Potentials

The first BCI that allowed for verbal communication with locked-in patients was controlled by slow cortical potentials (SCPs). This pioneering work is summarised in two contributions (Kübler et al., 1999; Birbaumer et al., 1999). Negative SCPs reflect the depolarisation level of cortical networks and, thus, their readiness for performance of a specific task. Positive SCP shifts follow task performance or reflect hyperpolarisation of cortical cell assemblies. SCPs are best measured at the central electrode Cz) (see Figure 2 for the naming and placement of the electrodes). Healthy subjects and those with severe neurological disease, such as epilepsy or amyotrophic lateral sclerosis, can learn to regulate the SCP amplitude voluntarily in a neuro-feedback paradigm wherein positive and negative SCP shifts are positively reinforced. Feedback can be provided visually or audibly; a

Figure 3. Experimental protocol used by Birbaumer's team to measure slow cortical potentials

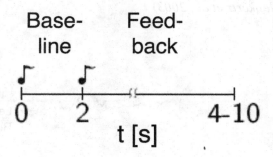

complete description of the procedure with different types of feedback modalities can be found in the work of Hinterberger and colleagues (Hinterberger et al., 2004). As depicted in Figure 3, a trial typically involves a two-second preparatory phase in which the cursor remains stationary on the screen and a baseline is recorded. In the following, active feedback phase, lasting 2–8 s, the cursor moves at constant speed from left to right and the vertical deflection corresponds to the SCP amplitude. The onsets of these two phases are indicated by a high- and a low-pitched tone, respectively. For each trial, the user is required to produce either a negative or a positive SCP shift. The SCP amplitude shifts are referenced to the SCP value of the last 500 ms of the two-second preparatory phase. At the end of the feedback phase, the SCP shift is classified as a negative or positive response according to the integral of the SCP shift across the feedback period. This BCI allows for binary choices (i.e., yes or no), which is the minimum output necessary for communication.

Another possibility is to monitor slow premovement potentials such as the Bereitschaftspotential (BP), or readiness potential. As shown in Figure 4, BP is a slow negative shift over the controlateral motor cortical area starting 500–600 milliseconds before the onset of the movement. As this is a slow potential, its dynamics are better

Figure 4. Grand averages of event-related movement potentials from self-paced left and right finger movements. Lateralisation of the BP is clearly visible, a contralateral negativation, for electrodes C3 and C4 over the motor cortex (see Figure 2), left and right, respectively (adapted from the work of Blankertz et al., 2003)

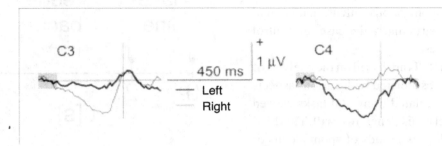

observed if a low-pass filter – say, below 4 Hz – is applied before analysis of the EEG. Also, it is not necessary to use any baseline for computing it, which accelerates the classification of outcome.

Rhythmic Activity

Variations of EEG rhythms in the frequency domain are also widely used as the BCI input signal. Populations of neurons can form complex networks via which feedback loops are responsible for the generation of oscillatory activity. In general, the frequency of such oscillations becomes slower the larger the size of the synchronised neuronal assemblies. A particularly significant EEG rhythm

can be recorded from the central region of the scalp overlying the sensorimotor cortex during the imagination of body movements.

Pfurtscheller's team work with event-related desynchronisation (ERD) (Pfurtscheller & Neuper, 2001). ERD is the basis of a number of BCIs, such as the ones described by Babiloni et al. (2000) and by Blankertz, Dornhege, Krauledat, Müller, and Curio (2007). Imagery of hand movement gives rise to amplitude suppression – ERD – of Rolandic μ rhythm. This rhythm is typically found in the frequency band 8–12 Hz. The amplitude suppression is usually observable in the central β rhythm (frequency range: 13–28 Hz). Both rhythms are measured over the contralateral primary hand mo-

Figure 5. Grand average ERD/ERS curves recorded over left and right motor cortex (electrodes C3 and C4, respectively; see Figure 2) during imagined hand movements. Positive and negative deflections, with respect to the reference, represent a band power increase (ERS) and decrease (ERD), respectively. The alpha band corresponds to the Rolandic μ rhythm. This figure shows negative deflections (ERD). Figure adapted from the work of Blankertz et al. (2008a)

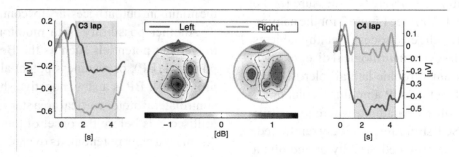

Figure 6. The cue stimulus in the form of an arrow indicates the type of imagination. The reference period used as a baseline for calculation of ERD/ERS is indicated

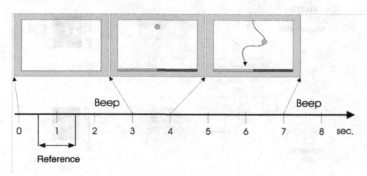

tor cortical area (Pfurtscheller & Neuper, 1997). As shown in Figure 5, this imagery-related ERD shows different time courses in the two bands. In the µ band (between 8 and 12 Hz), the ERD returns to baseline level within a few seconds. On the other hand, the central β activity displays a brief ERD followed by an amplitude increase – event-related synchronisation (ERS).

In Pfurtscheller and Neuper's teams, the ERD is computed at fixed time intervals after the subject is required to imagine specific movements of the limbs. Figure 6 illustrates the typical protocol (Pfurtscheller & Neuper, 2001). The experimental task is to imagine either right-hand or left-hand movement, depending on a visually presented cue. Subjects fixate on a computer monitor 150 cm in front of them. Each trial lasts 8 s and starts with the presentation of a fixation cross at the centre of the monitor, followed by a short warning tone (beep) at 2,000 ms. At 3,000 ms, the fixation cross has an arrow superimposed on it for 1,250 ms, pointing either to the left or to the right. The subject is instructed to imagine, depending on the direction of the arrow, a movement of, for example, the left or right hand. Recognition of the mental task executed is performed in a fixed time window, from 3,250 to 4,250 ms. The sequence of 'left' and 'right' trials, as well as the duration of the breaks between consecutive trials (between 500 and 2,500 ms), is randomised throughout each

experimental run. Finally, to compute the ERD/ERS, the EEG is first band-pass filtered and the band power is estimated – by means of, for instance, the Welch periodogram algorithm or an autoregressive model. Then, the power components are referred to the corresponding values of the band power of the reference baseline and transformed to dB – i.e., the logarithm of the division is taken.

Another approach is to extract ERD/ERS with CSP applied as a spatial filter. For the computation of CSP filters, the signal is band-pass filtered in an appropriate subject-specific band, then the optimal time interval where ERD/ERS can be found is estimated. After that, optimal linear mixtures of channels are found with CSP. With this method, no baseline is needed, and the ERD/ERS is estimated continuously with the help of the spatial filters, which enhance these effects between different locations of the scalp. This technique requires recording a calibration measurement of around 30 minutes for the optimisation. Then, the session can start with appropriate feedback for the control of applications. This information is summarised in Figure 7. For more information on how to use CSP, please refer to the tutorial (Blankertz, Tomioka, Lemm, Kawanabe, & Müller, 2008).

Alternatively, continuous changes in the amplitudes of the µ (8–12 Hz) or β (13–28 Hz)

Figure 7. The scheme of the Berlin BCI at work

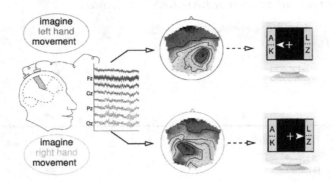

rhythms can be used as the input signal for BCI control. As with the CSP technique, it is not necessary to refer the band power amplitude to any baseline, thus speeding up the decision process. People learn to control μ or β rhythm amplitude and use that amplitude to move a cursor in one or two dimensions to targets on a computer screen. A linear equation translates μ (or β) rhythm amplitude into a cursor movement. Figure 8 illustrates the control achieved by a well-trained user. In each trial, lasting several seconds, users move the cursor in a randomly selected direction and trials are interleaved with short rest periods (e.g., 1 s). An example of this type of BCI can be found in the work of Wolpaw, McFarland, and Vaughan (2000). Kübler and colleagues showed that people with amyotrophic lateral sclerosis are able to control this BCI with motor imagery despite severe degeneration of motor cortical neurons (Kübler et al., 2005).

Finally, in addition to motor-related rhythms, other cognitive mental tasks can also be explored for modulating the EEG. This approach is grounded in a number of neurocognitive studies that have found that different mental tasks – such as mental rotation of geometric figures, arithmetic operations, or language – activate local cortical areas to differing extent. In particular, continuous variations of EEG rhythms can be analysed in a broad frequency range. This approach aims

at discovering task-specific spatio-frequency patterns embedded in the continuous EEG signal – i.e., EEG rhythms over local cortical areas that differentiate the mental tasks. One remarkable example can be found in work by Millán et al. (2002).

Evoked-Potential-Based BCIs

BCIs based on evoked or event-related potentials (ERPs) depend on the brain's response to external stimulation. Two types of evoked potentials

Figure 8. Frequency spectra of EEG recorded over the sensorimotor cortex of a trained subject when the target is at the bottom (red) or at the top (blue) of the video screen. The main difference between the two spectra is in the 9–12 Hz rhythm band and, to a lesser extent, in a 20–26 Hz rhythm band. Figure adapted from the work of Blankertz et al. (2008a)

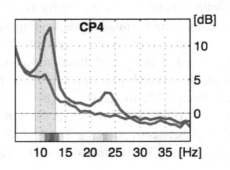

have been widely explored in the field of BCIs: the endogenous ERP P300 and the exogenous steady-state visual evoked potential (SSVEPs).

P300

The P300 component of the evoked potentials can be elicited in an oddball paradigm in which standard visual or auditory stimuli are interspersed with deviants (the 'oddball') of lower probability (ratio, e.g., 80:20). The P300 can be measured best at centro-parietal locations along the midline of the scalp (see Figure 2 for details of EEG electrodes placement). As illustrated in Figure 9, it is an ERP of positive polarity peaking between 250 and 600 ms after the oddball. The delay depends on the cognitive effort that has to be invested for detection of the oddball, the focus of attention, and (in patients with neurological disease) possible neurodegeneration. The amplitude of the P300 depends on the frequency of stimulus occurrence – less frequent stimuli produce larger responses – and task relevance. It can be elicited by a visual, auditory, or haptic stimulus.

To evoke a visual P300, subjects are given a sufficiently large number of options (e.g., letters of the alphabet or icons) from which they choose one. Then, options are visually enhanced (e.g., flashed or rotated) several times, in random order. Finally, it is possible to determine which choice the subject intended as a target simply by selecting the stimulus that elicits the largest P300. Compared to the BCI approaches using voluntary modulations of slow cortical potentials and sensorimotor rhythms (SMRs), the 'P300 Matrix Speller' (see Farwell & Donchin, 1988) holds the promise of allowing considerably higher information transfer rates.

Traditionally, the P300 has been used with visual stimuli to develop virtual keyboards (ibid.). Visual P300 potentials have also been the basis for brain-actuated control of several applications, such as an Internet browser, a brain painting program, and a virtual reality system, and of a wheelchair.

Figure 9. Grand average evoked potentials across many trials and subjects over the CPz and PO7 electrodes (see Figure 2). Time 0 is stimulus onset. Note the large P300 peak (actually occurring at around 400 ms) for the desired infrequent choice that does not appear for undesired choices. Figure adapted from the work of Acqualagna, Treder, Schreuder, and Blankertz (2010)

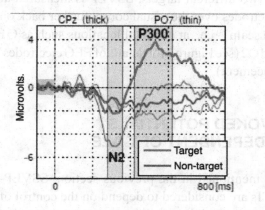

Please refer to the list of additional reading to find the related references.

SSVEPs

Visual evoked potentials (VEPs) reflect electrophysiological mechanisms underlying the processing of visual information in the visual cortex in the occipital lobe of the brain and vary in response to changes in visual stimuli. Steady-state visual evoked potentials are VEPs located over the visual cortex and induced by repeated stimuli. SSVEPs are composed of a series of components whose frequencies are harmonics (exact integer multiples) of the stimulus frequency. The strongest SSVEP signals are obtained during the fixation of a stimulus flashing at 6–30 Hz.

To operate an SSVEP-based BCI, multiple targets are placed on a visual panel, each flickering at a different frequency. When a subject gazes at a certain target, an SSVEP is induced in the visual cortex whose fundamental frequency is equal to the flickering frequency of the target; therefore, one can determine the target on which the BCI user is focusing for selection. This implies that SSVEP-based BCI paradigms depend on muscular control of gaze direction for their operation. Figure 10 shows an example of SSVEPs induced by two different targets. SSVEP is measured at electrodes over the visual cortex further back on the scalp – i.e., at occipital locations such as O1 and O2 (see Figure 2 for details of EEG electrodes' placement).

EVOKED POTENTIALS INDEPENDENT OF GAZE

As mentioned in the previous section, SSVEP-BCIs are considered to depend on the control of muscular activity to direct gaze to the attended target. These interfaces have been criticised by several authors (e.g., Kübler, Kotchoubey, Kaiser, Wolpaw, & Birbaumer, 2001; Wolpaw, Birbaumer, McFarland, Pfurtscheller, & Vaughan, 2002), who have described the limitation of this approach for

Figure 10. SSVEPs induced by visual stimulation. The frequency of the stimulation can be measured from the EEG. The peaks at these frequencies, as well as at their second harmonics, are clearly identified. Figure adapted from the work of Zhu, Bieger, Garcia-Molina, and Aarts (2010)

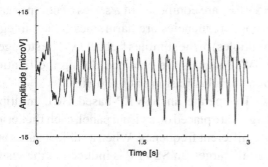

severely motor-impaired patients. Although eye or lid movements are typically the last remaining voluntary movements for patients diagnosed with a progressive neurodegenerative disease such as ALS, patients without eye-movement control may be encountered, for which non-visual BCIs have to be provided.

For these patients in a so-called complete locked-in state (CLIS), communication is very difficult to achieve. Patients in a CLIS are aware and awake but cannot move or communicate, because of complete paralysis of all voluntary muscles, including gaze control. All BCI approaches described above have been realised also for non-visual operation. Nijboer and colleagues presented a comparison of visual and auditory SMR-controlled BCI (Nijboer et al., 2008); Hinterberger and colleagues compared visual and auditory feedback and a combination of both for the SCP-BCI (Hinterberger et al., 2004); Müller-Putz and colleagues demonstrated the proof of principle with a steady-state sensorily evoked potential BCI (Müller-Putz, Scherer, Neuper, & Pfurtscheller, 2006); and, finally, Furdea and colleagues transferred the P300 spelling matrix to the auditory modality (Furdea et al., 2009) and Kübler and colleagues demonstrated its feasibility for patients with ALS (Kübler et al., 2009). In all these studies, the information transfer rate was lower for the auditory as compared to the visual modality. Currently, the auditory modality is subject to more intensive exploration (e.g., Schreuder. Blankertz, & Tangermann, 2010; Höhne, Schreuder, Blankertz, & Tangermann, 2010; Halder et al., 2010). Another approach, described below, might be to use the remaining visual capacity by reducing the spatial area on which the BCI user has to focus visual attention.

Covert Visual Attention with the P300

The visual P300 matrix speller is clearly dependent on control of one's gaze and – depending on the matrix size – on control of head movement. A recent study (Treder & Blankertz, 2010) demonstrated that performance with a P300-based BCI depends on event-related components of the visual cortex, which require overt fixation on the target. This result was verified by other BCI groups (e.g., Bianchi et al., 2010). Accordingly, for patients with oculomotor impairment, novel approaches to ERP-based spellers are required. Depending on the size of the matrix, letters are either small or located in the periphery of (or even outside) the visual field. However, the rapid decline of spatial acuity in the visual periphery makes it hard to resolve the symbols visually. Moreover, the deployment of attention is hampered by the crowding effect, which implies that it is hard to deploy attention to an object in the visual periphery when it is surrounded by other, similar objects (Strasburger, 2005). To alleviate this problem, Treder and Blankertz (2010) proposed an alternate speller design, based on the Hex-o-Spell formerly used in motor imagery paradigms (Williamson, Murray-Smith, Blankertz, Krauledat, & Müller, 2009). The ERP Hex-o-Spell breaks the selection process into two stages. The target symbols were six discs placed around the fixation point. In the first stage, the discs contained symbol groups (e.g., 'ABCDE'). Upon choice of a symbol group, the symbols in the chosen group expanded on the other discs, and the desired symbol could be selected. With covert attention, a performance increase of 50% from the result with the Matrix speller was observed.

So far, most visual spellers have been based on spatial attention alone. However, there are other forms of attention that can be exploited by visual spellers. For instance, humans can selectively attend to particular features such as colour and motion. To exploit this in a follow-up study, Treder, Schmidt, and Blankertz (submitted) used three variants of the Hex-o-Spell wherein the six different targets were also tagged by a unique colour and/or a unique shape. The targets appeared all in the centre of the screen, but their colours and shapes varied and the users paid attention to one

of them. Mean online classification performance, which was based both on the P300 component and on visually evoked potentials, was as high as 97%.

In another approach, Acqualagna, Treder, Schreuder, and Blankertz (2010) used rapid serial visual presentation (RSVP) of symbols. The stimulus consisted of rapid bursts (83 ms or 133 ms between successive symbols) of symbols at the central fixation location. Offline classification in the best setting revealed a mean accuracy over eight participants of 90% for selection of one out of 30 symbols. These approaches demonstrate that if innovative visual designs other than the classical row/column layout are considered, gaze-independent high-accuracy visual ERP spellers can be realised.

Covert Visual Attention with SSVEPs

Recently, BCI research started to integrate general results from visual attention research into the design of SSVEP-based interfaces. Kelly, Lalor, Finucane, and Reilly (2004) proposed an approach that seems applicable for CLIS patients if they have lost gaze control but maintained eyesight. In this study, healthy subjects were asked to keep their gaze on a central fixation cross while flickering stimuli (alternating checked patterns) in the left and right exterior visual field were constantly present. Without shifting their gaze direction to the flickering targets, the subjects moved their attention to the target of interest. In fact, this so-called covert attention strategy elicited stronger SSVEPs for the attended stimulus as compared to the unattended one, although the discriminative power of the approach was clearly less than with the use of strategies of overt attention with gaze shifts: in particular, the classification accuracy of the covert strategy was reduced by 20% in comparison to the overt strategy. Interestingly, the authors identified an active suppression mechanism at the contralateral hemisphere of the visual cortex during unattended stimuli as the main effect of discriminability.

Attention-Selected Overlapping SSVEPs

Other contributions to addressing the problem are the studies reported by Allison et al. (2008) and Zhang et al. (2010), both with healthy subjects. The authors experiment with two overlapping target stimuli that flicker at different frequencies but that both are located in the central visual field. By design, both targets were simultaneously visible without the need for a gaze shift. Partly transparent, neither of the two targets completely covered the whole central field. In the work of Allison et al. (2008), the stimuli were superimposed gratings and with half of the subjects the differences in SSVEP activity produced by the overlapping stimuli could yield to BCI control. Zhang et al. (2010) chose two superimposed dot patterns, rotating in opposite directions, as stimuli and obtained classification accuracies of above 70% for 10 out of 18 participants.

Visuo-Spatial Attention

In the work of Galán et al. (2007), an approach different from the ones presented before was investigated. In this work, they take advantage of the fact that it is possible to modulate EEG in subject-specific frequency bands (alpha to gamma – i.e., 8–35 Hz) by orienting visuo-spatial attention. Their goal was to allow BCI users to, for instance, turn a wheelchair just by orienting their attention (without any eye movement) to some location in the visual field. They show that it is possible to recognise the user's voluntary modulation of EEG rhythms associated with visuo-spatial attention in experiments carried out with two users, in which they are asked to attend covertly to two different locations, achieving classification rates above 80%.

All of the above-described new approaches to visual BCIs that require reduced or no gaze shifts await testing with the target patient group.

CURRENT APPLICATIONS

BCI systems are being used to operate a number of brain-actuated applications that augment people's communication capabilities, provide new forms of entertainment, and also enable the operation of physical devices. There exist virtual keyboards for selecting letters from a computer screen and writing a message (e.g., Kübler et al., 2001a). BCI-based games have been developed as well. For example, Millán (2003) illustrates the operation of a simple computer game based on the Pac-Man idea. In this game, two mental tasks are enough to control the game (turn left/right). The character changes direction of movement whenever one of the mental tasks is recognised twice in a row. In the absence of commands, Pac-Man moves forward until reaching a wall, where he stops and waits for instructions Another 'brain game' is brain pinball; for more details, the reader is referred to the work of Tangermann et al. (2009).

It is also possible to make a brain-controlled hand orthosis open and close, an example being that of Pfurtscheller's group as described by Pfurtscheller and Neuper (2001) or Kübler et al. (2001a). Wolpaw and McFarland (2004) demonstrate how subjects can learn to control two independent EEG rhythms and move a computer cursor in two dimensions. Despite these achievements, EEG-based BCIs are still considered too slow for controlling rapid and complex sequences of movements. But recent work (Millán, Renkens, Mouriño, & Gerstner, 2004a, 2004b) has shown for the first time that asynchronous analysis of EEG signals is sufficient for humans' continuous control of a mobile robot – emulating a motorised wheelchair – along non-trivial trajectories requiring fast and frequent switches between mental tasks. Two human subjects learned to drive the robot mentally between rooms in a house-like environment, visiting three or four rooms in the desired order.

HYBRID BRAIN-COMPUTER INTERFACES

As this book shows, the rapid development of eye tracking techniques has provided new avenues for the exploration of eye movements in different environments and research is no longer restricted to artificial laboratory experiments. New paradigms can now be developed and applied to more natural tasks and environments. Especially in the field of human–computer interfaces (HCI), the analysis of eye movements is becoming more important for the design of interfaces and the exploration of usability. However, one of the major problems of eye-tracking HCI remains: differentiation between eye movements serving visual orientation and the subject's intent to select an interface object. This is known in the eye tracking community as the Midas touch problem, and it is discussed in the chapter 'Computer Control by Gaze', in Section III. In recent years, interesting approaches have been proposed to overcome this effect. The solutions can be divided into two main groups. Firstly, there are systems that try to recognise selection by using only eye information, through fixation dwell time or blinking, such as the one described by Velichkovsky and Hansen (1996). Secondly, there are systems that combine eye movement with other physiological signals, such as voice control or electromyographic (EMG) signals, to activate selection – i.e., use of multi-modal interfaces. Another idea is to combine eye tracking and EEG, the feasibility of which has recently been demonstrated by Baccino and Manunta (2005) in reading tasks, and by Graupner, Velichkovsky, Pannasch, and Max (2007) during free exploration of visual scenes.

One of the aims of BCI interfaces is the restoration of motor and communicative functions for patients challenged by severe paralysis. In the most strongly affected patients, the 'locked-in' group, there is only residual motor ability and in CLIS patients there is no motor ability. As there are no other means available for those patients to communicate with the outside world, both invasive and non-invasive BCI use is warranted, within the limits set by patient consent and surgical risks. Fortunately, the number of these cases is rare. As the clinical causes of impairment can be very different and so can the residual level of motor ability, the need for assistive technology is different for every patient, and a good interface should assure use of all possible reliable signals for its control. In many cases (e.g., those of spinal-trauma-induced tetraplegia, in which arm function is lost but facial and eye muscle control remain intact), non-invasive means of restoration of motor function promise to offer significant benefits at limited risk and cost. In the case of patients who have limited control of gaze, one could explore the potential of this residual ability to augment the performance of non-invasive BCI-based spelling (i.e., communication) paradigms with the use of an eye tracker. From the current applications of BCI systems, those dedicated to communication, such as spelling devices, might be the most relevant for patients.

Despite the high speed and accuracy of eye tracking interfaces, some subjects, unfortunately, cannot benefit from this type of system, because of insufficient gaze control. Apart from the design of new interfaces based on covert attention, one way to overcome this issue could be to design hybrid interfaces wherein, for example, BCIs are used to supplement a gaze-tracking-based interface. Human–computer interaction interfaces for severely disabled people should use the remaining capabilities of each person and be designed to compensate for lost abilities, combining all useful physiological signals. Hybrid BCIs are currently being developed and extensively tested within the framework of TOBI (see http://www.tobi-project.org/).

Although the idea of combining eye tracking and EEG is attractive, not much research has been published in this direction. Some works that have addressed the design of such an interface are those of Danoczy, Fazli, Grozea, Müller, and Popescu

(2008); Popescu, Badower, Fazli, Dornhege, and Müller (2006); and Vidaurre et al. (2006). Vidaurre et al. (2006) proposed a framework for the use of EEG and eye tracking techniques in a single interface. Popescu et al. (2006) designed a hybrid interface for typing by means of EEG and gaze tracking signals, combining the Berlin BCI with an eye and head tracker. The task studied was typing via gaze directed at keys on a virtual keyboard, with a data information transfer rate of 60 bits/s, demonstrating that non-invasive BCI with gaze tracking can provide a useful, albeit limited, means of communication for paralysed patients. However, the number of subjects taking part in the study was low, and none of them were impaired. In the work of Danoczy et al. (2008), the same research group performed experiments with two non-impaired subjects using a multi-modal interface that consisted of a robot arm driven by a 3D eye tracker and an EEG-based BCI.

In conclusion, although the number of studies in the field of EEG gaze tracking interfaces is low, these have appeared promising. We would like to encourage researchers to pursue the development of such multi-modal interfaces with the combination of the very reliable gaze tracking techniques and other signals to complement them when and where necessary.

OTHER ASPECTS OF BCI RESEARCH

Currently, the field of BCI is attracting significant attention from an increasing number of research laboratories, around the world. However, fast decision-making is still a problem for BCI systems. Therefore, controlling devices such as robots, prostheses, or orthoses directly with brain signals is a very challenging application in BCI research.

A critical issue is how to improve the robustness of BCIs with the goal of making this a more practical and reliable technology. A first avenue of research is online adaptation of the interface to the user in order to keep the BCI constantly tuned to its owner. The point here is that, as subjects gain experience, they develop new capabilities and change their brain activity patterns. In addition, brain signals change naturally over time. In particular, this can be seen from one session (with which data the classifier is trained) to the next (where the classifier is applied). Therefore, online learning can be used to adapt the classifier throughout its use and keep it tuned to drifts in the signals it is receiving in each session. Preliminary results show the feasibility and benefits of this approach. Particularly significant results are that online adaptation makes it possible to complete the task of driving a wheelchair down a corridor while avoiding obstacles from the very first trial (Millán et al., 2006) or gives BCI control to users who otherwise would not be able to use a BCI (Vidaurre & Blankertz, 2010).

The second line of research involves the analysis of neural correlates of high-level cognitive and affective states such as errors, alarm, attention, frustration, and confusion. Information about these states is embedded in the EEG along with the mental commands intentionally generated by the user. Ability to detect and adapt to these states would enable the BCI to interact with the user in a much more meaningful way. One of these high-level states is the awareness of erroneous responses, whose neural correlate arises in the millisecond range. Accordingly, the user's commands could be executed only if no error is detected in this short time. Recent results have shown satisfactory single-trial recognition of errors that leads to significant improvement in BCI performance (Ferrez & Millán, 2005, 2006). In addition, this new type of error potential – which is generated in response to errors made by the BCI rather than by the user – may provide performance feedback that, in combination with online adaptation, could allow us to improve the BCI while it is being used.

A third issue is how to get a better picture of electrical activity all over the brain with high spatial accuracy without implanting electrodes

– by using instead a non-invasive estimation from scalp EEG signals. Local field potentials (LFPs) are produced from the electrical activity of small groups of neurons. LFPs have proved to be as efficient in predicting animals' behaviour or cognitive states as the information carried by the spike rate of individual neurons (Mehring et al., 2003; Pesaran, Pezaris, Sahani, Mitra, & Andersen, 2002). Recent developments in electrical neuroimaging allow the transformation of scalp-recorded EEG into estimated local field potential (eLFP) signals as if they were directly recorded within the brain (Grave de Peralta, Murray, Michel, Martuzzi, & González Andino, 2004). Non-invasive eLFP has the potential to unravel scalp EEG signals, attributing to each brain area its own temporal (spectral) activity. Preliminary results have shown significant improvements in the classification of bimanual motor tasks when eLFP is used with respect to scalp EEG (Grave de Peralta, González Andino, Perez, Ferrez, & Millán, 2005; Grave de Peralta, González, Millán, & Landis, 2006). Also, for a couple of patients with whom it was also possible to record intracranial potentials directly, eLFP and intracranial potentials had similar predictive power (Grave de Peralta et al., 2006). Finally, it is worth noting also that through this technique we can also gain better understanding of the nature of the brain activity driving the BCI.

Still a fourth issue is the nature and role of feedback for brain-actuated control. A particularly key open question is the use of multiple feedback modalities (visual, auditory, haptic, and vestibular) to accelerate user training and facilitate accurate control of the robots. The rationale behind this is that it is well known that disabled people (and healthy people too) learn better manipulation skills (among others) if they are provided with multiple sources of feedback – in particular, haptic. An additional benefit of the use of haptic feedback is freeing of visual and auditory attention to follow the process the user is controlling. This could open the way for broader use of brain-actuated devices that are able to preserve the visual and auditory processes usually engaged in normal brain surveillance activity. In this way, we hope, users will get a more precise sense of the capabilities of the robot in undertaking a task as well as of what the robot is doing, which will facilitate both the acquisition of better mental commands and conveyance of faster corrective mental commands in the event of undesired actions by the robot. Initial unpublished results seem to indicate that haptic feedback is as effective as standard visual feedback for user training.

Finally, a limiting factor of current EEG-based BCIs is the use of recording technology that requires gel for improving the conductivity of the electrical signals generated in the brain. This is a cumbersome procedure, as the right amount of gel has to be smeared on each electrode. However, recent advances in so-called dry electrodes, which require only good contact with the scalp for recording of brain signals, promise to change the situation in the coming years and enable the easy use of a large number of electrodes directly integrated into a helmet.

ACKNOWLEDGMENT

This work has been funded by the Bundesministerium fuer Bildung und Forschung (BMBF) (FKZ 01IBE01A/B); by the German Science Foundation (DFG), contract MU 987/3-1; by the EU's IST Programme under the PASCAL2 Network of Excellence, IST-216996; by the EU's Marie Curie grant number MEIF-CT-040666; and by the EU's ICT Programme under TOBI, ICT-224631, and MUNDUS. This publication only reflects the authors' views. Funding agencies are not liable for any use that may be made of the information contained herein.

REFERENCES

Acqualagna, L., Treder, M. S., Schreuder, M., & Blankertz, B. (2010). A novel brain–computer interface based on the rapid serial visual presentation paradigm. *Proceedings of the 32nd Annual International IEEE EMBS Conference.*

Allison, B. Z., McFarland, D. J., Schalk, G., Zheng, S. D., Jackson, M. M., & Wolpaw, J. R. (2008). Towards an independent brain–computer interface using steady state visual evoked potentials. *Clinical Neurophysiology, 119,* 399–408. doi:10.1016/j.clinph.2007.09.121

Babiloni, F., Cincotti, F., Lazzarini, L., Millán, J. R., Mouriño, J., Varsta, M., & Marciani, M. G. (2000). Linear classification of low-resolution EEG patterns produced by imagined hand movements. *IEEE Transactions on Rehabilitation Engineering, 8,* 186–188. doi:10.1109/86.847810

Baccino, T., & Manunta, Y. (2005). Eye-fixation related potentials: Insight into parafoveal processing. *Journal of Psychophysiology, 19,* 204–215. doi:10.1027/0269-8803.19.3.204

Bauernfeind, G., Leeb, R., Wriessnegger, S. C., & Pfurtscheller, G. (2008). Development, set-up and first results for a one-channel near-infrared spectroscopy system. *Biomedizinische Technik, 53,* 36–43. doi:10.1515/BMT.2008.005

Bianchi, L., Sami, S., Hillebrand, A., Fawcett, I. P., Quitadamo, L. R., & Seri, S. (2010). Which physiological components are more suitable for visual ERP based brain–computer interface? A preliminary MEG/EEG study. *Brain Topography, 23*(2), 180–185. doi:10.1007/s10548-010-0143-0

Birbaumer, N., Ghanayim, N., Hinterberger, T., Iversen, I., Kotchoubey, B., Kübler, A., & Flor, H. (1999). A spelling device for the paralysed. *Nature, 398,* 297–298. doi:10.1038/18581

Blankertz, B., Dornhege, G., Krauledat, M., Müller, K.-R., & Curio, G. (2007). The non-invasive Berlin brain–computer interface: Fast acquisition of effective performance in untrained subjects. *NeuroImage, 37,* 539–550. doi:10.1016/j.neuroimage.2007.01.051

Blankertz, B., Dornhege, G., Schäfer, C., Krepki, R., Kohlmorgen, J., Müller, K.-R., & Curio, G. (2003). Boosting bit rates and error detection for the classification of fast-paced motor commands based on single-trial EEG analysis. *IEEE Transactions on Neural Systems and Rehabilitation Engineering, 11,* 127–131. doi:10.1109/TNSRE.2003.814456

Blankertz, B., Losch, F., Krauledat, M., Dornhege, G., Curio, G., & Müller, K.-R. (2008a). The Berlin brain–computer interface: Accurate performance from first-session in BCI-naive subjects. *IEEE Transactions on Bio-Medical Engineering, 55,* 2452–2462. doi:10.1109/TBME.2008.923152

Blankertz, B., Tomioka, R., Lemm, S., Kawanabe, M., & Müller, K.-R. (2008). Optimizing spatial filters for robust EEG single-trial analysis. *IEEE Signal Processing Magazine, 25,* 41–56. doi:10.1109/MSP.2008.4408441

Buch, E., Weber, C., Cohen, L. G., Braun, C., Dimyan, M. A., Ard, T., & Birbaumer, N. (2008). Think to move: A neuromagnetic brain–computer interface (BCI) system for chronic stroke. *Stroke, 39,* 910–917. doi:10.1161/STROKEAHA.107.505313

Danoczy, M., Fazli, S., Grozea, C., Müller, K.-R., & Popescu, F. (2008). Brain2Robot: A grasping robot arm controlled by gaze and asynchronous EEG BCI. *Proceedings of the 4th International Brain–Computer Interface Workshop and Training Course,* 355–360.

Dornhege, G., Millán, J. R., Hinterberger, T., McFarland, D., & Müller, K.-R. (2007). *Towards brain–computer interfacing.* Cambridge, MA, USA: MIT Press.

Farwell, L. A., & Donchin, E. (1988). Talking off the top of your head: Toward a mental prosthesis utilizing event related brain potentials. *Electroencephalography and Clinical Neurophysiology, 70,* 510–523. doi:10.1016/0013-4694(88)90149-6

Ferrez, P. W., & Millán, J. R. (2005). You are wrong! – Automatic detection of interaction errors from brain waves. *Proceedings of the 19th International Joint Conference on Artificial Intelligence.*

Ferrez, P. W., & Millán, J. R. (2006). Error-related EEG potentials in brain–computer interfaces. In Dornhege, G., Millán, J. R., Hinterberger, T., McFarland, D., & Müller, K.-R. (Eds.), *Towards brain–computer interfacing* (pp. 291–302). Cambridge, MA, USA: MIT Press.

Furdea, A., Halder, S., Krusienski, D. J., Bross, D., Nijboer, F., Birbaumer, N., & Kübler, A. (2009). An auditory oddball (P300) spelling system for brain–computer interfaces. *Psychophysiology, 46,* 617–625. doi:10.1111/j.1469-8986.2008.00783.x

Galán, F., Palix, J., Chavarriaga, R., Ferrez, P. W., Lew, E., Hauert, C. A., & Millán, J. del R. (2007). *Visuo-spatial attention frame recognition for brain–computer interfaces.* Proceedings of the 1st International Conference on Cognitive Neurodynamics.

Graupner, S. T., Velichkovsky, B. M., Pannasch, S., & Max, J. (2007). Surprise, surprise: Two distinct components in the visually evoked distractor effect. *Psychophysiology, 44,* 251–261. doi:10.1111/j.1469-8986.2007.00504.x

Grave de Peralta, R., González, S. L., Millán, J. R., & Landis, T. (2006). Local field potentials estimation from the EEG for the study of neural oscillations and the development of direct non-invasive brain computer interfaces. *Proceedings of the 11th International Conference on Functional Mapping of the Human Brain.*

Grave de Peralta Menendez, R., González Andino, S., Perez, L., Ferrez, P. W., & Millán, J. R. (2005). Non-invasive estimation of local field potentials for neuroprosthesis control. *Cognitive Processing, 6,* 59–64. doi:10.1007/s10339-004-0043-x

Grave de Peralta Menendez, R., Murray, M. M., Michel, C. M., Martuzzi, R., & González Andino, S. L. (2004). Electrical neuroimaging based on biophysical constraints. *NeuroImage, 21,* 527–539. doi:10.1016/j.neuroimage.2003.09.051

Halder, S., Rea, M., Andreoni, R., Nijboer, F., Hammer, E. M., Kleih, S., & Kübler, A. (2010). An auditory oddball brain–computer interface for binary choices. *Clinical Neurophysiology, 121,* 516–523. doi:10.1016/j.clinph.2009.11.087

Hinterberger, T., Neumann, N., Pham, M., Kübler, A., Grether, A., Hofmayer, N., & Birbaumer, N. (2004). A multimodal brain-based feedback and communication system. *Experimental Brain Research, 154,* 521–526. doi:10.1007/s00221-003-1690-3

Hochberg, L. R., Serruya, M. D., Friehs, G. M., Mukand, J. A., Saleh, M., Caplan, A. H., & Donoghue, J. P. (2006). Neuronal ensemble control of prosthetic devices by a human with tetraplegia. *Nature, 442,* 164–171. doi:10.1038/nature04970

Höhne, J., Schreuder, M., Blankertz, B., & Tangermann, M. (2010). Two-dimensional auditory P300 Speller with predictive text system. *Proceedings of the 32nd Annual International IEEE EMBS Conference.*

Jasper, H. H. (1958). The ten-twenty electrode system of the International Federation. *Electroencephalography and Clinical Neurophysiology, 10,* 371–375.

Kauhanen, L., Nykopp, T., & Sams, M. (2006). Classification of single MEG trials related to left and right index finger movements. *Clinical Neurophysiology, 117,* 430–439. doi:10.1016/j.clinph.2005.10.024

Kelly, S. P., Lalor, E., Finucane, C., & Reilly, R. B. (2004). A comparison of covert and overt attention as a control option in a steady-state visual evoked potential-based brain computer interface. *Proceedings of the 26th Annual International Conference of the EMBS* (pp. 4725–4728).

Kennedy, P. R., Bakay, R., Moore, M. M., Adams, K., & Goldwaithe, J. (2000). Direct control of a computer from the human central nervous system. *IEEE Transactions on Rehabilitation Engineering, 8,* 198–202. doi:10.1109/86.847815

Kübler, A., Furdea, A., Halder, S., Hammer, E. M., Nijboer, F., & Kotchoubey, B. (2009). A brain–computer interface controlled auditory event-related potential (p300) spelling system for locked-in patients. *Annals of the New York Academy of Sciences, 1157,* 90–100. doi:10.1111/j.1749-6632.2008.04122.x

Kübler, A., Kotchoubey, B., Hinterberger, T., Ghanayim, N., Perelmouter, J., Schauer, M., & Birbaumer, N. (1999). The thought translation device: A neurophysiological approach to communication in total motor paralysis. *Experimental Brain Research, 124,* 223–232. doi:10.1007/s002210050617

Kübler, A., Kotchoubey, B., Kaiser, J., Wolpaw, J. R., & Birbaumer, N. (2001). Brain computer communication: Unlocking the locked in. *Psychological Bulletin, 127,* 358–375. doi:10.1037/0033-2909.127.3.358

Kübler, A., & Müller, K.-R. (2006). An introduction to brain–computer interfacing. In Dornhege, G., Millán, J. D. R., Hinterberger, T., McFarland, D., & Müller, K.-R. (Eds.), *Towards brain–computer interfacing* (pp. 1–25). Cambridge, MA, USA: MIT Press.

Kübler, A., Neumann, N., Kaiser, J., Kotchoubey, B., Hinterberger, T., & Birbaumer, N. (2001a). Brain–computer communication: Self-regulation of slow cortical potentials for verbal communication. *Archives of Physical Medicine and Rehabilitation, 82,* 1533–1539. doi:10.1053/apmr.2001.26621

Kübler, A., Nijboer, F., Mellinger, J., Vaughan, T. M., Pawelzik, H., Schalk, G., & Wolpaw, J. R. (2005). Patients with ALS can use sensorimotor rhythms to operate a brain–computer interface. *Neurology, 64,* 1775–1777. doi:10.1212/01.WNL.0000158616.43002.6D

Lal, T. N., Schröder, M., Hill, J., Preissl, H., Hinterberger, T., Mellinger, J., & Schölkopf, B. (2005). A brain computer interface with online feedback based on magnetoencephalography. In L. De Raedt & S. Wrobel (Eds.), *Proceedings of the 22nd International Conference on Machine Learning* (pp. 465–472).

Mehring, C., Rickert, J., Vaadia, E., Cardoso de Oliveira, S., Aertsen, A., & Rotter, S. (2003). Inference of hand movements from local field potentials in monkey motor cortex. *Nature Neuroscience, 6,* 1253–1254. doi:10.1038/nn1158

Mellinger, J., Schalk, G., Braun, C., Preissl, H., Rosenstiel, W., Birbaumer, N., & Kübler, A. (2007). An MEG-based brain–computer interface (BCI). *NeuroImage, 36*(3), 581–593. doi:10.1016/j.neuroimage.2007.03.019

Millán, J. del R. (2003). Adaptive brain interfaces. *Communications of the ACM, 46,* 74–80. doi:10.1145/636772.636773

Millán, J. del R., Buttfield, A., Vidaurre, C., Krauledat, M., Schögl, A., Shenoy, P., & Müller, K.-R. (2006). Adaptation in brain–computer interfaces. In Dornhege, G., Millán, J. R., Hinterberger, T., McFarland, D., & Müller, K.-R. (Eds.), *Towards brain–computer interfacing* (pp. 303–326). Cambridge, MA, USA: MIT Press.

Millán, J. del R., Mouriño, J., Franzé, M., Cincotti, F., Varsta, M., Heikkonen, J., & Babiloni, F. (2002). A local neural classifier for the recognition of EEG patterns associated to mental tasks. *IEEE Transactions on Neural Networks*, *13*, 678–686. doi:10.1109/TNN.2002.1000132

Millán, J. del R., Renkens, F., Mouriño, J., & Gerstner, W. (2004a). Brain-actuated interaction. *Artificial Intelligence*, *159*, 241–259. doi:10.1016/j.artint.2004.05.008

Millán, J. del R., Renkens, F., Mouriño, J., & Gerstner, W. (2004b). Non-invasive brain-actuated control of a mobile robot by human EEG. *IEEE Transactions on Bio-Medical Engineering*, *51*, 1026–1033. doi:10.1109/TBME.2004.827086

Müller-Putz, G. R., Scherer, R., Neuper, C., & Pfurtscheller, G. (2006). Steady-state somatosensory evoked potentials: Suitable brain signals for brain–computer interfaces? *IEEE Transactions on Neural Systems and Rehabilitation Engineering*, *14*, 30–37. doi:10.1109/TNSRE.2005.863842

Nijboer, F., Furdea, A., Gunst, I., Mellinger, J., McFarland, D., Birbaumer, N., & Kübler, A. (2008). An auditory brain–computer interface. *Journal of Neuroscience Methods*, *167*(1), 43–50. doi:10.1016/j.jneumeth.2007.02.009

Owen, A. M., Coleman, M. R., Boly, M., Davis, M. H., Laureys, S., & Pickard, J. D. (2006). Detecting awareness in the vegetative state. *Science*, *313*(5792), 1402. doi:10.1126/science.1130197

Pesaran, B., Pezaris, J. S., Sahani, M., Mitra, P. P., & Andersen, R. A. (2002). Temporal structure in neuronal activity during working memory in macaque parietal cortex. *Nature Neuroscience*, *5*, 805–811. doi:10.1038/nn890

Pfurtscheller, G., & Neuper, C. (1997). Motor imagery activates primary sensorimotor area in humans. *Neuroscience Letters*, *239*, 65–68. doi:10.1016/S0304-3940(97)00889-6

Pfurtscheller, G., & Neuper, C. (2001). Motor imagery and direct brain–computer communication. *IEEE Proceedings*, *89*, 1123–1134. doi:10.1109/5.939829

Popescu, F., Badower, Y., Fazli, S., Dornhege, G., & Müller, K.-R. (2006). EEG-based control of reaching to visual targets. In A. J. Ijspeert, J. Buchli, A. Selverston, M. Rabinovich, M. Hasler, W. Gerstner, D. Floreano (Eds.), *Dynamical Principles for Neuroscience and Intelligent Biomimetic Devices – Abstracts of the EPFL-LATSIS Symposium 2006*, Lausanne, Switzerland (pp. 123–124).

Schreuder, M., Blankertz, B., & Tangermann, M. (2010). A new auditory multi-class brain–computer interface paradigm: Spatial hearing as an informative cue. *PLoS ONE*, *5*(4), e9813. doi:10.1371/journal.pone.0009813

Sitaram, R., Zhang, H., Guan, C., Thulasidas, M., Hoshi, Y., Ishikawa, A., & Birbaumer, N. (2007). Temporal classification of multichannel near-infrared spectroscopy signals of motor imagery for developing a brain–computer interface. *NeuroImage*, *34*(4), 1416–1427. doi:10.1016/j.neuroimage.2006.11.005

Strasburger, H. (2005). Unfocussed spatial attention underlies the crowding effect in indirect form vision. *Journal of Vision (Charlottesville, Va.)*, *5*, 1024–1037. doi:10.1167/5.11.8

Tangermann, M., Krauledat, M., Grzeska, K., Sagebaum, M., Blankertz, B., Vidaurre, C., & Müller, K.-R. (2009). Playing pinball with non-invasive BCI. [Cambridge, MA: MIT Press.]. *Advances in Neural Information Processing Systems, 21*, 1641–1648.

Treder, M. S., & Blankertz, B. (2010). (C)overt attention and visual speller design in an ERP-based brain–computer interface. *Behavioral and Brain Functions, 6*, 28. doi:10.1186/1744-9081-6-28

Treder, M. S., Schmidt, N. M., & Blankertz, B. (n. d.). *Gaze-independent high-accuracy brain–computer interfaces based on covert spatial attention and non-spatial feature attention.*

Velichkovsky, B. M., & Hansen, J. P. (1996). New technological windows into mind: There is more in eyes and brains for human–computer interaction. *Proceedings of the SIGCHI conference on Human factors in computing systems: common ground (CHI '96)*. New York, NY: ACM Press. doi:10.1145/238386.238619

Vidal, J. J. (1977). Real-time detection of brain events in EEG. *IEEE Proceedings, 65*, 633–664. doi:10.1109/PROC.1977.10542

Vidaurre, C., & Blankertz, B. (2010). Towards a cure for BCI illiteracy. *Brain Topography, 23*, 194–198. doi:10.1007/s10548-009-0121-6

Vidaurre, C., Villanueva, A., Scherer, R., Joos, M., Schlögl, A., Pannasch, S., & Cabeza, R. (2006). Multi-modal interface: Gaze-EEG-based system. *Proceedings of the 2nd Conference on Communication by Gaze Interaction (COGAIN 2006)* (pp. 50-54). Retrieved from http://www.cogain.org/conference

Williamson, J., Murray-Smith, R., Blankertz, B., Krauledat, M., & Müller, K.-R. (2009). Designing for uncertain, asymmetric control: Interaction design for brain–computer interfaces. *International Journal of Human-Computer Studies, 67*, 827–841. doi:10.1016/j.ijhcs.2009.05.009

Wolpaw, J. R., Birbaumer, N., McFarland, D. J., Pfurtscheller, G., & Vaughan, T. M. (2002). Brain–computer interfaces for communication and control. *Clinical Neurophysiology, 113*, 767–791. doi:10.1016/S1388-2457(02)00057-3

Wolpaw, J. R., & McFarland, D. J. (2004). Control of a two-dimensional movement signal by a noninvasive brain–computer interface in humans. *Proceedings of the National Academy of Sciences of the United States of America, 101*, 17849–17854. doi:10.1073/pnas.0403504101

Wolpaw, J. R., McFarland, D. J., & Vaughan, T. M. (2000). Brain–computer interface research at the Wadsworth Center. *IEEE Transactions on Rehabilitation Engineering, 8*, 222–226. doi:10.1109/86.847823

Zhang, D., Maye, A., Gao, X., Hong, B., Engel, A. K., & Gao, S. (2010). An independent brain–computer interface using covert non-spatial visual selective attention. *Journal of Neural Engineering, 7*, 016010. doi:10.1088/1741-2560/7/1/016010

Zhu, D., Bieger, J., Garcia Molina, G., & Aarts, R. M. (2010). A survey of stimulation methods used in SSVEP-based BCIs. *Computational Intelligence and Neuroscience*, article ID 702357. doi:10.1155/2010/702357

Chapter 13
Gaze–Aware Systems and Attentive Applications

Howell Istance
De Montfort University, UK

Aulikki Hyrskykari
University of Tampere, Finland

ABSTRACT

In this chapter, we examine systems that use the current focus of a person's visual attention to make the system easier to use, less effortful and, hopefully, more efficient. If the system can work out which object the person is interested in, or is likely to interact with next, then the need for the person to deliberately point at, or otherwise identify that object to the system can be removed. This approach can be applied to interaction with real-world objects and people as well as to objects presented on a display close to the system user. We examine just what we can infer about a person's focus of visual attention, and their intention to do something from studying their eye movements, and what, if anything, the system should do about it. A detailed example of an attentive system is presented where the system estimates the difficulty a reader has understanding individual words when reading in a foreign language, and displays a translation automatically if it thinks it is needed.

INTRODUCTION

In this chapter, we will examine how knowledge of what a person is currently interested in or attending to can be used to make computer-based systems easier to deal with, less effortful, and – it is hoped – more efficient to use. As we don't

want a person to keep telling the system what the object of current interest is, we will try to infer this by monitoring the users as they use the system. There are many clues we can use, such as contextual information on what they are doing, what they have just done, or what they usually do at this time of day. However, as we saw in the first chapter in this section (Chapter 11 by Mulvey and Heubner), the most reliable way of getting

DOI: 10.4018/978-1-61350-098-9.ch013

information about the current focus of someone's attention is by monitoring gaze behaviour. This can be supplemented by additional information, with brain activity – the topic of the second chapter of this section (Chapter 12 by Vidaurre, Kübler, Tangermann, Müller, and Millán) – being one of the future possibilities.

We will use the term '*attentive system*' to describe a computer system that changes state on the basis of inferences about what the user of the system is currently attending to and, in some cases, intending to do as a consequence. An attentive system uses real-time measurement of gaze position and possibly of other physiological indicators to do this. This doesn't mean that the system second-guesses what the user will do and takes some action on the user's behalf automatically, although in certain circumstances this might be appropriate. It may simply mean that the action the user is most likely to want to perform next is offered as a default command.

We should consider other similar terms used to describe computer systems to clarify where the similarities and the differences lie. The term '*adaptive systems*' refers to systems that make use of knowledge of the tasks a person is performing in order to modify or adapt the current state of the system. To do this, these often make reference to a model of individual user preferences, and of similar tasks undertaken previously. Knowledge of the tasks is obtained from a log of commands the user has entered into the systems at different times. *Affective systems* typically try to take account of a user's current emotional (or affective) state. This state can be inferred from a variety of input modalities or sources, including facial expression, voice, heart rate, and pressure on a keypad during its use. This could be used to make feedback from the system appear to be sensitive or responsive to the current state of the person using it.

The term '*ubiquitous computing*' refers to computation embedded in basic objects, environments, and activities of our everyday lives in such a way that no-one will notice its presence (Weiser, 1999). This includes the idea of *tangible user interfaces*, where input and output devices are integrated with *real-world* objects (rather than the familiar dedicated devices) that someone can pick up, squeeze, shake, move around, and so on. These objects are also candidates to be made gaze-aware and attentive.

The term '*context-aware systems*' is a broad term that generally incorporates all of the above. It appears in different fields of computer systems research and development, not least in mobile technologies, which we will further examine below.

Importantly, in all of the above-mentioned types of system, there are two distinct phases: 1) determining what the current state of the person using the system is and 2) deciding what, if anything, to do with that information. The boundaries between the systems described by the terms used above are blurred, and these often overlap. The focus of this chapter will be on systems that make active use of a person's gaze position and eye movements.

Context-Awareness and the Importance of Context

Mobile devices (including phones) are equipped with the capability of continually sending information back to central computers. Importantly, this includes information about where the person is in relation to places and other people. This information allows different types of context to be defined and built for a person's current activity. Mobile devices are often equipped with accelerometers, which can detect motion. Integrating this information with, say, a person's online calendar can enable inferences to be drawn about the person's current activity. If, for example, the position of the device is changing rapidly, as indicated by the GPS sensor in the device, but the device is not bouncing up and down, it is likely that, if the time is before 9am and it is a work day, the person is driving or being driven, say, to work. Mobile services can then be adapted to be sensitive to the user's current context. An example frequently given of adaptation to what a person is currently doing is call management. If the device thinks the user is in a meeting, it can automatically put the phone function in silent mode, except if the caller has been identified as an exception, such as a family member. There are many, different contexts in which to consider a person's activity (Huuskonen, Salminen, & Lehikoinen, 2010). There is the *work* context: what tasks should be in progress now? There is the *social* context: where are the person's social networking 'friends' now? Is one just around the corner? There is an *information* context consisting of Web pages, e-mail, weather reports, and restaurant reviews, all of which may be retrieved to the device, depending on the person's current activity (to support, say, being able to check a bank balance when about to buy something). There are also *environmental*, *spatio-temporal*, *device*, *network*, and *service* contexts. In all of this passive monitoring of a person's context, gaze-aware attentive systems can be seen as part of this picture. We can think of attentive systems as the real-time 'right now' subset of context-awareness.

From a very early stage in consideration of user interface design, the importance of *context* has been recognised. Why ask the user to specify an instruction fully if the computer can use default values on the basis of what the user is currently doing? Even early on, pressing F1 would often cause help to be displayed about whatever the user happened to be doing at the time. Context has become a fundamental aspect of interface design whereby the command set available is determined by the application object that is currently being used. Since the late 1980s, CAD systems have configured the user interface to restrict the commands available at any one time to the phase of the job currently in progress. Since the early 1990s, desktop applications have used a pop-up menu. When the right mouse button was pressed over an object, the menu showed only those commands that could be applied to the particular object in focus. Microsoft have taken the principle of context much further in their Fluent interface to Microsoft Office products, and the whole interface is reconfigured (as opposed to just the contents of a pop-up menu) according to the currently active object. Microsoft's motive in this has been to make the user aware of functionality that is relevant in a particular context that otherwise may not have been discovered.

TOWARD ATTENTIVE SYSTEMS

Changing Perspectives of Computer Use: How Hard Should it be?

In the early 1970s, mainframe-based administrative systems were used by large numbers of office workers. There was often a question of how scarce computing resources should be utilised: for processing and increased functionality, or for improving the user interface and consequently the ease of use of those systems. Paying attention to the design of the user interface was sometimes seen as an optional extra, particularly when office workers had no choice in the system they used at work. Ease of use of these systems became an occupational health concern, alongside the ergonomics of workstation design.

The advent of personal computing in the late 1970s and early 1980s changed this perception dramatically. Initially, the IBM PC specification made computers available for home and office use. The users of these, however, still had to master operating system command languages in order to manage programs, which in themselves were very different in the way they worked. The release of the Macintosh by Apple (1984) and its graphical user interface (GUI) changed perceptions of how easy using a computer could be, through good and careful design of the user interface.

By comparison, command languages, such as MS-DOS and UNIX, were difficult to use and error-prone, even if they were a more expressive and powerful means of interaction. Early adaptive systems were attempts to improve the usability of these command languages. If, for example, the computer detected that the user was carrying out the same command over and over again, perhaps deleting single files, one at a time, automatic suggestions could be made about shortcuts, command parameters, or wildcard characters. The purpose was to make the users aware of easier ways of doing the job, by informing them of possibilities they might not know existed. The essence of these systems was to make inferences about what the user wanted to do on the basis of patterns of input commands, then take some automatic action to help the user do it. Of course, there was a considerable penalty if the system got it wrong and took some action that the user would then have to undo.

The user interface to automatic adaptive behaviour requires very careful design, to ensure that it is not intrusive to the user's normal work. If it is, then there is considerable risk that the user will be irritated and disable the adaptive functionality entirely. The application of artificial intelligence techniques to carry out these tasks, and the encapsulation of these into standalone software, resulted in what we now know as intelligent interface agents. These agents have generally routine tasks delegated to them. Now the design challenge is to ensure sufficient transparency that human users know what the agent is doing on their behalf.

The proliferation of personal computing resulted in the cost of hardware declining. More processing power and computer resources could be dedicated to the user interface. At the same time, the market for different software products was increasing, and the importance of usability or 'user-friendliness' as a marketing feature of products grew. The perception of the computer was transformed gradually from a technically complex machine that somehow had to be mastered into a tool that people expected to be able to use for an increasing variety of activities related to work,

education, and leisure. Now, as the phenomenal success of Apple's iPhone testifies, the quality of the user interface can be the most important feature of a computer product.

Changing Computing Platforms

Several trends over the last two decades have implications concerning the feasibility and utility of attentive systems.

First, there has been a move away from desktop monitors and keyboards as the main means of communicating with computers towards more diverse platforms of input and output devices. Input devices can now measure much of the user's physical activity, for example, whether a person is walking or standing still; detect gestures; measure eye position; and so on. Multi-touch gestures are becoming a common means of interaction with smartphones and tablet devices. Output devices can be dedicated monitors as before, either standalone or an integral part of a laptop or netbook; flexible and wearable displays embedded in clothing; multipurpose displays such as flat-screen television sets; or single-purpose consumer electronics devices such as cameras and projectors. They can provide haptic feedback (i.e., feedback related to touch) as well as visual and auditory feedback.

Second, the widespread use of mobile technology has led to the integration of voice and data communications and computing services into small hand-held devices.

Third, mobile autonomous robots are emerging as platforms through which intelligent software agents undertake tasks on behalf of human users. These tasks range from routine jobs such as cleaning hospital corridors to providing entertainment in the form of toy-like animals that respond to speech and touch. Interaction with these autonomous robots can include a user's gaze direction if the robot can sense when a human user is looking at it. This can make the robot appear to be responsive, and interaction with it appears to be more natural.

The implications for gaze-based attentive systems are that miniature video camera technology has reached the stage where embedding even several cameras in display devices such as mobile smartphones, netbook computers, and head-mounted displays is not expensive. This provides the potential for some form of eye tracking, depending on the cameras' field of view and resolution. The downside for effective monitoring of gaze is that computing devices can now be used in a wide variety of locations and lighting conditions. The display areas of mobile devices are small when compared with desktop monitors, and, consequently, the range of eye movements for looking from one side of the device to the other is also small. A hand-held display surface can be moved in relation to the user's head, which means that calibration of any gaze tracker mounted in the device itself would need to incorporate some element of measuring its own position.

It is highly unlikely that the accuracy of gaze tracking in the use of hand-held mobile devices will approach that currently obtained with fixed large desktop monitors. It may well be that attentive responses will be based only on the knowledge that the user is looking at the display, rather than where on the display the user is looking. Alternatively, some approximate gaze position within the display may be calculated, or relative changes in gaze direction may be detected ('looks up', 'looks left', etc.). Miluzzo, Wang, and Campbell (2010) describe a system mounted in a smartphone that enables detection by gaze of a cell from a 3 x 3 grid displayed on the phones screen. Mobile gaze tracking systems could be used to provide some form of attentive response, particularly as part of a larger context-aware system.

Changing User Populations

The last 20 years have also seen revolutionary changes to the user population of computer systems. Internet access of households in Europe has been growing rapidly in recent years. In 2009, 70%

of all households in the UK and 78% in Finland had Internet access, which was an 11% and 6% increase from the previous year's level, respectively, and 63% of UK households and 70% of Finnish households had a broadband connection to the Internet. This level of access to the Internet has had a huge impact on our day-to-day life, with nearly all aspects being influenced in some way – social computing, games, changing views of entertainment, shopping, etc. It has also led to a much greater level of sophistication within the general public in terms of ability to use software applications and expectations concerning the usability of different software products.

It is worth noting too that increased user sophistication in terms of using software applications doesn't mean that people have greater technical insights into computer systems and the way they work. However, the high expectations that users in general have of the quality of interaction with the software they use will impose great demands on the design of attentive systems. If an attentive system 'gets it wrong' in anticipating what a person is interested in doing, then any automatic response that is not considered to be useful is likely to be disabled quickly by the person using it.

BACKGROUND TO DESIGN AND BUILDING OF ATTENTIVE SYSTEMS

Command vs. Non-Command-Based Interaction

Since the early days of interactive computing, command-based interaction has been the predominant paradigm. The person using the system gives the computer a command, and the computer attempts to complete the instruction and gives the user some sort of feedback about how successful this has been. Many different interaction techniques have evolved to support giving the computer commands and to display system feedback. The underlying principle, though, is the same: the commands are explicit, and interaction with the computer is deliberate. However, even back in the early 1990s, people were looking toward a *non-command-based* means of interaction (Nielsen, 1993), wherein the computer would adapt its behaviour on the basis of its knowledge of what the user was currently doing.

A simple example given then was that the computer could display the text on the screen in a large font if the user was standing in the room but at some distance from the monitor. The user would be unlikely to give an explicit command to display text in a large font for time spent away from the desk. Nielsen talked about 12 dimensions of interaction, but the most significant was the computer's role, changing from 'obeying orders literally' to 'interpreting user actions and doing what it deems appropriate'.

A couple of years earlier, Jacob (1991) presented a series of eye-gaze-based interaction techniques. He dismissed the notion of controlling a mouse pointer by gaze and using gaze to generate deliberate mouse click events, since eye movements, he argued, are made unconsciously. He advocated instead more natural forms of interaction wherein the information displayed would respond to the user's gaze position automatically. For example, in a situation display of ship targets, information about the ship that the user is currently looking at could be retrieved and displayed automatically, without the user having to request this. Another example was that the contents of a window could be scrolled upward if previous gaze behaviour suggested that the user had read to the bottom of what was currently being displayed. The assumption was made that the user was probably going to scroll the contents upward. This is a very apposite technique, as, even today, usability problems arise when people aren't aware that there is more information below that currently visible, as they don't attend to the scrollbar.

An Early Attentive System

One of the earliest examples of a gaze-based attentive system was a 'self-disclosing gaze-responsive' display by Starker and Bolt (1990). In this system, a person looked at a virtual world displayed on a screen containing objects associated with a story. This story was *The Little Prince* by de Saint-Exupéry, and the objects included a planet, stairs, and the prince himself (see Figure 1).

As the user looked at different objects, an index of interest was assigned to each and the spoken commentary from the system to the user was modified according to an assumed level of user interest in the displayed objects. Looking at several objects resulted in a moderate index of interest being assigned to each, and the system gave a general commentary about those objects.

Figure 1. Starker and Bolt's self-disclosing display and a gaze path of a subject observer looking about a temporarily stopped planet (Starker & Bolt, 1990). © 1990 ACM. Reprinted with permission

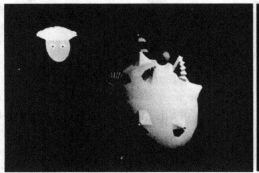 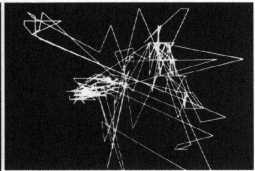

Figure 2. Components of an attentive system. © 2010 Istance and Hyrskykari. Used with permission

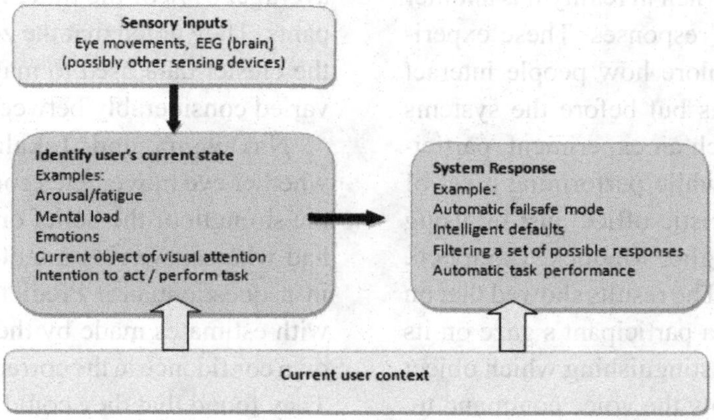

Looking at one object in particular resulted in a high index of interest being assigned to that object and the spoken commentary was modified to concentrate on that object. The system made assumptions about what the person was interested in on the basis of information about what that user was looking at, and modified its behaviour accordingly. This is the essence of attentive systems.

Components of an Attentive System

We can think of attentive systems as having the components shown in Figure 2.

There are four main components in an attentive system. First, there is a means of sensing a person's current state while they are using the system. The attentive systems we are describing rely mainly on visual attention, sensing where a person is looking at any given time. This may be supplemented in the future by additional information about brain activity. Second, depending on the purpose of the system in question, some assessment of the current state of the user can be made. At a low level, this may simply be an assessment of fatigue or arousal levels. At a higher level, inferences may be made about what objects the person is currently attending to. At a higher level still, predictions may be made about the user's intention to perform a particular task.

Third, an appropriate response is formulated on the basis of what the purpose of the system is and the current user state. Fourth, these stages can be mediated by a wider knowledge of the current context surrounding the person's activities.

IDENTIFYING THE CURRENT STATE OF A USER OF AN ATTENTIVE SYSTEM

The measurement of a person's gaze position has been covered elsewhere in this book. We will now look at what inferences we can make about the person's current state.

Focus of Attention

In the first chapter in this section, we saw that our gaze is directed by things that we are attending to, have just attended to, or are about to attend to. We also saw that gaze fixations are generally accepted as the most accessible indication of the object of our visual attention and that there is a close coupling between changes in visual attention and changes in what we fixate on.

Looking at the target of the next action is a natural behaviour in many situations. A 'Wizard of Oz' experiment creates an illusion that a system is doing something automatically (such as answering questions) when in reality it is another person generating the responses. These experiments are used to explore how people interact with computer systems but before the systems have been built. In such an experiment, participants were observed while performing a set of office tasks in a 'futuristic office' just by using voice commands (Maglio, Matlock, Campbell, Zhai, & Smith, 2000). The results showed that on 98% of the occasions a participant's gaze on its own was enough for distinguishing which object the user wanted to apply the voice command to. Users naturally looked at the target device when giving – often before and sometimes during – the commands. Oh et al. (2002) found the same result, showing how glances were a natural way of indicating the object of a command in another Wizard of Oz experiment when addressing 'Sam', an animated agent.

Intention to Act

The focus of a person's gaze already gives us a rough prediction that some action may be initiated at that location. We can record changes in this focus over time in the form of a list of gaze fixations, or the 'gaze path'. Combined with other information available about the environment and the user, and the logic of the application, this may enable us to predict what the person will do next, or, in other words, the person's intentions in the very near future.

Logging and analysis of gaze data may reveal consistent patterns prior to a particular task being carried out, and these patterns can then be used to predict whether or not a person will do something. Goldberg and Schryver (1993) investigated whether eye movements could be used in this way to classify which of three actions were performed (to zoom in, zoom out, or do neither) while participants were performing tasks involving information retrieval using a graphical user interface. They found that the best single metric derived from analysis of clusters of gaze points was

able to classify the command chosen correctly, on average, 61% of the time, for individual participants. They noted that the zones used to separate the cluster data used to make the classifications varied considerably between participants.

Nakayama and Takahasi (2006) studied whether eye movements could be used to predict the strength of the belief or confidence a person had when answering a multiple-choice question in a questionnaire. Predictions were compared with estimates made by the participants of their own confidence in the correctness of their answer. They found that they could make correct predictions of either high or low confidence 68% of the time solely on the basis of analysis of gaze paths

Another system (Bee, Prendiger, Nakasone, André, & Ishisuka, 2006) looked at making predictions about which necktie a person would choose when given a number of alternatives designs to choose from as part of a laboratory experiment. This is more a question of estimating an emotional or affective response when a person is asked to express a preference. The pattern of fixations followed what the authors described as a 'cascade effect', where the preferred object gradually received more and more attention in terms of fixations until it was finally selected. In one experiment, the system chose the tie that it was expected a person would like on the basis of analysis of gaze scan paths, and the participant was to confirm whether this was indeed the preferred tie. The success rate here was 81%. However this dropped to 72% when participants were asked to make a choice themselves and the estimate was made independently.

Gaze isn't necessarily the best indicator of intention to act. In one study of driver behaviour, head movements rather than eye movements were found to be a better predictor of the intention to change lanes while one was driving (Doshi & Trivedi, 2009).

There are two issues here: first, the extent to which single metrics based on gaze data can consistently predict that a person will take a particular action and, second, how far in advance of that action such a prediction can be made.

Mental Load and Fatigue

The possibility of identifying mental load when performing computer-based tasks without disturbing the human user can be very valuable, say, in the case of control systems. If the mental load increases to a threshold level, the application could take some action, perhaps by giving appropriate warnings, or by offering to take some tasks under automatic control.

As we saw in the first chapter in this section, mental load and fatigue do affect several eye movement measures. Studies have indicated that mental load affects fixation duration, saccade amplitude and velocity, blinking rate, and pupil size. However, using these measures for detecting situations where the mental load exceeds some pre-set alert level is not very easy. A number of factors make this complicated. For example, the effect of increased mental load on duration of gaze fixations depends on task characteristics. In tasks requiring rapid responses, such as driving a car or flying, the fixation duration decreases as mental load increases. However, in cognitively intensive tasks without time constraints, such as reading complex text or performing complicated tasks on-screen, increasing work load is accompanied by an increase in fixation duration. Measuring changes in saccade amplitudes requires a higher sampling rate than those normally available from commonly used eye trackers (they are typically 60 or 120 Hz).

In general, even if mental load has been found to affect several eye-movement-related measures, the experiments showing this have usually been conducted in controlled environments. There will be additional confounding factors when this is attempted in real-world settings, such as trying to separate the cognitive influences on eye movement from non-cognitive influences (such as lighting conditions). However, this may be solvable with more research, as the latency of

cognitively induced pupil response is less than the response resulting from changes in lighting conditions (see the first chapter in this section).

Trials at Mercedes-Benz to develop a reliable indicator of driver fatigue in cars led to the conclusion that observation of individual measures alone did not allow for reliable detection of tiredness. The measures they used included blinking rate (DaimlerChrysler, 2006).

Emotional State

Whether we are in a positive mood or a bad one is likely to determine how we respond to feedback we receive from a computer program. Consider, for example, an educational interactive application that includes a software agent helping the learner go through the new material and aiding the learner in performing the exercises. It could well benefit the learning process if the behaviour of the agent could take account of the learner's emotional responses and current mood. Studies reviewed by Mulvey and Heubner show that people in a positive mood are more likely to demonstrate flexible thinking, be creative, and be open to new and alternative information (see Chapter 11). One could equally imagine that if the system detects that the learner is frustrated and about to give up, some remedial action could be taken.

Again, it seems that recognising emotions solely on the basis of the data acquired by an eye tracker is not feasible. Eye movement behaviour has not been able to reveal any mood-specific data. Pupil size responds to emotional arousal, but the pupil can dilate as a result of both positive and negative arousal, so additional information would be needed for judging what the current situation is (Partala & Surakka, 2003).

Identification of Current State, in Summary

In conclusion, eye movement data are very good at revealing the object of our attention, particularly in terms of objects that we want to interact with

Figure 3. Categorisation of gaze-aware attentive systems (adapted from work by Hyrskykari, Majaranta, and Räihä, 2005). © 2010 Istance & Hyrskykari. Used with permission

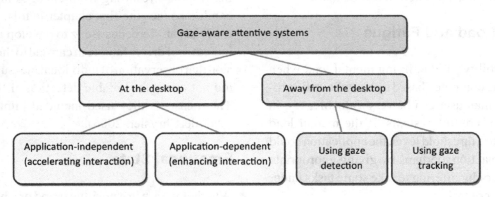

or apply commands to. However, attempts to use eye movement data to make inferences about our intentions, beliefs, preferences, and even fatigue levels have been less successful. We will see below, however, an example of successful use of gaze data to predict reading difficulties.

We have now looked at what we can infer about a person's current state from knowledge of eye movements. Next we look at how this information has been used in various examples of attentive systems.

APPROPRIATE SYSTEM RESPONSES: EXAMPLES FROM ATTENTIVE SYSTEMS

Most existing gaze-aware attentive applications are research prototypes and demonstrator systems. Eye trackers are generally too expensive to be deployed permanently as part of dedicated attentive systems. This situation is likely to change, particularly as video cameras become included more often with computer displays.

We categorise attentive systems as shown in Figure 3. The main division is between attentive systems that are integrated into a desktop environ-

ment, and remote systems where the object of a person's visual attention is away from the desktop.

In desktop applications, the input device is typically a keyboard and a mouse, and the display is usually a fairly large desktop monitor, which remains stationary during its use. The monitoring of gaze position is provided by an eye tracker, either fixed to the desktop or mounted in the bezel of the display screen. This category is split further into attentive interaction techniques, which are independent of a particular software application, and application-dependent systems, wherein the attentive element is integrated with the application itself. The other main category is interaction with objects or other people in the near environment, away from the desktop. In this case, tracking of eye movements is much more challenging.

Application-Independent Techniques: Accelerating Desktop Interaction

We have seen that gaze provides a reliable means of identifying the object at the interface to which a command action is directed – in other words, to infer the context for an action to be performed.

Focus of Visual Attention as the Context for Action

Improving the efficiency of operations that are very frequent in use of desktop applications, such as activating windows, pointing and clicking, or scrolling, has potential to yield substantial cumulative benefits. Simply using the focus of visual attention to identify the most likely target for action eliminates the need for manually moving the pointer onto the target.

MAGIC (Manual And Gaze Input Cascaded) (Zhai, Morimoto, & Ihde, 1999) pointing is a good example of an attention-aware pointing technique and demonstrates several relevant issues in making use of the focus of attention. The strength of using eye tracking data in the interface is the extreme speed of eye movements (when compared to a mouse, for example), but the weakness is the inherent inaccuracy of the tracked point of gaze. MAGIC pointing moves the cursor automatically into the focus (or to near the focus) of the user's attention. Because of the inaccuracy in measurement of the point of gaze by an eye tracker, the actual target is likely to be within about one or two degrees of the measured point of gaze and the fine correction of the cursor position is then done with the mouse.

Figure 4. The two MAGIC pointing techniques (Zhai, Morimoto, & Ihde, 1999). © 2010 Istance & Hyrskykari, used with permission

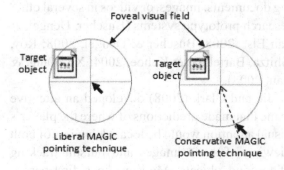

The importance of feedback is highlighted in the implementation of MAGIC pointing. In its original implementation, the cursor is moved close to every target the user looks at. The cursor may feel 'overactive', often jumping close to an object with which the user has no intention to interact. Zhai, Morimoto, and Ihde called this *Liberal* MAGIC pointing. They designed an alternative technique called *Conservative* pointing. In Figure 4, the crosshairs denote the measured position of the point of gaze, and the circle the sharp, foveal visual field within which the actual focus of attention lies. In the Liberal MAGIC pointing on the left, the cursor *warps* to the measured point of gaze, from which the small correction to the actual target is performed manually with the mouse. In the Conservative MAGIC pointing (as shown in Figure 4), the 'warping' action is not initiated before the mouse moves. Additionally, since the cursor appears when the mouse already is moving, the cursor is displayed not at the position of the measured point of gaze but on the border of the foveal vision field. The bias is created intelligently to the direction from which the mouse is moving. The dotted line in the picture shows the trajectory of the mouse movement.

The empirical evaluation of these techniques didn't show significant differences in selection times. Even so, the participant's subjective evaluations were very positive. The Liberal technique was slightly faster than traditional mouse pointing, while the Conservative technique was slightly slower. However, subjectively, the participants thought that both of the MAGIC pointing techniques were faster than using a hand-held mouse.

Zhai et al. reported that some subjects had the feeling that the system 'magically knows what I mean'. This is quite common with participants experimenting with different kinds of gaze-based techniques, and it encourages the idea that with careful design these techniques can feel very natural.

It is possible that the performance benefits of this type of attentive cursor movement would be more apparent on larger or multiple display surfaces (Räihä & Špakov, 2009), which are far more common now than they were in 2000 when the experiments with MAGIC pointing were done. Different kinds of general-purpose attention-aware techniques have been tried for activation of windows (Bolt, 1981; Fono, & Vertegaal, 2005) and for automatic scrolling (Kumar & Winograd, 2007; see also Chapter 9 by Skovsgaard, Räihä, and Tall in section 3 of the book)

Application-Dependent Systems: Enhancing Desktop Interaction

The examples cited above used the tracked focus of visual attention to accelerate general-purpose interaction techniques that can be used with any application without the need for the application itself to be gaze-aware. If eye trackers establish themselves as standard input devices, then applications can start making use of them as an additional input channel. The information about the user's focus of attention would be available in exactly the same way as the keyboard input stream or the position of the mouse.

The application can then interpret gaze paths in the context of the task being performed and adapt its state to the user's behaviour. In some cases, the adaptation may simply use the object at the user's focus of attention, as seen in the examples given above. In other cases, it can be an interpretation of gaze behaviour in relation to the contents of the application window over a longer period of time.

One early application that interpreted the gaze path was the 'automatic narrator', in the Little Prince Application (Starker & Bolt, 1990), which was referred to earlier in this chapter. A similar idea was used in the *iTourist* (Qvarfordt & Zhai, 2005), an experimental electronic travel agent consultant, which provided the user with recorded speech and images according to where the focus of visual attention was on a map. The

feedback from the iTourist users was very positive, regardless of occasional mistakes, as most of the time iTourist was able to give information about places that users were really interested in.

Maglio and Campbell (2003) developed *Suitor*, a framework for building attentive agents, which was used for specific attentive functions, such as task-specific help or Web navigation assistance. The main component of the system is a 'blackboard', or shared memory, which gathers information from the user and on the state of the world. According to what is on the blackboard, 'reflector agents' then make inferences, possibly to maintain a model of the user, and 'actors' receive posted information and take appropriate actions, such as notifying the user. In this framework, eye tracking was used to monitor reading activity on Web pages in order to infer what kind of topics the user was interested in. This information was then used to display peripheral information, such as headers of related articles, on a scrolling ticker display, located at the margin of the user's main screen.

Ohno's *EyePrint* (Ohno, 2004) made use of gaze path history to support searching through documents, images, or videos. It records the gaze path when a person looks at a document for the first time. Then, on subsequent visits, highlighting provides direct information on which parts of the document received different levels of attention during the previous visits. By reminding the user of the previous visits, the system makes it easier to find the parts of the documents searched for. Similar ideas have been applied to aid in revisiting documents, images, or videos in several other research prototype systems (Buscher, Dengel, & van Elst, 2008; Buscher & Dengel, 2008; Roy, Ghitza, Bartelma, & Kehoe, 2004; Xu, Jiang, & Lau, 2008).

Jie and Clark (2008) developed an attentive game that made predictions of where the player's visual attention would be located, in view of both viewing of static images and pursuit tracking of moving objects. Monsters in a first-person shooter game were created or 'spawned' such that they would be either easy or difficult to detect, depending on where the hypothesised focus of attention was. There was a significant difference in the participant's scores, with lower scores being obtained in the difficult condition. The entertainment value of the game can be increased through incorporation of a model of the player's attention. Game flow could, for example, be affected by whether a character in the game thinks the player is looking at it.

There are important issues to be addressed in the design of the way the application responds to inferences made about the user. We will discuss these design principles in the context of iDict (Hyrskykari, 2006), a reading aid that helps non-native speakers who are reading English text.

A Case Study: iDict, a Gaze-Aware Reading Aid

iDict tracks the reader's gaze behaviour and recognises the situations wherein the reader has problems in understanding the text. When this occurs, iDict automatically consults the dictionaries embedded in the system and displays a tooltip translation over the problematic word or phrase.

The idea is that the reader is able to glance at the translation very quickly, without serious interruption to the reading process. Readers who then want more information can just look at the dictionary frame area on the right and the whole dictionary entry appears (see Figure 5).

Identifying the Current State of the User: Uncertainty about a Word or Phrase

The challenge here is to identify when a person has trouble understanding a word or a phrase on the basis solely of real-time interpretation of the eye movements during reading. We studied several indicators that may reflect comprehension difficulties, including the length of fixations on a word,

the number of fixations on the word, regressions back to the word, and the total time spent on a word. In these studies, problematic words were identified right after the reading session by asking readers to point out the words in the passage that they had problems understanding.

We found that total time was the best predictor for comprehension difficulties; when the total time spent on a word exceeded a set threshold, the tooltip was presented. The frequency of a word's occurrence in English was taken into account when the time threshold was set for the word; rare words triggered the help function sooner than common ones did. There is a trade-off between missing or not giving translations for problematic words, on one hand, and 'false alarms' – i.e.,

Figure 5. The two-level help provided by iDict. The system has detected abnormal gaze behaviour from reading of the word 'regaled'. Linguistic analysis of the text informs the system that the word is a past-tense form from the infinite form 'to regale'. iDict gives a tooltip translation for the word in Finnish and displays it right above the word. The reader has turned the eyes to the dictionary frame, since the complete translation for the word has appeared there (on the right). © 2010 Istance & Hyrskykari, used with permission

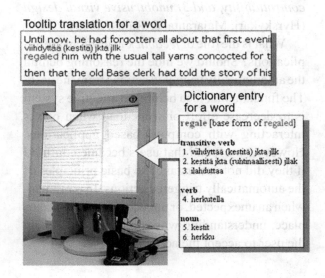

187

giving translations where they were not needed. We observed that, when using iDict, the users very quickly, and partly unconsciously, adopted the habit of deliberately prolonging their gaze slightly when they wanted to get help for a word. Consequently, our goal was primarily to *filter out* the 'false alarms', so that unwanted tooltips would not disturb the reader yet the problematic words would still trigger the help.

We were able to set the thresholds such that, in an experiment where participants read text without any automatic translations being displayed, about 30% of problematic words would have triggered the help function automatically but under 1% of non-problematic words would have caused a false alarm. When iDict with automatic translations available was then tested with those thresholds, the system triggered help for 91% of the words considered to be problematic and for 2.4% of the non-problematic words. This resulted from the change in reading behaviour to cause translations to appear, once users understood how the system worked.

Designing the Attentive System Response

The three main principles applicable to attentive systems in general are *1) appropriate feedback, 2) controllability, and 3) unobtrusive visual design* (Hyrskykari, Majaranta, & Räihä, 2003).

What is the role of *feedback* in gaze-aware applications? Should we hide the reasoning behind the automatically triggered actions from the user? The fundamental idea behind an attentive system is to decrease effort or work load when one is interacting with computer-based applications. However, we found that users became confused if they did not understand the basic principles of the automatically triggered actions. In particular, when an unexpected, or unnecessary, action takes place, understanding why it happened will help the user to accept the action.

In iDict, we tried to make the logic behind the triggered translations transparent by providing different feedback options – namely, by displaying the gaze point or by highlighting the active line, or the active word, as reading proceeds, or doing none of these. Of course, the feedback has to be designed sensitively so that it does not distract from reading of the text but is available if the reader wishes to use it. This aids in understanding of situations in which the system does not respond as expected – for example, because of the eye tracker's failure to follow the reader's gaze position.

The second of these issues is *controllability*: the user should not experience loss of control. In addition to understanding the causes of the automatic actions, the user should be able to influence the application's behaviour.

Incomplete mapping of fixations to target words is one reason the user may feel a loss of control. The reader can be given the ability to interactively correct the mistakes the background interpreter algorithms make. If iDict made a mistake in interpreting which line was currently being read, the reader could adjust this with the up or down arrow key. Similarly, the word assumed to be being read could be corrected horizontally to the previous or next one by pressing of the left or right arrow key.

By *unobtrusive design,* we mean that the costs of wrong decisions in giving translations can be minimised via careful visual design. The human visual system is sensitive to changes in the visual field (Bartram, Ware, & Calvert, 2003). Studies of *change blindness* have shown that, for conscious perception of a change in the visual field, the observer's focus of attention should be at where the change takes place (Simons & Rensink, 2005). When reviewing the videos of their reading sessions, many of the test users of iDict reported that they did not notice the appearance of tooltip translations that they did not need. Change blindness and the fact that the tooltip translations were designed to appear smoothly, without visual noise, probably together account for this. The location of the unnecessary tooltip translation was usually outside the focus of the user's visual attention, since reading had already continued beyond the point at which the system erroneously decided to take action. Additionally, Henderson and Hollingworth (1999) found that a change is more likely to go unnoticed if it occurs during a fixation orienting away from, rather than toward, the point of change.

There have also been studies indicating that change blindness is not only affected by the focus of visual attention; the relevance of the changed information to the task being performed also has a strong effect on the perception. Triesch, Ballard, Hayhoe, and Sullivan (2003) found that a change in the appearance of an object, even if it has visual focus, may go unnoticed if the changed attribute of the object is not relevant for performance of the primary task. Roda and Thomas (2006) make a similar observation on the basis of their interpretation of Grossberg's Adaptive Resonance Theory (ART); they state that '*intentions reflect expectations of events that may (or may not) occur*' and '*the user's attention will be focused on information that matches their momentary expectations*'. In the context of iDict when tooltip translations were given unnecessarily, the fact that a user is not expecting a translation to occur can easily account for the reports of users not perceiving these events.

Overall, there are two main factors on which a system such as iDict can be judged. The first is how well the system can make inferences about the current state of the user – in this case, how many problematic words in English were identified automatically. Second is how useful the system's response to this state was perceived to be. We were able to predict 91% of the problematic words correctly, with false alarms in only 2.4% of cases. An experiment to compare subjective preferences between manual selections of words for translation (using a mouse) with automatic selection by gaze showed a preference for the manual condition.

However the satisfaction ratings for gaze-based selection were also high. We believe that this was, in part at least, due to participants' familiarity with the mouse as an input device.

In this section, we have seen how gaze can be used to make interaction techniques attentive. We have also looked at a variety of examples of attentive applications and discussed three important design principles, related to appropriate feedback, controllability, and unobtrusive design. Next, we look at how objects away from the desktop can be made 'gaze-aware' and elicit an 'attentive' response.

Away from the Desktop

'Remote' attentive systems recognise when someone is looking at an object (or another person). The system can take some action related to the object without the person having to identify it explicitly for the system. This action may simply be pre-fetching of some information about the object in case the person wants to see it. Alternatively, if a person with disabilities looks at an object in the living space, the current state of that object and commands to interact with it can be displayed, without the person having to request this explicitly. This is very similar in principle to the early interaction technique proposed by Jacob for the ship situation display described in the introduction to this chapter. The attentive system configures the user interface with information or commands for the object the user is currently looking at, in case the user wants this. If not, nothing is lost. A significant question is how to detect which object (or person) the user of the remote attentive system is looking at. There have been different approaches to this issue.

Gaze Detection

One option developed by the Human Media Lab at Queens University in Canada has been to fit each candidate object with an eye contact sensor

Table 1. Categories of remote system

Gaze detection	
Put the camera and the light source on the remote object	Eyepliances incorporating Eye Contact Sensors (Shell et al., 2004) Eyebox (Xuuk, 2010)
Put the camera on the person's head and the light source on the remote object	ViewPointer (Smith, Vertegaal, & Sohn, 2005) Attentive hearing aid (Hart, Onceanu, Sohn, Wightman, & Vertegaal, 2009)
Gaze tracking	
Put the gaze tracker camera near the person, and use object recognition from a scene camera image to identify the remote object	Attention Responsive Technology (Shi, Gale, & Purdy, 2007)
Put the gaze tracker camera on the remote object	Interactive guide board and robot (Yonezawa, Yamazoe, Utsumi, & Abe, 2008)

(ECS). There is no intention here to track the user's gaze position; the idea is simply to detect whether or not the person has looked at the sensor. This sensor consists of a small camera and an infrared light source mounted together. When someone looks directly at the sensor, the position of the eyes can be detected by means of retinal reflections (familiar from flash photography as the 'red eye' effect), in combination with a glint of light reflected from the cornea (Shell et al., 2004). Importantly, the glint appears in the centre of the pupil when the viewer is looking straight at the sensor.

The limiting factors with this approach are, first, the range at which detection is effective (i.e., how far away from the person the ECS can be located); second, that the glint from one ECS reflected from a person's cornea can interfere with that from another ECS unit if the two units are close enough together; and, third, the number of people that can be detected at any one time if they are all in the ECS's field of view. This technique has enabled various real (as opposed to software) devices to be made 'gaze-aware'. The proposed applications of this vary with the actual appliance, so, for example, a video playback system could automatically pause when the viewer looks away, or an interface to switch a desk lamp on or off could be displayed to a person in a wheelchair on a local display whenever the person looks at the desk lamp. This idea could also be extended to other objects in a smart home.

This approach was later developed into a commercial product called the Eyebox (Xuuk, 2010), which has an array of infrared light sources mounted around a central camera. One of its uses is said to be as part of an advertising display in order to make it 'attentive', as the unit would be able to detect when someone is looking at it. This information could be used either to log how much attention people have paid to the display, to evaluate its effectiveness, or to make the display change or respond in some other way when someone looks at it.

The approach described above was subsequently modified such that the camera detecting the infrared glint was mounted on the head of the person using it, in a device called ViewPointer (Smith, Vertegaal, & Sohn, 2005). Small infrared light sources or 'tags' could be placed on remote objects. Eye contact with the tag is considered to be made when the glint appears in the centre of the pupil image (see Figure 6).

The function of the tags can be extended to incorporate binary identification codes that, since they use infrared rather than visible light, will not be visible to the wearer. However, the longer the code, the longer the viewer has to fixate on the target to ensure that the code is received via the camera. As soon as the user 'has' to do something,

Figure 6. ViewPointer – head-mounted camera (left); glint created by IR tag (right) (Smith, Vertegaal, & Sohn, 2005). © 2005 ACM. Reprinted with permission

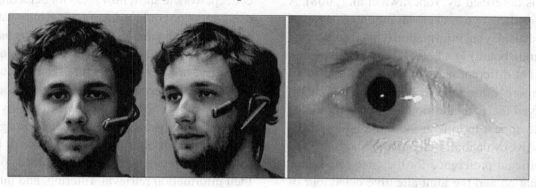

the attentive element of the system is diminished if gaze is being used deliberately to cause something to happen. As we saw with iDict, this can happen when the user understands how the attentive element of the system works.

One big advantage with the ViewPointer approach is that both the tagged object and the person viewing the object can now be mobile, whereas with the ECS approach, the viewer can be mobile while the source object cannot. The ViewPointer approach has been used to create an attentive hearing aid, AHA (Hart et al., 2009). In a conversation, it is usual to look at the person you are talking to. The IR tag is extended to include a small microphone, which is worn on the lapel of people with whom the person using the system may want to talk. The system uses identification of the location of the person being spoken to as the means of amplifying the output from a microphone. This enables distracting background noise to be cut down. Evaluation trials showed advantages in both objective performance and subjective feedback for the AHA in comparison with a system based on manual switching between people who were being listened to.

Gaze Tracking

This approach to the issue of identifying which object a person is looking at involves tracking the gaze point in the environment. Using an eye tracker can give people with mobility problems the ability to select objects in their immediate environment in order to interact with them in some way. Many eye tracker systems provide a facility to record a video image of the scene in front of the person who is using the system and then superimpose a marker showing the gaze point on top of this. One system (Shi, Gale, & Purdy, 2007) that uses this approach carries out image processing to recognise objects in the scene image and to extract their co-ordinates. The object intersected by the gaze vector provided by the eye tracker can then be determined. Then the current state of the object and controls for changing it can be displayed in a place that is easily accessible to the person concerned. The advantage of this approach is that the objects in the remote space are not actively emitting any signal and therefore there is no interference when several objects are detected in the same space. The disadvantage is that a far more sophisticated eye tracking system is needed, which must be calibrated for a particular user, and the objects in the living space must have been registered with the system already for object recognition purposes.

The final approach is to put an eye tracker on each object that we want to be able to detect a person's attention. A system to investigate the impact of joint attention between a human viewer and a guide robot in the form of a stuffed toy robot is described by Yonezawa et al. (2008). A single-camera eye tracker was mounted on top of a board displaying information (called an interactive guide board) in a hotel lobby. As the person looked at different parts of the board, the robot gave more information about the information displayed there. In addition, the robot turned its head to appear to look at the same information. Subjective evaluation with 25 participants showed a significant preference for the gaze-responsive information and the joint attentive behaviour of the robot. Importantly the eye tracker operated without any calibration. The authors reported an eye tracking accuracy of about 3.5° horizontally and about 6° vertically when people stood in front of the display.

We have seen different approaches to the question of how to detect when someone looks at an object in the vicinity. This is the main issue that has to be resolved. The attentive action taken as a result will depend very much on the circumstances, and at present is a secondary issue. As miniature cameras are made with higher resolution, embedding these within objects for either gaze tracking or gaze detection becomes a more flexible proposition. It is also possible that wearing some kind of head-mounted camera or display will become socially acceptable, particularly in response to the need to use mobile computing services hands-free. In that case, solutions such as ViewPointer become feasible for this type of system.

SUMMARY

Attentive systems aim to make active use of the current focus of someone's attention for a variety of purposes. These include making computers easier and less effortful to use, and safer to operate. They can be used to make games more challenging, and they can make interaction with robots appear to be more natural. They also have the potential to make advertising displays more effective.

Much of the work to date has been proof-of-concept work to show how ideas for detecting and using attention could be incorporated into systems. The future in this area looks very promising indeed. There is a needs-related pull and a technological push. Eye tracker manufacturers have recently produced compact and mobile glasses-mounted systems (Tobii, 2010). Augmented-reality systems enable objects in mobile video images to be aligned with objects in the real world. If the momentary focus of attention is added to this, then information retrieval, filtering, and interaction with real remote objects can take on a much wider dimension than has been possible so far. Initial work on inferring the relevance of objects for augmenting a dynamic real view of a scene on the basis of gaze-tracked data has already been carried out (Kandemir, Saarinen, & Kaski, 2010). The inclusion of attention can be extended further into game-playing, both outdoor location-based gaming and desktop gaming. Industrial and transport control systems can incorporate safety checks on the basis of whether the human operator has attended to important information or not. In-car safety systems may indeed make more active use of the focus of the driver's attention by integrating this with information from sensors inside and outside the car. In addition, smart homes can make more use of the attention of both elderly and disabled residents, to improve opportunities for independent living and greater quality of life. Clearly, gaze-based attentive systems have much to offer society in the years to come.

REFERENCES

Bartram, L., Ware, C., & Calvert, T. (2003). Moticons: Detection, distraction and task. *International Journal of Human-Computer Studies, 58,* 515–545. doi:10.1016/S1071-5819(03)00021-1

Bee, N., Prendinger, H., Nakasone, A., André, E., & Ishizuka, M. (2006). Automatic preference detection by analyzing the gaze 'cascade effect'. *Proceedings of the 2nd Conference on Communication by Gaze Interaction* (*COGAIN 2006*) (pp. 61–64). Turin, Italy: Politecnico di Torino. Retrieved from the COGAIN website: http://www.cogain.org/conference

Bolt, R. A. (1981). Gaze-orchestrated dynamic windows. *Proceedings of the 8th Annual Conference on Computer Graphics and Interactive Techniques* (*SIGGRAPH '81*), Dallas, TX, USA (pp. 109–119). New York, NY: ACM. doi:10.1145/800224.806796

Buscher, G., & Dengel, A. (2008). Attention-based document classifier learning. *Proceedings of the 8th IAPR Workshop on Document Analysis Systems* (*DAS'08*), Nara, Japan (pp. 87–94). Washington, DC., USA: IEEE Xplore.

Buscher, G., Dengel, A., & van Elst, L. (2008). Query expansion using gaze-based feedback on the subdocument level. *Proceedings of the 31st Annual International ACM SIGIR Conference on Research and Development in Information Retrieval* (*SIGIR'08*), Singapore (pp. 387–394). New York, NY: ACM Press. doi:10.1145/1390334.1390401

DaimlerChrysler. (2006). Fatigue at the wheel: Mercedes-Benz developing warning system for motorists. *Automotoportal*, Retrieved from http://www.automotoportal.com/article/fatigue-at-the-wheel-mercedes-benz-developing-warning-system-for-motorists

Doshi, A., & Trivedi, M. (2009). On the roles of eye gaze and head dynamics in predicting driver's intent to change lanes. *IEEE Transactions on Intelligent Transportation Systems Archive, 10*(3), 453–462. doi:10.1109/TITS.2009.2026675

Fono, D., & Vertegaal, R. (2005). EyeWindows: Evaluation of eye-controlled zooming windows for focus selection. *Proceedings of the SIGCHI Conference on Human Factors in Computing Systems* (*CHI'05*), Portland, OR, USA (pp. 151–160). New York, NY: ACM Press. doi:10.1145/1054972.1054994

Goldberg, J., & Schryver, J. (1993). Eye gaze control of the computer interface: Discrimination of zoom intent. *Proceedings of the 37th Annual Meeting of the Human Factors and Ergonomics Society in Seattle, Washington, October 11–15*.

Hart, J., Onceanu, D., Sohn, C., Wightman, D., & Vertegaal, R. (2009). The attentive hearing aid: Eye selection of auditory sources for hearing impaired users. *INTERACT 2009, 5726*(2009), 19–35. *LNCS, 2009*. doi:10.1007/978-3-642-03655-2_4

Henderson, J., & Hollingworth, A. (1999). The role of fixation position in detecting scene changes across saccades. *Psychological Science, 10*, 438–443. doi:10.1111/1467-9280.00183

Huuskonen, P., Salminen, I., & Lehikoinen, J. (2010). *Context Awareness: Essential Technology for Next Generation Smart Systems*. Hoboken, NJ: John Wiley & Sons.

Hyrskykari, A. (2006). Eyes in attentive interfaces: Experiences from creating iDict, a gaze-aware reading aid. (Dissertations in Interactive Technology 4, Department of Computer Sciences, University of Tampere). Retrieved from http://acta.uta.fi/pdf/951-44-6643-8.pdf

Hyrskykari, A., Majaranta, P., & Räihä, K.-J. (2003). Proactive response to eye movements. In M. Rauterberg, M. Menozzi, & J. Wesson (Eds.), *Proceedings of INTERACT 2003* (pp. 129–136). Amsterdam, The Netherlands: IOS Press.

Hyrskykari, A., Majaranta, P., & Räihä, K.-J. (2005). From gaze control to attentive interfaces. *Proceedings of HCI International 2005*. Erlbaum.

Jacob, R. J. K. (1991). The use of eye movements in human–computer interaction techniques: What you look at is what you get. *ACM Transactions on Information Systems, 9*, 152–169. doi:10.1145/123078.128728

Jie, L., & Clark, J. J. (2008). Video game design using an eye-movement-dependent model of visual attention. *ACM Transactions on Multimedia Computing, Communications, and Applications, 4*(3), 1–16. doi:10.1145/1386109.1386115

Kandemir, M., Saarinen, V.-M., & Kaski, S. (2010). Inferring object relevance from gaze in dynamic scenes. *Proceedings of the 2010 Symposium on Eye-Tracking Research & Applications (ETRA '10)*, Austin, Texas (pp. 105–108). New York, NY: ACM. doi:10.1145/1743666.1743692

Kumar, M., & Winograd, T. (2007). Gaze-enhanced scrolling techniques. *Proceedings of the 20th Annual ACM Symposium on User Interface Software and Technology (UIST '07)*, Newport, Rhode Island, USA (pp. 213–216). New York: ACM. doi:10.1145/1294211.1294249

Maglio, P. P., & Campbell, C. S. (2003). Attentive agents. *Communications of the ACM, 46*(3), 47–51. doi:10.1145/636772.636797

Maglio, P. P., Matlock, T., Campbell, C. S., Zhai, S., & Smith, B. A. (2000). Gaze and speech in attentive user interfaces. *Proceedings of the 3rd International Conference on Advances in Multimodal Interfaces* (ICMI 2000), 1–7. Berlin-Heidelberg, Germany: Springer.

Miluzzo, E., Wang, T., & Campbell, A. T. (2010). EyePhone: Activating mobile phones with your eyes. *Proceedings of the 2nd ACM SIGCOMM Workshop on Networking, Systems, and Applications on Mobile Handhelds (MobiHeld '10)* (pp. 15–20). New York, NY: ACM. doi:10.1145/1851322.1851328

Nakayama. M., & Takahasi, Y. (2006). An estimation of certainty for multiple choice responses using eye-movement. *Proceedings of the 2nd Conference on Communication by Gaze Interaction (COGAIN 2006)* (pp. 67–72). Turin, Italy: Politecnico di Torino. Retrieved from the COGAIN website: http://www.cogain.org/conference

Nielsen, J. (1993). Noncommand user interfaces. *Communications of the ACM, 36*(4), 82–99. doi:10.1145/255950.153582

Oh, A., Fox, H., Van Kleek, M., Adler, A., Gajos, K., Morency, L.-P., & Darrell, T. (2002). Evaluating Look-to-Talk: A gaze-aware interface in a collaborative environment. *Extended Abstracts on Human Factors in Computing Systems (CHI '02)* (pp. 650–651). New York, NY: ACM Press. http://doi.acm.org/10.1145/506443.506528

Ohno, T. (2004). EyePrint: Support of document browsing with eye gaze trace. *Proceedings of the 6th International Conference on Multimodal Interfaces (ICMI '04)*, State College, PA, USA (pp. 16–23). New York, NY: ACM Press. doi:10.1145/1027933.1027937

Partala, T., & Surakka, V. (2003). Pupil size variation as an indication of affective processing. *International Journal of Human-Computer Studies, 59*(1–2), 185–198. doi:10.1016/S1071-5819(03)00017-X

Qvarfordt, P., & Zhai, S. (2005). Conversing with the user based on eye-gaze patterns. *Proceedings of the SIGCHI Conference on Human Factors in Computing Systems (CHI '05)* (pp. 221–230). New York, NY: ACM Press. doi:10.1145/1054972.1055004

Räihä, K.-J., & Špakov, O. (2009). Disambiguating Ninja cursors with eye gaze. *Proceedings of the 27th International Conference on Human Factors in Computing Systems (CHI '09)* (pp. 1411-1414). New York, NY: ACM Press. doi:10.1145/1518701.1518913.

Roda, C., & Thomas, J. (2006). Attention aware systems: Theories, applications, and research agenda. *Computers in Human Behavior, 22*(4), 557–587. doi:10.1016/j.chb.2005.12.005

Roy, D., Ghitza, Y., Bartelma, J., & Kehoe, C. (2004). Visual memory augmentation: Using eye gaze as an attention filter. *Proceedings of the 8th International Symposium on Wearable Computers* (pp. 128–131). Washington, DC., USA: IEEE Computer Society. doi:10.1109/ISWC.2004.47

Shell, J. S., Vertegaal, R., Cheng, D., Skaburskis, A. W., Sohn, C., Stewart, A. J., & Dickie, C. (2004). ECSGlasses and EyePliances: Using attention to open sociable windows of interaction. *Proceedings of the Symposium on Eye Tracking Research & Applications* (pp. 93–100). New York, NY: ACM Press.

Shi, F., Gale, A. G., & Purdy, K. (2007). *A new gaze-based interface for environmental control* (LNCS 4555, pp. 996–1005). Berlin-Heidelberg, Germany: Springer.

Simons, D. J., & Rensink, R. A. (2005). Change blindness: Past, present, and future. *Trends in Cognitive Sciences, 9*(1), 16–20. doi:10.1016/j.tics.2004.11.006

Smith, J. D., Vertegaal, R., & Sohn, C. (2005). ViewPointer: Lightweight calibration-free eye tracking for ubiquitous handsfree deixis. *Proceedings of the 18th Annual ACM Symposium on User Interface Software and Technology (UIST '05)*, Seattle, WA, USA (pp. 53–61). New York, NY: ACM. doi:10.1145/1095034.1095043

Starker, I., & Bolt, R. A. (1990). A gaze-responsive self-disclosing display. *Proceedings of the SIGCHI Conference on Human Factors in Computing Systems (CHI '90)* (pp. 3–9). New York, NY: ACM Press.

Tobii (2010). *Tobii glasses eye tracker*. Retrieved from http://www.tobii.com/market_research_usability/products_services/eye_tracking_hardware/tobii_glasses_eye_tracker.aspx, and demonstration video at http://www.tobiiglasses.com/marketresearch/

Triesch, J., Ballard, D. H., Hayhoe, M. M., & Sullivan, B. T. (2003). What you see is what you need. *Journal of Vision (Charlottesville, Va.), 3*(1), 86–94. doi:10.1167/3.1.9

Weiser, M. (1999). The computer for the 21st century. *SIGMOBILE Mobile Computing and Communications Review, 3*(3), 3–11. doi:10.1145/329124.329126

Xu, S., Jiang, H., & Lau, F. C. (2008). Personalized online document, image and video recommendation via commodity eye-tracking. *Proceedings of the 2008 ACM Conference on Recommender Systems (RecSys '08)*, Lausanne, Switzerland (pp. 83–90). New York, NY: ACM Press. doi:10.1145/1454008.1454023.

Xuuk (2010). *Eyebox2*. Retrieved from https://www.xuuk.com

Yonezawa, T., Yamazoe, H., Utsumi, A., & Abe, S. (2008). Evaluations of interactive guideboard with gaze-communicative stuffed-toy robot. *Proceedings of the 4th Conference on Communication by Gaze Interaction (COGAIN 2008)* (pp. 53–58). Prague, Czech Republic: Czech Technical University. Retrieved from the COGAIN website: http://www.cogain.org/conference

Zhai, S., Morimoto, C., & Ihde, S. (1999). Manual and gaze input cascaded (MAGIC) pointing. *Proceedings of the SIGCHI Conference on Human Factors in Computing Systems (CHI '99)*, Pittsburgh, PA (pp. 246–253). New York, NY: ACM Press. doi:10.1145/302979.303053

Section 5
Methods and Measures

Chapter 14
Methods and Measures:
an Introduction

John Paulin Hansen
IT University of Copenhagen, Denmark

Hirotaka Aoki
Tokyo Institute of Technology, Japan

ABSTRACT

Understanding users' behaviour is one of the most crucial aspects in successful design of human–computer interaction. Experiments with prototypes of gaze interaction systems provide valuable quantitative measurement of performances in terms of such factors as speed, error, and accuracy, in addition to the comments and suggestions we may get from users. We will introduce some of the research methods, metrics, and measures that have emerged within the field associated with the design of gaze interactive systems. Many of the methods and measures are inherited from an engineering approach to system design that can be found within the human factors tradition. Others are unique to gaze interaction, taking advantage of the extra information that can be gained when one knows where the user is looking. In this chapter, our focus will mainly be on efficiency measures for gaze performance.

INTRODUCTION

Understanding users' behaviour is one of the most crucial aspects in successful design of human–computer interaction (e.g., Nielsen, 1993). Experiments with prototypes of gaze interaction systems provide valuable quantitative measure-

ment of performances in terms of such factors as speed, error, and accuracy, in addition to the comments and suggestions we may get from users. This contributes to deeper understanding of the potential and challenges of gaze interaction, and experiments may guide developers to better designs.

Gaze interaction is a new technology. In this part of the book, we will introduce some of the

DOI: 10.4018/978-1-61350-098-9.ch014

research methods, metrics, and measures that have emerged within the field associated with the design of gaze interactive systems. Many of the methods and measures are inherited from an engineering approach to system design that can be found within the human factors tradition. Others are unique to gaze interaction, taking advantage of the extra information that can be gained when one knows where the user is looking.

Within the next few years, gaze interactive systems are expected to become commodity hardware and not just for use in labs or by a few people with special needs (Hansen, Hansen, & Johansen, 2001). Introducing gaze interaction to a mass market may be quite a challenge, since the majority of people have no previous experience with gaze interaction that they can relate to. This is somewhat different from introducing other physical pointing devices – e.g., for a game console – that utilise well-established motor-control schemes for the hands, fingers, and arms; even head-pose pointing seems to be a natural human capacity that people readily pick up (Hansen, Johansen, Torning, Itoh, & Aoki, 2004). Gaze interaction is quite different from conventional interaction devices, because the motor control of the human eye is all geared toward acquiring information, not to manipulating the outside world. Consequently, the use of eyes for interaction activities such as typing, clicking, and entering commands may be rather confusing, at least in the very beginning. Many experiments have been focusing on the first encounter with gaze interaction, and some studies have been conducted as learning experiments to follow the effect of familiarisation (e.g., Tuisku, Majaranta, Isokoski, & Räihä, 2008).

The most basic gaze data formats are just raw co-ordinates (x,y) on the plane – for instance, the monitor – that people are looking at. The co-ordinates are then analysed in time series as fixations and saccades. The co-ordinate data can be recorded through continuous logging, and several of the professional gaze tracking systems have facilities for this. The body of data generated can be quite massive, dependent on the sampling rate. Most systems sample eye co-ordinates more than 25 times per second, and some do so more than 250 times a second. Now, how do we elicit meaningful information from this large quantity of data to address the design questions we might like to ask?

Some of the questions that we may wish to ask could be:

- How *efficient* is the application of different gaze interaction principles? What design elements will have significant impact on efficiency? For instance, there is a major impact on typing speed if users of dwell time selection are given the ability to adjust the dwell time directly via the typing interface and not just in the general settings of the system (Majaranta, Ahola, & Špakov, 2009).

- How *difficult* is it to use gaze interaction for a prolonged time? What kinds of problems are transient, and which problems are persistent? Do people feel comfortable when using gaze as input – once they have become familiar with it?

- How hard (strenuous) is it to use gaze interaction as compared to, for example, mouse or head pointing? Although eye movements are natural and fast, there are indications that it can be hard to stare at an object to make it respond if the activation time is too slow (Aoki, Itoh, Sumitomo, & Hansen, 2003).

- What is the *accuracy* of different gaze tracking systems, and how does accuracy affect interaction performance? Even the most accurate gaze tracking systems seems to be less precise than the mouse pointer, making it difficult to hit the smallest targets in a windowing environment (Skovsgaard, Hansen, & Mateo, 2008).

- What are the most *enjoyable* parts of gaze interaction? Can we facilitate user experiences that will make gaze interaction fun to use in, for instance, a computer game?

- How can gaze interaction be *integrated* with other input modalities? People with severe motor disability have been the pioneering user group for gaze interaction. Some of them need additional input channels to supplement or substitute for gaze interaction. Researchers within COGAIN are trying to combine gaze pointing with EMG selections (e.g., Mateo, San Agustin, & Hansen, 2008). Several other researchers have investigated how best to supplement gaze pointing with mouse pointing (e.g., magic pointer) or key activation (e.g., Kumar, Paepcke, & Winograd, 2007).

In this chapter (Chapter 14), our focus will mainly be on efficiency measures for gaze performance. Later chapters in this part of the book will present research trends related to evaluation of eye tracking systems for computer input (Chapter 15), gaze data analysis (Chapter 16), usability evaluation of gaze interaction (Chapter 17), and user-focused methods for user trials with people with disabilities (Chapter 18).

COMMON METRICS IN GAZE INTERACTION STUDIES

Text entry tasks performed by gaze input have been the preferred way to measure effectiveness of gaze input, for several reasons. First and foremost, this is the most common task performed on any personal computer. Secondly, it is the most important task that people with severe motor challenges will perform. Since they are the pioneers of gaze interaction, it makes good sense to focus on, for example, improvements to basic interaction features applied to this specific task. Thirdly, typing is a complex task in contrast to hitting a simple target on the screen. It requires that the subjects perform several cognitive sub-tasks – for instance, spelling and searching for a target key. Finally, since the early days of human computer psychology, typing has been the favourite task for studying and modelling (Card, Moran, & Newell, 1986).

The research endeavour to develop new typing metrics within gaze interaction is partly motivated by the potential for gaze performance measurements to be collected automatically in a user's home and sent off to, for example, a communication specialist when users are online. Such remote monitoring of user progress could aid communication specialists in timing of their advice or visits. For instance, it may be recognised when a user has reached a stable but sub-optimal level of performance, and better strategies could then be suggested to him or her. A disease such as ALS/MND may suddenly affect the ability to gaze type. Eye trackers may fail partly without the user discovering this. Early detection of deterioration in performance could warn the communication specialist that help is required.

Remote data collection (see Drey & Siegel, 2004) seems particularly relevant for the design of AAC systems for individuals with a mobility problem and for user groups that are relatively low in their numbers, and thus spread widely in the community. Remote data collection can provide a large quantity of data without intruding on the users. Several researchers and usability practitioners have emphasised the advantages of remote data collection (e.g., Ivory & Hearst, 2001; Lecerof & Paterno, 1998).

When evaluating gaze interaction systems, researchers would be able to benchmark gaze typing interfaces or eye tracking systems against each other in actual use, given user data from large populations. Collection of data from a significant number of users of a particular system reduces the influence from a few individuals with exceptionally slow performance. On the other hand, the possibility of identifying those few users with exceptionally fast typing could provide very useful inspiration that might help others improve.

Text data from people's personal communication must be treated with confidentiality.

Therefore, the performance metrics should be calculated locally on the user's PC, and only the metrics, not the text itself, should be submitted, for protection of the user's privacy.

Metrics for Studies of Gaze Typing

(1) Typing Speed Metrics

Words per minute (WPM): This metric refers to how many words are entered per minute. A word is standardised to five characters, including the spaces between words (i.e., the space is treated as just a normal character). So, the definition of the WPM metric is

$$WPM = \frac{Number\ of\ Characters}{Time\ Spent\ for\ Typing(min.) \times 5}$$

There are some variations of this WPM metric, depending on languages, because WPM cannot be applied to languages with a different character system, such as many of the Asian languages. In non-Latin languages, the number of keystrokes needed to enter a single character may vary quite a lot, depending on the information-richness of each character, which influences the numbers of keystrokes required to produce a specific character. Instead, a character-based typing speed metric, such as characters per minute (CPM), can be applied.

(2) Error Metrics

Keystrokes per character (KSPC) is a widely used metric representing how efficiently sentences are typed (MacKenzie, 2002; Soukoreff & MacKenzie, 2003). The definition of this metric is

$$KSPC = \frac{Number\ of\ Keystrokes}{Number\ of\ Characters\ Typed}$$

Error-free typing of text in lowercase on a QWERTY keyboard results in a KSPC value equal to 1. The KSPC figure becomes higher when the user produces errors that are corrected (e.g., via the backspace key). It also becomes higher than 1 if uppercase is used (requiring the activation of a Shift key) or if any special-character components, such as an accent mark, require an additional keystroke. On the other hand, some of the on-screen keyboards used by people with special needs offer word-completion, full-word prediction, or even full phrases that can be entered with just one keystroke. In this case, the KSPC value may become less than 1. So the minimal (error-free) KSPC figure is a factor of the keyboard design. Often, the best way to establish this minimum will be to run a simulation that measures the KSPC value from perfect typing of a sample of several sentences.

Minimum-string-distance-based, or MSD-based, error rate is an error metric obtained by comparing the text typed and the corresponding error-free target text (Soukoreff & MacKenzie, 2001, 2003). The MSD is the minimum number of editing primitives – insertions, deletions, or substitutions – needed to transform the text typed into the error-free text. The generic definition of MSD-based error rate is

$$MSD - Based\ Error\ Rate$$
$$= \frac{MSD}{Number\ of\ Characters\ Typed} \times 100\%$$

The reason for reporting the MSD-based error rate is that it reveals how many errors are left in the text, while some other measures – such as overproduction rate (see below) or rate of backspace activation (see below) – capture only errors discovered and corrected. So, often research papers report both the MSD error rate and one of the other error measures.

Overproduction rate (OR): The OR metric represents the ratio of the actual number of inputs to the minimum number of inputs needed (Hansen, Johansen, Hansen, Itoh, & Mashino, 2003; Itoh, Aoki, & Hansen, 2006). The concept of this metric can be described as follows:

$$\text{Overproduction Rate} = \frac{\text{Number of Keystrokes}}{\text{Minimum Number of Keystrokes}}$$

If the minimum number of keystrokes matches the number of characters (i.e., the error-free total), the value of the OR calculated is similar to the KSPC value. OR should be considered for use if several keystrokes are needed to input one character – for instance, in analysis of input in Asian typing systems.

Rate of backspace activations (RBA) is a quite simple indication of the rough error frequency, counting the number of times the Backspace or Delete key is used (Itoh et al., 2006). The metric is expressed as

$$\text{Rate of Backspace Activations}$$
$$= \frac{\text{Number of Keystrokes for 'Backspace' or 'Delete'}}{\text{Number of Characters Typed}}$$

RBA has the advantage of being easy to calculate. However, some of the alternative keyboards for gaze typing offer full-word prediction. Quite often, people will choose a full word with a wrong ending (e.g., 'motorcycling' instead of 'motorcyclist') and then just delete the wrong ending ('ng') to replace it with the correct one ('st'). In this case, the error count will increase, while 'Minimum Number of Keystrokes' in the OR value should take into account that this was, in fact, the most efficient strategy to use.

(3) Metrics specific to gaze interactive displays

Since gaze tracking provides information unique to each user's eye movements, it is also possible to include gaze data in the analysis. For instance, do people look in the 'right' places, or do they look at irrelevant elements? The majority of results from experiments with gaze interaction systems have been obtained from analysis with the traditional measures described above, but relatively little research has focused on measures including gaze behaviour itself (e.g., Aoki, Itoh, & Hansen, 2006). One of the few studies adopting eye movement patterns for evaluation of gaze interaction is the work by Majaranta MacKenzie, Aula, and Räihä (2006). They used a metric termed 'Number of Read Text Events per Character', measuring how frequently a user directed his or her gaze toward the text field. This metric has no direct relation to the accuracy of gaze interaction as such but may be regarded as an indirect measure, since people are more likely to look at the text they have produced when they are uncertain whether it has been typed correctly. The definition of this metric is

$$\text{Number of Read Text Events per Character}$$
$$= \frac{\text{Number of Gazes to Text Field}}{\text{Number of Characters Typed}}$$

Attended But Not Selected Rate (ANSR): ANSR (Aoki, Hansen, & Itoh, 2009; Aoki, Hansen, & Itoh, 2006) counts the number of keys that are gazed at but not entered. The definition of this metric is

$$\text{Attended But Not Selected Rage}$$
$$= \frac{\text{Number of Keys Gazed But Not Selected}}{\text{Number of Characters Typed}}$$

Table 1. Summary of gaze typing metrics

Class of metrics	Metrics
Text-focused metrics	Words per minute (WPM) Keystrokes per character (KSPC) Minimum string distance (MSD) (target text needed)
Gaze-focused metrics	Read text event (RTE) rate Attended But Not Selected Rate (ANSR) (applicable to dwell-time-based gaze typing)
Key-activation-focused metrics	Rate of backspace activations (RBA) Overproduction rate (OR) (target text needed)

Aoki et al. (2009) examined the correlation coefficients of the ANSR with the actual error frequency in gaze typing and found it to be very high – namely, 0.915. This suggests that ANSR could be an easy and anonymous way to estimate the error frequency in gaze-activated systems.

GENERAL DISCUSSION

Table 1 gives a brief summary of the gaze typing metrics cited, by class of metrics.

Outside the laboratory, the user is likely to be distracted during typing. Frequently, the user may sit for a while and think deeply on what to write or may just be waiting for others to reply to a question before typing of the next sentence. In order to include time-based measures in the remote metrics, one must filter out those breaks. The WPM (and the CPM) figure obviously includes a time factor, but none of the eye-movement-related metrics suggested in this paper includes time. In collection of user data from larger populations outside experimental rooms, performance metrics are needed that can be derived while the user types his or her own free text in real-life situations without the strict control of typing conditions that some of the traditional metrics require. In remote real-life conditions, users' behaviour during typing cannot be controlled. This makes it impossible to obtain metrics such as an 'overproduction' rate (e.g., Hansen et al. 2004; Itoh et al., 2006) that require comparisons

between the actual typed text and the optimal input stream for the target text. The user may type idiosyncratic words and abbreviations that will be understandable only to the people who know him or her well. Since this kind of personal text cannot be compared to any general dictionary standard, the quality of the productions cannot be judged by counting, for instance, the number of spelling errors. Even if this were possible, users differ enormously in their ability to spell. Whatever text the user produces, it has to be accepted as the target text.

Fortunately, gaze typing systems have unique advantages in collection of data 'at home', since it is known where the user is looking. The Attended But Not Selected Rate metric can be measured without knowledge of what the user intended to type and independently from what was actually typed. It correlates very well with the actual error rate according to the experimental results presented by Aoki et al. (2009). The metric could be submitted by the end of the day and would be a single, highly informative indication of the certainty the user had shown in his or her gaze operation of the relevant system.

The ANSR metric is inspired by the 'Principles of Motion Economy' (e.g., Barnes, 1968). These principles include guidelines for efficient manual work that conserve human energy. It is suggested here that this also applies to eye movements during skilled gaze typing. Although the 'energy cost' of an eye movement is very small, the cumulated cognitive cost of all unnecessary fixations during routine operations can be very high. This cost is expected to be a strong predictor of long-term user satisfaction and perceived work load. The results reported confirm that ANSR values are highly correlated with erroneous selections since every key that is unnecessarily fixated upon also risks becoming a wrong selection – c.f. the 'Midas touch' problem.

A metric such as WPM (or CPM) can be measured with any text entry system and is device-independent, while the eye-movement-related metrics suggested in this paper requires an eye tracker device. At first, this may restrict them to uses in tests of gaze typing systems only. However, if the metrics turn out to be as informative for keyboard design research as ANSR seems to be, then gaze recording could become a standard procedure in the design of typing systems for all kinds of input devices. The relationship between elements attended per selection and error rate may even hold for other interfaces than just on-screen keyboards: The more (selectable) places people look at in an interface before they make a selection, the higher the risk of the selection being wrong.

REFERENCES

Aoki, H., Hansen, J. P., & Itoh, K. (2006). Towards remote evaluation of gaze typing systems. *Proceedings of the 2nd Conference on Communication by Gaze Interaction (COGAIN 2006)* (pp. 94–101). Turin, Italy: Politecnico di Torino. Retrieved from the COGAIN website: http://www.cogain. org/conference

Aoki, H., Hansen, J. P., & Itoh, K. (2009). Learning gaze typing: What are the obstacles and what progress to expect? *Universal Access in the Information Society, 8*(4), 297–310. doi:10.1007/ s10209-009-0152-5

Aoki, H., Itoh, K., & Hansen, J. P. (2006). Usability evaluation of gaze interface based on scanpath analysis. *Proceedings of the 16th World Congress on Ergonomics*, Maastricht (CD-ROM).

Aoki, H., Itoh, K., Sumitomo, N., & Hansen, J. P. (2003). Usability of gaze interaction compared to mouse and head-tracking in typing Japanese texts on a restricted on-screen keyboard for disabled people. *Proceedings of the 15th Triennial Congress of the International Ergonomics Association*, Seoul, South Korea (pp. 267– 270).

Barnes, M. (1968). *Motion and time study*. New York, NY: John Wiley and Sons.

Card, S., Moran, T., & Newell, A. (1986). *The psychology of human–computer interaction*. Hillsdale, NJ, US: Lawrence Erlbaum Associates.

Drey, S., & Siegel, D. (2004). Remote possibilities? International usability testing at a distance. *Interactions, 11*(2), 10–17.

Hansen, J. P., Hansen, D. W., & Johansen, A. S. (2001). Bringing gaze-based interaction back to basics. In C. Stephanidis (Ed.), *Universal Access in HCI (UAHCI): Towards an Information Society for All – Proceedings of the 9th International Conference on Human–Computer Interaction (HCI '01)* (pp. 325–328). Mahwah, NJ, US: Lawrence Erlbaum Associates.

Hansen, J. P., Johansen, A. S., Hansen, D. W., Itoh, K., & Mashino, S. (2003). Command without a click: Dwell time typing by mouse and gaze selections. In M. Rauterberg et al. (Eds.), *Human–computer Interaction (INTERACT '03)* (pp. 121–128). Zürich, Switzerland: IOS Press.

Hansen, J. P., Johansen, A. S., Torning, K., Itoh, K., & Aoki, H. (2004). Gaze typing compared with input by head and hand. *Proceedings of the 2004 Symposium on Eye Tracking Research & Applications (ETRA 2004)* (pp. 131–138). New York, NY: ACM Press. doi:10.1145/968363.968389

Itoh, K., Aoki, H., & Hansen, J. P. (2006). A comparative usability study of two Japanese gaze typing systems. *Proceedings of the 2006 Symposium on Eye Tracking Research & Applications (ETRA 2006)* (pp. 59–66). New York, NY: ACM Press. doi:10.1145/1117309.1117344

Ivory, M. Y., & Hearst, M. A. (2001). The state of the art in automating usability evaluation of user interfaces. *ACM Computing Surveys, 33*(4), 470–516. doi:10.1145/503112.503114

Kumar, M., Paepcke, A., & Winograd, T. (2007). EyePoint: Practical pointing and selection using gaze and keyboard. Proceedings of the SIGCHI Conference on Human Factors in Computing Systems *(CHI '07)* (pp. 421–430). New York, NY: ACM Press. doi:10.1145/1240624.1240692

Lecerof, A., & Paterno, F. (1998). Automatic support for usability evaluation. *IEEE Transactions on Software Engineering, 24*(10), 863–888. doi:10.1109/32.729686

MacKenzie, I. S. (2002). KSPC (keystrokes per character) as a characteristic of text entry techniques. *Proceedings of the 4th International Symposium on Human–Computer Interaction with Mobile Devices* (LNCS 2411, pp. 195-210). Heidelberg, Germany: Springer-Verlag.

Majaranta, P., Ahola, U.-K., & Špakov, O. (2009). Fast gaze typing with an adjustable dwell time. *Proceedings of the 27th International Conference on Human Factors in Computing Systems (CHI '09)* (pp. 357–360). New York, NY: ACM Press. doi:10.1145/1518701.1518758

Majaranta, P., MacKenzie, I. S., Aula, A., & Räihä, K.-J. (2006). Effects of feedback and dwell time on eye typing speed and accuracy. *Universal Access in the Information Society, 5*(2), 199–208. doi:10.1007/s10209-006-0034-z

Mateo, J. C., San Agustin, J., & Hansen, J. P. (2008). Gaze beats mouse: Hands-free selection by combining gaze and EMG. *Extended Abstracts on Human Factors in Computing Systems (CHI '08)* (pp. 3039–3044). New York, NY: ACM Press. doi:10.1145/1358628.1358804

Nielsen, J. (1993). *Usability engineering.* San Diego, CA, US: Morgan Kaufmann.

Prague, Czech Republic (n. d.). *Prague, Czech Republic: Czech Technical University.* Retrieved from the COGAIN website: http://www.cogain.org/conference

Skovsgaard, H. H. T., Hansen, J. P., & Mateo, J. C. (2008). How can tiny buttons be hit using gaze only? *Proceedings of the 4th Conference on Communication by Gaze Interaction (COGAIN 2008)* (pp. 38–42).

Soukoreff, R. W., & MacKenzie, I. S. (2001). Measuring errors in text entry tasks: An application of the Levenshtein string distance statistic. *Extended Abstracts of the ACM Conference on Human Factors in Computing Systems (CHI '01)* (pp. 319–320). New York, NY: ACM Press. doi:10.1145/634067.634256

Soukoreff, R. W., & MacKenzie, I. S. (2003). Metrics for text entry research: An evaluation of MSD and KSPC, and a new unified error metric. *Proceedings of the ACM Conference on Human Factors in Computing Systems (CHI '03)* (pp. 113–120). New York, NY: ACM Press. doi:10.1145/642611.642632

Tuisku, O., Majaranta, P., Isokoski, P., & Räihä, K.-J. (2008). Now Dasher! Dash away! Longitudinal study of fast text entry by eye gaze. *Proceedings of the 2008 Symposium on Eye Tracking Research and Applications (ETRA 2008)* (pp. 19–26). New York, NY: ACM Press. doi:10.1145/1344471.1344476

Chapter 15
Evaluating Eye Tracking Systems for Computer Input

I. Scott MacKenzie
York University, Canada

ABSTRACT

When a human uses an eye tracker for computer control, the eye is called upon to do 'double duty'. Not only is it an important sensory input channel, it also provides motor responses to control the computer. This chapter discusses methods of evaluating the interaction. When an eye tracker is used for computer input, how well does the interaction function? Can common tasks be carried out efficiently, quickly, accurately? What is the user's experience? How are alternative interaction methods evaluated and compared to identify those that work well, and deserve further study, and those that work poorly, and should be discarded? These are the sorts of questions that can be answered with a valid and robust methodology for evaluating eye trackers for computer input.

INTRODUCTION

The eye is a perceptual organ. In the normal course of events, the eye receives *sensory stimuli* from the environment. The stimuli are processed in the brain as 'information' and decisions are formulated on appropriate actions. The normal course of events also calls for the human's decisions to yield *motor responses* that effect changes in the environment. If the environment is a machine or computer, then the sensory stimuli come from *displays* and the motor responses act on *controls*. This scenario mirrors the classical view of the human–machine interface.

Figure *1* provides a diagram.

Although visual displays are the most common, it is also valid to speak of 'auditory displays' or 'tactile displays'. These are outputs from the machine or computer that stimulate the human sense of hearing or touch, respectively. Human

DOI: 10.4018/978-1-61350-098-9.ch015

Figure 1. Classical view of the human–machine interface (Chapanis, 1965, p. 20)

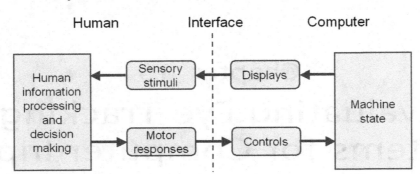

motor responses come by way of our fingers, hands, arms, legs, feet, and so on, and are used to control the machine or computer. Of course, speech and articulated sounds are also human responses and may act as controls to issue commands to the computer or machine. They are motor responses since the sound originates through movement in a human's larynx, or voice box.

Today, computing technology is pervasive and ubiquitous. Computers are used by humans for work and pleasure, in tasks both complex and trivial, and for pursuits mundane, challenging, and creative. Eye trackers are just one example of a computing technology that offers tremendous potential for humans. Applications for eye trackers can be divided along two lines. In one application, an eye tracker is a passive instrument that mea-

sures and monitors the eyes to determine where, and at what, the human is looking. In another, the eye tracker is an active controller that allows a human, through his or her eyes, to interact with and control a computer. When a human uses an eye tracker for computer control, the 'normal course of events' changes considerably. The eye is called upon to do 'double duty', so to speak. Not only is it an important sensory input channel, it also provides motor responses to control the computer. A revised diagram of the human–computer interface is shown in Figure 2. The normal path from the human to the computer is altered. Instead of the hand providing motor responses to control the computer through physical devices (set in grey), the eye provides motor responses that control the computer through 'soft controls'

Figure 2. The human–computer interface. With an eye tracker, the eye serves double duty, processing sensory stimuli from computer displays and providing motor responses to control the system

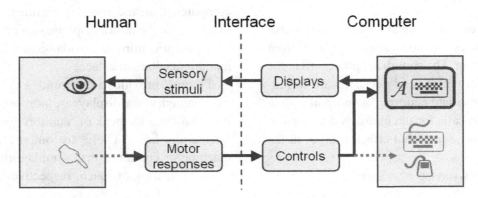

– virtual or graphical controls that appear on the system's display.

This chapter is focused on the second of these two applications – the use of an eye tracker for computer input. Our concern is with methods of evaluating the interaction. When an eye tracker is used for computer input, how well does the interaction function? Can common tasks be carried out efficiently, quickly, accurately? What is the user's experience? How are alternative interaction methods evaluated and compared to identify those that work well, and deserve further study, and those that work poorly, and should be discarded? These are the sorts of questions that can be answered with a valid and robust methodology for evaluating eye trackers for computer input.

COMPUTER INPUT

As a computer input device, an eye tracker emulates a computer mouse. Much as point-select operations with a mouse do, the eye can 'look-select' and thereby activate soft controls, such as buttons, icons, links, or text. Evaluating eye trackers for computer input, therefore, requires a methodology that addresses both the conventional issues for computer input using a mouse and the unique characteristics of the eye and the eye tracking apparatus.

In 1978, Card, English, and Burr undertook the first comparative evaluation of the mouse (Card, English, & Burr, 1978). Using tasks that combined cursor positioning with text selection, they compared a mouse to a joystick and two keying methods. Their study clearly established the superiority of the mouse. Many follow-on studies confirmed their findings. However, the methodologies used in the studies, taken as a whole, vary considerably, and this makes comparisons difficult. In view of this, a technical committee of the International Organization for Standardization (ISO TC159/SC4/WG3) undertook an initiative in the 1980s to standardise the testing methodology for computer pointing devices (Stewart, 2000). Draft versions were disseminated and assessed in the 1990s, with the final standard published in 2000 (ISO, 2000). Of interest here is Part 9, 'Requirements for Non-Keyboard Devices' (ISO 9241-9).

ISO 9241-9 lays out the methodology for assessing both performance and user comfort with input devices, such as mice, trackballs, touchpads, joysticks, and pens. Since an eye tracker emulates a mouse for computer input, it falls within the scope of the standard. The standard specifies seven performance tests, as described in Table 1.

Most pointing devices are capable, to varying degrees, of performing all of the tasks in Table 1. The unique challenge in using an eye tracker for

Table 1. Seven performance tests specified in ISO 9241-9 for non-keyboard input devices

Test	Test procedure
One-directional tapping	Manoeuvring a tracking symbol (e.g., a cursor) between two targets of width W separated by distance D and select the targets, using the device's selection method (e.g., pressing a button).
Multi-directional tapping	Acting similarly to in one-directional tapping, except using a circular arrangement of targets.
Dragging	Clicking and dragging, as in selection of an item in a pull-down menu or dragging of an object (e.g., a file icon) from one window to another.
Path-following	Moving an object (such as a circle) of width B between the borders of two parallel lines of length D separated by distance K without touching the boundary lines.
Tracing	Moving an object of width B within a track of width K formed by two concentric circles of radii R and $R+K$ without touching the boundary lines.
Free-hand input	Writing legible symbols (e.g., letters or digits) along a horizontal line of boxes of a specified dimension.
Grasp-and-park	Using the same hand, performing a series of simple pointing tasks while operating a key on the keyboard between tasks.

computer input is apparent in consideration of these same tasks. While 'look-select' is naturally suited to eye input, controlling the movement of an object or cursor along a path is not. The eyes move by saccades – quick movements of the point of gaze from one location to another. It is not feasible, for example, to use an eye tracker for path-following, tracing, or free-hand input – tasks easily done with a mouse or pen.

The test most commonly used for performance comparisons is the tapping task, either one-directional or multi-directional. Although traditional measures of speed and accuracy always serve as points of evaluation and comparison, the primary performance metric specified in the standard is 'throughput' (*TP*) in bits per second (bits/s). Throughput is a composite measure that includes both speed and accuracy of performance. Evidence suggests that a user's predisposition to emphasise speed vs. accuracy does not affect throughput (MacKenzie & Isokoski, 2008). Thus, differences in throughput are less susceptible to variation in the measures of speed or accuracy alone and are more likely due to inherent properties in the test conditions. This is an important and worthwhile property of throughput as a human performance metric.

The equation for throughput is Fitts' 'index of performance' (Fitts, 1954) except using an effective index of difficulty (*ID$_e$*). Specifically:

$$TP = \frac{ID_e}{MT} \tag{1}$$

where *MT* is the mean movement time, in seconds, for all trials within the same condition and:

$$ID_e = \log_2\left(\frac{D}{W_e} + 1\right) \tag{2}$$

ID$_e$, in bits, is calculated from *D*, the distance to the target, and *W$_e$*, the 'effective target width'. *W$_e$* is calculated as:

$$W_e = 4.133 \times SD_x \tag{3}$$

where SD_x is the standard deviation in the selection co-ordinates measured along the axis from the home position to the centre of the target. If multi-directional tapping is used, the data are first transformed, to effectively treat each trial as one-dimensional along the *x* axis. Using the effective target width allows throughput to incorporate the spatial variability in human performance. Thus, throughput includes both speed and accuracy (MacKenzie, 1992).

If one considers mouse evaluations in research *not* following the standard, throughput ranges from about 2.6 bits/s to 12.5 bits/s. Studies conforming to the standard report mouse throughputs from about 3.7 to 4.9 bits/s (Soukoreff & MacKenzie, 2004). The narrower spread in the ISO-conforming data is a clear sign that application of ISO 9241-9 improves the quality and comparability of device evaluations.

ISO 9241-9 assesses comfort by means of a questionnaire soliciting Likert-scale responses to 12 items (see Table 2). Items 1 through 7 are considered 'general indices', while items 8 through 12 are considered 'fatigue indices'. The questionnaire items are generally modified to suit the device condition under testing. In assessment of an eye tracker, for example, the items for finger, wrist, and arm fatigue are probably not relevant. An item may be used in their place for 'eye fatigue', instead.

EYE INPUT

Rather than controlling a cursor and moving it to a location, the eye simply looks at the location. However, unlike a mouse or other pointing device, the eye is not capable of moving a cursor or fixation point smoothly along a path. Changing the eye fixation point involves a rapid distance-traversing movement known as a saccade. Furthermore, the eye is incapable of fixating on a single pixel on a

Table 2. ISO 9241-9 questionnaire to assess device comfort

Force required for actuation:						
Very uncomfortable						Very comfortable
1	2	3	4	5	6	7
Smoothness during operation:						
Very rough						Very smooth
1	2	3	4	5	6	7
Effort required for operation:						
Very high						Very low
1	2	3	4	5	6	7
Accuracy:						
Very inaccurate						Very accurate
1	2	3	4	5	6	7
Operation speed:						
Unacceptable						Acceptable
1	2	3	4	5	6	7
General comfort:						
Very uncomfortable						Very comfortable
1	2	3	4	5	6	7
Overall operation of input device:						
Very difficult						Very easy
1	2	3	4	5	6	7
Finger fatigue:						
Very high						Very low
1	2	3	4	5	6	7
Wrist fatigue:						
Very high						Very low
1	2	3	4	5	6	7
Arm fatigue:						
Very high						Very low
1	2	3	4	5	6	7
Shoulder fatigue:						
Very high						Very low
1	2	3	4	5	6	7
Neck fatigue:						
Very high						Very low
1	2	3	4	5	6	7

computer display, to the exclusion of other pixels. Herein lies a significant challenge in use of an eye tracker for computer input. The problem (if we may call it that) is due to the part of the eye responsible for sharp central vision – the fovea. The fovea is the area of highest spatial resolution in the eye. It performs visual perception in tasks where detail is paramount, such as reading, driving, or sewing. Although it is often noted that the fovea captures *only* about two degrees of the visual field (a region about twice the width of a thumb at arm's length) (Duchowski, 2007, p. 14; Kammer, Scheiter, & Beinhauer, 2008; Komogortsev & Khan, 2006; Law, Atkins, Kirkpatrick, & Lomas, 2004; Tien & Atkins, 2008), a reverse perspective is more revealing: *because* the fovea's visual field is about two degrees, single-pixel sensing of the eye's fixation point on a computer display is simply not possible. This limitation is compounded by the inherent jitter in eye fixation (Law et al., 2004; Wobbrock, Rubinstein, Sawyer, & Duchowski, 2008). The eye's point of gaze is never perfectly still. Small jumps in the estimated co-ordinates of fixation are inherent with eye tracking systems, through no fault of the technology.

Target selection is another challenge for eye input to computers. While a computer mouse includes both movement tracking and selection capabilities, there is no equivalent or inherent 'button click' capability for the eye. Using an eye tracking system for computer input, therefore, requires an additional and satisfactory implementation of the select operation that typically follows pointing. One possibility is to use a separate physical switch for selection. The hand, a head action, or even a sip-and-puff straw can activate the switch. Speech is another potential modality for selection. Of course, these are not viable options if the goal is eyes-only input. Other possibilities engage the eye tracking technology in some manner. The most common method is dwell-time selection – maintaining the point of fixation on a selectable target for a pre-determined time interval (e.g., 700 ms). Dwell-time selection has performance

implications. Too long and the user is frustrated. Too short and unintended selections occur. Blinks, winks, or nods are other selection possibilities, if the eye tracking system includes the requisite image processing capabilities.

It is clear from the brief characterisation of eye input above that eye tracking systems present significant challenges when used for computer input. There are a myriad of parameters that are ripe for experimental testing. Whether one is considering the selection method; the duration of dwells or blinks for selection; or techniques to filter, alias, or smooth a noisy data stream, a methodology that allows for the empirical evaluation and comparison of alternatives is necessary. Two example evaluations involving eye trackers are elaborated upon below. Both embrace the ISO-standardised testing methodology for pointing devices in the context of eye tracking for computer input.

EXAMPLE 1: DWELL-TIME VS. KEY-BASED SELECTION

In the first example, three selection methods for an eye tracker are compared (portions of this example are based on work by Zhang and MacKenzie, 2007). A fourth condition – a mouse – serves as a baseline condition. The idea of a baseline condition is to include a technique that is commonly known and has been used with previous experimental testing of a similar nature. If the results for the baseline condition match those for the same condition in previous research, the methodology 'checks out', so to speak.

Participants

Sixteen paid volunteer participants (11 male, 5 female) were recruited from the local university campus. Participants ranged from 22 to 33 years (mean = 25). All were daily users of computers, reporting 4–12 hours of usage per day (mean = 7). None had prior experience with eye tracking.

All participants had normal vision, except one who wore contact lenses. Nine participants were right-eye-dominant, seven left-eye dominant, as determined by means of an eye dominance test (Collins & Blackwell, 1974).

Apparatus

An Arrington Research (http://www.arringtonresearch.com/) *ViewPoint* head-fixed eye tracking system served as the primary input device (3). The eye tracker was connected to a conventional desktop PC running Microsoft *Windows XP*. The system's display was a 19" 1280 × 1024 LCD. The tracker sampled at 30 Hz with an accuracy of a 0.25–1.0° visual arc, about 10–40 pixels with the configuration used.

The experimental software was a discrete-task implementation of the multi-directional tapping test in ISO 9241-9, as described in Table 1. It is similar in operation to the experimental software in an early ISO-conforming evaluation for pointing devices (Douglas, Kirkpatrick, & MacKenzie, 1999). Raw eye data and event data were collected and saved for follow-up analyses.

Procedure

Participants were briefed on the purpose and objectives of the experiment and on the operation of the eye tracker and the selection methods employed. They sat at a viewing distance of approximately 60 cm from the display. Calibration was performed before the first eye technique, with recalibration as needed.

At the start of each trial, a home square appeared at the centre of the screen. See Figure 4a. At the same time, the circle for the designated target was outlined in blue, with a blue dot in the centre. The home square disappeared after participants dwelled on it, pressed the SPACE key, or clicked the left mouse button, depending on the interaction technique. To exclude physical reaction time, positioning time started when the eye or mouse first moved after the home square disappeared. The task was to select the target circle. When the target circle received focus, it became white with a red dot in the centre (see Figure 4b). The dot helped participants fixate at the centre of the target. The grey background was designed to reduce the eye stress caused by colours, such as a white background. For the three eye techniques, the mouse pointer was hidden, to reduce visual distraction.

Figure 3. Experimental set-up

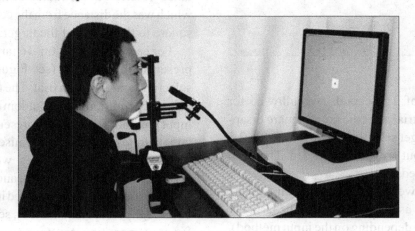

Figure 4. Multi-dimensional target selection task. Gaze on home square with target identified (b) Gaze on target

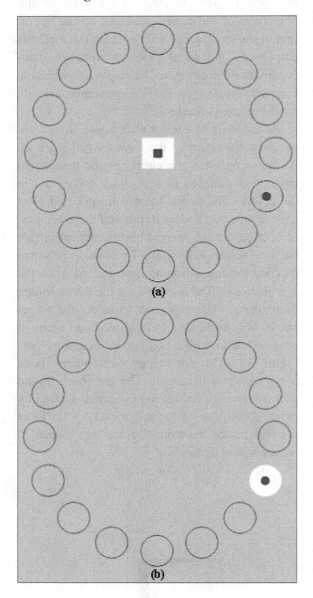

An interval of 2.5 seconds was allowed for completion of a trial after the home square disappeared. If no target selection occurred within 2.5 seconds, a timeout error was recorded. Then, the next trial followed.

Participants were instructed to point to the target as quickly as possible (look at the target or move the mouse, depending on the input method),

then select the target as quickly as possible (dwell on the target, press the SPACE key, or click the left mouse button, depending on the input method). After finishing the trials, the participants were interviewed and completed a questionnaire.

Design

The experiment wasa 3 × 2 × 2 within-subjects design. Independent variables and levels were as follows:

Input method: ETL, ETS, ESK, mouse
Target width: 75, 100 pixels
Target distance: 275, 350 pixels

The Eye Tracker Long (ETL) input method required participants to look at an on-screen target and dwell on it for 750 ms for selection. The dwell time was 500 ms for the Eye Tracker Short (ETS) technique. The Eye+SPACE Key (ESK) technique allowed participants to 'point' with the eye and 'select' by pressing the SPACE key upon fixation. To minimise learning effects, the four input methods were counterbalanced by means of a 4 × 4 balanced Latin square.

The two additional independent variables were included as recommended in ISO 9241-9 to ensure that the trials covered a reasonable and representative range of difficulties. Target width was the diameter of the target circle. 'Target distance' referred to the radius of the layout circle, which was the distance from the centre of the home square to the centre of the target circle.

For each test condition, 16 target circles were presented for selection (see Figure 4), with each selection constituting a trial. The target width and distance conditions were randomised within each input method. The order of presentation of the 16 target circles was also randomised.

The dependent variables were throughput (bits/s), movement time (ms), and error rate (%). As movement time is represented in the calculation of throughput (see Equation 1), separate analyses for movement time are not presented here.

Figure 5. Throughput (bit/s) by input method. Error bars show ±1 SD

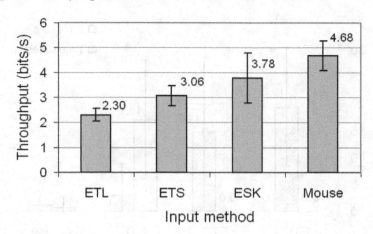

Results and Discussion

Throughput

As is evident from Figure 5, there was a significant effect of input method on throughput ($F_{3,45} = 47.46$, $p < .0001$). The throughput for the mouse of 4.68 bits/s is in the range cited earlier for ISO 9241-9 mouse evaluations (Soukoreff & MacKenzie, 2004), thus verifying the methodology. The 500 ms dwell time with the ETS technique seemed just right. The ETL condition had a lower throughput than ETS did. This is in part due to the 250 ms difference in the settings for dwell time. ESK was the best of the three eye tracking techniques. This is attributed to participants effectively pressing the SPACE key immediately upon fixation on the target. This eliminated the need to wait for selection. The throughput of the ESK technique was 3.78 bits/s, which approaches the 4.68 bits/s for the mouse. Given that the mouse has the best performance among non-keyboard input devices (ibid.), the ESK technique is very promising. As the user must press the SPACE key (or another key), this observation is tempered by acknowledgement

The total number of trials was 16 participants × 4 interaction techniques × 2 distances × 2 widths × 16 trials = 4,096.

that the ESK technique is appropriate only where an additional key press is possible and practical.

Error rates and Timeout Error

For the ETL and ETS techniques, participants selected the target by dwelling on it. Thus, the outcome was either a selection or a timeout error. Therefore, the error rates for ETL and ETS were zero, as shown in *Figure 6*. The timeout errors for the ETL, ETS, and ESK techniques were mainly caused by eye jitter and limitations in the eye tracker's accuracy. The more time taken to perform a selection, the greater the chance of a timeout error. ESK had 2.9% timeout errors, a figure substantially less than those for the other eye conditions, and, accordingly, approaches the 1.1% timeout errors for the mouse.

The ESK method had a high error rate. This is a classic example of the speed–accuracy trade-off. Here, it is attributed to participants pressing the SPACE key just before fixating on the target, or slightly after the eye moved outside the target area. Because no participant had prior experience with eye tracking, few could proficiently perform the co-ordinated task of eye pointing and manual pressing of the SPACE key. The error rate for the ESK technique varied a great deal across participants (SD = 11.4, max. = 35.6, min. = 3.1).

Figure 6. Error rate and timeout error figures by input method

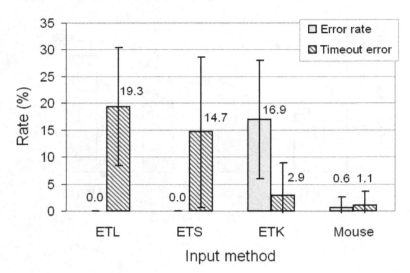

Participants would likely demonstrate lower error rates if further training were provided and improved feedback mechanisms were considered and tested.

The Questionnaire

The device assessment questionnaire consisted of 12 items, modeled on the response items suggested in ISO 9241-9 (see *Table 2*). The questions pertained to eye tracking in general, as opposed to a particular eye tracking selection technique. Each response was rated on a seven-point scale, with 7 as the most favourable response, 4 the midpoint on the scale, and 1 the least favourable response. Responses for seven of the 12 items are shown in *Figure 7*.

As seen, participants generally liked the fast positioning time of the eye tracker. For operation speed, the mean score was high, at 6.2. However, eye fatigue was a concern (3.5). Participants complained that staring at so many targets made

Figure 7. Eye tracker device assessment questionnaire. Response 7 is the most favourable, response 1 the least favourable

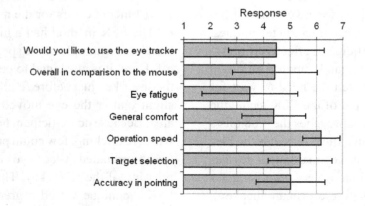

their eyes dry and uncomfortable. Among all of the questions, eye fatigue received the lowest score. Participants gave eye tracking a modest favourable response overall of 4.5, just slightly higher than the midpoint. Discussions following the experiment revealed that participants liked to use eye tracking and believed it could perform similarly to the mouse. Of the three eye tracking techniques, participants expressed a preference for the Eye+SPACE Key technique. Concerns were voiced, however, about the likely expense of an eye tracking system, the cumbersome calibration procedure, and the uncomfortable requirement of maintaining a fixed head position.

EXAMPLE 2: BLINK-BASED VS. DWELL-TIME SELECTION

The second example evaluates and compares dwell time versus blink for target selection. The evaluation also pushes the limits of eye tracking technology by using small targets.

Participants

Twelve volunteer participants (9 male, 3 female) were recruited from the local university campus. None had prior experience with use of an eye tracker, but all were experienced mouse-users. Vision was normal for all participants except for one who wore glasses and another who wore contact lenses during the experiment.

Apparatus

The eye tracker was an EyeTech Digital Systems (see http://www.eyetechds.com/) *TM3* eye tracker working with *Quick Glance* version 5.0.1 software. Unlike the device used in the previous study, the TM3 is reasonably portable, as there is no chin rest. It is also less cumbersome to set up and calibrate. The device uses infrared emitters that illuminate the eyes to create reference points

Figure 8. Quick Glance software displaying crosshairs on the user's eyes for reference points

for tracking of eye position and movement. The tracker confirms proper detection of the user's eyes through crosshairs on the image of the face (Figure *8*).

Calibration presents 16 circles on the display, with the user looking at the centre of each for 1.5 seconds, when the next target appears. The procedure returns a numeric score for each eye, where a lower score means less estimated deviation from the point of fixation to the centre of the target. Before the start of the experiment, the eye tracker was calibrated iteratively to achieve a score no higher than 4.0 for each eye, with no more than a 0.4 deviation between each eye. Calibration took an average of six minutes per participant.

Dwell-time-based selection uses a default dwell area of 20 mm; the fixation point must remain within the designated area for a specified amount of time before a click event occurs. We used the smallest allowable size, 5 mm, as the setting in the experiment. An error was logged if the computed fixation point was outside the target at the end of the dwell interval. An audible click was heard at the same time as a selection event. Cursor movement was smoothed with a smoothing factor of 10, as set in the software.

The camera operates at 30 frames per second, with a 16 × 12 cm field of view and a pixel density of 64.6 pixels/cm. The host computer was a Lenovo *3000 N100* laptop with a 15" screen running Microsoft *Windows XP*. The eye tracker was placed in front of, and below, the screen, with the angle adjusted accordingly.

Procedure

Following a briefing on the goals and objectives of the experiment, participants were asked to sit in front of the laptop with their head approximately 60 cm in front of the display and eye tracker (*Figure 9*). They were asked to sit comfortably and to try not to move their head during the experiment.

After successful calibration, the experimental software was launched. The software was a Java application implementing a serial-task version of the multi-dimensional tapping test specified in ISO 9241-9. Participants were instructed in how to select with the eye tracker and on the presence of the 'click' auditory feedback. They were allowed as much practice as desired before beginning the experiment. When participants were ready to start, the software was launched in data collection mode. They were instructed to begin each block of trails by selecting the red target 'as

Figure 9. Experiment set-up. The EyeTech TM3 eye tracker is seen below the LCD

quickly and accurately as possible'. This triggered the start of time measurement.

After the experiment was finished, each participant completed a questionnaire, designed to solicit qualitative responses concerning their experience with the eye tracker.

Design

The experiment was a 3 ×2 × 2 × 4 within-subjects design. The independent variables and levels were as follows:

Input method: Blink (eye tracker), dwell (eye tracker), mouse
Target width: 16, 32 pixels (6, 12 mm)
Target distance: 256, 512 pixels
Block 1, 2, 3, 4

The eye tracker conditions differed by selection technique. For both blink and dwell time, the duration was set to 500 ms. The target width conditions are at the extreme limit of the capabilities of eye tracking technology for selection of small targets. Therefore, one would expect the results to be somewhat poorer than those with larger targets.

For each target distance and width condition, the participant was presented with 17 circular targets, arranged in a circle. The diameter of the layout circle is the target distance. The diameter of the target circle is the target width. Figure 10 shows an example with the order of target selection indicated. The first trial begins with the first selection (circle in red). Each arrangement of 17 targets creates 16 trials. On each selection, the next target is highlighted in red.

The dependent variables were throughput (bits/s), movement time (ms), and error rate (%). As with the example detailed above, analyses for movement time are not presented here.

The order of administration of the input method conditions was counterbalanced. Given the overhead in calibration of the eye tracker, a nested

Figure 10. Sample block with order of target selection

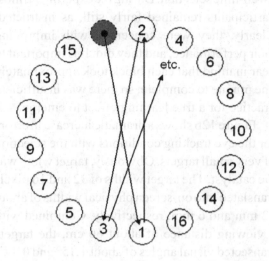

eye-mouse counterbalancing scheme was used, with three participants in each group:

Blink, dwell, mouse
Dwell, blink, mouse
Mouse, blink, dwell
Mouse, dwell, blink

After each block was completed, a dialog box displayed the participant's results for the block. Participants were encouraged to rest before continuing to the next block. After all four blocks were completed; a final dialog displayed their overall results.

The total number of trials in the experiment was 12 participants × 3 input methods × 2 widths × 2 distances × 4 blocks × 16 trials/block = 9,216.

Results and Discussion

Throughput

As Figure 11 depicts, and as expected, the mouse had a much higher throughput than either eye tracking condition ($F_{2,11} = 159.36$, $p < .0001$). The throughput for the mouse was 4.79 bits/s,

Figure 11. Throughput (bits/s) by input method

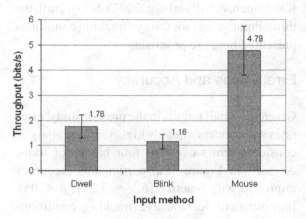

which was very close to the value of 4.68 bits/s reported in the previous study (using a different host computer and different software). This alone is testimony to the consistency ISO 9241-9 brings to pointing device evaluations.

In comparison of the eye tracking conditions, dwell-time selection was seen to have a much higher throughput. The throughput of 1.79 bits/s with dwell-time selection was 51.6% higher than the throughput of 1.16 bits/s observed when blink-based selection was used. These values are low when compared to those with the mouse and in comparison to the eye tracking evaluation presented in the preceding section. However, it is important to keep in mind at least two factors. One is the use of a fixed-head tracking system with the Arrington Research ViewPoint, which inherently simplifies the eye tracking problem. The other is the very stringent target conditions in the present evaluation. Error rates were (understandably) high and somewhat erratic, as discussed further in the next section. This, no doubt, played a significant role in the low values for throughput. Notably, throughput values below 2 bits/s are common, even in studies applying ISO 9241-9. Examples include a remote pointing device at 1.4 bits/s (MacKenzie & Jusoh, 2001), a touchpad at 1.8 bits/s (Douglas et al., 1999), a touchpad at 1.0 bits/s (MacKenzie & Oniszczak,

1998), and a joystick at 1.8 bits/s (MacKenzie, Kauppinen, & Silfverberg, 2001). So, overall, the throughput values for the eye tracking conditions presented here are promising.

Error Rates and Accuracy

Given the small targets in the present study, error rates were understandably high. Our first analysis considers errors over the four blocks of trials. As seen in Figure 12a, participants' accuracy improved with practice ($F_{3,10}$ = 3.247, $p < .05$). Improvement for the eye tracking conditions was most significant with dwell-time selection. Nevertheless, even on the fourth block, error rates

Figure 12. Error rates (a) by block and input method and (b) by input method and target width. Error bars show ±1 SD

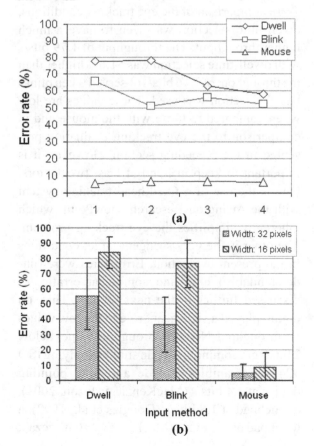

were high: 52.2% for blink selection and 58.3% for dwell-time selection. During the experiment, most participants remained fairly still, as instructed. Clearly, they were concerned with improving their performance, and they did. It is important to bear in mind that each block took approximately one minute to complete; so there was insufficient practice for a true learning effect to emerge.

Figure 12b shows a dramatic increase in errors for the eye tracking conditions with the selection of very small targets. Obviously, target width was the catalyst. The target widths of 32 and 16 pixels translated into on-screen physical widths of about 12 mm and 6 mm, respectively. Combined with a viewing distance of about 60 cm, the targets transected visual angles of about 1.15° and 0.57°, respectively. Thus, the target sizes taxed the limits related to the physiology of the eye. Given the eye's constant micro-saccades and the fovea size, even a 'perfect' eye tracker limits selection to targets transecting ≈1° of visual angle (Barcelos & Morimoto, 2008). Therefore, the results in Figure 12 are expected.

To provide further insight on the eye tracking experience, Figure *13* traces the changes in eye fixation for one block of trials using dwell-time selection with target distance = 512 pixels and target width = 16 pixels. Saccades are evident in the straight-line segments. At the end of each trail, most traces reveal a stream of fluctuations in the estimated point of gaze. The final selection co-ordinate (small red circle) was slightly off the target in most cases.

In the research literature, many creative solutions have been proposed and tested to accommodate the accuracy and jitter problems that arise with the use of an eye tracker for computer input. An example is shown in Figure 14a. Two ideas are proposed: an expansion factor (EF) and grab-and-hold selection (Miniotas, Špakov, & MacKenzie, 2004). Using an expansion factor means that a selectable target is automatically assigned a larger, expanded area according to an expansion factor set in the software. The ex-

Figure 13. Multi-directional test using an eye tracker with dwell-time selection. The targets are circles with diameter 16 pixels, or about 6 mm as measured on the display. Viewing distance was about 60 cm

Figure 14. (a) Virtual expansion of the target area to facilitate selection (Miniotas et al., 2004). (b) The target from the 7 o'clock position in Figure 13. An error becomes a correct selection with an expansion factor (dotted line)

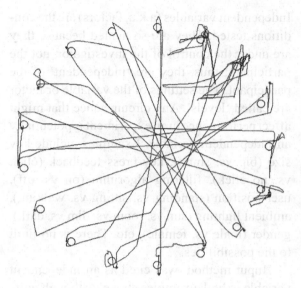

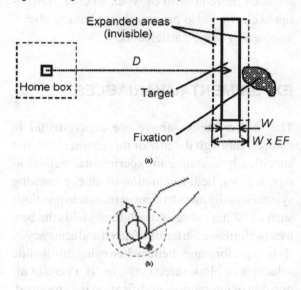

panded area is not seen by the user but is used in the interface to create a virtual expansion to the targeted region. The idea has been used successfully in conventional graphical user interfaces (Grossman & Balakrishnan, 2005; McGuffin & Balakrishnan, 2002) and may also work with eye tracking interfaces. Grab-and-hold is a technique to improve dwell-time selection. As soon as a fixation point is detected within the target or the target's expanded area, the target is grabbed and the dwell timer is started. Provided that there is no saccade during the dwell interval, the target is selected at the end of the dwell interval, even if the fixation points exhibit drift or jitter and never actually enter the target. This is seen in the fixation area in Figure 14a.

Figure 14b shows one of the target selections logged as an error in Figure *13*. A hypothetical expanded area is shown around the target. Had the experimental software used the expanded area and grab-and-hold selection, the result would likely be correct selection. The example above is

given mainly to acknowledge the sort of research initiatives that can be explored with an evaluation methodology of the likes presented in the two examples here and as offered in ISO 9241-9.

Questionnaire and Interviews

The eye tracker assessment questionnaire administered at the end of the experiment included 11 items asking participants about their overall experience, preferences, eye tracking performance, and fatigue. The rating was done on a five-point Likert scale with 1 the least favourable response and 5 the most favourable. The midpoint score was 3.

Participants were impressed with the performance of the eye tracker – in particular, with its smoothness (3.6) and operation speed (3.7). Eye fatigue was the biggest concern (1.2). In the discussions after the experiment, participants said that they enjoyed using the eye tracker but still preferred to use a standard mouse. There was concern about the long calibration process, keeping the head still for so long, and maintaining a specific distance from the eye tracker. Participants generally preferred blink-based selection to dwell-time selection, as they felt that the former afforded more control of when to click. Dwell-time selection also produced involuntary clicks, as noted by some participants.

EXPERIMENTAL VARIABLES

The two examples above are experimental in nature. Although the title of this chapter does not specifically reference an experimental methodology, it is implied. Evaluation of an eye tracking system usually aims to answer research questions such as 'What value of dwell time yields the best user performance in terms of speed and accuracy?', 'Is user performance better when using dwell-time selection or blink selection?', or 'If a certain algorithm or interaction modification is introduced, does user performance improve?'. These questions are best answered via a controlled experiment; two examples were given above. One advantage of control experiments is that conclusions of a 'cause and effect' nature are possible. If, for example, the experiment involved comparing two or more dwell-time selection intervals and user performance was best with a particular interval, then it is possible to conclude that the improvement was due to, or caused by, the dwell-time selection interval – provided that the experiment was designed and conducted according to an established methodology for experimental research with human participants. This is precisely the sort of information researchers are pursuing in their investigations.

While a complete tutorial on experiment design is beyond the scope of this chapter, some final comments are offered on the two primary variables in experimental research. Whether the experiment engages an eye tracker for computer input or tests some other aspect of the human–computer interface, the *independent variables* and the *dependent variables* set the tone for the entire experiment.

Independent Variables

Independent variables (a.k.a. factors) are the conditions tested. They are so named because they are under the control of the investigator, not the participant; thus, they are 'independent' of the participant. The settings of the variable or factor are called 'levels'. Any circumstance that might affect performance in an experiment is potentially an independent variable. Examples include key size (big vs. small), key-press feedback (click vs. no click), filtering algorithm (on vs. off), user position (standing vs. sitting vs. walking), ambient lighting (sun vs. room vs. dim vs. dark), gender (male vs. female), etc. There is no limit to the possibilities.

'Input method' was cited as an independent variable in both examples above. Although quite broad, the term served to encompass the levels, which were 750 ms dwell time vs. 500 ms dwell time vs. key press selection vs. mouse in the first example and dwell time vs. blink vs. mouse in the second. Both examples investigated methods of selection; however, as a mouse condition was included, 'input method' is a reasonable name for the factor.

In experimental evaluations of eye tracking systems, numerous other independent variables appear in the literature. A few examples are given in Table 3. Note that there is both a name for the independent variable (left column) and a delimitation of two or more levels of the variable (right column).

The last entry in Table 3, feedback mode, is a typical example of an aspect of eye tracking interaction well suited to experimental testing. Providing users with feedback about the state of the system is a long-held principle of good user interface design (e.g., Norman, 1988, p. 17). The same holds true for eye tracking systems – even more so, in fact. Even though eye tracking systems

Table 3. Examples of independent variables from experimental evaluations of eye tracking systems

Independent variable	Study	Description
Cursor redressment method	Zhang, Ren, & Zha, 2008	Comparison of four methods to improve the stability of the eye cursor by counteracting eye jitter. The methods were force field, speed reduction, warping to target centre, and no action.
Prediction mode	Zhang & MacKenzie, 2007	Comparison of letter prediction and word prediction in eye typing using a soft keyboard.
Algorithm	Zhai, Morimoto, & Ihde, 1999	Comparison of two settings of an algorithm to improve target selection by warping the eye cursor's area to encompass the target.
Fisheye mode	Ashmore, Duchowski, & Shoemaker, 2005	Comparison of four fisheye techniques to improve target selection. The techniques were no action, always on, and appearing only after fixation begins (with and without a grab-and-hold algorithm).
Typing system	Itoh, Aoki, & Hansen, 2006	Comparison of three eye typing systems for Japanese text entry. The systems were Dasher and two variants of GazeTalk (positioning the text window either at the top left or in the centre of the display).
Feedback mode	Majaranta, MacKenzie, Aula, & Räiha, 2006	Comparison of four feedback modes for keys on a soft keyboard used for text entry. The modes were visual only, click+visual, speech+visual, and speech only.

are often configured to emulate a mouse, an on-screen tracking symbol typically is not used, as it is distracting to the user and reduces the naturalness of look-select interaction. If dwell-time selection is used, pre-selection feedback helps to inform the user that the point of gaze is on a selectable item (and that selection is imminent!).

The feedback-mode example in Table 3 compared four types of feedback: visual only, click+visual, speech+visual, and speech only. The three visual modes indicated the progress of the dwell interval via a shrinking letter, which turned red on final selection. This is shown in Figure 15a. The idea of a shrinking letter is to 'draw in' the user's vi-

Figure 15. Pre-selection and dwell-time feedback. Pre-selection begins in the second frame. Dwell status is indicated by means of (a) a shrinking letter (Majaranta et al., 2006) or (b) a progress bar (Hansen, Hansen, & Johansen, 2001)

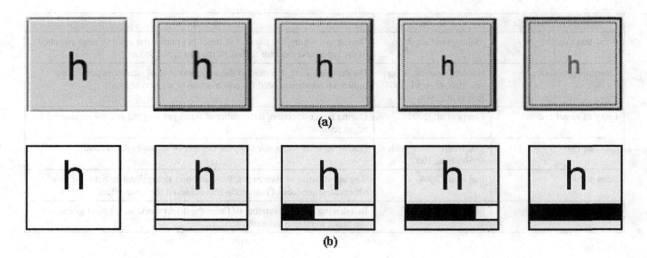

(a)

(b)

sual attention during the dwell time, and thus improve the stability in the point of gaze. An alternative is a simple progress bar, as shown in *Figure 15*b. The idea was a success. Text entry speed was significantly higher with the shrinking-letter feedback. Of the three visual feedback modes, the best performance was seen with the addition of auditory feedback using a 'click' sound on selection.

Dependent Variables

Dependent variables are the measured behaviours of participants. They are dependent in that they 'depend on' what the participants do. The most common dependent variables are related to the speed and accuracy with which participants perform tasks in the experiment. In the case of text entry using eye typing, speed is usually reported in words per minute or characters per minute. However, in interactions such as basic pointing and selecting, speed is usually reported in its reciprocal form, the time to complete a task. Beginning with ISO 9241-9 and with related work on computer pointing devices, throughput (bits/s) is also becoming widely used as a dependent variable. As noted above, throughput is a composite measure including both the speed and accuracy in participants' responses.

Besides coarse measures of speed, accuracy, and throughput, researchers often devise new dependent measures as appropriate for the interaction technique under investigation. In fact, any observable, measurable aspect of the interaction is a potential dependent variable, provided that it offers insight into human performance with an interaction technique. Some examples from the eye tracking literature are given in Table 4.

It is easy to imagine how the dependent variables in Table 4 can elicit a finer granularity of insight into participant behaviour. They provide information not just on the overall responses for trials but on aspects of the interaction that are present during trials.

In most research papers, the independent and dependent variables come together in the results section in statements of the form 'there was a significant effect of {independent variable} on {dependent variable}'. The statement is typically accompanied with the supporting statistical test, such as an analysis of variance. Consult any of the papers cited in Figure 15 and Table 4 for examples.

Table 4. Examples of dependent variables in experimental evaluations of eye tracking systems

Dependent variable	Study	Description
Read-text events	Majaranta et al., 2006	During eye typing, the number of times per phrase the point of gaze switched to the typed text field for review of the text typed so far.
Overproduction rate	Hansen, Tørning, Johansen, Itoh, & Aoki, 2004; Itoh et al., 2006	During eye typing, the ratio of the actual number of gaze selections to the minimum number needed for construction of a given sentence.
Entry of target events	Zhang et al., 2008	During target selection, the number of times per trial the eye cursor entered the target region.
Saccade rate	Takahashi, Nakayama, & Shimizu, 2000	During an audio-response task, the number of saccades per second.
Scan paths	Pan et al., 2004	During viewing of Web pages, the minimum string distance between two observed sequences of scan paths that achieved the same effect.
Off-road glances	Sodhi et al., 2002	In a driving task, the number of times the driver made an off-road glance (at the radio, mirror, or odometer).

CONCLUSION

The central issues in evaluation of eye trackers for computer input have been presented, along with two examples of experimental evaluations. One evaluation used the Arrington Research head-fixed eye tracker ViewPoint (see Figure 3); the other used an EyeTech Digital Systems TM3 (see *Figure 9*). The examples included 'input method' as the main independent variable. The methods included different settings of the time interval for dwell-time selection (500 ms and 750 ms) and a comparison of dwell-time with blink selection. Another method combined eye pointing with key selection. In both evaluations, a mouse was included as a baseline condition. The main dependent variable was throughput (bits/s) as stipulated in ISO 9241-9 – the 2000 ISO standard for evaluating and comparing non-keyboard input devices. The eye tracking conditions yielded throughput values in the range of 1.16 bits/s to 3.78 bits/s. These were, as expected, lower than the values of about 4.7 bits/s seen with the mouse. Overall, the eye tracking conditions show considerable promise for providing an alternative input modality for human interaction with computers.

ACKNOWLEDGMENT

Thanks are offered to research assistants William Zhang and Matthew Conte. This research has been sponsored by the Natural Sciences and Engineering Research Council of Canada. Thanks are also extended to EyeTech Digital Systems for the loan of a TM3 eye tracker.

REFERENCES

Ashmore, M., Duchowski, A. T., & Shoemaker, G. (2005). Efficient eye pointing with a fisheye lens. [Toronto, Canada: Canadian Information Processing Society.]. *Proceedings of Graphics Interface, 2005*, 203–210.

Barcelos, T. S., & Morimoto, C. H. (2008). GinX: Gaze-based interface extensions. *Proceedings of the ACM Symposium on Eye Tracking Research and Applications (ETRA '08)* (pp. 149–152). New York, NY: ACM.

Card, S. K., English, W. K., & Burr, B. J. (1978). Evaluation of mouse, rate-controlled isometric joystick, step keys, and text keys for text selection on a CRT. *Ergonomics, 21*, 601–613. doi:10.1080/00140137808931762

Chapanis, A. (1965). *Man–machine engineering*. Belmont, CA, US: Wadsworth Publishing Company.

Collins, J. F., & Blackwell, L. K. (1974). Effects of eye dominance and retinal distance on binocular rivalry. *Perceptual and Motor Skills, 39*, 747–754.

Douglas, S. A., Kirkpatrick, A. E., & MacKenzie, I. S. (1999). Testing pointing device performance and user assessment with the ISO 9241, Part 9 standard. *Proceedings of the ACM Conference on Human Factors in Computing Systems (CHI '99)* (pp. 215–222). New York, NY: ACM.

Duchowski, A. T. (2007). *Eye tracking methodology: Theory and practice*. Berlin-Heidelberg, Germany: Springer.

Fitts, P. M. (1954). The information capacity of the human motor system in controlling the amplitude of movement. *Journal of Experimental Psychology, 47*, 381–391. doi:10.1037/h0055392

Grossman, T., & Balakrishnan, R. (2005). The bubble cursor: Enhancing target acquisition by dynamic resizing of the cursor's activation area. *Proceedings of the ACM Conference on Human Factors in Computing Systems (CHI '05)* (pp. 281–290). New York, NY: ACM.

Hansen, J. P., Hansen, D. W., & Johansen, A. S. (2001). Bringing gaze-based interaction back to basics. *Proceedings of HCI International 2001* (pp. 325–328). Mahwah, NJ, US: Erlbaum.

Hansen, J. P., Tørning, K., Johansen, A. S., Itoh, K., & Aoki, H. (2004). Gaze typing compared with input by head and hand. *Proceedings of the ACM Symposium on Eye Tracking Research and Applications (ETRA '04)* (pp. 131–138). New York, NY: ACM.

ISO. (2000). *Ergonomic requirements for office work with visual display terminals (vdts) – Part 9: Requirements for non-keyboard input devices (ISO 9241-9) (report code ISO/TC 159/SC4/WG3 N147)*. International Organization for Standardization.

Itoh, K., Aoki, H., & Hansen, J. P. (2006). A comparative usability study of two Japanese gaze typing systems. *Proceedings of the ACM Symposium on Eye Tracking Research and Applications (ETRA '06)* (pp. 59–66). New York, NY: ACM.

Kammer, Y., Scheiter, K., & Beinhauer, W. (2008). Looking my way through the menu: The impact of menu design and multimodal input on gaze-based menu selection. *Proceedings of the ACM Symposium on Eye Tracking Research and Applications (ETRA '08)* (pp. 213–220). New York, NY: ACM.

Komogortsev, O., & Khan, J. (2006). Perceptual attention focus prediction for multiple viewers in case of multimedia perceptual compression with feedback delay. *Proceedings of the ACM Symposium on Eye Tracking Research and Applications (ETRA '06)* (pp. 101–108). New York, NY: ACM.

Law, B., Atkins, M. S., Kirkpatrick, A. E., & Lomas, A. J. (2004). Eye gaze patterns differentiate novice and experts in a virtual laparoscopic surgery training environment. *Proceedings of the ACM Symposium on Eye Tracking Research and Applications (ETRA '04)* (pp. 41–48). New York, NY: ACM.

MacKenzie, I. S. (1992). Fitts' law as a research and design tool in human–computer interaction. *Human-Computer Interaction, 7*, 91–139. doi:10.1207/s15327051hci0701_3

MacKenzie, I. S., & Isokoski, P. (2008). Fitts' throughput and the speed-accuracy tradeoff. *Proceedings of the ACM SIGCHI Conference on Human Factors in Computing Systems (CHI '08)* (pp. 1633–1636). New York, NY: ACM.

MacKenzie, I. S., & Jusoh, S. (2001). An evaluation of two input devices for remote pointing. *Proceedings of the 8th IFIP Working Conference on Engineering for Human–Computer Interaction (EHCI '00)* (pp. 235–249). Heidelberg, Germany: Springer-Verlag.

MacKenzie, I. S., Kauppinen, T., & Silfverberg, M. (2001). Accuracy measures for evaluating computer pointing devices. *Proceedings of the ACM Conference on Human Factors in Computing Systems (CHI '01)* (pp. 119–126). New York, NY: ACM.

MacKenzie, I. S., & Oniszczak, A. (1998). A comparison of three selection techniques for touchpads. *Proceedings of the ACM SIGCHI Conference on Human Factors in Computing Systems (CHI '98)* (pp. 336–343). New York, NY: ACM.

Majaranta, P., MacKenzie, I. S., Aula, A., & Räihä, K.-J. (2006). Effects of feedback and dwell time on eye typing speed and accuracy. *Universal Access in the Information Society, 5*(2), 199–208. doi:10.1007/s10209-006-0034-z

McGuffin, M., & Balakrishnan, R. (2002). Acquisition of expanding targets. *Proceedings of the ACM Conference on Human Factors in Computing Systems (CHI '02)* (pp. 57–64). New York, NY: ACM.

Miniotas, D., Špakov, O., & MacKenzie, I. S. (2004). Eye gaze interaction with expanding targets. *Extended Abstracts of the ACM Conference on Human Factors in Computing Systems (CHI '04)* (pp. 1255–1258). New York, NY: ACM.

Norman, D. A. (1988). *The design of everyday things*. New York, NY: Basic Books.

Pan, B., Hembrooke, H. A., Gay, G. K., Granka, L. A., Feusner, M. K., & Newman, J. K. (2004). The determinants of Web page viewing behavior: An eye-tracking study. *Proceedings of the ACM Symposium on Eye Tracking Research and Applications (ETRA '04)* (pp. 147–154). New York, NY: ACM.

Sodhi, M., Reimer, B., Cohen, J. L., Vastenburg, E., Kaars, R., & Kirschenbaum, S. (2002). Off road driver eye movement tracking using head-mounted devices. *Proceedings of the ACM Symposium on Eye Tracking Research and Applications (ETRA '02)* (pp. 61–68). New York, NY: ACM.

Soukoreff, R. W., & MacKenzie, I. S. (2004). Towards a standard for pointing device evaluation: Perspectives on 27 years of Fitts' law research in HCI. *International Journal of Human-Computer Studies*, *61*, 751–789. doi:10.1016/j.ijhcs.2004.09.001

Stewart, T. (2000). Ergonomics user interface standards: Are they more trouble than they are worth? *Ergonomics*, *43*, 1030–1044. doi:10.1080/001401300409206

Takahashi, K., Nakayama, M., & Shimizu, Y. (2000). The response of eye movement and pupil size to audio instruction while viewing a moving target. *Proceedings of the ACM Symposium on Eye Tracking Research and Applications (ETRA '00)* (pp. 131–138). New York, NY: ACM.

Tien, G., & Atkins, M. S. (2008). Improving hands-free menu selection using eye gaze glances and fixations. *Proceedings of the ACM Symposium on Eye Tracking Research and Applications (ETRA '08)* (pp. 47–50). New York, NY: ACM.

Wobbrock, J. O., Rubinstein, J., Sawyer, M. W., & Duchowski, A. T. (2008). Longitudinal evaluation of discrete consecutive gaze gestures for text entry. *Proceedings of the ACM Symposium on Eye Tracking Research and Applications (ETRA '08)* (pp. 11–18, 281). New York, NY: ACM.

Zhai, S., Morimoto, C., & Ihde, S. (1999). Manual gaze input cascaded (MAGIC) pointing. *Proceedings of the ACM Conference on Human Factors in Computing Systems (CHI '99)* (pp. 248–253). New York, NY: ACM.

Zhang, X., & MacKenzie, I. S. (2007). Evaluating eye tracking with ISO 9241 – Part 9. *Proceedings of HCI International 2007* (pp. 779–788). Heidelberg, Germany: Springer.

Zhang, X., Ren, X., & Zha, H. (2008). Improving eye cursor's stability for eye pointing tasks. *Proceeding of the 26th Annual SIGCHI Conference on Human Factors in Computing Systems (CHI '08)* (pp. 525-534). New York, NY: ACM.

Chapter 16
Gaze Data Analysis:
Methods, Tools, Visualisations

Oleg Špakov
University of Tampere, Finland

ABSTRACT

Analysis of gaze data collected during experiments is an essential part of any study that deals with eye tracking. In turn, analysis of gaze data is not a trivial procedure, on account of the nature of eye movement, peculiarities of human vision, and the imperfection of the measurement tools. In this chapter, we first draw out the most common issues that researchers are trying to resolve for analysis of gaze data, then present in detail the well-known methods and procedures of gaze data analysis, and finally point to the latest achievements in this field. The chapter contains a specification of the most promising directions in this field of research. We finish with a brief description of the most well-known academic and commercial tools that have been developed for gaze data visualisation and analysis. This chapter is based on an updated version of work originally published by Špakov in 2008.

INTRODUCTION

It has been suggested that visualisation tools are necessary for facilitating understanding of large volumes of data because the visual cortex dominates perception. Moreover, the key parts of the perception process occur rapidly without conscious thought (Zeki, 1992). The quantity of data collected during experiments makes researchers who study gaze behaviour eager to embrace data visualisation tools. There has been a steady stream of improvements to analyse and visualise eye movement data while one is observing static 2D stimuli (Lankford, 2000b; Wills, 1996; Wooding, 2002).

DOI: 10.4018/978-1-61350-098-9.ch016

Some researchers also have been outspoken about the tools they wish to have to help them in their gaze data analysis. Many of them have developed prototype systems to illustrate their individual approaches (Halverson & Hornof, 2002; Reeder, Pirolli, & Card, 2001). Some academic prototypes, such as GazeTracker and NYAN, have evolved into commercial systems that are becoming very popular.

While 2D observations already have strong support in analysis tools, improvements regarding gaze data processing and visualisation for dynamic stimuli are still in the early stages. Most techniques are based on frame-by-frame analyses of video data, although some recent findings in this field, such as 'bee swarm' and dynamic heat-map visualisations, are implemented in most of the modern commercial tools. However, it would not be too inaccurate to say that nobody has come up with a simple and intuitive way to visualise gaze data for dynamic stimuli so far.

The meaning of eye movement is impossible to interpret according to set rules, as there is very little evidence of gaze behaviour that could aid in distinguishing between a meaningless fixation such as an unintentional one and a deliberate or purposeful one (Posner, 1980). Evaluation of the efficiency and usefulness of existing visualisation methods remains a difficult problem. However, some researchers have illustrated that the application of work-load assessment methodologies (Hart & Wicken, 1990) to data comprehension tasks can provide a highly useful method for distinguishing among the effectiveness levels of various visualisations (Ramloll, Brewster, Yu, & Riedel, 2001). Eye tracking systems are often effective tools only in the hands of specialists who have had significant practice in the use of the technology. An experimenter new to this technology will frequently face several issues: 1) eye tracking devices are not plug-and-play; 2) the data gathered are not always reliable, because of the lack of data validity; and 3) making of meaningful inferences from the high volume of gaze data is difficult.

Another issue with eye tracking systems is that – while tools for processing, visualising, and analysing gaze data are being developed and improved continuously – these tools usually are highly dependent on the tracker system because of the raw data format and the data-gathering method. Therefore, it is often the case that gaze data visualisation software needs to be developed from the ground up for the eye trackers used in many laboratories utilising eye tracking devices. This state of affairs usually leads to duplication of effort in software development for each specific eye tracker. Typically, eye tracker manufacturers sell both hardware and associated software. Thus, the commercially available gaze data visualisation and analysis tools each are, as might be expected, designed for a specific tracker. The industry is showing great progress in developing electronic devices; accordingly, there is an increasing tendency for analysis and visualisation tool development efforts to be dissociated from eye tracker hardware implementation processes. This trend actually can be beneficial for both researchers and manufacturers.

The division of labour leads to a new software/ hardware equilibrium, as has happened with other modern standard devices (mouse, keyboard, joystick, etc.). This will pressure visualisation tool developers to give high priority to development of interoperability features necessary to enable their software to access as many raw data formats of eye tracker devices as possible. On the other hand, there is still hope that manufacturers will standardise on a universal raw data format and its means of access.

The COGAIN Network of Excellence has involved preparation of recommendations concerning raw gaze data format for manufacturers as one of its milestones. Deliverable 2.3 (Bates & Spakov, 2006) describes these recommendations, so it is expected that in the very near future the marketing objectives most probably will match the gaze data visualisation tool objectives – in

Figure 1. X and Y plot against time (iComponent)(@ 2008 Oleg Špakov. Used with permission)

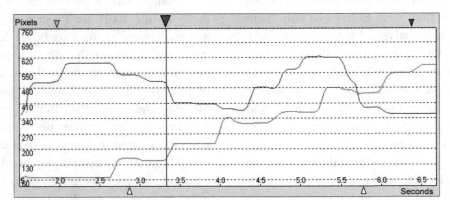

line with the recommendations made – and the interoperability issues will sort themselves out.

CLASSIFICATION OF VISUALISATION TECHNIQUES

The quantity of data produced by eye tracking devices is huge. Every second, a piece of data recording software receives from 30 to 4,000 gaze-landing points. Usually, all data are stored in files for further off-line analysis. In plotting of every position of gaze as a small dot, the view becomes less clear as recording duration increases. Therefore, the data analysis becomes complicated. Usually, only a few areas of the image are observed heavily by subjects, with tens of secondary-interest areas (if we consider multiple recordings for the same stimuli), but the number of gaze points may obscure this fact. A variety of visualisation techniques can be used for highlighting some aspects of the collected data.

Below, we first look at various temporal graphs that plot the data against time. Typically they do not show the stimulus in the visualisation, since it would clutter the view. However, keeping the stimulus in the visualisation is a common need, because the resulting visualisation is then easier to understand than are purely time-based presentations. We continue with examples of several two-dimensional visualisation techniques. Many of the techniques that we cover in this chapter share certain properties; for instance, they support selecting a particular time interval from the data for further analysis, or looking at the fixations in one part of the original stimulus.

Temporal Graphs

Many tools developed thus far provide visualisation by simply plotting gaze co-ordinates (X and Y of the point of gaze on the screen, and Z, torsional rotation, if available), against time (see Figure 1). This is one of the first types of gaze data visualisation ever undertaken by researchers. Regardless of its simplicity, researchers still use it to detect repeating patterns in users' stimulus observation behaviour.

Most video-oculography (VOG, based on analysis of video frames) eye trackers measure pupil size; therefore, visualisations plotting pupil size against time are usual for many tools. Plots with time shown on the X axis can include variables derived from movement, such as velocity and acceleration, as well as non-gaze data that change over time, such as mouse or head movement or continuation of some environmental events. This kind of visualisation can provide deep insight aiding in understanding the distribution of the subject's attention and focus of activity. It has appeared in tools developed recently.

Since a recording can cover a long time, a plot that contains all data may look very messy. A range bar to pare down the time period can be used. The time addressed can be called the period of interest. The range bar allows specification of a start and end time for the data in which the researcher is interested. Usually, researchers are allowed to adjust other graph properties, such as curve colour and width.

Showing several data curves on the same graph often serves to make it more informative and present correlations between these data. For example, changes of pupil size are not so informative on their own, but in combination with system and environmental events they may assist in detection of correlation between these events and the emotional state of the user.

Another one-dimensional visualisation presents the history of area-of-interest (AOI) observations in a very useful manner. In such visualisations, fixations in AOIs can be presented as horizontal bars. The time range that a subject has spent observing a certain AOI is given a unique colour (see Figure 2).

The coloured parts of bars (except the last) do not overlap (as each bar corresponds to a certain object in focus, or an absence of such). 'Temporal AOIs' is a row used for selecting a specific time interval for analysis to allow zooming the timeline in and out. The advantage of such visualisation is that a bar need not be only an AOI observed by gaze; it could be some other type of area/data combination (say, AOI visited by mouse). The disadvantage is the limitation of the number of bars that can be used while retaining a readable visualisation.

The visualisation of the reading and translation process developed most recently by Špakov and Räihä (2008) extends the idea of showing related and non-related events on horizontal panels against time by adding event-related details to each panel. The tool KiEV builds this kind of visualisation utilising the pre-processed gaze data, where detected fixations are linked to the corresponding word in the text (see Figure 3). It creates a visualisation with five horizontal panels on the same time line to present events of focusing on words in the source text and in the target (translated) text, the progress of typing the target text, pupil size dilations, and EEG data. Each panel contains blocks that represent a collection of uninterrupted

Figure 2. AOIs vs. time (Lessing & Linge, 2002) (@ 2002 Lessing Simon. Used with permission)

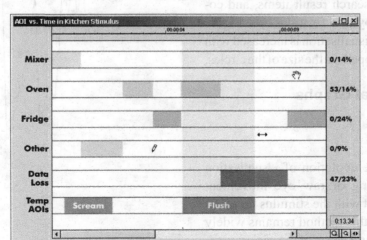

Figure 3. Visualisation of reading and translation processes in the KiEV tool(@ 2008 Oleg Špakov. Used with permission)

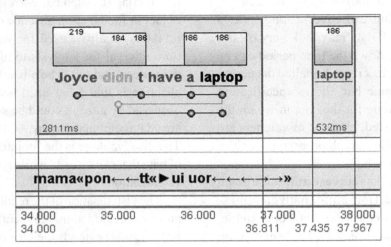

events. Each block starts at the time the first event occurred within this block and ends at the time its last event ended. The blocks of events in the source and target text panels cannot overlap. Each block of a source or target text panel consists of text, word bars above it, and the reading progress below it. Highlighting is used widely to pop up unusual or attention-requiring data and events.

Aula and her colleagues, who studied patterns in reading of Web search results, used a similar idea to build a one-dimensional visualisation based on the Y-co-ordinates in the subject's gaze path (Aula, Majaranta, & Räihä, 2005). Here AOIs are replaced with Web search result items, and coloured time ranges by true fixations (see Figure 4). The value of the visualisation is increased with fixation duration mapped via the size of the circles.

Two-Dimensional Graphs

Pure Scan Path

A further step in the evolution of visualisation techniques is plotting of raw eye movement data on an X–Y chart with the stimulus image as background. Again, this method remains widely used by researchers and is one of the easiest visu-

alisation techniques to implement. If a recording is made that uses an image (stimulus) slide show, all data are divided according to stimulus. Tools that visualise such data have a control to select

Figure 4. Observed items against time (Aula, Majaranta, & Räihä, 2005) (@ 2005 Anne Aula. Used with permission)

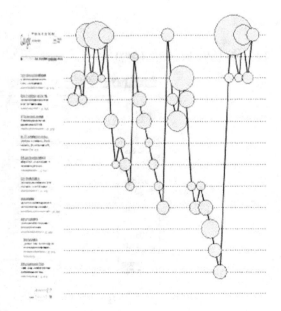

Figure 5. Pure scan path over image (constructed from the work of Yarbus, 1967) (@ 2009 Oleg Špakov. Used with permission)

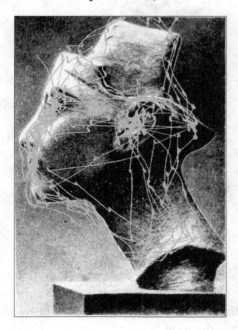

an image. After an image is selected, only those data that correspond to it are visible.

The first known visualisations in 2D space were made with Javal in 1879 (Huey, 1968); however, these and all other early visualisations, including the well-known techniques of Yarbus (1967), had

no initial stimuli underneath. An example of the simplest such visualisation, scan path, is shown in Figure 5; the image was created by overlapping the scan path from one of Yarbus's studies over stimuli. This scan path is continuous; however, all modern eye tracking devices provide gaze data as a sequence of samples; therefore, modern scan plots usually consist of numerous dots (sometimes connected by lines).

Many visualisation tools have time range limitation controls for plotting of data for just the period of interest. Some also show a certain effect for unobserved parts of stimuli (for example, hiding these parts or applying a blurring effect).

Fixations–Saccades Plot

Since a pure scan path blurs too much, some data clustering aids in providing more explicit visualisation. Here, fixation detection algorithms are used to convert raw data into a set of fixations. Traditionally, fixations are represented by circles, which may be connected by lines (saccades). Visualisation of a fixation can be as simple as a circle of fixed size over a stimulus image (see Figure 6).

To show the observation order, fixations must be connected by saccades. Usually, saccades are visualised as straight lines (see Figure 7), but

Figure 6. Visualisation of fixations (iComponent) (@ 2010 Oleg Špakov. Used with permission)

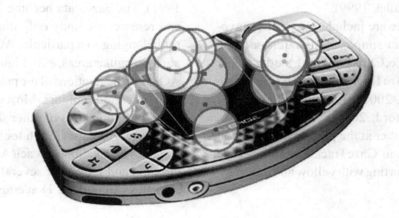

Figure 7. Visualisation of fixations and saccades (iComponent). @ 2010 Oleg Špakov. Used with permission

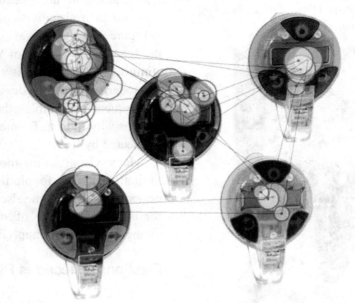

some tools show the pure scan path between fixations.

Nowadays, almost all tools map a fixation's duration to its circle radius. Usually, researchers may adjust scaling rate (ms to pixels) as well as other circle parameters (such as colour, transparency, and arc width).

The popularity of this kind of visualisation is determined in part by the many tools available for visualisation of numerical data in 2D charts. One example might be the 1998 study by Aaltonen and colleagues in which gaze data were analysed with IVEE Corporation's Spotfire software (Aaltonen, Hyrskykari, & Räihä, 1999).

Specialist software includes more eye movement features than simple 2D fixation–saccade charts. For example, Chris Lankford, the developer of the famous GazeTracker software (Lankford, 2000a; Lankford, 2000b; Lankford et al., 1997; Redline & Lankford, 2001), created 2D views with fixation number at the place where fixation occurs. Saccades in GazeTracker are lines on a colour gradient starting with yellow and progress-

ing through a set range of colours in line with saccade duration.

Other shapes are used to represent fixations, but quite seldom. An example is the study by Spence and colleagues where fixations are visualised as squares with the letter 'F' inside the box (Spence, Witkowski, Fawcett, Craft, & De Bruijn, 2004).

As with all types of visualisations already mentioned, a fixation–saccade plot may be simplified by selecting a period of interest. As they get more complex, analysis tools include the possibility to specify AOIs, as Charlier and Buquet, for example, did in their software (Charlier & Buquet, 1991). The gaze data become clustered by AOI, and researchers study only that part of the data set belonging to a particular AOI. Usually, AOIs are rectangular areas, as in Figure 8 with its seven AOIs and the fixations of the participants drawn in them in various colours. Most of the recent tools allow defining AOIs of other shapes, some even freely drawn shapes. Such tools usually provide statistics on fixations of each AOI within a given duration and for one or several participants. The statistics can include 1) average, minimum, and

Figure 8. Fixations in AOIs in iComponent (@ 2010 Oleg Špakov. Used with permission)

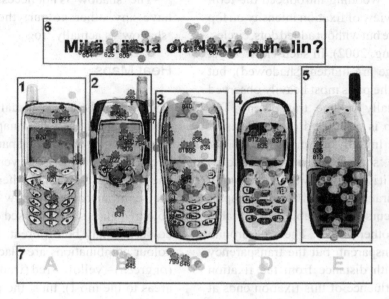

maximum fixation duration; 2) standard deviation of fixations' duration; 3) number of fixations in the AOI; 4) number of 'entries' by gaze into the AOI; 5) absolute and relative time spent observing the AOI; and 6) a list of system and environmental events occurring during observation of the AOI.

Clustering Fixations

The order of fixations in a scan path is not always important. Sometimes researchers need just a quick look to detect areas observed by users. In this case, only fixations are important, without saccades and individual samples. Researchers may want to define areas themselves to determine the intensity of stimulus observation in these areas. In both cases, it is not enough just to show circles (fixations) and remove all other visualisation objects: including a great many fixations can make the visualisation hard to grasp. Some clustering algorithms must be applied to group fixations. An example of such clustering is the visualisation by iComponent in Figure 9. Each small red circle represents the cumulative fixation duration, and

the red boundaries around the objects show roughly the area where the fixations are distributed.

Fixation Maps

Increasing the number of fixations on the same image brings about a worse overall view and less

Figure 9. Visualisation of observation duration (as red circles) in manually created AOIs (iComponent) (@ 2010 Oleg Špakov. Used with permission)

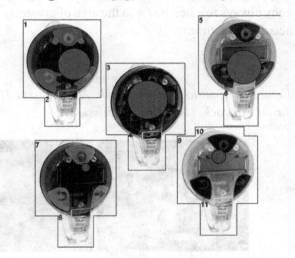

ready perception. Wooding introduced the term 'fixation map', a view of fixation intensity on top of a stimulus image but without added dots, circles, and lines (Wooding, 2002). In such views, most parts of the image are hidden (shadowed), but the areas around the parts most heavily observed by subjects gradually become 'transparent'. The transparency map is calculated on the basis of fixation duration. Initially, an image has 0% (or a bit more, if the 'shadow' is not fully opaque) transparency; i.e., it is completely black. A fixation of one-second duration 'adds' 10% of transparency where it occurs (the variable is adjustable and can have another value). The area around also becomes transparent, but the transparency rate decreases with distance from the fixation point (say, the influence of this fixation ends at a distance of 20 pixels). The two most popular transparency estimation methods are linear and Gaussian. The linear method decreases transparency linearly (the 3D function visualisation would look like a cone). With the Gaussian method, the transparency function's visualisation resembles a cone with a rounded top (Babcock, Pelz, and Fairchild, 2003; see Figure 10). This visualisation method has one serious disadvantage – when the total transparency reaches 100%, other fixations add no further transparency (however, they can stretch the transparent area, or the time-to-height mapping scale can be normalised so that transparency always reaches 100% in the area of greatest accumulated time).

The 'shadow' is not necessarily black; it may have any other colour; therefore, the white 'shadow' is actually 'fog'.

Heat Maps

The modern 'heat map' visualisation was derived from fixation maps. A heat map is a similar view to a fixation map, but the transparency (and shadow) becomes 'coloured'. However, the term 'transparency' is not quite suitable here, since colours in the semitransparent shadow have the effect of coloured glass superimposed over an image. The colouring may be different, but quite common colour combinations are black (or grey) – blue (or green) – yellow – red (from the least observed areas to the most); thus, the colour temperature increases with the duration of observation. The initial colour is black or blue, so at first the image looks very dark. The rest of the colours in the heat map are light, so 'heated' parts of the image look less shadowed than initially; nevertheless, the level of transparency of each colour may be the same.

Heat maps provide a better level of observation intensity separation than fixation maps do. For example, the visualisation in Figure 11 has a grey – blue – green – red colouring map. The red colour here denotes very long cumulative observation. Most probably, the Wooding fixation map would have red areas totally transparent, and the grey/blue/green areas would be gradually semi-transparent if created with the same gaze data.

Figure 10. Fixation maps: stimuli, 2D map, and 3D map (from http://www.jasonbabcock.com/) (@ 2002 Jason Babcock. Used with permission)

 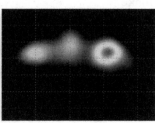 

Figure 11. Heat map with fixation marks (iComponent)(@ 2010 Oleg Špakov. Used with permission)

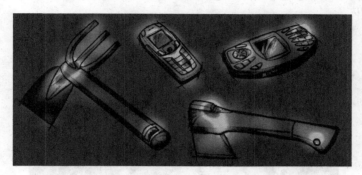

Some tools create opaque heat maps with no shadow over unobserved areas (for example, SMI BeGaze). However, this kind of visualisation hides details of the stimulus image and can prove inconvenient for precise analysis.

Semitransparent Fixations

Fixations can be presented not only as objects of a certain shape (e.g., circles as shown in the previous examples) but through image (stimulus) changes. Schiessl and colleagues have developed the software EyeSquare, where the area around fixations appears in the image as semitransparent spots painted as with an airbrush (Schiessl, Duda, Thölke, & Fischer, 2003). Researchers can select the brush colour before creating a view. Moreover, the visualisation tool allows separating data via some criteria and using different brushes for every chunk of data (similar visualisation can be created in an image editor, using two heat maps; see Figure 12). Many recordings can be loaded and analysed together. These features are very valuable in studying a large set of data involving many recordings in the same research project.

Three-Dimensional Visualisations

All analysis and visualisations discussed above were conducted in 2D space. However, some researchers have extended their consideration to 3D space, or 'virtual reality', as they term it.

Among them is Andrew Duchowski, who developed a method for visualisation of gaze path via 3D views using binocular eye tracking data (Duchowski et al., 2002). Actually, the visualisation itself shown in Figure 13 differs little from the scan-path visualisations presented above (e.g., Figure 7), but now every gaze data point has a 'depth' parameter.

The GazeTracker application can create a true 3D visualisation (Lankford, 2000b). It builds a topographic map with mountains where observation was longer than in other regions. The computation and logic are exactly the same as in fixation maps. The 3D map usually is rotated such that mountains can be easily detected at a glance

Figure 12. Cumulative gaze data separated by gender (constructed from data by Christopher Huang[1]) (@ 2010 Oleg Špakov. Used with permission)

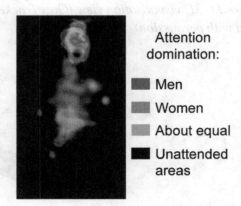

Attention domination:

■ Men
■ Women
■ About equal
■ Unattended areas

Figure 13. 3D view with superimposed gaze path (Duchowski et al., 2002) (@ 2002 Andrew Duchowki. Used with permission)

(see Figure 14). However, some image areas, located on the other side of the mountains and at the bottom of valleys, are hidden or inaccessible for detailed view because of the small view angle and the distortion.

The same gaze data analysis tool produces another kind of 3D visualisation where the observed areas pop up over the rest of the image (see Figure 14). The areas are flat squares and facilitate observation by the viewer. The amount of rise depends on the total time the subject spent looking at the element. Researchers may specify areas of interest manually, but a sophisticated image analysis algorithm can extract the most noteworthy ones automatically. Automatic AOI extraction can be performed for Web pages since

GazeTracker analyses the HTML structure of each page.

One more kind of 3D visualisation has been presented, by Ramloll and colleagues in 2004 (Ramloll, Trepagnier, Sebrechts, & Beedasy, 2004). In their research, 3D models of objects were used as stimuli. The visualisation view consisted of both initial and flattened shapes of the model with the usual scan path superimposed on it (see Figure 15).

Stellmach, Nacke, and Dachselt (2010) have developed a gaze analysis tool called SVEETER that presents a 3D scene, records the gaze path, and creates several visualisation with 3D objects (see Figure 16). One visualisation displays camera path and gaze direction in the 3D world (the

Figure 14. 3D visualisation view (GazeTracker, from http://www.gazetracker.com/) (@ 2007 Eyetellect. Used with permission)

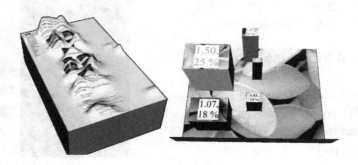

Figure 15. Initial and flattened 3D model with scan path (Ramloll et al., 2004) (@ 2004 Rameshsharma Ramloll. Used with permission)

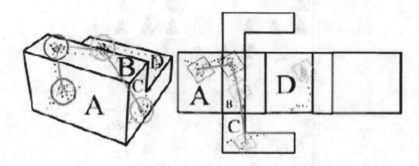

Figure 16. Screen-shots of SVEETER (@ 2010 Sophie Stellmach. Used with permission)

tool has four views, from various angles, of the 3D scene, as many CAD applications do). Another visualisation shows 3D objects coloured according to the attention received: the developers call this an object-based heat map. In a surface-based attentional map, each object is covered by a heat map.

Dynamic Visualisations (Replays)

All visualisations described thus far are for static images, which can be used as stimuli and later serve as the visualisation view background. But sometimes researchers need to investigate observations of dynamic stimuli, which cannot be represented by static images. A video file is recorded along with gaze data during such an experiment. The target of video capture is a screen or PC monitor (with

capture by any third-party software) or the physical environment around the participant as captured by a camera. Some researchers have even captured screen data with a separate digital camera (e.g., Cowen, Ball, & Delin, 2002) for further replay, but now applying ordinary screen capture tools or a commercial toolkit is more common.

During analysis, the video file is replayed with a moving gaze cursor over it. At any given moment, only the current gaze position is visible. The gaze cursor can be any shape or object as long as it is small enough to represent the 'current position' of the gaze and big enough to be noticed easily by observers. The gaze cursor also can have a 'tail' that consists of the last several replay points, in order to hold in view several previous gaze positions. For example, Witkowski,

Figure 17. 'Bee swarm' replay in Tobii Studio (@ 2010 Oleg Špakov. Used with permission)

Arafa, and deBruijn (2001) implemented replay with such a gaze 'tail'.

The gaze path replay can be performed over static images as well. The latest replay method known to be developed uses data from multiple subject recordings in the same experiment. It shows as many gaze points as there are records involved in the replay. Initially developed by scientists in the lab, it now has been implemented in the Tobii Studio software (see Figure 17). This visualisation is known as the bee swarm replay.

The same idea (conversion of static visualisation into dynamic) has been used to transform a static heat map into a dynamic one. In such replays, the heat-map-generating algorithm uses data from multiple recordings, for the last 1–2 seconds (e.g., in the IICap software developed at the University of Lund; Lessing & Linge, 2002).

The replay can be applied to several types of data. For example, if mouse movement is recorded simultaneously with gaze data, the two tracks can be replayed at the same time. Data that do not continue over time can be presented in replay as well. These can be system or environment events – mouse clicks, keystrokes, etc. For example, Bauer and Hollan mixed gaze and touch data in replay, where the gaze was presented via a wide red moving dot (Bauer & Hollan. 2003).

Other Kinds of Visualisations

Transition Map

One of the most widely known types of visualisations where no gaze point information is presented is the transition map for AOIs. The map consists of objects that represent AOIs. Each AOI is presented as a circle with observation time relative to total observation time; each line has an associated probability of transition between nearby AOIs (see Figure 18). The actual objects viewed by the subject can be shown in the map, though then it is not possible to indicate their relative importance via changes of size as with the circles. Note that the sum of probabilities of all outgoing transition from a single AOI is usually less than 100%, since some transitions lead to the outside-the-screen area.

EYE MOVEMENT DATA CLUSTERING

Some techniques for reducing the quantity of data are usually applied in the creation of a visualisation view (2D graphs). The most common techniques of this type use various algorithms for data (gaze point) clustering. The number of algorithms for

Figure 18. Two transition maps (Lessing & Linge, 2002) (@ 2002 Lessing Simon. Used with permission)

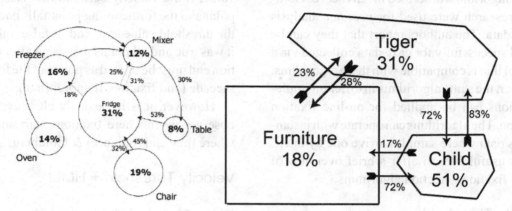

clustering points in 2D space is rather large (Santella & DeCarlo, 2004). However, most of them are not suited to gaze data analysis, because of slowness issues (hundreds of thousands of points may be stored in a single tracking file) and the need to know the number of clusters in advance. Therefore, researchers today use only a few selected algorithms to cluster gaze data.

There are at least two levels of clustering: for samples (individual gaze points) and for fixations. The results of sample clustering are fixations, and the results of fixation clustering are 'superfixations'. The latter consist of one or more fixations, which are treated now as an interrelated standalone group.

However, not all clustering algorithms are equivalent, and some can produce different results (there is no strict definition of how samples should be separated into saccade-related and fixation-related; broader discussion of this issue is found in Chapter 17 by Heikkilä and Ovaska). All algorithms have some variables to be adjusted by researchers in order to ensure meaningful results, and the values of these variables can be crucial for the data analysis. For example, fixations could be too wide or too tiny, thus biasing the interpretation of the data (Salvucci & Goldberg, 2000). Therefore, we need some knowledge of existing

algorithms in order to determine which are more suitable for data analysis in particular research.

Fixation Detection Algorithms

Fixation detection algorithms have different bases. Several of those selected as the most suitable for gaze data clustering (in terms of accuracy and robustness) have been described in Salvucci & Goldberg's research on identification of fixations and saccades (ibid.). Five algorithms were separated into classes, three groups; an additional, recently introduced algorithm by Olsson (2007) forms the fourth group. The separation criterion was the method of data clustering:

- Velocity-based algorithms: 1) velocity-threshold and 2) based on Hidden Markov Models (HMMs)
- Dispersion-based: 1) dispersion threshold and 2) maximum spanning trees
- Area-based: 1) area of interest
- Olsson filter

Most algorithms for fixation detection that are used by eye tracker manufacturers and researchers are variations on these types and may feature some additions and improvements (e.g., filtering).

The algorithms described in Salvucci & Goldberg's research were used for *post hoc* analysis of raw data. The authors report that they can be applied successfully for gaze data collected via a protocol that is compatible with these algorithms. However, the same algorithms in different implementations can be applied for on-line fixation detection. The algorithms can operate with instantaneous data where samples arrive one by one.

It is useful here to offer a brief overview of on-line fixation detection algorithms.

Velocity Threshold

To implement this algorithm, a buffer for unfinished-fixation inter-point velocities must be initialised. At the outset, the algorithm waits for the first point. With every new gaze direction point received by the software, the following calculations occur:

- The velocity of the new point is calculated and placed in a buffer.
- If the velocity obtained is below the threshold, the point belongs to the fixation. The algorithm sends notification of fixation start if the previous point was the saccade point, then clears the buffer, leaving the last point.
- Otherwise, the point belongs to the saccade. The algorithm sends notification of fixation end if the previous point was the fixation point; then, it clears the buffer, leaving the last point. If the fixation duration is below a given threshold (e.g., 100 ms), the algorithm sends a fixation cancellation message.

This simple algorithm can be improved to avoid accidental 'saccades' that can appear on account of variance in gaze direction computed by eye tracker software or hardware. The simplest way to do this is to wait for several further points to arrive, if the velocity is greater than the threshold value. If the velocity between the 'last' fixation point and the forthcoming point falls back below the threshold value, the 'end' is false; otherwise, it was true and all points that came after the fixation end must be treated as points of the following saccade (and fixation, if appropriate).

However, it is not exactly clear even to the observer when/where fixations start and when/where they end (Salvucci & Goldberg, 2000).

Velocity Threshold + HMM

Hidden Markov Models can be applied to improve the velocity-threshold algorithm's robustness. Such an algorithm is nearly as described above, but the probability of transition from fixation to saccade and back is determined by a two-state HMM.

Dispersion Threshold

The dispersion threshold algorithm uses a buffer that holds at least the last three gaze positions. On collection of the minimum number of gaze positions required, the algorithm starts computing dispersion when a new point arrives. The following calculations occur:

- The dispersion of the set of collected points is calculated.
- If the dispersion obtained is less than the threshold value, the point belongs to the fixation. The algorithm sends notification of a fixation start if the previous point was the saccade point.
- Otherwise, the point belongs to the saccade. The algorithm sends a notification of fixation end if the previous point was the fixation point; if fixation duration is below a given threshold (e.g., 100 ms), the algorithm sends a fixation cancellation message.

The set of points grows until the end of fixation. The last point in the set becomes the first point of the following saccade.

Maximum Spanning Trees (MST)

The next type of fixation identification is based on the algorithm for finding the minimal length of the tree created from the connections between the collected gaze points. The algorithm is not supposed to be used on-line, but it may serve for fixation re-identification during off-line analysis. A brief description of the algorithm is given by Goldberg and Schryver (1995). The main idea of the algorithm is to use one of the methods of data search optimisation to find a pair of adjacent samples, separated by a distance greater than a given threshold, thus identifying saccades.

Area of Interest

The AOI algorithm identifies fixations only in *post hoc* analysis. First, researchers must specify target areas (for example, words in a piece of text). Every gaze point hitting the area within the targets becomes a fixation point; the remaining points are not taken into account. Each target area is presented by a single fixation, which has its centre at the mass centre of all points inside the target area. The algorithm removes fixations with a duration below the predefined threshold. This kind of clustering is intermediate between clustering into fixations and into 'super-fixations'.

Olsson Filter

The Olsson filter has two implementations: for on-line and off-line cases. The on-line filter is a digital low-band filter expressed by the following formula:

$$c(n) = \frac{s(n) + ac(n-1)}{1 + a}, \qquad a = \frac{T}{h} \qquad (1)$$

where $s(n)$ is the measured gaze position, $c(n)$ is the filtered gaze position, T is the time constant of the filter, and h is the sampling interval. By choosing a large enough T, one can reduce the measurement noise to an acceptable level. However, large values of T result in slow stabilisation after a saccade. This issue may be eliminated by making T dynamic: if the difference between the means of $\{s(n), s(n-1), \ldots, s(n-k)\}$ and $\{s(n-k), s(n-k-1), \ldots, s(n-m)\}$ exceeds a threshold, an alarm is generated and T is set to a low value, T_{fast}; otherwise, T is set to a high value, T_{slow}. The time window (value of $k = m/2$) must be sufficient to cover at least two gaze samples. A value of 300 ms for T_{slow} was found to attenuate the noise during fixations sufficiently, and a value of 10 ms for T_{slow} was found sufficiently fast following saccades.

The Olsson off-line algorithm is designed to treat those differences between spatial means of adjacent (in time) groups of samples that exceed some threshold h as signals of saccades. Obviously, the number of samples in each group ('time window') must be greater than 1 but small enough not to span several saccadic motions within a single averaging window (max.: 80 ms). After all peaks in these differences greater than h are found, all samples are separated into 'fixations', although some of these samples belong to saccades. The location of each fixation is calculated as the median of all its samples. During the next step, the algorithm unites adjacent fixations if they are close enough to each other (closer than h). However, this algorithm does not search for the first and last fixation sample, so it lacks an additional step that removes fixation samples that were produced during saccadic motion.

Fixation Clustering Algorithms

One of the first attempts to cluster fixations was made by Scinto and Barnette (1986), who proposed a simple algorithm of grouping fixations into clusters on the basis of minimum number of fixations in a cluster and maximum distance between each pair of fixations in a cluster. This project was continued by Ramakrishna, Pillalamarri, Barnetfe,

Birkmire, and Karsh (1993), who used several methods to calculate the centre of a cluster: 1) simple mean of fixations $\{x,y\}$, 2) weighted (by duration) mean of fixations $\{x,y\}$, and 3) centre of the convex polygon that encompasses the fixations of the cluster.

The latest results in achieving the best clustering of this kind were described by Santella and DeCarlo (2004). The algorithms here were separated into two groups: 1) distance threshold and 2) mean shift.

Distance Threshold

Distance threshold is a quite simple data-driven method of clustering. It clusters fixations on the basis of the predefined maximum distance. The algorithm considers two points to be in the same cluster when they are closer than this specified distance. In brief, the algorithm's logic is:

- Take a fixation and assign it to a new cluster if it is not yet in any cluster.
- Calculate distances to the fixations not analysed yet (i.e., those that were not involved in the first step), and add to the same cluster those of them that are within the predefined distance.
- If the added fixation belongs to other groups already, join these groups to the current one.
- Repeat this step until all fixations are analysed.

The weakness of this algorithm is that it may create large clusters if the number of fixations is large and they cover an image heavily such that almost all intermediate clusters have at least one shared fixation.

Mean Shift

The mean shift algorithm does not have the above-mentioned disadvantage. There are two implementations of the algorithm, the main difference being that one clusters all close fixations

without regard for time and the other does the same but considers their distribution in time (all fixations in the same cluster have occurred in sequence). We can consider the latter the improved version of distance-based clustering that includes a pre-processing stage. The algorithm involves two steps:

- Move points into denser positions until they can be separated easily into clusters.
- Apply a clustering algorithm that uses a distance threshold (such as those described in the previous sections).

The mean shifting algorithm moves fixation points $F(X_i, Y_i)$ to a new location $S(X_i, Y_i)$. The result of shifting is the weighted mean of nearby points based on kernel function K (ibid.), which is a multivariate Gaussian function with zero mean and covariance σ:

$$K(X_i, Y_i) = \exp(-\frac{X_i^2 + Y_i^2}{\sigma_s^2}) \qquad (2)$$

Usually, σ is less than the distance between two image (stimulus) features. The algorithm proceeds several times, iteratively moving all points toward a location of higher density until all of them are relatively close to the weighted centres of clusters. The cluster centres are the points of moving convergence. The typical number of iterations is 5–10 and resolves the convergence to within 0.1% change across iterations.

Since the algorithm input data are fixations F, better clustering may be achieved by applying weights W for each fixation. The fixation duration can be used as the weight. The weights may decrease the number of iterations by as many as two:

$$S_{FIX}(F) = \frac{\sum_j W_j K(F - F_j) F_j}{\sum_j W_j K(F - F_j)} \qquad (3)$$

With all points collected at nodes, a clustering method that uses a distance threshold is safe. The same covariance σ can be used as the distance threshold for this final clustering. After all, clusters with a low total fixation duration can be discarded, as they are typically outliers.

Other researcher are successfully applying this method while creating their own fixation clustering tool (for example, Heminghous and Duchowski, 2006).

SOME COMMON COMMERCIAL TOOLS

ERICA: GazeTracker

The GazeTracker recording and analysis tool is becoming more and more popular among manufacturers of eye tracking devices (see http://www. gazetracker.com/). This powerful tool builds both static visualisations and dynamic ones (video). The main advantage of this software is that it records not only eye tracker data but also many other external events to bind all together for further analysis.

The GazeTracker software collects data from 1) the operating system (mouse and keyboard events, document scrolling, Web page URL, window sizing, etc.), 2) questionnaires, 3) the eye tracker, and 4) external video. All events and the test set-up reside in a common database, which can be used to extract recordings on request, according to particular conditions.

Another noticeable advantage of GazeTracker is that it allows Web page analysis based on HTML parsing. While recording gaze data, the application stores observed URLs and provides statistics about gaze activity in connection with page layout for Web page analysis. For example, it counts how many links were observed, how long each part of the page was viewed, and so on. Researchers do not need to define those areas (AOIs) manually in this case.

The playback function provides replaying of image or video observation progress by subject at either actual or reduced speed. The red cross shows the current position of the gaze. Mouse movement may be replayed simultaneously.

In fixations–saccades visualisation, fixations are plotted as circles and saccades as lines. Plots have ordinal number and duration of fixation near the circles. Line colour indicates saccade duration – from blue for long to red for short.

'LookZones' (AOIs) of any shape and size can be specified for generation of statistics on a particular part of the image (total time, total fixation duration, average fixation duration, number of fixations, number of entries to the AOI, and mouse clicks). The tool provides information about the order of observation of AOIs. AOIs can be specified for video analysis also. Once an AOI is defined, the software tracks the movement of AOI objects during video replay and corrects AOI position as long as the specified region can be recognised (see Figure 19).

Several graph types serve for data analysis; many are automated Microsoft Excel graphs. GazeTracker plots pupil size changes over time. One of the distinguishable graph types is the topographical graph, where the most heavily observed portions of the image are shown as mountains and other parts of the image as valleys.

Figure 19. Replay with bound AOI (GazeTracker, from http://www.gazetracker.com/) (@ 2007 Eyetellect. Used with permission)

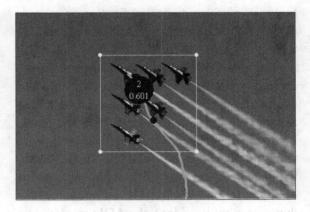

Another graph has raised 3D bars indicating AOIs. The rise height depends on the total time spent on the corresponding AOI. The 'LookZone Order' graph depicts a timeline showing the order in which a subject observed each AOI (with observation duration).

Several recordings can be plotted and analysed simultaneously. The tool can export eye movement data to a Microsoft Excel sheet or to an ASCII (comma-delimited) file.

SMI: BeGaze 2.0

The BeGaze tool supports data collected with the latest versions of the SMI eye trackers (see http://www.smi.de/). It can be used for all steps in a study: stimulus creation, monocular or binocular data recording, and further visualisation and analysis. The developers claim that it can be used in reading research, psychology, neurology, cognitive neuroscience, marketing research, and usability testing. Moreover, the software can be integrated easily with various stimulus presentation packages. The tool's built-in database stores all data, stimulus images, analysis graphs, and subject demographics collected during recording.

It is possible to compare data from multiple trials or multiple subjects by using this tool. A built-in fixation detection algorithm can be used to create a list of fixations and saccades. Saccade and fixation detection parameters can be adjusted for individual trials or the whole experiment. The tool may perform dedicated fixation or saccade analysis automatically, depending on experiment type.

The tool shows either raw data or a scan path created by fixations and saccades superimposed over a stimulus. Researchers may create a rectangular, elliptical, or polygonal AOI and obtain both statistics and either graphical analysis or temporal allocation of visual attention. Alternatively, researchers may allow automatic creation of AOIs. In analysis of gaze data produced for dynamic stimuli (video), the AOIs created on a snapshot of a certain video frame are moving and being transformed as the video playback proceeds (see Figure 20). The AOI transition matrix of visual attention thus generated can be exported to an ASCII file.

Clicking on a data plot provides detailed information and statistics on the selected data events. All analysis graphs are customisable and can be exported to other applications. Gaze data used for visualisation creation can be filtered by several parameters, such as subject gender or age. The developers claim that more than 100 statistical variables can be computed with BeGaze 2.0 (e.g., first fixation duration, number of glances, the pupils' size, and blink frequencies).

Focus-map and heat-map visualisation can be created with either static or dynamic stimuli. In the latter case, the cumulative attention distribution of many subjects appears as 'moving clouds' (see Figure 20). 'Bee swarm' is the alternative dynamic visualisation for attention-tracking. All kinds of dynamic visualisations can be exported to an AVI video file.

The tool builds a 1D graph showing the X and Y co-ordinates of gaze and pupil size dilation against time.

Figure 20. Screenshot of replay of a heat map with a dynamic AOI in BeGaze (SMI, from http://www.smi.de/) (@ 2009 SensoMotoric Instruments. Used with permission)

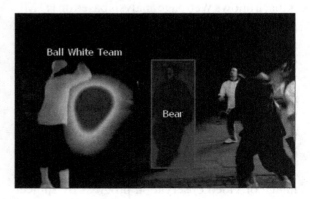

In cases of comparative analysis of the scan paths of several subjects, the tool builds a graph that shows send-by-second changes in the relative observation time of AOIs (summed for all users). For example, it might report that in the first second, 41% of users observed the AOI shown in red, 22% observed the AOI denoted in blue, and the rest of the users observed something else (none of the AOIs specified).

Tobii Technologies: Tobii Studio 1.5

The Tobii Studio tool supports the Tobii eye trackers developed by Tobii Technologies (see http://www.tobii.com/). In addition to gaze data, the tool records mouse clicks and keystrokes, and in analysis mode it allows addition of custom events. During analysis, gaze data may be filtered by time intervals, AOIs, and subject-related features (age and gender). It builds a classic scan-path view or heat-map view and plays back recorded data for single or multiple subjects (so-called bee swarm).

The tool has a built-in algorithm for detection of fixations from raw data. Before researchers create a view or start playback, they must specify whether to use fixations instead of raw data. The

fixation detection algorithm requires a maximum fixation radius (the maximum distance, in pixels, between any two samples in a fixation) and a minimum duration parameter to be set. Researchers can adjust the time range of the data visualised, via a range bar.

In the classic view, fixations are circles connected by lines of a certain level of transparency. Each fixation has a corresponding ordinal number nearby. If the fixation detection algorithm is disabled, only small dots (raw data) are shown superimposed on the image.

Researchers can define AOIs here and receive statistics on associated quantitative data (time to first fixation, fixation counts and gaze time distribution, observation length, observation count, fixations before, and percentage of participants). The statistics may accumulate data grouped by selected recordings or participants, AOIs, and images. The statistical values are the minimum, maximum, mean, median, cumulative, and standard deviation values (see Figure 21). Researchers also may limit the data used in statistical calculations by narrowing down the time range.

The heat-map view uses red to depict the areas most visited by gaze, and those less visited are in

Figure 21. Statistics in Tobii Studio(@ 2010 Oleg Špakov. Used with permission)

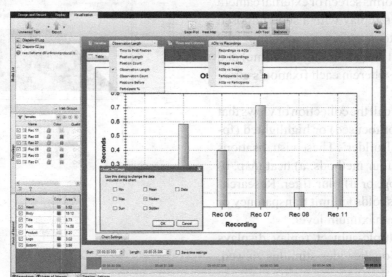

green. The rest of the view can be partly shadowed. Researchers can adjust the sensitivity of the heat map by means of the track bar below the view. Several recordings can be used to create a heat-map view.

The tool allows automatic fixation clustering. Each cluster features an indicator of the percentage of participants whose fixations are located within this cluster.

The replay plays back recorded data by using fixations or samples of raw data as points of the gaze cursor. Researchers are able to start playback from any moment. In a single-subject replay, the growing circle (the fixation detection algorithm is enabled) moves over the video, leaving about a one-second tail (lines). Any frame in the video file can be captured for visualisation in static views.

Interactive Minds: NYAN 2.0XT

The NYAN tool supports data collected by the EyeGaze eye tracker (from LC Technologies). The tool uses Web pages (with dynamic context separated from static), pictures (single or slideshow), text, video, or custom stimuli during recording (see http://www.interactive-minds.com/). Keystrokes, mouse movement, stimulus scrolling events, and custom events are recorded along with eye movement. The unit performs screen or external camera recording for use in replay with a superimposed gaze cursor. The tool creates a gaze–time plot (gaze x,y and pupil size values against time) and a classic gaze path wherein each fixation's circle is semitransparent.

The developers call the collection of views that show obscured (not focused) or highlighted (focused) areas 'Sinn Builder'. These visualisations implement one of four methods: a) heat map, b) transparency, c) fog, or d) blur filter. Researchers may apply thresholds to limit transparency or highlighting of the maximum level.

Single- or multiple-subject replay displays the gaze's position on the video stimulus viewed.

Researchers may define AOIs (or allow the tool to do so automatically) and see how long (in seconds or relative to total observation time) a subject observed areas inside it. Also, the tool provides the following statistical values for each AOI: a) time to first fixation, b) fixation count, c) mean fixation duration, c) AOI hit rate, and d) many other stimulus-dependent values (such as Web page visiting time). The tool creates a visualisation of navigations between Web pages with the basic transitions statistics.

The 3D view of the fixation map ('attentional landscapes') is the first 3D visualisation available with this tool (see Figure 22). The second is somewhat similar but allows single-subject and group comparison analysis. For instance, it uses different colours to paint regions where men spend more attention than women or vice versa. All data can be exported to various formats, such as Excel, XML, and ASCII.

Figure 22. 'Attentional landscapes' in NYAN (Interactive Minds, from http://www.interactive-minds.com/)(@ 2008 Markus Joos, Interactive Minds. Used with permission)

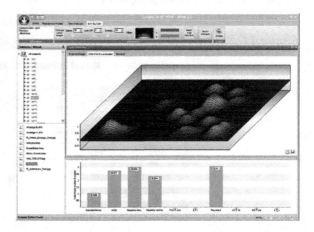

TOOLS DEVELOPED IN LABORATORIES

Bielefeld University: EyeDataAnalyser

Researchers from Bielefeld University developed many tools to support their studies on using eye trackers for human–computer interaction. They do not stress the eye trackers used, but in several publications they mention SR Research EyeLink and LC Technologies EyeGaze trackers.

The researchers have concentrated on graphical stimulus image analysis in order to predict the objects and 'layers' (areas) most important to the observer. Most of their tools build classic views with scan path superimposed over an image, where fixations are shown as circles connected by lines, with radius proportional to fixation duration. The set of visualisations is available on the Web page of this group and refers to the work done by Pomplun, Ritter, and Velichkovsky (1995). It is one of the earliest implementations of mapping of gaze data to transparency of a shadow superimposed over stimulus image ('fixation maps'), which later was transformed into the 'heat map' approach. The visualisations include gradually transparent areas over a shadowed, foggy, or blurred image (see Figure 23).

Other tools developed by the group provide more sophisticated solutions. For example, one tool clusters an image into regions and highlights the clusters most visited by the eye. Fixations are visualised as circles of a constant size in the same view. Another tool builds a heat map and creates fixation clusters. The heat map uses the data only within manually created AOIs.

The VDesigner tool was developed by researchers in this group to plan and run tests, but no mention was made of whether it presents the data in any way.

However, EyeDataAnalyser was developed for analysis and visualisation purposes. It supports SMI EyeLink I data format and creates classic scan-path and heat-map views. Developers report that it shows some 'trial-related data' also, which could be mouse clicks, mouse movement, key-presses, etc. Style and colours of graphical objects (fixations and saccades) are customisable. The views generated can be exported to JPEG image files. During analysis, researchers may add additional events ('user-defined messages'). Data can be corrected manually if drift is evident. Researchers can generate some gaze data statistics, which include number of fixations and average and cumulative fixation durations for user-defined AOIs. All data can be replayed in real time (fixations only, not raw data).

University of Tampere: iComponent

The iComponent software was developed at the Gaze Lab of the University of Tampere (Špakov, 2008). iComponent has a highly flexible architecture, which allows easy development of dynamic plug-in modules to support eye tracking devices

Figure 23. Fixation map visualisations (created from work by Pomplun, Ritter, & Velichkovsky, 1996) (@ 1995 Marc Pomplun. Used with permission)

Figure 24. Visualisation of same data in an iComponent fixation plot (@ 2008 Oleg Špakov. Used with permission)

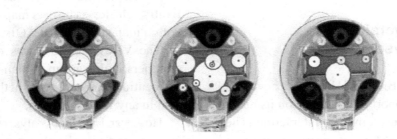

and experimental software. The unique data format and data transfer interfaces were developed on the basis of careful analysis of existing hardware.

iComponent has four types of 2D gaze data visualisation, three of which can include eye movements of several subjects, and one type of 1D visualisation. The 2D visualisations are superimposed over stimuli. These were observed during recording of eye movement. The visualisation called 'Classic' shows the gaze path in classic style: fixations are shown as circles, and saccades appear as lines connecting these circles. The 'Heat map' visualisation shows the stimulus dimmed, but the areas observed by subjects are graded in their transparency and are coloured according to observation duration. The 'Clustering' visualisation shows close fixations clustered into single units. Finally, the 'Replay' visualisation replays eye movement.

From among all such tools, this tool probably has the highest level of customisation of all kinds of visualisations. Researchers are allowed to adjust almost all features of the visualisations they create: colours, sizes, transparency, fonts, gaze-data-to-object mapping parameters, etc. It is unique that each data attribute can be mapped onto each visualisation object property, separately or using several properties to highlight some attribute (for example, see Figure 24). This gives researchers freedom in searching for the best way to visualise gaze data according to the task in mind.

Moreover, researchers can combine the visibility of each group of visualisation objects indi-

vidually and according to appropriate conditions. Thus, fixations, saccades, and samples are the targets for such manipulations. Navigation between fixations and samples provides deeper insight into the temporal order of gaze events and gaze data quality. The object in focus during navigation also serves as a window to raw data to be visualised.

Most of the iComponent visualisations allow simple interaction by displaying a hint with a summary of gaze data values over the object that is hit by the mouse cursor. Additionally, in this way researchers may retrieve all gaze data related to the object being analysed. Researchers may correct data (gaze positions) manually, using convenient view zooming and panning tools to increase the precision.

The visualisation of heat maps was improved also by a new kind of heat distribution (linear+sine) and various colour schemes (see Figure 25). Three approaches for smooth distribution of heat and transparency added new possibilities for improving gaze data perception via this visualisation method.

The method proposed in iComponent for visualising the contribution of stimulus observation for each participant, presenting fixation clusters as pie charts, makes it unique among the known methods for visualisation of fixation clusters (see Figure 26). This visualisation is particularly effective in comparing gaze paths of several subjects. The visualisation is enhanced by displaying transitions between clusters.

Figure 25. Comparison of Gaussian (left) and 'linear+sine' (right) distributions of transparency(@ 2008 Oleg Špakov. Used with permission)

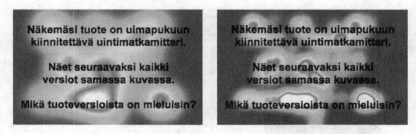

Figure 26. Automatic cluster creation: inspection of quality (left) and visualising pie charts (right)(@ 2008 Oleg Špakov. Used with permission)

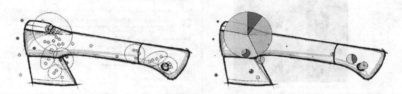

Figure 27. Manual clustering (by AOIs): AOI creation (left) and cluster visualisation (right) (@ 2008 Oleg Špakov. Used with permission)

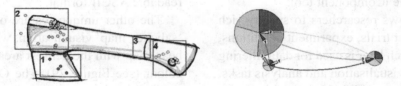

Automatic clustering does not always result in the best visualisation. Sometimes gaze data will contain so many fixations that it is not possible to set an appropriate distance threshold. In this case, it is better to draw areas of interest and let iComponent create clusters based on them (see Figure 27).

Researchers can select for analysis a subset of fixations according to their ordinal number, location, duration, timestamp, and preceding saccade angle. The iComponent system provides convenient means for selection creation, editing, and management.

Freie Universität Berlin: Open Gaze and Mouse Analyzer 2.0

The tools Open Gaze and Mouse Analyzer 2.0 were developed by Adrian Voßkuehler and colleagues, and published under the name OGAMA (Voßkühler, Nordmeier, Kuchinke, & Jacobs, 2008). They have a module-based architecture, with eight modules for visualisation, one for presentation of stimuli, and one for communication with devices (so far, all Tobii devices and mouse emulation are covered, as is data import from files recorded by SMI iViewX and ASL 504). The level of visualisation customisation is very high, and researchers may play around with numerous visualisation settings, searching for the

Figure 28. Multiple visualisations in OGAMA (from http://www.ogama.net/) (@ 2010 Dr Adrian Voßkühler. Used with permission)

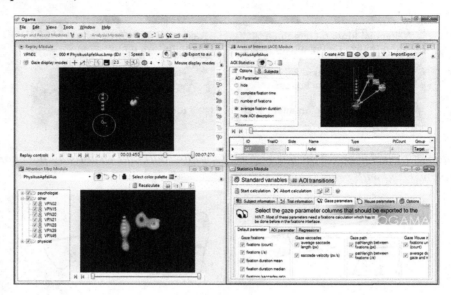

best view. In its key features, the OGAMA tool is very similar to the iComponent tool.

This tool allows researchers to specify rich information about trials, experiment conditions, and subjects, which later is used for data filtering and grouping in visualisation and analysis tasks. The ability to show multiple visualisations at the same time is a feature unique to OGAMA (see Figure 28)

Fixations (as circles), samples (as dots), or both are used during replay. Lines that connect adjacent replay points may be visible. If the replay mode is 'Spotlight', the portion of the image far from replay point(s) is shadowed. The replay can be exported into an AVI file.

The 'attention map' is implemented via a Gaussian distribution of the fixation data and a grey/coloured/transparent heat map. Another 2D visualisation is the classic scan path, wherein fixations are presented as circles with the radius dependent on their duration.

Researchers may create AOIs and get 'a lot of parameters useful for further analysis' by using

this tool. All statistics can be exported into SPSS-readable ASCII format.

The other unique feature of this tool is the 'saliency map' visualisation, which appears as a heap map with the densest areas denoted by red colour (see Figure 29). The OGAMA tool can predict the scan path on the basis of this map.

Figure 29. Salience map with fixations superimposed (OGAMA, from http://www.ogama.net/) (@ 2010 Dr Adrian Voßkühler. Used with permission)

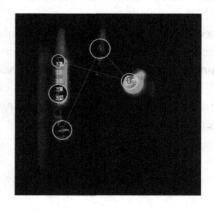

CONCLUSION

The tools listed in this chapter were selected mainly because of the unique visualisations they can create or because they are the first to implement a particular kind of gaze data visualisation. Figure 30 gives a short summary of the main features of these tools.

ACKNOWLEDGMENT

Special thanks go to Harri Rantala, and his colleagues in the "Perception of Design" project, who kindly provided gaze data collected in their experiments that was used for creating some of the visualizations in the iComponent application.

Figure 30. Common and unique visualisations among tools

Tool	1D: x,y / pupil size vs. time	Scan plot	Fix.–sacc. plot	Heat map	Clustering	Re-play: Plain	Re-play: Bee swarm	Re-play: Heat map	3D	Transition maps	External (e.g., MS Excel)	Uniqueness
GazeTracker (ERICA)	+		+			+			+	+	+	Unique visualisations: - 3D bars One of the first visualisations: - AOI tracking in replays - 3D hills and valleys
BeGaze 2.0 (SMI)	+	+	+	+		+	+	+			+	Unique visualisations: - AOI observation percentage second by second
NYAN 2.0 (Interactive Minds)	+		+	+		+	+			+		Unique visualisations: - Heat maps with colour scheme dependent on certain criteria
Tobii Studio (Tobii Technologies)		+	+	+		+	+	+			+	One of the first visualisations: - Bee swarm - Comprehensive built-in statistical tool
EyeData-Analyzer (Bielefeld University)			+	+	+							One of the first visualisations: - Various 'fixation maps' – Automatic separation of the screen into zones (AOIs) and highlighting of the most observed zones
iComponent (University of Tampere)	+	+	+	+	+	+	+				+	Unique visualisations: - Various gaze data parameters' mapping to various visual object features - Extended selection paradigm: fixation ordinal number, duration, timestamp, and preceding saccade angle in addition to location (AOI) One of the first visualisations: - Fixations that cluster the cluster visualisation as pie charts
OGAMA (Freie Universität Berlin)			+	+		+						Unique features: - 'Saliency map' with the fixations superimposed - Multiple visualisations in the same view (in parallel)

REFERENCES

Aaltonen, A., Hyrskykari, A., & Räihä, K.-J. (1998). 101 spots, or how do users read menus. *Proceedings of the SIGCHI conference on Human factors in computing systems (CHI '98)* (pp. 132–139). Los Angeles, CA: ACM.

Aula, A., Majaranta, P., & Räihä, K.-J. (2005). Eye-tracking reveals the personal styles for search result evaluation. In M. F. Costabile, & F. Paterna (Eds.), *Human–Computer Interaction (INTERACT '07)* (LNCS 3585, pp. 1058–1061). Berlin, Germany: Springer.

Babcock, J. S., Pelz, J. B., & Fairchild, M. D. (2003). Eye tracking observers during color image evaluation tasks. *Proceedings of SPIE, Human Vision and Electronic Imaging 5007* (pp. 218–230). San Jose, CA, US: SPIE.

Bates, R., & Spakov, O. (2006). *Implementation of COGAIN Gaze Tracking Standards.* (Deliverable D2.3. Communication by Gaze Interaction (COGAIN), Project IST-2003-511598). Retrieved from the COGAIN Association website: http://www.cogain.org/wiki/COGAIN_Reports

Bauer, D., & Hollan, J. D. (2003). IRYS: A visualization tool for temporal analysis of multimodal interactions. *Proceedings of the ACM International Conference on Multimodal Interfaces (ICMI '03)* (pp. 285–288). Vancouver, Canada: ACM.

Charlier, J., & Buquet, C. (1991). Experience with an eye tracker in visual communication evaluation. In Schmidt, R., & Zambarbieri, D. (Eds.), *Oculomotor control and cognitive processes: Normal and pathologicalaAspects* (pp. 457–464). Amsterdam, New York: Elsevier Science Publishers.

Cowen, L., Ball, L., & Delin, J. (2002). An eye movement analysis of Web page usability. In X. Faulkner, J. Finlay, & F. Detienne (Eds.), *People and Computers XVI - Memorable yet Invisible: Proceedings of the HCI 2002* (pp. 317–335). London, UK: Springer-Verlag.

Duchowski, A. T., Medlin, E., Cournia, N., Gramopadhye, A., Melloy, B., & Nair, S. (2002). 3D eye movement analysis for VR visual inspection training. *Proceedings of the 2002 Symposium on Eye Tracking Research & Applications (ETRA '02)* (pp. 103–110). New York, NY: ACM.

Goldberg, J. H., & Schryver, J. (1995). Eye-gaze contingent control of the computer interface: Methodology and example for zoom detection. *Behavior Research Methods, Instruments, & Computers, 27*, 338–350. doi:10.3758/BF03200428

Halverson, T., & Hornof, A. (2002). VizFix software requirements specifications. *Computer and Information Science, University of Oregon.* Retrieved on 1.10.2008 from http://www.cs.uoregon.edu/research/cm-hci/VizFix/

Hart, S., & Wicken, C. (1990). Workload assessment and prediction. In H. R. Booher (Ed.), *MANPRINT, an Approach to Systems Integration*, 257–296. New York, NY: Van Nostrand Reinhold.

Heminghous, J., & Duchowski, A. T. (2006). iComp: A tool for scanpath visualization and comparison. Poster presented at *the Symposium on Applied Perception in Graphics and Visualization.* Boston, MA, US.

Huey, E. (1968). *The psychology and pedagogy of reading.* Cambridge, MA, US: MIT Press. (Original work published 1908)

Lankford, C. (2000a). Effective eye-gaze input into Windows. *Proceedings of the 2000 Symposium on Eye Tracking Research & Applications (ETRA '00)* (pp. 23–27). Palm Beach Gardens, FL, US: ACM.

Lankford, C. (2000b). GazeTracker: Software designed to facilitate eye movement analysis. *Proceedings of the 2000 Symposium on Eye Tracking Research & Applications (ETRA '00)* (pp. 51–55). Palm Beach Gardens, FL, US: ACM.

Lankford, C., Shannon, P., Beling, P., McLaughlin, P., Israelski, E., Ellis, S., & Hutchinson, T. (1997). Graphical user interface design using eye gaze tracking and pupil response with ERICA. *Proceedings of Human Factors and Ergonomics Society 41ˢᵗ Annual Meeting*, 1371. Santa Monica, CA: HFES.

Lessing, S., & Linge, L. (2002). *IICap – A new environment for eye tracking data analysis*. (Master's thesis, University of Lund, Sweden). Retrieved from the Lund Humanities Lab website: http://www.humlab.lu.se/resources/publications/studentpapers/SimonLudvig_01.pdf

Olsson, P. (2007). *Real-time and offline filters for eye tracking*. Master's thesis, KTH Electrical Engineering, Stockholm. Retrieved from the KTH Royal Institute of Technology website: https://eeweb01.ee.kth.se/upload/publications/reports/2007/XR-EE-RT%202007:011.pdf

Pomplun, M., Ritter, H., & Velichkovsky, B. (1996). Disambiguating complex visual information: Towards communication of personal views of a scene. *Perception, 25*(8), 931–948. doi:10.1068/p250931

Posner, M. (1980). Orienting of attention. *The Quarterly Journal of Experimental Psychology, 32*, 3–25. doi:10.1080/00335558008248231

Ramakrishna, S., Pillalamarri, B., Barnetfe, D., Birkmire, D., & Karsh, R. (1993). Cluster: A program for the identification of eye fixation-cluster characteristics. *Behavior Research Methods, Instruments, & Computers, 25*(1), 9–15. doi:10.3758/BF03204444

Ramloll, R., Brewster, S., Yu, W., & Riedel, B. (2001). Using non-speech sounds to improve access to 2D tabular numerical information for visually impaired users. *Proceedings of the 3ʳᵈ International Workshop on Human–Computer Interaction with Mobile Devices* (pp. 515–530). Lille, France: Springer Verlag.

Ramloll, R., Trepagnier, C., Sebrechts, M., & Beedasy, J. (2004). Gaze data visualization tools: Opportunities and challenges. *Proceedings of IEEE 8ᵗʰ International Conference on Information Visualization* (pp. 173–180). London, UK: IEEE Computer Society Press.

Redline, C., & Lankford, C. (2001). Eye-movement analysis: A new tool for evaluating the design of visually administered instruments (paper and Web). Paper presented at *the Annual Meetings of the American Association for Public Opinion Research* (pp. 67–71). Montreal, Canada.

Reeder, R. W., Pirolli, P., & Card, S. K. (2001). WebEyeMapper and WebLogger: Tools for analyzing eye tracking data collected in Web-use studies. *Extended Abstracts of the ACM Conference on Human Factors in Computing Systems* (pp. 19–20). Seattle, WA, US: ACM.

Salvucci, D. D., & Goldberg, J. H. (2000). Identifying fixations and saccades in eye-tracking protocols. *Proceedings of the 2000 Symposium on Eye Tracking Research & Applications (ETRA '00)* (pp. 71–78). New York, NY: ACM.

Santella, A., & DeCarlo, D. (2004). Robust clustering of eye movement recordings for quantification of visual interest. *Proceedings of the 2004 Symposium on Eye Tracking Research & Applications (ETRA '04)* (pp. 27–34). New York, NY: ACM.

Schiessl, M., Duda, S., Thölke, A., & Fischer, R. (2003). Eye tracking and its application in usability and media research. *MMI-interaktiv Journal, 6*, 15–23.

Scinto, L., & Barnette, B. (1986). An algorithm for determining clusters, pairs or singletons in eye-movement scan-path records. *Behavior Research Methods, Instruments, & Computers, 18*, 41–44. doi:10.3758/BF03200992

Špakov, O. (2008) *iComponent – Device-independent platform for analyzing eye movement data and developing eye-based applications* (Doctoral dissertation, University of Tampere). Retrieved from the University of Tampere website: http://acta.uta.fi/teos.php?id=11064

Špakov, O., & Räihä, K.-J. (2008) KiEV: A tool for visualization of reading and writing processes in translation of text. *Proceedings of the Symposium on Eye Tracking Research & Applications* (*ETRA '08*) (pp. 107–110). New York, NY: ACM.

Spence, R., Witkowski, M., Fawcett, C., Craft, B., & De Bruijn, O. (2004). Image presentation in space and time: Errors, preferences and eye-gaze activity. *Proceedings of the International Conference on Advanced Visual Interfaces* (*AVI '04*) (pp. 141–149 + plate). New York, NY: ACM.

Stellmach, S., Nacke, L. E., & Dachselt, R. (2010). 3D attentional maps - Aggregated gaze visualizations in 3-dimensional virtual environments. *Proceedings of the International Conference on Advanced Visual Interfaces* (*AVI '10*) (pp. 345–348). New York, NY: ACM.

Voßkühler, A., Nordmeier, V., Kuchinke, L., & Jacobs, A. M. (2008). OGAMA (Open Gaze and mouse mnalyzer): Open-source software designed to analyze eye and mouse movements in slideshow study designs. *Behavior Research Methods, 40*(4), 1150–1162. doi:10.3758/BRM.40.4.1150

Wills, G. (1996). 524,288 ways to say 'This is interesting'. *Proceedings of the IEEE Symposium on Information Visualization* (*InfoVis '96*) (pp. 54–61). Washington, DC: IEEE Computer Society.

Witkowski, M., Arafa, Y., & deBruijn, O. (2001). Evaluating user reaction to character agent mediated displays using eye-tracking equipment. *Proceedings of AISB '01 Symposium on Information Agents for Electronic Commerce* (pp. 79–87). York, UK: AISB Convention.

Wooding, D. S. (2002). Eye movements in large populations: II. Deriving regions of interest, coverage, and similarity using fixation maps. *Behavior Research Methods, Instruments, & Computers, 34*(4), 518–528. doi:10.3758/BF03195481

Yarbus, A. (1967). *Eye Movements and Vision*. New York, NY: Plenum Press.

Zeki, S. (1992). The visual image in mind and brain. *Scientific American, 267*(3), 42–50. doi:10.1038/scientificamerican0992-68

ENDNOTE

[1] Gaze Data: Viewing Portraits. Retrieved from http://www.cs.bc.edu/~syu/artvis/course/project/viewportrait/index.html in December 2010.

Chapter 17
Usability Evaluation of Gaze Interaction

Henna Heikkilä
University of Tampere, Finland

Saila Ovaska
University of Tampere, Finland

ABSTRACT

This chapter provides practical advice on how to run tests with eye tracking devices in a laboratory environment and underlines some potential problems that the use of eye tracking equipment may create in test design. Examples of test settings used in design projects for gaze-based systems help the researcher decide what kind of procedure to use in their study. In addition, the authors discuss how to apply eye tracking in usability evaluations to augment understanding of the user experience and how to utilize gaze data when studying users' behavior.

INTRODUCTION

The purpose of this chapter is to present practical guidelines for running tests in a laboratory environment when using an eye tracking device in the test. These tests can range from very informal first trials ('diagnostic tests' (Dumas & Reddish, 1999) aimed at finding flaws in new interface design ideas) to more formally conducted research experiments aimed at publication as empirical research

studies. We point out some potential pitfalls and caveats in test design that are introduced by eye tracking, and we give examples of the various test settings used in design projects for systems that apply gaze interaction.

In the early phases of design projects, all user feedback on the design ideas is valuable, even in situations where the interaction method is not fully functional. Especially in the case of applying a novel interaction technique such as gaze interaction, the developers of software applications often need to collect informal feedback on

DOI: 10.4018/978-1-61350-098-9.ch017

their ideas very early in the process, so that they better understand the implementation challenges involved in meeting user needs. Because of the Midas touch (Jacob, 1991) and other problems with using eyes for control, evaluation and design iterations are needed in every development project. The small details of how to react to the user's gaze and how to give feedback on the eye movements that seem to control the system are hard to design correctly (i.e., in a way that works for the user) in the first iteration. As Jacob and Karn (2003) point out, designing systems that respond (and not over-respond) to eye movement input is much more challenging than designing for traditional, intentional mouse-based input. Currently, no standard interaction techniques for gaze-based systems have emerged, but designers are still trying to find the techniques that seem most natural for the eyes. For users, the challenges of first-time use are much bigger with a novel technology such as eye tracking than, for instance, with a mouse-based design.

The goal of the system developer is objective evaluation of whether the suggested interaction technique is usable by the test participants. In this chapter, we discuss practical usability evaluation guidelines for system designers who are considering adopting gaze interaction techniques in their software either as the only modality or as one of the modalities with which the system is used.

Our emphasis is on the guidelines for running usability tests for gaze interaction; that is, the input from the user's eyes is not aimed at post-test usability analysis but is used already during the test to control the functionality of the software system. Many usability studies discuss collecting eye gaze data for usability evaluation of Web sites or other software systems. The practical guidelines for tests that we present in this chapter apply to such tests too. Still, our focus is mostly on the usability evaluation of the interaction techniques themselves.

It is outside the scope of this chapter to discuss how to design gaze-interaction-based applications or Web sites that are highly usable and accessible,

but we want to point out that these issues are extremely important for users with disabilities if they are to use the same resources as other users, with the aid of their assistive tools. While some of the assistive tools (for instance, screen readers such as Jaws) are not related to gaze control in any way, assistive tools that are used with an eye tracker have been developed for those special user groups who access Web content with their eyes only. Examples range from systems like MyTobii P10 (2011) to special browser extensions such as the Accessible Surfing Extension, a Firefox 2.0 browser extension (ASE, 2009) described by Castellina and Corno (2007). Their functionality is described by Skovsgaard, Räihä, and Tall in this volume. For these assistive tools to work, it is important to follow the standards of the World Wide Web Consortium (W3C) when creating Web sites, since assistive tools transform the appearance of the Web site into a more gaze-control-friendly format through the mark-up language of the site. The assistive tools rely upon adherence to standards in the mark-up, but still the actual content of Web sites should be designed with usability and accessibility in mind, too.

It is also beyond the scope of this chapter to discuss the evaluation of the actual technology used to track eye gaze. However, one should note that eye tracking devices vary quite a lot in their design and implementation. Only some of the various eye trackers have been empirically compared (Cheng & Vertegaal, 2004; Špakov, 2008). In reality, the usability of the device itself is a key concern for increasing adoption rates.

GAZE RESEARCH AND USABILITY EVALUATION

In this section, we offer definitions for the term 'usability' and discuss the issue of utilising a usability test to analyse the usability of gaze interaction. We also address the issue of how well the results gathered in a laboratory compare to real-world use.

Definitions of Usability

Usability is defined in the standard ISO 9241-11 (1998) as 'the extent to which a product can be used by specified users to achieve specified goals with effectiveness, efficiency and satisfaction in a specified context of use'. However, commonly not all aspects of usability are discussed in gaze interaction studies. Instead, the studies often emphasise various quantitative measures that focus on one particular aspect of usability (often efficiency), and the measures selected are derived from the field of application.

For instance, in the field of text-entry systems (including eye typing), WPM (words per minute) and CPM (characters per minute) are measures that describe the efficiency of use (see the work by Hansen and Aoki in this volume for a description of these common metrics used in eye typing). By measuring these with longitudinal tests, researchers can hypothesise as to how efficiently users eventually could use their system, since typically participants learn to master the technique and the numbers get better in time until a threshold is reached. Such numbers are important for those who want to compare methods with each other, and, as standardised measures, they form a baseline for the evaluation of the interaction techniques.

Several reasons for not considering aspects of usability apart from efficiency can be found. For instance, when one works with able-bodied users in the laboratory environment, the question of satisfaction with the novel interaction method is somewhat cursorily addressed, since the whole test set-up overrides personal preferences. For those who are able to operate a computer with the keyboard and mouse, gaze interaction is not a practical option, in view of the cost of eye tracking devices and, for example, poor text entry rates in comparison with other input devices. Additionally, subjective satisfaction is highly dependent on the background of the participant. A person with disabilities, typing a letter by herself with the help of eye tracking for the first time in her life, may value an eye typing system more than

an able-bodied user who would achieve better results more quickly by using a keyboard. The eye tracking devices still need to be developed to make gaze interaction possible and a viable alternative in the everyday computing arsenal with basic computer set-ups.

Furthermore, the concept of usability can be defined in various ways, as Hornbæk (2006) points out in a survey of 180 usability studies. Some of the studies included in the survey do not even mention 'usability' but look at some specific aspect of 'quality-in-use'. Similar observations apply also in the field of gaze interaction studies: many of them do not mention 'usability' as one of their key concepts but directly focus on more easily quantifiable constructs, such as the WPM and CPM measures mentioned above. As pointed out by Hornbæk, selecting measures for usability is a difficult task, and in that selection, one also decides what the important aspects of the situation are, and how they should be evaluated. That is why one should stop to think about what kind of evaluation needs to be done and how to learn about 'quality-in-use' with the measures chosen.

While the division of usability into effectiveness, efficiency, and satisfaction is commonly accepted and is also used by Hornbæk (2006) as a starting point, he points out that the concepts actually overlap. Hornbæk suggests that one should evaluate outcomes, the actual interaction process, and user experience, and all of these from both an objective and a subjective standpoint. For instance, how well has the user reached the intended outcomes, and how satisfied is the user with them? How fluent is the interaction process? The actual interaction process can encompass measures such as enhanced efficiency of text input over time, but equally important is to look at the subjectively experienced time and workload during the process – though Hornbæk claims such measures are not commonly applied in usability studies. Users' attitudes and experiences can be measured from an objective standpoint with, for instance, physiological measurements, or one might resort to a (standardised) questionnaire for collection of opinions. Many of the measures collected by Hornbæk are relevant in the evaluation of gaze-controlled interaction.

Also, studies related to gaze interaction techniques have proposed other ways of breaking down 'usability'. Among others, the set of usability attributes promoted by Nielsen (1993) has been adopted by some researchers – for instance Itoh, Aoki, and Hansen (2006) – and adapted in creation of measures that are relevant for gaze interaction techniques. One of the key aspects of usability in work with gaze interaction is learnability, or ease of learning. Being easy to learn is an important quality in all systems, as the cognitive load that the user experiences decreases when the user becomes more fluent in using the system. Ease of learning is even more important in gaze interaction as the interaction becomes smoother and faster when the user learns the technique.

Usability Evaluation in Laboratory Settings

An eye tracking device can provide data for usability analysis of any kind of software with a graphical user interface. According to usability research practitioners (e.g., Bojko, 2006), the eye tracker device itself does not compromise the ecological validity of the test, since modern eye trackers are not complicated laboratory analysis devices anymore. When the eye tracker is used for controlling the application, the situation becomes challenging for the user: the eyes are usually used only to get input from the environment, and the user is not used to applications that react to eye gaze. Long fixations on screen elements or certain movement patterns from one part of the screen to another may cause something to happen on the screen. If the user is unprepared for eye-based control, the actions launched may be a surprise. That is why the usability test settings need to be carefully planned in advance, so that the test participant is introduced to the goals of the test and, at the same time, too much isn't revealed.

Although gaze interaction is often targeted at supporting persons with disabilities, the design of interaction techniques and user interface details commonly still starts with able-bodied persons; nearly all the work cited in this chapter has been done with able-bodied users. They are often more readily available to serve as test participants. If we can find a baseline design that works for able-bodied users, it can provide a design that suits the disabled – at least when tailored to their specific needs. However, when working with able-bodied users in the laboratory conditions, one cannot learn about the specific contextual factors that affect usability evaluation in the user's context (see the Chapter 18 by Donegan, Gill, and Oothuizen in this volume for more information about working with disabled users).

The tests often require finding a balance of expertise in the application area and in eye tracking, so that feedback can be collected on the suggested interaction technique itself in the application area. For instance, if we are developing tools for gaze control in online virtual worlds, our test participants need experience in how to act in the virtual world with the conventional input techniques (mouse and keyboard) if they are to be able to comment on the alternate input method of gaze interaction.

How Do the Findings Compare with Reality?

When the user starts using the software for real, the lab conditions do not hold anymore. For instance, there will be delays and pauses for thinking needed when one is spontaneously entering text via eye typing (Aoki, Hansen, & Itoh, 2009), whereas in the test all of the phrases to be written are given to the participant, so no thinking time is needed. To ensure the validity of the findings in the laboratory, it is important to focus on tasks that are similar to the real-world behaviour. However, a total match is impossible to achieve; the laboratory is always different from the field.

When the test participant is asked to work on a task – say, read text on the screen – the motivation to work on the task is extrinsic, provided by the test moderator. It is not easy to achieve concentration on the test task (Hyrskykari, 2006); instead, the participant might start to mimic the behaviour asked for, moving the eyes cursorily over the text but not understanding it fully. In this case, the gaze-aware tool does not really work, since it would require the user to aim for comprehension of the text. Common usability test guidelines – for instance, those given by Dumas and Reddish (1999) – point out that the wording of the task scenarios has an impact on how the participant starts working on them. Hyrskykari (2006) observed that the participants were trying to 'do well in the reading task' instead of applying their natural reading behaviour, and they changed the way they read the text and how they moved their eyes. This compromises the findings of the reading test on the basis of which the designer was hoping to develop the gaze-aware tool.

Often the baseline for evaluation comes from another input device or modality, such as mouse and keyboard (Bates, Vickers, & Istance, 2010), or other devices not so commonly used yet in practice – for instance, a hand-held Polhemus tracker (Tanriverdi & Jacob, 2000) for interacting in a 3D virtual world. However, the comparison is not always fair, since the participants do not know the basics of the novel interaction style and have not gained any experience in its use. The novel method will easily fail in all comparisons, even if it has potential with better design of the eye tracking device and algorithms for reacting to the eyes. When the user becomes unsure of how to control the device with the eyes, resorting to the old, well-known interaction styles is a tempting option.

Even having to calibrate the eye tracker or having to wear it on one's head or use a chin rest to make the head more stable can affect the behaviour of the participant. The test settings may apply a chin rest to ensure perfect calibration, while such an unnatural posture would not be accepted in practice. As we pointed out earlier, the methods applied and results obtained in the lab do not necessarily hold in practice; we need to consider the specific user needs and tailor the interaction method and settings accordingly. However, tests in the laboratory still have a purpose to serve: with them, designers can collect initial feedback on their designs, and if they are aiming for controlled experiments, laboratory settings allow this well – the conditions are fully under the researcher's control, which is never true in the field.

PRACTICAL GUIDELINES FOR USABILITY TESTING

In this section, we describe issues that need to be taken into account in planning and running of a usability test involving a gaze interaction system. We wish to note that the guidelines compiled in Table 1 and discussed in this section deal with issues that need to be addressed especially when eye trackers and gaze interaction systems are used in usability tests. We do not offer advice on how to design test tasks in general, since these depend on the actual system being tested; instead, we discuss the issue of how the test task should be given to the test participant without affecting the results. Further guidelines on how to run usability tests can be found, for example, in the books listed in the 'Additional Readings for Section 5'.

Preparing for the Tests

Nothing is more frustrating for the test participant than trying to work on tasks with an application that is full of technical problems. If the goal of the tests is to find possible usability problems with the application, some technical problems are acceptable. However, the presence of numerous technical issues may hide the real usability problems if the user needs to beware of technical instability and cannot work normally with the application.

Table 1. Guidelines for usability testing of gaze interaction

Guidelines for test settings	Detailed questions
Be prepared for the test well in advance.	Is your system stable enough to be tested by outsiders?
Recruit people who fit your target population and the goals of your test. If time is scarce, screen the participants carefully.	Do you expect problems in calibration? Can the participants be almost anybody, or do you need to find people who match your target group?
Decide on the test procedure.	How many minutes does each phase require? Will the participant require breaks in between? What is the best way to give the test tasks to the participant? Should you use the retrospective think-aloud method to gather insights from the participants?
Reserve time for each participant for playing around with gaze interaction.	How extensive introduction is needed before the test? Do you need another application in the test as the practice bed? What level of experience should the participant have gained in the practice rounds before starting for real?
Reserve time for calibration, and calibrate often.	Is it enough to calibrate once for the practice session and once for the actual test, or should you check even more often?
Obtain informed consent.	Do the participants understand the test settings and their rights in the test?
Collect subjective opinions and background data.	What aspects of usability are you interested in learning about? Will a questionnaire be enough, or are you looking for additional information that you can collect only through interviewing?
Plan in advance how to analyse your data.	What kind of analysis do you plan for the data? Will you require gaze-point-level analysis to learn about the usability of the interaction method you are designing?

Moreover, when the aim is to collect longitudinal experimental data, the application should not have usability problems anymore. Otherwise, the participants may be too distracted by the usability problems and the data will not show any clear results concerning the participants' learning curve.

Recruiting the Test Participants

In usability testing (Dumas & Reddish, 1999), it is emphasised that the participants recruited should match the intended user population of the software application being tested. The demographics of the participants are equally important in gaze-based interaction tests, but still, it is often impossible to recruit people from the group who will benefit the most, those with motor control disabilities making hand and mouse movement hard or impossible. Running experiments with able-bodied student participants is commonplace in university research.

However, when recruiting the participants for an eye tracking study, one should bear in mind that the tracking of the eyes is not always possible even with modern technology. Eyeglasses or contact lenses can make calibration hard or cause loss of calibration during the test. Some eyes are shaped in such a way that tracking them is difficult. Some people find it hard to sit still in front of the computer, even though movement can endanger calibration. For one reason or another, some will not succeed in using the system. Also, especially in testing of applications that use 3D, no participants who are predisposed to migraines, motion sickness, or epileptic fits should be recruited for the test if there is any danger that the application could trigger an episode. Therefore, it would be good to know of potential problems in advance and, if needed, recruit additional participants. Pernice and Nielsen (2009) describe their screening procedure and present a screening questionnaire with questions about the eyes that allows those participants who match the target population but might cause problems in eye tracking to be masked out.

An issue raised often in usability tests is the number of participants. Usually gaze interaction researchers prefer to use about 10 participants in their tests. In most cases, the participants are novices in eye tracking. When one is trying to find usability problems with any application, quite a small number of test participants is enough, since after only a few participants the researcher is already able to point to the most critical usability problems. Sometimes even only two or three experienced participants may give the results needed (e.g., Istance, Bates, Hyrskykari, & Vickers, 2008). If the goal is to find out how well the users can perform with the application, more participants are needed if one is to achieve statistically significant results. All in all, no general rule can be given, especially since the goals of tests vary so much.

Deciding on the Test Procedure

The use of gaze for controlling the computer may be fatiguing for the participants if they are not used to using their eyes as an input method. A participant unfamiliar with eye trackers may find the test tiring for the eyes and may suffer from dry eyes. Novices often try to control their eyes more precisely, and they also may (consciously or unconsciously) avoid blinking during the test. These things limit the time that can be used to perform the tasks.

If a long test is needed, one should consider offering breaks between tasks. For instance, Majaranta, Aula, and Räihä (2004) ran a test where participant typed 30 phrases in total. They offered a short break (a few minutes) after every 10 phrases. During the break, the feedback method of the application was changed. The downside of the breaks during the test is that the calibration may shift if the participants change their position or leave the chair. Then recalibration is needed. At least, the quality of the calibration should be checked with a calibration-checking screen after a longer break. In all tests, the tasks should be designed in a way that the participants have the possibility of resting their eyes between tasks.

When one is designing a test, it needs to be decided whether the experimenter will accompany the participant in the test room or whether the participant is to be left alone in the test room. The presence of the experimenter may cause difficulties during the tasks if the participant's attention is drawn to the experimenter. The participant may also feel a need to turn toward the experimenter or start to talk with the experimenter in the middle of the task. These behaviours might cause problems with calibration and with performance measurements. However, if the performance measures are not essential, talking during the task performance may offer additional information about the ease of use and on usability problems. The think-aloud method is still not recommended in tests where eye tracking is used (Bojko, 2006; Pernice & Nielsen, 2009). A better method for collecting this kind of information is the retrospective think-aloud method, introduced later in this chapter.

Wherever the experimenter is situated during the test, the easiest way to deliver the test tasks is to present them on the screen (see Figure 1 for an example). This decreases the possibility of the calibration shifting when the participant reaches for the task paper and reads it. Another way is for the experimenter to read the phrases out loud as Itoh et al. (2006) did in their tests. However, for some participants, it may be harder to memorise the phrases by hearing them than by reading them. Also, emphasis is placed on participants' spelling abilities if the participant cannot check the correct spelling when writing. However, having the task available during performance slows down the participant, and some careful typists might check the correct spelling unnecessarily often. Finally, in some test situations there is no room on the screen for the task description when the task is in progress. In these situations, the application and task descriptions need to be separately controlled, which may require using the mouse or keyboard

Figure 1. An easy and unobtrusive way to supply tasks (or here, example text for Dasher) for the participants is to present them on the screen

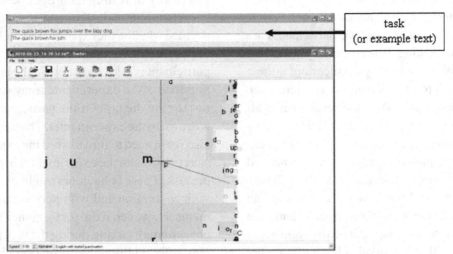

for advancing between tasks while the application itself is controlled by eye gaze.

Practising the Interaction Method

An introduction to the laboratory, test set-up, and devices in use is needed so that the participant feels comfortable in the laboratory environment. The depth of introductions depends on the study goals: for instance, when the goal is to learn about problems related to first-time use, the introduction should give only the essential information but not detailed guidance in how to use the gaze interaction techniques. However, participant briefings concerning how the eye tracker captures eye movements and how the interaction techniques work are important so that the participant understands what to expect from the test.

When the user tries out the application for the first time, the situation triggers problems that are related to the unfamiliar functioning of the application. When the user learns the basic principles that underlie the functioning of the application, these kinds of problems will disappear. Usually researchers are more interested in how well the users will perform with the application in the long

run than how well the users perform when they use the application for the first time. Although a longitudinal test set often would be the best way to learn about the application, long test sets are seldom possible, because of limitations in resources. With the participants trying out the test application before the tasks, first-time use factors should have less effect on the results.

A short practice period before the actual tasks can be useful especially if the participants are not familiar with gaze interaction. Even 5–10 minutes of practice with the eye tracker may help to reduce the problems that occur if the participant does not know how gaze interaction works. Depending on the nature of the test and the test application, the practising can be completed with the test application itself, with a special practice application, or with some other application that uses functions similar to those of the test application (for example, a game of Solitaire trains one in dwelling and moving an object with the eyes). Next, we will give some examples of how the need for practicing has been handled in studies.

In their tests of eye typing applications, Majaranta et al. (2004) let the participants practise with three phrases before recalibration and presentation of the actual test phrases. The practice period, as short as it was here, let the participants familiarise themselves with the eye typing application and so made the test data less sensitive to the effect of first-time use. Also, when Wobbrock, Rubinstein, Sawyer, and Duchowski (2008) piloted their longitudinal study of the gaze-gesture-based EyeWrite application, the test procedure included two practice periods. First, they let the participant practise with the application (EyeWrite or an on-screen keyboard, depending on the participant group) for 20 minutes. This practice was unguided. After a five-minute break, the participant wrote given sentences similar to the test phrases for 10 minutes and had another five-minute break before writing the actual test phrases as quickly and accurately as possible.

When the only goal is to evaluate the gaze interaction and the application to be tested contains novel interaction elements (for instance, a new virtual keyboard layout and menu organisation for eye typing), one should ensure that the participant understands the intended functionality (Aoki et al., 2009). If the interaction elements used in the application are unfamiliar to the participant, tackling these elements may affect the participant's performance. Poor performance may lead to the conclusion that the use of gaze interaction is not useful in that particular application even if the reason for the poor performance was the problems the participants experienced with the unfamiliar interaction element. Though this seems surprising for testing of a new gaze-based application, participants should practise first by using the on-screen keyboard with a mouse or another conventional input device (if at all possible) so that they understand what to expect when working with the gaze modality.

In their longitudinal study, Wobbrock et al. (2008) used a special practice session, which was the first session in the participant's test set. During the practice session, the participant practised the EyeWrite gaze gestures with pen and paper. The goal was to memorise the gaze gestures.

The participant also wrote two practice phrases with the actual application. This practice session lasted about an hour. In the other sessions in the longitudinal study, the participant first warmed up with two practice phrases before completing eight test phrases.

Repeated practice periods are often needed also during a longitudinal study. A short practice period before each session helps the participant to warm up. By using these practice periods, the researcher can assure that the time between the tests does not affect the learning curve. For example, in their longitudinal study of GazeTalk, Itoh et al. (2006) used a 10-minute practice period at the beginning of the test set and a five-minute warm-up period at the start of the other sessions. Here, a short, five-minute warm-up period was enough to allow the participants to familiarise themselves with the application again.

Calibrating the Eye Tracker

The better the calibration is, the more accurately the device knows where the user is looking. Calibration is done by asking the participant to focus on calibration points on the screen one at a time. The number of points is commonly nine or more but can be lower; for instance, De Luca, Weiss, and Drewes (2007) used only two positions in the calibration for gesturing up and down movement with the eyes. The quality of the calibration can be enhanced by adding more on-screen calibration points. Usually, eye tracker manufacturers provide instructions and recommendations that work for their device. Overall, calibration should be done as normally as possible, without any tricky adjustments. When not in the laboratory environment, users will not follow instructions exactly anyway.

Surprisingly simple factors can hamper calibration. For instance, if the participant relaxes after the calibration, already the changed posture can cause loss of calibration. A good rule of thumb is to check the quality of the calibration before starting the test tasks. An easy way to do this is to show the participant a grid of points on the screen and ask him or her to look at each point in turn. If the gaze data points gathered are off by too much, the eye tracker should be recalibrated if this is needed. For example, Hyrskykari (2006) used a test window containing 12 points, and the participants were asked to look at each of the points in turn. Similar calibration checking should be done after the test, so that the researcher can be sure that the results are not affected by poor calibration quality.

Asking for Informed Consent

Informed consent is an essential part of any test. Before participants sign an informed consent form, they need to be informed about the test set-up and the test procedure. If the test will be recorded, the participant needs to be informed of that as well. Furthermore, the participants need to know that they can stop the test if they so desire. The participants may have some fears concerning the devices and the laboratory environment, and the experimenter should make it clear beforehand that nothing in the test can harm the participant.

The best way to obtain informed consent is to ask the participants to fill in an informed consent form after the test procedure has been explained to them. However, if the participant is a minor or for some other reason has a guardian (for example, because of mental handicap), both the actual participant and the guardian (usually a parent) need to give their consent. Also, if the participant needs the assistant to be present during the test and if the test will be recorded, permission to record has to be obtained from the assistant as well. Model informed consent forms can be found in the work of Donegan et al. (2006). The examples include forms for disabled adults and for both disabled children and their guardians.

Asking for Subjective Opinions

It is common to collect quantitative and qualitative evaluations and feedback from the participants after the test by means of questionnaires. Questionnaires are used to collect subjective feedback on the devices used, the interaction technique itself, and the experiences of the user. Douglas, Kirkpatrick, and MacKenzie (1999) point out the need for having an additional, open-ended questionnaire for comfort-related questions.

Itoh et al. (2006) used a questionnaire to collect feedback on GazeTalk. The questionnaire had questions about perceived typing speed, perceived likelihood of error, interface preference, satisfaction with the system, perceived fatigue, and experience of motion sickness. In their longitudinal study, Wobbrock et al. (2008) used a very short questionnaire wherein the participants were asked to estimate the ease of use, speed, and fatigue. In both cases, the participants were asked to answer the questions on a five-point Likert scale.

Often the questionnaires used in the studies cited here have been compiled for the specific study being conducted. Questions are selected on the basis of the researchers' information needs. These self-made questionnaires can convey useful information, for example, for iteration, but their flaw is that they do not yield results that are generalisable or comparable with other research, as do the standardised questionnaires. So far, no standardised questionnaire has been developed with solely gaze interaction in mind. However, standardised questionnaires that measure comfort, effort, fatigue, or workload are available, and they can be used for gaze interaction evaluation as well. Next, we briefly introduce two standardised questionnaires suitable for evaluating gaze interaction applications: the ISO 9241-9 questionnaire and the NASA-TLX questionnaire.

The ISO 9241-9 standard (2000) includes a questionnaire intended for assessment of the performance, effort, and comfort of a non-keyboard pointing device, such as a mouse or a pen. The

Table 2. NASA-TLX evaluation scales (NASA-TLXNASA-TLX: Task Load Index, 2010)

Dimension	Detailed questions
Mental Demand	How much mental and perceptual activity was required in the task?
Physical Demand	How physically demanding was the task?
Temporal Demand	How hurried or rushed was the pace of the task?
Performance	How successful were you in accomplishing what you were asked to do?
Effort	How hard did you have to work to accomplish your level of performance?
Frustration	How insecure, discouraged, irritated, stressed, and annoyed were you?

questionnaire includes scales to assess mental and physical effort, general comfort, and fatigue, to name a few elements. MacKenzie (in this volume) presents this ISO 9241-9 questionnaire and introduces how it can be utilised in gaze interaction research.

The NASA Task Load Index, or NASA-TLX for short (Hart & Staveland, 1988), is a tool for assessing subjective workload. A list of the dimensions affecting subjective workload is presented in Table 2. Each dimension is rated on a line divided into 20 equal intervals along a low–high continuum (or, for the Performance item, good–poor). With this questionnaire, users can assess their own performance, effort, and frustration levels as well as how demanding the system under evaluation is in mental, physical, and temporal respects, either for each task in the test or after completion of the test. To assess workload, the dimensions are weighted separately according to subjective perception of important factors contributing to workload. The ratings collected can be used without the weighting process as 'Raw TLX', or RTLX, which makes the evaluation process simpler: the ratings are averaged or added to create an estimate of overall workload (Hart, 2006).

The NASA-TLX tool is often used in laboratory-based experimental studies, though there is no general consensus concerning its superiority. For example, Öquist & Lundin (2007) compared four text presentation formats covering the aspects of NASA-TLX. Often, the NASA-TLX dimensions are taken as part of a separately tailored

questionnaire. Kammerer, Scheiter, and Beinhauer (2008) used a modified NASA-TLX questionnaire to measure cognitive load in their comparative study of two menu designs. They left out the Effort dimension. Also, Bates and Istance (2002) tailored their questionnaire by combining the ISO 9241-9 questionnaire questions with NASA-TLX dimensions. However, they changed the scale into a seven-point fully labeled scale. As these examples indicate, there is no consensus on the dimensions to evaluate, let alone the scales to use, in assessment of subjective experiences.

For longitudinal studies, repetitive questionnaires offer the possibility to compare subjective impressions between sessions. To compare the first impression and the impression after longer use, Itoh et al. (2006) asked the participants to fill in the same questionnaire after the first and the last session in the longitudinal study. In the study of Wobbrock et al. (2008), the participants were asked to complete the questionnaire after each session (not including the first session, which was the training session), for a total of 14 times.

Another way to collect subjective feedback is to interview the test participants. Tuisku, Majaranta, Isokoski, and Räihä (2008) used short interviews after the last session in their longitudinal study of Dasher. They asked for participants' preference as regards two different text input methods (Dasher and an on-screen keyboard). They were also interested in problems that occurred during the sessions and ideas the participants had for improving Dasher.

Analysing the Collected Data

Often there is a need to understand the interactions between the user, the eye tracking device, and the software acting on the basis of the user's eye gaze in great detail. This means that dedicated data collection routines need to be planned and implemented (the software is 'instrumented') such that data will be collected as log data from within the actual running software application. In this respect, running usability tests with collection of gaze data only to support usability analysis is different from testing gaze-aware applications, since there are various analysis packages available for the eye tracker data collected, as explained by Špakov in the previous chapter. For instance, analysing a writing tool such as Dasher (see Majaranta in this volume for description of Dasher) would not be possible with the common analysis package tools, since when writing with Dasher, the eyes stay relatively constant while the letters move on the screen.

Careful planning of data analysis before one conducts the test set helps when the time comes for actual analysis of the data. For instance, in evaluation of the usability of an eye typing application, certain metrics (WPM or CPM, error rate, etc.) are used. Implementation of counters that during the test count the data items needed for calculation of the metrics can save a lot of time and effort when the researcher begins to analyse the data. Without these counters, the researcher would need to refer to the eye tracker's massive gaze data files or to videos in order to calculate the metrics.

Questionnaires and videos (including the participants' comments about the application during the tasks and the interviews) give the most useful information to support the usability analysis. Said data will help to reveal the usability problems. If the purpose of the test set is to test the application against another application, then more precise metrics are needed. To get what is needed for these metrics, the researcher needs data, for example, from the selections the participants did during the tests. For this purpose, combination of the eye tracker's gaze data files and the researchers' own implementations of loggers or counters can be highly useful.

We will briefly return to the issue of analysing the data collected, when we describe the use of eye trackers in ordinary usability tests to gather additional information.

EXAMPLES OF USABILITY EVALUATION STUDIES FOR GAZE INTERACTION

In this section, we look at usability evaluations for some systems that utilise gaze-based interaction. The systems covered here include eye typing with on-screen keyboards, attentive interfaces, games and virtual worlds, and gaze gestures. We will discuss the evaluation process and describe the challenges the researchers faced when designing and evaluating the usability of these systems.

Eye Typing

In eye typing, the goal is to produce text using the focus of the eye as input (Majaranta, MacKenzie, Aula, & Räihä, 2006). Usually the text appears in a window on the computer screen, from which it becomes a part of a text document, completes a field in a form, or contributes the user's turn in a chat. In addition to actual character entry, the functionality of deleting, scrolling, and positioning of the text cursor in the text can be required, but there seldom is a need to manipulate the text as text objects (as in graph drawing, where one must be able to position text objects in relation to each other). Typically, the software for eye typing has only basic text entry capabilities and the on-screen keyboard can fill the whole screen. When the user focuses on an individual letter to select it, it gets highlighted and, after a dwell time, selected and entered in the text entry field. It is common for the user to check what was entered, and also correct the error immediately if a wrong key was selected. The shorter the dwell time on a key that is required, the more error-prone the system is, although faster text entry is possible. By contrast, increasing the dwell time makes the system slower to use, and users find this uncomfortable.

Majaranta et al. (2006) have pointed out the importance of proper feedback design for eye typing. In addition to feedback presented visually on the screen, auditory feedback (similar to a mouse click after the selection of a key) can make the process faster. But when the letter selected is spoken aloud, the user becomes distracted from the writing process. When a short dwell time is used, simple feedback is preferred. However, Majaranta et al. point out that users need means to adjust the feedback parameters, since their subjective preferences vary. For instance, adjusting dwell time according to one's pace of writing increases the text entry rate. In a longitudinal study of 10 sessions, the text entry rate increased from under seven, in the first session, to almost 20 words per minute, in the tenth session (Majaranta, Ahola, & Špakov, 2009).

Eye typing is an area of application for gaze interaction that is relatively straightforward. As the work of Majaranta and her co-workers shows, even minor user interface details have an effect on both speed and accuracy. To understand the needs of the users, careful design of experimental research settings with dozens of users is required.

Attentive Interfaces

'Gaze-aware' software is designed to react to the user's eye movements proactively so that the user does not need to wait for the dwell time to pass in order to launch a command explicitly. Instead, the software seems to work according to the user's intentions.

iDict (Hyrskykari, 2006; see Chapter 13 by Istance and Hyrskykari in this volume for a description of iDict) is an example of such ap-

plications. It is a tool for people reading text in a foreign language. When the user encounters a difficult word, the reading process slows down, and the eye tracker shows that the eyes fixate on a word or move back in the text to the part of the sentence where difficulties began. The tool tries to help the user automatically by giving the translation of the difficult word as a tooltip next to the word. However, if the basic translation is not enough, the user can ask for the dictionary entry by moving the eyes to the other frame in the window.

The usability evaluation of iDict was carried out in several iterative steps where collection of feedback from users was followed by design iterations. In the first concept trial tests, the designers collected only eye tracking data for the eye movements when a user was reading text. In these tests, the participants were asked to press a button or say aloud that they had encountered a difficult word, and the test moderator would then provide help with that word, acting as 'human dictionary'. Hyrskykari (2006) reports that this solution was not an optimal one, since attending to secondary tasks even as simple as pressing a hardware button or addressing a person during the test immediately corrupts the eye tracking data.

The first prototypes of the tool were designed to find a long fixation on a word and give the tooltip only after the eye tracker software indicated that there indeed was a long fixation. However, the users felt that the software seemed to freeze: even though they looked at a word, they could not get a tooltip for it before moving their eyes away. After this finding, the software needed to be completely changed and the data collection of data on fixation length had to be done within iDict itself so that it could react better to ongoing fixations.

The sensitivity for giving tooltip help is an important design decision, too. If it appears too easily, the software starts annoying the users. Istance and Hyrskykari (in this volume) tell more about the challenges of designing proactive gaze-aware applications.

Games and Virtual Worlds

A three-dimensional game world such as Second Life involves controlling and moving one's avatar in the world, operating the menus of the software, acting with in-world objects, and communicating with the other users (or their avatars) in the world. While all of this can be done with a mouse and keyboard, using only gaze interaction for those purposes is much more demanding and requires careful design of the functionality and interaction technique. It is a commonly accepted starting point for design to look at the control-related requirements for the tasks involved (e.g., Bates et al., 2010; Tanriverdi & Jacob, 2000). However, if one separates out just one part of the task, such as handling of objects (Tanriverdi & Jacob, 2000), and works on improving its design, fluent interaction within the virtual world as a whole is not guaranteed. Working, by contrast, on the design as a whole is a challenge too, since the evaluation of what works and what does not is non-trivial, because of the complexity and information-richness of the virtual world.

The first trial evaluations of new interaction techniques (e.g., the Snap Clutch of Istance et al., 2008) are best done by recruiting expert users who are experienced and familiar with the relevant virtual world as participants (Bates et al., 2010; Istance et al., 2008); otherwise the findings can be distorted. The first gaze interaction trials with expert users in Second Life (Bates et al., 2010) simply mapped the mouse control and eye gaze. However, even the first trials revealed that the existing controls in the mouse-operated interface are not suitable for gaze interaction: when one is controlling, for example, an online tool palette for camera movements, the feedback appears far from the actual control, forcing extensive eye movements between the scene and the control. Furthermore, the need to dwell on the control is unsuitable for fast interaction; other options, including gaze gestures, might provide a faster interaction style. Research into gaze interaction techniques suitable for virtual worlds is ongoing, and the fast-paced activities required in the control

of one's avatar in a virtual world continue to pose challenges for interaction designers.

Gaze Gestures

Gaze gestures are a fairly new concept in gaze interaction. A gaze gesture is a sequence of eye movements that causes an action when performed. Since they free screen space of buttons and menus, gaze gestures are most useful when screen space is very limited. Gaze gestures are often offered as a solution to problems that the use of dwell time causes, such as Midas touch and accuracy problems (Drewes and Schmidt, 2007). However, according to the survey by Heikkilä and Räihä (2009), most researchers still use dwell time in some form in their gaze gesture applications.

In recent research, the most common field of application for gaze gestures has been in text entry, as a substitute for on-screen keyboards. In EyeWrite, by Wobbrock et al. (2008), the user makes letter-like gaze gestures one by one in a writing window. Porta and Turina (2008) used a very similar approach in their Eye-S, with the distinction that in Eye-S the user makes the gaze gestures not in a separate writing window but in the whole screen area. Drewes and Schmidt (2007) created gaze gestures that can be used to control an application (in their case, a music player). Their gaze gestures combined strokes in eight directions. Compared to the gaze gestures from EyeWrite and Eye-S, the gaze gestures studied by Drewes and Schmidt were more complex and not directly based on familiar shapes.

Learnability (ease of associating a gesture with a command) and memorability (ease of retaining the associations from memory) are always issues when one is designing gesture sets. In graphical interfaces, toolbars and menus are used to offer the selection of functions to the user. When these elements are removed from the visible interface and replaced with gestures, the user must first learn the gestures by heart and then recall them when needed. The more complex the gestures are, the more learning and the more memory capacity are needed.

To aid in the learning and recall process, Wobbrock et al. (2008) as well as Porta and Turina (2008) used gaze gestures that resemble letters of the Roman alphabet. As results from their longitudinal test set, Wobbrock et al. reported that the learning curve showed strong improvement over sessions. They also reported a significant decline in the total error rate over sessions, which indicates that the user had memorised the gaze gesture set well. This suggests that by connecting the gaze gestures to common alphabets, gestures are easier to learn and to remember. However, despite the use of gaze gestures that resemble numbers, De Luca et al. (2007) reported that the gaze gestures were less intuitive and were harder to learn than the techniques to which they were compared. In these tests, the gaze gesture technique was also slower, though much less error-prone.

Proper feedback can enhance learning and improve the efficiency of gaze gestures. For example, Wobbrock et al. (2008) decided to draw a stylised arch from corner to corner according to the user's eye movements. The character that the gaze gesture corresponds to appears in the corner where the last stroke is made. This way, the application gives feedback on the progress, when the user makes the gaze gesture. Showing the progress of the gaze gesture helps the user to learn the gesture alphabets. Also, efficiency increases when the user sees the progress and is able to avoid errors.

In addition to the feedback, the shapes of the gestures need to be designed carefully. Heikkilä and Räihä (2009) learnt that round shapes are hard to make with the eyes, and hitting exact points with the gaze is challenging. Users also differ quite a lot in their behaviour: some are more careful than others when making gestures. These findings from early tests with participants provide information for design of gesture sets and the interaction method in general. However, the detailed analysis at gaze point level that is required in comparison of the various gesture ideas is tedious and time-consuming, and it often is not part of the design process where one is aiming for direct implementation.

COLLECTING GAZE INFORMATION TO SUPPORT USABILITY ANALYSIS

Until now, our focus has been on gaze-based interaction. Last, but certainly not with the least practical application, we look at applying eye tracking in usability tests as one source of information about how the participant approaches the system being tested. In 2003, Jacob and Karn highlighted the potential for applying eye tracking in usability engineering as 'highly promising for many years but progress has been slow'. Since those days, it has become common in the usability engineering profession, partly because more usability laboratories have acquired eye trackers, and software tools assisting in analysis of the collected data have become available.

A usability test is commonly recorded for further analysis. The recording of the test session usually includes screen events and mouse movements, often augmented with a video overlay of the participant's face, and audio recordings of the think-aloud. Additionally, it may contain an overlay of the participant's gaze path shown moving on the screen as the test progresses, if an eye tracker was used during the test. However, adding the gaze-path visualisation to the recording requires use of a special tool such as Tobii Studio in the test arrangements.

The advantage of gathering gaze data during an ordinary usability test is that the gaze path may reveal things that the participant's speech or mouse movements cannot show. For instance, the participant may report that a certain function is missing even though the recorded gaze path may show that actually the participant did look at the right function several times but did not use it. Instead of a change in its position on the screen, perhaps better naming would be in order. The gaze data will reveal where participants looked first and also where they did not look at all, both unattainable with other testing methods (Breeze, 2010).

When an eye tracker is used to collect additional data during an ordinary usability test, the procedure is basically the same as without use of an eye tracker during the test; only brief calibration is needed at the beginning of the test. At least, this is the case from the participant's standpoint. The researcher, however, needs to prepare the tests in such a way that the collection of gaze data is possible. For example, Tobii offers a tool for recording and analysing usability tests with the Tobii eye tracker. At this point, we will not offer any special advice on how to run a usability test wherein an eye tracker is used to collect additional data but refer to the practical guidelines we gave earlier, since they are valid also here.

Next, we describe the retrospective think-aloud method, which is recommended in preference to an ordinary think-aloud method for use when one is tracking the gaze. Last, we discuss analysis of the collected data and the pitfalls of analysis.

Different Think-Aloud Methods

In usability studies, the think-aloud method is often used to collect data from the participants. In the think-aloud method, the participant is asked to verbalise his or her thoughts (or to think aloud) while completing the test tasks. Think-aloud is used to achieve better understanding of a participant's mental models and to gain additional information about the participant's actions and choices. However, as mentioned earlier, when the test participant is asked to think aloud during the test, the behaviour in the test changes, as does the way of looking at the screen (Bojko, 2006). A well-known fact is that verbalising of thoughts may slow down performance, and many participants feel that thinking aloud is unnatural (Nielsen, 1993; van Someren, Barnard, & Sandberg, 1994). Additionally, in testing of a gaze-aware application, the use of a think-aloud method may cause unintended actions, since while trying to verbalise, the participant may stare in one place or the gaze may wander. Nielsen and Pernice (2009) point out that when asked to comment on a Web page, people read the text more carefully than they would during normal use, and they focus more on design elements and advertisements than they

would in real life. With such effects, one cannot reliably know anymore how the participant looked at the various parts of the interface. To avoid compromising data collection during the test with think-aloud, the retrospective think-aloud method is recommended as more suitable for cases where the participant's full attention is needed for performance of the given tasks.

In the retrospective think-aloud method for usability tests, the video recording of the test situation is reviewed with the participant after the test tasks are done. While reviewing the recording, the participant is asked to think aloud or to comment on his or her actions. The use of recordings and gaze path data to evoke comments is sometimes called cued retrospective think-aloud (Hyrskykari, Ovaska, Majaranta, Räihä, & Lehtinen, 2008; Elling, Lentz, & de Jong, 2011).

When they see a video replay of their gaze path overlaid on the screen being tested, participants seem to remember their thoughts and the potential usability problems encountered. However, seeing the gaze replay can be distracting at first to the participant, since the blue dots indicating fixations and lines for saccades between fixations appear at such a fast pace on top of the screen display. Each participant needs to be briefed about the visualisation and told that such rapid movement is normal for eyes (Pernice & Nielsen, 2009).

The weakness of the retrospective think-aloud method is that participants might not remember exactly what they were thinking of while performing the tasks, and they might come up with new explanations for their actions if they cannot remember their thoughts correctly (van Someren et al., 1994; Pernice & Nielsen, 2009). Although the participant's memory may fail in places, the retrospective comments are considered to be fairly truthful, because the recording helps the participants to remember their actions better. Nevertheless, postponing all questions and commentary until after the test (instead of using the concurrent think-aloud method) lets the participant concentrate on the task at hand and so reduces unintended actions and errors, which is especially important in the case of testing of gaze-aware applications.

Yet another variation of using gaze data to better understand what is going on is the "triggered think-aloud" method (Freeman, 2011) where the test moderator views the participant's scan path in real time while the task execution is ongoing. Gaze data can be used to help the moderator determine when to pause the task execution for more information. This reduces the need for memory recall but also might endanger the reliability of data collection by interrupting the participant's thought processes.

Although the retrospective think-aloud method originated in connection with ordinary usability tests of graphical user interfaces and Web pages, the method is useful for tests of gaze-controlled applications, too. It allows for obtaining the participants' comments on the interaction sequences, and perhaps some explanation concerning difficult tasks, after the test. However, if the gaze cursor or other feedback on gaze position is shown on the screen during the test and captured in the recording, showing the gaze path overlaid on the screen probably is not necessary. The gaze replay might make the replay screen too noisy, especially if the screen elements being looked at react to the eye gaze by expanding or shrinking.

Though getting participant comments about the test is important, it makes the test session longer than without a retrospective think-aloud session,

a trade-off to be considered in test settings. Most analysis is done after the usability test participant has left. A video replay of the test situation together with the scan path can be helpful for the analysis even without the participant. Usually, though, further analysis is based on different kinds of visualisations of the collected data.

Analysing the Collected Data

One of the challenges related to usability analysis based on eye tracking data stems from the fact that eye trackers collect so large quantities of data that it is not easy to find the important aspects (Jacob & Karn, 2003). For instance, the Tobii T60 eye tracker produces 60 data points each second for each eye in the raw gaze data set. Visualisations, such as heat maps and fixation maps, can help with this challenge (see Špakov's work in this volume for more examples). However, the visualisations depend on the default settings for fixation detection, and those need to be discussed first.

The gaze data analysis and visualisation tools usually let the researcher adjust certain parameters, such as the minimum length of a fixation and the radius of the area from which individual gaze points are counted as belonging to the same fixation. To be considered a fixation (displayed as a circle in the gaze path visualisation, for instance, in Figure 2), the consecutive data points need to be close enough to each other spatially (as determined by the radius parameter, measured in pixels

Figure 2. The same data look different when the fixation radius parameter is modified (scan-path visualisation screenshots generated with Tobii Studio; courtesy of Selina Sharmin)

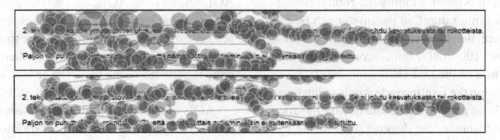

or in degrees of visual angle) and temporally (as determined by the minimal duration parameter, measured in milliseconds). In some analysis tools, temporally close but not consecutive data points can be counted in one fixation, especially if some data points in the middle are missing. One should be aware that a change in these parameters has an effect on the results and the visualisation, and it might bias the conclusions as well. For example, Shic, Scassellati, and Chawarska (2008) demonstrate how a change in the fixation duration parameter can affect the results and therefore the conclusions drawn from the (biased) results.

Next, we show an example of how adjusting the fixation radius parameter affects the visualisation. The screenshots in Figure 2 are from a test where the participant was asked to read a piece of text that appeared on the screen letter by letter. The visualisations look quite different though the underlying data points are the same. The size of the circles changes most noticeably, which makes one think that the participant has focused on the text more in the upper example; it is not evident that the data sample is the same in both. The difference in the fixations is caused by one changed parameter in analysis: the radius setting in the lower panel is 30 and in the upper panel 45 pixels; the fixation duration is kept constant (80 ms). In the visualisation fragment, calibration is a little off, especially toward the end of the line. It is not clear which line of text is being read.

Short fixations are excluded from the analysis through raising of the minimum duration threshold; the reasoning behind exclusion of shorter-than-threshold-value fixations is that it is not clear if the participant has actually attended to the stimulus at this point. Finding the right threshold for the minimum duration parameter can be difficult, since the theoretical minimum duration varies from 100 to 400 milliseconds, depending on the nature of the task (Blignaut, 2009).

Expanding the fixation radius helps with those people whose gaze is not stable during the fixations. For instance, the degeneration of the eye

due to ageing or illness and some diseases, such as Alzheimer's disease and ADHD, makes the gaze jitter and can hinder the capability to fixate properly (Blignaut & Beelders, 2010). According to Blignaut and Beelders, the recommended threshold for the fixation radius varies from 0.25° to 1.6° of the visual angle, depending on the nature of the task. As Shic et al. (2008) point out, selecting the correct threshold both for fixation duration and also for fixation radius is not enough. The interaction between the parameters and their effect on the results are equally important aspects of the decisions on which algorithms, parameters, and thresholds to use.

An approach often used for analysis is the use of areas of interest (AOIs). AOIs are (usually rectangular) areas on the screen that are in some way interesting in the study. For example, a researcher might want to know how many of the participants look at a search function on the tested Web site, and that small area can be set as an AOI for the analysis. The process of determining the AOIs takes place after the test, and it can be iterated at will if that is needed. From the standpoint of fixation analysis, an AOI collects all fixations in that larger area, not only those data points that hit within the fixation radius. If the centre of the fixation hits the area of the AOI, the fixation is included in the analysis. Even with AOIs, one should understand that the fixation duration parameter and the fixation radius parameter are used in selection of which data points belong to the data analysis and which are left out. Furthermore, not all fixations that should be in the counts are included in them, if the calibration is so far off that the fixation is deemed to land outside the AOI. Usually the AOIs are therefore defined to be somewhat larger than the actual objects on the screen. Fortunately, modern software toolkits can follow the defined AOI shape even when the Web page is scrolled in the test. The resolution is not good enough for definition of small AOIs, though.

AOIs are used in combination with different measures. Usually the researchers are interested in how many fixations landed within the AOIs. Also, the cumulative duration of the fixations inside an AOI tells how carefully the AOI was looked at during the test. Depending on the goal of the test, the researcher might also be interested in knowing how long it took before the participant looked at a certain AOI for the first time or how often during the test a certain AOI was looked at. In addition to looking at all collected data, the analysis can be done on the level of one participant or a subgroup, if there are different target user groups to consider, and some specific test tasks. Selecting from among the various measures and metrics for analysis is demanding.

Jacob and Karn (2003) describe 21 usability studies that have been conducted with eye tracking with various measures and point out that the selection of the measures to use depends on the research setting: top-down, from a cognitive theory or design-hypothesis, or bottom-up, starting with an analysis of the actual data collected. When one aims at finding potential usability problems in the user interface, both methods can provide interesting results. Having AOIs as a starting point of analysis requires a background theory concerning where the problematic areas are located. However, on many occasions, such a theory is not available and the raw data constitute the only source of information.

The goal of the research study from which Figure 2 is taken is to study which of two text presentation formats works better for a specific user group and use situation. Unfortunately, in this kind of analysis, the visualisations do not really help. It is not possible to discern the two text presentation conditions just by looking at the visualisations, though it was first presumed that the eyes behave differently if the text is shown letter by letter instead of word by word. To proceed with the analysis, the researchers need to examine the raw data set with specially tailored methods.

For our final recommendation, we want to emphasise the importance of understanding the basics of eye gaze behaviour and the collection of

eye tracking data to support analysis. In particular, wrong settings for the radius or the duration of fixation can lead to incorrect conclusions. For instance, the Tobii Studio settings are discussed by Špakov in this volume. One should study the default settings in the analysis software and experiment by changing them and by looking at the raw data points. Research papers should report the settings applied in the analysis, so that the research community can repeat the experiments if this is needed.

Finally, one should approach eye tracking studies with attention to the parameters and measures applied in the research. For instance, it is possible to report among the conclusions of an eye tracking study that most people notice a certain advertisement on a Web page if one considers the percentage of participants fixating on the advert area at some point in the test. However, it might be that many of these people have just briefly glanced at the advert and not spent time reading it. Without knowing the actual metrics applied, one cannot judge the reliability of a result.

FROM USABILITY ANALYSIS TO UNDERSTANDING BEHAVIOUR PATTERNS

Eye tracking during usability tests has been used mainly in the testing of Web sites to support their usability analysis, but the gaze data can also reveal behavioural patterns of use: what areas of the Web site users are commonly attending to and what kinds of strategies and behavioural patterns in search and reading emerge. For instance, Nielsen and Pernice (2008) report their collective findings of a large-scale eye tracking Web usability study. They were interested in how the test participants look for information from Web pages as determined by their task. They found, for example, that users with a specific search task scanned the navigation elements first when they entered the Web site and that they were able to tune out the adverts when they were on a mission to find some specific information.

Likewise, from the analysis of eye tracking data collected during usability tests, Nielsen (2006) found that the heat-map visualisation of a reading task resembles the letter 'F'. The F-shaped pattern of reading emerges as the user reads the first couple of lines or paragraphs of the text more thoroughly and then skims through the rest, reading only some of the words, perhaps reading another paragraph or some lines on the way down the text page. Recent work by Buscher, Biedert, Heinesch, and Dengel (2010) suggests that within long documents, the resulting heat-map shape of user attention is more like a 'T' shape rotated 90° to the left, with scanning for the correct paragraph or relevant information making up the top bar and reading of the relevant text in full forming the stem.

Behavioural patterns for reading of search results have also been studied with eye tracking. On search result pages, the result titles and short summaries given by the search engine are the only information given for decision on whether to click a result link or not, and people have different strategies for reading through them. From a gaze-path analysis, Aula, Majaranta, and Räihä (2005) found that the participants in their study had two different styles for evaluation of search results: an exhaustive evaluation style, wherein the participants carefully read all results shown before making their decision, and an economic evaluation style, in which the users looked carefully at only the first few results before making their decision. By recording the gaze paths, Rodden, Fu, Aula, and Spiro (2008) studied how users use their eyes and the mouse when determining which result to follow from search results. They found that some users use their mouse to mark a promising result while they still are evaluating the result page further or go back to re-evaluate the already dismissed results. Such analysis makes it possible to understand what parts of the screen the user has attended to, which is relevant information for content designers but also may give rise

to ideas for gaze-enhanced functionality (e.g., in Web browsers).

While the gaze data can reveal usability problems and support learning about patterns of behaviour, one should always keep in mind that the data collection procedures applied in the laboratory will have an effect on user behaviour and, ultimately, on the gaze paths. Therefore, for instance, tests in which the experimenter accompanies the participant in the laboratory or the participant is encouraged to think aloud while working on the task may compromise the data. The approach might still be useful for analysis of usability problems, but one should take care not to build models of behavioural patterns on its basis.

CONCLUSION

In this chapter, we tackled the question of how to evaluate the usability of a gaze-based system with a laboratory study. When a gaze-based system is being developed, the interaction techniques that are adopted need careful design and evaluation with users, and for that purpose lab tests are one possibility (though they perhaps lack ecological validity). We advised the reader on how to design usability testing for these systems by discussing the issues arising from the use of eye tracking systems during the tests. Toward the end of the chapter, we described the process of design and evaluation of several systems to show how different issues arise from different application areas. Last, we discussed the use of eye tracking during ordinary usability tests in order to gather additional information, along with the retrospective or triggered think-aloud method, which seem more suitable for tests utilising eye tracking than is the otherwise commonly applied concurrent think-aloud method.

Some of the advice given in this chapter will be useful when one is designing any kind of test set-up that utilises an eye tracker, whether as an input device or to gather information about the user's gaze point. For example, the challenges related to recruiting of test participants are the same, since these arise from the limitations of the eye trackers. In planning of any test set-up, finding the perfect balance between the goals of the study, the limited resources, and the right methods can be tricky. Every study needs to be planned carefully. Tasks, questionnaires, and interview questions should always reflect the goals of the study, and every test set-up needs to be pilot-tested at least once before the actual test set starts. Only then is it possible to spot and remove elements in the settings that might compromise data collection. Even using data from an eye tracker in the analysis phase requires special attention, since the decisions made for selection of thresholds, methods, and measures can bias the results and the conclusions.

ACKNOWLEDGMENT

We wish to thank Selina Sharmin and Oleg Špakov, from the Visual Interaction Research Group at the University of Tampere, for their contributions to this chapter.

REFERENCES

Aoki, H., Hansen, J. P., & Itoh, K. (2009). Learning gaze typing: What are the obstacles and what progress to expect? *Universal Access in the Information Society*, 8, 297–310. doi:10.1007/s10209-009-0152-5

ASE. (2009). *Accessible surfing extension*. Retrieved from Politecnico di Torino website: http://elite.polito.it/research-mainmenu-33/accessibility-mainmenu-79/17-gaze-tracking/66-ase

Aula, A., Majaranta, P., & Räihä, K.-J. (2005). Eye-tracking reveals the personal styles for search result evaluation. In M. F. Costabile, & F. Paternò (Eds.), *Human–Computer Interaction (INTERACT '05)* (LNCS 3585, pp. 1058–1061). Berlin, Germany: Springer-Verlag. doi:10.1007/11555261_104

Bates, R., & Istance, H. (2002). Zooming interfaces! Enhancing the performance of eye controlled pointing devices. *Proceedings of the 5th International ACM Conference on Assistive Technologies (ASSETS 2002)* (pp. 119–126). New York, NY: ACM. doi:10.1145/638249.638272

Bates, R., Vickers, S., & Istance, H. O. (2010). Gaze interaction with virtual on-line communities: Levelling the playing field for disabled users. *Universal Access in the Information Society*, 9(3), 261–272. doi:10.1007/s10209-009-0173-0

Blignaut, P. (2009). Fixation identification: The optimum threshold for a dispersion algorithm. *Attention, Perception & Psychophysics*, 71(4), 881–895. doi:10.3758/APP.71.4.881

Blignaut, P., & Beelders, T. (2009). The effect of fixational eye movements on fixation identification with a dispersion-based fixation detection algorithm. *Journal of Eye Movement Research*, 2(5):4, 1–14. Retrieved from http://www.jemr.org/

Bojko, A. (2006). Using eye tracking to compare Web page designs: A case study. *Journal of Usability Studies*, 3(1), 112–120. Retrieved from http://www.upassoc.org/upa_publications/jus/.

Breeze, J. (2010). Eye tracking: Best way to test rich app usability. *UX Magazine*, 19 March 2010. Retrieved from http://uxmag.com/technology/eye-tracking-the-best-way-to-test-rich-app-usability

Buscher, G., Biedert, R., Heinesch, D., & Dengel, A. (2010). Eye tracking analysis of preferred reading regions on the screen. *CHI '10 Extended Abstracts on Human Factors in Computing Systems (CHI '10)* (pp. 3307–3312). New York, NY: ACM. doi:10.1145/1753846.1753976

Castellina, E., & Corno, F. (2007). Accessible Web surfing through gaze interaction. *Proceedings of the 3rd Conference on Communication by Gaze Interaction* (*COGAIN 2007*) (pp. 74–77). Leicester, UK: De Montfort University. Retrieved from the COGAIN Association website: http://www.cogain.org/wiki/COGAIN_Conference

Cheng, D., & Vertegaal, R. (2004). An eye for an eye: A performance evaluation comparison of the LC technologies and Tobii eye trackers. *Proceedings of the 2004 Symposium on Eye Tracking Research & Applications (ETRA '04)* (p. 61). New York, NY: ACM. doi:10.1145/968363.968378

De Luca, A., Weiss, R., & Drewes, H. (2007). Evaluation of eye-gaze interaction methods for security enhanced PIN-entry. *Proceedings of the 19th Australasian Conference on Computer–Human Interactions (OZCHI '07)* (251, pp. 199–202). New York, NY: ACM. doi:10.1145/1324892.1324932

Donegan, M., Oosthuizen, L., Bates, R., Istance, H., Holmqvist, E., Lundalv, M., & Signorile, I. (2006). *Report of user trials and usability studies.* (Deliverable D3.3. Communication by Gaze Interaction (COGAIN), Project IST-2003-511598). Retrieved from the COGAIN Association website: http://www.cogain.org/wiki/COGAIN_Reports

Douglas, S. A., Kirkpatrick, A. E., & MacKenzie, I. S. (1999). Testing pointing device performance and user assessment with the ISO 9241, Part 9 standard. *Proceedings of the SIGCHI Conference on Human Factors in Computing Systems (CHI '99)* (pp. 215–222). New York, NY: ACM.

Drewes, H., & Schmidt, A. (2007). Interacting with the computer using gaze gestures. In C. Baranauskas, P. Palanque, J. Abascal, & S. D. J. Barbosa (Eds.), *Human–Computer Interaction (INTERACT '07)* (LNCS 4663, pp. 475–488). Berlin, Germany: Springer-Verlag. doi:10.1007/978-3-540-74800-7_43

Elling, S., Lentz, L., & de Jong, M. (2011) Retrospective think-aloud method: using eye movements as an extra cue for participants' verbalizations. *Proceedings of the 2011 Annual Conference on Human Factors in Computing Systems (CHI '11)* (pp. 1171–1174). New York, NY: ACM. doi:10.1145/1978942.1979116

Freeman, B. (2011). Triggered think-aloud protocol: using eye tracking to improve usability test moderation. *Proceedings of the 2011 Annual Conference on Human Factors in Computing Systems (CHI '11)* (pp. 1171–1174). New York, NY: ACM. doi:10.1145/1978942.1979117

Hart, S. G. (2006). NASA-Task Load Index (NASA-TLX); 20 years later. *Proceedings of the Human Factors and Ergonomics Society 50th Annual Meeting* (pp. 904-908). Santa Monica, CA: HFES.

Hart, S. G., & Staveland, L. E. (1988). Development of NASA-TLX (Task Load Index): Results of empirical and theoretical research. In Hancock, P. S., & Meshkati, N. (Eds.), *Human Mental Workload* (pp. 139–183). Amsterdam, The Netherlands: North Holland Press. doi:10.1016/S0166-4115(08)62386-9

Heikkilä, H., & Räihä, K.-J. (2009). Speed and accuracy of gaze gestures. *Journal of Eye Movement Research, 3*(2):1, 1–14. Retrieved from http://www.jemr.org/

Hornbæk, K. (2006). Current practice in measuring usability: Challenges to usability studies and research. *International Journal of Human-Computer Studies, 64*(2), 79–102. doi:10.1016/j.ijhcs.2005.06.002

Hyrskykari, A. (2006). *Eyes in attentive interfaces: Experiences from creating iDict, a gaze-aware reading aid.* (Doctoral dissertation, University of Tampere, Finland). Dissertations in Interactive Technology, Number 4. Retrieved from http://acta.uta.fi/pdf/951-44-6643-8.pdf

Hyrskykari, A., Ovaska, S., Majaranta, P., Räihä, K.-J., & Lehtinen, M. (2008). Gaze path stimulation in retrospective think-aloud. *Journal of Eye Movement Research, 2*(4):5, 1–18. Retrieved from http://www.jemr.org/

ISO 9241-9 (2000). Ergonomic requirements for office work with Visual Display Terminals (VDTs) – Part 9: Requirements for non-keyboard input devices. Geneva, Switzerland: International Organization for Standardization.

ISO 9241-11 (1998). Ergonomic requirements for office work with Visual Display Terminals (VDTs) – Part 11: Guidance on usability. Geneva, Switzerland: International Organization for Standardization.

Istance, H., Bates, R., Hyrskykari, A., & Vickers, S. (2008). Snap Clutch, a moded approach to solving the Midas touch problem. *Proceedings of the 2008 Symposium on Eye Tracking Research & Applications (ETRA '08)* (pp. 221–228). New York, NY: ACM. doi:10.1145/1344471.1344523

Itoh, K., Aoki, H., & Hansen, J. P. (2006). A comparative usability study of two Japanese gaze typing systems. *Proceedings of the 2006 Symposium on Eye Tracking Research & Applications (ETRA '06)* (pp. 59–66). New York, NY: ACM. doi:10.1145/1117309.1117344

Jacob, R. J. (1991). The use of eye movements in human–computer interaction techniques: What you look at is what you get. *ACM Transactions on Information Systems, 9*(2), 152–169. doi:10.1145/123078.128728

Jacob, R. J., & Karn, K. S. (2003). Eye tracking in human–computer interaction and usability research: Ready to deliver the promises. In Hyönä, J., Radach, R., & Deubel, H. (Eds.), *The mind's eye: Cognitive and applied aspects of eye movement research* (pp. 573–605). Amsterdam, The Netherlands: Elsevier Science B.V.

Kammerer, Y., Scheiter, K., & Beinhauer, W. (2008). Looking my way through the menu: The impact of menu design and multimodal input on gaze-based menu selection. *Proceedings of the 2008 Symposium on Eye Tracking Research & Applications (ETRA '08)* (pp. 213–220). New York, NY: ACM. doi:10.1145/1344471.1344522

Majaranta, P., Ahola, U., & Špakov, O. (2009). Fast gaze typing with an adjustable dwell time. *Proceedings of the 27th International Conference on Human Factors in Computing Systems (CHI '09)* (pp. 357–360). New York, NY: ACM. doi:10.1145/1518701.1518758

Majaranta, P., Aula, A., & Räihä, K.-J. (2004). Effects of feedback on eye typing with a short dwell time. *Proceedings of the 2004 Symposium on Eye Tracking Research & Applications (ETRA '04)* (pp. 139–146). New York, NY: ACM. doi:10.1145/968363.968390

Majaranta, P., MacKenzie, I. S., Aula, A., & Räihä, K.-J. (2006). Effects of feedback and dwell time on eye typing speed and accuracy. *Universal Access in the Information Society, 5*(2), 199–208. doi:10.1007/s10209-006-0034-z

MyTobii P10 (2011). *MyTobii P10 product description.* Retrieved on 27 January 2011 from Tobii Technology website http://www.tobii.com/en/assistive-technology/global/products/hardware/mytobii-p10/

NASA-TLX: Task Load Index (2010). Retrieved from http://humansystems.arc.nasa.gov/groups/TLX/

Nielsen, J. (1993). *Usability engineering.* Boston, MA: Academic Press.

Nielsen, J. (2006). F-shaped pattern for reading web content. *Jakob Nielsen's Alertbox,* 17 April 2006. Retrieved from http://www.useit.com/alertbox/reading_pattern.html

Nielsen, J., & Pernice, K. (2009). *Eyetracking web usability.* Berkeley, CA: New Riders Press.

Öquist, G., & Lundin, K. (2007). Eye movement study of reading text on a mobile phone using paging, scrolling, leading, and RSVP. *Proceedings of the 6th International Conference on Mobile and Ubiquitous Multimedia (MUM '07)* (284, pp. 176–183). New York, NY: ACM. doi:10.1145/1329469.1329493

Pernice, K., & Nielsen, J. (2009). *Eyetracking methodology: How to conduct and evaluate usability studies using eyetracking.* Nielsen Norman Group, August 2009. Retrieved from http://www.useit.com/eyetracking/methodology

Porta, M., & Turina, M. (2008). Eye-S: A full-screen input modality for pure eye-based communication. *Proceedings of the 2008 Symposium on Eye Tracking Research & Applications (ETRA '08)* (pp. 27–34). New York, NY: ACM. doi:10.1145/1344471.1344477

Rodden, K., Fu, X., Aula, A., & Spiro, I. (2008). Eye-mouse coordination patterns on Web search results pages. *Extended Abstracts on Human Factors in Computing Systems (CHI '08)* (pp. 2997–3002). New York, NY: ACM. doi:10.1145/1358628.1358797

Shic, F., Scassellati, B., & Chawarska, K. (2008). The incomplete fixation measure. *Proceedings of the 2008 Symposium on Eye Tracking Research & Applications (ETRA '08)* (pp. 111–114). New York, NY: ACM. doi:10.1145/1344471.1344500

Špakov, O. (2008). *iComponent – Device-independent platform for analyzing eye movement data and developing eye-based applications.* (Doctoral dissertation, University of Tampere, Finland). Dissertations in Interactive Technology, Number 9. Retrieved from http://acta.uta.fi/pdf/978-951-44-7321-0.pdf

Tanriverdi, V., & Jacob, R. J. (2000). Interacting with eye movements in virtual environments. *Proceedings of the SIGCHI Conference on Human Factors in Computing Systems (CHI '00)* (pp. 265–272). New York, NY: ACM. doi:10.1145/332040.332443

Tuisku, O., Majaranta, P., Isokoski, P., & Räihä, K.-J. (2008). Now Dasher! Dash away! Longitudinal study of fast text entry by eye gaze. *Proceedings of the 2008 Symposium on Eye Tracking Research & Applications (ETRA '08)* (pp. 19–26). New York, NY: ACM. doi:10.1145/1344471.1344476

Van Someren, M. V., Barnard, Y. F., & Sandberg, J. A. C. (1994). *The think aloud method: A practical guide to modelling cognitive processes.* London, England: Academic Press.

Wobbrock, J. O., Rubinstein, J., Sawyer, M. W., & Duchowski, A. T. (2008). Longitudinal evaluation of discrete consecutive gaze gestures for text entry. *Proceedings of the 2008 Symposium on Eye Tracking Research & Applications (ETRA '08)* (pp. 11–18). New York, NY: ACM. doi:10.1145/1344471.1344475

Chapter 18
A Client–Focused Methodology for Gaze Control Assessment, Implementation and Evaluation

Mick Donegan
ACE Centre, UK

Lorna Gill
ACE Centre, UK

Lisa Ellis (Oosthuizen)[1]
Tobii Technology, Sweden

ABSTRACT

This chapter addresses challenges involved when working with people whose involuntary eye or head movements make it difficult for a gaze-controlled computer to accurately interpret their eye movements. The chapter introduces the methodology we adopted for the ACE Centre user trials, which we have described as the 'KEE' approach to trialling and implementing gaze control technology: Knowledge-based, End-user focused, and Evolutionary. In our experience, this approach has been found to enhance the chances of success for even the most complex end-users.

INTRODUCTION

During the COGAIN project, the ACE Centre has aimed to address the access needs of people who have the most complex and severe disabilities. Some individuals have experienced nystagmus and/ or the ability to move their eyes in only a horizontal or vertical plane; whilst others have experienced Athetoid Cerebral Palsy, causing severe involuntary movement. In these particular cases, it has been quite a challenge for gaze control systems to accurately interpret their eye movements. The ACE Centre has asserted that, by modifying gaze control systems in order to meet the needs of those who have the most severe and complex difficulties, it should be possible to meet the needs of a far wider range of people.

DOI: 10.4018/978-1-61350-098-9.ch018

This chapter discusses the methodology that has been adopted for the COGAIN end-user trials, which can be summarised as the 'KEE' approach (Donegan & Oosthuizen, 2006). In our experience, adopting the KEE methodology increases the chances of success for even the most severely disabled participants.

THE KEE METHODOLOGY

The 'KEE' approach incorporates a combination of methods:

- **Case Study:** In case studies, the emphasis is placed on exploration and description. Our own approach has been to examine the interplay of as many variables as possible, in order to build up as complete an understanding of the individual's needs, and the means to meet these needs. A process by Geertz (1973), known as 'thick description', is one in which the researcher not only aims to explain the entity under investigation, but its context as well, such as: the specific circumstances; the specific characteristics; and the nature of the community in which the research is based. During a gaze control assessment, factors identified include the purpose of using the gaze control system i.e., for social communication and environmental control, etc; and the wider social and physical context of the user.

For our own investigations, there were several advantages in selecting a case-study-based approach, over other methods. Through adopting a case-study-based approach, researchers are able to "generate their own analysis of the problems under consideration, develop their own solutions and practically apply their own theoretical knowledge to these problems" (Boyce, 1993).

Often, for those people who have physical disabilities, using a gaze control system is a simple speedy and straightforward process. For example, for the well-motivated and literate person, who has good head control and visual acuity, they are generally able to 'eye type' on more or less any of the currently commercially available systems in a matter of minutes. However, for others, the process is not so straightforward. This is true for individuals who have profound and multiple learning difficulties; visual difficulties; and/or severe involuntary movement. This is why a flexible case-study-based approach was adopted. With this approach, researchers have..."the power to analyse and to master a tangled circumstance by identifying and delineating important factors; the ability to utilise ideas, to test them against facts and to throw them into fresh combinations..." (Merseth, 1991)

- **Grounded Theory:** Primarily qualitative research methods were applied. These methods owe a great deal to 'Participatory Design'; the 'Grounded Theory' approach of Glaser and Strauss (1967); and 'Comparative Analysis'.

The Comparative Analysis of cases takes us beyond the notion of the case study being illustrative. When data from similar situations are compared, common themes and patterns can be elicited, hypotheses generated and theory developed. The examination of themes is important in all case studies, but particularly important if the research demands Comparative Analysis. (Edwards and Talbot, 1994, p. 45)

Over time, by comparing the results of several individual case studies we found that, themes emerged which, if applied, could enhance the chances of success for both the initial assessment and subsequent implementation.

- **Participatory Design:** As well as understanding the individual's access difficulties; it was important to identify the activities the individual wished to undertake. Hence, the individual was consulted at each stage in relation to what their needs were, and how effectively their needs were being met. A principle of Participatory Design is "to see the current ways that work is done as an evolved solution to a complex work solution that the designer only partially understands" (Greenbaum and Kyng, 1991, p4). Our challenge was to develop a deeper understanding of the individual's needs so that their needs could be met, and by cross referencing our results across case studies to discover themes, through Comparative Analysis.

During this process, it was necessary to consider the following: the pre-assessment process; the calibration process; the assessment activities; and the implementation activities. These are described as follows:

The Pre-Assessment Process

Firstly, we gathered detailed information about the abilities and interests of the individual; secondly, we clarified the individual's expectations of the assessment; and thirdly, we prepared all aspects of the social and physical environments.

- **Background Information:** In order to tailor the assessment to the user, the assessor has to apply their understanding of the individual's physical, visual, communication and cognitive abilities; and relate the assessment to their personal interests

- **Managing Expectations:** In advance, it should be conveyed to the individual that it is not their fault if the assessment is unsuccessful; rather, the fault lies with the assessor and/or the currently available technology. This is hopefully reassuring and helpfully deters any potential feelings of disappointment, should the assessment not fulfil their expectations. Such feelings can certainly hinder future assessments.

- **The Social Environment:** Beware, the more attendees there are at a gaze control assessment, and the more intense is the pressure on the individual to succeed. Difficulties are more likely to arise. So, simply be alert to minimising attendee numbers. Moreover, attendees need to be unobtrusive, especially during the calibration process

- **The Physical Environment:** The ability of the device to register eye movement is affected by lighting conditions, including daylight. Ideally, before the assessment, the assessor should identify problems by testing the system out themselves. Where difficulties transpire, for any reason, the assessor should deal with these; and even anticipate holding the assessment in another room. When considering individuals who have a 'startle reflex', extra care ought really to be taken, especially during the calibration process.

The Calibration Process

The gaze control system acquires data regarding the individual's eye movement via the calibration process. The individual gazes at a number of on-screen targets. The more successful the calibration is, the more accomplished the individual will be. Knowing the physical and cognitive abilities of the individual guides where the calibration is to be specially adapted (i.e., in the use of a one or two eye calibration, auditory feedback, and customized targets, etc).

Assessment Activities

It has been our experience that the chances of a successful assessment are increased through good preparation, planning and a customised initial trial, i.e. one designed for the specific needs and abilities of the individual.

Figure 1. The MyTobii Utility by Tobii Technology to enable the user to try different cell sizes

- **Before Starting:** in addition to preparing the environment appropriately before the assessment even begins, it is also very important to prepare the client, too. The individual and those supporting them, often wish to try gaze control because all other options have failed or, indeed, because there is no other option. Because of this, hopes can be high. Once more, on the day it is important to be clear that it is not the fault of the individual if the assessment is not successful; rather, the fault lies with the assessor and/or the currently available technology. As reiterated above, once this is understood, not only is the individual more likely to relax for the current assessment, but, it is also more likely that the individual will adopt a positive attitude for any future eye control assessments

- **Introductory 'Warm-Up' Activities:** Once a successful calibration has taken place, the next step is to present activities which are not too cognitively demanding. For example, even if the client is literate and one of their aims is to be able to use the computer to write, it is important not to rush into this kind of activity. Many people who have complex physical difficulties are unable to control a pointer directly, so they need to utilise the grid that has cells which are the appropriate size. In this case, the first thing to investigate is the size of cell that they are comfortably and reliably able to access. The MyTobii, for

example, provides support with this process (Figure 1). The assessor is able to try out a number of grids with cells of different sizes.

Depending on the client's abilities and level of motivation, it can be helpful to provide a personalized set of grids at this stage; and the more motivating the better. For example, activities that include characters from the client's favourite television programs, family and friends, etc. might be helpful in encouraging them to persevere while the assessor is trying to establish the optimal cell size for the client. It is important that these grids are failure proof. In other words, whilst these grids should be enjoyable and engaging, the cognitive demands should be low so that, from the assessor's point of view, the client's ability to successfully access a cell is not being confused with their cognitive ability.

Most gaze control systems now offer the opportunity to make a selection either by blinking, pressing a switch, or dwelling on an item for a specific length of time. The concept of dwelling is unfamiliar to most people, and it can be very disconcerting to make unexpected or unwanted selections. Presenting the client with undemanding activities, therefore, such as playing musical notes by looking at the screen, can provide an effective way of enabling the client to learn this new concept.

After the Assessment: Implementation Activities

The 'implementation period' is the period of time during which the system is adapted and personalised to meet the individual needs of the client. Whilst the purpose of an assessment is to establish whether or not there is a gaze control system that is of any potential benefit to the client, the purpose of the implementation process is to try to ensure that this potential benefit is realized. A carefully planned progression of personalized activities can enhance the chances of a successful and positive experience for the individual during this period.

During our initial trials, we regarded it as our role to explore whether or not gaze control could potentially be achieved and, if not, to adjust or modify the software and/or hardware available to us in order to enhance the chances of success in subsequent trials. If necessary, this might have involved working in partnership with manufacturers and developers. As a result, changes could be made with the aim of making the system more accessible to a specific user. In the best traditions of action research methodology, this is an 'evolutionary', cyclical process where each modification or set of modifications is re-trialled with the user involved, with the ultimate aim of acquiring a personalized gaze control system for the user involved.

THE KEE APPROACH

Donegan and Oosthuizen (2006) refer to the Pre-assessment, Assessment and Post-assessment processes described above as the 'KEE' approach to trialling and implementing eye control technology:

- Knowledge-based: founded on what is known of the end-user's physical and cognitive abilities.
- End-user Focused: designed to meet the end-user's interests and needs.

- Evolutionary: ready to change in relation to the end-user's response to eye-control technology and software provided.

The 'KEE' approach provides a method through which a personalized solution can be explored and found for each user. Someone who is able to control the mouse pointer directly by gaze control might prefer to use their eye movement in the same way that others might use a mouse. However, people with more complex physical and/or visual difficulties are likely to need a personalized grid that will need to evolve over time. A good example of a client with whom we successfully used the approach described above is Russell.

Case Study: Russell

Following a stroke, Russell (Figure 2) is unable to speak or reliably control any part of his body, other than his eyes. Whilst he had a very good low-tech system based on raising his eyes to confirm letters of the alphabet spoken out by his communication partner, he wanted to be able to communicate and to control his environment independently. He is only able to move his eyes up and down. His visual difficulties are exacerbated by the fact that he has involuntary eye movement, nystagmus. His eyes are not affected equally by the nystagmus, which results in slightly blurred vision.

Figure 2. Russell using a gaze control system

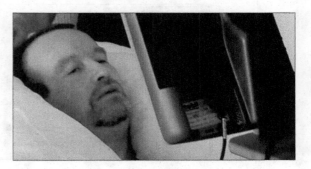

In keeping with our Participatory Design approach, we began by finding out the best size and position for his writing cells on the screen. Due to his vertical eye movement, the cells had to be positioned vertically. By using a program that enabled Russell to play music using his eyes during our initial trials, we found that the number of cells that he could reliably access was five or six. We therefore designed a grid that enabled Russell to write by selecting from five cells positioned vertically (Figure 3). Once selected, each letter and word was read out for Russell to minimize the need for him to read what he had written. We began by trialling a range of foreground and background colours and Russell chose red letters against a white background.

The next decision was how to position his 'writing cells'. Initially, we tried positioning them to the left of the screen (Figure 3). We also gave Russell the opportunity to try them positioned to the right of the screen and in the middle. He de-

cided on the middle of the screen (Figure 3). However, once he had decided that his writing cells should be in this position, he used his low-tech system to explain that, whilst he wished his text box to remain red on white, he wondered if he might find it easier to differentiate and target his writing cells if they each had a different colour (Figure 4).

Having modified the grid, as requested, Russell commented that, while differentiating the colours was an improvement, he also wished to make two further improvements to the grid. The first was to position his writing cells right across the screen, with the letter repeated several times. The second improvement he requested was for the text he had written to be positioned at the bottom of the screen. Russell could not describe why repeating the letters across the screen in this way helped him and, because such a request was unexpected, it took a little while for us to understand exactly what he was asking for. However,

Figure 3. Sensory Software Grid 2 examples demonstrating different layouts

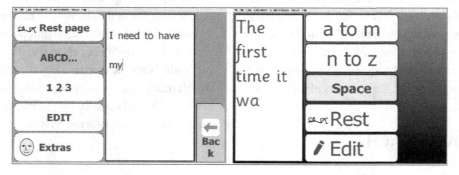

Figure 4. Sensory Software Grid 2 examples tailored for a user with impaired eye control

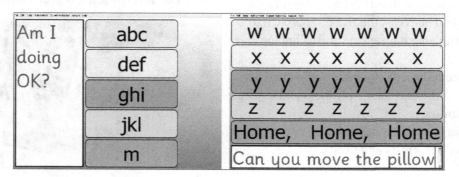

once this had been done, Russell trialled the system once more and was finally satisfied with the grid layout.

CONCLUSION

Whilst the KEE approach has evolved as a method for finding optimal ways for each individual to utilize gaze control technology as effectively as possible, the process also enables a comparison of what has been learnt through a process of comparative analysis across case studies. As a result, several common themes have emerged.

There is no such thing as 'the best gaze control system'. The system should be selected on the basis of how effectively it meets the individual's physical and visual/cognitive needs:

- e.g. for some, a system that is able to accommodate involuntary head movement might be required. For others, this facility might be unnecessary.

Appropriate mounting and positioning of the system is critical in relation to the client's needs:

- the system must be positioned so that it provides optimal comfort, function and visibility for the specific user. Safety is also a factor here and size and weight needs to be considered in relation to the user's needs, too, particularly if it is to be positioned on a wheelchair.

Appropriate on-screen visual representation (pictures, symbols, text, foreground/background colours, etc):

- visual images should be presented in a way that is most clearly visible and comprehensible to the client.

Appropriate auditory support and feedback:

- consideration must be given in relation to any additional support that might provide valuable feedback to the individual (e.g., should the system speak out the symbols, letters, words or pictures?).

In general, most of the people we have worked with that have involuntary head movement preferred to use dwell selection, rather than a switch or blinking. The choice must be their own. Whilst we had been told that several of the clients could only move their eyes either up-down or left-right, we found that, given time, they could visually scan the whole screen and could therefore achieve a full calibration. However, when actually using the system for written communication, most were unable or unwilling to deviate from a strict up-down or left-right movement. Therefore, all of the functional cells needed to be positioned in a straight line. For those clients who could not visually scan the whole screen during the calibration process, the calibration points needed to be adjusted to fit within the area of the screen that the client could scan. Whilst the speed of using the gaze control system is extremely important, it has emerged that many users value the reduced pain and/or effort experienced in comparison with other control methods even more highly.

REFERENCES

Boyce, A. (1993). *The case study approach for pedagogists*. Annual Meeting of the American Alliance for Health, Physical Education, Recreation and Dance, Washington, DC., USA

Donegan, M., & Oosthuizen, L. (2006). The 'KEE' Concept for eye-control and complex disabilities: Knowledge-based, end-user-focused and evolutionary. *Proceedings of the 2nd Conference on Communication by Gaze Interaction (COGAIN 2006)*, Turin, Italy (pp. 83–87). Retrieved from http://www.cogain.org/conference

Edwards, A., & Talbot, R. (1994). *The hard pressed researcher*. London, UK: Longman Group.

Geertz, C. (1973). *The interpretation of cultures*. New York, NY: Basic Books.

Glaser, B., & Strauss, A. (1967). *The discovery of grounded theory*. Chicago, IL: Aldine.

Greenbaum, J. M., & Kyng, M. (1991). *Design at work: Cooperative design of computer systems*. Hillsdale, NJ: Lawrence Erlbaum.

Merseth, K. K. (1991). *The case for cases in teacher education*. (RIE. 42p. ERIC). Washington, DC., USA: American Association for Higher Education and American Association of Colleges for Teacher Education.

ENDNOTES

[1]   Lisa's surname changed from Oozthuizen to Ellis after this chapter was written.

Section 6
Building an Eye Tracker

Chapter 19
Introduction to Eye and Gaze Trackers

Dan Witzner Hansen
IT University of Copenhagen, Denmark

Arantxa Villanueva
Public University of Navarre, Spain

Fiona Mulvey
IT University of Copenhagen, Denmark

Diako Mardanbegi
IT University of Copenhagen, Denmark

ABSTRACT

In the previous chapters of the book, you will have seen multiple applications for using (and the benefits of using) a gaze tracker. In this chapter, you will be given more insight into how an eye tracker operates. Not only can this aid in understanding the eye tracker better, it also gives important information about how future applications might improve on current ones, by using more of the information available from the eye tracker: as we shall see, an eye tracker can often provide you with more information than just coordinates on a screen. This chapter gives an overview of the components of an eye tracker and introduces basics of gaze modelling. It helps in understanding the following chapters which each provide some details of how to build an eye tracker. This section has technical content, but it is our hope that also readers not particularly interested in the details of eye and gaze trackers will gain some useful insights.

INTRODUCTION

In this chapter, you will be given more insight into how an eye tracker operates. This section has technical content, but it is our hope that also readers not particularly interested in the details of eye and gaze trackers will gain some useful insights. Each chapter provides some details of how to build an eye tracker, but for a comprehensive review of different techniques for eye and gaze tracking we refer the reader to the work of Hansen and Ji (2010).

A person's gaze direction is determined by eyeball position and orientation. A person can change his or her gaze direction by rotating the eyeball (and consequently also the pupil) while

DOI: 10.4018/978-1-61350-098-9.ch019

keeping the head stationary. Similarly, a person can change gaze direction by moving the head while keeping the eye stationary relative to the head. Usually a person moves the head to a comfortable position before orienting the eye. Head pose therefore determines the coarse-scale gaze direction while the eyeball orientation determines the local and detailed gaze direction Hansen and Ji (2010).

A gaze tracker is a device for detecting and tracking eye movements and may provide information about the point of regard (PoR) or gaze direction. The PoR is the intersection of the gaze direction with an object in space, such as the screen. While eye trackers vary in the technologies they employ, in this chapter we will focus only on eye detection and gaze tracking in video-based eye trackers (a.k.a. video-oculography).

A general overview of the components of eye and gaze trackers is given in Figure 1. Eye and gaze tracking systems obtain information from one or more cameras (*image data*). The eye location in the image is detected and is either used directly in the application or subsequently tracked over frames. The gaze direction or PoR can be estimated on the basis of the information obtained from the eye region and possibly, but not necessarily, through head pose data. This information is then used by gaze-based or gaze-attenuated applications in, for example, positioning of a mouse pointer for gaze-driven control.

In addition to choice of the most appropriate hardware, there are two main considerations for eye and gaze tracking – namely, eye localisation in the image and gaze estimation. For eye detection there are three sub-tasks to consider. One is to detect the presence of eyes in the image, another is to interpret eye positions in the images accurately, and the third (for video images) is to track the detected eyes from frame to frame. The eye position is commonly measured according to the pupil or iris centre. The gaze estimation method uses the information obtained in the images of the eyes to estimate and track where a

Figure 1. Components of video-based eye detection and gaze tracking. Adapted from the work of Hansen & Ji (2010)

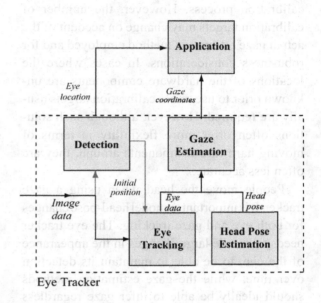

person is looking (e.g., on the screen). In the subsequent discussion, we will use the terms 'eye detection' and 'gaze tracking' to differentiate between the components, where eye detection represents eye localisation in the image while gaze tracking means estimating gaze paths. Calibration is an important issue when one is using a gaze tracker and is performed by having the user look at a set of on-screen targets. The purpose of calibration is to infer the parameters needed to estimate gaze. The main reason for having calibration is that our eyes are inherently different and the parameters for each person need to be determined if one is to obtain reliable results from the system. Another reason is that information about the geometric relationships of hardware components needs to be encoded for gaze estimation. In some gaze estimation methods, most of the parameters for encoding geometric relationships are known prior to use. This is the most likely situation in commercial gaze trackers. The producers have spent time and money to fix the locations of the hardware such that their geometric relationships are known. If these parameters are known, then fewer parameters need to be inferred by the calibration process. However, the number of calibration targets may change on account of the actual gaze estimation method employed and for robustness considerations. In cases where the locations of the hardware components are unknown prior to use, more calibration targets usually are required. However, although such solutions often offer more flexibility in terms of moving hardware components around, they are often less accurate.

People move the head when using a gaze tracker. It is important to model head-pose changes for both eye and gaze tracking. The eye tracker needs to handle large changes in the appearance of the eye, to be able to maintain its detection over time, while the gaze estimation methods should ideally be able to infer gaze regardless of head orientation. A few methods use explicit head pose estimation methods in combination with a gaze estimation method to estimate gaze; however, the usual way to deal with head movements is to employ one or more cameras placed either remotely or mounted on the head and in conjunction with IR (infrared) light sources (see Figure 2). IR illumination is the most common

approach for obtaining good eye images for eye trackers (both remote and head-mounted eye trackers). IR light enhances image contrast, making image analysis simpler. The reflections of IR light sources on the cornea can be used to stabilise gaze estimation. Intuitively one can think of the reflections as serving the same purpose as stars used for navigation (i.e., fixpoints). However, although IR light is invisible to humans, shining IR light (or any other kind of light) onto the eye may have an impact on human eye safety and is subject to restrictions of international safety standards. The use of IR light is differently limited in head-mounted and remote eye trackers, as light intensity decreases with distance. Throughout this section, we will describe the various aspects of gaze tracker development (e.g., eye tracking, gaze estimation, and safety issues) while mindful of the distinction between head-mounted and remote eye trackers.

The outline of this section follows the components shown in Figure 1. The most commonly used physical components used in eye trackers are cameras, light sources, a computer, a monitor, and – of course – an eyeball. The number of physical components used in a given set-up changes, but all components must operate together in order to track the eye and gaze. In gaze

Figure 2. Basic types of eye tracking systems. (a) Head-mounted eye tracker (Mardanbeigi & Hansen, 2010), (b) experimental remote eye tracker (Droege et al, 2007)

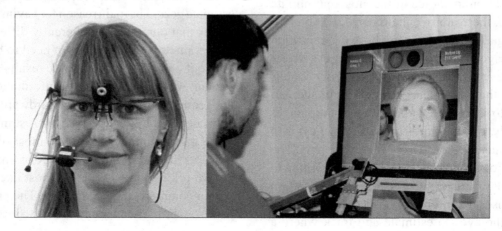

control systems, we track not only the moving eye but also the point in space (e.g., something on the computer screen) where the eye is focused. This is the defining factor, which differentiates *eye tracking* from *gaze tracking*. Usually, gaze trackers provide only a direction or a point on the screen. In some sense, this is misleading, since human gaze is defined over an area. As with any system that includes a biological component, absolute accuracy is hard to obtain. There is always some 'noise' or random information inherent in eye behaviour that needs to be dealt with in such a way that accuracy in calculation of gaze is maximised. Other factors limiting accuracy include the fact that digital images are discrete (i.e., each is composed of 'pixels'), no light source is small or sharp enough to produce a single point (i.e., a gaze position so small that it has no area!) on the eye, and no eye is perfectly or uniformly curved. Beyond these physical limiting factors, the system's ability to track gaze position accurately is further influenced by the mathematical methods applied to synthesise the data available from the various components, the camera frame rate, the amount of illumination and hence the quality of the image produced, the processing speed of the computer, the use of lenses or filters, and indeed aspects of the individual's actual eye. In order to integrate components, we need mathematical representations of the various components and software, which will apply these mathematical models to the various data streams. For the user, these mathematical models will not be obvious or visible in the same way the 'specs' of hardware components may be; however, they are nonetheless the determining factors for the usability and accuracy of a system. Without optimal mathematical models, even the most impressive hardware will not produce an optimal gaze tracking system. It is tempting to reduce accuracy to a single reported value of degrees of vision, implying that a system will track gaze position to, for example, within 1°, but this is misleading. Because of the complexity of the system, the inherent sensitivity to ambient light conditions, and the variability of hardware configuration and individual eye shape and colour, no system is consistently accurate. The goal of this part of the book is to explain the role and operations of each of the components in gaze trackers as well as introduce the mathematical procedures involved in analysing the images and estimating gaze. Such an understanding will be useful not only to developers but also to any researcher seeking to match a system (which will have its relative strengths and weaknesses) to his or her needs and also to a user attempting to figure out which system to buy.

The end result of a gaze tracker is to be able to determine gaze. The basic concepts and definitions used for gaze estimation in order to impose a common frame of reference for the intermediate steps that leads to an estimated gaze position are described below. The core software components – namely, analysing images of eyes and determining gaze – are discussed in Chapter 20 by Droege and Chapter 21 by Villanueva, Cabeza and San Agustin, respectively. A detailed description of the design of eye tracking hardware is provided in Chapter 22 by Daunys. The choice of hardware components such as lenses, cameras, and external light sources may have an impact on various safety issues. Safety issues are described in Chapter 23 by Mulvey, Villanueva, Sliney, Lange, and Donegan. In Chapter 24, Hansen, Mulvey and Mardanbegi summarise and conclude with additional perspectives on eye tracking.

BASICS OF GAZE MODELLING

In this section, a basic introduction to relevant facts related to mathematical modelling of gaze is provided. Models are needed to estimate gaze. Gaze can be defined either by gaze position or by gaze direction. Several gaze estimation methods use geometric representations of the eyeball. These models contribute to gaze direction estimation and

Figure 3. Refraction and reflection effects

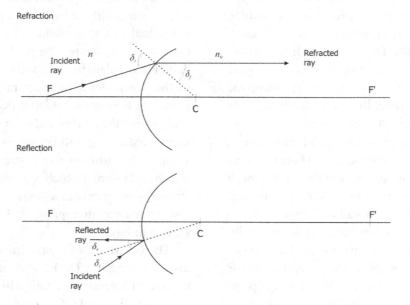

provide the basics of the phenomena observed by the eye camera. The following sections describe important aspects of the eye, its physiology, and its geometry. The objective is to highlight those features most relevant to eye tracking and gaze estimation, leaving the details to subsequent chapters.

PHYSIOLOGY AND KINEMATICS OF THE EYE

The pupil and the cornea are core in the making of a gaze tracker. Pupil orientation is important since it is related to the direction of gaze relative to the head or IR light sources. The relative nature of the pupil position may be constrained by reflections on the cornea surface, for example, allowing for point of regard estimation on the screen. The cornea also causes refraction of light and alters the perception of any object inside the cornea, such as the pupil. The cornea is a highly transparent structure with a thickness of 0.5–0.6 mm composed of multiple lenses. A thin layer of lacrimal fluid covers the anterior face. The cornea

is often regarded as a single spherical surface, although some models model it as an ellipsoid (Beymer & Flickner, 2003; Guestrin & Eizenman, 2006). Light from IR sources is reflected on the cornea by the same angle as the incoming visible light (see Figure 3). Refraction occurs when a ray of light traverses the boundary between two media having different refractive indices. Refraction is described by Snell's law, which states that $n \sin(\delta_i) = n_0 \sin(\delta_f)$ where n and n_0 are the refractive indices of air and the other medium, respectively. δ_i and δ_f are the angles of the incident and refracted rays. It is the aqueous humour, liquid inside the cornea, that causes the refraction.

Figure 4 shows a geometric model of the eye and the entities commonly used for gaze estimation. The eyeball centre, the pupil centre, and the centre of the cornea are key elements in this model and are used to define the optical and visual axis. The optical and visual axes are separated by horizontal and vertical angular offsets (see Figure 5). The optical and visual axis are also known as (approximations of) the line of gaze (LoG) and the line of sight (LoS), respectively.

Figure 4. Schematic diagram of the eyeball model, showing its most relevant features

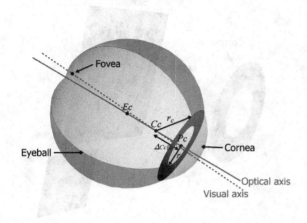

The fovea is the region of the retina with the highest density of cones, responsible for sharp vision, and is slightly displaced from the anterior pole of the eye. The optical axis is defined by the (imaginary) line joining the centres of the eyeball, cornea, and pupil, while the visual axis of the eye is defined by the line connecting the fovea and the corneal centre. Under the assumption that gaze can be modelled as a single axis, it is likely the visual axis that is the most accurate approximation of gaze direction.

IMAGE FORMATION

This section describes the geometric principles for the formation of eye images e.g., the pupil and glints. A gaze tracking system normally consists of one or more cameras and often some infrared light sources. These infrared light sources are used to illuminate the eye while the camera captures the images of the eye. The images captured contain features that can be used to detect the eye and to calculate gaze. The features used most often in gaze trackers are the pupil and the image of the reflections produced by an infrared light source on the corneal surface (a.k.a. glints).

The position of the elements of the gaze tracking system, such as the illuminators, the screen, and the user's eyeball, is aligned with respect to the camera reference system (see Figure 6). For the sake of simplicity, we consider the camera to be the origin of the world co-ordinate system (WCS), but the WCS may equally well be defined on the screen. This difference does not matter much, since these co-ordinate systems are usually related by a fixed rigid transformation. A WCS defined on the screen is useful when the gaze system is used for interaction. For gaze trackers with more than one camera, any of the cameras can be used as the main reference system; in fact, any convenient WCS can be used.

Points in 3D space are projected to the two-dimensional (2D) image plane through the camera.

Figure 5. The geometric relationship between optical and visual axes

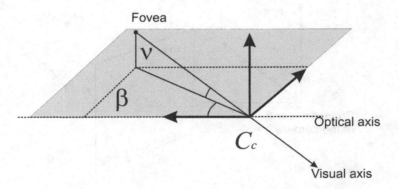

Figure 6. The camera is considered to be the centre (of the WCS); the remaining elements are positioned with respect to the camera

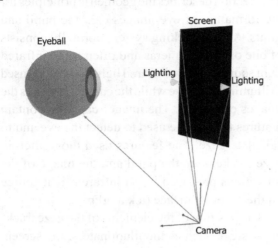

Figure 7. 3D to 2D projection in the image plane

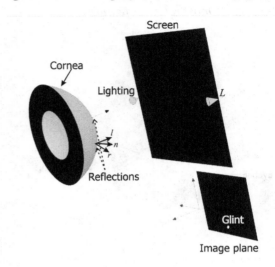

The projection of a point in space to image planes is usually modelled by means of pinhole camera models as depicted in Figure 6.

Corneal Reflections

Figure 7 shows the process of how corneal reflections (the glints) are produced in the image. The cornea reflects light from its surroundings, and some of the reflected light rays may intersect the

camera centre. As a consequence of the reflection law, it turns out that an incident ray from a light source, its reflected ray, and the normal at the point of incidence are coplanar. Consequently, the light source, the projection centre of the camera, the corneal centre, the reflection point, and the glint are coplanar. This fact becomes important when one is deriving information about gaze.

Figure 8. The light sources produce rays in different directions. Each ray is reflected according to the reflection law at the corneal surface. The reflected ray crossing the projection centre of the camera produces the glint in the image plane

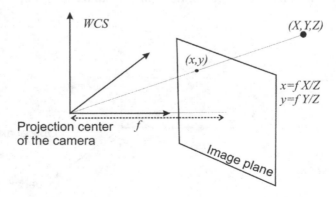

Figure 9. The pupil shape is altered and scaled as a result of corneal refraction. For image-modelling purposes, each pupil-contour point is analysed separately. Different rays coming from the same point deviate differently because of refraction. The ray reaching the projection centre of the camera produces the image of the corresponding contour point in the camera plane

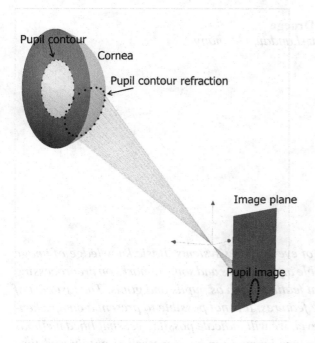

Pupil Image

The pupil is core in most methods used for gaze estimation. The image of the pupil is caused by light reflected on the retina passing through the pupil and reaching the camera. The pupil is almost circular; therefore, after a projection through the camera, it appears elliptical in the image. The image of the pupil is also affected by a non-linear refraction process. Consequently, the image of the pupil centre is not the same as the centre of the pupil shape in the image. However, a good approximation (and even fully valid under certain conditions) is to assume these to be equal (Guestrin & Eizenman, 2006).

DISCUSSION

This chapter served to give an overview of eye trackers and their components and how they are related. The chapter also provided some insight into the physics of how images of eyes and glints are produced. This will come in handy in discussion of how images are processed and gaze estimated. The subsequent chapters should, therefore, be more easily approachable and coherent after reading this introductory chapter.

REFERENCES

Beymer, D., & Flickner, M. (2003). Eye gaze tracking using an active stereo head. *CVPR '03: Proceedings of the 2003 Conference on Computer Vision and Pattern Recognition* (vol. 2, p. 451). Los Alamitos, CA, USA: IEEE Computer Society.

Droege, D., Geier, T., & Paulus, D. (2007). Improved low cost gaze tracker. In Istance, H., & Bates, R. (Eds.), *COGAIN 2007* (pp. 37–40).

Guestrin, E., & Eizenman, M. (2006). General theory of remote gaze estimation using the pupil center and corneal reflections. *IEEE Transactions on Bio-Medical Engineering, 53*(6), 1124–1133. doi:10.1109/TBME.2005.863952

Hansen, D. W., & Ji, Q. (2010). In the eye of the beholder: A survey of models for eyes and gaze. *IEEE Transactions on Pattern Analysis and Machine Intelligence, 32*(3), 478–500. doi:10.1109/TPAMI.2009.30

Mardanbeigi, D., & Hansen, D. W. (2010). *Reflections of head mounted systems for domotic control (IT Technical Report)*. Copenhagen, Denmark: IT University of Copenhagen.

Chapter 20
Image Analysis

Detlev Droege
University of Koblenz-Landau, Germany

ABSTRACT

This chapter focuses on the image processing part of eye tracking systems. Basic knowledge of image processing is assumed. After an overview of the possible input images and some remarks on preprocessing of the images, we will focus on the detection relevant features such as pupils and glints. The last part of this chapter focuses on estimating positions of these features. It is not possible to present a comprehensive solution for an eye tracker in this chapter; however, we will indicate possible yet simplified methods in the different steps of processing and demonstrate how images can be processed to obtain real-time performance. The program code is given in Matlab (Octave) language for clarity.

INTRODUCTION

This chapter focuses on the image processing part of eye tracking systems. Basic knowledge of image processing is assumed. The reader might want to refer to books established as references in this field, such as those of Jain (1989) and Jähne (2005), for more in-depth background.

The organisation of this chapter is as follows. After an overview of the possible input images

in "What is in the image?", and some remarks on "Preprocessing", we will focus on "Detection relevant features" such as pupils and glints. The last part of this chapter focuses on "Estimating positions" of these features.

As almost always with real-time tasks, efficiency is to be considered for all steps, since image processing is a computationally expensive task. As the user's system usually not only runs the eye tracking software but primarily handles the user's application programs, the tracking system must not consume all available CPU resources.

DOI: 10.4018/978-1-61350-098-9.ch020

Figure 1. (a) Eye image from Li et al. (2005), as produced by common eye tracking systems, (b) face image from image series used by Schmidt (2008)

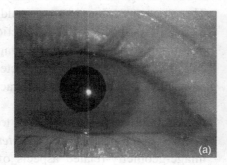 

An extensive overview of the topic of eye detection and the algorithms published can be found in the work of Hansen and Ji (2010). Only some of them are mentioned in this chapter.

It is not possible to present a comprehensive solution for an eye tracker in this chapter; however, we will indicate possible yet simplified methods in the different steps of processing and demonstrate how images can be processed to obtain real-time performance. The program code is given in *Matlab (Octave)* language for clarity.

WHAT IS IN THE IMAGE?

Depending on the eye tracker set-up, the camera usually provides images of either faces or only eyes. Systems working with eye images allow for more accuracy while those showing the whole face allow for a larger range of head movements.

Head-mounted eye trackers, as shown in Figure 2 (a) of Chapter 19 by Hansen and colleagues, have the camera very close to the eye and usually produce images showing the eye only, similarly to Figure 1 (a). Remote eye trackers as shown in, for example, Figure 2 (b) in Chapter 19, are generally much less intrusive; however, this imposes some costs. Using a camera with a narrow field of view (FOV) requires the user to keep the head in a rather fixed position. The resulting images are similar to those from head-mounted devices. A wide FOV is needed to allow greater freedom of head movement. Consequently, the camera images show the whole face as in Figure 1 (b) and – most importantly for the image processing – provide only much lower resolution to the image of the eye, making it more difficult to acquire accurate measurements.

Another question related to the set-up of the eye tracking system that has considerable impact

Figure 2. (a) Bright-pupil effect, (b) dark-pupil effect, both from Geier (2007)

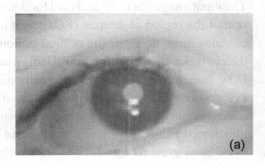 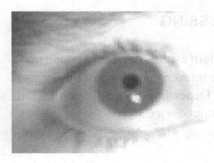

on the image processing is the position of the light source(s) with respect to the optical axis of the camera. These (usually infrared) light sources generate a reflection on the cornea whose position is of importance for subsequent calculations in the gaze tracking calculations. These light sources shine not only onto the eye but also into the eye, where they illuminate parts of the retina. If the light source is positioned very close to the optical axis of the camera, the light will be reflected back from the retina through the pupil, making the pupil appear bright (this is the same effect as the 'red-eyes' effect observed with small photo cameras where the flash light is close to the lens). Such systems are said to employ on-axis illumination, resulting in a bright-pupil effect as shown in Figure 2 (a). In contrast, systems positioning the light source at some distance from the camera employ 'off-axis' illumination, resulting in a dark pupil image.

The position of the pupil and of the glint(s) may be used for gaze estimation as described by Villanueva, Cabaeza and San Agustin in Chapter 21, and should, therefore, be determined accurately. However, several issues have to be considered if one is to achieve reasonable results. For instance, the reflections on the rim of the glasses in Figure 1 (b) should not be confused with the reflections on the cornea. The image in Figure 1 (a) shows usual artefacts such as visual noise and shining dust particles on the cornea, which likewise have to be considered. Furthermore, changing light conditions might alter the contrast as well as the image grey values.

PREPROCESSING

Numerous kinds of camera devices exist and may be used for eye trackers as described by Daunys in Chapter 22. Depending on the properties and quality of the input device and on the signal they produce, their images have to be (pre)processed.

Most algorithms for eye detection and tracking are designed to work on greyscale images. Therefore, any colour images would be converted in the first step. For face detection, however, one might consider taking advantage of the skin colour. Skin colour is easily detected in the HSV colour space by looking for a characteristic range of the H value.

After conversion of the input to a grey level image (sometimes also called *intensity image*), image-geometry-related aspects of the camera system used must be considered. For cameras delivering an interlaced (analogous) signal, a de-interlacing step has to be performed. In cases with significant distortion caused by the lenses, a resampling step correcting these could be performed (see Chapter 22 by Daunys). However, as the camera distortion parameters for a specific camera usually are known (possibly by means of geometric calibration during the initial system set-up), this could be deferred to a correction of the final results – unless the distortion interferes with the detection of geometric forms such as circles or ellipses.

Noisy signals can be smoothed by appropriate filtering (e.g., Gaussian or median filters). Faint signals could be amplified through adjustment of the intensity levels to fill the entire range available. However, such amplification also amplifies the noise, so it must be used with care.

DETECTION OF RELEVANT FEATURES

The input image has to be analysed for determination of the region of interest (ROI), as it usually contains more than just the desired region (e.g., the eye) relevant for eye tracking. Using a narrow-FOV camera puts the burden of positioning the eye properly toward the camera on the user. In some systems, the camera is mounted on a sophisticated pan-and-tilt unit to follow the user's eyes. Such systems can directly start with look-

Algorithm 1.

```
1   % main program for image processing
2
3   imgname = '271207_015.png';
4   inimg = imread (imgname);
5   if (length(size(inimg)) == 3) % RGB image, convert to grey
6     inimg = rgb2gray(inimg);
7   end
8
9   [omx omy obx oby] = findFaceCentreAndTop(inimg);
10
11 [plx, ply, prx, pry] = detectPupils (inimg, omx, omy, obx, oby);
12 [glx, gly, grx, gry] = detectGlints (inimg, plx, ply, prx, pry);
```

ing for the pupil. Wide-FOV systems, however, have to cope with a more complex situation, as not only the user's face but also a multitude of background objects might be visible and could disturb the detection.

The general layout of the image processing component is given in the Matlab code shown in Algorithm 1.

It first detects the position of the face in the image. It then uses this information to find the eyes and to determine the positions of the pupils and glints for further processing as described in the next chapter, on gaze estimation.

Detection of the Face

Face detection can be challenging, and several dozen approaches have been published (Kong et al., 2005). Face recognition isn't necessary if a good eye detector exists. Face detection may help to avoid false positives in eye detection.

The detection of regions with skin colour might be a first step when a colour camera is used. This limits the search space for subsequent methods so saves computing time.

Another approach, published by Viola and Jones (2001), employs a Haar feature cascade to perform the detection. A series of increasingly complex tests, based on statistical data derived from a large set of face images, is used to test for the presence and position of faces in an image. Unfortunately, this test proves to be computationally intensive and should not be applied to every input image. It does, however, provide a good starting point for subsequent face tracking based on simpler methods.

For a simplified walk-through, consider faces to be large, bright ellipse-shaped regions surrounded by a dark background. Given the image in Figure 1 (b) as a starting point, we translate the grayscale image to a binary image, using a threshold obtained with Otsu's algorithm (Otsu, 1979). As only large structures are relevant, we perform this operation on a scaled-down version of the input image. The function **findFaceCentreAndTop** (see Algorithm 2) then performs a morphological *closing* operation to obtain a uniform area. Via **findPrincipalAxis** (see Algorithm 3), the centre of gravity (CoG) and the main axis are determined. By 'walking' of this axis from the CoG, the border for the height of the area is determined.

The function **findPrincipalAxis** builds the covariance matrix of all co-ordinates of white pixels in the binarised low-resolution image. The

Algorithm 2.

```
1   function [mx my bx by] = findFaceCentreAndTop (inimg)
2      % image resize and greyscale-to-binary conversion
3   lowresscale = 10;
4   imsmall = imresize(inimg, 1/lowresscale, 'linear');
5   otsu_th = graythresh(imsmall);
6   imbw = im2bw(imsmall, otsu_th);
7      % apply morphological 'closing' operator
8   imcl = closing(imbw, ones(3));
9   [sh sw] = size(imcl);
10  [mx my dx dy] = findPrincipalAxis(imcl);
11  checkAngleRange(dx, dy);
12
13  % walk the principal axis from centre of gravity upward to find border
14  % remember: y axis increases downward, and we want to go upward
15  bx = mx;
16  by = my;
17  while (imcl(round(by),round(bx)) == 1)
18    by = by - 1;
19    bx = bx - dx/dy;
20  end
21  % one step back
22  by = by + 1;
23  bx = bx + dx/dy;
24
25  % everything was scaled down, so scale values up again
26  mx = mx * lowresscale;
27  my = my * lowresscale;
28  bx = bx * lowresscale;
29  by = by * lowresscale;
30  end
```

eigenvector for the largest eigenvalue of this matrix gives the longer axis of the ellipse.

The function **checkAngleRange** just performs some sanity checks to detect situations where no mainly upright ellipse was found (see Algorithm 4).

Detection of the Eyes

Most eye detection algorithms can be classified as *shape-based*, *appearance-based*, or a hybrid of the two (Hansen & Ji, 2010). Some incorporate face detection to improve stability.

In Algorithm 5 we take a very simple appearance-based approach wherein we take advantage of the fact that we have some rough estimate of the face centre and its orientation. We expect the eyes to occur in some band above the centre of the face, one to the left and one to the right. We simply give the sizes as values relative to the length of the upper half axis of the ellipse, calculated as **base** in the next step.

Algorithm 3.

```
1 function [mx my dx dy] = findPrincipalAxis(imcl)
2   % eigenvectors of the covariance matrices of all point co-ords with
f(x,y)=1
3   % km = sum of the ((x,y)' * (x,y))*f(x,y) with only 0 or 1 in f
4   [sh sw] = size(imcl);
5   [xx yy] = meshgrid([1:sw], [1:sh]);
6   m00 = sum(sum(imcl));
7   m10 = sum(sum(imcl.* xx));
8   m01 = sum(sum(imcl.* yy));
9   mx = m10 / m00
10  my = m01 / m00
11  xx = xx - mx;
12  yy = yy - my;
13  covmat = zeros(2,2);
14  covmat(1,1) = sum(sum(imcl.* xx.^2));
15  covmat(2,2) = sum(sum(imcl.* yy.^2));
16  covmat(1,2) = sum(sum(imcl.* xx.* yy));
17  covmat(2,1) = covmat(1,2);
18  [evec eval] = eig(covmat);
19  if (eval(1,1) < eval(2,2)) % exchange columns
20    evec = evec(:,[2 1]);
21    eval = eval(:,[2 1]);
22  end
23  dx = evec(1,1);
24  dy = evec(2,1);
25 end
```

Figure 3. Operations on the binarised low-resolution image. (a) Binarised, (b) after closing, (c) main axis of the head

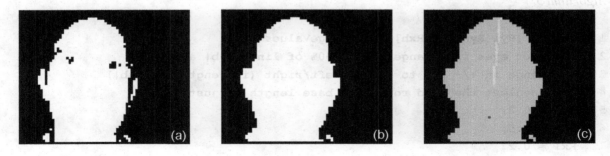

Algorithm 4.

```
1 function checkAngleRange(dx, dy)
2   if (abs(dx) > abs(dy))
3     error ('principal axis not mainly vertical');
4   end
5   incx = dx * sign(-dy);
6   incy = dy * sign(-dy);
7   maxbend = 20;
8   theta = atan2(incy, incx) / pi * 180;
9   if (theta < -90-maxbend || theta > -90+maxbend)
10     error('head is angled by more than 20 degrees');
11   end
12 end
```

Figure 4. Face regions

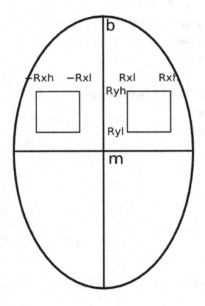

Algorithm 5.

```
1 function [Ryl Ryh Rxl Rxh] = setRangeValues()
2   % expect eyes in y range 20% to 50% of line |m,b| and in
3   % x range in +/- 20% to 50% to left/right (in length of |m,b|)
4   % we neglect the head rotation; base length is just  b - m
5   Ryl = 0.2;
6   Ryh = 0.5;
7   Rxl = 0.2;
8   Rxh = 0.5;
9 end
```

Figure 5. Eye regions for left and right eye, based on anthropomorphic averages

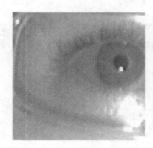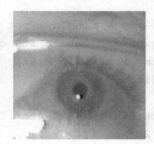

This procedure provides only a good guess as to where the eyes should be and may catch other regions than eyes. We rely on the next step (function **findDarkSpot**) to detect the pupil within the estimated areas of the image that are shown in Figure 5.

Detection of the Pupil

We might have to deal with either dark or bright pupils, depending on the system set-up, as described in "What is in the image?" above. We limit our example to the former case, so we now have to look for dark regions in the images in Figure 5. In the IR spectrum, the pupils clearly stand out as a dark region, as can be seen in Figure 6, where the grey levels are depicted as a height field. The 'cone' pointing downward in Figure 6 (b) represents the pupil pixels, but there may also be other regions in the image that are dark (e.g., nostrils or eyebrows).

Considering our given set-up, we estimate the pupil to have a diameter of approximately nine

pixels. Therefore, we expect roughly $9^2 / 4\cdot\pi \approx 64$ pixels to be part of the pupil. Using a grey level histogram, we look for the grey value such that 64 pixels are either as dark as or darker than this value. This value is given a 5% surplus to account for some tolerance and then used as a threshold for again binarising the corresponding sub-images. Note that the threshold may be different for each eye (see Algorithm 6).

As we did with the face ellipse, we use the first-order geometric moments to calculate the centre of gravity.

$$m_{10} = \sum_{x,y} x f(x,y) \quad , \quad m_{01} = \sum_{x,y} y f(x,y)$$

The binary images used in this step contain only grey level values of either 0 or 1 (the latter for the previously dark pixels). By directly using the image co-ordinates of the original image, not the sub-images, we directly obtain the result in co-ordinates of the input image.

Figure 6. Grey values of the right eye sub-image (Figure 5) as height field from different viewing angles

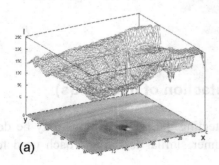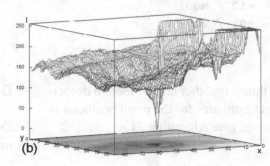

Algorithm 6.

```
1 function [cx, cy, im] = findDarkSpot (fullim, xmin, xmax, ymin, ymax, diam)
2    % find dark region and return its centre of gravity
3    im = fullim(ymin:ymax, xmin:xmax);
4    [eh ew] = size(im);
5
6    % number of dark pixels we expect for the spot
7    npixels = diam^2 * pi / 4.0;
8
9    % look for brightness of the npixels darkest pixels in the sub-image
10   lhisto = hist(reshape(im, ew*eh, 1), 256); % reshape for overall histogram
11   darkval = 0;
12   hsum = lhisto(1);
13   while (hsum < npixels)
14     darkval = darkval + 1;
15     hsum = hsum + lhisto(darkval+1);
16   end
17   darkval = darkval + 0.05*255; % add a 5% margin (values are 0...255)
18
19   % binarise to see pupil/glint only (hopefully)
20   imbw = 1-im2bw(im, darkval/255.0); % threshold expected in [0..1], inverted
21   if (diam > 3) % don't do opening if structure element is larger than spot
22     imcl = opening(imbw, ones(3,3));
23   else
24     imcl = imbw;
25   end
26   % imagesc(imcl); % display intermediate result
27
28   % find centre of gravity by building weighted mean
29   [xx yy] = meshgrid([xmin:xmax], [ymin:ymax]); % to get fullim co-ordinates
30   m00 = sum(sum(imcl));
31   m10 = sum(sum(xx.* imcl));
32   m01 = sum(sum(yy.* imcl));
33   cx = m10 / m00;
34   cy = m01 / m00;
35 end
```

We put things together in the function **detect-Pupils** to get estimates for the pupil positions in the input image (see Algorithm 7).

Detection of the Glint(s)

Detecting the glint positions may be done in a manner similar to the approach used for pupil

Algorithm 7.

```
1  function [lx ly rx ry] = detectPupils (inimg, omx, omy, obx, oby)
2     [Ryl Ryh Rxl Rxh] = setRangeValues();
3     base = abs(omy - oby);
4
5     % left eye sub-image border
6     lxmin = round(omx-Rxh*base); lxmax = round(omx-Rxl*base);
7     lymin = round(omy-Ryh*base); lymax = round(omy-Ryl*base);
8     % right eye sub-image border
9     rxmin = round(omx+Rxl*base); rxmax = round(omx+Rxh*base);
10    rymin = round(omy-Ryh*base); rymax = round(omy-Ryl*base);
11
12    pupdiam = 9;
13    [lx, ly] = findDarkSpot(inimg, lxmin, lxmax, lymin, lymax, pupdiam)
14    [rx, ry] = findDarkSpot(inimg, rxmin, rxmax, rymin, rymax, pupdiam)
15 end
```

Figure 7. Left and right iris sub-images

 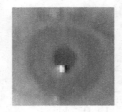

detection. First the search space is limited through selection of image areas around the pupils. With the given set-up, the corneal reflection will always occur within the iris or pupil. From the set-up we also know that the iris's diameter should be 30 to 40 pixels. Therefore, we use sub-images covering the range of ±20 pixels around the detected pupil centres. Within these sub-images as shown in Figure 7, the corneal reflection usually shows up as the highest spot.

Thus, we could employ the same method for glint detection as we did for the pupil centre but while looking for the brightest instead of the darkest spot (see Algorithm 8). We can even reuse the **findDarkSpot** function by simply inverting the input (sub-)images.

The function **findDarkSpot** does not just give a rough guess of the pupil centre. A comparison with other algorithms as in the work of Droege et al. (2008) shows that for low-resolution input such as face images as used in this example, such a simple algorithm provides results of comparable quality.

ESTIMATION OF POSITIONS

Several algorithms have been developed to estimate the positions of the pupil or iris centre and glint centre(s) as accurately as possible. While some work from the pure image intensity values, as the above function **findDarkSpot** does, a number of them work on values derived from these intensities.

The contour (ellipse) of the eye provides valuable information about the location of the iris. The contour can be detected through the local changes in the image – i.e., the gradients. Mathematically, gradients are the first derivative in space of the intensity values. The common way of calculating the gradients is to apply the Sobel operator to the

Algorithm 8.

```
1 function [glx gly grx gry] = detectGlints (inimg, plx, ply, prx, pry)
2    irisRadius = 20;
3
4    % left iris sub-image border
5    rlx = round(plx); rly = round(ply);
6    lxmin = round(rlx-irisRadius); lxmax = round(rlx+irisRadius);
7    lymin = round(rly-irisRadius); lymax = round(rly+irisRadius);
8
9    % right iris sub-image border
10   rrx = round(prx); rry = round(pry);
11   rxmin = round(rrx-irisRadius); rxmax = round(rrx+irisRadius);
12   rymin = round(rry-irisRadius); rymax = round(rry+irisRadius);
13
14   glintdiam = 2;
15   [glx, gly] = findDarkSpot(255-inimg, lxmin, lxmax, lymin, lymax, glint-
diam)
16   [grx, gry] = findDarkSpot(255-inimg, rxmin, rxmax, rymin, rymax, glint-
diam)
17 end
```

image, which for each pixel results in the local derivative in the horizontal and vertical direction. The Sobel operation is performed by convolving the image with the horizontal and the vertical Sobel mask:

$$\begin{bmatrix} -1 & 0 & 1 \\ -2 & 0 & 2 \\ -1 & 0 & 1 \end{bmatrix} \quad , \quad \begin{bmatrix} -1 & -2 & -1 \\ 0 & 0 & 0 \\ 1 & 2 & 1 \end{bmatrix}$$

These values are then used as orthogonal components to form the direction vector of the gradient. The vector's magnitude is given by the

Algorithm 9.

```
1 function [gradStrength gradAngle] = gradientImage(img)
2    centralDifference = [-1 0 1];
3    gaussMask = [1 2 1] / 4.0;
4
5    sobelHor = conv2 (gaussMask, centralDifference, img, 'valid');
6    sobelVer = conv2 (centralDifference, gaussMask, img, 'valid');
7
8    gradStrength = sqrt(sobelHor.^2 + sobelVer.^2);
9    gradAngle = atan2 (sobelVer, sobelHor); % 2-parameter variant of arctan
10 end
```

Figure 8. Gradients of the left iris sub-image (grey vectors are shortened for better visibility), from Droege and Paulus (2010)

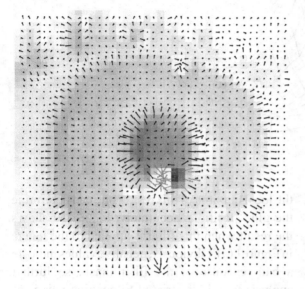

Euclidean distance; the direction angle can be calculated via the **arctan** function. For efficiency, the Sobel mask can be separated into a central difference mask and an elementary Gauss mask in the simple Matlab function **gradientImage**.

The gradients calculated according to this method are shown in Figure 8, superimposed on the (faint) image of the left iris sub-image (Figure 7 (a)). The strongest gradients, mostly around the glint, have been shortened for better visibility – those arrows are drawn in light grey. The image gives an idea of the derived values, which can be used for more advanced algorithms.

Determining the Pupil Centre

Numerous algorithms to find the co-ordinates of the pupil centre have been developed, for a multitude of eye tracking systems. For example, the algorithm described by Li et al. (2005) guesses the limbus by looking for gradients of a certain strength when travelling from a previously guessed centre in 18 radial directions. After refining of

this list of feature points via clever iterations, an ellipse is fitted to these points by means of the RANSAC algorithm.

In a similar way, the algorithms described by Daunys and Ramanauskas (2004) indirectly take the gradient into account to determine the pupil border. On the basis of these border points, the centre is estimated either by fitting a circle or through simple but effective weighted averaging.

Most of the published algorithms are used with images of fairly good quality, as delivered by head-mounted or narrow-FOV eye tracking systems. A selection of such algorithms can be found in the work of Hansen and Ji (2010) and Schmidt (2008).

Determining the Glint Position

Image processing algorithms often depend on the resolution of their input images. In low-resolution images, the glint diameter may be only 2–3 pixels, making the gradient information rather unreliable. As shown above ("Detection of the glint(s)"), the simple centre of gravity approach again is a good starting point. Similar techniques may be employed for accurately determining the position(s) of the glint(s) in the image. Gradient-based approaches are not suitable for low-resolution images, since the glint diameter is much smaller.

In the algorithm used in conjunction with Starburst (Li et al., 2005), glints are detected by looking for the brightest pixel in the image region around the pupil. These are very likely to belong to the glint, as the infrared light source pointing toward the eye causes very good reflections on the cornea. The brightest value found is chosen as an initial threshold, which is then lowered iteratively. All image regions exceeding the threshold are observed during the iterations. The region changing in size the most when the threshold is lowered is most likely a glint. Its centre is then chosen as the glint position.

Another approach is applied by Schian (1999), which is intended for use with medium- to high-

Figure 9. 19 X 19 glint filter mask by Schian (1999), as height plot

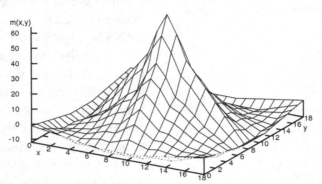

resolution pupil images. A filter mask is constructed with dimensions suitable for the expected size of the reflections. The mask is tailored such that it gives the best response for bright, glint-like regions surrounded by dark(er) pixels. It is shown in Figure 9 as a height plot. For this technique, it is important to know the expected size of the reflections, as the mask should enhance all bright pixels of the glint and attenuate the dark pixels. Schian constructed this mask with computational efficiency in mind, as it can be decomposed into the successive convolution with two smaller masks consisting of the values (- 1, 0, 1) only, thus avoiding floating point multiplications. Furthermore, one of the masks is a simple, separable mean filter.

Applying this mask gives good indications of where to look for the glints. By further evaluating

the local maxima of this result, one can determine the glint positions accurately. Figure 10 shows the result when this filter is applied to the image in Figure 1 (a). Obviously, negative values indicate a bad response of the filter mask, so further analysis may be restricted to positive values as shown in the right-hand image.

CONCLUSION

Determining accurate co-ordinates for pupils and glints is a crucial task for an eye tracker. This chapter has shown an exemplary implementation of the image processing component while pointing to alternative, usually more capable and complex approaches. Since a number of external factors

Figure 10. Figure 1 (a)(Li et al., 2005) filtered with mask shown in Figure 9. Left: all resulting values, scaled to grey values. Right: positive responses only, scaled to grey values

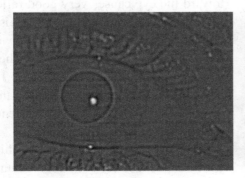
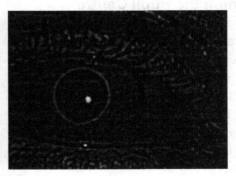

such as camera resolution, camera sensitivity, lens parameters, the camera's distance from the eyes, and light conditions, and numerous others, directly influence the choice of adequate algorithms, it is impossible to describe a general solution here. The implementation concept presented may, however, serve as a framework for one's experiments. The reader is encouraged to adapt the algorithms or replace them with ones more suitable for his or her specific set-up and needs. The co-ordinates found by this component then provide the input for the gaze estimation as described in the following chapter.

REFERENCES

Daunys, G., & Ramanauskas, N. (2004). The accuracy of eye tracking using image processing. *Proceedings of the 3rd Nordic Conference on Human–Computer Interaction* (*NordiCHI '04*) (pp. 377–380). New York, NY: ACM.

Droege, D., & Paulus, D. (2010). Pupil center detection in low resolution images. *Proceedings of the 2010 Symposium on Eye-Tracking Research & Applications* (*ETRA '10*) (pp. 169–172). New York, NY: ACM.

Droege, D., Schmidt, C., & Paulus, D. (2008). A comparison of pupil center estimation algorithms. *Proceedings of the 4th Conference on Communication by Gaze Interaction* (*COGAIN 2008*) (pp. 23–26). Prague, Czech Republic: Czech Technical University. Retrieved from the COGAIN website: http://www.cogain.org/conference

Geier, T. (2007). *Gaze-Tracking zur Interaktion unter Verwendung von Low-Cost-Equipment.* Master's thesis, Universität Koblenz-Landau, Campus Koblenz, Fachbereich 4 Informatik, Institut für Computervisualistik, Koblenz, Germany.

Hansen, D. W., & Ji, Q. (2010). In the eye of the beholder: A survey of models for eyes and gaze. *IEEE Transactions on Pattern Analysis and Machine Intelligence, 32*(3), 478–500. doi:10.1109/TPAMI.2009.30

Jähne, B. (2005). *Digital image processing* (6th ed.). Berlin/Heidelberg, Germany: Springer.

Jain, A. K. (1989). *Fundamentals of digital image processing.* Upper Saddle River, NJ, USA: Prentice Hall.

Kong, S. G., Heo, J., Abidi, B. R., Paik, J., & Abidi, M. A. (2005). Recent advances in visual and infrared face recognition: A review. *Computer Vision and Image Understanding, 97*, 103–135. doi:10.1016/j.cviu.2004.04.001

Li, D., Winfield, D., & Parkhurst, D. J. (2005). Starburst: A hybrid algorithm for video-based eye tracking combining feature-based and model-based approaches. *IEEE Computer Society Conference on Computer Vision and Pattern Recognition* (*CVPR '05*) (pp. 79–86). Washington, DC, USA: IEEE Computer Society.

Otsu, N. (1979). A threshold selection method from gray-level histogram. *Transactions on Systems, Man, and Cybernetics, 9*(1), 62–66. doi:10.1109/TSMC.1979.4310076

Schian, R. (1999). *Automatische Bildauswertung zur dynamischen Schielwinkelmessung bei Kleinkindern und Säuglingen.* PhD thesis, Universität Koblenz-Landau, Germany.

Schmidt, C. (2008). *Evaluation von Eye-Tracking-Teilalgorithmen* (Technical report/ Bachelor's thesis). Universität Koblenz-Landau, Fachbereich Informatik, Germany.

Viola, P., & Jones, M. J. (2001). Robust real-time face detection. *International Conference on Computer Vision, 2*, 747.

Chapter 21
Gaze Estimation

Arantxa Villanueva
Public University of Navarre, Spain

Rafael Cabeza
Public University of Navarre, Spain

Javier San Agustin
IT University of Copenhagen, Denmark

ABSTRACT

The main objective of gaze trackers is to provide an accurate estimate of the user's gaze by using the eye tracking information. Gaze, in its most general form, can be considered to be the line of sight or line of gaze, as 3D (imaginary) lines with respect to the camera, or as the point of regard (also termed the point of gaze). This chapter introduces different gaze estimation techniques, including geometry-based methods and interpolation methods. Issues related to both remote and head mounted trackers are discussed. Different fixation estimation methods are also briefly introduced. It is assumed that the reader is familiar with basic 3D geometry concepts as well as advanced mathematics, such as matrix manipulation and vector calculus.

INTRODUCTION

The main objective of gaze trackers is to provide an accurate estimate of the user's gaze by using the eye tracking information. Gaze, in its most general form, can be considered to be the line of sight (LoS) or line of gaze (LoG) as defined in the Introductory chapter (Chapter 19) to this Section, as 3D (imaginary) lines with respect to the camera, or as the point of regard (PoR) (also

termed the point of gaze, or PoG). The PoR is defined as the point of intersection between the LoS and the object being observed. In this chapter, it is assumed that the reader is familiar with basic 3D geometry concepts as well as advanced mathematics, such as matrix manipulation and vector calculus.

GAZE ESTIMATION TECHNIQUES

To calculate eye movements, a connection between the features provided by the technology (i.e., eye

DOI: 10.4018/978-1-61350-098-9.ch021

Figure 1. Gaze estimation attempts to find a relationship between image analysis results and gaze

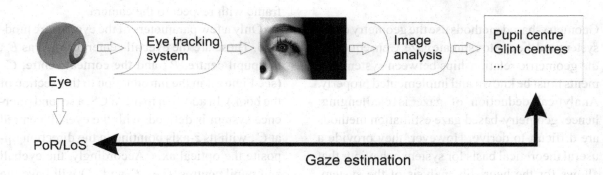

tracking results) and gaze must be established. Our eyes are constantly in motion. As we look around, the eyes perform different movements so that the informative parts of the scene are sensed by the fovea. When fixating on an object, the eye performs specific micro-movements from which the stable point of fixation can be deduced. Gaze estimation is defined as the function connecting eye image and gaze (PoR/LoS) (see Figure 1). The success of this task depends largely on the technology selected, on the algorithms used to extract the specific eye features from the image, on the gaze estimation method employed, and on the fixation-estimation algorithm used.

Gaze estimation is not a trivial task, and, so far, no single solution to the problem has emerged (i.e., a method for determining gaze that is clearly the best). An acceptable gaze estimation method should, preferably, be accurate (with an error of <1°), robust, and tolerant to head movement. The third characteristic in particular has been one of the most sought-after features in recent years. In head-mounted systems, head movement tolerance is not a problem, as the gaze tracking system moves with the head; however, there are other problems with head-mounted systems, as described later in this chapter, in the section 'Head-mounted Gaze Trackers'. Head movements are particularly important for remote eye tracking systems, in which the subject can move more freely with respect to the camera.

The connection between image and gaze is not self-evident, and different approaches have been proposed in recent decades. In attempting to find this connection two main approaches can be distinguished:

- Geometry-based methods
- Interpolation methods

Geometry-based methods express the relationship between the image and gaze in terms of the geometry of the gaze tracking system in combination with modelling of the visual fixation mechanism. Thus 3D models (for the eyeball and system framework) are constructed. In the same manner, the mathematical basis of the image-formation process must be explored. Alternatively, interpolation methods, largely arising during the last few decades, represent the relationship between the image and gaze via a general-purpose function, such as linear or quadratic polynomials, based on unknown (empirical) coefficients and a vector containing the image features and their possible products. For a more extensive description of this topic refer to the work of Hansen and Ji (2010).

In this chapter, the basic theory underlying gaze estimation methods is presented. Additional sections focus on the problems of head-mounted eye trackers and fixation-estimation methods.

GEOMETRY BASED METHODS

Geometry-based methods use the geometry of the system and the eye to estimate gaze. Consequently, the geometric relationships between system elements must be known and implemented properly. Analytical deduction of gaze is challenging; hence, geometry-based gaze estimation methods are difficult to derive. However, they provide a useful theoretical basis for system behaviour that allows for the heuristic analysis of the system. These kinds of methods permit the measurement of alternative factors of system performance, such as the sensitivity of the system to different variables (e.g., image resolution) and the possibility of quantifying errors theoretically, among other elements.

Knowledge of the relative positions of system elements, such as screen and light position or camera focal length, are often needed for geometry-based methods, but not always, as will be explained under 'Uncalibrated Set-ups'. Obtaining set-up parameters (hardware set-up calibration) is not a trivial task and requires recalibration each time any part of the hardware is moved or changed.

Here, we differentiate between user calibration and set-up calibration. Every user has different eyes, so, user calibration is needed to adjust the system for a certain subject, whereas set-up calibration is an additional process for deducing hardware parameters such as camera information and screen or illuminator data. Generally, set-up calibration precedes user calibration and it can be considered one-time calibration as long as the same hardware configuration is maintained. A basic geometric review of the gaze estimation problem is presented below.

Given a point $\bar{X} = \left(\bar{X}, \bar{Y}, \bar{Z} \right)$ in a known reference system (WCS), its coordinates with respect to the camera **X** can be calculated as $X = R\bar{X} + t$, where R is a 3 x 3 rotation matrix representing the orientation of the given co-ordinate frame with respect to the camera and **t** is the translation vector of the origin of the co-ordinate frame with respect to the camera.

Only a few parameters of the eyeball are modeled. These are the eyeball center denoted as E_c; the pupil centre, P_c; and the corneal centre, C_c, (see Figure 4 in the introduction to this section of the book). In addition to the WCS, a second reference system is defined, with the eyeball centred at C_c, with its z-axis pointing in the direction opposite the optical axis. Accordingly, the eyeball and pupil centres, (i.e., E_c and P_c) will have the coordinates $(0, 0, \Delta_{C_c E_c})$ and $(0, 0, -\Delta_{C_c P_c})$, respectively, in the eyeball reference system. The cornea is modelled as a sphere with radius r_c, and the radius of the pupil (considered a circular plane) is r_p. The gaze direction can be approximated by the visual axis of the eye. This axis is approximated as the line connecting the fovea and the corneal centre and presents horizontal and vertical angular offsets with respect to the optical axis of the eye, defined as β and ν, respectively. The visual axis can be defined with respect to the optical axis by means of a rigid transformation (translation + rotation) as shown in Figure 5 of the introduction to this section of the book. The reference system of the eye rotates and translates together with the eyeball with respect to the system camera, so all coordinates of the eyeball elements are preserved with respect to C_c.

According to Equation 1 in the introduction to Section VI of the book, to calculate the image of any 3D point for the camera it should be referenced to the camera co-ordinate system. Given a 3D point in the eyeball reference system $\left(\tilde{X}, \tilde{Y}, \tilde{Z} \right)$, one can calculate its image by using the matrix

$$P \begin{pmatrix} R & t \\ 0 & 1 \end{pmatrix} \begin{pmatrix} \tilde{X} \\ \tilde{Y} \\ \tilde{Z} \\ 1 \end{pmatrix} = P \begin{pmatrix} R_\theta R_\varphi & C_c \\ 0 & 1 \end{pmatrix} \begin{pmatrix} \tilde{X} \\ \tilde{Y} \\ \tilde{Z} \\ 1 \end{pmatrix} \qquad (1)$$

where $(R, \mathbf{t})$ represent the rigid transformation between eyeball and camera reference systems, being the rotation matrix $R = R_\theta R_\varphi$ where R_θ and R_φ are the rotation matrices with respect to the x and y axes of the WCS– in this case, the camera co-ordinate system and $\mathbf{t}$, the translation vector represented by the corneal centre position, C_c.

Figure 8 in Chapter 19 in this Section shows an LED illuminating the eye. According to the reflection law, the incident ray, the reflected ray, and the normal at the point of incidence are co-planar. This plane, denoted as $\prod_{L_1}$, can be calculated as a function of the LED position (i.e., L_1), the glint created by L_1 (i.e., c_1), and the projection centre of the camera.

$$\prod_{L_1} = L_1 \times c_1 \tag{2}$$

If a second light source is added to the system an additional plane, $\prod_{L_2}$, can be calculated, as

$$\prod_{L_2} = L_2 \times c_2 \tag{3}$$

where L_2 represents the second light source and c_2 the corneal reflection created by L_2. According to the reflection law, the corneal centre, C_c, is contained in both planes, and, therefore,

$$\prod_{L_2} \cdot C_c = \prod_{L_2} \cdot C_c = 0 \tag{4}$$

In other words, the corneal centre and projection centre of the camera both lie on the line formed by the resulting intersection of planes $\prod_{L_1}$ and $\prod_{L_2}$ (see Figure 2).

The function **EstimateCorneaLine** (see Function 1) outlines the procedure used to calculate the line containing the cornea.

Regarding the pupil image, according to the refraction law, the incident ray, refracted ray, and normal at the point of incidence are coplanar. If a ray is back-projected from the pupil image and its intersection with the corneal surface calculated, the refracted ray for that given point and the corresponding incident direction can be calculated, according to Ohno and Mukawa (2004) as

$$f_k = \left(\frac{n_0}{n}\right)\left[i_k - \left((i_k \cdot n_k) + \sqrt{\left(\frac{n_0}{n}\right)^2 - 1 + (i_k \cdot n_k)^2}\right)n_k\right] \tag{5}$$

where f_k and i_k represent the refracted light and the incident light directions, respectively; variables n_0 and n denote the refraction indices of the incident and refracted media, respectively; and n_k is the surface normal vector at the point of incidence.

In the following discussion, on the basis of their set-up calibration requirements, basic approaches are presented for two different types of systems: (a) fully (set-up-) calibrated and (b) uncalibrated.

Figure 2. According to the reflection law, the incident, reflected, and normal rays are contained in the same plane. Consequently, and the camera projection centre are contained in that plane. If two light sources are used, the corneal centre is contained in the intersection line of the planes

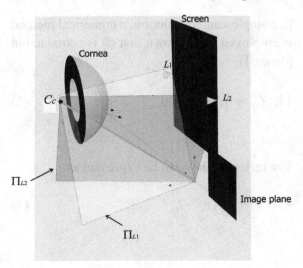

Function 1.

```
1 function cornealine=EstimateCorneaLine(c1,c2,L1,L2)
2 %a plane can be calculated for each glint-LED pair
3 % L1 3D position of LED 1, c1 3D glint position in the image plane
4 % L2 3D position of LED 2, c2 3D glint position in the image plane
5 ledplane1=LedGlintPlane(c1,L1);
6 ledplane2=LedGlintPlane(c2,L2);
7 % the 3D line containing the cornea is estimated as the intersection of
8 % the 2 planes
9 cornealine=Intersect(ledplane1,ledplane2);
10 end
```

A. FULLY CALIBRATED SET-UPS

In a fully calibrated set-up, all geometric relations related to the physical set-up are assumed to be known (e.g., camera-calibration parameters, screen size and position, and the locations of the light sources [the camera reference system is assumed to be the WCS]). The goal is to deduce the eyeball's 3D position by using 2D data extracted from the eye image. More specifically, the objective is to find the user's LoS with respect to the camera. The PoR (i.e., the point gazed at on the screen) can be calculated as the intersection between the 3D line represented by the LoS and the screen plane.

Geometrically, it is simpler to calculate the LoS as a function of the optical axis of the eye, as will be explained later in this section of the chapter. The optical axis of the eye is formed by three principal points: E_c, C_c, and P_c. The optical axis can be calculated if two of these three points are known. The simplest approach is to estimate the optical axis as the 3D line connecting the corneal and pupil centres.

Corneal Centre Estimation

We know from the previous analysis that a line containing C_c can be calculated if a camera and two light sources are used. Two scenarios can be proposed for a gaze tracking system with different geometric solutions.

Stereo Solution

In a stereo solution combining an additional camera with L_1 and L_2, another 3D line will be generated, containing C_c and the projection centre of the second camera. The intersection of the lines corresponding to the two cameras yields C_c (see Figure 3) (Shih and Liu, 2004).

The function **EstimateCorneaStereo** (Function 2) outlines the procedure for calculating C_c with a stereo set-up.

Single-Camera Solution

In a single-camera solution, a numerical method is employed. It is known that C_c is contained in planes $\prod_{L_1}$ and $\prod_{L_2}$:

$$\prod_{L_1} \cdot C_c = \prod_{L_2} \cdot C_c = 0 \qquad (6)$$

The reflection law can be expressed as

$$r_1 = 2\left(n_1 \cdot l_1\right)n_1 - l_1 \qquad (7)$$

Figure 3. In a stereo solution, can be estimated as the intersection of the lines from each of the cameras

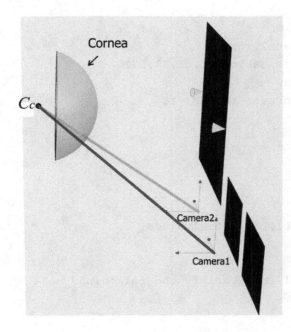

where r_1 is the unit vector in the direction c_1, l_1 is the unit vector in the direction $(L_1 - G_1)$, n_1 is the normal vector at the point of incidence in the direction $(G_1 - C_c)$, and G_1 represents the point of reflection at the corneal surface. The point G_1 can be expressed as a function of C_c if r_c is known (Villanueva & Cabeza, 2008).

$$d\left(G_1, C_c\right) = r_c \qquad (8)$$

The location of the corneal centre is deduced as the global optimum that fulfils Equations 6 to 8. The function **EstimateCorneaSingle** (Function 3) outlines the procedure for calculating C_c with a single camera in use.

Pupil Centre Estimation

Once the cornea location has been calculated, the estimation of the pupil centre, P_c, is simplified as the refraction of any back-projected ray from the image can be calculated at the corneal surface. For this, the corneal refraction index is assumed to be known. From the refraction law, it is known that an incident ray, its refracted ray, and the normal at the point of incidence are coplanar. Different approaches for calculating P_c can be found in the literature that are based on the pupil information contained in the image (Shih & Liu, 2004; Guestrin & Eizenman, 2006; Hennessey et al., 2006). A

Function 2.

```
1 function Cc=EstimateCorneaStereo(g1c1,g2c1,g1c2,g2c2,L1,L2)
2 %L1 LED 1's position in 3D with respect to WCS
3 %L2 LED 2's position in 3D with respect to WCS
4 % g1c1 glint position in 3D produced by L1 in Camera1 with respect to WCS
5 % g2c1 glint position in 3D produced by L2 in Camera1 with respect to WCS
6 % g1c2 glint position in 3D produced by L1 in Camera2 with respect to WCS
7 % g2c2 glint position in 3D produced by L2 in Camera2 with respect to WCS
8 % estimate the cornea line created via the information of Camera1
9 cornealine1=EstimateCorneaLine(g1c1,g2c1,L1,L2)
10 % estimate the cornea line created via the information of Camera2
11 cornealine2=EstimateCorneaLine(g1c2,g2c2,L1,L2)
12 % intersect the two lines to estimate the corneal centre
13 Cc=Intersect(cornealine1,cornealine2)
14 end
```

Function 3.

```
1 global ledplane1
2 global ledplane2
3 global rc
4 function F=funCc(Cc,G1, ledplane1, ledplane2,rc)
5% Cc is contained in cornealine=EstimateCorneaLine(g1,g2,L1,L2)
6% G1, Cc, and L1 satisfy the reflection law
7% the distance between Cc and G1 is the corneal radius, rc
8 F=[ledplane1.Cc-ledplane2.Cc;
9 Norm(G1-Cc,2)-rc;
10 Cc/Norm(Cc,2)-ReflectedRay(G1,L1,Cc)];
11 end
12
13
14 function Cc=EstimateCorneaSingle(c1,c2,L1,L2,initialvalues)
15 ledplane1=LedGlintPlane(c1,L1);
16 ledplane2=LedGlintPlane(c2,L2)
17% find the global optima points Cc and G1 that satisfy the following
18% constraints
19 fsolve(@funCc,initialvalues)
20 end
```

simpler approach approximates the centre of the pupil image as the image of point P_c.

Under this approximation, it can be shown that p and P_c will be contained in the plane formed by incident, refracted, and normal rays, termed $\prod_p$. The corneal centre too, C_c, will be contained in this plane, since it is contained in the normal at the point of incidence. Consequently, the optical axis formed by P_c and C_c of the eye is also contained in $\prod_p$; the equation for this plane can be expressed as a function of the previously calculated p and C_c as

$$\prod_p = p \times C_c \qquad (9)$$

Stereo Solution

If a stereo system is used, one plane can be defined for each of the cameras containing the optical axis of the eye. The optical axis is calculated as the intersection of the two planes. Note that in this stereo approach the pupil centre, P_c, is not specifically calculated; instead, the optical axis of the eye is (Shih and Liu, 2004).

The function **EstimatePupilStereo** (Function 4) gives the procedure for calculating the optical axis in a stereo system.

Single-Camera Solution

In a single-camera approach, point p is back-projected and its intersection with the corneal surface calculated using Equation 5.

Once the refracted ray is calculated, P_c is estimated as the point on the refracted ray at distance $\Delta_{C_c P_c}$ from C_c (Guestrin and Eizenman, 2006).

However, in a more accurate approach, P_c cannot be calculated from p, because they are not corresponding points. A common approach, there-

Figure 4. The pupil centre is numerically calculated as a point contained in a plane perpendicular to vector and as the centre of the circle constructed from the intersections of the refracted rays with that plane

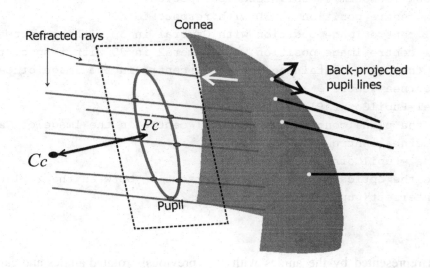

fore, is to use pupil boundary points in the image as input features, which increases the complexity of the task. Each point can be back-projected and refracted individually according to Equation 5. Once the refracted rays have been calculated as 3D lines $\{f_i\}_{i\,=1..n}$ inside the cornea (see Figure 4), pupil shape constraints can be established as follows.

The pupil is contained in plane Π and is perpendicular to C_cP_c, with a distance $\Delta_{C_cP_c}$ from C_c.

$$\frac{(C_c - P_c)}{\Delta_{C_cP_c}} \cdot (x - C_c) + \Delta_{C_cP_c} = 0 \qquad (10)$$

The intersections of the refracted lines $\{f_i\}_{i\,=1..n}$ with plane Π will generate a set of points $\{P_i\}_{i\,=1..n}$, which lie on the pupil contour. The pupil radius, r_p, can vary in the course of a tracking session because of dilation and contraction of the pupil. As the pupil changes size during the tracking session, we may use the fact that the

pupil is circular. For any two points of pupil contour, P_i and P_j, their distance to the pupil centre P_c is the same, so the circular shape constraint can be established as

$$d(P_i, P_c) = d(P_j, P_c)_{(i,j)=\{1..n\}, i \neq j} \qquad (11)$$

The location of the pupil centre, P_c, can be solved for numerically by finding the global optimum for equations 10 and 11 (Villanueva and Cabeza, 2008) (see Figure 4). Having three pupil contour points suffices for estimating a circle and therefore also finding P_c. However, in practice, using more points will reduce the effect of noise and outliers in the image and increase the accuracy of the estimation of P_c (Hennessey et al., 2006).

The function **EstimatePupilSingle** (Function 5) is the procedure used to calculate the optical axis with a single camera.

Once P_c has been calculated, the optical axis of the eye is estimated as the line connecting P_c and C_c (i.e., the position [rotation and translation] of the optical axis of the eye with respect to the camera can be calculated). The rotation of the

Function 4.

```
1 function OpAxis=EstimatePupilStereo(pc1,pc2,Cc)
2% Cc cornea centre position in 3D with respect to WCS
3% pc1 pupil centre image position with Camera1 in 3D with respect to WCS
4% pc2 pupil centre image position with Camera2 in 3D with respect to WCS
5% estimate the plane containing the pupil centre in the image of Camera1
6% and the cornea centre
7 pupilplane1=PupilCorneaPlane(pc1,Cc);
8% estimate the plane containing the pupil centre in the image of Camera2
9% and the cornea centre
10 pupilplane2=PupilCorneaPlane(pc2,Cc);
11% estimate the optical axis as the intersection between the 2 planes
12 OpAxis=Intersect(pupilplane1, pupilplane2);
13 end
```

optical axis is represented by the angles with respect to the x and y axes of the camera co-ordinate system, φ and θ. When the eye moves from one position to another, it makes a single rotation about an axis perpendicular to the plane containing the visual axis in both positions – i.e., before and after rotation (Listing's law). However, in modelling of eye position, the rotation is normally decomposed in two consecutive rotations about different axes of the WCS: (φ and θ). The same 3D position of the eye can be achieved through the use of alternative decompositions (φ and θ pairs); however, the degree of torsion can be different. Moreover, the eye orientations for different combinations of composed rotations resulting in the same final position of the optical axis can differ; these may also differ from the actual position. This fact disagrees with Donder's law (i.e., given a 3D position of the eyeball with respect to a WCS, its orientation is the same regardless of the path used to reach it). To compensate for this 'error', an additional torsion should be included in the modelling of eye movement. This rotation, termed 'false torsion' (Fry et al., 1947), is formally defined as a rotation about the visual axis of the eye, and it is a function of the previously rotated angles and can be calculated as

$$\tan\left(\frac{\alpha_v}{2}\right) = \tan\left(\frac{\theta_v}{2}\right)\tan\left(\frac{\varphi_v}{2}\right) \qquad (12)$$

where a_v is the value of the torsion around the visual axis and θ_v and φ_v are the rotation angles of the visual axis with respect to the camera. However, in practice, the 'false torsion' is approximated by a rotation about the optical axis of the eye, which considerably simplifies the modelling of the gaze tracking system as

$$\tan\left(\frac{\alpha}{2}\right) = \tan\left(\frac{\theta}{2}\right)\tan\left(\frac{\varphi}{2}\right) \qquad (13)$$

where α is the value of the torsion around the optical axis and, φ and θ are the rotation angles of the optical axis with respect to the camera.

In this manner, the eyeball orientation resulting from the geometric model of the eye agrees with the physiological orientation. Equation 1 therefore becomes

Function 5.

```
1 global points
2 function F=funPc(Pc,points)
3% the distances of all contour points to the centre should be equal
4% the number of equations can be altered using a minimum of 3
5 F=[(points(1)-Pc)-(points(2)-Pc);
6 (points(1)-Pc)-(points(3)-Pc);
7 (points(1)-Pc)-(points(4)-Pc);
8...
9 (points(k-1)-Pc)-(points(k)-Pc)];
10 end
11
12 function OpAxis=EstimatePupilSingle(pupilimage,Cc,na,nb,deltaCP,initialvalu
es)
13% find the global optima points Pc that satisfy the following constraint:
14% for each pupil contour point
15% calculate refracted ray inside the cornea, using refraction law
16 refract(i)=RefractedRay(pupilimage(i),Cc,na,nb);
17% calculate the intersections of the refracted rays with the pupil plane
18 points(i)=PupilPlaneIntersect(Cc,Pc,deltaCP,refract(i));
19% find the global optima points Pc that satisfy the following constraints
20 fsolve(@funPc,initialvalues)
21 OpAxis=Pc-Cc;
22 end
23% as initialvalues corneal centre could be selected
```

$$P \begin{pmatrix} R_\alpha R_\theta R_\varphi & C_c \\ 0 & 1 \end{pmatrix} \begin{pmatrix} \tilde{X} \\ \tilde{Y} \\ \tilde{Z} \\ 1 \end{pmatrix} \qquad (14)$$

where R_α represents the rotation matrix of the eye around itself.

Thus, the eyeball orientation (degree of torsion) can be calculated by applying the corresponding torsion (14). Once the orientation of the eyeball co-ordinate system orientation has been calculated, the angular offsets can be applied at C_c to find the visual axis (i.e. β and ν).

Note that the methods presented above require not only data about the hardware but also the subject's unique eyeball parameters; the number of parameters needed varies with the set-up selected. Optical-axis estimation does not require any user parameters if a stereo system is used, whereas r_c and $\Delta_{C_c P_c}$ are needed in a single-camera system. However, to calculate the LoS from the optical axis of the eye, β and ν are required for both stereo and single-camera systems. To this end, user calibration is normally needed.

The following figure summarises the geometry-based methods just described, using a block diagram and considering both single-camera and stereo frameworks (see Figure 5).

Figure 5. Summary of geometry-based methods using stereo and single-camera set-ups

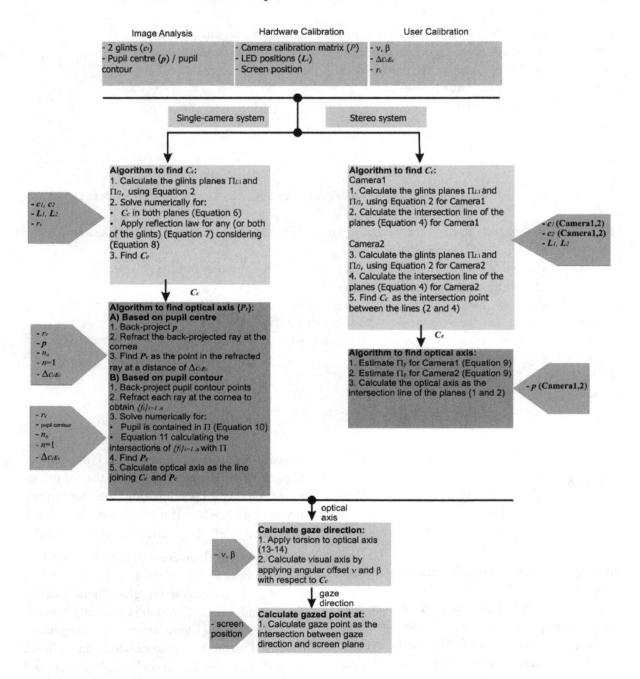

B. UNCALIBRATED SET-UPS

Set-up calibration is complex and time-consuming. Moreover, it has to be repeated every time a hardware element is moved or changed. Some methods have been designed in an attempt to eliminate the set-up calibration requirement from the gaze estimation method. These methods are considered to be within the scope of geometry-based methods because they incorporate system geometry and eyeball information to some extent, but they are normally limited to 2D gaze estimation (PoR on the screen). However, their simplicity makes these models useful in many practical applications (Hansen & Pece, 2005).

If we assume the cornea to be a planar surface, the gaze estimation problem can be approximated through projection between planes: screen–cornea–image. In this scenario, planar projective geometry can be applied.

When the user looks at the screen, we can consider the point gazed at to be projected onto the corneal plane by the same projection with which the light sources are projected onto the corneal reflections. The objective of these methods is to use projective invariants to estimate gaze. Well-known examples can be found in the literature, such as the cross-ratio method of Yoo and Chung (2005).

Four points are sufficient for estimation of the homography between two planes related by a projection. A method based on homographies between planes is described by Hansen et al. (2010) in which the positions of four LEDs on the screen is the only hardware information to be known.

INTERPOLATION METHODS

The interpolation-based methods represent an alternative to the complex derivation of geometry-based methods since no hardware information is required. In engineering, when a function is too complex to be modelled, a number of data points are sampled and a function is constructed that fits these data points. It is assumed that this function closely approximates the behaviour of the process even for unsampled points. The quality of the interpolation depends to a large extent on the function and data points selected.

Interpolation methods have been widely applied in the context of gaze estimation systems. The possible data points are normally contained in a perfectly defined area, such as a screen. Therefore, sample data points are sampled by means of regular 3 x 3 or 4 x 4 grid points covering the gazing area.

The data obtained from the sampled points (i.e., image features) are used as variables in a function to deduce image coordinates. This function is composed of image features and their possible combinations with unknown (empirically determined) coefficients and can be generally expressed as

$$P_0 = C_0 \cdot F_\theta \tag{15}$$

where, P_0 represents the gaze point (p_x, p_y), or PoR, on the screen; F_θ represents the image feature vector (glints, pupil centre, etc.) and their possible combinations; and C_0 represents the coefficient vector.

Eye images contain alternative features that can be used and combined in a function. Normally, a relative measure of pupil information and glints is used with the assumption that this compensates for any head movements. This is not formally true, but it results in functions that are more tolerant of head movement than those based exclusively on pupil centre or glint. One of the most well-known features used is the pupil centre – corneal reflection vector, the PCCR. This can be easily obtained from the image as $p - c$. If more glints are used, the number of possible features increases and more versatile functions can be constructed.

Another important issue to resolve is the function to be used; as any function can be approximated by a polynomial, polynomials are normally used, with quadratic functions employed most often. There is no function accepted as yielding the best performance. A review by Cerrolaza et al. (2008) presents a classification of possible functions, according to the possible image features, degrees of polynomials, and number of terms, among other elements. For the present work, it was concluded that there is no unique function that excels among the rest, but general conclusions about interpolation functions for gaze estimation are given.

Once the function is selected, the unknown coefficient vector needs to be determined, to generate a completely defined function. To this end, sample data are compiled and the coefficients deduced. These coefficients are different for each user and are calculated by means of a user-calibration process consisting of asking the user to gaze at certain known points on the screen (P_0). These points are normally placed in a 3 x 3 or 4 x 4 uniform grid of points covering the screen that constitute the sample data for the interpolation function.

HEAD-MOUNTED GAZE TRACKERS

Head-mounted gaze trackers, in contrast to remote systems, are based on mounting the camera on the user's head while pointing it at the eye. Most often, the camera is attached to a helmet or a pair of glasses to keep it fixed with respect to the head. As the user might have to wear the headgear for a long time, physical limitations associated with the hardware that can be used should be taken into account. For example, the cameras used in head-mounted systems are usually lightweight, to make the user more comfortable while wearing the equipment. These limitations have an impact on eye tracking performance. For example, lighter and smaller cameras usually offer lower frame rates and lower resolution than the cameras used in remote eye tracking.

Remote tracker systems are based on a camera placed on the desktop or screen in front of the user. Therefore, the head can move with respect to the camera. Depending on the gaze estimation technique employed, the estimated screen coordinates may be affected by head movements (i.e., when the system is not head-pose-invariant). In head-mounted gaze tracking systems, the camera is mounted on the user's head. On the assumption that the camera is firmly attached, the relative position of camera and head is fixed, meaning that, ideally, head-mounted systems don't need to model head movements. In practice, however, the headgear used to mount the camera may slip as the user moves; therefore, robust gaze estimation methods are required.

A fully (set-up-) calibrated remote system requires the relative positions of camera, light sources, and screen to be known. In remote systems, where all components are fixed, these measurements need to be calculated only once. Conversely, in head-mounted systems, the location of the camera changes from user to user, and also other camera parameters, such as the focus, may need to be modified. Therefore, these systems are usually uncalibrated, and interpolation methods are often used to estimate gaze. Depending on whether infrared light is used, the pupil centre or the iris centre is used. To improve robustness against slippage, one or more corneal reflections can be used to normalise the pupil or iris centre.

A few head-mounted systems have been described in the literature. A standard head-mounted system is presented by Babcock and Pelz (2004) that uses two cameras, one pointing at the eye and a second to record the scene in front of the user. Both cameras are mounted on the frame of a pair of security glasses. An infrared LED is also located off-axis of the eye tracking camera, providing a corneal reflection. Calibration is performed by means of nine points projected by a laser, allowing for a mapping from eye position to scene camera in post-session analysis. Li et al. (2006) followed a similar approach to hardware implementation in their construction of a head-mounted eye tracker called openEyes. Their system works in real time, and all of the hardware diagrams and software source code were made publicly available.

A straightforward application of head-mounted gaze tracking is interaction via head-mounted displays where other interaction is needed for additional tasks or when using a mouse or a keyboard for interaction might be difficult. Gaze interaction has potential to provide a convenient, hands-free pointing technique.

FIXATION ESTIMATION

Our eyes are constantly in motion (Salvucci and Goldberg, 2000). As we look around, they perform different movements so that the interesting parts of the scene are sensed by the fovea. Basic eye movements can be divided into three categories: fixations, saccades, and smooth pursuit movements. A fixation occurs when we stare at an object of interest and is usually considered to have a duration of at least 100 ms. It is during a fixation that we gather data from our surroundings. A saccade is a rapid ballistic movement that occurs between two fixations and which allows the eye to reposition itself so that the object of interest is projected onto the fovea. During a saccade, the eye rotates at over 300 degree/sec. Smooth pursuit movements take place when our eyes track a moving target.

In most video-based gaze tracking systems, the estimated gaze coordinates suffer from jitter when the user is fixating on a single point. This noise has two sources: inaccuracy in the estimation of eye features, such as the pupil centre or corneal reflections, and small eye movements that occur during a fixation, such as microsaccades and tremors. As a consequence of this noise, the pointer does not remain steady during a fixation, which might distract the user.

Because of this inherent noise in the estimated gaze coordinates, gaze-based interaction may benefit from smoothing of the cursor position using the information from the last N images rather than only the last one, thus reducing the jitter and making the cursor more stable. This is usually achieved by means of a fixation-detection algorithm that can differentiate between fixations and saccades. When a fixation is detected, the cursor position is averaged over time, reducing the apparent noise perceived by the user. Once the fixation is finished and a saccade is detected, the algorithm stops smoothing the cursor position, to avoid the 'lag-behind' effect.

The literature regarding algorithms for real-time fixation identification is scarce. Salvucci and Goldberg, (2000) presented a taxonomy of fixation-detection algorithms based on spatial and temporal characteristics. They classified the algorithms according to five criteria: velocity, dispersion, area, whether or not the algorithm is duration-sensitive, and whether it is locally adaptive. They proposed five representative algorithms, from which the main facts are described below.

Velocity-Based Algorithms

Velocity-based algorithms use eye velocity as the criterion to identify a fixation, proceeding from the fact that during a fixation the eye has a low velocity while during a saccade the velocity is very high. For each given pair of coordinates, the speed is calculated with respect to the previous point. A simple threshold is used to classify the point as belonging to a fixation or to a saccade: if the velocity is below the threshold, it is considered a fixation; otherwise, it is considered a saccade. The value of this threshold depends on the characteristics of the gaze tracker and, more specifically, on the amount of noise in the estimated gaze coordinates: higher noise levels result in higher speeds during a fixation, and the threshold must be adjusted to account for the noise.

Dispersion-Based Algorithms

Dispersion-based algorithms use the spatial information of the cursor location to identify a fixation. When a fixation occurs, all of the estimated gaze coordinates are clustered together in a small region. By specifying a maximum allowed distance between points, one can identify consecutive samples as belonging to the same fixation. Usually, a minimum duration of 100 to 200 ms is considered before assumption that a fixation occurs. As with the velocity-based algorithms, the maximum dispersion threshold depends on the noise level of the gaze tracking system.

Area-Based Algorithms

Area-based algorithms identify fixations only when they occur within specified regions of interest – for example, interactive elements such as buttons or icons. Points outside these target areas are labelled as saccades. A benefit of this method is that when a fixation is detected in a region of interest, the cursor can be placed at the centre of the region, removing all of the jitter coming from the noisy gaze coordinates. However, the fixation-detection algorithm must be supplied with the locations of the regions of interest in every application, and this information might not be provided by the operating system.

LIST OF SYMBOLS

The symbols used in this chapter are listed below.

r_c: Corneal radius
r_p: Pupil radius
P_c: Pupil centre
C_c: Corneal centre
E_c: Eye centre
L: LED position
β: Horizontal angular offset of optical and visual axes
v: Vertical angular offset of optical and visual axes
c: Glint in the image
p: Pupil centre in the image

CONCLUSION

In recent years, geometry-based gaze estimation has been one of the most challenging aspects of eye tracking technology. The field has attracted numerous researchers, and the number of published works has increased considerably. Although interpolation-based methods provide a simple and valid framework, the most sought-after objective is to construct robust gaze estimation methods providing head movement tolerance and minimal set-up calibration requirements. In the near future, gaze estimation should also consider the orientation of the technology toward Web-camera-based technologies in which the resolution of the eye image decreases and for which new gaze estimation methods are required.

REFERENCES

Babcock, J. B., & Pelz, J. B. (2004). Building a lightweight eyetracking headgear [sic]. *Proceedings of the Symposium on Eye Tracking Research & Applications (ETRA'04)* (pp. 109–114). San Antonio, TX, US: ACM Press.

Cerrolaza, J., Villanueva, A., & Cabeza, R. (2008). Taxonomic study of polynomial regressions applied to the calibration of video-oculographic systems. *Proceedings of the Symposium on Eye Tracking Research & Applications (ETRA'08)* (pp. 259–266). Savannah, GA, US: ACM Press.

Fry, G. A., Treleaven, C. L., Walsh, R., Higgins, E. L., & Radde, C. A. (1947). Definition and measurement of torsion. *American Journal of Optometry and Archives of American Academy of Optometry, 24*, 329–334.

Guestrin, E., & Eizenman, M. (2006). General theory of remote gaze estimation using the pupil center and corneal reflections. *IEEE Transactions on Bio-Medical Engineering, 53*(8), 1124–1133. doi:10.1109/TBME.2005.863952

Hansen, D. W., & Ji, Q. (2010). In the eye of the beholder: A survey of models for eyes and gaze. *IEEE Transactions on Pattern Analysis and Machine Intelligence, 32*(3), 478–500. doi:10.1109/TPAMI.2009.30

Hansen, D. W., & Pece, A. E. (2005). Eye tracking in the wild. *Computer Vision and Image Understanding, 98*(1), 155–181. doi:10.1016/j.cviu.2004.07.013

Hansen, D. W., San Agustin, J., & Villanueva, A. (2010). Homography normalization for robust gaze estimation in uncalibrated setups. *Proceedings of the Symposium on Eye Tracking Research & Applications (ETRA'10)* (pp. 13–20). Austin, TX, US: ACM Press.

Hennessey, C., Noureddin, B., & Lawrence, P. (2006). A single camera eye-gaze tracking system with free head motion. *Proceedings of the Symposium on Eye Tracking Research & Applications (ETRA'06)* (pp. 87–94). San Diego, CA, US: ACM Press.

Li, D., Babcock, J., & Parkhurst, D. J. (2006). OpenEyes: A low-cost head-mounted eye tracking solution. *Proceedings of the Symposium on Eye Tracking Research & Applications (ETRA'06)* (pp. 95–100). San Diego, CA, US: ACM Press.

Salvucci, D. D., & Goldberg, J. H. (2000). Identifying fixations and saccades in eye-tracking protocols. *Proceedings of the Symposium on Eye Tracking Research & Applications (ETRA'00)* (pp. 71–78). Palm Beach Gardens, FL, US: ACM Press.

Shih, S. W., & Liu, J. (2004). A novel approach to 3-D gaze tracking using stereo cameras. *IEEE Transactions on Systems Man, and Cybernetics. Part B, 34*(1), 234–245.

Villanueva, A., & Cabeza, R. (2008). A novel gaze estimation system with one calibration point. *IEEE Transactions on Systems, Man, and Cybernetics. Part B, 38*(4), 1123–1138.

Yoo, D. H., & Chung, M. J. (2005). A novel nonintrusive eye gaze estimation using cross-ratio under large head motion. *Computer Vision and Image Understanding, 98*(1), 25–51. doi:10.1016/j.cviu.2004.07.011

Chapter 22
Eye Tracker Hardware Design

Gintautas Daunys
Šiauliai University, Lithuania

ABSTRACT

Designing an eye tracker involves choosing the most appropriate hardware components. A variety of hardware components are available for building an eye tracker, but it is not obvious which ones are the most appropriate. The common factors to consider are: sensitivity to low light, conditions, camera speed, camera fidelity, weight, the working distance of the user, light emission levels (for safety), and cost. This chapter discusses the hardware components used in most eye trackers. It is our hope that the overview provides sufficient understanding of the hardware components that it could be used to make your own eye tracker.

INTRODUCTION

Designing an eye tracker involves choosing the most appropriate hardware components. A variety of hardware components are available for building an eye tracker, but it is not obvious which ones are the most appropriate. Common factors to consider are:

- Sensitivity to low light conditions
- Camera speed
- Camera fidelity
- Weight
- The working distance of the user
- Light emission levels (for safety)
- Costs

Manufacturers of commercial eye trackers do not provide detailed information about their hardware, but their choices most likely aim to optimise certain (perhaps unknown) goals. High accuracy under head movement conditions and minimisation of user calibration are usually optimised. By contrast, researchers exploring low-cost eye

DOI: 10.4018/978-1-61350-098-9.ch022

tracking solutions publish their hardware selection (Fritzer, Droege, & Paulus, 2005; Hansen & Pece, 2005; Hansen, San Agustin, & Villanueva, 2010; San Augustin et al., 2010; Winfield, Li, Babcock, & Parkhurst, 2005). However, these systems often have different parameters to optimise – for example, being designed for minimal price and increased flexibility. Each system has its hardware design choices that influence the usability and price of the system. This chapter discusses the hardware components used in most eye trackers. It is our hope that the overview provides sufficient understanding of the hardware components that it could be used to make your own eye tracker.

CAMERA

Image Sensor

The purpose of the image sensor is to convert optical information into an electrical signal. Many technical features of the camera arise from the image sensor. For example, the sensor material has significant influence on the performance of the sensor. Almost all image sensors are made from silicon, but a few sensors used for infrared light sensing are made from other semiconductors, such as indium antimonide (InSb) or indium gallium arsenide (InGaAs). This chapter only focuses on sensors made from silicon, as they are sensitive to photons in the visible and near-infrared spectra.

There are two methods for scanning the pixel matrix: progressive scan and interlaced scan. During a progressive scan, all pixels are read in order. In an interlaced scan, only every second line of the pixel matrix is read. In the latter case, a frame consists of two fields: a first field with odd lines and a second field with even lines. Interlacing was a convenient feature for old analogue interfaces and video displays because it reduced flicker, but it is not particularly convenient for computer vision applications. When interlaced images are used, image analysis can either be done for every field (even and odd) or combine the two fields into a single frame. Using every field in sequence results in reduction of the vertical resolution by a factor of two. Using the combined fields reduces the temporal resolution by a factor of two but increases the spatial resolution. However, a combined odd + even image may have artefacts due to the two images being obtained at different times. For example, when eye image are registered during eye movement, the differences between odd and even lines can be significant. The subsequent processing may therefore fail to localise the eye in the image, as a result of severe distortions.

There are two rival types of image sensors: CCD (*Charge-Coupled Device*) and CMOS (*Complementary Metal-Oxide-Semiconductor*). CCD or CMOS image sensors are pixelated metal-oxide-semiconductor devices. The sensing part of the sensor is an array of photodetectors. The sensors accumulate the signal charge in each photodetector, proportional to the local illumination intensity. When the exposure is complete, a CCD transfers each charge packet sequentially to a common output structure, which converts the charge to a voltage, buffers it, and sends it off-chip. Every voltage value, obtained from a charge packet, corresponds to pixel brightness. The main functional difference of a CMOS imager is such that the charge-to-voltage conversion takes place in each pixel instead of through the use of sequential charge transfers. The absence, or the ability to create signals, of colour information allows for either **black and white** or **colour sensors**. Colour sensors are covered by micro-filters of three types, each with maximal sensitivity in specific wavelength regions (red, green, or blue). All of the micro-filters when viewed together as a single object are called a Bayer filter (see Figure 1). The figure shows that there are twice as many photodetectors for green colour as for red or blue, to enhance visualisation. However, this choice creates additional constraints when one is processing the images.

Figure 1. Bayer filter

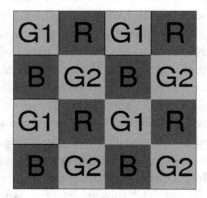

Image resolution characterises the size of the image sensor array. Typically, sensor resolution is expressed as the number of pixels in the horizontal and in the vertical direction (length and height). A higher resolution often means better image quality but may be technologically challenging to produce. Increasing the number of photodetectors either requires the chip (sensor) to become larger or decrease the size of each photodetector. Larger chips with more photodetectors increase complexity and manufacturing costs. Smaller photodetectors must have increased sensitivity if they are to be able to capture the same amount of light; otherwise, noise can offset the expected benefits. Another issue is that higher-resolution sensors need more storage space to store and transmission capacity to transfer the

data acquired. Common resolution standards are listed in Table 1.

Interpolating the pixels can increase the resolution. However, interpolation does not add any new information to the image; it just increases the quantity of data. A colour image consists of three brightness values for each pixel (e.g., red, green, and blue components [RGB]). Interpolation is often used to obtain the same number of pixels in the image as pixels in the image sensor. In interpolation, the intensities of colour components are obtained through averaging of neighbouring values.

A parameter related to resolution is the image sensor format. Common formats and their image geometries are given in Table 2.

Sensitivity and dynamic range. There are several characteristics of a sensor that together determine how appropriate it is for eye tracking (for instance, how sensitive it is to specific wavelengths). The following paragraphs provide common descriptors of the performance of a given camera sensor and its capability. Some image sensors are characterised by their sensitivity, which is defined by the voltage generated for a specific light exposure. The output voltage depends on the chip construction and its signal conditioning stage. A more objective evaluation of sensor sensitivity is obtained when the spectral characteristics are examined in combination with the

Table 1. Commonly used resolutions of image sensors

Abbreviation	Name	Width, pixels	Height, pixels	Number of pixels
QCIF	Quarter Common Intermediate Format	176	144	25,300
QVGA	Quarter Video Graphics Array	320	240	76,800
CIF	Common Intermediate Format	352	288	101,400
VGA	Video Graphics Array	640	480	307,200
MPEG2 ML	MPEG2 Main Level	720	576	414,720
SVGA	Super Video Graphics Array	800	600	480,000
XGA	Extended Graphics Array	1,024	768	786,400
720p or i	High Definition TV with 720 lines	1,280	720	921,600
1080p or i	High Definition TV with 1080 lines	1,920	1,080	2,073,600

Table 2. Geometry with various image sensors

Sensor format	Height, mm	Width, mm
1"	9.6	12.8
2/3"	6.4	8.8
1/2"	4.8	6.4
1/3"	3.2	4.8
1/4"	2.4	3.2
1/6"	1.6	2.4

dynamic range. The dynamic range is defined by the ratio between the maximum light the photodetector can accept (saturation level) and the minimum needed to provide a signal (noise level). The dynamic range is described in either decibels or the effective number of bits. The last way aids in selection of the right number of bits for pixel values representation.

CCDs have an advantage of about a factor of two in comparison to CMOS when the dynamic range is taken into account. The reason is that CCDs benefit from having less on-chip circuitry, an inherent tolerance to bus capacitance variations, and common output amplifiers with transistor geometries that can be easily adapted for minimal noise. Even external coddling of the image sensor through cooling, better optics, higher resolution, or adapted off-chip electronics cannot make CMOS sensors equivalent to CCDs.

Different technological innovations have been made for increased sensitivity. The examples from Sony Corporation are the HAD and Super HAD structures for photodetectors. A recent breakthrough that provides extended sensitivity in the infrared spectrum is back-side illumination (BSI) technology. Hence, mention of the BSI feature on a camera data sheet can mean benefits for your tracker in terms of camera selection, especially for near-infrared tracking using CMOS sensors.

Windowing and shuttering are two additional parameters that characterise image sensors. Windowing applies only to CMOS sensors and is the capability to read a selected region of interest

(ROI) from the image sensor. Windowing allows fewer pieces of data to be transferred from the image sensor and, thereby, an increased frame rate. Shuttering controls the duration of light exposure of the pixels, in which time the conversion of light photons into a charge in pixels occurs. A longer shutter time ensures that more light is passed to the sensor. However, these slow shutter speeds are problematic if the target moves too rapidly in comparison to the shutter speed. During a saccade, the eye moves rapidly and a long exposure may therefore create blurring in the direction of movement. Hence, the exposure time, frame rate, and illumination conditions must be optimised simultaneously. More flexible electronic shuttering is possible only for CMOS image sensors.

INTERFACE

Image data from a camera then will be transferred via an interface to the computer. The most important requirements for the interface involve transfer rate, transfer types, latency, errors or distortions, and whether it can supply power for cameras. The transfer rate must be high, to ensure that all frames are transferred to the computer. Eye trackers require a real-time image streaming interface for interactive purposes, and one should therefore be careful, since some camcorders or digital still cameras do not offer real-time streaming. Even interfaces with high transfer rates are not necessarily appropriate if they do not deliver the images sufficiently quickly. Almost all Web cams, camcorders, and digital still cameras transmit compressed images to allow for fast image transfer. Some compression methods, such as JPG format, throw away image information (lossy compression) in favour of high compression rates. Lossy compression techniques may introduce image distortions that can influence subsequent image processing but may not be visible to the naked eye.

Cameras can be either analogue or digital. Only a computer equipped with a framegrabber can acquire images from an analogue camera. The framegrabber transforms the analogue signal into a digital image frame by frame. Framegrabbers are connected to a computer either as a PCI extension card for desktop computers or as pluggable 'PC cards' for notebooks. Framegrabbers are usually limited to the resolution of standard television (e.g., 720 x 576 for PAL). As they are directly connected to the internal system bus, they usually do not need to compress the images. Analogue signals can be distorted or interfered with by noise when being transferred from the camera to the framegrabber. Cameras with an analogue interface are still used for eye trackers because they are relatively cheap. The drawback of analogue interfaces is the need to use a framegrabber and the added noise created since the signal has to be transferred through a cable. Digital signals should arrive without distortion and are therefore also more common in recent eye trackers. The features of the image sensor and the interface are the main criteria in selection of a camera of machine vision type. The cameras of other domains have their specific properties.

Analogue interfaces. Analogue interfaces are inherited from analogue television. There are four main standards: CCIR, PAL, EIA-170, and NTSC. CCIR and EIA-170 are monochrome (black and white) video standards, while PAL and NTSC are colour video standards. All analogue standards deliver interlaced video. CCIR and PAL have a frame rate of 25 Hz with 625 lines per image. Forty-nine lines are used for synchronisation, which results in 576 lines per image frame and 288 lines in every field. The pixels are sampled every 68 ns. This leads to 768 pixels per line. These two formats, therefore, have a resolution of 768 x 576. By contrast, EIA-170 and NTSC have a frame rate of 30 Hz with 525 lines per image, and 45 lines are used for synchronisation. The image frames under these standards have 480 lines, so there are 240 lines in every field. Pixels are sampled every 82 ns. This leads to 640 pixels

per line. Therefore, the format's resolution can be described as 640 x 480 (VGA).

There are several digital interfaces that can be applied for eye trackers. The most common are USB, FireWire, GigE Vision, and Camera Link.

USB (Universal Serial Bus) was designed to replace old serial interfaces (e.g., those based on the RS-232C standard) and is found in most recent computers for interfaces with peripheral devices (e.g., mouse, scanner, Web camera, printer, and external drives). Cameras based on USB are very popular and are core to many low-cost eye trackers. The USB interface has a master–slave architecture, wherein the computer is the master device and the connected device is the slave. This means that the host controller initiates all transfers. USB supports 5 V voltage and can deliver up to 500 mA of electrical current for a device. The USB standard defines four transfer rates:

- Low speed (LS), at 1.5 Mbps, USB 1.0
- Full speed (FS), at 12 Mbps, USB 1.1
- High speed (HS), at 480 Mbps, USB 2.0
- Super speed (SS), at 5.0 Gbps, USB 3.0

There are currently many cameras with FS and HS USB transfer capabilities. So far, only one camera has been based on the USB 3.0 standard; however, this is likely to change within the foreseeable future. The bus speeds describe the rate at which information travels on the bus. Note that all peripherals share the same bus. In addition to data, the bus must carry status, control, and error-checking information. Therefore, the rate of data transfer that an individual peripheral can expect will be less than the bus speed. The theoretical maximum rate for a single data transfer is about 53 MB/sec with high-speed USB and 1.2 MB/sec with full-speed USB. Each image can be, at most, about 2 MB when high-speed USB is used at a frame rate of 25 fps.

FireWire (IEEE-1394). FireWire (IEEE 1394a) is a standard that provides a similar bandwidth to that of USB 2.0 (nominal 400 Mbps) and has been the typical connection for digital video cameras. The newer standard IEEE 1394b allows for 800 Mbps. FireWire has a higher degree of standardisation than does USB. Many computers include built-in FireWire ports, and, as with USB, there is no need for an additional framegrabber. If the computer does not have a built-in FireWire port, then a PCI or Cardbus FireWire interface can easily be installed. There is also a standardised software interface for cameras, called DCAM or IIDC, in addition to the standardised hardware interface. This interface standard facilitates use in which any compliant driver can operate any compliant camera and therefore reduces integration problems and provides true plug-and-play operability. FireWire cameras are quite common for both commercial and low-cost solutions.

GigE Vision. Gigabit Ethernet, also called GigE, is a serial computer network standard that allows for one-gigabit-per-second communication bandwidth. GigE is relatively low-cost, because of its widespread use in computer networking hardware. To support high-bandwidth data transfer, the GigE Vision standard is based on the User Datagram Protocol (UDP), since it uses ports to allow application-to-application connections. The GigE Vision Control Protocol (GVCP) and the GigE Vision Streaming protocol (GVSP) have been added to GigE Vision to overcome the challenges with UDP as well as to add plug-and-play features. The GVCP is an application-layer protocol that relies on UDP IPv4. The main task of the GVCP is to add mechanisms that guarantee the reliability of image transmission. The GVSP allows applications to receive image data, image information, and other information from a device through the LAN cable. The main benefit of GigE Vision is high transfer bandwidth.

Camera Link. The Camera Link protocol was developed specifically for high-speed digital image transfer from camera to framegrabber. The standard defines three configurations, with different transfer rates:

- Basic with maximal bandwidth, 2.04 Gbps
- Medium, 4.08 Gbps
- Full, 5.44 Gbps

The interface is based on National Semiconductors Channel Link technology and uses its serialiser chips.

In the case of Camera Link Basic configuration, it uses one serialiser; Medium configuration employs two serialisers, and Full configuration uses three serialisers.

The Camera Link interface uses a standard cable ending with two 26-pin MDR connectors. Because computers do not have a Camera Link connector, a framegrabber is necessary for acquiring video data.

OPTICAL SYSTEM

The purpose of using a lens in eye trackers is to get a focused close-up image of the eye. The lenses are complex systems consisting of simple lenses and mechanical and/or electromechanical mechanisms for controlling these. The main parameters for selection of a lens are focal length (F), f-number, and the type of mounting.

Focal Length

The focal length may intuitively be understood as how much the lens zooms. The focal length therefore determines how far the user has to be from the eye tracker camera in order for the system to obtain clear images. In this context, it is useful to know about the rear focal point and the front and rear nodal points. The rear focal point (RFP in Figure 2) of an optical system has the property that rays entering the system parallel to the optical axis are focused such that they pass through the rear focal point.

The front and rear nodal points (FNP and RNP in Figure 2) have the property that a ray aimed at one of them will be refracted by the lens such that

Figure 2. Image formation and the cardinal points of the lens

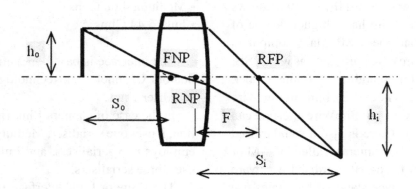

it appears to have come from the other, and with the same angle with respect to the optical axis.

The focal length, *F*, is the distance between the rear nodal point and the rear focal point. The focal length can be derived from equation

$$\frac{1}{S_o} + \frac{1}{S_i} = \frac{1}{F} \qquad (1)$$

where S_o refers to the distance from the object to the front nodal point and S_i refers to that from the rear nodal point to the plane where the image of the object is best focused. The focal length can therefore be determined through

$$F = \frac{S_o S_i}{S_o + S_i}. \qquad (2)$$

and can be used to determine the optimal focal length when one knows the distance from the eye to the front nodal point and the distance from the rear focal point to a plane of an image sensor.

Aperture, F-Number, and Image Depth

Aperture is a parameter that depends on the opening of the lens and describes the degree of collimation of the light rays entering the lens. Light rays become more collimated when the opening is small and therefore forms a sharp image. When the opening is larger, the image becomes more blurred. The aperture often is characterised by the f-number (FN). The f-number is a function of the focal length and the diameter of the lens opening, D_{op}:

$$FN = \frac{F}{D_{op}} \qquad (3)$$

Larger apertures therefore have lower f-numbers. Lenses with larger apertures are described as being 'faster' because the shutter speed can be made faster for the same exposure. Additionally, a smaller aperture means that objects can be in focus over a wider range of distances, a concept also termed the depth of field. In the case of an eye tracker, we obtain wider depth of field when we use a lens with a higher f-number. However, in that situation, the light-gathering area becomes smaller and we need to increase the lighting or exposure time in order to obtain an image with a wide enough dynamic range.

LEDS, FILTERS, AND CAMERA MOUNTS

IR light is used in most eye and gaze trackers. Often, that light comes from LEDs. Cameras are able to capture light of many wavelengths; however, not all wavelengths are relevant for eye and gaze trackers. Filters are used to attenuate the wavelength ranges of uncontrolled light sources (e.g., the monitor or sunlight) while retaining those wavelengths that are of use (e.g., from the LEDs).

LEDs have particular spectral characteristics such as their peak wavelength, the radiation angle, and the output as a function of the wavelength (spectral characteristic). For the LED shown in Figure 3, the peak wavelength is 880 nm. This wavelength is considered a good choice for silicon-based image sensors. The distance between the two points where the characteristic curve drops to 50% of the maximal value is called the bandwidth.

A filter is properly characterised by the transmittance spectral characteristic. Every filter reflects some of the incident light; therefore, the transmittance is lower than 100% even in the pass region. The main parameter of the filter is cut-on wavelength, which separates the filter's pass region from its stop region.

There are some standards for mounting the lens on the camera, with the most common being the C-mount and CS-mount. C-mount lenses provide a male thread, which mates with a female thread on the camera. The distance from the lens mount flange to the focal plane is 17.526 mm for a C-mount, while the distance for the CS-mount is 12.52 mm. Other parameters are identical. A C-mount lens can be mounted on a CS camera by means of a 5 mm extension ring.

ADDITIONAL HARDWARE

Eye trackers are usually deployed with a standard PC, and, therefore, the tracking software and the application share the resources of the computer. An

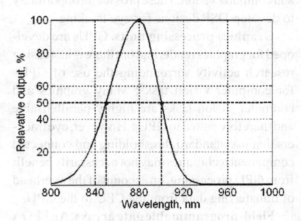

Figure 3. Spectral characteristic of an LED

alternative approach is to perform image analysis on a separate computer by using, for example, the following:

- General-purpose processors (GPPs)
- Digital signal processor (DSP)
- Graphics processing unit (GPU)
- Field-programmable gate array (FPGA)
- Smart camera chips or image processors

General-purpose processors are those found in most standard computers. A GPP has a fixed instruction set and expects a program that is executed in a sequential manner. In their features, GPPs are nearest the CPU, processors used in PCs. Of course, modern CPUs have multiple pipelines; therefore, they process multiple instructions concurrently. Two computers may be connected through a network connection, which can solve some of the problems with shared resources but introduces other issues, such as delays and added costs.

Digital signal processors. A DSP's instruction set is optimised for digital processing of signals, where the main operations are multiplication and accumulation. DSPs have deep pipelining and expect a linear program flow with infrequent conditional jumps. Most manufacturers offer DSP development boards specific to image processing and computer vision. These provide an opportunity to develop DSP designs for eye tracking.

Graphics processing units. GPUs are developed for graphics rendering, but there is increasing research activity surrounding the use of GPUs for computer vision tasks. Many graphics and computer vision tasks are highly parallelisable and therefore suited to GPUs. However, eye trackers that use standard thresholding and connected component techniques may not necessarily benefit from GPU processing, on account of the overhead of transferring data from the CPU to the GPU.

Field-programmable gate arrays. An FPGA is a semiconductor device in which the actual logic circuit can be modified, allowing for high degrees of parallel processing. An FPGA is more flexible than a processor is, since FPGAs allow for creation of a processor dedicated to a specific application. Eye trackers based on FPGAs have been described by Amir et al. (2005) and Kolodko et al. (2005).

Smart camera chips and image processors. A limitation of FPGAs is that only a few of their elements can be used in specific designs. An image sensor can be combined with electronics for image processing. using an ASIC (application-specific integrated circuit). However, this is cost-effective only for large production volumes.

DYNAMIC VISION SENSOR

Dynamic vision sensors are an attempt to create a new type of image sensor. Conventional image sensors see the world as a series of frames. Successive frames contain enormous amounts of redundant information, necessitating more memory access, RAM, disk space, energy consumption, computation power, and use of time. In addition, each frame imposes the same exposure time on every pixel, making it difficult to deal with scenes containing very dark and very bright regions. The dynamic vision sensor is inspired by the human visual system. Instead of wasteful sending of entire images at fixed frame rates, only the local pixel-level changes caused by movement in a scene are transmitted, at the time when they occur. The result is a stream of events at microsecond time resolution, equivalent to or better than conventional high-speed vision sensors running at thousands of frames per second. Dynamic range from a typical value of 50 dB can be increased to 120 dB. For more information, see the work of Liu and Delbrük (2010).

DISCUSSION

There are many parameters and design issues to take into account when choosing hardware suitable for an eye tracker (which camera, how far the user usually is from the eye tracker, costs, weight, etc). This chapter has provided basic knowledge of the essential hardware components used in current eye trackers. New technological developments (increasing an image sensor's number of pixels, back-side illumination of an image sensor chip, dynamic vision sensors, and GigE Vision and Camera Link interfaces) may allow for better eye trackers. There is no doubt that hardware will become faster and smaller, and it is therefore obvious that eye trackers are likely also to follow these trends. However, it would be interesting to see whether new hardware can alter the way eye trackers are built, so that they can become more versatile, inexpensive, and more mobile.

REFERENCES

Amir, A., Zimet, L., Sangiovanni-Vincentelli, A., & Kao, S. (2005). An embedded system for an eye-detection sensor. *Computer Vision and Image Understanding*, *98*(1), 104–123. doi:10.1016/j.cviu.2004.07.009

Fritzer, F., Droege, D., & Paulus, D. (2005). Gaze tracking with inexpensive cameras. *Proceedings of the 1st Conference on Communication by Gaze Interaction* (*COGAIN 2005*) (pp. 10–11). Copenhagen, Denmark: IT University of Copenhagen. Retrieved from the COGAIN website: http://www.cogain.org/conference

Hansen, D. W., & Pece, A. E. (2005). Eye tracking in the wild. *Computer Vision and Image Understanding*, *98*(1), 155–181. doi:10.1016/j.cviu.2004.07.013

Hansen, D. W., San Agustin, J., & Villanueva, A. (2010). Homography normalization for robust gaze estimation in uncalibrated setups. *Proceedings of the 2010 Symposium on Eye Tracking Research & Applications* (*ETRA '10*) (pp. 13–20). New York, NY: ACM.

Kolodko, J., Suzuki, S., & Harashima, F. (2005). Eye-gaze tracking: An approach to pupil tracking targeted to FPGAs. *Proceedings of the IEEE/RSJ International Conference on Intelligent Robots and Systems* (*IROS 2005*) (pp. 344–349).

Liu, S. C., & Delbrück, T. (2010). Neuromorphic sensory systems. *Current Opinion in Neurobiology*, *20*(3), 288–295. doi:10.1016/j.conb.2010.03.007

San Agustin, J., Skovsgaard, H., Mollenbach, E., Barret, M., Tall, M., Hansen, D. W., & Hansen, J. P. (2010). Evaluation of a low-cost open-source gaze tracker. *Proceedings of the 2010 Symposium on Eye-Tracking Research & Applications* (*ETRA '10*) (pp. 77–80). New York, NY, USA: ACM.

Winfield, D., Li, D., Babcock, J., & Parkhurst, D. J. (2005). *Towards an open-hardware open-software toolkit for robust low-cost eye tracking in HCI applications* (Technical report ISU-HCI-2005-04). Iowa, USA: Iowa State University, Department of Psychology.

Chapter 23
Safety Issues and Infrared Light

Fiona Mulvey
IT University of Copenhagen, Denmark

Arantxa Villanueva
Public University of Navarre, Spain

David Sliney
CIE International Commission on Illumination, USA

Robert Lange
Technical University of Dresden, Germany

Michael Donegan
ACE Centre, UK

ABSTRACT

Infrared light is the most common choice for illumination of the eye in current eye trackers, usually produced via IR light-emitting diodes (LEDs). This chapter provides an overview of the potential hazards of over-exposure to infrared light, the safety standards currently in place, configurations and lighting conditions employed by various eye tracking systems, the basics of measurement of IR light sources in eye trackers, and special considerations associated with continuous exposure in the case of gaze control for communication and disabled users. It should be emphasised that any eye tracker intended for production should undergo testing by qualified professionals at a recognised test house, in a controlled laboratory setting. However, some knowledge of the measurement procedures and issues involved should be useful to designers and users of eye tracking systems.

DOI: 10.4018/978-1-61350-098-9.ch023

INTRODUCTION: EYE TRACKERS AND INFRARED LIGHT

Infrared light is the most common choice for illumination of the eye in current eye trackers, usually produced via IR light-emitting diodes (LEDs). As we previously discussed, IR light is particularly suited to eye tracking because it is not visible to the human eye and is therefore comfortable for the user. IR light doesn't cause the pupil to contract and can also provide an image with sufficient contrast and quality for image analysis. Since levels of exposure to light can have various effects on the health of the structures of the eye, all light-emitting and eye protection products are subject to international safety standards. Infrared light levels must fall within safe exposure limits, set according to type and intended use. These levels are decided upon and continuously updated by international standardising bodies. In this chapter, we will look at how light affects the eye, potential hazards, rudimentary measurement of IR sources in eye trackers, and currently applicable standards. In the case of eye tracking, the usual hardware set-up involves one or more IR LEDs directed toward the eyes. These can be mounted on or beside the eye cameras but may be elsewhere or additionally mounted beside head cameras. Light source position, number, brightness, size, and distance from the eye all have a bearing on the safety calculations, so safety calculations must be made for all possible set-up variations, with worst-case scenarios assumed (e.g., the shortest possible distance between the eye and camera during normal operation) and with a single-fault criterion (i.e., assuming at least one failure or fault within the system).

This chapter provides an overview of the potential hazards of over-exposure to infrared light, the safety standards currently in place, configurations and lighting conditions employed by various eye tracking systems, the basics of measurement of IR light sources in eye trackers, and special considerations associated with continuous exposure in the case of gaze control for communication and disabled users.

It should be emphasised that any eye tracker intended for production should undergo testing by qualified professionals at a recognised test house, in a controlled laboratory setting. However, some knowledge of the measurement procedures and issues involved should be useful to designers and users of eye tracking systems.

LIGHT AND THE EYE

The eye is designed by evolution to be biologically sensitive to natural light energy; indeed, this is the basis of vision. Therefore, the various structures and tissues of the eye are designed to collect and focus light on the retina. These structures and tissues are affected in various ways by light, and at intense levels, this effect may be adverse. Because of this, any light source intended for human use must be carefully tested and conform to safety regulations.

Natural Defence Mechanisms and Photobiological Effects

The eye is well adapted to protecting itself against overly intense broad-band optical radiation from the natural environment (i.e., ultraviolet, visible, and infrared radiant energy), and mankind has learned to use protective measures, such as hats and eye-protectors, to shield against the harmful effects on the eye from very intense ultraviolet radiation (UVR) and the blue light present in sunlight over snow or sand. The eye is also protected against bright light by the natural aversion response to viewing bright visible light sources. The aversion response includes blinking and/or head movements to avoid strongly perceived light. It normally protects the eye against injury from viewing bright light sources such as the sun, arc lamps, and welding arcs, since this aversion limits the duration of exposure to a fraction of a second (about 0.25 s).

The infrared LEDs employed in most infrared LED eye trackers do not, however, produce a strong aversion response, as they are barely visible to the human eye, and the spectral emission is limited to the near-infrared (IR-A, 780–1400 nm) spectral band. If a conventional incandescent lamp or discharge lamp that has been filtered to block most visible light and transmit IR-A is employed, some emissions of note are possible outside the IR-A range and must be evaluated separately.

Potential Hazards

In general, optical radiation safety guidelines identify at least five separate types of potential hazards to the eye from intense optical sources that normally must be independently evaluated to assure optical safety:

1. Ultraviolet photochemical injury to the cornea (photokeratitis) and lens (cataract)

of the eye (180nm to 400nm): with separate measurements to be made in relation to each

2. Thermal injury to the retina of the eye (400nm to 1400nm)

3. Blue-light photochemical injury to the retina of the eye (principally 400nm to 550nm; unless aphakic, 310nm to 550nm)

4. Near-infrared thermal hazards to the lens (approximately 800nm to 3000nm)

5. Thermal injury (burns) to the cornea of the eye (approximately 1400nm to 1mm)

In the case of the LEDs and IR-A filtered lamps used in most infrared eye trackers, only aspects (b) and (d) are relevant. There should be no detectable ultraviolet or blue light from the LEDs, and the far-infrared (thermal) radiant energy emitted is insignificant. The retinal thermal injury hazard (b) normally requires optical radiance values characteristic of intense xenon-arc lamps if visible light is present and the hazard criterion is limited to exposures of 10 seconds or less; however, in the case of a near-infrared source with a weak visual stimulus, special retinal thermal

Figure 1. The different photobiological effects of optical radiation are generally limited to specific spectral bands. The photobiological bands designated by the International Commission on Illumination (CIE) are shown at the top. The hazard criteria listed in (a) through (e), above, generally apply to only one or two spectral regions

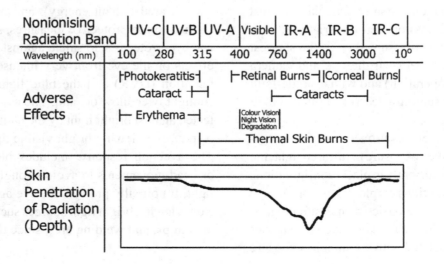

hazard criteria exist for continuous viewing. Therefore, this retinal thermal effect (b) and the infrared hazard to the lens (d) should be evaluated in detail for each system. To prove beyond any doubt that UVR is of no concern, aspect (a) can also be quickly checked by measurement. Any blue-light emissions would be readily detectable (and annoyingly bright) if it were of concern in any system.

The following section provides basic knowledge of key concepts in radiometry and photometry for readers not familiar with the topic. The terms and concepts included are directly applicable in the calculation of levels of exposure to IR light in eye tracking. Readers familiar with this introductory material may wish to skip ahead to Measurement Considerations.

INTRODUCTION TO RADIOMETRY: KEY TERMS AND CONCEPTS

Introduction to Radiometric Measurements

Solid Angle Ω

The solid angle itself is not a radiometric quantity but, rather, a unitless ratio defined in three dimensions, comparable to the radian in two dimensions. In other words, the solid angle is to the surface of a sphere what a normal angle segmenting a circle is to the circumference of that circle. The solid angle is part of the radiometric quantities radiant intensity and radiance.

Definition

The solid angle describes the geometrical distribution of a volume that extends (expands) linearly from one point of origin. It is calculated as the product of 4π and the ratio of the area of intersection between this volume and an imaginary sphere

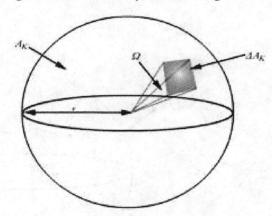

Figure 2. Illustration of the solid angle

with the same point of origin ΔA_K to the total area of the same sphere A_K (see Figure 2).

It is noteworthy that the shape of the area of intersection ΔA_K is arbitrary (for example, circular or rectangular). Depending on the physical properties to be described with the solid angle, we assign one or more certain properties to this volume, which makes it different from the ambient space. For purposes of describing the spatial distribution of radiation from a certain source, one assigns to the volume the property of limiting the radiation-containing space.

$$\Omega = 4\pi \frac{\Delta A}{A_K} \tag{6.1}$$

or with $A_K = 4\pi r^2$

$$\Omega = \frac{\Delta A_K}{r^2} \tag{6.2}$$

Unit

For practical purposes, the auxiliary SI unit the steradian (*sr*) is assigned to the (actually unitless) solid angle Ω.

For a common type of solid angle, the *canonical* one, the following *transformation* to the angle φ can be employed (see Figure 3):

Figure 3. Illustration of transformation of the canonical solid angle Ω to the angle φ

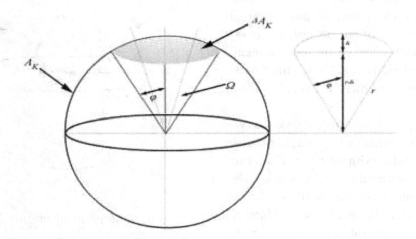

The size of the spherical cap ΔA_K is

$$\Delta A_K = 2\pi rh \qquad (6.3)$$

From this it follows that

$$\Delta A_K = 2\pi r^2 (1 - \cos\varphi) \qquad (6.4)$$

Insertion of the value from Equation 6.4 into Equation 6.2 leads to

$$\Omega = 2\pi(1 - \cos\varphi) \qquad (6.5)$$

Radiant Energy Q

Definition
Radiant energy corresponds to the energy that is emitted by an object in all directions or received by an object from all directions.

Unit
The SI unit of radiant energy Q is the *J(oule)*.

Radiant Power Φ

Definition
The radiant power (also called radiant flux) is the quantity of energy ∂Q emitted by an object per unit of time ∂t in all directions or received by an object per unit of time from all directions.

$$\Phi = \frac{\partial Q}{\partial t} \qquad (6.6)$$

Unit
The SI unit of radiant power is the *W(att)*.

Radiant Intensity I

Definition
Radiant intensity is defined as radiant power $\partial\Phi$ per unit solid angle $\partial\Omega$ of a *point source* (see the definition of a point source below). If the intensity is the same in all directions, the source is 'isotropic'. Whenever a source does not have the same power in all directions, it is said to be 'anisotropic'.

$$I = \frac{\partial \Phi}{\partial \Omega} \tag{6.7}$$

Unit

The SI unit of radiant intensity is $\frac{W}{sr}$.

Radiance L

Definition

Radiance is defined as radiant power $\partial \Phi$ per unit solid angle $\partial \Omega$ and per unit projected source area $\partial \Omega \cos\theta$ of an *extended source*. Thereby θ is the projection angle between the surface normal and the specified direction (see Figure 4).

$$L = \frac{\partial^2 \Phi}{\partial \Omega \partial A \cos\theta} \tag{6.8}$$

Unit

The SI unit of radiance L is $\frac{W}{m^2 sr}$.

Radiance is an important measure in eye safety standards. The reason for its suitability as a quantity for exposure limits is that it can be used to calculate how much of the radiant energy emitted by an extended source can be concentrated by an optical system (i.e., lenses or reflectors) that is directed toward this source under the projection angle θ. In the case of the eye directed at a light source, the solid angle of interest is the area of the pupil.

Conservation of Radiance

A given radiance cannot be increased by an optical system, although *irradiance* is increased when the optical system focuses an image onto a smaller plane. Radiance, however, is a constant, and, provided that no light is absorbed by the lens, radiance will be at least the same at the light source as it is when the image is passed through the lens and focused on the retina.

Figure 4. Radiance of an extended source

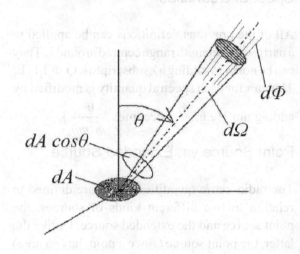

Irradiance E

Definition

This is the radiant power $\partial \Phi$ on a surface per surface unit ∂A from all directions of a hemisphere.

$$E = \frac{\partial \Phi}{\partial A} = \int L \cos\Phi \partial\Omega = \frac{\partial I}{\partial d^2} \tag{6.9}$$

Unit

The SI unit of irradiance E is $\frac{W}{m^2}$. which can be otherwise expressed as Wm⁻².

Inverse Square Law

The inverse square law states that the irradiance produced on a surface by a point source is inversely proportional to the square of the distance (see Figure 5).

$$E_{A1} = \left(\frac{d_2}{d_1}\right)^2 E_{A2} \tag{6.10}$$

Spectral Quantities

All of the previous definitions can be applied to a narrow wavelength range centred around λ. They can be noted by adding a λ subscript as: $Q_\lambda \Phi_\lambda I_\lambda L_\lambda E_\lambda$ The unit for each spectral quantity is modified by adding nm^{-2} (e.g. $\frac{W}{m^2}$ becomes $\frac{W}{m^2 nm}$).

Point Source vs. Extended Source

The radiometric quantities above are defined in relation to two different kinds of sources, the point source and the extended source. Unlike the latter, the point source (since a point has no area) exists only as a useful theoretical construct. If the extension of an extended source is one tenth of its distance from the target object or less, one can regard it as a point source. In terms of the eye, the definitions above, which are restricted to point sources, can be used for real sources if the distance between the light source and the eye is at least 10 times the size (extension) of the light source. If the light source is larger, then it cannot be considered a point source in the calculation of irradiance.

Figure 5. Illustration of the inverse square law

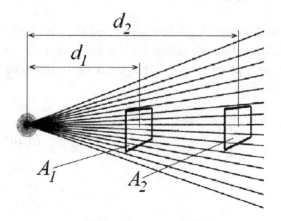

MEASUREMENT CONSIDERATIONS

Exposure of the Eyes at Reference Points and for Normal Use

In measurement of exposure levels, irradiance should be measured at a reference distance corresponding to the closest viewing distance realistically possible when the system is in operation. The actual intended use viewing distances will normally be greater, but for the calculation of safety standards the maximum exposure during operational use should be measured. Although, for accurate measurement, a controlled laboratory setting (e.g., in a recognised testing house) is essential, in designing a system and deciding on IR sources, measurements within a reasonably large margin of error within safety limits can initially be usefully taken with hand-held devices. Measurements of total irradiance at the locations where the eyes would be exposed to one or more LEDs should be made at line-of-sight (LoS) positions. Measurements should be made with and without a calibrated 10% transmission filter to check for detector linearity and assure that the detector is not saturated; however, a comprehensive test for detector saturation and maximal detector alignment is not possible in a non-laboratory setting. It must, therefore, be emphasised that values recorded in this way may not always accurately reflect the emissions of the device tested. Therefore, it is essential to ensure more accurate measures prior to a product release.

Exposure of the Eyes at the Closest Points of Exposure

To assure worst-case measurements (i.e., irradiance at close distances) and to simplify alignment of the radiometer detector, any infrared window enclosure can be removed to maximise the emission levels measured. In a laboratory setting, the detector would be positioned for measurement of a part of an LED array, or an entire array for a multiple-LED source. Furthermore, with an array, a mask would typically be employed to block the emissions of all but one LED at 20 cm. This permits the measurement of the irradiance from a single LED at the distance recommended by IEC 62471 / CIE S 009 (Photobiological Safety of Lamps and Lamp Systems) and ANSI/IESNA RP27.2-02.

Measurements of Ultraviolet Radiation (UVR)

Although there may be no reason to expect that the infrared LED illuminators would emit optical radiation outside the IR-A spectral region, routine checks can be made to detect the presence of UVR. To assure that there is no shorter-wavelength ultraviolet radiation emitted from the illuminators, measurements can be made with a UV Hazard detector head and with the UV-A detector.

MEASUREMENT OF SOURCE CHARACTERISTICS

In this section, we will look at how the various hardware set-ups you will have seen in previous chapters should be considered for performance

of safety calculations. Eye trackers use various arrangements of LEDs as light sources. Some have only one or a few LEDs, other have arrays, and still others use two widely separated arrays. Some LED packages actually consist of compact arrays of up to 60 surface-emitting gallium-aluminum-arsenide (GaAlAs) chips with a collimating lens to concentrate the infrared output as desired for the application. The LED array can be imaged via digital photography. To illustrate the technique, Figure 6 shows some images of an infrared light source mounted on eye tracking cameras, on-access and slightly off-access. The apparent source moves around, depending upon the position of the viewer. To provide a very conservative hazard analysis and to maximise the calculated radiance, the effective emission area of only the central bright spot is routinely used for measurements and calculations. This permits calculation of the highest radiance. Furthermore, to assure worst-case calculations, the angular subtense α of the source for safety calculations can be based on the outside dome dimension at the 20 cm reference distance. In most eye trackers, the emission is in a very diffuse ('Lambertian') pattern, or slightly tighter beam. Some beams could be more collimated if directed by the eye

Figure 6. These images were taken on-axis and off-axis. When one knows the dimensions of the window, or any element in the image that is on the same plane as the light, the actual source size can be quickly determined. A ruler can be placed adjacent to the source for more direct calibration. This method supports routine tests during product development: once a large margin of error is used, for conservative estimates, it is a useful method. Any product intended for the market should undergo testing at a recognised testing house

tracker. Estimation of the source size under these conditions is quite limited.

Head-Mounted vs. Remote Systems

Head movements are a challenge for gaze tracking purposes when the cameras are mounted remotely. Some eye trackers mount the cameras and IR sources on a headband or cap, so that the cameras move with the head. In such systems, the IR sources are closer to the eye, and this has a bearing on levels of irradiation of the eye structures. Because the light source is closer to the eye, the apparent source size is larger. If the extension of the source is more than one tenth of the minimum distance to the eye, it can no longer be considered a point source in irradiance calculations but must, instead, be deemed an extended source.

On- and Off-Axis Positioning

The relative position of the camera illuminating the eye with reference to the eye itself results in different locations of the glint in the eye image and can have different photobiological effects on eye structures. One of the most frequently applied distinctions is classification of the IR light position as on-axis or off-axis (where 'axis' refers to the optical axis of the camera). Thus, the light source can be placed coaxially to the camera or not coaxially to the camera.

Using on-axis lighting also affects image processing (i.e., leading to bright or dark pupil images). Placing the light sources far from the camera axis does not generate a bright pupil effect, making the pupil appear dark in the image. However, this does not mean that the light is not reaching the retina; it merely indicates that it is being reflected in another direction than the camera position.

Single LED vs. Array

The light sources employed in eye tracking can be composed of single LEDs or composed of arrays of LEDs, arranged in various manners. The objective of using arrays of LEDs is to generate more powerful point sources and larger glints in the image, reducing the imprecision of the glint position in the eye image. If the array is such that the beams of light emitted overlap at the eye, there may be a cumulative effect on irradiance measurements.

There is no maximum number of LEDs used in eye tracking systems: some systems use arrays of between 30 and 40 LEDs. As we shall see, the number of LEDs used will also have a bearing on safety calculations.

Use of Lenses and Filters

Additional hardware elements can be used to modify the effects of the IR light in eye tracking systems. The use of lenses in front of the IR source can modify the light pattern. Some systems make use of lenses to increase the apparent size of the source. This will result in larger glints in the image and, consequently, greater precision in glint location. Such lenses change the 'spread' of the light from the source and will need to be taken into account in the calculation of emissions.

Some cameras filter out visible light and capture just the image resulting from the IR emission. However, such filters on the cameras themselves do not affect the exposure of the eye to the light; they only affect the quality of the image to be analysed. Note that this is not the case if broadband light sources are filtered to emit only IR light; tests must be carried out for emissions outside the IR range in this case.

CHARACTERISTICS OF THE LIGHT EMITTED

In this section, we describe additional aspects of the use of IR light in eye tracking from the standpoint of the characteristics of the emitted light. Although we cannot envisage exact numbers or ranges, we will point out some of the most important aspects of the light emitted.

The wavelengths commonly used in eye trackers are in the portion of the near-infrared range from 820 to 950 nm. However, this statement is not based on an exhaustive review of the available systems, and each system must be assessed individually.

Pulsed and Continuous Light

IR sources can remain on constantly during tracking or can be pulsed at variant frequencies. Continuous light describes the light remaining on in the same conditions during the tracking session. In contrast, pulsed light describes either switching the lights on and off, using alternative synchronisation patterns, or regularly reducing and increasing the amount of light emitted. The pulse frequency varies from one system to another, depending on the objectives. Many of the systems present a frequency synchronised with the camera acquisition rate, so that they keep the lights on during part or all of the period of image acquisition and switch the lights off until the next image starts to be acquired. There are also cases in which different pulse frequencies are used for different point light sources. Although the reasons for pulsing light depend on the image analysis methods used, one possible advantage is that its use makes it easier for the system to differentiate between system IR light and ambient IR light such as that found in daylight.

In all cases, pulsed light is subject to further safety calculations, which we will come to later in the chapter. This is related to the rate at which the light energy can be dispersed across the surfaces it falls on in the eye, in comparison to the rate at which the light is pulsed and the amount of micro eye movements that can be assumed for a normal eye during fixation.

Mixed Lighting Conditions

A particular case of pulsed light is the use of mixed light conditions. In these kinds of systems, on- and off-axis lights are applied with different lighting frequencies or continuous light is used for off-axis lighting and pulsed light for on-axis lighting. Regardless of whether the light is on- or off-axis, the essential point of this technique is the use of pulsed light for the on-axis light source. This is known as the image difference method. Ideally, on the assumption that there is a sufficiently fast sample rate that eye movements between two consecutive frames are minimal, the most important difference between the images would be the intensity level of the pupil. In the first of the images, we would have a bright pupil and in the second one a dark pupil. Then, calculating the difference between the two frames will result in an image in which the blob with the highest intensity, among the blobs greater than a specified size, is going to be the pupil area. Since eyes are usually peculiar in the image in that they will change from dark to bright with high-contrast differences as the lighting conditions change and that the sampling rate is fast enough to catch these changing light effects, subtracting one image from the next will locate the pupil quite reliably. In this manner, the pupil can be located easily (Ebisawa, 1995). For safety calculations, the single-fault condition must be used in calculating emissions. Therefore, alternate lighting patterns and pulses may require an additive measure if it is possible that a single fault of the system may cause all or several lights to appear concurrently.

OPTICAL RADIATION SAFETY STANDARDS AND GUIDELINES

Having considered the lighting conditions usually employed for eye tracking, we will now look at some existing standards for the use of infrared light and assess their applicability to eye tracking scenarios. It should be noted that at the time of printing, the development of a safety standard specifically for eye tracking is underway through the work of a technical committee in the CIE. However, until this work is published as a standard, there are a number of relevant general standards for infrared light exposure that are applied.

Hazard Criteria

Several national and international organisations provide guidelines for human exposure to optical radiation and recommend exposure limits for the eye and skin. The most prominent are the American Conference of Governmental Industrial Hygienists (ACGIH) in North America and the International Commission for Non-Ionizing Radiation Protection (ICNIRP). In the European Union, the Optical Radiation Directive employs the ICNIRP exposure limits for use in the workplace. Other organisations recommend product-safety emission limits. Currently, there are only two types of product safety standards that apply to the use of lamps including solid-state lamps (LEDs) worldwide. These are listed below.

The CIE Lamp Safety Standard

CIE Standard S 009/E-2002, Photobiological Safety of Lamps and Lamp Systems, which was based upon an earlier edition of American National Standard ANSI RP-27.1-2005, Recommended Practice for Photobiological Safety for Lamps and Lamps Systems: General Requirements, published by the Illuminating Engineering Society of North America, is the first set of documents in a series of standards and employ ocular exposure limits that are essentially identical to the guidelines for human exposure published by the International Commission on Non-Ionizing Radiation Protection, which, in turn, are essentially the same as the threshold limit values (TLVs) for broad-band optical radiation published by the American Conference of Governmental Industrial Hygienists. The ACGIH and ICNIRP materials differ slightly in the UV-A spectral region but not for visible radiation and near-infrared. Also, the ICNIRP recommend that these guidelines for incoherent and non-laser-light sources be applied to LEDs. One of the IESNA standards included specific guidelines on methods of measurement at realistic viewing distances – not closer than 20 cm – that are not issued by the ACGIH but were adopted by CIE S009. It should be noted that these standards are constantly updated, so the first step in choosing which standard to apply to any particular system should be a thorough check for updates, revisions, or new standards being in place. At the time of printing, a safety standard specifically for eye trackers is in preparation within the CIE.

The IEC/CIE Lamp Safety Standard

International Electrotechnical Commission (IEC) 62471 / CIE S 009-2006, Photobiological Safety of Lamps and Lamp Systems, which is identical to CIE S 009/E-2002, became a joint-logo standard in 2006. It provides guidance to manufacturers on classification of lamps and lamp systems into one of four risk groups but gives no requirements for labelling, etc. Work on a draft IEC technical report, IEC TR 62471-2, called 'Photobiological safety of lamps and lamp systems - Part 2: guidance on manufacturing requirements relating to non-laser optical radiation', is currently in progress, with potential completion and publication in 2011.

The EN 60825-1 Laser Product Safety Standard

In Europe, a laser safety standard issued by CENELEC also applied until recently to LEDs: EN 60825-1:1994 (+ corr. Feb. 1995) +A1:2002 + A2:2001 (+ corr. Apr. 2004); Amendment 2 to Safety of Laser Products - Part 1: Equipment Classification, Requirements, and Users' Guide. This was based on IEC 60825-1 (Safety of Laser Products - Part 1: Equipment Classification, Requirements, and Users' Guide), the international laser product standard from the IEC. The inclusion of LEDs by IEC Technical Committee TC-76 (which developed the standard) in 1993 was largely to deal with the specific use of infrared LEDs in optical-fibre communication systems. The many, different geometries of other LED products were not properly considered, and subsequent amendments attempted to correct some of these problems in 1996 and 2001. Since national and international experts considered this application of laser limits to incoherent sources as overly conservative, the IEC's TC-76 voted to eliminate the inclusion of LEDs in the second edition of IEC 60825-l, which was published in March 2007. Although IEC 60825-lno longer applies to the LEDs in eye tracker systems, IEC 62471:2006 does apply.

Human Exposure Limits for Hazard Evaluations

The ICNIRP recommended guidelines for limiting human exposure to optical radiation may be updated for retinal thermal limits in the future. But for now, the following limits for ocular exposure to broad-band visible and infrared radiation are recommended by the ICNIRP for use in analysis of the potential optical radiation hazards to the retina from lamps and LEDs: The ACGIH issued a Notice of Intent to Change for its limits (that is, TLVs) in 2008.

Exposure Guidelines for IR-A Radiant Energy

Both the ICNIRP and the ACGIH provide exposure limits for near-infrared optical radiation. If the emitting areas of adjacent LED sources are separated by at least 100 milliradians (5.7 degrees) (i.e., by 2 cm at the standard 20-centimetre assessment distance) then from the retinal hazard standpoint, they are considered completely independent. However, for assessment of the risk to cornea and lens, they are all additive in the infrared band.

Infrared Corneal (Lens) Thermal Hazard

The ACGIH and ICNIRP recommend a maximal daily corneal exposure of 10 mW/cm² total irradiance for wavelengths 770–3,000 nm (EIR only) for day-long, continuous exposure, which could be applied to the sum of the average irradiance of all of the infrared LEDs as

$$E_{IR\text{-}only} = 0.01\,W \cdot cm^{-2} \text{ average for } t > 1{,}000s \tag{6.11}$$

This is termed the 'infrared radiation hazard limit' in the ANSI/IESNA and CIE/IEC lamp safety standards. Higher irradiances are permitted for exposure durations of less than 1,000 s (~16.6 minutes):

$$E_{IR\text{-}only} = 1.8t^{0.75}\,Wcm^{-2}\,210\,W\,cm^{-2} \text{ as an example for a single 1,800 µs pulse} \tag{6.12}$$

However, since the peak irradiances would be only increased by the reciprocal of the duty cycle, the peak irradiance may not be the limiting case. For a repetitively pulsed system, also the peak power must be evaluated.

Retinal Thermal Hazard

Before assessing the retinal thermal hazard from an IR light source, one must first confirm that no UV light is emitted. Once it has been ascertained that only IR light is involved, the CIE/IEC international standard IEC/CIE 62471 / S 009E-2006 and the ANSI RP27.1-2006 lamp safety standards follow the ACGIH TLV and ICNIRP guideline for protecting the human retina against the retinal thermal hazard, as well as the 'infrared lens hazard'. The TLV for lengthy viewing (i.e., for $t > 1,000s$ is:

$$L_{NIR} = \Sigma L_\lambda \cdot R\lambda \cdot \Delta\lambda \le 0.6/\alpha W \cdot cm^{-2} \cdot sr^{-1} \text{ for } t > 810$$

$$= 6.0 W \cdot cm^{-2} \cdot sr^{-1} \text{ for } \alpha = 100 \text{ } mrad = 0.1 \text{ } radian \tag{6.13}$$

where the value of R(λ) between 700 nm and 1,100 nm is

$$R(\lambda) = 10^{[(700nm-\lambda)/500nm]} \tag{6.14}$$

which, for example, has a value of 0.60 for a wavelength of $810nm$, but since an $800nm$ LED would typically have a $30nm$ emission bandwidth (FWHM), it is customary to use the Rλ value that applies at the shorter edge of the bandwidth measured at 50% of peak (i.e., at 795 nm, where Rλ is 0.65). Thus, when the measured radiance is multiplied by the R(?) factor, the effective radiance becomes less. For example $(0.066W / (cm^2 \cdot sr)) \cdot (0.65) = 0.043W / (cm^2 \cdot sr)$ effective, which is only about 0.6% of the limit for $t > 810$ and even the peak radiance for a 0.8 ms pulse does not exceed the long-term continuous exposure limit. The limiting radiance provided by the ACGIH for $t < 810$ and all pulsed exposures is

$$L_{NIR} = \Sigma L_\lambda \cdot R(\lambda) \cdot \Delta\lambda \le 3.2/(\alpha \cdot t^{0.25}) \text{ W/cm}^2 \cdot sr^{-1}$$
for t < 810s $\tag{6.15}$

For example, for an emitter with a 0.8 ms pulse and an angular subtense of 90 mrad, the exposure limit would be

$$L_{NIR} \le 3.2/[(0.09 \text{ '[radian]})(0.0008 \text{ [s]})^{0.25}] \text{ W/cm}^2 \cdot sr^{-1} = 19 \text{ W/cm}^2 \cdot sr^{-1}$$

which is 29% of the limit L_{NIR}. This is a 3.5 fold safety factor. Greater safety factors actually exist, since the conservative application of a smaller source size was used to determine radiance. With current technology, bare LEDs project a CW radiance less than $L \sim 10W / (cm^2 \cdot sr)$; however, this is not biologically weighted. With normal viewing, micro-saccadic and saccadic eye movements blur the retinal image area for multiple-pulse exposure. This is one reason that the limits vary with exposure duration. An open question, which may apply to chronic exposure over a lifetime, is whether there exist any individuals who are particularly sensitive, such as individuals with impaired circulation, who have larger pupil sizes, or who are on medication that might alter susceptibility to some biological effects. We will look at this question again later in this chapter.

Maximum Permissible Exposure Limits for Laser Radiation at 810nm

Just for comparison, it may be informative to compare the exposure limits that apply to laser radiation, which have additional safety factor because of the nature of laser systems. This may also be useful because of the earlier attempts to include LEDs under the IEC laser product safety standard. American National Standard Z136.1-2007 (ANSI, 2007), the laser guidelines of the International Commission on Non-Ionizing Radiation Protection (ICNIRP, 2000), and the international Electrotechnical Commission standard IEC 60825-1.2007 all have the same maximum permissible exposure (MPE) limit at $810nm$. The appropriate MPE is found in Table 5b, page 75 of

ANSI Z136.1-2007. This is normally expressed as an irradiance E_{MPE}:

$$E_{MPE} = 1.8 C_A \cdot C_E \cdot T_2^{-0.25} mW.cm^{-2} \text{ for exposure}$$
duration exceeding T_2 (6.16)

where C_A is a spectral correction factor [ ], $C_A = 1 / R(\lambda)$ which is 1.66 at $810nm$, C_E is a correction factor for extended sources that have an angular subtense α (in mrads) that is greater than α_{min} and less than α_{max} and is expressed as

$$C_E = \alpha / \alpha_{min} \quad (6.17)$$

where $\alpha_{min} = 1.5 mrad$ and $\alpha_{max} = 100 mrad = 0.1$ radian and T_2 is

$$T_2 = 10 \times 10^{(\alpha - 1.5)/98.5} = 100s \text{ for } \alpha > \alpha_{max}, \text{ where}$$
$T_2^{-0.25} = 0.316$ (6.18)

The maximum value of C_E occurs at α_{max} and is 66.7. Therefore, at $\alpha = \alpha_{max}$:

$$E_{MPE} = 1.8(1.66) \cdot (66.7) \cdot (0.316) mW \cdot cm^{-2} =$$
$63 mW \cdot cm^{-2}$ for $t > T_2$ (6.19)

but this is only for $\alpha = 0.1 rad$, where the corresponding solid angle $\Omega = \pi \cdot \alpha^2 / 4 = 0.00785 sr$. Therefore, if we divide the irradiance MPE by Ω, then the MPE can be expressed as radiance:

$$L_{MPE} = 8W \cdot cm^{-2} \cdot sr^{-1} \text{ for } t > 100s \quad (6.20)$$

Therefore, for all sources exceeding an angular subtense $\alpha > 100 mrad (\sim 5.7°)$ the MPE can be expressed as a constant radiance of approximately $8W \cdot cm^{-2} \cdot sr^{-1}$ and this is confirmed by referring to one standard that actually presents the limit for large sources in terms of radiance (i.e., in Figure 11 on page 78 of ANSI Z136.1-2007). Hence, no matter whether one stares at the source at close range or from further away, if the time-averaged radiance of the source remains below this, the system would be safe for viewing. The time-averaged source radiance of an eye tracking system most typically will be much less. For an eye tracker employing repetitive pulses, in our example of a pulse width of $800\mu s$ ($t = 0.8ms$), the value of L_{MPE} would be increased by the ratio of $t^{-0.25} / t_2^{-0.25} = (5.95) / (0.316) = 18.8$, since all other correction factors remain the same. Hence,

$$L_{MPE} = 151 W \cdot cm^{-2} \cdot sr^{-1} \text{ for } t = 0.8ms$$
(single pulse) (6.21)

However, the single-pulse laser limit has a multiple-pulse correction factor C_P not applied in the incoherent exposure limits. For example, consider an LED source with a pulse repetition frequency (PRF) of 100 Hz. The correction factor $C_P = N^{-0.25}$ where N is the number of pulses in a train. Because of normal eye movements, the laser-safety guidance is to limit the pulse integration time to a $10s$ maximum, as applied in accordance with the standard. For a $10s$ exposure at a PRF of $100Hz$, N is 1,000. And, $C_P = 1000^{-0.25} = 0.178$, which would reduce the pulse radiance MPE to $L_{MPE} = (0.178)(151) = 27 W \cdot cm^{-2} \cdot sr^{-1}$ for a $100Hz$ train of $0.8ms$ pulses for a period of $10s$ or greater. It is important to recognise that the laser limits apply most directly to point-source viewing conditions as the default condition of exposure, hence the added effort to convert the limits to radiance. The ICNIRP clearly points out that the MPEs for incoherent sources should apply to all lamps such as LEDs, and not laser limits. Furthermore, the US federal laser product performance standards do not apply to LEDs.

Retinal Irradiance

If the apparent source size subtends an angle a of the order of 100 milliradians or greater at a distance $r = 100$ to $200mm$, the radiance approach to measurement remains the best approach for assessing retinal hazards of an eye tracker. A source with diameter of $2cm$ will produce an image diameter d_r at the retina of approximately $1.7mm$ in diameter, since

$$d_r = f \cdot \alpha \qquad (6.22)$$

where f is the effective focal length (in air) of the relaxed normal eye.

As noted previously, the radiance L measured at any distance from an extended source does not change. However, because typical infrared eye trackers may have an array of LED sources, with overlapping irradiance patterns in the area of the face, the number of LEDs seen as bright sources and the appearance of the bright areas within each LED will vary somewhat with viewing position. As we have also noted previously, the retinal irradiance E_r is related to the source radiance L as

$$E_r = 0.27L \cdot \tau \cdot d_\theta^2 \qquad (6.23)$$

where τ is the transmittance of the ocular media, which can be up to 0.9, and d_θ is the pupil diameter in cm. This formulation (Sliney and Wolbarsht, 1980) assumes that E and L have units of $W \cdot cm^{-2}$ and $W \cdot cm^{-2} \cdot sr^{-1}$, respectively. The exposures typical of LED eye trackers are typically below MPE limits and therefore well below actual retinal injury thresholds. The best available data for retinal injury thresholds for large-image exposure at $810nm$ come from work published by Ham and Mueller (1989). The thresholds for visible retinal injury were several times greater than for exposures from an argon laser in the visible spectrum. The special conditions that apply to ophthalmic-instrument exposure require special consideration, but for the infrared eye tracker application, if we assume the individual is awake and task-oriented, viewing a display above or adjacent to the infra-

red eye tracker source while directing his or her gaze at specific instructions on the display, it is unlikely that the eye will be fully dark-adapted. It should be noted that medications or particular illnesses may dilate a pupil, and this will be considered below for the case of gaze control for users with physical impairment. However, a computer monitor is considered sufficiently bright for normal working conditions at a luminance of $10cd \cdot m^{-2}$ (see ISO 9241-3), which is relatively low indoor lighting, so if one assumes some level of dark-adaptation, the pupils could be larger than those typical with indoor illumination. Therefore, the underlying assumption of a dark-adapted ($7mm$) pupil employed in the derivation of the retinal safety limit provides a conservative limit. The question remains whether the chronic exposure characteristic of gaze-directed communication is more extensive than was anticipated in the derivation of the ICNIRP limits. This question is currently being addressed within the CIE in the development of a safety standard for eye trackers.

MEDICAL ISSUES AND SPECIAL POPULATIONS

Special Cases of Eye Control as a Communication Aid

People without disabilities might use a computer for work and leisure purposes. For many people with disabilities, a computer offers the only possible means of carrying out work and leisure activities and is also the only means of communicating socially. Let us take, for example, Keith, a person with ALS/MND who is unable to move any part of his body voluntarily. His eye control system is a) the only means by which he can complete his tasks at work; b) the only way in which he can independently enjoy his leisure time by, for example, surfing the Web, e-mailing friends, and playing games; and c) an essential means by which he has been able to communicate socially and independently since losing the ability to speak. To an extent, he can achieve communication and control by means other than eye control. However, eye control offers him the only means by which he can achieve these things independently. Therefore, as do many people with disabilities who are eager to use this technology for communication and control, Keith chooses to use the system for up to 12 hours per day. In addition to the length of exposure involved with this infrared illuminated eye tracker, another factor is that Keith finds it impossible to blink or close his eyes, and as a result he is unable to lubricate his eyes in the same way as other people. Keith's extensive use of his assistive technology is by no means atypical among people with disabilities who are completely reliant on their system for all of their communication and control needs. Current infrared safety standards are, of course, designed for a range of devices to which the user is not usually exposed for long periods of time or at such close proximity. For example, in the case of a television remote control, the device will be used for a matter of mere seconds each day and even then directed away from the eye to control the television as opposed to pointing directly at the eye in order to pick up eye movements. Hence, a safety standard specifically addressing the eye tracking situation is desirable and under preparation within the CIE.

Physical Impairments Leading to Change in the Exposure Situation

Today, users of eye control technology are often people with severe disabilities and degenerative conditions (for example, ALS/MND) (Donegan et al., 2005). People with severe disabilities or degenerative conditions are more vulnerable to the risk of infection and injury. Not only that, but infection or injury is potentially more debilitating. Donegan et al. identified a range of user groups

who benefit from eye control technology. With the exception of people with repetitive strain injury, these groups include people with neurological conditions. Some of the physical impairments experienced by people with neurological conditions that lead to a change in the exposure situation include reduced mobility, sensation problems, poor nutritional status, fatigue, visual impairment, and decreased cognitive ability. Reduced mobility restricts people's ability to change their position or that of their computer independently. Consequently, they have difficulty moving away from the source of infrared light independently. Unlike people who are mobile and who frequently change their position, they instead rely on having the ability to pause or switch off the equipment. Furthermore, any muscular degenerative condition can also affect the muscles of the eyes and may reduce the microsaccadic as well as saccadic movements, which normally 'spread' irradiance across a greater area of the retina.

The eyelids protect the eyes by removing debris and spreading moisture (tears). Tears are rich in both antibodies and nutrients and spread oxygen to the cornea. However, when the eyelids aren't functioning normally or, because of muscular degeneration, the person is blinking less often, the cornea is at risk of becoming infected, drying out, or being injured. This poses more of a risk for someone who is dehydrated or undernourished in consequence of difficulties in eating or drinking. The level of hydration of the eye is also a factor in reducing the effects of light on the lens. Abnormal eye sensation such as pain can intensify through increased exposure to visible light. Whether this also applies to invisible light such as infrared is unknown. Fatigue is associated with certain neurological conditions; tasks can take longer, so more time is spent at the computer. However, because eye control technology is so effective as an access and communication tool, people with severe disabilities and degenerative conditions who do not have any other means of computer control or communication may hold a view different from that of a non-disabled person about the benefits of pacing oneself and taking regular breaks. All of these issues affecting eye tracker users with disabilities must be considered in order to ensure that the system is as safe as possible. Simple design considerations such as incorporating a means of reducing emitted light when full power is not needed, turning off light sources when no eye movement is detected, or otherwise limiting the exposure to what is necessary for good functioning may greatly reduce any adverse effects of long-term usage.

Finally, some people are simply more sensitive to light than others are, and also our sensitivity to light increases as we grow older. All of these aspects of user characteristics that are related to safety could be usefully included in systems' supporting information or FAQs and should, ideally, be made known to all people with a disability who are making the decision on use of an eye tracker, as well as their carers or the medical professionals treating them.

Medications that Affect Light-Sensitivity

A wide range of medications heighten light-sensitivity. Only a small number of examples are given here. These medicines range from tetracycline (a common antibiotic) to digitalis (used to treat heart failure) to tropicamide or cyclopentolate (found in eye drops to dilate the pupil). Even Plaquenil, which is prescribed for rheumatoid arthritis, may have such effects. Some medications affect the eyes in other ways. For example, 'dry eyes' is a side effect of certain common non-steroidal anti-inflammatory drugs, and pupil dilation is a common side effect of many drugs. However, a medical opinion is required in order to determine how significant the effects of the medication in question are upon sensitivity to light, especially when taken in specific doses and over certain periods of time.

CONCLUSIONS

It remains an open question whether there exist any individuals who are particularly sensitive, such as individuals with impaired circulation, with larger pupil sizes, or on medication that might alter susceptibility to some biological effects of chronic infrared exposure. Individuals who use eye control technology do so in all likelihood for many hours per day, have a severe physical disability or degenerative condition, and take medication. Current safety standards do not explicitly take into account this kind of exposure, so it is recommended that light emissions be kept to a minimum as a priority in the design of eye trackers. As with all new technologies, the standards are constantly being updated to account for real-world hardware and usage situations. Although there is little reason to expect any damage to the eye from long-term usage of an eye tracker, anyone with abnormal eye movements, or taking medications that heighten sensitivity to light, should discuss possible adverse effects with a qualified medical practitioner or ophthalmologist.

EXAMPLES AND EXERCISES

Assume the following specification of an LED:

Estimate the irradiance and the radiance if a user is sitting at $d=55mm$ from the LED. Do the values remain under the permissible limits? Assume standard eyeball values.

Suppose now that an array of LEDs (4 x 4) is used for lighting. How are the values from question 1, above modified?

Normally, more than one array of LEDs is used for the lighting of the eye. Calculate the radiance and irradiance if two lighting points are used in our system, one at either side of a $300 \times 300mm$ screen for a user sitting at $500mm$ from the screen. Are the values within permissible limits?

Table 1.

Parameter	Symbol	Condition	Value	Units
Central wavelength	λp	If= 50mA	850	nm
Spectral bandwidth	$\delta\lambda$	If= 50mA	20	nm
Beam width (-3dB)	$\theta_{1/2}$	If= 50mA	6	
Radiated power	P_W	If= 50mA	7	mW
Source size	D_L		1.5	nm

DISCUSSION

Eye and gaze tracking have a long history, but only recently have gaze trackers become robust enough for use outside laboratories (Hansen and Ji, 2010).

We have provided a guided tour through various aspects of eye tracker development and have described the basic hardware equipment and how it is used in eye trackers. On the basis of this, we provided a gentle introduction to how eye images can be processed in order to obtain relevant feature parameters, such as the iris and pupil ellipses and glint locations. Through the feature descriptors, it is possible to estimate the gaze of the user. We described different approaches to determining gaze in both calibrated and uncalibrated set-ups as well as in remote and head-mounted systems. These methods are fundamentally different, and there seems to be room for several new directions for improving both eye detection and gaze estimation methods. We showed throughout this chapter that IR light plays an important role in current eye trackers, but it also poses issues with glasses and if not carefully considered also user safety. The chapter was rounded off with a thorough explanation of hardware issues and discussion of various aspects of eye and gaze tracker safety issues.

Finally, below, we discuss future perspectives on eye and gaze tracking. The precision of current gaze trackers is sufficient for many types of applications.

Both high accuracy and few calibration points are desirable properties, but they are not neces-

sarily the only parameters to be addressed in a gaze tracker (Scott and Findlay, 1993). Price is obviously another salient issue, yet it is one that may be resolved through current technological developments. Regardless of these advances, in some situations it would be convenient if light sources, cameras, and monitors could be positioned according to particular needs rather than being constrained by manufacturer specifications (Hansen et al., 2010). If they could also work well in both indoor and outdoor scenarios while allowing robust gaze results, eye trackers could become more widespread. Future directions for eye and gaze trackers include the following, noted by Hansen and Ji (2010).

- **IR light:** IR light is useful for eye trackers, mainly because it is not visible to the user but also because it can be used for controlling light conditions, obtaining higher-contrast images, and stabilising gaze estimation. A practical limitation of systems using IR light is that they are not necessarily reliable when used outdoors. Methods that either avoid the use of IR light or can provide more robust detection of features would be needed.

- **Head mounts:** While significant emphasis has been placed on remote gaze tracking, head-mounted gaze trackers might be experiencing a renaissance due to both the challenges facing remote eye trackers and the increased interest in mobile eye tracking and small head-mounted displays.

- **Flexible set-up:** Many current gaze trackers require calibration of the camera(s) and the geometric arrangement. At the theoretical level, this is quite a well-understood domain (Guestrin and Eizenman, 2006). A major limitation of fully calibrated set-ups is that they require exact knowledge of the relative positions of the camera, light sources, and monitor. The calibration is tedious and time-consuming to perform, and it also means that a slight unintended movement of part of the system may result in significantly decreased accuracy. Accuracy is difficult to maintain unless a rigid set-up is employed. Such requirements add to the cost of the system. However, avoiding external light sources or allowing users to change the zoom of the camera to suit their particular needs would be desirable in some situations. Gaze models that support flexible set-ups eliminate the need for rigid frames that keep individual components in place. For example, this would benefit eye trackers intended for mobility and the mass market, as avoidance of the rigid frames may result in more compact, lightweight, adaptable, and inexpensive eye trackers. If the models employed in the gaze trackers required no more than a few calibration targets and could maintain accuracy while avoiding the need for light sources, then eye tracking technology would take an important step toward being more flexible, mobile, and convenient for the general public. Use of multiple light sources has to some extent facilitated uncalibrated and partially calibrated set-ups and provides fairly accurate gaze estimates (Coutinho and Morimoto, 2006; Hansen et al., 2010; Yoo and Chung, 2005).
- **Limit calibration:** Current gaze models either use a strong prior model (hardware calibration) with little session calibration or apply a weak prior model but more calibration points. Another future direction will be to develop methods that do not require any calibration. This does not seem to be possible, given current eye and gaze models. New eye models and theories need be developed for achieving calibration-free gaze tracking.
- **Costs:** The costs of current eye tracking systems remain too high for general public use. The main reason for this is the cost of parts, especially high-quality cameras and lenses; the cost of development; and the relatively small market. Alternatively, systems may opt for standard or even off-the-shelf components such as digital video and Web cameras and exploit the fast development in this area (Hansen et al., 2003; Hansen and Pece, 2005; Li et al., 2005). While advances in camera and sensor technology may add to the continuing progress in the relevant fields, new theoretical developments are needed if accurate gaze tracking with low-quality images is to be possible.
- **Degree of tolerance:** Tolerance for eyeglasses and contact lenses is a practical problem that has been solved only partially. The use of several light sources, synchronised according to the user's head movement relative to the camera and light source, may remove some of the associated problems. However, more detailed modelling such as modelling of glasses themselves may be needed if eye trackers are to be used outdoors, where light conditions are less controllable.

The trend of producing mobile and low-cost systems may multiply the ways in which eye tracking technology can be applied to mainstream applications but may also lead to less accurate gaze tracking. While high accuracy may not be needed for such applications, mobile systems must be able to cope with higher noise levels than do eye trackers for indoor use. While it would be desirable to have a 'calibration-free high-accuracy' system, it is not obvious that one could be obtained. The discussion should perhaps be redirected to focus on how to adapt gaze tracking systems to the particular situation.

ACKNOWLEDGMENT

This chapter is based on the COGAIN Deliverable D5.4 on "Exploration of safety issues in Eyetracking" (available at the COGAIN website, www. cogain.org). We would like to thank people who contributed to the original report: Markus Joos (Interactive Minds Dresden), Michael Heubner (TU Dresden) Gintautas Daunys (Šiauliai University), Olga Štěpánková (Czech Technical University), Detlev Droege (University of Koblenz-Landau), Mårten Skogö (Tobii Technology), Jacques Charlier (Metrovision), Dixon Cleveland (LC Technologies), Boris Velichkovsky (TU Dresden).

REFERENCES

American Conference of Governmental Industrial Hygienists (ACGIH) (2007). *Documentation for the threshold limit values* (2007 edition). Cincinnati, OH, US: American Conference of Governmental Industrial Hygienists.

American Conference of Governmental Industrial Hygienists (ACGIH) (2008). *TLV's, threshold limit values and biological exposure indices for 2007*. Cincinnati, OH, US: American Conference of Governmental Industrial Hygienists.

American National Standards Institute / Illuminating Engineering Society of North America (ANSI/IESNA) (2005). *Photobiological safety of lamps and lighting systems, RP27. 1. New York, NY: IESNA.*

American National Standards Institute / Illuminating Engineering Society of North America (ANSI/IESNA) (2007). *Photobiological safety of lamps and lighting systems – Risk group classification and labeling, RP27.3-07*. New York, NY: IESNA.

American National Standards Institute / Illuminating Engineering Society of North America (ANSI/IESNA). (1996). *Photobiological safety of lamps and lighting systems, RP27.3*. New York, NY: IESNA.

American National Standards Institute / Illuminating Engineering Society of North America (ANSI/IESNA). (2000). *Photobiological safety of lamps and lighting system – Measurement systems – Techniques, RP27.2-00*. New York, NY: IESNA.

American National Standards Institute / Illuminating Engineering Society of North America (ANSI/IESNA). (2005). *Photobiological safety of lamps and lighting systems – General requirements, RP27.1-05*. New York, NY: IESNA.

Amir, A., Zimet, L., Sangiovanni-Vincentelli, A., & Kaoc, S. (2005). An embedded system for an eye-detection sensor. *Computer Vision and Image Understanding, 98*(1), 104–123. doi:10.1016/j.cviu.2004.07.009

Babcock, J. S., & Pelz, J. B. (2004). Building a lightweight eyetracking headgear. *Proceedings of the 2004 Symposium on Eye Tracking Research & Applications* (ETRA '04) (pp. 109–114). New York, NY: ACM.

Beymer, D., & Flickner, M. (2003). Eye gaze tracking using an active stereo head. *Proceedings of the 2003 Conference on Computer Vision and Pattern Recognition* (CVPR '03) (vol. 2, p. 451). IEEE Computer Society.

Böhme, M., Dorr, M., Graw, M., Martinetz, T., & Barth, E. (2008). A software framework for simulating eye trackers. In K.-J. Räihä & A.T. Duchowski (Eds.), *Proceedings of the Eye Tracking Research & Application Symposium (ETRA 2008)* (pp. 251–258). New York, NY: ACM.

Böhme, M., Meyer, A., Martinetz, T., & Barth, E. (2006). Remote eye tracking: State of the art and directions for future development. *Proceedings of the 2nd Conference on Communication by Gaze Interaction (COGAIN 2006)* (pp. 10–15). Turin, Italy: Politecnico di Torino. Retrieved from the COGAIN website: http://www.cogain.org/conference

Borchert, M., Lambert, J., & Sliney, D. (2006). Validation of ICNIRP estimates of toxicity thresholds for NIR (785 nm) light in the retinas of pigmented rabbits. *Health Physics, 90*(1), 3–10. doi:10.1097/01.HP.0000175146.94650.4e

CENELEC. (2002). *EN 608025-1/A11, Amendment 11 to safety of laser products - Part 1: Equipment classification, requirements, and users- guide*. CENELEC.

Center for Devices and Radiological Health (CDRH). (1985). *Laser product performance ptandard, title 21, code of Federal regulations, Part 1040*. Washington, DC, US: Government Printing Office.

Cerrolaza, J., Villanueva, A., & Cabeza, R. (2008). Taxonomic study of polynomial regressions applied to the calibration of video-oculographic systems. *Proceedings of the Eye Tracking Research & Application Symposium (ETRA '08)* (pp. 259–266). New York, NY: ACM.

Commission Internationale de l'Eclairage, the International Commission on Illumination (CIE) (2002). *CIE Standard S-009E-2002, Photobiological safety of lamps and lamp systems*. Vienna: CIE. Adopted as a joint-logo standard by the International Electrotechnical Commission in 2006, as IEC 62471 / CIE S 009-2006.

Coutinho, F. L., & Morimoto, C. H. (2006). Free head motion eye gaze tracking using a single camera and multiple light sources. In M. Oliveira Neto & R.L. Carceroni (Eds.), *Proceedings of the 19th Brazilian Symposium on Computer Graphics and Image Processing (SIBGRAPI '06)*. Washington, DC., USA: IEEE Computer Society.

Daunys, G., & Ramanauskas, N. (2004). The accuracy of eye tracking using image processing. *Proceedings of the 3rd Nordic Conference on Human–Computer Interaction (NordiCHI '04)* (pp. 377–380). New York, NY: ACM.

Droege, D., Schmidt, C., & Paulus, D. (2008). A comparison of pupil center estimation algorithms. *Proceedings of the 4th Conference on Communication by Gaze Interaction (COGAIN 2008)* (pp. 23–26). Prague, Czech Republic: Czech Technical University. Retrieved from the COGAIN website: http://www.cogain.org/conference

Fry, G., Treleaven, C., Walsh, R., Higgins, E., & Radde, C. (1947). Definition and measurement of torsion. *American Journal of Optometry and Archives of American Academy of Optometry, 24*, 329–334.

Geier, T. (2007). *Gaze-Tracking zur Interaktion unter Verwendung von Low-Cost-Equipment*. Master's thesis, Universität Koblenz-Landau, Campus Koblenz, Fachbereich 4 Informatik, Institut für Computervisualistik, Koblenz, Germany.

Guestrin, E., & Eizenman, M. (2006). General theory of remote gaze estimation using the pupil center and corneal reflections. *IEEE Transactions on Bio-Medical Engineering, 53*(6), 1124–1133. doi:10.1109/TBME.2005.863952

Ham, W. T. Jr, & Mueller, H. A. (1989). The photopathology and nature of the blue light and near-UV retinal lesions produced by lasers and other optical sources. In Wolbarsht, M. L. (Ed.), *Laser applications in medicine and biology* (pp. 191–246). New York, NY: Plenum Publishing Corp.

Hansen, D. W., Hansen, J. P., Nielsen, M., Johansen, A. S., & Stegmann, M. B. (2003). Eye typing using Markov and active appearance models. *IEEE Workshop on Applications of Computer Vision* (pp. 132–136).

Hansen, D. W., & Ji, Q. (2010). In the eye of the beholder: A survey of models for eyes and gaze. *IEEE Transactions on Pattern Analysis and Machine Intelligence, 32*(3), 478–500. doi:10.1109/TPAMI.2009.30

Hansen, D. W., & Pece, A. E. C. (2005). Eye tracking in the wild. *Computer Vision and Image Understanding, 98*(1), 155–181. doi:10.1016/j.cviu.2004.07.013

Hansen, D. W., San Agustin, J., & Villanueva, A. (2010). Homography normalization for robust gaze estimation in uncalibrated setups. *Proceedings of the 2010 Symposium on Eye-Tracking Research & Applications (ETRA '10)* (pp. 13-20). New York, NY: ACM.

Hartley, R. I., & Zisserman, A. (2003). *Multiple view geometry in computer vision* (2nd ed.). Cambridge, UK: Cambridge University Press.

Hennessey, C., Noureddin, B., & Lawrence, P. (2006). A single camera eye-gaze tracking system with free head motion. *Proceedings of the 2006 Symposium on Eye Tracking Research and Applications (ETRA '06)* (pp. 87–94). New York, NY: ACM.

International Commission on Non-Ionizing Radiation Protection (ICNIRP). (1996). Guidelines on limits for laser radiation of wavelengths between 180 nm and 1,000 μm. *Health Physics, 71*(5), 804–819.

International Commission on Non-Ionizing Radiation Protection (ICNIRP). (1997). Guidelines on limits of exposure for broad-band incoherent optical radiation (0.38 to 3 μm). *Health Physics, 73*(3), 539–597.

International Commission on Non-Ionizing Radiation Protection (ICNIRP). (2000). ICNIRP statement on light-emitting diodes (LEDs) and laser diodes: Implications for hazard assessment. *Health Physics, 78*(6), 744–752. doi:10.1097/00004032-200006000-00020

International Electrotechnical Commission (IEC). (2007). *IEC 60825-1, 2nd edition - Safety of laser products - Part 1: Equipment classification and requirements*. Geneva, Switzerland: International Electrotechnical Commission.

Jähne, B. (2005). *Digital image processing* (6th ed.). Berlin/Heidelberg, Germany: Springer.

Jain, A. K. (1989). *Fundamentals of digital image processing*. Upper Saddle River, NJ: Prentice Hall.

Kisačanin, B., Bhattacharyya, S. S., & Chai, S. (Eds.). (2009). *Embedded computer vision* (1st ed.). Berlin/ Heidelberg, Germany: Springer. doi:10.1007/978-1-84800-304-0

Li, D., Babcock, J., & Parkhurst, D. J. (2006). openEyes: A low-cost head-mounted eye-tracking solution. *Proceedings of the 2006 Symposium on Eye Tracking Research & Applications (ETRA '06)* (pp. 95–100). New York, NY: ACM.

Li, D., Winfield, D., & Parkhurst, D. J. (2005). Starburst: A hybrid algorithm for video-based eye tracking combining feature-based and model-based approaches. *IEEE Computer Society Conference on Computer Vision and Pattern Recognition (CVPR '05)* (pp. 79–86). Washington, DC., USA: IEEE Computer Society.

Otsu, N. (1979). A threshold selection method from gray-level histogram. *Transactions on Systems, Man, and Cybernetics, 9*(1), 62–66. doi:10.1109/TSMC.1979.4310076

Räihä, K.-J., & Duchowski, A. T. (Eds.). (2008). *Proceedings of the Eye Tracking Research & Application Symposium (ETRA 2008)*. New York, NY: ACM.

Salvucci, D. D., & Goldberg, J. H. (2000). Identifying fixations and saccades in eye-tracking protocols. *Proceedings of the 2000 Symposium on Eye Tracking Research & Applications (ETRA '00)* (pp. 71–78). New York, NY: ACM.

Schmidt, C. (2008). *Evaluation von eye-tracking-teilalgorithmen (Technical report). Universität Koblenz-Landau.* Fachbereich Informatik, Germany: Studienarbeit.

Scott, D., & Findlay, J. (1993). *Visual search, eye movements and display units. Human Factors Report.* Durham, UK: University of Durham.

Shian, R. (1999). *Automatische Bildauswertung zur dynamischen Schielwinkelmessung bei Kleinkindern und Säuglingen* (PhD thesis). Germany: Universität Koblenz-Landau.

Shih, S. W., & Liu, J. (2004). A novel approach to 3-D gaze tracking using stereo cameras. *IEEE Transactions on Systems, Man, and Cybernetics, 34*(1), 234–245. doi:10.1109/TSMCB.2003.811128

Sliney, D. H. (1997). Laser and LED eye hazards: Safety standards. *Optics and Photonics News, 7*(9), 31–37. doi:10.1364/OPN.8.9.000031

Sliney, D. H., Aron-Rosa, D., DeLori, F., Fankhauser, F., Landry, R., Mainster, M., & Wolffe, M. (2005). Adjustment of guidelines for exposure of the eye to optical radiation from ophthalmic instruments: A statement from the International Commission on Non-Ionizing Radiation Protection (ICNIRP). *Applied Optics, 44*(11), 2162–2176. doi:10.1364/AO.44.002162

Sliney, D. H., & Wolbarsht, M. L. (1980). *Safety with lasers and other optical sources.* New York, NY: Plenum Publishing Corp.

Villanueva, A., & Cabeza, R. (2008). A novel gaze estimation system with one calibration point. *IEEE Transactions on Systems, Man, and Cybernetics. Part B, 38*(4), 1123–1138.

Viola, P., & Jones, M. J. (2001). Robust real-time face detection. *International Conference on Computer Vision, 2,* 747. Washington, DC., USA: IEEE.

World Health Organization (WHO). (1982). *Environmental Health Criteria No. 23, lasers and optical radiation,* a joint publication of the United Nations Environmental Programme, the International Radiation Protection Association, and the World Health Organization. Geneva, Switzerland.

Yoo, D. H., & Chung, M. J. (2005). A novel nonintrusive eye gaze estimation using cross-ratio under large head motion. *Computer Vision and Image Understanding, 98*(1), 25–51. doi:10.1016/j.cviu.2004.07.011

Chapter 24
Discussion and Future Directions for Eye Tracker Development

Dan Witzner Hansen
IT University of Copenhagen, Denmark

Fiona Mulvey
IT University of Copenhagen, Denmark

Diako Mardanbegi
IT University of Copenhagen, Denmark

ABSTRACT

Eye and gaze tracking have a long history but there is still plenty of room for further development. In this concluding chapter for Section 6, we consider future perspectives for the development of eye and gaze tracking.

DISCUSSION

Eye and gaze tracking have a long history, but it is only relatively recently that gaze trackers have become sufficiently robust for use outside laboratories (Hansen & Ji, 2010). This development, alongside the ongoing reduction in price and increase in number of manufacturers, opens up many more application domains.

In the previous chapters of this Section 6, we have provided a guided tour through various aspects of eye tracker development and have described the basic hardware equipment and how it is used in eye trackers. Proceeding from this, we provide a gentle introduction to how eye images can be processed in order to obtain relevant feature parameters, such as the iris and pupil ellipses and glint locations. Through the feature descriptors it is possible to estimate the gaze direction, and

DOI: 10.4018/978-1-61350-098-9.ch024

hence the gaze location of the user. The different approaches to determining gaze in both calibrated and uncalibrated set-ups, as well as in both remote and head-mounted eye trackers are outlined. These methods are fundamentally different, and there seems to be room for improvement along several dimensions, to improve both eye detection and gaze estimation methods. For example, few systems have managed to cope well with reflections from eyeglasses.

The previous chapters have described the important role played by infra red (IR) light in current eye trackers and the special properties that make IR light particularly suitable for illuminating the eye. As with any light source, user safety must be carefully considered in terms of the effect on eye structures. The foregoing discussion concluded with a thorough explanation of hardware issues and safety considerations.

FUTURE PERSPECTIVES

In the following discussion, we consider future perspectives for eye and gaze tracking. The precision of current gaze trackers is sufficient for many types of applications. Both accuracy and having few calibration points are desirable properties, but they are not necessarily the only parameters to be addressed in a gaze tracker (Scott & Findlay, 1993). Price is obviously an issue, but it is one that may be resolved through current technological developments. In some situations, however, it would be convenient if light sources, cameras, and monitors could be positioned according to particular needs rather than being constrained by manufacturer specifications (Hansen, San Agustin, & Villanueva, 2010). It seems likely that the high accuracy required to measure eye movement parameters beyond simple fixation position would not be possible without fixed hardware geometries; however, many applications do not require exact measurement of further parameters of eye movements. If eye trackers can also function reliably

in both indoor and outdoor scenarios, they are likely to become more widespread and diverse in their application. Current and future topics for eye and gaze tracker hardware development include the following, outlined by Hansen and Ji (2010).

Illuminating the Eye

IR light is useful for eye trackers, mainly because it is not visible to the user but also because it can be used for controlling light conditions, obtaining higher-contrast eye images, and stabilising gaze estimation. A practical limitation of systems using IR light is that they are not necessarily reliable when used outdoors, although pulsing the light or alternating between on- and off-axis lighting can eliminate many aspects of the problems associated with erroneous light sources. However, tracking outdoors is problematic regardless of the type of light used to illuminate the eye. There is room for improvement and methods that can provide more robust detection of relevant features.

Head-Mounted Systems

While significant emphasis has been placed on remote gaze tracking, head-mounted gaze trackers could be applied to interactive scenarios in the future, because of both the challenges facing remote eye trackers and the increased interest in mobile eye tracking and tiny head-mounted displays. For future technologies, head trackers may also offer a means of tracking several users while they look at the same screen, whereas remote eye trackers imply one user per screen.

Flexible Hardware Set-Up

Many current gaze trackers require calibration of the camera(s) and the geometric arrangement. This is a quite well understood domain theoretically (Guestrin & Eizenman, 2006). A significant limitation of fully calibrated set-ups is that they require precise knowledge of the relative positions of the camera, light source(s), and monitor. The calibration procedures are tedious and time-consuming, and they also mean that a slight unintentional movement of an element in the system may result in a significant decrease in accuracy; clearly, accuracy is difficult to maintain in a non-rigid set-up. Such requirements may add to the cost of the system, also making the system more prone to damage and less robust. However, avoiding external light sources or allowing users to change the zoom of the camera to suit their specific needs would be desirable in some situations for the best possible eye image under varying lighting conditions. Gaze models that support flexible set-ups eliminate the need for rigid placement of individual components. This would benefit eye trackers intended for mobility and the mass market, as it results in more compact, lightweight, portable, adaptable, and inexpensive eye trackers. If the models employed in gaze trackers needed no more than a few calibration targets and simultaneously maintained accuracy while avoiding the need for light sources, eye-tracking technology would take an important step toward being more flexible, mobile, and convenient for the general public. The use of multiple light sources has to some extent facilitated uncalibrated and partially calibrated set-ups and provides fairly accurate gaze estimates (Coutinho & Morimoto, 2006; Hansen et al., 2010; Yoo & Chung, 2005); however, multiple light sources mean more light, and this must be achieved within safe limits for light exposure.

Calibration Procedures

Current gaze models either use a strong prior model (hardware calibration) with little session calibration or employ a weak prior model and a larger number of calibration points (Hansen et al., 2010). Another future direction will be to develop methods that do not require any calibration. This does not seem to be possible in view of current eye and gaze models. New eye models and theories need be developed if we are to realise calibration-free gaze tracking. There also seem to be plenty of room for methods that make the calibration procedure implicit and more entertaining.

Cost of Components

The cost of eye tracking systems, although falling dramatically in recent years, remains too high for use by the general public. The main reasons for this are the cost of parts (especially high-quality cameras and lenses), the cost of development, and the relatively small market. Alternatively, systems may opt for standard or even off-the-shelf components such as digital video cameras and Web cameras and exploit the rapid development in this area (Hansen et al., 2003; Hansen & Pece, 2005; Li et al., 2005; Winfield et al, 2005, San Augustin et al, 2010; Fritzer et al, 2005). While advances in camera and sensor technology may contribute to the progress in the field, theoretical developments are needed if accurate gaze tracking can be performed with low-quality images. Price is obviously an issue, but low cost should not be the only consideration, since the cost issue will most likely be resolved inevitably with technological developments. Today, even cheap Web cameras are of sufficient quality (in terms of both spatial and temporal resolution) to provide reliable gaze tracking for, to take an example, point-and-click interaction purposes. However, for the time being, their temporal resolution is insufficient for the analysis of many of the eye movement parameters, such as saccade velocity. Eye trackers use cameras and external light sources as their main system components – neither of which need necessarily imply high cost. Gaze trackers have, in fact, not changed much for the last 30 years in terms of hardware components – one may even argue since the 'Dodge Photochronograph'. Besides the use of computers, it is mainly the quality and the price of the hardware components that have changed significantly. What may negatively influence the cost of current systems is the need for dedicated hardware such as rigid frames, specialised electronics, and rapid pan-and-tilt units. Low-cost components can make eye and gaze tracking more widespread in the short term, but, since the cost of adequate components will decrease with time in any case, it seems less important for the future to reduce cost than it will be to obtain system flexibility and robustness. The more flexible the system can be, the more adaptable it will be to changes in component cost and quality and indeed expansion in application domains.

Tolerance

Tolerance with respect to glasses and contact lenses is a practical problem that has been solved only partially or with particular systems. The main interference from glasses or other lenses involves the reduced amount of light getting to the eye, as well as the possibility of erroneous pupil-like reflections on the glass being mistaken for pupil reflections by the eye model. Such reflections are common from fingerprints on glasses. If such a reflection is mistaken for the pupil, any tracking at all is impossible until the reflection is removed either physically or by changing the eye–camera–light-source geometry. The use of several light sources, synchronised according to the user's head movement relative to the camera and light source, may remove some of the associated problems but increases the amount of light, which has its safety considerations. These problems are particularly pronounced in low-cost or low-performance eye trackers suitable for point-and-click interaction only. Eye trackers of higher quality, such as those used in research, are less likely to mistake the reflection for a pupil, on account of their higher eye image resolution, and overcome these problems through more complex eye models or by modelling eye behaviour with selection criteria for possible pupil reflections in the eye image. However, other approaches, such as modelling the glasses themselves, could be useful,

particularly for more inexpensive systems, which usually work with a reduced-quality eye image.

CONCLUSION

While high accuracy may not be a priority for all applications, mobile systems must be able to cope with less predictable and more extreme light levels than eye trackers used indoors do. While it would be desirable to have a 'calibration-free high-accuracy' system, it is not obvious that one could be obtained..

REFERENCES

Coutinho, F. L., & Morimoto, C. H. (2006). Free head motion eye gaze tracking using a single camera and multiple light sources. In M. Oliveira Neto & R. L. Carceroni (Eds.), *Proceedings of the 19th Brazilian Symposium on Computer Graphics and Image Processing* (*SIBGRAPI '06*). Washington, DC., USA: IEEE Computer Society.

Fritzer, F., Droege, D., & Paulus, D. (2005). Gaze tracking with inexpensive cameras. *Proceedings of the 1st Conference on Communication by Gaze Interaction* (*COGAIN 2005*) (pp. 10–11). Copenhagen, Denmark: IT University of Copenhagen. Retrieved from the COGAIN website: http://www.cogain.org/conference

Guestrin, E., & Eizenman, M. (2006). General theory of remote gaze estimation using the pupil center and corneal reflections. *IEEE Transactions on Bio-Medical Engineering, 53*(6), 1124–1133. doi:10.1109/TBME.2005.863952

Hansen, D. W., Hansen, J. P., Nielsen, M., Johansen, A. S., & Stegmann, M. B. (2003). Eye typing using Markov and active appearance models. *IEEE Workshop on Applications of Computer Vision* (pp. 132–136).

Hansen, D. W., & Ji, Q. (2010). In the eye of the beholder: A survey of models for eyes and gaze. *IEEE Transactions on Pattern Analysis and Machine Intelligence, 32*(3), 478–500. doi:10.1109/TPAMI.2009.30

Hansen, D. W., & Pece, A. E. (2005). Eye tracking in the wild. *Computer Vision and Image Understanding, 98*(1), 155–181. doi:10.1016/j.cviu.2004.07.013

Hansen, D. W., San Agustin, J., & Villanueva, A. (2010). Homography normalization for robust gaze estimation in uncalibrated setups. *Proceedings of the 2010 Symposium on Eye-Tracking Research & Applications (ETRA '10)* (pp. 13-20). New York, NY: ACM.

Li, D., Winfield, D., & Parkhurst, D. J. (2005). Starburst: A hybrid algorithm for video-based eye tracking combining feature-based and model-based approaches. *IEEE Computer Society Conference on Computer Vision and Pattern Recognition (CVPR '05)* (pp. 79–86). Washington, DC., USA: IEEE Computer Society.

San Agustin, J., Skovsgaard, H., Mollenbach, E., Barret, M., Tall, M., & Hansen, D. W. (2010). Evaluation of a low-cost open-source gaze tracker. *Proceedings of the 2010 Symposium on Eye-Tracking Research & Applications (ETRA '10)* (pp. 77–80). New York, NY: ACM.

Scott, D., & Findlay, J. (1993). *Visual search, eye movements and display units. Human factors report*. Durham, UK: University of Durham.

Winfield, D., Li, D., Babcock, J., & Parkhurst, D. J. (2005). *Towards an open-hardware open-software toolkit for robust low-cost eye tracking in HCI applications* (Technical report ISU-HCI-2005-04). Iowa, USA: Iowa State University, Department of Psychology.

Yoo, D. H., & Chung, M. J. (2005). A novel nonintrusive eye gaze estimation using cross-ratio under large head motion. *Computer Vision and Image Understanding, 98*(1), 25–51. doi:10.1016/j.cviu.2004.07.011

Section 7
Future Directions

Chapter 25
Conclusion and a Look to the Future

Mick Donegan
ACE Centre, UK

Päivi Majaranta
University of Tampere, Finland

John Paulin Hansen
IT University of Copenhagen, Denmark

Aulikki Hyrskykari
University of Tampere, Finland

Hirotaka Aoki
Tokyo Institute of Technology, Japan

Dan Witzner Hansen
IT University of Copenhagen, Denmark

Kari-Jouko Räihä
University of Tampere, Finland

ABSTRACT

Gaze-controlled computers had already been utilized successfully for well over two decades before the COGAIN project started. However, those actually benefitting from the technology were comparatively few compared to the numbers who needed it. During the five year course of the project, however, systems, software and strategies were developed that made this technology potentially available, given appropriate support and technology, to groups who might not have even considered eye control a possibility. As a result, gaze control technology was opened up to a much wider group of people. In this final chapter, we sum up research presented in this book and close it by presenting some future trends and areas with high potential for applied use of eye tracking and gaze interaction.

DOI: 10.4018/978-1-61350-098-9.ch025

INTRODUCTION

Even though eye tracking has a long history, only recently have the systems matured to a level usable and robust enough to be used beyond the lab (Hansen & Ji, 2010). However, those actually benefitting from the technology were comparatively few compared to the numbers who needed it (Donegan et al., 2005; Jordansen et al., 2005). During 2004–2009, the COGAIN Project (www. cogain.org) was a catalyst in moving gaze control forward as a computer access method. The range of beneficiaries and numbers of people using the technology increased dramatically, both in Europe and globally. A key development that took place during COGAIN's five years was the creation of gaze control systems that, combined with appropriate software, could potentially enable people with a much wider range of disabilities to use the technology than ever before.

Prior to COGAIN, the limitations of gaze controlled technology restricted it to clients who were primarily literate, well motivated, had good vision and who had very little or no involuntary movement, such as that suffered by people with ALS/MND. During the course of the project, however, systems, software and strategies were developed that made this technology potentially available, given appropriate support and technology, to groups who might not have even considered eye control a possibility, such as those with severe involuntary head movement or visual difficulties (see Features of Gaze Control Systems by Donegan in Section 2). As a result, gaze control technology was opened up to a much wider group of people, including a significant proportion of the 2.5 million people categorized in Table 1.

The thematic sections of this book presented an overview of the research and development concerning the involvement and special needs of users with varying needs and abilities; key features of gaze control systems targeted at people with disabilities; and interaction design issues of gaze-controlled and gaze-aware systems. We have also learnt about methods and measures for the evaluation and analysis of gaze-based interfaces, or how eye tracking may benefit usability evaluation in general. Finally, we had an in-depth look into the operating principles of a gaze tracking system and learned what it takes to build one of your own. Below, we present some future trends and areas with high potential for applied use of eye tracking and gaze interaction.

Table 1. Groups who could potentially benefit from gaze control technology, with a rough estimate of the prevalence and total number in Europe. (In July 2005, the estimated total population of the EU was 457,000,000.) (Adapted from Jordansen et al., 2005.)

Target groups	Prevalence	Estimated total number in EU
Amyotrophic lateral sclerosis (ALS) / motor neuron disease (MND)	6 per 100,000	27,000
Multiple scleroses (MS)	30 per 100,000	135,000
Cerebral palsy (CP)	200 per 100,000	900,000
Spinal cord injury (SCI)	8 per 100,000	36,000
Spinal muscular atrophy (SMA)	12 per 100,000	54,000
Rett syndrome	6.66 per 100.000	29,970
Muscular dystrophy (MD)	28 per 100.000	126,000
Brainstem stroke	153 per 100,000	688,500
Traumatic brain injury (TBI)	150 per 100.000	675,000
Total		2,671,470

FUTURE IMPROVEMENTS FOR GAZE-BASED ASSISTIVE TECHNOLOGY

Environmental Control

Not only has great progress been made in terms of communication for this very complex group, but also in terms of environmental control. In fact, environmental control is an integral part of a range of gaze control-compatible applications such as The Grid 2 (Sensory Software, 2010), Tobii Communicator (Tobii, 2010), iABLE (2010) and GazeTalk (2010).

At present, the gaze-based environmental control systems that are available commercially require the user to look at an interface on a gaze-controlled screen. However, efforts to eliminate the need for a screen interface are being pursued by a number of researchers, including COGAIN partners.

For example, Shi, Gale, and Purdy (2007) at Loughborough University are investigating the process of the user looking directly at electrical items in order to operate them, thereby removing the need for an on-screen interface for those who do not need one. One clear advantage here is that the screen does not hinder the view of the user, which is important for household electrical appliances such as a TV.

Corno, Gale, Majaranta, and Räihä (2010) and Chapter 10 by Bates and colleagues in this book review the different approaches to environmental control.

Gaze Control for Powered Mobility

Whilst great progress has been made with gaze controlled communication, computer control and environmental control, the use of gaze control for powered mobility remains a key area for further development. Big steps forward have, however, already been taken in this area, as reported by Bates and colleagues in Chapter 10 of this book.

Current systems allow the wheelchair to be 'steered' by following the direction of gaze, or by applying an intelligent mobility control system that can automatically navigate to predefined locations in closed (safety assured) environments. However, there is still some way to go before gaze controlled mobility can be freely used by people with disabilities because of the health and safety issues involved. For example, Matsumoto, Ino, and Ogasawara (2001) achieved a precision level of 3 degrees with their wheelchair-mounted tracking system. They had concerns that the user's attention may easily be distracted in dynamic environments and when surrounded by other pedestrians, making it dangerous to gaze-drive a wheelchair. Canzler and Kraiss (2004) experienced problems with unpredictable lighting conditions (e.g. sunlight and neon lights shining into the camera). Vibrations from the rolling wheelchair also complicated gaze tracking. Wästlund, Sponseller, and Pettersson (2010), on the other hand, conducted a clinical trial with a modern, reliable gaze tracking device. The two users in their trial both mastered – and highly appreciated – the ability to control a powered wheelchair by gaze.

There are three different design approaches to controlling a vehicle by gaze:

1. Directly, by looking in the drive direction (e.g., Matsumoto et al., 2001).
2. Indirectly, by gazing at on-screen buttons that execute commands such as "forward," "stop," etc. (e.g., Novák, Krajník, Přeučil, Fejtová, & Štěpánková, 2008).
3. By gazing at an image of the front-view (a live view of the scene on the screen).

Tall et al. (2009) investigated the third option using an unmanned vehicle for conducting safe trials with (remote) gaze-driven locomotion. A screen showing live images from a forward-facing camera mounted on the vehicle was found to be a natural interface for locomotion control. The live image interface offered additional interaction design features. For instance, the further ahead (i.e. up) in the image the user fixated, the faster the vehicle travelled, while looking away from the image would cause it to brake immediately, providing an intuitive "panic button".

There seems to be a high level of need for development of gaze-driven locomotion and opportunities for intensified research. Some of this research may also lead to new ways of controlling mobile cameras used for industrial inspection and for remote exploration of hazard areas. New robot toys, such as the driving Rovio (2010) or the flying AR.DRONE (2010), could have in-built mobile cameras that could be controlled remotely. A primary target group for this research would be disabled children. Controlling robot toys by gaze would allow these children to explore and interact with locations that they would not otherwise have access to, such as rough nature areas, for instance.

For the use of gaze control for powered mobility, the challenges that still remain are:

- to develop *failsafe* gaze controlled mobility interfaces for people with a wide range of physical, visual and learning disability, and
- to develop a gaze controlled system that can be used reliably out of doors.

The importance of taking safety issues into account with powered mobility cannot be overestimated. If a computer-based application such as word processor crashes, the result can be annoying; if an eye-powered mobility system crashes the consequences could be fatal. The huge potential and challenges of gaze-based environmental control and mobility are discussed in more detail in Chapter 10.

Alternatives for Limited or Deteriorating Eye Control

As a result of the COGAIN project, several users described as having locked-in syndrome were able to use a gaze control system successfully, even if they had involuntary eye movement and could only move their eyes in one direction. However, it was found that a small number of people with locked-in syndrome were unable to use a gaze control system due to technical issues.

The essential problem was that many gaze controlled computers require the entire pupil to be visible to the camera. With some locked-in users, and a small number of other users, their eyelids partly covered their pupils. Whilst the LC system, for example, has a 'droopy eyelid compensation' feature designed to overcome this problem, there were still some users whose eye movement was difficult to recognize. For many people with locked-in syndrome, even though they might be paralyzed and find controlling their eye movement difficult, one skill that they *do* retain is the ability to look in a single direction. This movement is often used as an affirmation. For example, Russell (in Figure 1), is extremely quick and effective at using an upward eye movement for his low-tech communication. As his carer goes through the alphabet, Russell looks up when his communication partner speaks the letter he wants. Whilst Russell's pupil is clearly visible when he looks up, with many other users the pupil disappears behind the eyelid, making the use of a gaze control system difficult to use for this purpose.

Figure 1. Russell looking up

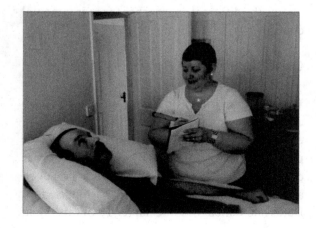

It is strongly recommended that, in future, gesture recognition of such deliberate movements is fully investigated in order to capitalize upon what is, for many people with such disabilities, a quick, effective, deliberate and easy movement. It is encouraging to see that work is already being done in this area. Istance, Vickers, and Hyrskykari (2009), for example, are utilizing gaze gestures to simulate the controls of popular computer games for quick and efficient computer control (see Figure 2).

Even though eye or lid movements are typically the last remaining voluntary movements for patients diagnosed with progressive neurodegenerative diseases, some patients are devoid of any eye movement control. For these patients in a so-called completely locked-in state (CLIS), communication is very difficult to achieve. By means of a brain-computer interface (BCI), subjects can learn as a response to provided information to deliberately increase or decrease brain activity and changes in behaviour can be measured accordingly. Usually, the provided information is visual. Chapter 12 by Vidaurre and colleagues refers to studies in which auditory information

has been successfully used as a substitute for visual information in BCI based communication. Auditory information and feedback could thus be achieved in CLIS cases, although in all of the studies the information transfer rate was lower for auditory information compared to visual information.

Evaluation

As noted above, gaze control is becoming a realistic option for an increasing number of users. Close involvement of the end users in all stages of the research, design and implementation processes therefore remains essential. However, involving users with complex disabilities in the design process can be challenging, as there often is considerable variability between individuals depending on the stage and severity of their condition (Donegan et al., 2009). The researcher needs to carefully consider the current and evolving abilities of the user and be ready to adjust their evaluation methods to suit the characteristics of the participants (Hornof, 2008; Lepistö & Ovaska, 2004). Nevertheless, further work is required

Figure 2. Gaze gesture interface in the Blizzard Entertainment's World of Warcraft. The numbered lines (not seen by the player) illustrate an example gaze gesture path. (Adapted from Istance, Vickers, & Hyrskykari, 2009. © 2009 Istance et al. Used with permission.)

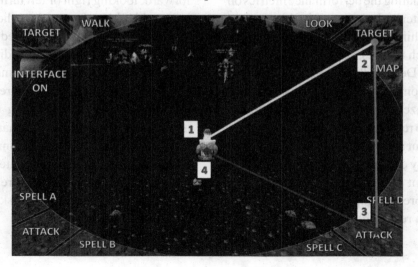

to develop research methods that enable better involvement of people with disabilities.

Apart from a few exceptions, gaze control research has continued to rely heavily on controlled experiments with able-bodied participants. Although the results give indicative information on system usability and efficiency, they may not be directly applicable to the target users. Conducting controlled experiments with people who have serious medical conditions presents a series of challenges. For instance, it may not be practical or safe to transfer the participants to a laboratory environment. Furthermore, in the case of rare conditions, potential participants can be few and far apart. Aoki, Hansen, and Itoh (2006) suggest using remote evaluation as a means of collecting large quantities of data ecologically in the user's normal environment. This would enable benchmarking of eye tracking or gaze typing systems in actual use. The remote evaluation concept raises questions concerning the measures used to evaluate user gaze performance which, while being effective at eliciting user behaviour from large amounts of eye movement data, are subject to strict limitations due to user privacy. Aoki et al. suggest the use of measures which preserve user privacy by not revealing the content of user communication, but which still transfer useful information on their progress. This can be implemented by calculating the performance metrics on the local computer and sending only this result to the remote machine for further examination (for examples of such metrics, see e.g. Aoki, Hansen, & Itoh, 2009). Despite the great importance of remote evaluation, the development of measures that represent gaze behaviour in actual use and that are applicable to remote evaluation has been slow. The development and validation of measures that can be efficiently calculated from large quantities of eye movement data obtained in natural conditions is, therefore, an important area for future gaze interaction research.

Games and Toys

For people with severe motor disabilities, playing games and taking part in virtual communities can be especially important (Vickers, Bates, & Istance, 2008). Participation can be challenging and fun, but in addition, multi-player online games (MOG) give opportunities for social interaction, and the extent of the player's disability need not be apparent to other players. This kind of interaction, where the player is often playing against the clock, poses additional demands on gaze interaction techniques (Istance, Hyrskykari, Vickers, & Chaves, 2009).

One new branch of research aims to design software devices that enable gaming for users who are not able to use traditional keyboard/mouse/gamepad input devices. There are already a number of games that can be played by eye control alone. SpecialEffect (specialeffect.org.uk) maintains a game base for gamers with disabilities. Information on the supported control methods, gaze pointing included, is provided for each game.

Gaze can also be used to remotely control toys. Fejtová, Figueiredo, Novák, Štěpánková, and Gomes (2009) have developed a toy car that can be remotely steered by eye movement: a central eye position (looking directly ahead) keeps the car stationary; a glance up causes the car to move forward; looking right or left turns the car right or left; and looking down drives the car in reverse.

These studies into gaze-based leisure applications for disabled users are seeding ideas for the use of point of attention in games for all. They may well be regarded by future generations as pioneering work in improving the quality and naturalness of interaction in many future applications, including those of the mainstream video games industry. Adding gaze interaction to existing games can make them more immersive and more fun for any player (Isokoski, Joos, Špakov, & Martin, 2009).

EYE TRACKING FOR ALL

The focus of this book is on how to use eye gaze to assist users with special needs and varying abilities. However, eye gaze has a major potential role to play in the development of applications that are easier and more natural for everybody to use (Hansen, Hansen, Johansen, & Elvesjö, 2005; Kumar, Paepcke, & Winograd, 2007). If this eye tracking potential were to be realised in software and hardware industries, ordinary people in both the disabled and the wider community would benefit. The increased demand for good quality web cameras capable of eye tracking would decrease the manufacturing costs of more demanding eye trackers for disabled users and, vice versa, average users would benefit if applications were made smarter with an embedded 'attention tracker'. Examples of such gaze-aware mainstream applications include hands-free mobile phones (Miluzzo, Wang, & Campbell, 2010; Nagamatsu, Yamamoto, & Sato, 2010) or eye-enhanced laptops (Tobii, 2011).

Attentive Interfaces

Measuring the point of fixation by following eye movement has the unique capability of revealing the user's focus of attention, if not definitively, at least to a very high degree of reliability. The opportunities that this information presents for future applications could be immense.

An eye tracker can consist of a standard input device that provides an application with information on the user's attentional state. In addition to revealing the user's focus of attention, the device might also provide indications of their intentions, mental load, fatigue or even their emotional state. Eye movements alone provide an effective indicator of the user's focus of attention and, to some extent, intentions, but they are limited with respect to determining the user's mental load, fatigue, or emotional state. Brain signal measurement offers the potential for direct access to information on

these states. When an application receives information on the user's attentional state, the response can vary widely depending on the circumstances. At the bottom end of the scale, this information might trigger a subtle adjustment of system default values, or the pre-fetching of information for possible later use by, for example, modifying the way the application behaves subsequently, or, at the other extreme, it could be translated into direct commands. Between the extreme approaches, gaze data can be used to produce implicit information retrieval queries based on the user's interest inferred from the gaze patterns (Ajanki, Hardoon, Kaski, Puolamäki, & Shawe-Taylor, 2009; Ajanki et al., 2010).

In the future, gaze-awareness might not be limited just to desktop applications, but any number of objects around us could be gaze-aware and responsive to our attention (Vertegaal, 2003). Gaze awareness may be embedded in the objects themselves or on the user (e.g. by having her wear a portable head-mounted gaze tracker). Everyday objects in the home and office could change their current state when attended, or systems could react by recognizing which object(s) the user is attending. In this book (see e.g. Chapter 13 by Istance and Hyrskykari), we presented a number of possible ways in which to detect when the user is attending an object. The development of high performance miniature cameras is making a variety of solutions viable, which makes the future for this area look very promising indeed (see Chapter 24 by Hansen and colleagues for discussion of the future development of gaze tracking systems).

Above, we discussed the safety issues involved in gaze-based control of a powered wheelchair. In contrast, adding eye tracking capability to a car can potentially bring substantial improvements to automotive safety. For example, an 'attentive car' can detect driver drowsiness or fatigue based on slow blinking and alert the driver (Grace et al., 1998). It has also been suggested that gaze pointing combined with a button on the wheel could replace a touch screen in communication and infotainment applications in modern cars; if the display is projected onto the windscreen, the driver can keep their eyes on the road and their hands on the wheel (e.g., Kern, Mahr, Castronovo, Schmidt, & Müller, 2010). Human attention can, however, be easily distracted. The user might be deep in thought or engrossed in conversation – the driver's eyes may be on the road, but their attention may be elsewhere (Sodhi et al., 2006).

Videoconferencing

Videoconferencing technology has proven an invaluable tool for business communication, and one-to-one video chat systems have millions of users worldwide. Being able to see the people you are communicating with makes a difference and can substantially enhance the communication process. The value of this is even more apparent for people with mobility limitations. In multi-channel video meetings where each participant is presented via an individual video stream, the image of the person being currently regarded may be updated most frequently and the audio from this person prioritized. This could help overcome the bandwidth challenges of live video transmissions and retain the smoothness of conversational exchanges in groups of people seated around a table, even though they occupy different physical locations. With the exception of GAZE-2 by Vertegaal, Weevers, and Sohn (2002), there has been little research into gaze-interactive videoconference systems. A universally accessible interface with the Skype video chat system CanConnect (2010), which allows gaze control, has recently been released and this may generate more interest in the field.

Wearable Displays

Technological developments often spark unpredictable market developments. We expect gaze interaction via wearable displays to have a major impact on the spread of gaze interaction in the mainstream market. Wearable displays, although rarely used yet, are likely to become lightweight and discrete, minimising their power consumption. Developers of gaze tracking systems have also begun exploring this avenue (e.g. San Agustin, Hansen, Hansen, & Skovsgaard, 2009). Besides augmentative and alternative communication (AAC) and mainstream applications, gaze interaction via wearable displays may be of relevance to a range of professionals. Doctors, for instance, could interact with medical records and images by gaze-attentive technology while examining a patient (Lewis, 2004). Everyday gaze interactive wearable displays would replace the majority of activities that we currently perform with our fingers on a mobile phone, only there would be no need to pick it up or search for it in a pocket – the display would be right before our eyes and our hands would be free. Sony (2010) has showcased an interesting mobile application for Lifelog: a forward facing camera records the scene in front of the user and a gaze tracker records what the user is paying attention to. The application can recognize English characters and collect character data from the text that the user is viewing, such as a book title. Instant translation of fixated words or characters would be another obvious application for this kind of tool (cf. iDict introduced in Chapter 13, and Hyrskykari, 2006).

Certain interesting features of tracking systems may in themselves promote the combination of gaze control with wearable displays. For example, the ability to mount a tracking camera and display together on the head eliminates the need to compensate for head movement and overcomes the field of view limitations of remote stationary cameras. The result for the user is total freedom of orientation and position. Secondly, disturbing reflections on glass lenses can be eliminated by locating (micro-) cameras inside glasses. Finally, the short distance between the eye and the display provides an observable reflection of the screen image on the cornea, which Hansen, San Agustin, and Villanueva (2010) have been able to utilize in a new, robust gaze tracking method.

CONCLUSION

Eye tracking continues to be an important tool for usability testing, market research and the medical science, as well as any other discipline where knowledge of human visual attention can be beneficial. However, as this book shows, its importance for interactive technology is growing rapidly. Gaze control technology is particularly beneficial for people with special needs, but there is also huge potential for its applied use in a wide variety of everyday systems that might benefit from knowledge of the user's attention. It remains to be seen which "killer application" will finally launch eye tracking into the mainstream market and put it on a price par with other specialized input devices, such as game controllers.

The cost of gaze control, which is still relatively high compared to many other control methods, may still be the main barrier to accessing this new technology. Our work with those people who have had the opportunity to use gaze control in their everyday life nevertheless clearly shows that gaze control can, indeed, have a positive impact on posture, pain reduction, speed, academic success, quality of life, and employability (Donegan, 2010). Weighed against these benefits, almost any cost can begin to appear cheap.

All in all, while much has already been achieved, there is still a great deal of work to do to make sure that as many people as possible whose preferred, or only, method of computer control is eye movement are ensured access to this empowering technology. It is sincerely hoped that future work will continue to put the user at the heart of the research and development process. Without the enthusiasm, patience and determination of the users who have been so closely involved, the great strides that COGAIN made between 2004–2009 would never have been possible.

REFERENCES

Ajanki, A., Billinghurst, M., Järvenpää, T., Kandemir, M., Kaski, S., Koskela, M., et al. (2010). Contextual information access with augmented reality. *IEEE International Workshop on Machine Learning for Signal Processing (MLSP '10)* (pp. 95–100), Kittilä, Finland. doi:10.1109/MLSP.2010.5589228

Ajanki, A., Hardoon, D. R., Kaski, S., Puolamäki, K., & Shawe-Taylor, J. (2009). Can eyes reveal interest? Implicit queries from gaze patterns. *User Modeling and User-Adapted Interaction*, *19*(4), 307–339. doi:10.1007/s11257-009-9066-4

Aoki, H., Hansen, J. P., & Itoh, K. (2006). Towards remote evaluation of gaze typing systems. *Proceedings of the 2nd Conference on Communication by Gaze Interaction (COGAIN 2006)* (pp. 96–103). Turin, Italy: Politecnico di Torino. Retrieved from the COGAIN website: http://www.cogain.org/conference

Aoki, H., Hansen, J. P., & Itoh, K. (2009). Learning gaze typing: What are the obstacles and what progress to expect? *Universal Access in the Information Society*, *8*(4), 297–310. doi:10.1007/s10209-009-0152-5

AR. DRONE (2010). Retrieved December, 2010, from http://ardrone.parrot.com/parrot-ar-drone/en/

CanConnect. (2010). Retrieved December, 2010, from http://www.canassist.ca/EN/main/programs/technologies-and-devices/human-computer/can-connect.html

Canzler, U., & Kraiss, K. F. (2004). Person-adaptive facial feature analysis for an advanced wheelchair user-interface. In P. Drews (Ed.), *Conference on Mechatronics & Robotics 2004* (*MechRob 2004*) (vol. Part 3, pp. 871–876). Aachen, Germany: Sascha Eysoldt Verlag.

Corno, F., Gale, A., Majaranta, P., & Räihä, K.-J. (2010). Eye-based direct interaction for environmental control in heterogeneous smart environments. In H. Nakashima, H. Aghajan, & J. C. Augusto (Eds.), *Handbook of ambient intelligence and smart environments* (pp. 1117–1138). New York, NY: Springer. doi:10.1007/978-0-387-93808-0_41

Donegan, M. (2010). Gaze controlled technology – How far have we come? Where are we going? In Wilson, A., & Gow, R. (Eds.), *The eyes have it! The use of eye gaze to support communication* (pp. 3–6). Edinburgh, UK: CALL Scotland, The University of Edinburgh.

Donegan, M., Morris, D. J., Corno, F., Signorile, I., Chió, A., & Pasian, V. (2009). Understanding users and their needs. *Universal Access in the Information Society, 8*(4), 259–275. doi:10.1007/s10209-009-0148-1

Donegan, M., Oosthuizen, L., Bates, R., Daunys, G., Hansen, J. P., & Joos, M. …Signorile, I. (2005). *User requirements report with observations of difficulties users are experiencing.* (Deliverable 3.1. Communication by Gaze Interaction (COGAIN), Project IST-2003-511598). Retrieved from the COGAIN website: http://www.cogain.org/wiki/COGAIN_Reports

Fejtová, M., Figueiredo, L., Novák, P., Štěpánková, O., & Gomes, A. (2009). Hands-free interaction with a computer and other technologies. *Universal Access in the Information Society, 8*(4), 277–295. doi:10.1007/s10209-009-0147-2

GazeTalk. (2010). Retrieved December, 2010, from http://www.cogain.org/wiki/Gazetalk

Grace, R., Byrne, V. E., Bierman, D. M., Legrand, J.-M., Gricourt, D., & Davis, B. K. …Carnahan, B. (1998). A drowsy driver detection system for heavy vehicles. *Proceedings of the 17th AIAA/IEEE/SAE Digital Avionics Systems Conference (DASC '98)* (vol. 2, I36/1–I36/8). doi:10.1109/DASC.1998.739878

Hansen, D. W., & Ji, Q. (2010). In the eye of the beholder: A survey of models for eyes and gaze. *IEEE Transactions on Pattern Analysis and Machine Intelligence, 32*(3), 478–500. doi:10.1109/TPAMI.2009.30

Hansen, D. W., San Agustin, J., & Villanueva, A. 2010. Homography normalization for robust gaze estimation in uncalibrated setups. *Proceedings of the 2010 Symposium on Eye-Tracking Research & Applications (ETRA '10)* (pp. 13–20). New York, NY: ACM. doi:10.1145/1743666.1743670

Hansen, J. P., Hansen, D. W., Johansen, A. S., & Elvesjö, J. (2005). Mainstreaming gaze interaction towards a mass market for the benefit of all. *Proceedings of the 11th International Conference on Human-Computer Interaction (HCII '05),* (VOL 7, CD-ROM). Mahwah, NJ: Lawrence Erlbaum Associates, Inc.

Hornof, A. (2008). Working with children with severe motor impairments as design partners. *Proceedings of the 7th International Conference on Interaction Design and Children (IDC '08)* (pp. 69–72). New York, NY: ACM. doi:10.1145/1463689.1463721

Hyrskykari, A. (2006). *Eyes in attentive interfaces: Experiences from creating iDict, a gaze-aware reading aid.* Dissertations in Interactive Technology 4, University of Tampere, Finland. Retrieved from the University of Tampere website: http://acta.uta.fi/pdf/951-44-6643-8.pdf

iABLE (2010). Retrieved December, 2010, from http://www.iable.ca/web/

Isokoski, P., Joos, M., Špakov, O., & Martin, B. (2009). Gaze controlled games. *Universal Access in the Information Society, 8*(4), 323–337. doi:10.1007/s10209-009-0146-3

Istance, H., Hyrskykari, A., Vickers, S., & Chaves, T. (2009). For your eyes only: Controlling 3D online games by eye-gaze. In T. Gross, J. Gulliksen, P. Kotzé, L. Oestreicher, P. Palanque, R. O. Prates, & M. Winckler (Eds.), *Human–Computer Interaction (INTERACT 2009)* (LNCS 5726, pp. 314–327). Berlin, Germany: Springer-Verlag. doi:10.1007/978-3-642-03655-2_36

Istance, H., Vickers, S., & Hyrskykari, A. (2009). Gaze-based interaction with massively multiplayer on-line games. *Extended Abstracts of the 27th International Conference on Human Factors in Computing Systems (CHI '09)* (pp. 4381–4386). New York, NY: ACM. doi:10.1145/1520340.1520670

Jordansen, I. K., Boedeker, S., Donegan, M., Oosthuizen, L., di Girolamo, M., & Hansen, J. P. (2005). *Report on a market study and demographics of user population.* (Deliverable 7.2. Communication by Gaze Interaction (COGAIN), Project IST-2003-511598). Retrieved from the COGAIN website: http://www.cogain.org/wiki/COGAIN_Reports

Kern, D., Mahr, A., Castronovo, S., Schmidt, A., & Müller, C. (2010). Making use of drivers' glances onto the screen for explicit gaze-based interaction. *Proceedings of the 2nd International Conference on Automotive User Interfaces and Interactive Vehicular Applications (AutomotiveUI '10)*, Pittsburgh, PA. Retrieved from http://www.auto-ui.org/10/proceedings/p110.pdf

Kumar, M., Paepcke, A., & Winograd, T. (2007). EyePoint: practical pointing and selection using gaze and keyboard. *Proceedings of the 25th International Conference on Human Factors in Computing Systems (CHI '07)* (pp. 421–430). New York, NY: ACM. doi:10.1145/1240624.1240692

Lepistö, A., & Ovaska, S. (2004). Usability evaluation involving participants with cognitive disabilities. *Proceedings of the 3rd Nordic Conference on Human-Computer interaction (NordiCHI '04)* (vol. 82, pp. 305–308). New York, NY: ACM. doi:10.1145/1028014.1028061

Lewis, J. R. (2004). In the eyes of the beholder. *IEEE Spectrum, 41*(5), 24–28. doi:10.1109/MSPEC.2004.1296010

Matsumoto, Y., Ino, T., & Ogasawara, T. (2001). Development of intelligent wheelchair system with face and gaze-based interface. *Proceedings of 10th IEEE International Workshop on Robot and Human Communication (ROMAN '01)* (pp. 262–267). Washington, DC., USA: IEEE. doi:10.1109/ROMAN.2001.981912

Miluzzo, E., Wang, T., & Campbell, A. T. (2010). EyePhone: activating mobile phones with your eyes. *Proceedings of the 2nd ACM SIGCOMM workshop on Networking, systems, and applications on mobile handhelds (MobiHeld '10)* (pp. 15–20). New York, NY: ACM. doi:10.1145/1851322

Nagamatsu, T., Yamamoto, M., & Sato, H. (2010). MobiGaze: development of a gaze interface for handheld mobile devices. *Proceedings of the 28th International Conference on Human Factors in Computing Systems (CHI '10)* (pp. 3349–3354). New York, NY: ACM. doi:10.1145/1753846.1753983

Novák, P., Krajník, T., Přeučil, L., Fejtová, M., & Štěpánková, O. (2008). AI support for a gaze controlled wheelchair. *Proceedings of the 4th Conference on Communication by Gaze Interaction (COGAIN 2008)* (pp. 46–49). Prague, Czech Republic: Czech Technical University. Retrieved from the COGAIN website: http://www.cogain.org/conference

Rovio (2010). Retrieved December, 2010, from http://www.wowwee.com/en/products/tech/telepresence/rovio/rovio

San Agustin, J., Hansen, J. P., Hansen, D. W., & Skovsgaard, H. H. T. (2009). Low-cost gaze pointing and EMG clicking. *Extended Abstracts of the 27ᵗʰ International Conference on Human Factors in Computing Systems (CHI '09)* (pp. 3247–3252). New York, NY: ACM. doi:10.1145/1520340.1520466

Sensory Software. (2010). *The Grid 2*. Retrieved December, 2010, from http://www.sensorysoftware.com/thegrid2.html

Shi, F., Gale, A., & Purdy, K. (2007). A new gaze-based interface for environmental control. In C. Stephanidis (Ed.), Universal access in human-computer interaction. Ambient interaction, *Proceedings of the 4ᵗʰ International Conference on Universal Access in Human-Computer Interaction (UAHCI 2007)*, Part II (LNCS 4555, pp. 996–1005). Berlin, Germany: Springer-Verlag. doi:10.1007/978-3-540-73281-5_109

Sodhi, M., Reimer, B., Cohen, J. L., Vastenburg, E., Kaars, R., & Kirschenbaum, S. (2002). On-road driver eye movement tracking using head-mounted devices. *Proceedings of the 2002 Symposium on Eye Tracking Research & Applications (ETRA '02)* (pp. 61–68). New York, NY: ACM. doi:10.1145/507072.507086

Sony (2010). *Sony prototypes eye-tracking glasses for lifelog*. Retrieved December, 2010, from http://techon.nikkeibp.co.jp/english/NEWS_EN/20100604/183197/

Tall, M., Alapetite, A., San Agustin, J., Skovsgaard, H. H. T., Hansen, J. P., Hansen, D. W., & Møllenbach, E. (2009). Gaze-controlled driving. *Extended Abstracts of the 27ᵗʰ International Conference on Human Factors in Computing Systems (CHI '09)* (pp. 4387–4392). New York, NY: ACM. doi:10.1145/1520340.1520671

Tobii (2010). *Tobii Communicator*. Retrieved December, 2010, from http://www.tobii.com/en/assistive-technology/global/products/software/tobii-communicator/

Tobii (2011). *Tobii unveils the world's first eye-controlled laptop*. Press release, March 1, 2011. Retrieved June, 2011, from http://www.tobii.com/en/group/news-and-events/press-releases/

Vertegaal, R. (2003). Attentive user interfaces. *Communications of the ACM, 46*(3), 30–33. doi:10.1145/636772.636794

Vertegaal, R., Weevers, I., & Sohn, C. (2002). GAZE-2: An attentive video conferencing system. *Extended Abstracts of Human Factors in Computing Systems (CHI '02)* (pp. 736–737). New York, NY: ACM. doi:10.1145/506443.506572

Vickers, S., Bates, R., & Istance, H. (2008). Gazing into a Second Life: Gaze-driven adventures, control barriers, and the need for disability privacy in an online virtual world. *Proceedings of the 7ᵗʰ International Conference on Disability, Virtual Reality and Associated Technologies (ICDVRAT 2008)*, Maia, Portugal. Retrieved from http://www.icdvrat.reading.ac.uk/2008/abstracts.htm

Wästlund, E., Sponseller, K., & Pettersson, O. (2010). What you see is where you go: Testing a gaze-driven power wheelchair for individuals with severe multiple disabilities. *Proceedings of the 2010 Symposium on Eye-Tracking Research & Applications (ETRA '10)* (pp. 133–136). New York, NY: ACM. doi:10.1145/1743666.1743699

Additional Reading

ADDITIONAL READINGS FOR SECTION 1

Bates, R., Donegan, M., Istance, H. O., Hansen, J. P., & Räihä, K.-J. (2007). Introducing COGAIN: communication by gaze interaction. *Universal Access in the Information Society, 6*(2), 159–166. doi:10.1007/s10209-007-0077-9

Findlay, J. M., Walker, R., & Kentridge, R. W. (Eds.). (1995). *Eye movement research. mechanisms, processes and applications. North-Holland.* Elsevier Science.

Gale, A. G., & Johnson, F. (Eds.). (1984). *Theoretical and applied aspects of eye movement research.* Amsterdam, The Netherlands: Elsevier Science Publishers B.V.

Gregory, R. L. (1997). *Eye and brain, the psychology of seeing* (5th ed.). NJ, USA: Princeton University Press.

Haber, R. N., & Hershenson, M. (1973). *The psychology of visual perception.* London, UK: Holt, Rinehart and Winston.

Hyönä, J., Radach, R., & Deubel, H. (Eds.). (2003). *The mind's eye: Cognitive and applied aspects of eye movement research.* Amsterdam, The Netherlands: Elsevier Science.

Lens, A., Coyne Nemeth, S., & Ledford, J. K. (2008). *Ocular anatomy and physiology* (2nd ed.). NJ, USA: SLACK Inc.

Loshin, D. S. (1991). *The geometrical optics workbook.* London, UK: Butterworth-Heinemann.

Snowden, R., Thompson, P., & Troscianko, T. (2006). *Basic vision: An introduction to visual perception.* Oxford, UK: Oxford University Press.

Van Buren, J. M. (1963). *The retinal ganglion cell layer.* Springfield, Illinois: Charles C. Thomas.

ADDITIONAL READINGS FOR SECTION 2

Calvo, A., Chiò, A., Castellina, E., Corno, F., & Farinetti, L. …Vignola, A. (2008). Eye tracking impact on quality-of-life of ALS patients. *Computers Helping People with Special Needs (ICCHP '08)* (LNCS 5105/2008) (pp. 70–77). Berlin, Germany: Springer.

Donegan, M., Morris, D. J., Corno, F., Signorile, I., Chió, A., & Pasian, V. (2009). Understanding users and their needs. *Universal Access in the Information Society, 8*(4), 259–275. doi:10.1007/s10209-009-0148-1

Garbe, J. (2006). *Typing quickly and relaxed with the eyes. A case study comparing switch based and Gaze Controlled Input Methods*. Handout for the COGAIN PhD Course on Eye-Computer Interaction: Eye performance and interface design, 6-8 September 2006, Turin, Italy. Retrieved from the COGAIN website: http://www.cogain.org/wiki/ COGAIN_Camp_2006 _PhD_Course

Hornof, A. (2008). Working with children with severe motor impairments as design partners. *Proceedings of the 7th International Conference on Interaction Design and Children (IDC'08)* (pp. 69–72). New York, NY: ACM Press. doi:10.1145/1463689.1463721

Hornof, A. J. (2009). Designing with children with severe motor impairments. *Proceedings of the 27th International Conference on Human Factors in Computing Systems (CHI '09)* (pp. 2177–2180). New York, NY: ACM Press. doi:10.1145/1518701.1519032

Hornof, A. J., & Cavender, A. (2005). EyeDraw: Enabling children with severe motor impairments to draw with their eyes. *Proceedings of the SIGCHI Conference on Human Factors in Computing Systems (CHI'05)* (pp. 161–170). New York, NY: ACM Press.

Joos, M., Malischke, S., Pannasch, S., Storch, A., & Velichkovsky, B. M. (2007). Comparing two gaze-interaction interfaces: A usability study with locked-in patients. *Proceedings of the 3rd Conference on Communication by Gaze Interaction (COGAIN 2007)* (pp. 82–88). Leicester, UK: De Montfort University. Retrieved from the COGAIN website: http://www.cogain.org/conference

Wilson, A., & Gow, R. (2010). *The Eyes have it! The use of eye gaze to support communication*. CALL Scotland, University of Edinburgh, Edinburgh, Scotland. (The book can be purchased online at http://www.callscotland.org.uk/shop.)

ADDITIONAL READINGS FOR SECTION 3

Barea, R., Boquete, L., Mazo, M., & Lopez, E. (2002). System for assisted mobility using eye movements based on electro-oculography. *IEEE Transactions on Neural Systems and Rehabilitation Engineering, 10*(4), 209–218. doi:10.1109/TNSRE.2002.806829

Barreto, A. B., Scargle, S. D., & Adjouadi, M. (2000). A practical EMG-based human-computer interface for users with motor disabilities. *Journal of Rehabilitation Research and Development, 37*(1), 53–64.

Bates, R., Istance, H. O., & Vickers, S. (2008). Gaze interaction with virtual on-line communities. In P. Langdon, J. Clarkson, & P. Robinson (Eds.), *Designing inclusive futures* (pp. 149–162). London, UK: Springer. doi: 10.1007/978-1-84800-211-1_15

Charlier, J., Buquet, C., Dubus, F., Hugeux, J. P., & Degroc, B. (1997). VISIOBOARD: A new gaze command system for handicapped subjects. *Medical and Biological Engineering and Computing, 35,* 416 supplement D90.OS1.03.

Corno, F., Gale, A., Majaranta, P., & Räihä, K.-J. (2010). Eye-based direct interaction for environmental control in heterogeneous smart environments. In H. Nakashima, H. Aghajan, & J. C. Augusto (Eds.), *Handbook of ambient intelligence and smart environments* (pp. 1117–1138). New York, NY: Springer. doi:10.1007/978-0-387-93808-0_41

Duchowski, A. T., & Vertegaal, R. (2000). *Eye-based interaction in graphical systems: Theory and practice.* Course 05, SIGGRAPH 2000. Course Notes. New York, NY: ACM. Retrieved December, 2010, from http://vret.ces.clemson.edu/sigcourse/

Garbe, J. (2006). *Typing quickly and relaxed with the eyes. A case study comparing switch based and gaze controlled input methods.* Handout for the COGAIN PhD Course on Eye-Computer Interaction: Eye performance and interface design, 6-8 September 2006, Turin, Italy. Retrieved from http://www. cogain.org/wiki/ COGAIN_Camp_2006_PhD_Course

Hori, J., Sakano, K., & Saitoh, Y. (2006). Development of a communication support device controlled by eye movements and voluntary eye blink. *IEICE Transactions on Information and Systems, 89*(6), 1790–1797. doi:10.1093/ietisy/e89-d.6.1790

Milekic, S. (2003). The more you look the more you get: Intention-based interface using gaze-tracking. In *Museums and the Web 2003: Selected Papers from an International Conference.* Toronto, Canada: Archives & Museum Informatics. Retrieved from http://www.archimuse.com /mw2003/papers/milekic/milekic.html

Miniotas, D., Špakov, O., & Evreinov, G. E. (2003). Symbol creator: An alternative eye-based text entry technique with low demand for screen space . In Rauterberg, M., Menozzi, M., & Wesson, J. (Eds.), *Human–Computer Interaction – INTERACT 2003* (pp. 137–143). Amsterdam, The Netherlands: IOS Press.

Monden, A., Matsumoto, K., & Yamato, M. (2005). Evaluation of gaze-added target selection methods suitable for general GUIs. *International Journal of Computer Applications in Technology, 24*(1), 17–24. doi:10.1504/IJCAT.2005.007201

Nakano, Y., Nakamura, A., & Kuno, Y. (2004). Web browser controlled by eye movements. *Proceedings of the IASTED International Conference on Advances in Computer Science and Technology (ACST '04),* 93–98.

Shi, F., Gale, A., & Purdy, K. (2006). Helping people with ICT device control by eye gaze. In K. Miesenberger, J. Klaus, W. Zagler, & A. Karshmer (Eds.), *Computers Helping People with Special Needs* (ICCHP 2006) (LNCS 4061, pp. 480–487). Berlin, Germany: Springer-Verlag. doi:10.1007/11788713_72

Shi, F., Gale, A., & Purdy, K. (2007). A new gaze-based interface for environmental control. In C. Stephanidis (Ed.), *Universal Access in Human-Computer Interaction. Ambient Interaction* (UAHCI 2007) (LNCS 4555, pp. 996–1005). Berlin, Germany: Springer-Verlag. doi:10.1007/978-3-540-73281-5_109

Špakov, O., & Majaranta, P. (2009). Scrollable keyboards for casual eye typing. *PsychNology Journal, 7*(2), 159–173.

Surakka, V., Illi, M., & Isokoski, P. (2003). Voluntary eye movements in human–computer interaction . In Hyönä, J., Radach, R., & Deubel, H. (Eds.), *The mind's eye: Cognitive and applied aspects of eye movement research* (pp. 473–491). Amsterdam, The Netherlands: Elsevier.

Tien, G., & Atkins, M. S. (2008). Improving hands-free menu selection using eyegaze glances and fixations. *Proceedings of the Symposium on Eye Tracking Research & Applications* (*ETRA '08*) (pp. 47-50). New York, NY: ACM. doi:10.1145/1344471.1344482

Velichkovsky, B., Sprenger, A., & Unema, P. (1997). Towards gaze-mediated interaction: Collecting solutions of the "Midas touch problem" . In Howard, S., Hammond, J., & Lindgaard, G. (Eds.), *Human–Computer Interaction – INTERACT '97* (pp. 509–516). London, UK: Chapman and Hall.

Wang, J., Zhai, S., & Su, H. (2001). Chinese input with keyboard and eye-tracking: an anatomical study. *Proceedings of the SIGCHI Conference on Human Factors in Computing Systems* (CHI '01) (pp. 349–356). New York, NY: ACM. doi:10.1145/365024.365298

ADDITIONAL READINGS FOR SECTION 4

Abrams, R. A., & Christ, S. E. (2003). Motion onset captures attention. *Psychological Science, 14,* 427–432. doi:10.1111/1467-9280.01458

Allison, B. Z., & Pineda, J. A. (2003). ERPs evoked by different matrix sizes: Implications for a brain computer interface (BCI) system. *IEEE Transactions on Neural Systems and Rehabilitation Engineering, 11,* 110–113. doi:10.1109/TNSRE.2003.814448

Anderson, C. W. (1997). Effects of variations in neural network topology and output averaging on the discrimination of mental tasks from spontaneous EEG. *Journal of Intelligent Systems, 7,* 165–190. doi:10.1515/JISYS.1997.7.1-2.165

Babiloni, F., Cincotti, F., Bianchi, L., Pirri, G., Millán, J. R., Mouriño, J., & Marciani, M. G. (2001). Recognition of imagined hand movements with low resolution surface Laplacian and linear classifiers. *Medical Engineering & Physics, 23,* 323–328. doi:10.1016/S1350-4533(01)00049-2

Bailey, B. P., Konstan, J. A., & Carlis, J. V. (2001). The effects of interruptions on task performance, annoyance, and anxiety in the user interface. *Proceedings of the International Conference on Human–Computer Interaction (INTERACT'01)* (pp. 593–601). IOS Press.

Bayliss, J. D. (2003). Use of the evoked potential P3 component for control in a virtual environment. *IEEE Transactions on Neural Systems and Rehabilitation Engineering, 11,* 113–116. doi:10.1109/TNSRE.2003.814438

Birch, G. E., Bozorgzadeh, Z., & Mason, S. G. (2002). Initial on-line evaluation of the LF-ASD brain–computer interface with able-bodied and spinal-cord subjects using imagined voluntary motor potentials. *IEEE Transactions on Neural Systems and Rehabilitation Engineering, 10,* 219–224. doi:10.1109/TNSRE.2002.806839

Blankertz, B., Dornhege, G., Krauledat, M., Schröder, M., Williamson, J., Murray-Smith, R., & Müller, K.-R. (2006). The Berlin Brain–Computer Interface presents the novel mental typewriter Hex-o-Spell. *Proceedings of the 3rd International Brain–Computer Interface Workshop and Training Course 2006* (pp. 108–109). Verlag der Technischen Universität Graz.

Buttfield, A., Ferrez, P. W., & Millán, J. R. (2006). Towards a robust BCI: Error recognition and on-line learning. *IEEE Transactions on Neural Systems and Rehabilitation Engineering, 14*, 164–168. doi:10.1109/TNSRE.2006.875555

Carmena, J. M., Lebedev, M. A., Crist, R. E., O'Doherty, J. E., Santucci, D. M., Dimitrov, D. F., & Nicolelis, M. A. L. (2003). Learning to control a brain-machine interface for reaching and grasping by primates. *PLoS Biology, 1*, 193–208. doi:10.1371/journal.pbio.0000042

Chapin, J. K., Moxon, K. A., Markowitz, R. S., & Nicolelis, M. A. L. (1999). Real-time control of a robot arm using simultaneously recorded neurons in the motor cortex. *Nature Neuroscience, 2*, 664–670. doi:10.1038/10223

Chochon, F., Cohen, L., van de Moortele, P. F., & Dehaene, S. (1999). Differential contributions of the left and right inferior parietal lobules to number processing. *Journal of Cognitive Neuroscience, 11*, 617–630. doi:10.1162/089892999563689

Derryberry, D., & Reed, M. A. (2002). Anxiety-related attentional biases and their regulation by attentional control. *Journal of Abnormal Psychology, 111*(2), 225–236. doi:10.1037/0021-843X.111.2.225

Franconeri, S. L., & Simons, D. J. (2003). Moving and looming stimulicapture attention. *Perception & Psychophysics, 65*, 999–101. doi:10.3758/BF03194829

Galley, N. (1993). The evaluation of the electrooculogram as a psychophysiological measuring instrument in the driver study of driver behaviour. *Ergonomics, 36*(9), 1063–1070. doi:10.1080/00140139308967978

Gao, X., Dingfeng, X., Cheng, M., & Gao, S. (2003). A BCI-based environmental controller for the motion-disabled. *IEEE Transactions on Neural Systems and Rehabilitation Engineering, 11*, 137–140. doi:10.1109/TNSRE.2003.814449

Graimann, B., Huggins, J. E., Schlögl, A., Levine, S. P., & Pfurtscheller, G. (2003). Detection of movement-related desynchronization patterns in ongoing single-channel electrocorticogram. *IEEE Transactions on Neural Systems and Rehabilitation Engineering, 11*, 276–281. doi:10.1109/TNSRE.2003.816863

Hayhoe, M., & Ballard, D. (2005). Eye movements in natural behavior. *Trends in Cognitive Sciences, 9*, 188–194. doi:10.1016/j.tics.2005.02.009

Hinterberger, T., Schmidt, S., Neumann, N., Mellinger, J., Blankertz, B., Curio, G., & Birbaumer, N. (2004). Brain–computer communication and slow cortical potentials. *IEEE Transactions on Bio-Medical Engineering, 51*, 1011–1018. doi:10.1109/TBME.2004.827067

Iturrate, I., Antelis, J. M., Kübler, A., & Minguez, J. (2009). A noninvasive brain-actuated wheelchair based on a P300 neurophysiological protocol and automated navigation. *IEEE Transactions on Robotics, 25*, 614–627. doi:10.1109/TRO.2009.2020347

Jacobs, R. J. K. (1990). What you look at is what you get: Eye movement-based interaction techniques. *Proceedings of the SIGCHI Conference on Human Factors in Computing Systems*, 11–18.

Kalcher, J., Flotzinger, D., Neuper, C., Gölly, S., & Pfurtscheller, G. (1996). Graz brain–computer interface II. *Medical & Biological Engineering & Computing, 34*, 382–388. doi:10.1007/BF02520010

Kornhuber, H. H., Becker, W., Täumer, R., Hoehne, O., & Iwase, K. (1969). Cerebral potentials accompanying voluntary movements in man: Readiness potential and reafferent potentials. *Electroencephalography and Clinical Neurophysiology, 26*(4), 439.

Land, M. F., & Lee, D. N. (1994). Where we look when we steer. *Nature, 369*(6483), 742–744. doi:10.1038/369742a0

Lang, P. J., Bradley, M. M., & Cuthbert, B. N. (1999). *International Affective Picture System (IAPS): Technical manual and affective ratings.* Gainesville, FL, USA: University of Florida, Center for Research in Psychophysiology.

Lemm, S., Blankertz, B., Curio, G., & Müller, K.-R. (2005). Spatio-spectral filters for improved classification of single trial EEG. *IEEE Transactions on Bio-Medical Engineering, 52,* 1541–1548. doi:10.1109/TBME.2005.851521

Leuthardt, E. C., Schalk, G., Wolpaw, J. R., Ojemann, J. G., & Moran, D. W. (2004). A brain–computer interface using electrocorticographic signals in humans. *Journal of Neural Engineering, 1,* 63–71. doi:10.1088/1741-2560/1/2/001

Maglio, P. P., Barrett, R., Campbell, C. S., & Selker, T. (2000). SUITOR: An attentive information system. *Proceedings of the 5th International Conference on Intelligent User Interfaces (IUI '00)* (pp. 169–176). ACM Press.

McFarland, D. J., McCane, L. M., David, S. V., & Wolpaw, J. R. (1997). Spatial filter selection for EEG-based communication. *Electroencephalography and Clinical Neurophysiology, 103,* 386–394. doi:10.1016/S0013-4694(97)00022-2

Middendorf, M., McMillan, G., Calhoun, G., & Jones, K. S. (2000). Brain–computer interfaces based on the steady-state visual-evoked response. *IEEE Transactions on Rehabilitation Engineering, 8,* 211–214. doi:10.1109/86.847819

Millán, J. R. (2002). Brain–computer interfaces . In Arbib, M. A. (Ed.), *Handbook of brain theory and neural networks* (pp. 178–181). Cambridge, MA, USA: MIT Press.

Millán, J. R. (2004). On the need for on-line learning in brain–computer interfaces. *Proceedings of the International Joint Conference on Neural Networks.*

Morgan, S. T., Hansen, J. C., & Hillyard, S. A. (1996). Selective attention to stimulus location modulates the steady-state visual evoked potential. *Proceedings of the National Academy of Sciences of the United States of America, 93,* 4770–4774. doi:10.1073/pnas.93.10.4770

Mouriño, J. (2003). *EEG-based analysis for the design of adaptive brain interfaces.* PhD thesis. Barcelona, Spain: Centre de Recerca en Enginyeria Biomèdica, Universitat Politècnica de Catalunya.

Mouriño, J., Millán, J. R., Cincotti, F., Chiappa, S., Jané, R., & Babiloni, F. (2001). Spatial filtering in the training process of a brain computer interface. *Proceedings of the 23rd Annual International Conference of the IEEE.* Engineering in Medicine and Biology Society.

Muenssinger, J. I., Halder, S., Kleih, S. C., Furdea, A., Raco, V., Hoesle, A., & Kübler, A. (2010). Brain painting: First evaluation of a new brain–computer interface application with ALS patients and healthy volunteers. *Frontiers in Neuroscience, 4.*

Mugler, E. M., Ruf, C. A., Halder, S., Bensch, M., & Kübler, A. (2010). Design and implementation of a P300-based brain–computer interface for controlling an Internet browser. *IEEE Transactions on Neural Systems and Rehabilitation Engineering, 18,* 599–609. doi:10.1109/TNSRE.2010.2068059

Müller-Gerking, J., Pfurtscheller, G., & Flyvbjerg, H. (1999). Designing optimal spatial filters for single-trial EEG classification in a movement task. *Clinical Neurophysiology, 110,* 787–798. doi:10.1016/S1388-2457(98)00038-8

Müller, K.-R., Tangermann, M., Dornhege, G., Krauledat, M., Curio, G., & Blankertz, B. (2008). Machine learning for real-time single-trial EEG-analysis: From brain–computer interfacing to mental state monitoring. *Journal of Neuroscience Methods, 167,* 82–90. doi:10.1016/j.jneumeth.2007.09.022

Mussallam, S., Corneil, B. D., Greger, B., Scherberger, H., & Andersen, R. A. (2004). Cognitive control signals for neural prosthetics. *Science, 305,* 258–262. doi:10.1126/science.1097938

Neuper, C., Scherer, R., Reiner, M., & Pfurtscheller, G. (2005). Imagery of motor actions: Differential effects of kinesthetic and visual-motor mode of imagery in single-trial EEG. *Brain Research. Cognitive Brain Research, 25,* 668–677. doi:10.1016/j.cogbrainres.2005.08.014

Nicolelis, M. A. L. (2001). Actions from thoughts. *Nature, 409,* 403–407. doi:10.1038/35053191

Obermaier, B., Müller, G. R., & Pfurtscheller, G. (2003). 'Virtual keyboard' controlled by spontaneous EEG activity. *IEEE Transactions on Neural Systems and Rehabilitation Engineering, 11,* 422–426. doi:10.1109/TNSRE.2003.816866

Perrin, F., Pernier, J., Bertrand, O., & Echallier, J. (1989). Spherical spline for potential and current density mapping. *Electroencephalography and Clinical Neurophysiology, 72,* 184–187. doi:10.1016/0013-4694(89)90180-6 .

Perrin, F., Pernier, J., Bertrand, O., & Echallier, J. (1990). Corrigendum EEG 02274. *Electroencephalography and Clinical Neurophysiology, 76,* 565.

Petersen, S. E., Fox, P. T., Posner, M. I., Mintun, M., & Raichle, M. E. (1988). Positron emission tomographic studies of the cortical anatomy of single-word processing. *Nature, 331,* 585–589. doi:10.1038/331585a0

Prendinger, H., Hyrskykari, A., Nakayama, M., Istance, H., Bee, N., & Takahasi, Y. (2009). Attentive interfaces for users with disabilities: Eye gaze for intention and uncertainty estimation. *Universal Access in the Information Society, 8*(4), 339–354. doi:10.1007/s10209-009-0144-5

Rebsamen, B., Burdet, E., Teo, C. L., Zeng, Q., Guan, C., Ang, M., & Laugier, C. (2006). A brain control wheelchair with a P300 based BCI and a path following controller. *Proceedings of the 1st IEEE/RAS-EMBS International Conference on Biomedical Robotics and Biomechatronics.*

Roberts, S. J., & Penny, W. D. (2000). Real-time brain–computer interfacing: A preliminary study using Bayesian learning. *Medical & Biological Engineering & Computing, 38,* 56–61. doi:10.1007/BF02344689

Scherer, R., Müller, G. R., Neuper, C., Grainmann, B., & Pfurtscheller, G. (2004). An asynchronous controlled EEG-based virtual keyboard: Improvement of the spelling rate. *IEEE Transactions on Bio-Medical Engineering, 51,* 979–984. doi:10.1109/TBME.2004.827062

Schlögl, A. (2000). *The electroencephalogram and the adaptive autoregressive model: Theory and applications.* Aachen, Germany: Shaker Verlag.

Serruya, M. D., Hatsopoulos, N. G., Paninski, L., Fellows, M. R., & Donoghue, J. (2002). Instant neural control of a movement signal. *Nature, 416,* 141–142. doi:10.1038/416141a

Sheridan, T. B. (1992). *Telerobotics, automation and human supervisory control.* Cambridge, MA, USA: MIT Press.

Singer, W. (1993). Synchronization of cortical activity and its putative role in information processing and learning. *Annual Review of Physiology, 55,* 349–374. doi:10.1146/annurev.ph.55.030193.002025

Starker, I., & Bolt, R. A. (1990). A gaze-responsive self-disclosing display. *ACM, CHI90,* 3–9.

Surakka, V., Illi, M., & Isokoski, P. (2004). Gazing and frowning as a new human–computer interaction technique. *ACM Transactions on Applied Perception, 1,* 40–56. doi:10.1145/1008722.1008726

Sutter, E. E. (1992). The brain response interface: Communication through visually-induced electrical brain response. *Journal of Microcomputer Applications, 15,* 31–45. doi:10.1016/0745-7138(92)90045-7

Taylor, D. M., Helms Tillery, S. I., & Schwartz, A. B. (2002). Direct cortical control of 3D neuroprosthetic devices. *Science, 296,* 1829–1832. doi:10.1126/science.1070291

Velichkovsky, B. M., Sprenger, A., & Unema, P. J. A. (1997). Toward gaze-mediated interaction: Collecting solutions of the 'Midas touch problem . In Howard, S., Hammond, J., & Lindgaard, G. (Eds.), *Human–Computer Interaction: INTERACT'97.* London, UK: Chapman & Hall.

Vertegaal, R. (2002). Designing attentive interfaces. *Proceedings of the Symposium on Eye Tracking Research & Applications (ETRA '02)* (pp. 22–30). New York, NY: ACM Press.

Vertegaal, R. (2003). Attentive user interfaces. *Communications of the ACM, 46*(3), 30–33. doi:10.1145/636772.636794

Vertegaal, R., Dickie, C., Sohn, C., & Flickner, M. (2002). *Designing attentive cell phone using wearable EyeContact sensors. CHI '02 Extended Abstracts on Human Factors in Computing Systems* (pp. 646–647). New York, NY: ACM Press.

Vidaurre, C., Schlögl, A., Blankertz, B., Kawanabe, M., & Müller, K.-R. (2008). Unsupervised adaptation of the LDA classifier for brain–computer interfaces. *Proceedings of the 4th International Brain–Computer Interface Workshop* (pp. 122–127).

Vidaurre, C., Schlögl, A., Scherer, R., Cabeza, R., & Pfurtscheller, G. (2006). A fully on-line adaptive BCI. *IEEE Transactions on Bio-Medical Engineering, 53,* 1214–1219. doi:10.1109/TBME.2006.873542

Vidaurre, C., Schlögl, A., Scherer, R., Cabeza, R., & Pfurtscheller, G. (2007). Study of on-line adaptive discriminant analysis for EEG-based brain computer interfaces. *IEEE Transactions on Bio-Medical Engineering, 54,* 550–556. doi:10.1109/TBME.2006.888836

Vigário, R. (1997). Extraction of ocular artefacts from EEG using independent component analysis. *Electroencephalography and Clinical Neurophysiology*, *103*, 395–404. doi:10.1016/S0013-4694(97)00042-8

Westermann, R., Spies, K., Stahl, G., & Hesse, F. W. (1996). Relative effectiveness and validity of mood induction procedures: A meta-analysis. *European Journal of Social Psychology*, *26*(4), 557–580. doi:10.1002/(SICI)1099-0992(199607)26:4<557::AID-EJSP769>3.0.CO;2-4

Wickelgren, I. (2003). Tapping the mind. *Science*, *299*, 496–499. doi:10.1126/science.299.5606.496

Wolpaw, J. R., McFarland, D. J., Vaughan, T. M., & Schalk, G. (2003). The Wadsworth Center brain–computer interface (BCI) research and development program. *IEEE Transactions on Neural Systems and Rehabilitation Engineering*, *11*, 204–207. doi:10.1109/TNSRE.2003.814442

Yantis, S., & Jonides, J. (1990). Abrupt visual onsets and selective attention: Voluntary versus automatic allocation. *Journal of Experimental Psychology*, *16*(1), 121–134.

Yoshino, A., Inoue, M., & Suzuki, A. (2000). A topographic electrophysiologic study of mental rotation. *Brain Research. Cognitive Brain Research*, *9*, 121–124. doi:10.1016/S0926-6410(99)00046-4

ADDITIONAL READINGS FOR SECTION 5

Aula, A., & Rodden, K. (2009). *Eye-tracking studies: More than meets the eye*. Retrieved from http://googleblog.blogspot.com/ 2009/02/eye-tracking-studies- more-than-meets.html

Dumas, J. S., & Reddish, J. (1999). *A practical guide to usability testing*. Norwood, NJ: Ablex.

Goldberg, J. H., & Wichansky, A. M. (2003). Eye tracking in usability evaluation: A practitioner's guide . In Hyönä, J., Radach, R., & Deubel, H. (Eds.), *The mind's eye: Cognitive and applied aspects of eye movement research* (pp. 493–516). Amsterdam, The Netherlands: North-Holland.

Rubin, J., & Chisnell, D. (2008). *Handbook of usability testing, Second edition: How to plan, design, and conduct effective tests*. Indianapolis, IN: Wiley.

Strandvall, T. (2010). *EyeTracking.Me* – a blog by Tommy Strandvall. Retrieved from http://eyetracking.me/

Tullis, T., & Albert, W. (2008). *Measuring the user experience: Collecting, analyzing and presenting usability metrics. The Morgan Kaufmann Interactive Technologies series*. Amsterdam, The Netherlands: Elsevier.

Webb, N., & Renshaw, T. (2008). Eyetracking in HCI . In Cairns, P., & Cox, A. L. (Eds.), *Research methods for human–computer interaction* (pp. 35–69). Cambridge, UK: Cambridge University Press.

ADDITIONAL READINGS FOR SECTION 6

Axelson, J. (2009). *USB complete. The developer's guide* (4th ed.). Lakeview Research.

Benson, K. B., & Whitaker, J. C. (Eds.). (2003). *Handbook of video and television engineering*. New York, NY: McGraw-Hill.

Cieszynski, J. (2006). *Closed circuit television*. Newnes.

Eid, E.-S. (2001). Study of limitations on pixel size of very high resolution image sensors. *Proceedings of the 18th National Radio Science Conference* (NRSC 2001) (v. 1, pp. 15–28).

Fossum, E. R. (1997). CMOS image sensors: Electronic camera on a chip. *IEEE Transactions on Electron Devices, 44*(10), 1689–1698. doi:10.1109/16.628824

Gamal, A., & Eltoukhy, H. (2005). CMOS image sensors. *IEEE Circuits and Devices Magazine, 21*(3), 6–20. doi:10.1109/MCD.2005.1438751

Kisačanin, B., Bhattacharyya, S. S., & Chai, S. (Eds.). (2009). *Embedded computer vision* (1st ed.). Berlin, Germany: Springer. doi:10.1007/978-1-84800-304-0

Liu, D. (2008). Embedded DSP processor design: *Vol. 2. Application specific instruction set processors*. San Francisco, CA, USA: Morgan Kaufmann Publishers, Inc.

Magnan, P. (2003). Detection of visible photons in CCD and CMOS: A comparative view. *Nuclear Instruments and Methods in Physics Research Section A: Accelerators, Spectrometers, Detectors and Associated Equipment, 504*(1–3), 199–212. *Proceedings of the 3rd International Conference on New Developments in Photodetection.*

Mueller, S. (2007). *Upgrading and Repairing PCs* (18th edition). Indianapolis, IN, US: QUe Corp.

Ohta, J. (2008). *Smart CMOS image sensors and applications*. CRC Press.

Ting-Chung, P., & Taegeun, K. (2006). *Engineering optics with Matlab*. River Edge, NJ, US: World Scientific Publishing.

Winder, S. (2008). *Power supplies for LED driving*. Newnes.

About the Contributors

Päivi Majaranta is a researcher at the University of Tampere, where she also received her PhD in Interactive Technology in 2009. She has worked on several research projects related to eye tracking. She is especially interested in the application of eye tracking in gaze-controlled and gaze-aware interfaces.

* * *

Hirotaka Aoki is an Associate Professor at Tokyo Institute of Technology. He received his PhD in Engineering from Tokyo Institute of Technology. His current research interests lie in the application of eye tracking techniques to cognitive work analysis, usability engineering and consumer behaviour analysis.

Richard Bates is a Senior Research Fellow at De Montfort University, Leicester where he received his PhD in Eye Gaze Communication. His current research focuses on enabling creativity and communication for people with profound and multiple physical and learning disabilities through the application of technology, particularly in the fields of art and music. He has an ongoing interest in Assistive Technology and also works as a freelance consultant in the field.

Margret Buchholz is a Council Certified Specialist in Occupational Therapy at DART - Centre for Augmentative and Alternative Communication (AAC) and Assistive Technology (AT), Sahlgrenska University Hospital, Gothenburg, Sweden. She has worked in the field of AAC and AT since the mid 1990's and wrote her MSc and specialist degree in Occupational Therapy with emphasis on AT. She has worked on developing AT assessment methodology for users with severe physical impairments and complex communication needs in several projects, including early Swedish projects on eye-gaze-technology and the COGAIN project.

Rafael Cabeza received his PhD degree (with honors) in Telecommunications Engineering in 1996 from the Public University of Navarra, Pamplona, Spain. Since 1999, he has been an Associate Professor in the Department of Electrical and Electronics Engineering, Public University of Navarra, where, from 2000 to 2010, he has been the Head of the Signal Processing, Microelectronic, and Instrumentation Research Group. His current research interests include the area of signal and image processing, virtual instrumentation, and software tools.

Emiliano Castellina (PhD) is a research assistant in the e-Lite research group at the Department of Computer Science and Automation of Politecnico di Torino. His current research interests include computer assistive technologies (development of special software applications for disabled people) and domotic Systems. He has published several papers on the topic.

Fulvio Corno (PhD) holds an MSc in Electronic Engineering from the Politecnico di Torino in 1991 and a PhD in Computer Science Engineering from the same university in 1994. He is currently an Associate Professor at the Department of Control and Computer Engineering (Dipartimento di Automatica e Informatica) of Politecnico di Torino, and is enrolled in the Faculty of Management and Industrial Engineering (IV Facoltà di Ingegneria - Organizzazione d'Impresa e Ingegneria Gestionale). He has worked on computer-aided design for VLSI design, evolutionary algorithms for optimization problems, intelligent and semantic technologies for Web applications, and domotics and smart homes. His current research interests include semantic technologies, iIntelligent domotic environments, and interfaces for alternative access to computer systems.

Gintautas Daunys is an Associate Professor at Siauliai University, Lithuania. He received his PhD in electrical & electronic engineering from Kaunas University of Technology. He is interested in biomedical signal digital processing, computer vision for human-computer interaction. He has led research on video-based gaze and head tracking, and automatic gesture recognition. He is a member of international organizations: IEEE, ACM, EURASIP, ISCA, COGAIN Association.

Mick Donegan is the Founder and Director of SpecialEffect, a charity dedicated to providing enhanced opportunities for people with disabilities to access video games and express themselves through design and music. He was awarded a PhD by Birmingham University in 2006 for an investigation into the conditions for the successful use of Assistive Technology in mainstream education. He was the coordinator of the User Requirements element of COGAIN, a European gaze control and disability project and is currently an Advisor for TOBI, a European funded project on brain control and disability.

Detlev Droege received his diploma in computer science in 1988. He has worked since then at the University of Koblenz-Landau as a faculty member specialising in operating systems, computer graphics and image processing. His research concentrates on active vision systems, focusing on low cost gaze tracking systems in recent years. He participated in the COGAIN Network of Excellence and is now member of the COGAIN association.

Lisa Ellis (Oosthuizen) is the director of an AAC (Augmentative and Alternative Communication) and Assistive Technology company in South Africa. She completed her BSc in Linguistics and Industrial Psychology at Rhodes University in South Africa. Her areas of interest include eye control access to technology for people with disabilities, the application of AAC in a 3rd world and low resource environment and AAC training for rural teachers and therapists.

Laura Farinetti holds an MSc in Electronic Engineering from the Politecnico di Torino in 1990, and a PhD in Cognitive Science from the same university in 1996. She is currently a senior researcher and Assistant Professor at the Department of Computer Science of Politecnico di Torino. Her research interests include Information and Communication Technologies for open and distance education, Semantic Web, Web Intelligence, hypertext, multimedia and hypermedia systems, human-computer interaction and user modeling, knowledge management, ICT for accessibility, eInclusion and eAgeing.

Lorna Gill is a clinical psychologist currently working in a child and adolescents mental health service. She completed her doctorate at the University of Birmingham. She worked on the COGAIN user involvement trials from 2006-2007, at the ACE Centre, Oxford. She retains a keen interest in the application of Assistive Technologies in improving the quality of the lives for those with complex disabilities.

Dan Witzner Hansen is an Associate Professor within the Innovative Communication group at the IT University of Copenhagen, where is also received his PhD. He has been assistant professor at both ITU and the Technical University of Denmark and has been a visiting researcher at Cavendish laboratories, University of Cambridge, UK. His research interests are within computer vision and machine learning for interactive purposes with as special focus on eye tracking and gaze interaction in mobile scenarios. He is the author of several papers and patents related to eye and gaze tracking.

John Paulin Hansen is an Associate Professor at the IT University of Copenhagen. He received his PhD in psychology from Aarhus University. Hansen has a major interest in gaze interaction and Assistive Technologies. He has been pioneering the use of gaze tracking for usability studies and was one of the initiators of the COGAIN network. Hansen is now head of the Innovative Communication research group at IT University of Copenhagen

Henna Heikkilä (MSc) is a researcher at the University of Tampere. She is interested in gaze-based interaction, especially on how to utilize gaze gestures in gaze-controlled applications.

Michael Heubner completed his studies in psychology at Greifswald University. From 2006 to 2010 he was a member of the Applied Cogntive Research Unit at Technische Universität Dresden and the Department of Marketing at Tilburg University. His research has focused on gaze-controlled interfaces and the emotional influence on attentional processes. Currently, he holds a position as Senior Researcher at Millward Brown Healthcare, UK.

Eva Holmqvist is a Council Certified Specialist in Occupational Therapy at DART - Centre for Augmentative and Alternative Communication (AAC) and Assistive Technology (AT), Sahlgrenska University Hospital, Sweden. She has worked within the field of AAC and AT since 1989 and wrote her MSc and specialist degree with emphasis on AAC. She participated in early Swedish projects on eye-gaze-technology. In COGAIN she mainly worked with developing assessment methods and constructing user-friendly layouts for persons with severe disorders and a need of special training to be able to use eye gaze systems.

Aulikki Hyrskykari is a Lecturer in Computer Science at the University of Tampere. She obtained her Lic.Phil degree in Computer Science in 1995 and her PhD in Interactive Tecnology in 2006 at the University of Tampere. She worked as a coordinator in the EU FP5 IST Project iEye, a three year project which focused on studying gaze assisted access to information. She has also acted as a program and organizing committee member in several international HCI conferences, most recently as the program chair of the ACM Eye Tracking Research and Applications conference ETRA 2010.

Howell Istance is a Principal Lecturer in the Centre for Computational Intelligence at De Montfort University in Leicester, UK. He originally worked as an ergonomist on the human factors of industrial control systems, but later moved into computer science to work in HCI. His research interests are in the design of eye gaze communication techniques, particularly for use with computer games by people with physical disabilities. He has chaired a number of international eye tracking conferences; the COGAIN Conferences from 2005 to 2008 and the ACM Eye Tracking Research and Applications conference ETRA in years 2010 and 2012.

Andrea Kübler received her MSc in Biology and Psychology and the PhD in Biology at the University of Tübingen, Germany. She is currently Professor of Psychology at the University of Würzburg. Her research areas are the application of brain-computer interfaces in severely impaired patients and disorders of consciousness; addiction and eating disorders; and sleep disorders in children.

Robert Lange received his diploma in medical engineering in 2005 from the Saxon University of Cooperative Education. After working in the Department of Clinical Engineering in the hospital of Zittau, Saxony, he was employed for 6 month in the department of Engineering Psychology and Cognitive Ergonomics of the Technical University of Dresden to assist in the field of infrared radiation measurements in eyetracking settings. Currently he is taking a postgraduate course in biomedical engineering at the Martin Luther Univerity Halle and at the Anhalt University of Applied Sciences.

I. Scott MacKenzie's research is in human-computer interaction with an emphasis on human performance measurement and modeling, experimental methods and evaluation, interaction devices and techniques, alphanumeric entry, language modeling, gaming, eye tracking, and mobile computing. He has more than 120 publications in the field of Human-Computer Interaction (including more than 30 from the ACM's annual SIGCHI conference) and has given numerous invited talks over the past 20 years. Since 1999, he has been Associate Professor of Computer Science and Engineering at York University, Canada.

Diako Mardanbegi is a PhD student at IT University of Copenhagen. He received his MSc. In his Masters thesis he built and evaluated a low-cost head mounted eye tracking system for screen-based interaction. His current research is within mobile gaze tracking for control of home appliances.

José del R. Millán is the Defitech Professor at the Center for Neuroprosthetics of the Swiss Federal Institute of Technology in Lausanne where he explores the use of brain signals for multimodal interaction and the development of non-invasive brain-controlled neuroprostheses, bringing together the work of brain-machine interfaces (BMI) and adaptive intelligent robotics. He received his PhD in computer science from the Univ. Politècnica de Catalunya (Barcelona, Spain) in 1992. He was a research scientist at the Joint Research Centre of the European Commission in Ispra (Italy) and a senior researcher at the Idiap Research Institute in Martigny (Switzerland). He was Research Leader in 2004 by the journal Scientific American for his work on brain-controlled robots. He is the coordinator of several European projects on BMI and also is a frequent keynote speaker at international events. His work on BMI has received wide media coverage around the world.

Klaus-Robert Müller is Professor of Computer Science at TU-Berlin since 2006 and also directs the Bernstein Focus on Neurotechnology Berlin. He studied physics in Karlsruhe from 1984-89 and obtained his PhD in Computer Science at TU Karlsruhe in 1992. He was PostDoc at GMD FIRST in Berlin (1992-1994), a European Community STP Research Fellow at University of Tokyo (1994-1995). In 1995 he started the Intelligent Data Analysis (IDA) group at GMD FIRST (later Fraunhofer FIRST) and directed it until 2008. From 1999-2006 he was a Professor of Computer Science at University of Potsdam. In 1999, he was awarded the Olympus Prize by the German Pattern Recognition Society, DAGM and in 2006 he received the SEL Alcatel Communication Award. Since 2000 one of his main scientific interests has been to study the interface between brain and machine: non-invasive EEG-based BCI.

Fiona Mulvey worked as a postgraduate researcher in University College Dublin 2003-2006 and was a DAAD Fellowship holder in TU Dresden 2006-2009. She is currently at the IT University of Copenahagen, where she will complete her PhD in 2011. Her major research interest is in the cognitive neuropsychology of attention and eye movements and individual differences in cognition. She led research within COGAIN for the development of an international safety standard for infrared illumination in eye tracking and currently coordinates work within COGAIN towards an international standard for eye tracker accuracy.

Petr Novák is a research assistant in the NIT research group at the Department of Cybernetics of the Czech Technical University in Prague. His current research interests include computer Assistive Technologies, domotic systems and utilization of objective measurements for improving quality of medical diagnostics e.g. in opthalomology. He has published several papers on these topics.

Saila Ovaska is a Lecturer in Interactive Technology at the University of Tampere, where she obtained her Lic.Phil degree in Computer Science in 1997. She teaches various courses in human-computer interaction, user interfaces and computer-supported collaborative work. Her research interests are in Interaction Design and Usability Evaluation methods.

Valentina Pasian holds a BSc in Speech Therapy from Università di Torino since 2005. She is interested and active in alternative and augmentative communication and the related aids, including eye trackers. She currently collaborates with the Regional Centre for ALS in Torino and with the Child Neuropsychiatry Unit in Torino.

Kari-Jouko Räihä is a Professor of Computer Science at the University of Tampere. He received his PhD in 1982 at the University of Helsinki. He has done research in compiler construction, databases, and for the past 20 years in human-computer interaction. He is particularly interested in new interaction techniques for the desktop environment, and in the use of eye gaze for analyzing interaction and as an input channel. He has led tens of research projects, including the COGAIN Network of Excellence funded by the European Commission. He is currently the Dean of the School of Information Sciences at the University of Tampere.

Javier San Agustin holds a PhD from the IT University of Copenhagen, and an MSc in Telecommunication Engineering from the Public University of Navarra. His research interests are eye tracking, gaze-based interaction, and multi-modal interaction, with a special focus on the use of low-cost and off-the-shelf components on gaze tracking technology. He is currently employed as a Post Doc at the IT University of Copenhagen.

Isabella Signorile has a degree in Computer Engineering from Politecnico di Torino in 2001. She is interested in computer gaze interaction. Her thesis was titled "Study and achievement of an eye-gaze pc access system for motor disabled people". Currently she works at CeLM (Centre for e-Learning and Multimedia of Politecnico di Torino) and she coordinates activities and projects for distance students with disabilities.

Henrik Skovsgaard's research interests include Assistive and Accessible Technologies (e.g., alternative computer input), single and multimodal interface design, cognition, language modeling, virtual environments, programming languages and human performance (e.g., measurement and modeling). In 2008 he entered the PhD program at the IT University of Copenhagen, where he is currently employed.

David Sliney initially studied physics and radiological health, but obtained his PhD in biophysics and medical physics from the University of London, Institute of Ophthalmology. He worked for the US Army Medical Department for many years until retiring in 2007. He served as CIE Director of Division 6 on Photobiology for 12 years and as a CIE Vice-President, and served as President of the American Society for Photobiology during 2008-2009. His research interests focus on subjects related to vision, ultraviolet, infrared and intense light effects upon the eye, optical hazards from medical devices and lasers, laser-tissue interactions, photobiological/laser applications in medicine and surgery.

Oleg Špakov is a researcher in Tampere Unit for Computer-Human Interaction (TAUCHI), University of Tampere, and has worked in gaze data analysis and gaze-aware and gaze-controlled applications development. He received his PhD in Interactive Technology in 2008 focusing on investigation of target selection processes and algorithms in gaze-based applications. He was one of the authors of the recommendations for gaze data standardization in COGAIN, and implemented this standardization in a tool named ETU-Driver.

Olga Štěpánková is a Professor of Applied Cybernetics at the Czech Technical University at Prague and she is a vice-head of the Department of Cybernetics at the Faculty of Electrical Engineering of the Czech Technical University in Prague, which she joined in 1988. She graduated from the Faculty of Mathematics and Physics at the Charles University in Prague and she defended her doctoral degree in 1981. Her research has been focused on theoretical foundations of ICT situated on the border between mathematical logic and artificial intelligence, and on data mining, machine learning and their medical applications. Recently, she became deeply involved in the design of novel assistive tools and of tele-medical solutions. She is author or co-author of more than 100 conference and journal papers, co-author or co-editor of 10 books.

Martin Tall is an engineering research associate at Duke University, USA. His current work involves radiology and medical image perception research. Prior to Duke, Tall held the same position at Stanford University, USA. Before relocating across the Atlantic, Tall was a PhD student at the IT University Of Copenhagen working on gaze interaction interfaces. At ITU, collaboration with Dr. Javier San Agustin started on the open source GazeTracker which has since grown to a vibrant online community.

Michael Tangermann is a Postdoc Researcher at the Berlin Institute of Technology. He is a member of BBCI group of the Machine Learning Department of Professor Klaus-Robert Müller. After studies of computer science and biology he received his doctorate in 2007 at the University of Tübingen, Germany. His main fields of research are BCI approaches for patients, novel auditory ERP paradigms for BCI, motor imagery paradigms, machine learning methods in BCI for feature selection or artifact removal, mental state monitoring applications, workload analysis in real-time applications and EEG-based gaming.

Carmen Vidaurre is Senior Postdoc at the Computer Science at TU-Berlin since 2008. Her research fields are robust and adaptive systems, online learning, and learning under non-stationarities. She received her PhD at the Public Universtity of Navarra in 2006. She was Marie-Curie fellow of the EU at Fraunhofer FIRST (2006-2008), worked at the Center for Applied Medical Research in Pamplona, Spain (2005-2006). She is Telecommunication Engineer from the Public University of Navarra (Spain, 2000).

Arantxa Villanueva is an Associate Professor in the Department of Electrical and Electronics Engineering at Public University of Navarra, Pamplona, Spain. She received her PhD in Telecomunications Engineering in 2005 focusing on Mathematical Models for Video Oculography. Her current research interests are gaze tracking technology and computer vision. She is the leader of the Gaze Interaction Group at The Public University of Navarra.

Index